Change from the Inside

Change from the Inside:
My Life, the Chicano Movement, and the Story of an Era

By Richard Alatorre

With Marc Grossman

Berkeley Public Policy Press
Institute of Governmental Studies
University of California, Berkeley
2016

Copyright © 2016 by the Regents of the University of California. All rights reserved.

Library of Congress Cataloging-in-Publication Data

Names: Alatorre, Richard, author. | Grossman, Marc, 1940- author.
Title: Change from the Inside : my life, the Chicano movement, and the story of an era / by Richard Alatorre with Marc Grossman.
Other titles: My life, the Chicano movement, and the story of an era
Description: Berkeley, CA : Berkeley Public Policy Press, [2016]
Identifiers: LCCN 2016003890 | ISBN 9780877724513
Subjects: LCSH: Alatorre, Richard. | California–Politics and government–1951- | Legislators–California–Biography. | City council members–California–Los Angeles–Biography. | Los Angeles–Politics and government–20th century. | Chicano movement–California. | Mexican Americans–California–Politics and government. | Mexican Americans–California–Biography. | Addicts–California–Los Angeles–Biography. | Los Angeles–Biography.
Classification: LCC F8662. .A44 2016 | DDC 979.4/053092-dc23
LC record available at http://lccn.loc.gov/2016003890

Contents

Foreword: Why Me?	vii
Chapter 1: Where I Come From	1
Chapter 2: My Awakening	23
Chapter 3: Teaching and Learning	51
Chapter 4: Working from the Inside	85
Chapter 5: Fulfilling a Childhood Dream at the Capitol	115
Chapter 6: Dedicating Myself to Cesar's Cause	179
Chapter 7: The Speakership War	201
Chapter 8: Righting a Wrong	233
Chapter 9: Giving It All Up to Come Home	273
Chapter 10: Laying a Foundation for Decades	291
Chapter 11: I'm There to Do More Than Just Take Up Space	303
Chapter 12: The Godfather of the MTA	391
Chapter 13: Finding Redemption	413
Index	431

Foreword

Why Me?

Of the close friends I grow up with on the tough streets of East Los Angeles, many never reach their potential or accomplish much with their lives. A number of them start out in juvenile probation camps, graduate to the state Youth Authority, and then go on to just about every prison mankind ever builds. Some die violent deaths or meet their ends from drinking and narcotics.

I spend more than four decades in social and political activism, almost 30 of them in politics as a California state legislator and a Los Angeles city councilmember.

Often, I ask myself, why me? Today, I feel blessed to have achieved what I did despite the temptations of the neighborhoods where I'm raised.

I am around five years old when my mother, father, sister, and I move from Boyle Heights to the Belvedere neighborhood of East L.A. The people who immediately have the most influence over me are our next door neighbors—a big family named the Galindos—and, next door to them, another big family, the Cercedeses. Felix Galindo, at six, is my friend; I spend the most time with him even though I am younger. I am also close to Manual Cercedes, who at eight is a little older than Felix.

The two boys always protect me, maybe because I'm younger and live next door. Since they are both good athletes, they teach me sports: how to catch and throw a baseball, and how to play football, basketball, and kickball. Felix is pretty good at basketball. Manual's game is baseball; he can really hit. They are the friends I hang around with until I start playing basketball on the school playgrounds.

All the things you learn in adolescence I learn from Felix and Manuel, before adolescence. The three of us do everything together.

Felix is smart, streetwise, a good-looking guy. It is a tragedy that he never realizes his promise given everything he has going for him. I, too, could easily become another victim of my place and time. I experiment with grass, marijuana, but it doesn't settle well with me, so I stay away from it.

Felix also raises pigeons. I get a bird too. We fight them, pitting one against the other by putting them together in a cage. Sometimes they leave each other alone, but if one tries to assert himself, they battle it out and only one prevails. We learn the same lesson on the streets where we live.

Once elementary school begins, I walk to school, where I meet and become friends with Leonard Castellanos. His God-given talent is painting. He is a great artist who can draw anything. At 12, Leonard paints a still life of fruit on a table, oil on canvas. It is an amazing feat for a 12 year old. (He later graduates from Chouinard Art Institute in Los Angeles.) He and I are contemporaries. He is another naturally talented athlete, great at shot put and track. Bigger than me, he is well built and muscular. We become the best of friends through junior and senior high school. He gets married right out of high school. I am the best man at his wedding. I get married shortly after the start of college. He is my best man.

When I'm not with Felix and Manual as a kid, I am with Leonard. With Leonard, Richard Marquez, and his brother, Robert, we start a gang called the Cutdowns of Hoyo Mara, short for Maravilla, a big nearby neighborhood. The name Hoyo (from *el hoyo*, or hole) in bastardized Spanish comes from where Michigan Avenue follows east from our neighborhood in Belvedere and eventually goes down a hill, forming a sort of hole.

Several related gangs are associated with El Hoyo. The Dukes are older guys, mostly in their twenties, who graduate from junior gangs like ours. The Dukes are also guys who are going to or have recently returned from jail or prison for drugs, robbery, murder—you name it, they do it.

The Cutdowns are a big step down from the Dukes. We form out of the simple need for survival. My friends and I are going to catechism, Catholic religious instruction, when we come across a guy from a different gang around Indiana Avenue, not far away. They call him Dopey. He is older and bigger than all of us, already in high school. Dopey likes to intimidate us, threatening to beat us up. We get tired of it. So we start the gang and whenever anything comes down, when there is a perceived danger, we band together. Self-survival is an amazing thing.

When it comes to gangs, you can "jump in" or "jump out." That means you are either part of a gang or you learn how to run. I am never a fast runner. Getting initiated into the gang as a boy usually requires the rite of passage of getting the crap beat out of you. More ominous is the expression, "Blood In, Blood

Out," made famous by a 1993 film of the same name about three members of a Chicano family who join the same street gang in the 1970s and '80s. It accurately depicts young kids being initiated into a gang allegedly associated with the Mexican Mafia. The rule is you have to kill somebody to get in the gang and the only way to leave is to die (or get put into the federal witness protection program)—therefore blood in, blood out.

Another guy I grow up with, older than me by several years, is Rafael ("Chispas") Sandoval. Rafael grows up a block away from my house. There are maybe six or seven brothers in the Sandoval family. Rafael and Raymond are the most prominent. Raymond is my contemporary, but I look up to Rafael, Chispas. I know the family, especially the mother. I have a strong friendship with them. One of the kids is run over by a car on the street and almost dies when I am close by. I see it all.

Yet what really shakes me up is when Richard Marquez is killed. We call him Dickiebird. We go to elementary school together. He is smart, a good athlete; he has the ability to be somebody.

Richard dies because he goes to a party in the territory of another gang, called the White Fence, in Boyle Heights. They know Richard because he has a reputation. He gets into a fight at the party, a bunch of guys jump him, and he is stabbed to death.

In gang folklore there is always a payback, even if it takes years. It so happens that one of the other members of the gang is at the Cleland House Neighborhood Center when some guys from White Fence who jumped Richard show up in the territory of the El Hoyo gangs. Members of that gang decide on revenge. This guy beats the shit out of a few White Fence gang members. A few are hurt; one ends up dying. The guy from our gang gets his face opened up with a hook knife used in roofing. It takes him about three or four years, but one day while in prison the same guy spots the guy who cut up his face. There is a fight and the White Fence guy dies. No one knows who is responsible.

That is how gang culture works. It is all about territory. You know, "This is my barrio," they boast. Gang fights end up happening because somebody, like my friend Richard, violates the territory—or allegedly disrespects a woman belonging to another gang. That's how it starts—and it doesn't stop. You hit them and they come back and hit you. It goes back and forth like that. Somewhere along the way you forget how it got started.

As bad as it is back then, it's nothing compared to what it is now. Today, they don't fight with fists or knives; now they pull out guns and start shooting. When we grow up, there are values, as crazy as it may seem. Although gangs are known from their inception to the time I'm a kid for carrying on long-term feuds and members don't even remember why they are fighting because it goes on for so many years, there is honor among thieves. You never involve a family member who is not involved with the gang. You never attack or hurt a woman or go after the girlfriend of a rival gang member. You always respect parents and elders.

Whatever problem you have with a rival gang, it is not with the family or the girlfriend of the other gang members. That's the difference between the old, traditional established gangs and what we see today, where there is absolutely no respect for human life. A person may be a victim of gang violence and it has nothing to do with his or her membership in a gang; the person may just be standing with a gang member's family, at the wrong place at the wrong time. Everybody is a target.

It seems a lifetime ago, but when Richard Marquez dies, it is devastating for me. He is just starting junior high school. And he is my friend.

While I never advertise being in a gang around my mother and father because they will kill me, we are still the Cutdowns. This goes on until junior high school and then it is over for me. I start distancing myself from this crowd. A lot has to do with my family. I also know the gang culture doesn't lead anywhere I want to go. I don't want the gang to be the rest of my life.

Many of the guys I grow up among and go to school with from the gangs become drug addicts or alcoholics or close to it. One thing they don't do is recreational drinking; they drink to get drunk—regularly. Some things are hard to shake.

I am also exposed to and pick up some habits from being with my older friends, like drinking, that stay with me a long time after I decide to abandon the gang lifestyle. They come back to haunt me.

My greatest regret in life is that this addiction interferes with the things I want to do. I don't regret that I never attain higher political office because I don't have that kind of ambition. I'm not cut out for executive office. At one time, some of my friends want me to run for mayor of Los Angeles. I want to be a congressman, but when the time comes I don't choose to go in that direction. I love my time in the legislature and I learn to love my time on the city council. What I do at these two institutions where I serve best suits my interests and talents in helping to bring change to the people I care about.

My life is always spent jumping right up to the line and doing crazy things, but always keeping to the right side of the line. I learn early how to game the system and maneuver on the line while never crossing over it.

Still, a practice that carries through the rest of my life is that I know many guys from the old neighborhoods—even though I don't have anything to do with gang activity after my mid-teens. That's a fact various law enforcement agencies have a hard time accepting over the years, even when I serve in elected office, although eventually they do.

So now I look back on it all and ask the question, why me? Only one insight makes any sense: Although my life goes down a very different path than many of my friends, we really aren't much different. I certainly never think I am any better than they are. We band together at a young age out of camaraderie and devotion, relying on and protecting each other to survive in a rough place. Those experiences color our lives from then on.

They also shape my motivation for seeking a career in public life; my political career begins by getting involved in student government, just as my gang association ends. I sense from an early age that politics is about power: Who gets it? How much? How effectively do you use it and for what purpose?

I learn from my father growing up that Mexican Americans are often poorly served by the American political system, from the local to the national levels. Yet I come to believe in that system, but not blindly or naively. Power accrues to those who know how the system works and who work hard to make it respond to their needs. Essential to achieving power are a clear vision of where you are going, the commitment to work tirelessly for that vision, and the internal fortitude to sustain yourself during the struggle.

Therefore, I always believe the measure of a politician is what he or she accomplishes rather than what he or she says or how he or she says it. The contemporary fascination in American politics with image over substance and words over actions often puts me at a disadvantage and leads people to underestimate me since I am not seen as performing very well during debates or in front of audiences. Others are seen as more accomplished than me when it comes to those things.

From a personal standpoint, I don't have any worries. That's the nature of the political game that I choose as my life's vocation. But I like to think I best most of my colleagues behind the scenes in the day-to-day nitty-gritty of cutting deals, leveraging influence, counting votes, and forging compromise, which is where the real work of politics, at least legislative politics, takes place.

Too often reporters, pundits, and most ordinary people view the work of politicians—sometimes dismissed as "back-room" politics—as something undesirable and unseemly. What I do regret is the diminishing appreciation of how exciting and constructive politics can be. You can accomplish much for the public good. How ironic that the critics and commentators who don't dare expose their own personal lives to public scrutiny are so quick to pass glib judgment over those who choose to follow the path of public service.

So I always believed the goal of politics is to do something good for people. Achieving that goal requires the skills of negotiating and compromising with other politicians whose personal or constituent interests are not always the same as your own. That recognizes plain reality, the world as we find it. I am always impatient with so-called gadfly or maverick politicians who clamor about how they want to "empower" the people or with good-government do-gooders who brag about how "accountable" they are to the voters. Because they operate from an idealized illusion of reality, my experience is that their methods of political practice are less honest and more dangerous than those who deal and compromise for the sake of solving a real problem, righting a genuine grievance, or fulfilling an authentic social need. Because gadfly or good-government politicians also frequently can't be trusted to keep their word or fulfill a commitment, they can become ineffectual.

This book is about the improbable odyssey through American politics and government of one politician who proudly embraces the label. It also chronicles the journey over several decades of a community that is finally gaining maturity and strength and coming into its own in the political arena. Mostly, it's about how one politician learns how to make things happen and get things done, and why.

Chapter 1

Where I Come From

I am born on May 15, 1943 at the old White Memorial Hospital on First Street in Boyle Heights and raised in East Los Angeles, where I live until the age of 20. It's a place that changes ethnic hands several times in the last century and becomes, when I am growing up, a port of entry for Mexican and Central American immigrants and refugees.

Even today, you can quite successfully live in Boyle Heights without knowing a word of English or eating a crumb of what we know as American food. Mass is celebrated in Spanish as well as English, goods and services are advertised and delivered in Spanish, and entire lifetimes can be spent without having to speak English or assimilate into American culture. That is also what it is like in my day.

Before Latinos come to dominate the place, Boyle Heights is the port of entry in the West for immigrants arriving from Europe, especially Jews. East Los Angeles is the city's first Jewish community before the Fairfax District, the strip of real estate along Fairfax Avenue on the west side of L.A. where Canter's Restaurant and a bunch of Jewish businesses and shops cater to recently arrived Jewish immigrants or migrants from other parts of this country. Such establishments—kosher butcher shops, delis, bakeries, barber shops, book stores, and other retail outlets, including Zellman's Department Store—first take seed in L.A. around the corner of Brooklyn Avenue (now Cesar Chavez Avenue) and Soto Street and flourish there from around 1910 until the 1950s. There is every kind of business that a small thriving community needs. In the years after the Second World War, Jews begin moving west to the Fairfax District and into other West L.A. neighborhoods.

The last vestige of Jewish life in Boyle Heights is the Breed Street Shul or synagogue, which in its day is the center for the Jewish community at 247 North Breed Street. Services stop being performed at the Breed Street Shul in 1986, the structure is abandoned and it falls into disrepair. The rabbi who controls the property wants it demolished and turned into housing. I remember it well growing up in Boyle Heights during the '50s. Years later, as an L.A. city councilmember, I prohibit demolition, get it designated as an L.A. city historical landmark in 1988, and work on preserving the shul. It helps in 1998 when then-First Lady Hillary Clinton visits the shul and includes it in her Save America's Treasures campaign. At my urging, the Los Angeles City Council eventually turns the property over to the Jewish Historical Society of Southern California, which is rehabilitating it.

Nearby is the former Mount Sinai Clinic, which later evolves into the famed Cedars Sinai Medical Center in Beverly Hills. At 4th Street and Boyle Avenue is a neighborhood settlement center, a forerunner of the settlement houses that spring up throughout the country. It is there that Jewish immigrants turn for help to find housing, access social services, organize unions, and take civics classes to become U.S. citizens. Here the Committee to Protect the Bill of Rights is formed in the early 20th century by local activists; some of them are also members of the Communist Party. The location still serves today as a neighborhood center for seniors, now mostly Latinos.

A short distance away, across the street from Hollenbeck Park, is the Jewish Home for the Aged, which is still there and serving all area residents.

Jewish businesses and stores exist side by side with those that are owned by and cater to Latinos. I know all the little Mexican restaurants, *carnecerias* (meat stores), *panaderias* (bakeries), plus local mom-and-pop barbershops, drug stores, and other small businesses. The retail and eatery hub, the Latino business district for Boyle Heights, is concentrated on Brooklyn Avenue, from St. Louis Avenue on the west to just past Soto Street on the east.

I remember how some businesses that accommodate Latinos are actually owned by Japanese Americans. There is Brooklyn Market, a large grocery store also on Brooklyn Avenue, a block east of Soto, owned by the Inadomi family and targeting new immigrants who are Mexicans.

Boyle Heights and the City Terrace neighborhood, with modest homes set up and down a hill overlooking downtown L.A. to the west and California State University, Los Angeles to the north, are true examples at the time of the ability of divergent groups of people to live in close proximity and coexist generally peaceably with one another. When I am growing up there are still Jews living there, although most eventually move out. Immigrants from Armenia, Japan, Russia, and China replace them. Yet Mexicans populate the area in ever-greater numbers, and they eventually turn into Mexican Americans, who later call themselves Chicanos and now Latinos. (I'm still partial to Chicanos, the term popularized in the '60s and '70s, but that shows my age.) Today, Latinos still populate Boyle Heights, but the Mexican Americans are now in the minority; new immigrants from Mexico make up the majority today.

I recall Boyle Heights as a rich mosaic of many cultures and peoples. Some of the Jewish families who live there for years are still residents then or own and run businesses. Elderly Japanese Americans who inhabit Boyle Heights for decades before World War II are present. In fact, one of the largest retirement homes for Japanese Americans in California, perhaps in the nation, even now is located in Boyle Heights as is one of the biggest Chinese cemeteries in the country. The Japanese Home for the Aged is a topnotch place that still operates with support from the Japanese-American community and the government of Japan. Visitors to the home, the residents' children and grandchildren, now come from outside the area because very few live around there any longer. I guess the same is true for visitors to the Chinese cemetery.

This is where I am born and grow up. It is where I learn about people and about the streets. It is where my social and political aspirations and beliefs take root. This is where the Zoot Suit Riots take place during the Second World War, when Anglo sailors and marines set upon and severely beat young Latinos sporting the high-waist wide pants with tight cuffs at the ankles plus long coats with padded shoulders and wide lapels.

Boyle Heights is also the birthplace of the Community Service Organization, founded in the late 1940s by legendary community organizer Fred Ross and sponsored by Chicago-based Saul Alinsky and his Industrial Areas Foundation. CSO empowers barrio residents to register to vote, go to the polls, and seize political power to bring about much-needed changes in their communities. The group elects Edward R. Roybal to the L.A. City Council in 1949, the first Latino to serve on that body since the 19th century. (In 1986, I became only the second Latino, after Ed Roybal, to be elected to the council in the 20th century.) CSO also spearheads the response by the Latino community to Bloody Christmas in 1951, when seven Latino youths are savagely beaten by Los Angeles police officers. That response leads to the indictment of eight officers, the first time LAPD cops are prosecuted for beating Latinos. That is a big deal back then. I remember people talking about it when I am a kid.

CSO soon expands to cities across California, including San Jose in 1952, when Fred Ross recruits and trains a 25-year-old former migrant farmworker in the East San Jose barrio they call *Sal Si Puedes* (Get Out If You Can). Thus begins the remarkable organizing career of Cesar Chavez, who two decades later plays a huge role in my life. Cesar lives in Boyle Heights, directing the statewide CSO for three years before returning to Delano to found what becomes the United Farm Workers of America.

Boyle Heights is part of my old state assembly district (the 55th) and city council district (the 14th). To be sure, there are many other parts of the district I serve and that support me when I run for election and reelection. But Boyle Heights still tugs at my heart most strongly. It is always my political home ground. It is where I am born and where I live until about the age of five.

We live there on Rogers Street in back of the old Bravo Medical Clinic, which is at Soto and Rogers streets. Our house is a small, simple, wood-frame structure. Today it is probably considered a Craftsman home, with a tiny patch of lawn out in front and some short stairs leading up to a porch. The house is narrow in front, but deep, with two bedrooms, one bath, a little kitchen, and small sitting room. That is the place of my first memories with my family, my father, Jose Paz Alatorre, my mother, Maria Martinez Alatorre, and my sister, Cecelia, who I share a bedroom with.

My father is born in the border city of Juarez, Mexico, across from El Paso, Texas, where he lives until age 13. Like all border towns, Juarez is a difficult place to live. Yet it has a unique history. For several centuries Juarez is the gateway to the United States from Mexico, specifically to California and Los Angeles, for many Mexican immigrants. Many people, like my family, move from Juarez across the Rio Grande River to land in Isleta, a small Latino town on the U.S. side of the border in the outskirts of El Paso. It is through Juarez that Cesar Chavez's grandfather, Cesario, emigrates to the U.S. in the early 1880s from the Mexican state of Chihuahua, leading a wagon train drawn by oxen.

My grandmother brings my father to live in Isleta when he's a teenager. From there they move to East Los Angeles, probably in the early 1920s, and settle in the Belvedere area. My grandmother, being a strong and resourceful woman, runs her own grocery store and prospers by comparison to others in the community. My father attends Belvedere Junior High School, as I later do, but he doesn't graduate. As a young man he works for Cleland House, the neighborhood center run by the Presbyterian Church. Later, he is a final repairman for O'Keefe and Merritt, making sure completed appliances are properly built and correctly assembled before going out for sale. He works there for about 37 years, right up until his death.

The only one in the family who is regularly employed is my father. My mother is a trained cosmetologist, but my father, like most Mexican men, feels his wife's responsibility is to look after the home and raise the kids. Sometimes my mom takes over serving the clientele at my aunt's beauty shop, which she operates on the backside of her house, when my aunt takes her trips to Mexico. But that is only for limited periods of time. Otherwise, my father is a very traditional Mexican husband; he's the breadwinner of the family. I don't think my mother works full time from when she is married until my father dies, when I get her a job working for the Head Start program in East L.A. It is the first real steady job she has.

My father believes very strongly that the man rules the house. My mother always makes my father number one in the household. It takes me a long time to figure out that things aren't quite the way they seem. Whenever there is a decision to be made about whether I can do something important, my father, while he projects this image as head of the household, answers yes so long as my mother says it's okay. He goes to the bank every Friday after getting paid, deposits his check, takes money out, and gives it to my mother to do the shopping and pay all the bills. Despite what my father wants to pretend, it is essentially a matriarchal family where my mother plays a very important role.

Funny thing is, whenever I'm going to be punished by my father, I turn to my mother who tries to negotiate with my dad. Nevertheless, when it comes down to it, my father plays a very profound role in my life.

From my father I learn values, the work ethic, and a keen interest in civic and political affairs. Even though the family is not political, I remember my dad has us sit in front of the television set and watch Adlai Stevenson at the Democratic National Convention in 1956, my first recollection of witnessing a major political event. The next candidate who is nominated at a Democratic convention is John F. Kennedy, which happens in Los Angeles in 1960. That year my father takes me to my first political rally as a young man, for Kennedy's presidential campaign at East Los Angeles College. I never forget the day. I am a senior in high school. It is pouring rain. The college football stadium is packed with 20,000 people despite the poor weather. The candidate is two hours late.

I'm more interested in getting the fuck out of the rain, getting away, and being warm. My father says, "No, this is an historic event you will never forget." In his mind, the Kennedys represent the future. John Kennedy is the first major national politician who comes into our community seeking our votes and talking about the plight of the poor, making it part of his political agenda. My dad sees him as a politician who cares about the poor and wants to make life better for those who don't have a voice. Kennedy carries East L.A. by huge margins in the 1960 fall election. Eight years later in the California Democratic presidential primary, his brother, Robert F. Kennedy, wins East L.A. precincts with 99 and 100 percent of the vote. Like many from my generation, President Kennedy has the deepest impact on the way I view the world.

Among the things I identify with the Kennedy administration are creation of the Peace Corps, the struggle to get to the moon, the proposed Civil Rights Act that Lyndon B. Johnson passes in 1964, and establishment of the Office of Economic Opportunity that predates LBJ's War on Poverty. Most important is the idealism JFK brings to politics. That a rich family invests its time and energy to change things teaches me and many others that one person can make a difference. That is the genesis of my politics, which I come to see as a viable means to help the poor and disadvantaged.

I actually know relatively little about poverty in those days even though I live in an impoverished community with chronic high unemployment, low incomes, and high dropout rates. With all those negatives, my father has a regular job, provides a home and shelter, brings food to our table, clothes us, and stresses the importance of a good education. From those standpoints, I think we are rich compared to other families I know who live around me.

I also think we are rich because I believe my father makes a lot of money. You have to understand that we own our own home. My father actually owns two houses. There is the house we live in for part of my growing up and the bigger one we later move into next door. He buys the homes from his sister. My father religiously makes payments to my aunt every week, until he pays off the two places.

The home in Belvedere where we move into when I am five is a stucco house with a one-car attached garage, two bedrooms and one bath opening onto a hallway. There is a larger front lawn that I have to mow every Saturday. In the days before air quality control districts there is an incinerator in the backyard alongside a clothesline where we burn the household trash.

In the seventh grade, we move to the bigger house next door while my father rents the smaller one. It is two stories with two bedrooms upstairs. Downstairs is a living room, a formal dining room, laundry room and den. My sister and I share a bedroom upstairs. I consider it a mansion in comparison to what is around us. It is considered the nicest house in the neighborhood.

My parents make a conscious decision not to have more children so my sister, Cecelia, who is a year and a half older, and I can get the best possible education and other opportunities given my father's limited income. My father and mother decide it is better to have only two children and provide properly for them rather than raise a larger family where it is a lot more difficult to do a good job for their kids. That reasoning runs contrary to most Mexican couples that often produce very large families.

In fact, my father's greatest aspiration in life is to see Cecelia and me graduate from college and lead an easier and more fulfilling life than his job hands him. He hates his job, but it feeds the family so that is that. An incredibly likable and intelligent man, my father gives his all for us to be educated and to go out and serve our community. It is only through an education, he believes, that I will find a job or profession that I like and through which I can be a contributing member of society. Without an education, I'll have to be satisfied with working with my hands, which he determines early in my life I am not capable of doing.

It is because my father works for such a long period of time for one company that I think ours is a rich family, relatively speaking. We are really rich because of the fact that the greatest man I ever meet in my life is my father.

He influences me more than anyone. We eat at a certain time each day. At the dinner table there are discussions about what we do during the day. We discuss what is going on around us. My father is not a joiner of any organization as much as he is politically aware, well informed, and relatively sophisticated. He always votes; my mother does the same. I often hear them discuss the issues of the day. My dad ingrains in my mind from a very early age that you have a responsibility to give back for what you are being given.

There are many things my father teaches me that I am never able to ask him about because he dies too soon. I am never able to ask what he means when he says, "You make your bed and you lay in your bed." I think he means you accept responsibility. Or he says, "If something happens to you, it's nobody's business. It's up to you to figure it out." Or "Your business is your business; it stays within the family." I think he is saying to resolve your own problems and don't tell others about them.

He teaches me that if in your lifetime you can count your true friends on the figures of one hand, you should consider your life to be successful. He teaches

The parents of Richard Alatorre and his older sister, Cecelia Alatorre, decide to only have two children so they can offer them the best possible education.

me about friendship and the difference between true friends versus acquaintances and passersby.

For a man with only a seventh grade education, he is very well read, very concerned about the world and about his community, and a wise man. He instills in us the importance of obtaining an education and impresses on me the sad fact of politics that Mexicans don't have their own elected representatives who can better represent their interests.

Another profound impact on me is my grandmother, Francisca Alatorre. She dies at the age of 105, although it is more likely around 110. She is vain and never tells her real age. We can't get her to show us a birth certificate. She is 100 years old for five years. But she leads a fascinating life and is probably the most important source of my cultural upbringing as a Mexican American living in the United States.

She relates mesmerizing stories of going to dances and parties while living in Mexico where famed revolutionary General Francisco Pancho Villa is in attendance. My grandmother tells how she rides with him, which would make her one of the female companions who accompany Villa's troops during the Mexican Revolution. Although these *soldaderas*, or female fighters, are romanticized and portrayed in *corridos*, or ballets, such as La Adelita, they rarely fight in battles and are often wives or girlfriends of Villa's men.

It's unclear what role, if any, my grandmother plays with Villa during the revolution, but she does know him personally and tells powerful stories about what a great man he was and what he means to the people of Mexico, stealing from the rich and giving to the poor. She makes him into a modern day Robin Hood.

Most important, she teaches me about Mexico's past and about its culture. She insists we speak Spanish to her although she is fully fluent in English, even though she claims not to speak or understand it. I realize this fact because in those days there is no Spanish-language television. Yet my grandmother spends much of her time in front of the TV set watching Roller Derby, boxing, wrestling, and some soap operas, all of them in English. Still, she refuses to speak English and feels her language is Spanish. If you speak to her in English, she responds in Spanish. It is just her way. I don't believe she ever becomes an American citizen, even though she lives most of her life in the United States. My grandmother loves this country, but she loves Mexican history and culture more.

The Mexican part of me, and whatever language development I have in Spanish, comes from my grandmother due to her constant reinforcement. I start school speaking relatively little English. In class, the teachers chop off the Spanish. I quickly learn you don't speak Spanish, even on the playground. You get punished for using Spanish; they berate you for conversing in a foreign language and report you to the principal's office. You learn real fast what you can't do. As a result, like a lot of people from my generation I don't get to learn Spanish fully and actually have a hard time, and sometimes still do, speaking proper English.

I'm first put into EMR classes, for educationally mentally retarded children. I have a hard time speaking English because I'm nervous with the language, and I stutter. I know I'm not dumb or stupid. I resent being singled out when parents come to visit the classroom. The teachers stand me up to read and do stuff like that so they can show the parents, "What a good job we're doing with our kids."

My grandmother makes it a point of saying to us, and teaching us, that it is important to know our native language, Spanish. But because we live in this country and the language of this country is English, she says it is also important we learn English, even as we never lose sight of the importance of our first tongue. My father speaks Spanish at home, but also understands it is necessary to master English. Since my grandmother says it was so vital that we learn English, I once ask her why she doesn't speak it. She replies it doesn't apply to a lady of her age. Case closed. You never argue with my grandmother. She can be mean and tougher than shit. She doesn't exactly come of age in the glory times of life, when things are prosperous and plentiful. She can be very demanding on people, and that probably serves her well.

Francisca Alatorre lives the entire time I can recall in the same house across the street from where we live at Michigan Street and Herbert Avenue in the Belvedere part of East Los Angeles. Living in the same house as my grandmother is

Richard Alatorre, his grandmother Francisca Alatorre, his father Jose Alatorre, and his sister Cecelia. Richard's grandmother teaches him about Mexican culture and history.

my aunt Francis Benitez, who owns the home. Her husband, my uncle Juan Benitez, runs a little *joyeria*, or small jewelry store, on First Street in East L.A., where he fixes watches and designs and sells jewelry.

We assume he is a rich guy. He is the only man I knew in the neighborhood where I live who goes to work every day in a nice suit. He always has no more than a two-year old luxury car. But we never see customers in his *joyeria*. We theorize many things taking place in that little shop, from gambling to selling hot goods. Still, Uncle Juan is never in trouble with the law.

He doesn't have much to do with my side of the family because, coming from the Mexican state of Jalisco, he is light skinned and feels superior to darker-skinned Mexicans.

It turns out my aunt is the one with the money, made from the small beauty shop she runs in the back of her house where my mom sometimes fills in. She is able to accumulate property and money in the bank, enough to educate her children in whatever they want to do. They all go to Catholic schools from kindergarten through 12th grade; my cousin goes on to the University of Southern California.

Growing up, as much as my mother loves my grandmother, her husband's mother, she doesn't necessarily appreciate the fact that my father always goes to visit with his mother after work and before he comes home.

Every day of his working life, before he arrives home, my father stops and sees his mother, almost at the same time of day. They have a glass of wine, a beer, or a mixed drink together. He maybe spends an hour with her before walking across the street to his own home.

My mother never articulates any resentment; it is to her credit that she gets along so well with my grandmother. Getting a little bit older, I notice that when we are all going to Mass on Sunday—my grandmother goes to church with my father and our family when we go—if we want to go to an early service and my grandmother prefers a later Mass, we go later. I know my mother comes to love her as her own mother. But to my father, my grandmother is a guiding light and a source of strength.

My grandmother has a lot to do with me being raised in a family with a strong Mexican tradition. But ironically, her oldest son, my father's brother Antonio Alatorre, who has even darker skin than my father, compensates and chooses to survive in the larger society by assimilating as best he can. He feels this is an easier way to survive and raise his family in an Anglo-dominated society. During the entire time I remember him, he lives with his family in South Gate, then an almost all-white community southeast of downtown L.A.

My uncle Antonio works for 40 years at the American Can Company plant south of downtown. When workers try organizing their plant, my uncle isn't for the union. It isn't that he is anti-union; he just chooses to be a company man. He refuses to walk out during a strike. My father, who is strongly for unions, tells me about his brother, embarrassed by the fact Uncle Antonio isn't pro-union. My father finds it awkward that his brother tries so hard to assimilate. It doesn't make a difference at work; the company takes advantage of him and abuses him just the same.

One of my memories is traveling with my grandmother during the 1950s on the annual vacations we take by car to places like Ensenada, Baja California, or El Paso, Texas. We listen to her stories the entire way. There is the time as a young lady she gets to meet and dance with William H. Bonnie, also known by his alias, Billy the Kid, at a dance in El Paso, during the late 19th century. She says he is very handsome and that he has an infamous reputation when it comes to women, robbing banks, and other questionable enterprises. She enthralls us with stories of her youth and what life is like in El Paso before she moves with her family to Los Angeles.

I remember those trips for other reasons too. We never eat at most restaurants on the highways to Texas because they don't serve Mexicans. We either have to go to the back entrance or order our food to go. This is something that really bothers my father. It brings back an incident that happens during the Depression when he is working construction in Los Angeles.

He goes to have lunch at a local eatery one day and notices everyone is being served except him. When he insists on having his order taken, my father is told Mexicans are not served there. It is only then that he notices he is the only Mexican in the place. A proud man, he still insists on being served anyway and is arrested for his trouble. Not only is he humiliated, but also he loses his job since they take him to jail.

Racial discrimination is not an academic matter for my father when I am coming of age. Mondays through Thursdays my mother cooks meals at home. On Fridays, my father brings home food from one of several local restaurants. Saturdays we work around the house and maybe, once in a while, go to a relative's home for the afternoon and stay for dinner. By the time I'm in high school, on special occasions we sometimes venture out to a restaurant in nearby Montebello called the French Cafe.

My father never forgets the shame he experiences from racial bias in L.A. or on the road during our trips. Consequently, we rarely venture out of East Los Angeles for entertainment or to eat out.

I remember one time, for some special event, he drives out of East L.A. to take the family to eat. We drive up Sunset Boulevard and west into the Echo Park area. There is a French restaurant there called Taix. He drives around and around the block, trying to work up the courage to take us there for dinner. But I think the fear of being humiliated in front of his family the way he is arrested years before while standing up for his rights is too much for him. He never wants to expose us to such treatment. Anyway, we never do eat at that place.

The fear of racism dogs him in other places too. My father works at many things in L.A. before he marries my mother, and he is successful at most of them. For example, he works as a caddy on a golf course.

My father is a good golfer. At the time it is hard enough for him to be a caddy. You see very few Mexicans on golf courses in the city back then. Nevertheless, he often gives pointers to the golfers he is caddying for, advising them about the right golf clubs to use and correcting their swings. One of my dreams as a boy is when I get older taking up golf and playing together with my father. It never comes to pass because he dies early in life.

When we move to our new home in Belvedere from Boyle Heights, there is a neighborhood of single-family homes called Bella Vista, sandwiched between Belvedere (still considered East Los Angeles) and Monterey Park to the east. Many Chicanos see Bella Vista as a step up from East L.A. My father is thinking of maybe buying in Bella Vista because it is a better neighborhood and we can go to better schools.

I'll always remember one Saturday or Sunday in the early 1950s. We have a (relatively) new 1948 Dodge, and our family drives around, stopping when we see a "for sale" sign. My father has us stay in the car while he goes inside. Each time he comes back and says the house either costs too much money or has already been sold. Later we find out the owners don't want to sell to Mexicans. He tries keeping it from us; my mother tells us years later that is the reason.

Of course, Monterey Park or Montebello, communities adjacent to East L.A., are not even considerations. They are primarily white then and much too expensive for someone making $120 a week, even though my father has equity in the homes he owns.

My father does and doesn't want to move. He feels comfortable where he is in East L.A. When he dies, you can never get my mother out of there. She too feels comfortable and safe where she lives. Unlike others from that generation who encourage their children to "escape the barrio," my father always insists we give back to the community because of what we are able to achieve both on our own and with the community's help.

Even though we move to Belvedere from Boyle Heights when I am a young boy, the area is still considered gang-ridden and poverty-stricken. I attend Belvedere Elementary School, Belvedere Junior High School (the last school my father attends), and Garfield High School.

When he gets married to my mother, my father decides he will hold onto the job at the appliance company, regardless of how unsatisfying it is to him personally. Perhaps for that reason he constantly encourages his children to get an education so we'll be able to have a choice about where we work and what we do in life. He wants us to have the education he didn't get. My father believes getting an education is even more critical for me.

To my father's frustration, he and I find out early in life I'm not very good with my hands. They joke that I can't even screw in a light bulb. My father, on the other hand, is very handy around the house and everywhere else. My lack of skill is irritating because he tries to teach me. He has me help him. But whenever I try, it is a disaster.

My father can be verbally abusive. He has a voice that scares the shit out of everybody. Everyone in the neighborhood is afraid of him. You see, he has a strong personality. He wears a mustache and seldom smiles. Think about what it means going to work your entire adult life at a job you hate. He makes me feel like a dumb schmuck. In Spanish, he calls me *cabron*, bastard, or *pendejo*, which means asshole. Come Saturday and much of Sunday he'll be out doing things around the house. Like any kid, I want to work with my father. But invariably, I come running back into the house after my father yells at me because I haven't done something right. He finally tells me not to bother trying; he'll do it himself. I come running to my mother who says not to pay attention to my dad because he doesn't mean what he says.

Yet the lesson he hammers home is simple: you can't do any of this stuff. I try teaching you. You'll be a failure using your hands. What you have to do is use the brain that God gives you. Once again, his insistence is on getting a good education.

I leave the gang while still in junior high school, and start distancing myself from gang activities. But if I ever get into trouble, I know they will always be there for me. I don't need the help. Still, the guys of the gang are my friends. They support me. I play basketball with them, the only real sport I play in junior and senior high school.

There is a gym built on the junior high campus across the street from where we live. That is my safe haven. I spend much of my time playing basketball there. Most of the guys are older so I learn a lot playing with them.

My father insists I get good grades. I'm tracking in the academic program by that time. The classes I take eventually lead me towards the school's college-bound program even though I am a misfit. I don't exactly fit the mold of a good student. I get good grades by getting others, mostly girls, to do my work. I also get into student government.

Most gang members are not joiners of anything socially constructive. They are definitely not into academics. They disdain student government, concluding it's for sissies. I learn that by being in student government, I don't have to do certain school chores that make my life easier in junior high—something I replicate in high school.

For me, being in the gangs at one time supplies me with some valuable street wisdom; it teaches me how to survive in a hostile environment. The hostile environment gang members learn to navigate—to survive threats from rival gangs, the police, and generally being on the streets—I apply to the hostile environment most Chicanos endure in the public schools of the 1960s. Then, too many teachers and administrators develop—and act upon—stereotypes. The main one is that people who look like me aren't going anywhere so why waste your time on them?

So the skills I learn from the gang in order to make it through childhood—how to survive, not get picked on, and not get abused—I apply to making it through school.

I also work from an early age. As a young kid, I have a newspaper route. At age 15, I get a summer job working at a meatpacking plant in Vernon, a tough, gritty industrial area south of downtown L.A.

I am always fond of nice clothes and want to earn money on my own so I can buy outfits for school. We may be poor, but as I say I don't know it. The one thing my father does is always make sure we have a nice house to live in. He buys a car in 1948; I am five years old. We always have clothes—not expensive, but nice clothes. My father clothes us. We get new clothes at the beginning of the school term and they have to last for the rest of the school year.

Because I'm in elected class office, both in junior and senior high school, I think I have to wear suits. Since I want to look good, at first I buy what they call continental suits. Then three-piece suits become fashionable. That is what I am into. Ultimately, much later I graduate to Italian suits and nice accessories. My biggest vice is always nice clothes. I find the latest styles at Zieler & Zieler, a haberdashery across the street from Los Angeles City College. Seeing the advertising in the newspaper, I go there.

I learn the value of money and what it can get you at an early age. I save money from my paper route. Getting the job with Hoffman Packing Company, the Vernon meatpacking plant, is my choice. It isn't something my father insists on or forces me to do.

At first I want to be a box boy at a supermarket. Because it is unionized, you can become a union member and make decent money. I can't land the job. I apply and somebody else always seems to get it.

One day I'm talking with my uncle, Charlie Rico, a Teamsters Union organizer. Summer is coming soon and I tell my uncle I really want to get a job. He asks when I get out of school. I tell him. "How about I get you a job at one of the companies in Vernon?" he offers. "I'll talk to a friend of mine who's the owner at Hoffman Packing."

My uncle can get me work precisely because he knows the owner of the plant. Uncle Charlie organizes many of the big meat packing plants across the city of Vernon, which is, and remains, a tough place. At first, the companies don't want unions. The workers are rough guys: butchers, packers, truck drivers—and guys who work on the kill floors slaughtering animals. My uncle organizes all of them. He too is a big, tough guy, the muscle of the union. He lives and breathes the union. In later years, he organizes food caravans to support the Delano grape strikers and pickets and marches with Cesar Chavez, but he isn't into nonviolence.

My father once tells me Uncle Charlie is at a party with his first wife when some guy dances with her, pissing off my uncle. He calls the guy out, they get into a fight, the guy pulls out a hook and mangles his face. My uncle proceeds to beat the crap out of the guy with his hands.

When a strike hits the plant where my father works, Uncle Charlie goes to support the picket line. A trucker decides he is going to drive through the line. My uncle drags the guy out of his truck and tells him he isn't going to cross the picket line and if he sees him there again, things will get very unpleasant. The driver leaves and never comes back.

Once, in the midst of all the bad publicity about Jimmy Hoffa, president of the International Brotherhood of Teamsters, I ask Uncle Charlie about the union. His answer is very simple: "When you look at the Teamsters, look at all the rights and working conditions they won. Without Jimmy Hoffa, we would have nothing." Uncle Charlie is indicted for his union activities. He dies before he can stand trial, but he is always proud of everything he does on behalf of the workingman. He ingrains that pride into me.

They pay union wages at Hoffman. I work as a packer, loading trucks on the graveyard shift. I make cardboard boxes and pack them with meat. I work in the big refrigerated rooms where meat is stored. The men can never figure out how I get the job because I'm underage. I am about 15, but clearly look young, weighing maybe 100 pounds. Let's put it this way: if the wind is up, it carries me away.

Different assignments are given to me. The men can be chickenshit. They have me do things they know I can never handle, and then laugh at my misfortune. One day I'm in the cooler helping a butcher who's cutting up the meat. At first, I can't distinguish between different types of meat: one is rounds—big pieces of meat the butcher uses to cut sirloin steaks. The other is half a steer, which is when the cow is cut in half, so it weighs a lot. The butcher says, "Go get that piece of meat," and he points to half a cow. You have to lift it up and yank it off the hook where it is hanging from the ceiling. So I get a good handle on the half steer. It weighs more than me, 150 pounds or so. I lift it up on my shoulders and it starts taking me all over the place. Everyone starts laughing. Finally, one of the guys says, "You stupid asshole, you're going to hurt yourself."

Not long after that my Uncle Charlie swings by and sees me. I'm eating off by myself. "How you doing?" he asks.

"Not good," I reply.

"What's wrong?"

"These fucking guys—I'm trying to do my job. All they do is laugh at me." I relate the story about trying to lift the half a cow.

"Stay right here," my uncle says. "I'll be back."

The next thing I know is all the workers run into the big locker—the cooler—because they hear there's a fight. I don't go; my uncle tells me to sit there so I do. What I find out is Uncle Charlie enters the meat locker and proceeds to beat the shit out of this one guy who is giving me grief. My uncle comes back to where I am and says, "Rest assured, they won't give you another problem again."

These are all his men. They are loyal to him. Once everyone else finds out who I am, I have no more problems. I end up working as a butcher's helper at Hoffman.

I can't say it is enjoyable to work, but I make a lot of money over that summer. I don't realize until later, when I am 17 years old, that I am making more money in the summer I start at the meat packing plant than my dad earns at any point in his whole life. I am making more than $120 a week, which is a lot of money back then. My dad is only being paid about $110 a week at the time, after working more than 30 years for the same company.

It is with great reluctance, I learn much later, that my father drives me to work every evening by 11. We talk while he drives, but I find out later it breaks his heart. Here I am heading to work at 11 p.m. when he is returning home to go to sleep so he can get up early the next morning to go to his job. He hates to see me working those kinds of hours. It doesn't matter to me. It is like anything else: a means to an end, a way to make money during the summer months that can be put aside for school—and be spent on the nice clothes I like or on taking out girls. (I go with friends on weekends, taking a girl out to the movies or doing fast food—Stan's Drive-In or A&W Root Beer.)

I am nearly ready to get my driver's license at age 16, so my father is still driving me around. Talking about the job at Hoffman, he says, "You don't have to do it."

"Yes, you're right," I reply, "I don't have to do it. It's my choice. I need to save money for school, for clothes, and everything else."

My dad always keeps coming back to the importance of finding something I will like to do in my life, whatever it is I ultimately do. During one conversation, my father says he has labored for O'Keefe and Merritt for decades—and emphasizes there is nothing worse in life than having to work at a job and wake up in the morning and hating to go to work.

That conversation and the job at Hoffman reinforce what my father always impresses upon me: I find out what I don't want to do the rest of my life. It isn't as clear as to what I will eventually do. But the meat packing work impresses him in another way.

I make boxes outside the Hoffman plant in a big parking lot where trucks roll in, back up, unload, and pick up. To the side is where the staple machine is located. There are certain size boxes for different cuts of meat or meat products. Late one night after dropping me at work, my father, from a distance so I don't know he is there, watches me work and interact with my co-workers for hours.

My father comes home excited, relating to my mother that while he isn't sure just how good a worker I am, everyone seems to really like me. He is amazed that I seem to get along with people from every age, race, and national origin. That's who works at Hoffman: blue-collar workers, skilled and unskilled, from every walk of life. They are Latinos, blacks, and poor whites; you name it and they are there. Even at that young age, I'm not afraid to talk with people, kids or adults. By that time I have acquired a good gift of gab—the gift of bullshit. I learn how to do that.

I can take the easy way out by agreeing with what my father is saying and quitting my job. He would give me money every week if that's what I want. I guess he is impressed because I want to make my own money and help out the family and myself. I give my mother money every week after getting paid. I don't have to do that either. He is proud of me learning the work ethic: getting to work on time and working for the money they pay me. I suppose any father likes to see his son with good work habits, social skills, and the like.

Still, he feels guilty that his son has to take a job like that. There is a part of him that feels that as much as he tries, he can't give enough to his kids so that one of them has to work at this gritty, tough, manual labor in a meatpacking company in Vernon.

By the time I get home early in the morning, I'm dead tired; all I can think about is going to bed and sleeping. At least, from my parents' point of view, I don't have the time or strength to be out on the streets and getting into trouble. Even on weekends, at least Friday nights, I am still exhausted from the week's work. That doesn't stop me from going out on Saturday nights to do the things I shouldn't be doing, which I do. But my father probably thinks, at least he's only doing it one night out of the week.

Thinking back probably to the 12th grade, nearing graduation from high school, my dream in life is to eventually represent East Los Angeles, where I grow up, in some political office. The big daily newspapers, which my father reads, talk about what is going on citywide or in the state or nation. I try to read the local papers. They are my link to what is happening in the community.

Their editorial policies are fascinating. They are usually the opposite of how the community votes. There are the Kovner Publications. Kovner is more repre-

Richard and his father at his graduation from Garfield High School. Richard's dream even then is to someday represent East Los Angeles in public office.

sentative of the community, from a liberal Jewish Democratic tradition. But on many issues he is still fairly conservative.

The Citizen publications are part of Northeast Newspapers at the time and controlled by Oran Asa, an Anglo, who owns the local "throwaway" papers. One of Asa's papers is the *Belvedere Citizen* that targets my neighborhood. It's what I read every Thursday when it comes out and influences me the most since it is the only vehicle that gives you local news. The *Los Angeles Times* really ignores our community. The only paper that tries to half-ass cover Eastside affairs is the old *Herald Examiner*, an afternoon daily. (That's the paper I deliver as a kid.) There is also the *L.A. Mirror*, which is both a morning and afternoon newspaper. My father reads *La Opinion*, the Spanish-language daily, because he brings it home for my grandmother.

It always amazes me how reactionary the *Belvedere Citizen* is. What offends me most are the candidates it supports for political office, especially Republican presidential candidates. They are totally inconsistent with how most people in the community vote. The *Citizen* also always endorses Anglo over Chicano candidates seeking local or state legislative offices.

Eddie Diaz, a reporter and later editor at the *Citizen*, is kind of the Mexican front guy for the newspaper. He is a Republican himself, but at least he writes newspaper articles about things that are going on in the community. He does a fairly good job of doing that but a horrible job when it comes to political endorsements or coverage of economic issues, where, reflecting his boss, Oran Asa, he is squarely on the side of big business. I think Ed Roybal is about the only Democratic politician they support.

To my recollection, we Chicanos have no real representation when it comes to media coverage of our own community. That is consistent with what my father impresses upon me about how far behind our people are when it comes to political representation. I recall him explaining about gerrymandering and how Anglos use it to keep us politically impotent.

Look at East Los Angeles, my father will say. It is a relatively small area, but it's divided up between several different elected legislators, all Anglos. Politicians who draw legislative boundaries never want East L.A. to be placed into one district, he adds, because then we can more easily elect one of our own to office. Much later on I learn this is one of two major philosophies about gerrymandering and reapportionment. One theory, the status quo at the time, is the favorite of Democratic politicians: you dilute the Chicano vote by dividing Mexicans into a number of adjacent districts so they can help elect Anglo Democratic candidates against Republicans but never put a Chicano into office. The Republican preference is concentrating people from the same race or ethnicity into one district because, in the case of Mexicans, it means they cannot be used to tip the balance for Anglo Democrats in nearby districts.

My father makes it real clear that if we are ever to have people of our community representing us then things have to change. It is a lesson I get to apply later on.

That is why my father is a very profound man. Most people, if they think about these things at all, view problems in the abstract and come up with off-the-wall solutions. He looks at a problem in a basic and straightforward manner. And his solutions made common sense because they are about simple empowerment.

One of my teachers in the sixth grade tells me I will never make it, that I will be in jail by the age of 16. That's because I'm almost a social outcast. I obstruct the class or sometimes find a way of not going to school or spend time in the nurse or principal's offices.

But my father doesn't tolerate me screwing up at school. He kicks my ass if I do. He does that a few times when I am caught. He teaches respect for authority, teachers, and most of all, respect for education. If I mess up, he feels it is his job to straighten me out—real quick.

In those days we have corporal punishment at school. It seems like I spend a lot of time in junior high bending over and getting swatted because I am disruptive. Once, after I am the target of some abusive treatment, my father goes to school and tells the teacher, "You never touch my son again. If he does something wrong, you let me know and I'll take care of it. But that's not your job."

Still, thanks mostly to my father, I am always interested in history, government, and current events. And I love sports. In elementary school, I avidly pour over the *Weekly Reader*, all about current events. That follows in junior high school.

By the second semester of 10th grade, I pretty much check out of high school mentally, in terms of taking my studies seriously. I decide high school is nothing but bullshit.

Nevertheless, as disruptive as I may be I learn how to get good grades by putting in a minimum amount of work—and sometimes no work at all. I engage others to do my homework and term papers. They are almost exclusively girls since there aren't any guys willing to do anything for me and most of them can't do the work themselves anyway. My strategy is pretty successful because in high school, I am on the academic track to go to college. Don't ask me how I get there, but I am. That is where I am headed, to college, in my mind.

I learn other tricks. One of my fond recollections is taking this geometry class from a guy in his waning years as a teacher. I stand in front of him, with his attendance and grading sheets set out in front of him. I'm talking with him, having these long, involved conversations, while I change my grades on the weekly exams to reflect an "A" grade, which is what I ultimately get in the class.

One day I find out there is a teaching manual for the geometry class. I "borrow" it for a bit. It takes care of producing my geometry homework for a whole year. I procrastinate over taking Geometry II because I never learn the basis for Geometry I. I barely get a "D" in the Geometry II class.

I learn how to play the game so well. I know how to bullshit the teachers. I am very popular in school and do whatever it takes to get decent grades—or get others to do it for me. That really gets the teachers mad and resentful towards me because many of them want a reason to throw me out of their classes.

The teachers can be mean-spirited. Students are being considered for an honor society. I should be one of them. The day before the faculty interviews nominees, I go with the basketball team to play Huntington Park High School. The next day I show up at school and my coach asks, "How come you didn't show up this morning?"

"Show up for what?" I reply.

"The students who were nominated [for the honor group] were interviewed by the faculty."

"Nobody even told me," I add.

"That's chickenshit. You have to do something about it," the coach advises.

I ask the faculty sponsor why I'm not notified. If I am traveling for the game at Huntington High, why don't they tell my coach?

"Well, you know, it was an accident," the sponsor says.

I press the issue all the way up the line with the faculty and administration. Basically, everyone just says, "It's too bad. It's your fault."

I am very bitter. Nobody deserves it more than I do. Not only do my grades qualify me, but nobody is more involved with the student body and in the community.

It is a very dormant community in those days, before the start of the Chicano movement, which begins in East L.A. with the high school walkouts at campuses like Garfield. Dropouts are a big issue. But there is no social activism *per se*. The attitude by parents and other residents is kind of like whatever the school does, they know better. I guess most people conclude that whatever problems Chicanos have, they're our fault, not their fault.

Every time there is a school assembly, as student body president I have to go to the principal and tell him what I am going to say to the students. I never do that because he can never find me ahead of time. I just show up for the assembly without having consulted him. The reason is simple: my first assembly at the beginning of the semester I am president, I just roll and shit all over the teachers—that they aren't doing their jobs and everything else.

The principal calls me into his office real fast and informs me I can't do that. "What right do you have to criticize the teachers?" he says.

"Well, tell me what I said that was wrong" about the teachers. He can't tell me anything.

From that point on, I am pretty much censored. So I become more than a social misfit because I have a mouth and I freely express what I feel.

Much to the teachers' dismay, I am always in the academically motivated track that is going to college. Yet I always feel like an oddball in those classes because there are few kids I can relate to. The students in the college-bound classes are squares as far as I am concerned. The people I can relate to are primarily guys who mess up in school, guys who are into playing sports, guys who are in gangs. Initially the decision to go to college is made by my father. I don't decide until the tenth grade.

I am always being called out of class as a student body officer the whole time at Garfield High, and I'm student body president in the last semester of my senior year. I am also a good basketball player and am offered tryouts for the basketball team at California State University, Los Angeles when I go there; they have a great team then.

I have the grades to get into Cal State L.A., but I have some fundamental problems: I never test well. I can't read very well. I also have a hard time getting my high school transcripts sent to Cal State. Teachers say I am just going to drop out and they are doing me a favor by encouraging me to go to junior college. Since I am student body president at the time, I go to the principal and tell him, "They [the teachers] didn't send my grades. They didn't send my transcripts." I report the teachers and they get in trouble. So they are pretty much forced to forward my transcripts no matter what they think.

For me, the end of high school is the beginning of my preparation for my real life. There is no doubt in my mind that I am unprepared for college because

I have never been challenged in high school. Early on it is easy to blame it on the school for not doing a very good job of educating me, which is true. But on reflection, I avoid being challenged and applying myself because I learn I can avoid it—and I do.

Chapter 2

My Awakening

I graduate from Garfield High School in the winter of 1961 and am accepted at Cal State L.A. for the spring semester. By the summer of 1962, I need to get a job. There is an advertisement on the bulletin board at the student employment center on the Cal State campus. The job is working in a jewelry store, helping customers fill out credit applications and serving as a general clerk. I call and they give me an interview.

Having just turned 18, I walk into Birk's Diamond Company on Whittier Boulevard in East L.A. wearing a double-breasted suit. Louis Koransky, the owner, is impressed: here's a young Mexican. He thinks I speak better Spanish than I do, but at least I can speak and understand the language. And I am going to college. He is also impressed with the fact I was student body president in high school. Some people I know come into the store during the interview. He is impressed I know people and they know me. So he gives me the job. It is the beginning of something that carries me all the way through graduation from college in 1965.

I almost don't make it that far. After starting to take college classes, I nearly quit.

Cal State might as well be Harvard as far as I am concerned. I think our high school graduating class numbers 400 or 500 students. Only four of us go on to a four-year college or university. The rest either go to work or to East Los Angeles College, the local community college.

My first day of college, I take the bus and show up at Cal State. Everything is going well for the first three classes. Hal Fishman, the anchorman/news commentator at KTLA-TV, Channel 5, teaches the last class that day, in the Political Science Department. He is a misfit among the professors. He drives a Corvette, but is a bright son-of-a-gun.

You know what the first day of college is like. The professor says, "This is what the class is about, here's what we're going to do, and here's the list of books. Class dismissed."

Fishman comes in a little late. "Here are the books I want you to read," he tells us. "Pick them up after class. This is what we're going to do in class." Then he starts talking about government. Now, I am good in government. Despite my difficulty taking tests in high school, I still score in the 80th and 90th percentile when it comes to the part about government.

But then Fishman starts going around the class, asking questions of students. In high school, I sit in the back of the class. When I'm in college, I sit in the back too. I always try to disappear and get lost so nobody ever asks me questions. Fishman gets me. We are talking about communism. Shit, the only thing I remember studying about that is Karl Marx, who I know wrote the Communist Manifesto. That is the sum and substance of the knowledge I have at the time. After class I'm blown away about how stupid I feel and how smart these other kids in class are. Since it is an introductory class, most of the students are freshmen; it isn't as if I am in with a bunch of sophomores or juniors or seniors.

I'm not sure how much they really know, but they sure express it well. I remember taking the bus home and saying to myself, "I don't know how long I'm going to stay in college." That first day's experience is pretty devastating. First of all, the whole day I don't see a Chicano. I see blacks; blacks I can relate to because I look at them as just like me. But shit, I say to myself, "God damn." I feel so inferior, so insecure. And the feeling just keeps growing. I tell my father how I feel. He quickly hammers home that this is bullshit. "You're better than they are," he says, "and you can't let other people dictate your life." But man, I am feeling on and off the whole rest of the week. Friday I feel just as stupid as I feel on Monday.

After a week of going to college, I'm riding home on the RTD bus; I don't have a car so commuting on public transit is the only option. I'm thinking, maybe Cal State L.A. isn't the school for me. I am overwhelmed by my lack of preparation. I know no one at Cal State. There are very few Chicanos who are going there then. The student body at Garfield High is 95 percent Chicano and five percent others: Asians, some Armenians, and a handful of Anglos. I don't really know anything about what it is like to go to a school with anybody who isn't brown. My first week at Cal State is absolute culture shock. I feel lost. And among the students I do interact with in class, it is obvious how ill prepared I am to do the work.

That Friday, riding the bus home, I think this is going to be my last day at the college. The following day, I tell my father of my decision to drop out of Cal State L.A. and instead enroll at East L.A. College. It takes me a while to work up the courage to tell him while helping him do his work around the house on that Saturday. He says nothing at first; he just keeps on working. I wonder and think: he isn't even sympathetic to my problem.

Then, all of a sudden, he turns to me in his inimitable style and says, "So you decided today you're not going to Cal State L.A. When are you going to come to me and tell me maybe East L.A. College isn't such a good idea either?" I'm not impressed, at first. It is clear he doesn't understand what I am feeling.

Thinking it over, I conclude what he is trying to communicate to me is that if you give up on this today, you will give up on something else tomorrow and never end up accomplishing anything with yourself. He emphasizes for the 2,000th time that my only hope in life is using my mind because I have to abandon any hope of making a living based on my manual skills.

By the end of the day, I make up my mind that it will take me longer to study than others. It takes me three hours to study what somebody else can do in one hour. Although I resent the fact, it doesn't matter how much time it takes me to study for the classes I am taking; I'll put in the time. It just takes me more time than most of my fellow students to finish a day's assignment.

Every day, in between my classes, I'm at the library. Lunchtime I just grab something to eat by myself and run to the library. I stay on campus studying in the library until late at night. After it closes I continue studying at home until the wee hours of the morning—until I finish whatever I need to do. Friday is boys' night out; I head out with my friends drinking and going to dances. All of us have girlfriends and on Saturdays we take them all out somewhere. Sunday morning I head over to whatever university I can find that has an open library. I find it is hard to work at home. I need a place where I don't know anybody, where there will be no distractions. I initially go to the UCLA campus library, but it proves too far from the Eastside. So, until I graduate from college, I go every Sunday to the library at the much more prestigious California State Polytechnic University, Pomona. The library there has one gigantic room where students gather to study. I use that space and time to help prepare myself for classes on the following weekdays, doing reading or working on class projects. I am there until 7 or 8 p.m., when I return home and keep getting ready for that week's classes.

I always wonder when I have time, "Gee, what do other people think? Here's a guy by himself. Gee, I even feel sorry for this poor fuck, me." I never want someone to say that about me. But I make up my mind and tell myself: "Hey, fuck it. I'm going to do it come hell or high water." And I do.

By the end of my first semester, I develop something that totally escapes me in high school: the discipline to study. I become very disciplined in how to utilize my time. There is no choice if I want to graduate. I also discover something else useful, something my father has been telling me: the knowledge that I can compete with anybody.

More than for most freshmen students, for me the jump from high school to college is a huge transformation. An even bigger transformation awaits me as a sophomore.

Low and behold, a year and a half after starting college, I decide to get married to my high school sweetheart, Stella Daniels. And we are going to have our first son, Derrick. Stella and I meet going to junior and senior high school together.

At first, I work at Birk's jewelry store during that summer of 1962. Then I start working Fridays and Saturdays during the week while attending college. By the time college classes began again in the fall of '63, with my newfound family responsibilities, I have to find a full-time job. My employer, Louis Koransky, can't afford to give me what I need so I find employment in downtown L.A. working for Barry's Jewels, another jewelry store, as a credit collector. By that time I have learned how you collect money from people who are in arrears. I work in downtown L.A. until the following year, when Mr. Koransky calls and says he needs me back, at which time I go back with him on a full-time basis.

During my first semester as a sophomore, I take only one class because I am working a full-time job. The class is the history of Mexico. I think I'm going to die. The professor is this lefty guy, Tim Harding, who ends up starting a mariachi. I remember the day I take the final saying to myself, "I'm never going to make it this way."

I go to the financial aid office and find out about a student loan. I make up my mind it will take forever to graduate at this pace and decide the only way I can get through is to go to school full time and work full time too. That is possible because Mr. Koransky agrees to accommodate my class schedule. It takes me four and a half years, from start to finish, to get out of Cal State. I work 60 hours a week and take a full class load.

My daily schedule takes form around my school and work obligations. I start classes at 8 a.m. and finish by 11 a.m. Then I am off to Birk's jewelry store, where I work until 9 p.m. I start studying as soon as I get home, staying up until 2 or 3 a.m. I no longer have the luxury during the week of spending evenings at the library before heading home. That is my life the rest of my time in college. I see it as having two jobs: going to college and continuing my newfound academic discipline is my first job; but the real job that puts food on the table is working as a credit collector and ultimately credit manager at the store Mr. Koransky buys in the nearby city of Commerce, about a mile away from his original business.

We have a small one-bedroom apartment, not more than 700 square feet in Montebello. The beauty of it is this 15-unit complex is new. We live there until Derrick, our first son, is born. Then a friend of my father's buys a duplex nearby in Montebello, adjacent to the State Route 60 freeway, which is then under construction. We move into one of the duplex units, with two bedrooms. The second son, Darrell, is born while we are living there.

You can't imagine the pressure I feel. Stella doesn't work after our first week of marriage—or at any time throughout the period we are married. She stays home to take care of our first son and, soon thereafter, our second son. We have just one car, which I use to go to and from school and work. She feels cooped up in the apartment all day, with no outlets, family, or friends in the immediate neighborhood.

I come home later at night, usually around 9:30. After catching something to eat out so she doesn't have to cook late in the evening, I proceed to study until the early hours of the morning. Sundays I drop her off at her mother's house so I can spend all day at the library studying some more.

Throughout my college years I am never able to have the conventional college experience, the enjoyable and rewarding times most students spend on or around campus interacting with friends, fellow students, and professors. Seeking that experience is what draws me, in part, some years later to start teaching at the University of California, Irvine.

The realization of my responsibilities and all they entail can be overwhelming. To cope with the pressure and rigors of all of a sudden being confronted with having to act like a responsible adult, I start to drink. The drinking isn't debilitating; it never impairs my studying, working, or meeting other obligations. I never drink during the week. But as the years go on, it becomes easier to cope with life by drinking.

The day my oldest son is born, April 15, is the same day my father dies. It is devastating for me, really devastating, to know my father is never going to see my oldest son, his grandson.

It is six o'clock in the morning when Derrick is born. My mother wants to be at the hospital with me but by then my father is already very sick. By 9 a.m., I'm at my mom and dad's house. He's excited for me and for my son. He's still counseling me. It doesn't matter—the man is dying and he's telling me why now it is that much more important for me to finish college; that now I have the added responsibility of a child and how important that responsibility is. I haven't slept for a couple of days. Somehow, I manage to have both of my sons around finals time.

My dad tells me, "Go home and go to bed. You need some sleep."

"I'm going to stay with you in case you need to go to the doctor," I reply.

"I'll be fine," he says.

I remember going home and just passing out. The next thing I know, my mother is calling. "You have to take your dad to the hospital," she tells me. "The doctor told him he has to go in." So I take him. Before we leave he tells my mother that while he's in the hospital he wants her to look after my grandmother. Just before heading to the hospital, he makes me take him to my grandmother's—his mother's—house right across the street. He sits down. He's basically dying.

"I want you to know—I want you to take care of my wife and look after her," he tells his mother. "I'm going to be all right. Don't worry about me."

He has a glass of wine with her.

While I'm driving to the hospital, he's telling me about going to school and about me being a father and all about the things we are going to do together. He's dying to see my newborn kid. I get him into the hospital and no sooner do they roll him into a bed than he has his first heart attack. They put him on oxygen and everything else.

But I know he's all right, I tell myself, because he's pinching the nurse on the ass and kidding around. "Why don't you go home? Have you eaten?" he asks me.

"No, no," I say.

"Why don't you go get something to eat?" he tells me again.

I go get something in the cafeteria. When I walk back into his room he has his last heart attack. He's gone.

Just the Christmas before, for the first time I'm able to sit down with him as an equal, as a man, and let him know how I feel: "What you taught me has done me well," I say. "Don't worry. I'm a man regardless of the circumstances. I accept my responsibilities. School is too important to me, and you don't have to worry about that anymore." We spend four hours together. It's during a family gathering and everyone else is pissed off because the two of us sit in a corner and just talk. We never talk like that before. He's already sick, but we talk a lot about everything we are going to do with one another.

It takes many years for me to fully accept his death, and my feelings of guilt over it. I believe things I do are responsible for aggravating his illness—even though I now know there's nothing I could do about it; his illness is congenital, as we find out later. Still, one time some years before I get in a fight and he finds out about it. He gets sick because he is so worried about me. The circumstances of my marriage are another issue. Getting married all of a sudden makes him worry about me more. Six months later I find out from the doctor that he has to stop working. If he doesn't, he'll die. He chooses to work—and he chooses to die—because, as he tells me later, "I'm going to die anyway. I'll die from working, so I choose to do it this way."

My father's death hits the entire family, immediate and extended, and me very hard. It is the beginning of a cycle. My grandmother's first son dies from tuberculosis. My father dies of a heart attack. Her third son dies of cancer. Her grandson is killed in an automobile accident. She outlives them all.

When my father dies, that leaves me as the only man in a family with my mother and older sister. But the family is matriarchal; the women run it anyway.

At Birk's, the jewelry store, I begin as a credit clerk and end working as credit manager at one of Mr. Koransky's stores. It eventually allows me the flexibility of going to school full time while supporting a family.

Let me tell you, I hate my work. But for me it is a means to an end. I'm so good at working in the jewelry store; I can do it with my eyes shut. It is a family business. I learn a lot about Jews, especially the solid business ethic Mr. Koransky has. He's a shrewd businessman and isn't afraid to take chances when few others are willing to do so in East L.A. The reason is he knows what I know: Chicanos are basically honest and conscientious about meeting their obligations. They want to pay their bills. When nobody else gives them credit, Mr. Koransky does.

He bases it on risk and return. Many times the down payment and the first few regular payments he collects from customers are enough to cover his costs for selling a piece of merchandise. He's smart that way. Even if customers try to skip out, they usually move from one block to another in the same neighborhood and you can find them easily enough through neighbors and relatives. The only problem you have to worry about is overloading them by selling something they can't afford. What does it matter for Mr. Koransky since the money he already collects around the time of sale provides a clear profit. So he is willing to take risks that other merchants won't take.

At first I'm taking credit applications in the store. Later, they get me making calls and collecting money. I get very good at it and become credit manager at the second store he opens in Commerce. I feel badly for some of the people I have to collect money from. Others never give me a reason to feel bad. It's all anonymous since you never use your real name, especially over the phone.

Being nice to customers and getting to know them makes it easier if I have to show up later at their homes to collect. Then they feel bad about not paying the bill. They will always complain about how mean Mr. Torres, another collector, is. "Yeah, I know," I will agree, "he makes it hard for me." If you treat a person nice the first time and they don't live up to their commitment, then you're a little tougher the next time.

One time I go to a house to repossess. It's pretty hard to get things back. This time it's for a big diamond. I accuse the customers of pawning and selling the diamond. "No, it's here," they insist.

"Let me see it," I ask. "I'll be right back to check the serial number." As soon as I get in the car, I'm off.

Most people get behind because they are out of work or they become financially overloaded, as many Chicanos have big families to support. Even then they will pay $5 instead of $10, but they usually pay.

I get so good at it that I can sit down, take a person's credit application, and know whether or not he or she is going to pay. When I explain to the owner why I'm turning someone down, sometimes he insists that the sale go through anyway; he wants to sell. When the customer gets behind in making the payments, I tell Mr. Koransky, "I told you so."

He has a beautiful wife, a nice lady. His son-in-law is credit manager at one store. Mr. Koransky is short and overweight, with a gruff voice; he sounds mean. But he becomes a good friend, is always nice to me and my kids, and contributes to my campaign the first time I run for public office.

I learn how much of a cutthroat business it is. They never want me to be out on the floor selling because I will tell some customers not to buy. They are stupid for buying some of these things. You know how material things are so important to us—rings and stuff for our wives and mothers. Towards the end of my career in the jewelry business, I start to hate it.

One day, as graduation approaches in late 1965, I'm working on this term paper about the federal Head Start program, how it got started, and the formation of a group called the Foundation of Mexican American Studies. I need to interview the foundation's executive director, a guy named Phil Montes. Unbeknownst to me, my professor, a Chicano, hates Phil Montes and Phil Montes hates my professor. The professor thinks Phil is a radical. Phil thinks the professor is a *vendito*, a sellout. But the professor also believes Phil is the best person for me to turn to for my paper.

I show up at Phil's office, the Foundation for Mexican American Studies, at 1421 West Second Street, just west of downtown L.A. He's late. Who is there is Charlie Erickson, who has been working for the foundation with Phil. Charlie, who is the writer and the researcher, is a nice guy. "Sit down," he tells me, "Phil will be here."

Soon Phil walks in. He looks at me and says, "What the fuck do you want?"

I look at him. "Well, I'm Richard Alatorre, and I have an appointment with you."

"What the fuck do you want?" he repeats. Then adds, "Before you do that I have to drop off my car. We can talk on the way."

"I'm doing a term paper. My professor sent me." I name him and tell Phil what it is I'm doing with my term paper.

"Oh, that fucking *vendito*," and Phil starts shitting all over the guy, which kind of blows me away. "How do I know you're not a spy?" he asks.

"Wait, look," I explain, "I don't know why you dislike this guy. I don't like him either. I'm a senior trying to get through college. This is the term paper I decided to do and your name keeps coming up, and that's why I'm here. So don't hold it against me." I tell him my story: married, two kids, things are tough.

By that time we get back to his office, and we talk some more. He gives me the history of the foundation and tells me about another organization, the Association of Mexican American Educators, of which he is president and one of the founders.

I'm about two months away from graduating Cal State. By 1 or 2 p.m., he tells me, "So what are your plans when you graduate?"

"I really don't know. I got to get another job."

By that time Phil knows enough about me, my values, and everything else. I just like the guy. I like the way he talks. He's trying to blow up the Los Angeles Unified School District and Max Rafferty, the very conservative state superintendent of public instruction, over how they're treating, and abusing, Chicano students. I'm for that, given my own experiences with the public schools and school district administration in East L.A. I later find out Phil's building is the place anybody goes who wants to find out anything about Chicanos, education, and everything else. Aside from the studies they do—Charlie Erickson pretty much produces them—Phil and his groups are able to fund the first bilingual Head Start programs in Boyle Heights and the San Fernando Valley through the Council of Mexican American Affairs, a bunch of professionals involved in bilingual and bicultural education.

Richard gravitates toward Phil Montes, a prominent Chicano education and civil rights activist in the 1960s who becomes his mentor. Montes is pictured here in later years.

Phil is an extremely bright and streetwise guy who doesn't grow up in East L.A. His roots are in Gardena, in southern Los Angeles County. He's an educator and psychologist. When I meet him he is probably in his mid-to-late 30s, an effective speaker who is used to doing in-service training on bilingualism and biculturalism at major educational institutions and school districts. Everything I come to learn about the plight of young kids in public education, I learn from Phil and Charlie, and the people who work out of their place.

Phil is loyal to a fault with his friends, a quality I greatly admire. He is viewed by many people as being crude because he has a sharp tongue that borders on vulgarity. But you can't take away from him his knowledge and intellect. His manner of informally expressing himself is not intellectually profound. But when he speaks, it is obvious this is a man way ahead of his time.

He is also viewed by California's educational establishment as not mainstream enough and, in fact, way too far to the left. The status quo of public education affecting Latinos in the mid-1960s is that it's doing as good a job as humanly possible given what it is funded to do. The public schools are geared to the urban Anglo mentality and don't consider all the cultural and linguistic differences Chicano kids bring into the classroom just as they don't take into account the cultural and social differences of African-American kids. (Remember, when I am growing up and attending East L.A. public schools we are punished for speaking Spanish, even on the playground. The only language we are allowed to speak is English. Nothing has changed on the Eastside even as I'm getting ready to graduate from college.)

Back in the '60s, the great majority of kids in public schools are Anglos. Then, California is one of the top states in the nation when it comes to per pupil spending. White parents are generally satisfied with the school system, and their kids for the most part are performing well. Public education is doing a pretty good job by Anglo children so educators never think they should be doing anything differently for Latino or black kids. But the schools aren't doing such a good job for the kids I grew up with and the schools I attended, where the dropout rate is still more than 50 percent, more than twice the average for the state.

In Phil's mind, the tragedy of kids dropping out during my time in public school will continue until the system starts to take into account the fact it is dealing with a totally different cultural and linguistic reality. He is advocating at that time for bilingual education, which is viewed by most conventional educators as a radical, leftist, and revolutionary concept.

All this forms the basis for establishing the Association of Mexican American Educators, created in Los Angeles by Phil from his travels around California. It is dedicated to increasing the number of Chicano teachers—recruiting them, getting them promoted once they are in the classroom and elevating more of them into upper echelon positions as administrators and superintendents—all to bring about change within school systems, including bilingual and bicultural education in the classrooms. (The establishment at this time is into English as a Second Language—the emersion of Chicano kids in the English language.) The Association of Mexican American Educators is also the vehicle for attacking the status quo by pushing for textbook revisions, to make them more relevant to the Chicano experience. Doing all this means challenging and taking on the entire educational establishment, from state schools chief Rafferty (and later Wilson Riles) to local school district administrators and boards of education.

The founder of bilingualism and biculturalism is Dr. Marcos de Leon, a Ph.D. who teaches at Belmont High School. He becomes the association's second president. He and Phil are on the same side but where de Leon is the intellectual, Phil is the activist. De Leon's strength is the credibility of his advocacy; he is hard to argue with. You may disagree with him, but he presents it in a dignified and intellectual manner. He dresses well and is a very professional, grandfatherly figure. Phil is younger and dresses in suits, but is kind of disheveled. He has a charm about him, which can sometimes be disarming, but at the same time he is brusque and direct, in your face and fearing nothing. Phil Montes' approach is much more confrontational than Dr. de Leon.

As first president of the Association of Mexican American Educators, Phil has a platform to travel across the state forming local chapters and presenting his views before educational institutions, conferences, school districts, and community organizations. His background gives him both an educational and psychological perspective on the Mexican American-Chicano child. He becomes a hot property when it comes to getting out in front of people with a different point of view.

My Awakening

All this is what I'm exposed to about Phil. I become an appendage to him. He becomes like a father to me or the big brother I never have. He is my mentor during my early development as an activist.

The Association of Mexican American Educators has just been founded. Then there is this other collection of school administrators out of L.A. Unified made up of principals and district bureaucrats who want to perpetuate the status quo. At that time we refer to them as the *venditos*, or traitors, of the world. They want to take over the Association of Mexican American Educators. Working with the *venditos* are officials with the California Department of Education based in Sacramento, run by Max Rafferty, the right-wing Republican in the nonpartisan office of state schools superintendent who sternly resists the kind of philosophy Phil and the rest of us are espousing. We—Phil and the association leadership—are a thorn in the side of Rafferty, Wilson Riles, his successor, and school districts like L.A. Unified, which are always attacking us. Their purpose is to eliminate our association, which is beginning to mature and expand in local communities.

Phil, Charlie Erickson, and I end up traveling all over California, attending conferences and installations of local association chapter officers. Everywhere, Phil speaks and I serve as his associate. When people hear Phil speak and me talk, they say we must be brothers because we both use the same colorful language and are very direct and forceful in our advocacy styles.

Developments culminate in elections for new statewide association officers. We decide to run Dr. de Leon to succeed Phil as president. We also get wind that Max Rafferty wants to take control of our association by electing one of his guys, a Chicano named Dick Baca, who is director of migrant education in the California Department of Education. CDE is a crucial funding source for local school districts; Rafferty funds a lot of teacher training and other programs local districts rely on. Rafferty is prepared to use that financial influence to his advantage and his people think they can pressure local district administrators into backing Baca. That way Baca can be drafted and presented as the alternative to Marcos de Leon. The end result will be to make Baca the kiss-ass representative of Rafferty and undermine the effectiveness of our association. It is not an empty threat.

All this maneuvering is taking place under the table. The Rafferty faction thinks Phil and the rest on our side don't even know what's going on and that we'll be surprised when the vote results come out. But we do discover it. Phil devises a strategy to shove it right up Baca's ass.

The voting is set for an association conference to elect statewide officers at the Edgewater Marina Hotel in Long Beach. There's a cocktail reception ahead of the conference. Phil along with three or four of us corner and confront Baca at the reception, telling him it will be best for Baca not to stay for the conference because we know he is being put up to it by Rafferty. "All right, motherfucker, we know what you're doing," we tell him. If Baca stays, we threaten to expose and embarrass him in front of nearly 1,000 delegates as a tool of Max Rafferty. "Then we'll spend our every waking hour destroying your educational career.

We think it's in your best interest to go back to Sacramento." Within an hour, the guy leaves the conference and flies home to Sacramento, never to be heard from again in connection with the association.

We elect the second president of the association, who is Dr. de Leon, the godfather of bilingual and bicultural education. He is not as dynamic a leader in pursuing a proactive agenda, but he enjoys the attention and is a good speaker. More importantly, Phil keeps control of the association.

Phil and our crowd keep fighting with the state Board of Education, L.A. Unified School District, and the funding agencies for the War on Poverty. None of them is happy because we are bringing to their attention serious shortcomings.

When I admit during our first meeting that I don't know what I'm going to do after graduating from college, Phil puts a piece of paper in front of me. On it is an idea he has recently written down, setting up educational resource centers to work with what at the time is the federal War on Poverty program created by President Lyndon B. Johnson. The poverty program already sets up these teen posts across southern California, to keep young kids in poor and minority neighborhoods, including Latino neighborhoods, occupied and out of trouble. The teen posts are born out of the Watts Riots and other civil unrest and run through the Office of Economic Opportunity under Sargent Shriver, brother-in-law of President Kennedy and first director of the Peace Corps. His daughter later becomes California First Lady Maria Shriver.

Phil envisions running this educational program to compliment teen post activities wherever there are Chicano kids. "Why don't you write something up, a proposal, and I'll get it funded through the War on Poverty," he says. "Then, if we get it funded, you'll have a job."

All of Phil's qualities lead me to gravitate towards him. Soon, here's this young kid—me—just getting out of college and working out of Phil's office. I volunteer for about two months.

I hand back to Phil a one-pager, my proposal for the project. Two weeks later he calls me up and says he has it funded. Then he tells me, "How would you like to be the director of this?"

"What?" I say. "Director of what? Shit. I've just graduated from college."

"Don't worry about it," he replies. "Why don't you become the director of it? Why don't you write the budget?" The job pays eight hundred dollars a month. That's a lot of money at the time. I become director of it.

I create my own job title: Director of the Educational Resource Program of the Teen Posts of Southern California. It covers all over the city and county of Los Angeles, from the San Fernando Valley all the way to Pomona in eastern L.A. County.

So here I am. Phil says, "Let's sit down and see what your needs are." So we do a needs assessment, which means I meet with the directors of all the teen posts. David Lizarraga heads one of the teen posts I work with. He goes on to lead the East Los Angeles Community Union, TELACU. David says he needs tutorial programs. And he says, "I'd like to be able to teach kids how to participate in the political and community process—learn how to speak up for themselves and their community." Other directors want tutors for academic subjects, cultural enrichment, boxing or martial arts coaches—everything you can think of. We try to suit the individual needs of each teen post. You can always find coaches and athletic or PE teachers. But if students need math tutoring, we have to find someone who's competent.

I hire about 300 teachers with skills to match the needs identified by the teen post directors. We're paying $10 an hour then for part-time work, all after school or on weekends. Teachers also organize recreational activities. My propensity is to look for Mexican-American teachers, but we also have Anglos. We only hire teachers who give a shit about teaching. I interview all of them. What does a 23-year old kid know about interviewing people? Some of them have been teaching for 15 or 20 years. What I do know is when somebody wants to work with kids and enjoys working with them. Those are the ones I hire.

This is my first job out of college. It's a lot different than being credit manager at a jewelry store.

We run the program and pretty much everything else out of Phil's office, including the first bilingual Head Start program plus the Association of Mexican American Educators. With 300 teachers working for me, each teen post can get five or six of them doing different things, depending on the kids' needs and what we can recruit in terms of teachers geared to fulfilling those needs. On any given day each teen post can serve 50 or 60 kids; it goes up into the hundreds during the summer months. Some programs operate during the day, others in the late afternoon or evening.

We measure success by the number of programs established at teen post chapters and by the success of the teachers in working with the kids and developing leadership skills among the students. I notice that one of the things blacks are able to do very well is become very vocal and self-assured in exercising their rights in front of anybody. We want Latino kids to learn the same skills. We take them on field trips, to meetings of political bodies or governmental agencies so they can practice advocating for their interests in front of them. They appear before the board of directors of the EYOA, the Economic and Youth Opportunities Agency of Greater Los Angeles, a community action group that is the delegate agency for all War on Poverty funds being received in L.A. from Washington, D.C. They testify before school boards. We organize conferences so kids from all the teen posts can come together to share experiences and identify their needs and grievances plus come up with solutions to their problems.

We help avert gang fights by getting kids who belong to gangs involved in our programs. We will sit down young males from different gangs and work on getting them to resolve their differences peacefully instead out on the street, which is what kills my friend Richard Marquez when we are both in junior high.

One positive thing about the War on Poverty is the youth programs it funds, especially during the summer when there are a lot of kids with nothing to do and the greatest amount of gang activity. When these programs get underway, gang recruitment and violence remain stagnant and crime goes down, although it is short-lived because the Vietnam War is increasingly sucking up attention and treasure from the War on Poverty. While these programs last, the theory is if they employ kids who are in gangs or are vulnerable to them five days a week, they're too busy and tired at the end of the day to go gang banging. And if they have money in their pockets they're less likely to be involved in gang activity.

Thousands of kids benefit from the educational resource centers in the teen posts, which start in 1966 and go on for about a year. Then they fall victim to racial competition. The blacks in the L.A. War on Poverty decide to do the program in and get it defunded. The way they do it is by citing our activism—getting the kids to advocate for their rights before government agencies, which is what the blacks do too—to prompt an investigation over allegedly using federal funds for political purposes. They claim misappropriation of the money, arguing that when we train kids to appear before public bodies our goal is to really promote a political agenda. Some of the kids on their own later get involved in local political campaigns, but they are able to do so because we have turned them on to activism. None of the teen post resource center program monies go for political activities.

Even though Phil, the Foundation of Mexican American Studies, and the Association of Mexican American Educators are ostensibly educationally related, his office—through programs like mine—become involved in Community Service Organization-style social activism and advocacy because of the vacuum of political leadership plaguing the Chicano community in the mid- and late-'60s. Most organizations that do exist are situationally formed around protesting a particular incident or issue. Even those that try to define a broader agenda are stuck spending more time dealing with internal politics than affecting what they set out to do.

One of the fights brewing out of Phil's office near downtown is a classic war from the mid-'60s. (We lose a battle in that war when my education resource center funding is lost.) The war evolves from the disproportionate amount of federal antipoverty money flowing into South Central L.A., where there is the heaviest concentration of African Americans. The initial focus of the War on Poverty is coming to the aid of blacks, a reaction to the social unrest in Watts and other ghettos. Chicanos don't riot and there isn't the same kind of recognizable strife and impoverishment. So when it comes time to allocating antipoverty resources, Latinos are an afterthought. The challenge among Latinos is fighting for our fair share of the pie, meaning directing more money and services into Latino communities, which then pretty much covers East L.A. and the San Fernando Valley.

That means confronting the EYOA, the main agency handing out poverty program funds in L.A. If you want a program funded, you have to go to the EYOA. That isn't a problem for me. Nor is it a problem that the blacks are getting the lion's share of the funds. We just want to try to make sure the agency also takes into consideration the needs of Chicanos that are just as real.

I find opportunities on my own to join in the skirmishes.

Around this time there is a conference luncheon to discuss the state of poverty in Los Angeles at what's called the Jewish Pentagon, an imposing structure on Vermont Avenue just north of the Hollywood Freeway that is home to the Jewish Federation of Los Angeles, which encompasses most of the Jewish community organizations. Phil is supposed to be a main speaker. He can't make it so he sends me.

The status of politics in L.A. in that day is that when you talk about poverty and programs to fight it, the discussion is very one-sided—meaning it is all black. I'm the last speaker. My job is to talk about Chicanos. In all the discussions that come before I go on, no one says a thing about the problems confronting my people; it's all about problems facing blacks. It's like Chicanos don't even exist in Los Angeles. In the audience are leaders and decision-makers, mostly from Jewish groups that make up the building.

I get up. "Here lies the problem in Los Angeles," I declare. "I've been sitting here for several hours listening to people speak and ask questions. At no time was my community and its needs ever even mentioned. All efforts to confront poverty and exclusion from participation in democratic society are seen as a black-and-white issue. That also reflects the tenor of the whole country. The challenges African Americans face are all legitimate and is a good thing they are being highlighted."

I make the position Phil and I take simple: "I have no objection to whatever emphasis is being made for African Americans. But you have to recognize that the problem in L.A. is more than just black and white."

The response from the event organizers and the audience is that people are literally embarrassed. I point out a truth they have to acknowledge.

That is the dilemma and the state of the community we confront at the time I begin my social and political career—my awakening. Phil helps me shape my arguments and helps me speak on behalf of Chicanos, but never at the expense of blacks or anyone else. I never believe in doing that. Later, my closest political ally and friend in the legislature is a black man, Willie Lewis Brown Jr. He introduces me to legislative politics. First I'm with the Urban Affairs Institute legislative internship program funded by the Ford Foundation. I am indebted for what I learn from Mervyn Dymally, then a state senator and later lieutenant governor and U.S. congressman before returning to the state assembly. He is the first politician in Los Angeles who truly believes in coalition politics, and acts on his beliefs. This is also what is championed by Phil Montes, and it becomes my politics too throughout my service in the state legislature and on the L.A. City Council.

Phil, who grows up in South Central L.A. around blacks and attends black high schools, is not a racist. But he also believes the blacks can take care of themselves and we Chicanos need to learn from the effective way the black community functions politically.

My baptism in Chicano politics comes during the poverty wars by going up against African Americans. It is a constant battle. Any time funding for a new poverty program becomes available, the blacks try to take it over or resist sharing anything with anybody else. I have a great relationship with blacks because most of the students I can relate with in college are black. I hang around with them since there aren't very many Chicanos on campus.

It is never a matter of being antiblack as it is being pro-Chicano. "This is not the way it should be," I say to my black colleagues in the ranks of the antipoverty programs. "I'm not trying to take away from you, but how about us?" I ask them. It is a real bitter fight. Largely because of Phil Montes and others, Chicanos are becoming a real threat in competing for resources that are diminishing as the '60s drag on and LBJ becomes obsessed with Vietnam. Since Latinos get relatively little in comparison from the poverty programs, it is easier to fight another minority. Minorities have a much easier time fighting each other than going after the ones who're really pulling all the strings. Cesar Chavez calls them all "poverty warriors." Others call them "poverty pimps" because some people who make a very good living off these government programs do little or nothing to help the people they are supposed to assist.

Nevertheless, the War on Poverty does a lot for the poor by providing options other than poverty. It offers chances for education that lead to gainful employment of young black, Latino, and poor white people, many of whom have dropped out of school. Some are led up career ladders that will never otherwise be open to them. More importantly, it educates poor people, introducing them to social and political participation and leads to empowerment for themselves and their communities. Empowerment makes it possible for a lot of other things to happen because people use those skills to become activists in the best sense of the word. The rise of ethnic awareness fostered by the poverty programs, including our teen posts, starting in junior and senior high school, can't be dismissed.

I disagree with those who criticize the War on Poverty, those who say that the good from the poverty programs only lasts until the money runs out and that no systemic change results. Many human lives are saved during this period of time. Many of these programs have a positive influence, bettering individual kids who participate. We use those funds during those long hot summers to hire a lot of teachers to get a lot of kids doing something other than hanging out on the streets. That money helps keep the peace during a time when there is a lot of inner-gang rivalry and Chicano-on-Chicano violence. We start doing workshops and run football leagues. So from that standpoint, it pacifies and there aren't as many killings.

Many people who become successful professionals begin their careers with the War on Poverty, which, from my vantage point, is the beginning of enlightenment for poor and minority communities and the larger society.

A central figure at EYOA, L.A.'s antipoverty delegating agency, is Opal Jones, a black woman who is politically shrewd and very formidable in successfully navigating the antipoverty system. You have to put in a lot of hard work over many hours to get something over on that lady. We develop a very good relationship. A few years later I'm going out with a jazz singer, a mutual friend, who gets into a conversation about me with Opal Jones. Opal remembers me as "an outspoken loudmouth who at least was always consistent. He played fair," Opal tells her friend. I take it as high praise.

At the time, Latinos are neophytes; unlike blacks, we are not participating much organizationally.

The most effective and militant Latino activist group in Los Angeles is the Community Service Organization, begun in East L.A. during the late '40s. It is the CSO that elects Ed Roybal to the city council in 1949. It pioneers a lot of things, including reform of police brutality. But by the mid '60s, the CSO is in decline after Cesar Chavez leaves the organization in 1962, to form the farmworkers union.

The only other major Latino political group of any note back then is the Mexican American Political Association, MAPA, founded by Enrique "Hank" Quevedo and Bert Corona, who later becomes a giant in advocating for immigrant rights. Unlike CSO, which is a grassroots organization that can turn out hundreds of volunteers working precincts during elections or campaigning for other parts of its agenda, MAPA usually surfaces only during political campaign season. It has no real troops or influence in L.A. other than endorsing candidates. In other parts of the state, MAPA chapters get more involved in electing people and in the political and social affairs of their communities.

MAPA always pitches itself as a nonpartisan group, which I think is kind of stupid. Everybody knows it is mostly Democratic. MAPA basically stays under the control of Ed Quevedo. Then it is transferred over to Bert Corona and Abe Tapia.

While working with Phil Montes around 1967, I help form a group called the Mexican American Action Committee. It starts with a handful of guys. We see ourselves as the new breed of young 1960s activists. It's not so much from the standpoint of our militancy, but rather the fact that you—the established Latino political leaders—are the old and we are the new. We primarily come together around politics but then take on other jobs, like trying to help out our kids and be role models for them. Most of the guys in this group eventually become lawyers, business people, and professionals. In the short period of time we are active, we became the first ones to ever picket an L.A. County sheriff, Peter Pitches, over charges of police brutality when he is speaking at the Alexandria Hotel in downtown L.A. That is a no-no; you never take on the cops. We see things a little differently after some sheriff's deputies beat up some young Chicanos. We protest the abuse.

By then I am already out of Phil's office and working on civil rights issues with the NAACP Legal Defense and Education Fund, upon which the Mexican American Legal Defense and Education Fund is modeled. I meet these two women who are community relations representatives for the Sheriff's Department. I'm kind of interested in one of them who is a Latina. I meet them for lunch, ironically at the Alexandra Hotel. When the Latina opens her purse, a microphone falls out. "What the fuck?" I blurt out.

They are surveilling me. By that time I'm helping out with the East L.A. high school walkouts led by Sal Castro. Here I am trying to make a move on this woman and she's trying to put me in jail. It isn't very nice. And I think she likes me for my looks and intellect.

A lot is converging at the same time. Most activists are directing their efforts at police misconduct by the LAPD, including the antics of Chief William Parker and his associates and successors. The L.A. County sheriff, interesting enough, is pretty much being left alone. To do what we do in picketing the sheriff at the time is considered borderline communism in the eyes of law enforcement. Nobody likes being accused of condoning brutality. The sheriff hates negative publicity, as I find out later. He is truly one of the most powerful men in southern California.

(In the early 1970s, after I'm elected to the state assembly, Sheriff Pitches gets to like me. He is a tall, gregarious guy with a good tan—sort of a man's man. I head up a prison reform select committee in the assembly investigating Mexicans who are being beaten in the Orange County Jail. They beat the shit out of anybody who gets out of line. The Orange County sheriff hates me and issues some threats. Sheriff Pitches calls up to warn me. Later, I get invited to stop by his office and we are talking. "I was cleaning up my office and I found these pictures," the sheriff says, handing them over to me. They are of that protest demonstration at the Alexandria Hotel where he speaks back in the '60s. Until that day, nobody ever pickets the sheriff. What the fuck do we know at the time?

Several years earlier I meet a guy at the Rexall Pharmacy at First Street and Ditman Avenue in East L.A. Sol Monroy is his name. He becomes a good friend of mine when I'm in college. A longtime local pharmacist, he's right in the middle of different activities, in MAPA and before that with CSO—all the Chicano causes in East L.A. When my activism starts through Phil Montes, Sol confesses to me that he's a Communist, a card-carrying member of the Communist Party of the U.S.A. Sol assures me he's well connected in the party and close to well-known long-time party activists like Dorothy Healey. "It's one thing for you to come into the store," he warns me, "but if you ever see me in public don't you ever acknowledge me. If I'm ever doing something and I tell you, 'Don't hang around me,' do not ask any questions; just walk away." I tell him, "I don't care." I figure he doesn't want me to become the subject of investigations by law enforcement.

I lose track of Sol over time. One night in the early '70s I'm in Hollywood with my kids, driving up Highland Avenue. I come to a halt at a stoplight. Idling next to my car is an LAPD police cruiser. I turn around, look at the officer and it's Sol Monroy. I do a double take. Then I say to myself, "Oh shit!" He spots me too. All I do is shake my head and smile, as if to tell Sol it all makes sense now. Without any acknowledgement, he drives off as soon as the signal light changes.

A day or two later I put in a call to Eddie Diaz, the editor at the *Belvedere Citizen* newspaper. I know he is a close friend of Sol's. They're drinking buddies. I tell him about running into Sol. "I know he's LAPD," I tell him.

"Yeah," Eddie responds. After just having had a long talk with Sol, Eddie has also been wanting to call me about his friend, since by then I'm the state assemblyman representing our district. From what Eddie tells me and from what I learn from another reliable source, Sol had been in deep cover for some 25 years, after being recruited as a rookie cop just graduated from the police academy by Chief Parker to investigate the Communist Party and Latinos who law enforcement suspect of having Communist ties, including during the 1950s CSO and Cesar Chavez. What Eddie wants to tell me is that after so many years as a police spy, under a new LAPD chief, Ed Davis, who takes over the department in 1969, Sol is all of a sudden put back on duty in the streets as an entry-level patrol officer. Eddie explains how unfair it is for Sol, and how he feels Sol's life could be in jeopardy since his cover has been exposed. "I think it is chickenshit," Eddie remarks.

"I don't want to do anything that Sol wouldn't want me to do," I reply. "But I'm prepared to call Ed Davis, the new chief of police, and tell him I think it's outrageous. Here's a man who has been working undercover for I don't know how long. Outing Sol and exposing him to danger by putting him back out on patrol from one day to the next is the kind of crap I dislike about the LAPD."

Eddie tells me Sol is concerned somebody could kill him. But cops are typically not whiners or complainers. They just take whatever gets mete out to them. That's especially true of Chicano cops who have so much pride and don't want special favors from anybody.

I place a call to Chief Davis, who calls me back. "You guys are the most chickenshit people," I tell the chief. "You don't even protect your own. I know Sol Monroy was deep cover with the LAPD. Some people are going to be very upset when they find out for decades he served as an undercover officer. I know Sol. He lived in the community I represent. Whatever he did he did, but the department should have some sensitivity to what they made him do over a period of decades. This is totally unacceptable and I would hate for this to become an issue."

The chief says he will look into it. Within a day he calls back and thanks me for bringing the matter to his attention. "I've taken care of it as of today," he reports. "Sol Monroy is no longer on patrol." Sol is reassigned and is no longer working the streets.

I don't hear anything more until about a year later. I'm at a summer performance of Tchaikovsky's "Overture of 1812" at the Hollywood Bowl. Because of my background, I can spot undercover cops a mile away. I see two of them who are part of the dignitary protection detail for the visiting mayor of Jerusalem, who is in attendance. I go up to one of them. "Hey, Sol," I say. He introduces me to his partner.

"Can I see you for just a second?" Sol asks. We stroll out of earshot. "I want to thank you for what you did," he tells me. He knows about my intervention with the chief. "I never had a chance to call you," Sol adds.

"Brother, whatever you did, you were always very fair and helpful to me. You could have made my life very miserable" by informing his superiors about my activism during the '60s. "You were always a friend, and I believe in reciprocating friendship." Then we start laughing together. Since at one time I am a struggling college student working full time and with a family to support, at the pharmacy he fills my prescriptions at no cost. He tells me later he never puts my name in his reports to the LAPD even though he knows all about my political activities. Little do I know at the time how vulnerable I am making myself. Without Sol's help, I can easily become a target of the witch-hunts the LAPD wages against so many innocent people who, like me, are activists even though we are just exercising our constitutional free speech and association rights and are not violating the law.

All I know is that during my activist days, whenever I get into trouble—or am worried about getting into trouble—Sol is there for me. When I need advice I turn to Sol because he has been around for so long. He says, "Be careful with this person or be careful at this event. Don't talk to that person." When I ask Sol a question, he either answers me or says, "You don't need to know." I decide early on that clearly here's a good guy to know and confide in. Then it hits me: think about it, man, he is like Dorothy Healey's Mexican. I start thinking, What the fuck do I ever tell him? Can it come back to haunt me? But I never hear anything I talk with Sol about. My name never comes up in connection with anything I discus with Sol or any event where he sees me.

I vividly remember one example. Reverend Vahac Mardirosian is a Baptist minister from a church on the Eastside. He becomes chairman of a group of Chicano parent activists who serve as advocates for students and work for change in the L.A. schools. It is infiltrated by the LAPD. As I'm getting ready to be with Reverend Mardirosian's group, all I remember is Sol telling me, "You're going to be at this meeting tonight. Don't even come close to me." A half hour after the meeting is over, I find out the LAPD knows everything that goes on.

I guess Sol appreciates where I grow up and just likes me. That's the reason I go to bat for him later with the police chief.

Sol also introduces me back then to Rose Chernin, who is executive director of the Los Angeles Committee for the Defense of the Bill of Rights, founded in 1950 as the Los Angeles Committee for Protection of the Foreign Born. She's the one I turn to when all the Chicano militancy erupts and Sal Castro and others are indicted and need bail money out of the East L.A. high school walkouts in 1968. Actually, first I turn to Sol, who turns me onto Rose. I know the only place to quickly find money to help get people out of jail and get them a legal defense is the lefties. "Let me give you a name and number," Sol says. He calls Rose Chernin first and lets her know I'm going to be phoning. She comes through when we really need the help and there isn't anyone else.

When I get out of college, I see MAPA members—called *Mapistas*—as the old guard. The way they operate is telling politicians, "Hey, give me ten thousand dollars and we'll deliver the Chicano community." MAPA becomes a vehicle for a few people to make money in political campaigns in exchange for endorsements that are of questionable value anyway—but what the hell, there doesn't seem to be anyone else speaking for Mexicans and most Anglo politicians don't know the difference.

I remember taking on MAPA when my friends and I start the Young Citizens for Governor Brown in 1966. This is when Pat Brown, Jerry's father, is unsuccessfully running for reelection against Ronald Reagan. Through Phil Montes and the Association of Mexican American Educators, I meet another young activist named David Ochoa, a graduate of Claremont College going to law school at UCLA who is very involved in Pomona where he lives. I first meet him when he's director of a teen post when I am doing that program. Together, we get actively involved in the Chicano community with Governor Brown's reelection and see ourselves as a counterweight to MAPA. At least we decide we don't want to be associated with MAPA.

We campaign legitimately for Pat Brown, doing voter registration and speaking in public for the old man. The campaign likes us because we're not trying to shake them down or hustle them for money. We're just young guys interested in Democratic politics, part of the group of young Latinos I set up, the Mexican American Action Committee, which includes David Ochoa, Ralph Ochoa, and Antonio Rodriguez.

Both us young Turks and the older *Mapistas* have the rhetoric down. Don't get me wrong, Bert Corona is as charismatic as hell; the shit really flows. He has put a lot of years in and has a lot of knowledge. He's been in it early, stays in it—and does a lot of good things, and some things that aren't so good. He knows no boundaries. Me and my guys do crazy things, but we really work hard for the governor in the campaign.

Bert goes to the Brown people and does his usual thing: "Give me X amount of dollars and I'll deliver you the endorsement" of MAPA, and therefore the Chicano community.

The same thing happens two years later in the 1968 California Democratic Primary when Robert F. Kennedy campaigns for president. (I know this because I get it later from Frank Mankiewitz, RFK's press secretary in '68.) This time I'm co-chair of the Viva Kennedy campaign (the part of the campaign aimed at Latinos)—along with Bert Corona. But there's a new wrinkle.

That year also sees the "Chicano Blowouts," or walkouts by high school students protesting the lousy quality of education Latino kids are getting in East L.A., among other grievances. I'm in Fresno the weekend before the June 4 primary election, on Association of Mexican American Educators business. I get a call from the girlfriend of Sal Castro, the teacher who helps lead this milestone of the 1960s Chicano movement. She's the roommate of a woman I'm seeing; Sal is also a friend and we've been working together since before the walkouts begin.

Sal and 12 others, including Moctesuma Esparza (who later produces some major motion pictures, including "Gettysburg"), have been arrested at the behest of Evelle Younger, the Los Angeles County district attorney, for conspiring to commit a misdemeanor, which makes it a felony. The misdemeanor is for dis-

Richard becomes friends with Sal Castro, advises Castro when he helps organize the famed East L.A. high school walkouts in 1968, and arranges to bail out him and 12 others after they are arrested for conspiracy in connection with the protests.

rupting the public school campuses where the walkouts take place. The felony is for conspiring to tell kids to walk out of their classes.

It's Friday night and I turn around and drive back to L.A., arriving around 1 a.m. at a house in Lincoln Heights that is a focal point for activists, both kids and adults, involved in the walkouts. Also there is Oscar Acosta, the Chicano lawyer (and later author) who comes to represent Sal and his "co-conspirators." They become known as the Chicano 13. The pressing need seems to be raising money to get them bailed out of jail and to finance their legal defense.

I turn for advice to Sol Monroy. He already knows about everything, which I don't understand at the time. "I got to raise money," I tell him. "You have any ideas?"

"Yeah," Sol replies. "I'll make a phone call." By now it's Saturday morning. I call this Rose Chernin, the woman with the Committee for the Defense of the Bill of Rights, the one Sol turns me onto, telling her what has happened, that we need money and what it's for.

My Awakening

To bail out Sal Castro and the indicted East L.A. high school "conspirators" in 1968, as well as hundreds of protestors arrested during the 1970 Chicano Moratorium, Richard turns for help to Rose Chernin with the Committee for the Defense of the Bill of Rights. Here she testifies with her attorney before the House Un-American Activities Committee in 1956.

"How much money?" is all she wants to know. It comes out to more than $100,000 for all 13 of them. A half hour later she calls me back, "You've got the money," she informs me. But then I ask myself if it isn't better to use the funds for legal defense. The reason Sal and the rest are arrested at 5 p.m. on a Friday is they have to spend the whole weekend in jail before a hearing can be set on Monday—unless they get bailed out before then. At the time of the arraignment on Monday, the bail will be significantly reduced. I want the money to go instead for their legal defense.

Oscar, the attorney, and I talk it over and we make a decision. I tell Oscar he has to go talk to his clients in jail and tell them they have to stay there because we want to use the money to pay for their defense. He goes, also to make sure the 13 are all safe and they're not being roughed up. Some of them don't like being behind bars the whole weekend. But Oscar comes back and reports they're okay with it.

Tuesday, in three days, is the statewide primary election. I get a call from the campaign of Senator Eugene McCarthy, who's running against Robert Kennedy in the Democratic primary. They've seen the statewide and national news coverage of the arrests. "The senator is shocked and horrified, and wants to see if you need any assistance," I'm told. The McCarthy campaign is offering to contribute $100,000 or more for the legal defense fund of these poor Chicano students and adults who've been arrested.

Obviously, I accept the money real fast. The money is to be delivered by a representative of Senator McCarthy. There's just one thing, I'm told: all they want is for the senator to make a statement on Monday, the day before the election, at a news conference in L.A., so Gene McCarthy can show what a great American he is. Such a gesture could have a big impact on Chicano voters the day before they're heading to the polls to vote for president.

I'm vice chair with Bert Corona of the Kennedy campaign. So I go to Frank Mankiewitz, who I've met through our work. He's a good lefty, I figure, so I tell him about McCarthy and the news conference on Monday and the national—and local—impacts I'm sure the McCarthy campaign is hoping to get. "We have a problem," I warn Mankiewitz. "This can turn the election, man." What the fuck does he know. This is all my manufacturing. I tell Mankiewitz that we—the Kennedy campaign—have to respond in a likewise manner. "Well," I add, "what do you think we should do? McCarthy gave $100,000. At least we should do that." The Kennedy campaign agrees.

This is all on a weekend. The banks are closed. On Monday morning, I pick up a check at Kennedy campaign headquarters on Wilshire Boulevard. I'm not sure why Phil Montes is with me, but he is. "You better make sure this check is good because come Tuesday, this check isn't any good," Phil warns. Together we head off to the bank in Westwood where it's drawn. We get there to cash the check and turn it into a cashier's check. It comes back with insufficient funds.

I call Mankiewitz: "I'm here at the bank. What the fuck are you guys doing? You guys lied to me. You know this check isn't any good. We're having a news conference at 12 noon today and I'll have no choice but to renounce you guys and tell the public what you guys have done and that you lied to the community." I guess I do learn something from Bert Corona after all.

The Kennedy campaign sends someone from headquarters who hands me a cashier's check for $100,000.

In the course of three days, I raise $300,000 in cash money to aid the legal defense of the Chicano 13. That Monday afternoon they're arraigned at the Sheriff's station. Bail is lowered to $15,000 each. We only have to put up 10 percent of it to post bail through a bail bondsman. I get my friend, Ernie Camacho, who owns his own bail bonds agency, to bail them out. Later, Ernie is the principal guy I use in bailing out many other activists who are arrested in connection with advocating for Chicano causes on the Eastside.

I hit up Rose Chernin for every major Chicano rights demonstration that leads to incarceration of anybody, raising the bail money or legal defense funds. They include sit-ins at the L.A. Unified School District headquarters protesting the firing of Sal Castro that lead to the arrests of 35 adults and students. The last go-around is the Chicano Moratorium two years later, in 1970, when we bail out

700 to 800 people through a conglomerate of bail bonds agencies that Ernie organizes—all financed with contributions supplied by Rose Chernin and her committee.

She and I always speak on the phone. Whenever I talk with her and thank her, she explains the reason for helping us is the history of her organization and what it initially stands for: protecting and representing the interests of Jews and other immigrants who are facing problems like assimilation, acculturation, and discrimination. Rose and the committee have also become advocates for other downtrodden minority groups and union activists, including Mexicans, who are swept up in the anti-Communist witch-hunts of the McCarthy era. By the '60s, they're helping the Black Panthers, Angela Davis, and student antiwar activists. Now they are helping us.

You always wonder what they're going to ask you to do in return for their generosity. The only thing Rose ever asks me to do, shortly after the Chicano 13 are bailed out, is speak at the annual dinner of the Committee for the Defense of the Bill of Rights. I ask Sol Monroy what to do. She's a lovely lady. "Look at it this way," he advises. "They came through for you and all they're asking you to do is to thank them."

"I have no problem with that," I say. He just laughs. "Do you think the cops have it?" I ask. (In other words, do they know about my connection with Rose Chernin?)

"Probably," he responds.

I say, "Thank you."

Among those sitting with me at the head table for the committee dinner in a large ballroom at the Biltmore Hotel in downtown Los Angeles are Alprentice "Bunchy" Carter, a black activist, former gang member, and leader of the Black Panther Party who is shot to death a short time later at UCLA; Angela Davis, the UC Berkeley professor and Communist; one of the founders of Students for a Democratic Society; and one Mexican, me. I get up and acknowledge the entire head table. "I want to talk about a community that many of you in this room grew up with in places like Boyle Heights," I say. "But today that community is asking for recognition of inequities in education and the administration of justice." I recount the story of the East L.A. walkouts and thank them for supporting us. "We will never forget it," I affirm. Then I get out of there as fast as I can.

At 10 that night I'm watching the television news on KTLA, Channel 5. It's the George Putnam news, anchored by this right-wing guy. There I am live and in color. (I don't remember seeing any TV news cameras.) Putnam goes off talking about the "Red scare" and saying how, in the '60s, the Communist Party is still very prominent and mostly based out of a place called the "Red Hill," L.A.'s Echo Park neighborhood. Oh well.

That dinner is the first and last time Rose Chernin and I see each other. But she keeps coming through time and time again whenever I call, never questioning and never asking anything in return. Each time all she just wants to know is, "How can we help?" And then she adds, "We believe in what you're striving for."

It all starts with the Chicano 13 in 1968.

I meet Sal Castro through the Association of Mexican American Educators. Then, he's an activist teacher at Lincoln High School after being thrown out of Belmont High. At Lincoln he becomes athletic director because of his love for sports. He works with Chicano kids, trying to boost their motivation and pride. I am already involved in an annual youth leadership conference organized through the L.A. County Human Relations Commission by Mike Duran, a county probation officer. By the time I am showing up the conference is bringing together students from all over southern California to a camp in Malibu where they learn about ethnic pride, student activism, and educational problems. I'm a counselor and help out in workshops for the kids.

Through these leadership conferences I get to meet some students from Roosevelt High School. One of them is Vicky Castro; she later becomes a junior high school principal and is elected to the L.A. Unified school board. I get to know Moctesuma Esparza, who is going to Lincoln High. I come to meet other East L.A. high school kids through the teen posts. As head of the resource center programs in the teen posts, we organize student councils all over the place. That's how I first get to know Richard Polanco, later a state assemblymember, state senator, and political ally of mine. Clearly, though, leadership among the Chicano high school students is emanating from Lincoln High.

All these kids hang out at the Church of the Epiphany, an Episcopal church originally built in the old English Gothic Revival style in Lincoln Heights. It is a hotbed of Chicano movement activism on the Eastside during the '60s and '70s, from sheltering and supporting Cesar Chavez and the farmworkers to students organizing around educational equity issues. There is born *La Raza* newspaper, only the second underground publication in L.A., with Eliseo Risco as editor. *La Raza* becomes a voice for the Chicano community, covering what's really happening in the schools. In the midst of the push for change is the church's pastor, Father John Luce. We become very good friends, going out to have dinner, drink, and have a good time.

I raise some money to pay the rent for a nearby coffeehouse at Olympic Boulevard and Goodrich Avenue so the students can have a place to hang out and hold discussions. There is a former CHP headquarters on one side. In the building, where Tomayo's restaurant is today, kids and student activists all hold talk sessions and debate the state of the Chicano community. Cops tail people in and out and take pictures of most everyone coming and going. David Sanchez, founder of the Brown Berets, a group of self-described Chicano revolutionaries, also comes out of the Church of the Epiphany. The coffeehouse is where Sanchez hangs out and where the Brown Berets are formed. It is where student activism starts to unfold in East L.A.

When Phil Montes and I need kids to go testify about public education in East L.A. at a hearing in Washington, D.C. before the U.S. Commission on Civil Rights, we turn to students hanging out at the coffeehouse, especially Vicky Castro and Moctesuma Esparza. He's extremely articulate and blows the socks off the commissioners. I start in late 1967 and early 1968 working on the civil rights commission staff. Phil is the first state office director and later western regional director for the commission. After making their case before the commissioners, the kids come back and become even more outspoken, wanting more than ever to change the system.

The 1968 high school walkouts are caused by a combination of things. It comes down to the fact students are sick and tired of getting an inferior education. They draft their demands for change. It is clearly understood something is going to happen.

By this time, Sal Castro is *persona non grata* at Lincoln High School. I am going out with a young lady who is the roommate of his girlfriend. We periodically get together at a well-known Mexican watering hole, a restaurant and bar in West L.A., where we meet to drink and head off to sporting events. Sal and I aren't close friends, but we are friends.

It is March. We're at a meeting with a number of students from different high schools, primarily Lincoln High, in the basement of the Epiphany church the day before the walkouts begin. Everyone knows something is going to come down the next day. I tell them what they have to worry about. I explain they have to be careful. To walk out of classes and disrupt the school is a misdemeanor. But to conspire to disrupt the school can be seen as a felony. If it is viewed that two or more people get together to decide to commit an act that's illegal, even if it's just a misdemeanor, then it becomes a conspiracy to commit a misdemeanor, which is a felony.

I make the same point to Sal. I'm more worried about him. By then, everything going on is being blamed on Sal because of his entire history of educating Mexican-American kids and teaching them pride in themselves, their history and culture. He loves to make speeches, so I tell Sal, "I'm more worried about you because you're an adult and you're the first one they're going to go after." What Sal has to say, I tell him, when he's asked about his role in the walkouts is, "I am here because I'm concerned about the health and welfare of the kids, about protecting them."

On the first day of the walkouts, I march with the students all the way from Lincoln High School to the University of Southern California Medical School, which is adjacent to the area superintendent's office for L.A. Unified. All the way down, I'm warning Sal. "Sal," I say, "remember you're here to protect the health and welfare of the kids." He's excited for the students, as are all of us. These kids are really something. There are hundreds of them walking out of Lincoln High. At the same time there are walkouts at Roosevelt High too. Most of it is spontaneous, through word of mouth. It is an awesome experience. There are later walkouts, better organized and involving more students from more schools. But on that first day you get the feeling something momentous is happening.

No sooner do we turn the corner and arrive at where the rally is being held than news media microphones converge on Sal. He proceeds to indict himself by saying exactly what we tell him not to say, acknowledging the walkouts are all organized.

Ironically, the spark that begins to light the fire of change in our community doesn't come from the adults; it comes from the kids. You know what, the students embarrass the parents. By standing up and walking out, the kids are telling their elders, "Hey, we've had enough, man." Change begins to be seen because young people get involved in positive activities, meeting with one another through programs like the teen posts, finding out their problems are no different than anyone else's. They recognize the inferior quality education they are receiving, regardless of where they live or what schools they're attending. And they begin to speak out, and strike out, against the unequal education they're receiving.

A basic tenet of their demands is for more minority teachers. As a result, more Latinos and other minorities become teachers. The educational establishment recognizes that the outcry by students is not going to fade away, the problem is not going to disappear and that educators need to begin addressing the shortage of minority and bilingual teachers and the lack of ethnically and culturally relevant instruction. The East L.A. walkouts do bring about some changes in the way the schools do business. They also create a focal point for parents to get more involved in their children's schools.

They also bring people to question some hallmark assumptions of the civil rights movement. One is that segregation is inherently discriminatory against ethnic and racial minorities. This is absolutely correct. But what starts happening is kids are being bused, oftentimes for hours a day, away from where they live. Students have to get up at 5 a.m. to be somewhere to be picked up and bused to places like the San Fernando Valley. Integration is usually a one-way proposition since white kids from the San Fernando Valley are not being bused into East L.A. One result is parents have no relationship with their kids' schools. What is the purpose of busing kids from the dysfunctional schools they're attending on the Eastside where their cultural and educational needs are being ignored and making them travel for hours each day to other dysfunctional schools that also ignore their needs—but in a foreign environment where, because of the distance, there are even fewer opportunities for parent participation?

When Chicano kids start standing up for their rights, they begin talking about improving schools in the communities where they live by providing them with more resources and alternatives to the conventional way of doing things, including a faculty that is more reflective of the community plus more bilingual and bicultural instruction. That process also helps focus attention on other long-simmering grievances Chicanos have in East L.A.—and around the country.

Chapter 3

Teaching and Learning

I stay with the NAACP Legal Defense and Education Fund, which lets me keep involved in Chicano civil rights and education issues, from early 1968 through most of '69. In 1969, I also start teaching a class on Chicano studies at California State University, Long Beach. The job comes through my connections with the Chicano student movement, the East L.A. walkouts, and an outside role I play in the formation of UMAS (United Mexican American Students), a group of Latino college students that is a forerunner to MEChA (Movimiento Estudiantil Chicano de Aztlan, or Chicano student movement of Aztlan). I'm involved because many of the kids I meet and work with who walk out of East L.A. high schools go on to colleges and universities in California. They're also among the students who help create UMAS.

A few of these kids, including Fernando Hernandez, who goes to Banning High School in Wilmington, are now student activists at Long Beach State. They ask if I am willing to teach a 1969 fall semester class on their campus, which lasts into early 1970. I never pretend to be a great academician, but I guess I'm pretty popular because Chicano students from other colleges hear about the class, which is offered in the evening, and ask if they can sit in. I agree as long as there's room.

Several visiting students are from the recently opened campus of the University of California, Irvine, in nearby Orange County. Earlier, in 1969, I address their Cinco de Mayo celebration. In 1970, the same kids talk with me about whether I am interested in a full-time teaching position at UCI. It so happens that the dean of the School of Comparative Cultures, Dr. Joe White, is a black guy I know through Phil Montes. I meet with Irvine's chancellor, Daniel G. Aldrich.

The students come to me because within a four-year period of time since graduating from college, I'm connected, and often deeply involved, with almost every conceivable issue and landmark event in the still-young Chicano movement. This is through my work with the War on Poverty, the U.S. Civil Rights Commission, and the NAACP Legal Defense and Education Fund. The issues run the gamut: antipoverty programs impacting Latinos, education equity and the East L.A. high school walkouts, Cesar Chavez and the Delano grape strike, and even Reies Lopez Tijerina and his struggle to restore land grants to Latinos in New Mexico. I ask myself, so why don't I want to teach? If I'm teaching a class on contemporary Chicano subjects, all I have to talk about is what I've been personally involved with; I don't really need to bring in other materials for a class, although I end up doing it anyway. I figure I already have enough knowledge in a lot of fields to make for an interesting Chicano studies class focusing on civil rights and bilingual and bicultural education up until the present time.

I teach the first introductory courses on Chicano studies at UCI as a lecturer in comparative culture. African-American studies are already underway at Irvine. There is more of an interest among white students in the classes about blacks, but there's enough interest to fill my classes too. I have 200 to 300 students per class. It is mandatory for full-time instructors to teach four classes a year. In addition, I have to put in the time equivalent of another class to be available to meet with students during office hours. I move from Los Angeles to Huntington Beach, although throughout this period I still stay involved in L.A. politics and civil rights activism. By this time I'm divorced and doing my best to also be a weekend father.

Teaching is attractive since I need to work full time to support a family. But being on campus and working closely with students also stands in for the years I don't get to have the college experience as a student at Cal State L.A. At UCI, I'm now a teacher, father figure, and big brother—a multitude of roles I play for the Chicano kids; I also find out I have an impact on some of my black and Anglo students.

It's 1970. I'm 26 years old, but I guess wise beyond my years.

At Irvine, I don't have the same needs, or concerns, as many of my Chicano students, whose plight reminds me of myself during the first year of classes at Cal State L.A. Most are uprooted and come to UCI, primarily from East L.A., although there are others from different parts of California, including the Central Valley. Most have never been away from their home communities. They find themselves studying and living on a large, rambling campus designed by a team of renowned architects led by William Pereira in a contemporary style he calls "California Brutalist." For many of these young Chicanos, it seems like they're in a foreign country. UCI is snuggled into the hills of the Irvine Ranch on land donated to the state by the Irvine Corporation a few miles from existing devel-

Richard in a classroom while teaching ethnic studies and civil rights at the University of California, Irvine.

opment in the heart of Orange County. Then, when you drive to campus west from the Orange County airport you pass nothing but bean fields and grazing cattle. In those days, the county is predominantly Anglo, Republican, and anti-almost anything that at the time even hints at progressivism.

But for me, Irvine is a great opportunity. I help recruit many of the kids who take part in the Chicano walkouts at East L.A. high schools and convince them to go to UCI. Their activism motivates them to want to continue on and do something with their lives. They make up some of the first Chicano kids who attend Irvine.

I'm one of three Chicano professors at UCI. One of them, in the same department as me, is Carlos Munoz, who I already know from attending education conferences. Academically, he's the real thing. He's a scholar but he is also a pretty radical guy and has been a student activist himself, coming from UC Berkeley, where he eventually returns.

My first year at UCI is one of the most exciting periods for me. I have a basic philosophy: never stay on a job for more than a year. Irvine is the first job

I have in my adult life, other than working at the jewelry store to put myself through college, where I stay longer. I'm there for two years.

I teach both ethnic studies and civil rights at UCI. Pretty much the majority of the ethnic studies students are Anglo because the great majority of the student body at the Irvine campus in the middle of Orange County is Anglo. Chicanos, blacks, and maybe a few Asians make up the minority of students in my classes. For me the challenge is delivering subject matter and making it interesting. I think it'll be interesting for the Chicanos because many of them know very little about themselves. The real trick is making it so everybody feels they're getting something out of it. I'd say 70 or 80 percent of the students don't have the foggiest idea about anything to do with Chicanos, including some of the Chicanos. Actually, that's not surprising since the modern Chicano movement has really only been underway in earnest since the mid-1960s, only half a decade or so before.

There are Chicanos who resist or resent the label. I have a kid in one of my classes, a Chicano who grows up in San Marino, a wealthy and exclusive Anglo community, and goes to San Marino High School. He thinks the Chicano experience I'm talking about in class is bullshit because his experience in life is being protected by his family and surroundings where he is not really exposed to any depravation or discrimination. What I describe isn't reality to him. This young man is real light skinned. He's always very proud of his father, who grows up three or four blocks from where I am raised in East L.A. The father is a real success story: a Latino who I'm sure is subjected to discrimination, but gets an education, finds his way out of the barrio, becomes a professional, marries an Anglo woman and is able to provide well for his son, pretty well since I don't know many Chicanos who live in San Marino. This kid's reality is 180 degrees different than mine.

He sometimes disagrees with me in class and will make statements taking me on. I'm real tolerant, trying to get through to him that one day, when he least expects it, he will become the victim of prejudice or racism; something will happen that makes him understand the truth of what he is disagreeing with me about. "I just hope," I add, "that when it happens you remember the two people in your life, your parents, who are the most unselfish people you will ever meet and who have tried to provide a better life than they had and shield you from the hurt and discrimination they might have experienced, especially your father."

One day this student, who has an undeclared major, comes into my office and tells me he's applying to major in the School of Fine Arts at UCI. He wants to be a stage actor. "That's a pretty difficult department to get into," I say. "I hope you understand that in the eyes of many there's not a real big market for someone like you, even though you can change your name and use a stage name like Joe Smith, because you look like a Joe Smith."

He insists on applying to the school using his Spanish surname. The day of reckoning comes when they turn him down. In so many words, they explain why acting is the wrong major for this young man, that there isn't a market for Latino actors, that this is the wrong career choice for him and he should think of doing something else. He walks in my office absolutely devastated that the reality I talk about in my class has come home to him. Exactly what I warn him about occurs. Right away the young man starts blaming his father, who knows what the world is really like for Chicanos but never prepares his son for this day. He doesn't even want to speak with his father.

"I know your father tried to shield you from the things you experienced," I acknowledge. "That doesn't make him a bad father. I may disagree with what he did, but he thought he was doing the right thing by you. Instead of blaming your father, learn to accept the reality and do something about it." Then I work to get him into the school.

I make a call to the dean of the School of Fine Arts. I remind the dean that this Chicano kid is a good student with a high GPA, high SAT scores; he's a high achiever and I think the school is making a mistake in rejecting him. To which the dean basically tells me to go fuck myself, giving excuses why they aren't taking him. I always believe in trying to do things the easy way. If I can't accomplish what I want the easy way, then I elevate the level of discussion. "I respect your honesty," I tell the dean, "but the patronizing reason you used to turn him down defies reality: that a Chicano student should stay in the social science arena where he can do the most good."

I go directly to Dan Aldrich, UCI's chancellor: "Before I blow up this school, I thought I'd let you know what one of your stellar deans used as a reason to turn down this young man's major application." I bring the young man with me to meet with the chancellor. They talk. Aldrich says, "Thank you." The kid leaves. The chancellor is tall, with this deep voice and an imposing personality. He's the epitome of Mr. Brooks Brothers, sporting a certain look: button-down white shirts, Herringbone sports coats or pinstripe suits. Aldrich and I talk. "Dan, we're either going to do it this way [meaning he gets accepted] or if that doesn't happen we'll start exposing the racism of this department and when we're done with that we'll expose a few other departments that do the same thing. Dan, I'm your guy, but this is wrong. You know it's wrong, and I expect you to do something about it."

"Let me look into it," the chancellor says.

Two weeks later, the student comes back into my office. "I got accepted," he declares, all happy. "I don't know how to thank you."

"You got there because you deserve to be there," I reply. "Don't think they're just letting you in there and you're not qualified. But I want to make it real clear to you that you better damn well not fuck it up because if you do you'll ruin it for others who follow you."

The kid graduates from the School of Fine Arts. He also has a long conversation with his father. "Why didn't you tell me, prepare me?" the son asks.

"I thought I was doing right," the father answers. They talk about what happens to the father when he is growing up. It is a great conversation that leads to a closer relationship between father and son.

There are lots of success stories that my students go on to create. There's this one student, the last person you'd ever pick as likely to succeed, a farmworker kid from Orange County when there is still some agriculture there. He takes some of my classes at Irvine, graduates with some prodding from me, and ends up finishing law school. Now he's a member of the board of directors of a big bank in Santa Ana, which is a municipality now dominated by Latinos, a mark of how the county changes since the 1970s. I run into him every once in a while. Sometimes kids just need a little help—and a little push—at certain critical junctures in their lives. This kid is testimony to how it can work, one of many who make me proud of my brief tenure as a teacher.

Teaching seems like the continuation of what I've been doing since graduating from college—and I get to do it with kids who generally know nothing about their culture or history or even some of the important contemporary events that will eventually bring about revolutionary changes for Latinos. I know I can impart to them my last four or five years of intense experience, my activism and knowledge. I feel I can make a contribution.

I know I'm never going to be a full-time tenured professor. From the beginning, I realize I'm not there to publish or perish, the ritual for instructors seeking a career in academia at the university. I'm there to teach whatever courses I can, to provide assistance and guidance to Latino students, and to work with other kids who take my classes and need help. What I also have to offer is the fact I'm young. I'm an instructor, but in many ways I'm also the contemporary of many of them, given our life experiences. I don't particularly care about being loved by students; I'm more interested in being respected—and being a genuine person they can relate to.

For me the opportunity comes at a challenging time in my life. I like young people. I enjoy my first stint at teaching at Long Beach State. It is a logical transition from my involvement with student activism in the East L.A. high schools before, during, and after the walkouts. Some of the same kids who I know from those high schools move onto UCI. One of the things Sal Castro impresses on his students is that activism is important, but what our community really needs is for their young minds to be developed—and that means going on to higher education. So the kids I teach at Long Beach State and later Irvine are one of the first big waves of Chicano students, not just from L.A. but from across the state, who move onto college. Usually, like me, they're the first from their families to attend college.

What the campuses discover is how ill equipped many of them are to handle college-level work, something I can appreciate. It isn't enough to provide financial assistance. These kids need tutors and mentors—professors and staff that can capture their imaginations and help get them through college so they can develop their capacities.

I'm convinced effective teaching is about more than just communicating knowledge. So I'm not the traditional professor who is satisfied with simply lecturing, where communication is one way—my way. I allow and encourage interaction in class; in fact, I insist on it. I tell the students, "Look, I don't care if you agree with me or not. If you disagree, let me hear about it."

I have exchanges, sometimes heated discussions, with students. For those who, in my eyes, are ignorant, it's a great game. There is one Anglo student, a sophomore or junior majoring in humanities. I call him Nick Nolte because he looks like the actor, with long hair and a mustache. On the first or second day the class begins to discuss assimilation, cultural differences, and identity. I'm walking on campus after class when he comes up to me. "I want to talk with you." I say okay.

"Yeah, I think you're full of shit," he tells me.

"Well, maybe if you listen instead of making judgments, you'll understand what I'm talking about. The fact that you would make a statement like that after only the first lecture, I think you're full of shit." He's taken aback. He thinks he can get in my face and maybe back me down.

I say, "Hey brother, I don't know what kind of fucking teachers you're used to and maybe you can intimidate them. But I'm not going to be intimidated by a fool like you. Now, if you don't agree with me, take your time and be man enough to disagree with me in class. Then we can have a fair exchange. As I told the class, I don't expect any of you to totally agree with what I say. I won't hold it against you if you disagree with me, but you have to have a reason and make your case. That's what learning is all about."

"That sounds fair to me," he manages to get out. By the end of the semester, Nick Nolte becomes one of my converts. He stops by my office. Sometimes we go down to have lunch together. He's a smart kid and becomes a clear-thinking writer and probably one of my better students. I enjoy him.

My training teaches me that when you're in a situation with a lot of people you try to identify the ones who disagree with you or hate you the most. If you deal with them straight out, others will come into line too and understand they can disagree with you and still know you know what you're talking about. I can tell by studying the kids, looking into their faces when I'm lecturing. My thing is trying to get them to be part of it. I don't want to talk for an hour while they're taking notes and getting little out of it. My thing is to get into an exchange of ideas and differences. Some ask innocent questions out of ignorance. One of the things I learn in life is you can distinguish people's real feelings, from somebody who hates everything I stand for versus those who are genuinely trying to understand what I'm trying to say even if it is foreign to them. I'm interested in respecting people's ideas and opinions, but I also want my ideas to be respected.

I inform my students on the first day of class that grading is not all that relevant for me. "Everyone starts today with an A in this class," I declare. "Whatever you end up getting other than an A is because you didn't put in what you needed to do, didn't take the class seriously, didn't do the readings, or couldn't justify the positions you took. It's totally in your hands." And I really mean it. Grades are not that important for me. They become important if students think they're going to get an A for doing nothing, a mistake some of the Chicano kids make.

Besides teaching, the first year I'm also faculty sponsor for the Latino student organization MEChA. The Chicanos come to me for everything that involves them with the administration of the university and its programs, which is a lot. At the same time, protests against the war in Vietnam are reaching a feverish pitch across the nation, so this is a very active time in the history of the student movement, ethnically and otherwise. Like colleges and universities across America, the Irvine campus gets shut down by students responding with outrage against the May 4, 1970 massacre by National Guardsmen of four antiwar student demonstrators at Kent State University in Ohio.

This coincides with one of the seminal events in the early Latino movement, the Chicano Moratorium that takes place that summer. I remember it vividly. For weeks before the demonstration, a massive march down the streets of East L.A., preparations are underway, organized by the National Chicano Moratorium Committee co-chaired by Rosalio Munoz. Opposition to the war becomes an issue for more than just Anglos or lefties. It cuts across all lines. I remember Chicanos going to medical school in L.A. Latinos who want to become doctors. They're involved. Chicanos from all over the country make plans to come to the march. Critics can't dismiss or discredit the demonstrators as Communists trying to infiltrate the event. There are young and old people from everywhere participating in the moratorium.

Two weeks before the thing happens Phil Montes and I are frequenting the Redwood Room, a local watering hole for locals, including newspaper reporters, at Second Avenue and Broadway in downtown L.A. It's near the *Los Angeles Times* and the *Los Angeles Herald Examiner*, and not far from Phil's office. One of the guys we hang out with there is Ruben Salazar. He returns from being the *Los Angeles Times*' bureau chief in Mexico City and reporting from Vietnam, and starts writing columns about the Chicano experience in America. At first it seems like he's writing from the 50th floor looking down at Chicanos, from an ivory tower, with no real connection or understanding about the community he's writing about. Here's a guy who commutes to work at the *Times*' building in downtown L.A. from a great house in Orange County, a long way from the police brutality and other social and human ills of the Eastside. His wife is Anglo and isn't politically involved. She's content to care for the family and let Ruben do his thing as a journalist.

But over a short period of time, the more columns he writes the more he learns and the greater connection he makes. Ruben undergoes an evolution, the evolution of his own Chicano experience. I see it in his writings and in the conversations we have, mostly at the Redwood Room. It is the place to be, a serious drinking bar. Ruben likes to drink and I'm doing a lot of drinking too. Over time, I get to know him.

He is a fascinating man, well-schooled, well-travelled, and well-vested in international affairs. He is somebody you can't help but like. He's not outgoing, but a very genuine guy. Ruben is considered the Mexican at the *L.A. Times*; he's probably the first Mexican writing for a major white newspaper, fast gaining a national reputation, and therefore considers himself fortunate. He starts out, as people say, as a company man, but becomes his own person. His beliefs begin to be shaped by the developments he covers and the progress events are taking in Los Angeles, out of sight and mind from where he lives in Orange County: the student militancy, the Vietnam War, police misconduct, the farmworkers' struggle.

He writes about the LAPD, the L.A. Sheriff's Department and how they treat people in our community. One incident, the killing of an undocumented worker in one of the downtown skid row hotels, moves him. He gets into the plight of the undocumented, which isn't a big issue at the time. But it's a beginning of what we now know as the problem of immigration. It's a regional concern then, at best. Real change takes action at the national level, and there is little interest there. Ruben starts writing about this and other matters, and his change in perspective—and his insights—become very noticeable among those of us in the Chicano community and increasingly among the general public too.

Over time, he sees and understands the responsibility his job entails and consequently becomes very serious about the issues he's covering. He recognizes the power of the pen and the power of his column that comes out twice a week. It becomes just once a week when he branches out into Spanish-language television and becomes news director for KMEX-TV, Channel 34, now the flagship of the influential Univision network. The pioneering station manager, Danny Villanueva, a Republican and former L.A. Rams field goal star, hires Ruben to work in his news department. Ruben is becoming an extremely articulate guy.

We have a lot of conversations and some arguments—Phil Montes, Charlie Erickson, a former newspaper man himself, Ruben, and me. We'd laugh and joke with Ruben to his face, telling him he's a *vendito* and a sellout. But the rest of us realize that once Ruben starts practicing a harder-edged brand of journalism through the twin mediums of print and broadcast—his column and his work at Channel 34—he is becoming a threat to the establishment. More and more he is using the printed page and the airwaves to take up issues that are not complimentary to the educational establishment and the administration of justice. More people are starting to look twice at Ruben Salazar.

He writes about the skid row killing and the brutalization of several Chicanos in another incident, which leads to examining heavy-handedness by the LAPD and local law enforcement, including cracking down on students exercising their free speech rights during the walkouts and police infiltration of Chicano organizations by the police—what I later learn the LAPD orders Sol Monroy do for decades in East. L.A.

The police approach Ruben. "All this bullshit you're writing has to stop because you're inflaming the community with this writing," Ruben is bluntly told. He tells them to go fuck themselves and to get the hell out of his office.

That's when a couple of LAPD representatives meet with Danny Villanueva, Ruben's boss at KMEX. It is in Danny's best interest to fire Ruben because he is spewing subversive stories and creating mistrust, the officers communicate. Even Ruben thinks Danny is going to fire him. "I thought I was toast," he tells us. To Danny's credit, he looks at the cops, tells them the same thing Ruben says and throws them out of his office. "You can't tell me how to run my station and what my reporters should report," Danny says. That takes a lot of balls. The LAPD is always a very powerful institution, both in restraining crime but also in influencing public opinion. It is never really challenged, least of all by a Chicano reporter. And nobody is doing stories like Ruben is writing. I remember Danny relating that story of his meeting with the cops with a sense of great pride.

Ruben would be fired by the mainstream media of the era in L.A., if it ever let him do those stories in the first place. The only reason he can cover such subjects at the *Times* is the fact he's a columnist, not a reporter. The *Times*, thanks to its publisher, Norman Chandler, tells the cops to fuck off too. They go to everyone to try to shut Ruben up.

KMEX is a nothing TV station back then, with limited resources. It is unable to attract institutional advertising like the English-language stations. It is barely making it. Before Danny takes over, the level of reporting reflects the lack of resources. Danny's dream is to transform Channel 34 into a first-class television station with a bent towards reporting on the lives and experiences of Chicanos and Mexicans along with the news. Under his leadership, before he sells and gets out, KMEX ascends to the powerhouse it is today, the most popular television station in either language in Los Angeles. Ruben makes important early contributions to that transformation.

One evening three or four days before the moratorium is coming down, we're drinking with Ruben in the Redwood Room, talking about the upcoming protest. "I was in Mexico City for the student revolution during the Olympics of 1968," he says. "I've been in Vietnam as a war correspondent. All dangerous situations. But I fear for my life this coming Saturday, the day of the moratorium, more than I have ever feared before."

We start laughing. "What are you talking about?" one of us asks.

"I don't know if I'm going to make it," Ruben says. "I think something is going to happen."

"Just keep doing your work," we say. "You have the entire community supporting you."

I distinctly remember seeing him during the moratorium march on the back end of a truck with a camera crew from Channel 34, on the way to Laguna Park, as it is known then, where the big moratorium rally is happening. Tens of thousands of people are marching around him. "Ruben, how's it going?" I yell.

"Incredible!" he replies. He looks at ease, comfortable with himself. That is the last time I see Ruben Salazar alive.

I take this woman, Peg Cuthberston, with me to the moratorium. It's our first date; needless to say it isn't a normal date. A tall red head and a very smart lady, she is a deputy with U.S. Senator Alan Cranston's office, representing the senator at the march. She is supposed to speak for him at the rally. We meet two years earlier when she is working with Bobby Kennedy's press secretary, Frank

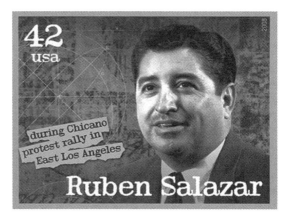

Richard develops a friendship with pioneering Chicano journalist Ruben Salazar, shown on the sidewalk in the bottom of the photo above, as he walks alongside the Chicano Moratorium march on August 29, 1970. A Los Angeles County sheriff's deputy kills Salazar a short time later. (Photo by Ralph Arriola) Image of Ruben Salazar on a U.S. postage stamp.

Mankiewitz. I'm seriously pursuing her. This is her inauguration to the Chicano community.

I remember telling her, "Walk this way if things go bad." I know how to behave during mass confusion. I get it from being in a big Vietnam War demonstration in Century City when the cops come in, tear gas and beat people. I learn how to get in and get out. I explain to Peg that if something happens on one side of the park, then the other side will be blocked off by parked buses. "People will freak out so you don't go that way," I say. "You'll get trampled on and never get out. If anything happens, this is where you go. This is how you get out of here because the natural tendency is for people to move a certain way, and you'll be trapped."

Peg doesn't want to speak on behalf of Senator Cranston, so I do it for her. I do my militant shit and get off the stage.

The Sheriff's Department, LAPD, and CHP are all assembled at, or nearby, Laguna Park. What happens is some guys rip off some beer at a liquor store near the park. From there they run into the park. The cops follow them. Given the tenor of the times and the tension of the day, law enforcement knows all hell will break lose. How could they not when there are 100,000 marchers bused in from far and wide, and at least 50,000 people still filling the streets in all directions from the park, which is very small?

Sure enough, all hell breaks out. First, you hear commotion. People start yelling as cops in riot gear and gas masks move in with batons. Then the tear gas starts.

My advice to Peg turns out right. Once the melee starts, the cops use tear gas and police lines to push people towards where all the buses are parked, where they are sandwiched. A lot of people get hurt. Hundreds are arrested.

We move out quickly to the north side of the park. We approach the stoplight at Ditman and Whittier. We run into Tom Brokaw, then with KNBC News, the local NBC affiliate. I know him from when he covers the high school walkouts, and we become friends. He turns to me, "Richard, what are you doing here?"

"What do you think I'm doing here?" I reply.

Then he turns around and sees Peg, whom he also knows. "Peg, what are you doing here?"

"I'm with him," and she gestures at me. Tom looks at me as if to say, You chickenshit guy. Why would you put her life in danger?

Her life in danger? I say to myself. She's fine with me. I will never put her life in danger.

The exchange turns into a running joke between us for years after that. Later, Tom asks me, "What does she see in you? I'm a TV guy, and that should count for something."

"I'm a Mexican, and that counts for a lot."

After we manage to get away from the police and back to my car that's parked a long way off, our eyes red from the tear gas that is everywhere, I have her drop me off at an office on Whittier Boulevard, where I spend the whole night arranging to get people bailed out of jail. "I can't take you home right now," I tell Peg. She lives in West L.A. I tell her how to get out of there while avoiding the area where the uproar is still going on. "I'll talk to you later this evening," I add. She takes my car home.

I'm up all night at the office on Whittier that serves as a command station for everything. Earlier we talk about making lawyers available in case of arrests. We arrange for a group of young Chicanos studying to be doctors, Chicanos for Creative Medicine, to provide medical assistance. A lot of ancillary things are organized ahead of time.

I am always in the background. I always believe that everybody has a role to play. If anyone gets busted, my role is to get them out of jail and find legal help, which is what I do during and after the walkouts. Personally, I have an aversion to getting arrested, but some people love it because it gives them a sense of identity. I don't need it.

Reports start coming into the command center. We hear about a shooting at the Silver Dollar, a dive bar on Whittier west of Atlantic Boulevard. I've been there. You walk in the front door, past a curtain, and then it's a room going straight ass back and around to the left. This is strictly a drinking bar—not a lot of cuisine. The day of the moratorium is a hot day. Reporters being what they are, Ruben Salazar takes his crew and finds a place to drink some beers. There is not a fucking thing going on inside that bar.

A sheriff's deputy fires a tear-gas canister into the bar. Ruben is hit in the head by the projectile and dies instantly. Cops come from every which way. It is maybe a quarter of a mile away from where we're working on Whittier. I know where I want to be and where I don't want to be. I don't want to be there because it isn't going to be very productive. And anyway, I'm up to my ass the whole night receiving information about mass arrests, about 700 people in all, mostly for disturbing the peace, assault on a police officer, interfering with a police officer. There are four or five charges they can choose from. When in doubt, the cops tag people with one or multiple charges and hope one of them ends up sticking. It's standard procedure for demonstrations.

I call Rose Chernin, with the Committee to Protect the Bill of Rights. "I don't know if you've heard what's happened at the moratorium?"

"Yes, sketchy stories," she says. "What happened?" I brief her.

"Oh, terrible," is her reaction.

"I don't have the slightest idea at this time who's been arrested or will be arrested," I continue. "But we'll need bail for them."

"Okay, let me call you back."

She calls back a short time later. "I've called around and we have 'X' number (I don't remember the exact count) of people prepared to put up their property in equivalency to what is needed." Never attempting to influence me or the cause I'm asking her to support, she just wants to support social activism by the Chicano community, which she thinks is good for the city. Her people are willing to put up their houses, some of them more than one, to raise money.

My friend, Ernie Camacho, and I coordinate with other bail bonds owners we know. We organize all of the bail bonds agents in East L.A. There's the mother of Mike Hernandez, later a member of the L.A. City Council. Another one, I affectionately call him Fat Albert, is an activist in Fresno and ends up being the biggest bail bonds agent in the state. We have to spend all night and into the next day, almost 24 hours, getting people bailed out, but we do it. The guys are held everywhere, from the county jail to the Hall of Administration to the city jail at Parker Center. The women are held at the Sybil Brand Institute, the women's jail in East L.A. Most have the charges against them dropped at some point along the line. Others they try to prosecute, but there isn't much traction for doing it. If you look at what happens, clearly any time there are such big crowds, it's easy for hysteria to take place. And clearly, there is a massive overreaction by the police.

More details come out about Ruben Salazar's death at the Silver Dollar. The official explanation is that a deputy shoots into the bar because it is suspected someone involved in a shooting is hiding inside, and he accidentally hits Ruben. I never believe that. You keep playing back in your mind what Ruben says the two weeks before, which I never forget: "I fear for my life this coming Saturday more than I have ever feared before."

We're soon back drinking at the Redwood Room in downtown L.A. Reporters and other friends of Ruben know it isn't an accident. They can't say it in their stories because they have to pretend they're objective journalists, but they feel there is foul play. That's my opinion too—and it still is. Towards the end of his life, Ruben Salazar becomes one of the most powerful opinion makers in Los Angeles on behalf of a community that is not well understood by the mainstream media or the general public. One of the reasons he is a threat to the establishment is the community he is writing about at the time doesn't have a lot of readers who get their news in English from the pages of the *L.A. Times*. The great majority of people who are reading his stuff are better educated Anglos, who he is influencing with his columns. Then Ruben discovers another constituency, Mexicans and Chicanos, whose main source of information and opinion comes from budding Spanish-language television. Since KMEX is the only game in town then, Ruben works at reporting the news there too. So his power emanates both from print and broadcast mediums, a powerful, and eventually unstoppable, combination, which is why he is a tremendous threat to the status quo in L.A. and why he is silenced.

At the same time I'm in the middle of the action in East L.A., there are regular protests going on against the war and activities at UCI where I'm involved around black and Chicano issues, with students pushing for change within the university. During my tenure as an instructor, I spend as much time in Chancellor Aldrich's office as anybody else on campus, advocating for the Latino students and their agenda. From where I'm at, it's a great time to be at a university.

I usually teach two classes a quarter. With all the office hours I put in meeting with students or other faculty, and the time spent working with student groups, I often don't leave campus until 7 or 8 p.m. By working with these kids over those two years, I get the college experience I don't have time for when I'm in college. For me, my life is fulfilled.

Dan Aldrich serves as the first chancellor at UCI from when it opens in 1965, until he leaves in 1984. He is a man of integrity, a firm believer in academic freedom. When anyone—usually right-wingers from Orange County—attacks members of his staff, professors, or administrators, he sides with his people until they are proven wrong. He also believes that a university education is not just for some, but for all.

The chancellor is very friendly towards blacks and Latinos, which is not necessarily consistent with the confines of his background, experience, and position, especially for a UC campus in one of the state's most conservative counties. He still has to rely for construction and research on the conservative Irvine Corporation, the huge family-controlled agricultural and development company in central and southern Orange County.

An early leader on campus of the radical SDS, Students for a Democratic Society, is Michael Chrisman. He's one of the brightest, most astute young men I meet up to that point who is Anglo, with great empathy for ethnic and racial minorities. Because of his close relationship with the chancellor, Aldrich hires him to be an administrator in charge of student affairs. The newspapers and politicians come down hard over Aldrich picking a guy with such a radical past. Remember the context: this is the height of student activism against the war and for civil and women's rights. Plus ethnic activists are seeking greater access to university resources and curriculum. All this strikes many people in Orange County as very threatening at the same time the chancellor is giving a young man with a leftist history a top position at the university. Things get pretty intense. At one point, Mike tells me, "I don't know if I can withstand the onslaught."

"You got to just stay in there," I reassure him. "I believe the chancellor will support you and will not give in to whatever amount of pressure comes down."

When he has problems, including how to handle the Chrisman controversy, Aldrich turns to me for help. My advice to him is simple: "If you blink, you're dead." I tell him that I sometimes question his political judgment, "but I don't question your resolve, and I believe [hiring Chrisman] is a good decision if it was anywhere but in Orange County because Chrisman is a man with integrity, not just the bomb thrower everyone thinks he is. He has good relationships with the student body and has their best interests in mind."

Dan Aldrich sticks to his guns. In the final analysis he makes the right decision because Mike serves the interest of UCI in an exemplary way. Later, he moves to Sacramento where he serves in top posts with the administration of Governor Jerry Brown.

One of the students in a class I teach on civil rights is Marc Grossman, who gets deeply involved with the United Farm Workers as an American history major at UCI. He impresses the hell out of me by writing a 70-page term paper on the legal aspects of the farmworkers' struggle. As a senior he starts teaching a class himself on farm labor organized through my colleague, Professor Carlos Munoz. Aldrich asks me what I think about the class. I tell him it's a good idea. Marc is well qualified and prepared for the class, isn't an ideologue, and doesn't impose his views on the students.

A brief news story about the class that appears in the university newspaper comes to the attention of the vice president for agriculture of the Irvine Corporation. The guy goes nuts, demanding that the chancellor kill the farm labor class. The chancellor refuses, mostly because it's an issue of academic freedom but also because before coming to Irvine, Aldrich is vice president for agriculture of the entire UC system. He observes that a one-time only undergraduate class introducing students to problems facing farmworkers isn't even a drop in bucket compared to the millions of dollars and the substantial resources the University of California spends every year benefiting the agricultural industry such as research on crop development, marketing, mechanization, and pesticides. The Irvine Corporation executive tries to go over Aldrich's head by appealing to the president of the nine-campus University of California, but Aldrich prevails. Marc goes on to become Cesar Chavez's longtime press secretary, speechwriter, and personal aide, and works for me at the state Capitol in the mid-'70s when the Agricultural Labor Relations Act, which I co-author, is passed.

Dan Aldrich always treats me very respectfully even though for a year all we do is fight. It seems like there's always an issue landing on his desk having to do with some facet of university life that impacts Chicanos or other minority students with grievances that I am bringing to the chancellor's attention. He also turns to me and asks for advice when there are problems with blacks. He knows I work in the past with the U.S. Civil Rights Commission and the NAACP legal defense fund.

When an issue comes up and it's severe enough, I go directly to the chancellor. That is also because many top administrators under Aldrich, deans and vice chancellors, are either indifferent or antagonistic when it comes to minorities; I run into my share of them at Irvine. Usually, I exaggerate the problem and the consequences of not resolving it with the chancellor. You have to understand the times: even though many in leadership positions may not care about people of color, everyone in leadership positions is sensitive to charges of racism and discrimination; such problems can have an impact on the administrator's reputation and ability to govern.

Aldrich is in a precarious position, in the middle of Orange County, which at the time could care less about the reality of the poor and minorities. What I discover about the chancellor during this process is he is a very fair-minded man who stands up for you if he thinks you're right and doesn't give into pressure. This is driven home to me by the stands he takes over Michael Chrisman and Marc Grossman.

A lot is also going on in and around campus capturing the imagination of Chicano students. There's the war in Vietnam and the disproportionate numbers of Latino kids who are dying over there. If you follow the history of participation by Latinos in America's wars, they are very patriotic, proud of their military service and are awarded a disproportionate number of decorations, including the Medal of Honor. I remember one or two of the big antiwar demonstrations at UCI. I was proud to be there, seeing the number of young people who are galvanized and come together expressing disagreement with their government's actions. Irvine becomes a focal point for the sit-ins and teach-ins that don't happen as much elsewhere in Orange County.

The international boycott of California table grapes begins in 1967, but really starts taking off by the time I'm at Irvine. It is another struggle that Chicano students at UCI and in Orange County, especially at Santa Ana Community College, get involved with in a serious way. By that time there are other Chicano causes going on: Rodolfo "Corky" Gonzales's Crusade for Justice in Denver and Reies Lopez Tijerina in New Mexico. But the grape boycott and the work of Cesar Chavez become very personal to them—and very symbolic. Cesar strikes a very special cord in all of us because he represents people who are powerless and voiceless, and before the UFW don't have anybody or any group to speak out for their rights. The other thing is that if you go back in the family history of most Chicanos, somebody worked out in the fields, whether it's in California, Arizona, or Texas. So the farmworkers, while far removed from the daily lives of most college kids who are largely from urban backgrounds, have a universal appeal.

The other reason is the man. Cesar is almost a mythic figure, a person who if you ever meet and listen to him has a special quality about him. He is part labor leader, part political leader, and part religious figure, but at the same time unaffectedly modest and self-effacing.

Ironically, of all of my students, the one who gets the most turned onto the farmworkers' cause—and makes it his life's work—is not Chicano at all, but Marc Grossman, the nice Jewish kid from West L.A. who graduates from Inglewood High School and lives in Ladera Heights with his mom and stepfather, Nathan Goldstein, a prominent dentist who practices in Brentwood. (I later become one of his patients, as does Cesar Chavez.) Marc is probably the first student I have who's better read and has a better grasp of the subject matter before he takes the course than anyone I have the good fortune of teaching.

Helping bring him along is worth it, I figure, because Marc is somebody who might spend a great deal of his life advancing the cause of ethnic and racial minorities. It's no wonder that he not only takes his class work seriously but also carries through on what he feels strongly about in the course of his career, spending many years working with the UFW for the grand total of $5 a week (later doubled to $10 a week), the same "pay" Cesar gets. He still continues with the farmworkers more than 50 years later. (He also marries two Latinas and has three "Mexi-Jew" sons, as he calls them.)

As a senior at UCI, almost ready to graduate, one day Marc comes to me saying he wants to quit college to go work full time with the UFW. "You've put this much time in and you're close to graduating," I advise. "Your value to the movement will be greatly enhanced by finishing your education." He finishes and goes on to graduate school in journalism at UCLA before returning to work with Cesar.

I also meet the current president of the SDS chapter at UCI, a white woman, when the Chicano students ask me to speak at their 1969 Cinco de Mayo event on the Irvine campus. After the speech, she comes up and introduces herself. Later on I find out she's close to Mike Chrisman and her father is president of Crown Zellerback Paper Company and a former U.S. ambassador to some European country. "I like your rap," she says, "but it seems you represent the establishment. Look at how you like to dress." I'm wearing my usual three-piece suit.

I look at her. "I don't know you," I respond. "You don't know me. If you're going to judge me by the way I'm dressed, that's your problem. But I'm not judging you by the way you're dressed because if I did, you look like some straggly piece of shit." Her reaction to me is a way for her to reject materialism, I keep going, which is really not what her background is about because more than likely she isn't born into poverty. "I'm not your parent or your government who you should be angry with." She looks at me. "Give me a shot," I ask her, "because I'm going to withhold judgment about you being a slob and not having much to offer except rhetoric, which is very prevalent in your social group. So you withhold judgment about me being a sellout.

"The difference between you and me is I grew up in a community with limited opportunities," I continue my little lecture. I go through a brief laundry list of some of the best parts of my life growing up in East L.A. "I'm not even going to embarrass you by asking for your background. I can make assumptions and more than likely my assumptions will be correct."

She says, "We'll see."

"Fine," I reply.

She ends up taking my first ethnic studies class. By the end of the quarter, she turns into a convert. Only after the class is over do I end up going out with her. She's one of many Anglo students I meet who come from privileged backgrounds and are rebelling against everything material, some of them with a hatred of their parents for whatever reason—because of what their parents stand for or maybe they come from dysfunctional families. That kind of attitude seems to fit in with the college setting of the day and age. Many of these affluent radicals are fascinated by the black and Chicano experiences. Most go on to successful and lucrative careers as business people or professionals. Few spend their lives living the convictions they profess during their radical college years.

Only after getting elected to public office a short time later do my long-held views on dressing well come into sharper focus with help from people like Willie Brown. Effectively presenting your overall politics means you also have to look presentable. Minority politicians such as Willie and I "knew they had to look good," observes our colleague Maxine Waters. "When they rolled out, they looked immaculate and did it with style."

"It serves you well, particularly for minorities," Maxine continues. "You go back to what your parents taught you. Minority parents said, 'Son, when you go downtown to shop, I want you to look good. Put on a nice shirt, nice pants; don't let them think you're somebody who doesn't have money or that you're there to steal something. Look nice and they'll treat you better.' Latino and black parents always said that to their children."

I spend much time counseling and becoming friends with many college students. Something that surprises me is how much hostility many kids who are Chicano, as well as Anglo, show towards their parents. They contrast the new things they're exposed to in college to the hypocrisy, the inconsistency of values, and the lack of tolerance they see in their parents. It's a little shocking. These are young people who are barely a generation removed from me. Maybe I too rebel against my mother and father. My father can be verbally abusive, but he is the greatest man I meet in my life in terms of what he instills in me, and I also recognize the love my parents feel for me.

Talking about their parents, I constantly tell the kids, "You will never find two people who have any greater interest than what's best for you even if they may not know how to love you the way you would like to be loved or the knowledge to help you get to where you want to go." This doesn't have anything to do with the students' academic careers. It happens anyway just because of who I am and the worries kids have about their lives when they are away from home for the first time in a strange environment. Students talk to me about things they can't talk about with their parents or even spouses.

I'm at a party in a professor's home in Laguna Beach when the husbands of two of my students, both Anglo women, separately take me aside. Their wives both take multiple classes with me. Outside of class, the women talk about their lives and marriages. I mostly listen. "I don't even know you, but I want to thank you," one husband tells me.

"For what?" I ask.

"You have really helped me and my wife in our marriage because you got her to see things more clearly and she has, in turn, gotten me to understand and resolve problems."

I know how both of my students feel because they express it on numerous occasions. Like the Chicano students, sometimes it's good to have someone to talk with.

I feel part of my responsibility at UCI is getting the Chicano kids to understand how four years in college can come and go quickly. In order for them to finish and graduate, I always reinforce the concept that while they're going to school everybody wants to play at being something they're not. People who want to be lawyers want to act like they're lawyers when they're not. Those who want to be leaders want to play at it when they still haven't finished their college educations. Some want to commit their entire lives then and there to the Chicano movement, which in my eyes is naive and adolescent. So I constantly instill in them the importance of going to class, concentrating on their studies, and then deciding what paths they want to take. Our community needs lawyers, I emphasize, not people who play at being lawyers. We need teachers, not people who play at being teachers. We need doctors, not people who play at being doctors.

The students' first job, I keep repeating, is to become what they want to become and then to become an asset to their community, family, and themselves.

Latino students at UCI really have it made. Their existence is largely subsidized, either by the government through grants and loans, or for some by their parents if they have the wherewithal. Their living conditions are better than most of them have ever known. Their only responsibility is going to classes and studying, and some have a hard time doing that. Others have a hard time being apart from what is familiar in their communities, which in my eyes is ridiculous because these Chicano kids have an opportunity most of their parents and peers never know. There's the opportunity of earning a degree from one of the most prestigious institutions of higher learning in the world. Then there's spending four years of their lives in a place, while foreign and to some hostile, is a short hop from communities like Newport Beach and Laguna Beach, and the beautiful Pacific Ocean. That doesn't seem real hard to me.

Relationships I develop with students on campus continue after they graduate and I leave UCI. I keep in touch with many of them and help them with their careers in future years. They turn out and work on my campaigns when I run for public office.

Meantime, my teaching career takes me to a very different setting not far away from the Irvine campus.

Phil Montes asks me to fill in for him by speaking about ethnic and minority relations at a conference of federal prison wardens being held at Idyllwild, California. I know a little about federal prisons from a black and brown perspective, which is that an increasingly disproportionate percentage of people incarcerated in them happen to be minorities, primarily blacks and Chicanos. And since the system knows little about these groups, consequently very little is being done to deal with the changing reality. That's what I talk about in Idyllwild.

In the audience are probably about 65 or 75 wardens and administrators with the Federal Bureau of Prisons. After the speech is over, a guy comes up to me. Lee Jett is the assistant warden, second in command, at the federal correctional institution at Terminal Island, near the entrance to the L.A. harbor between San Pedro and Long Beach. "I just want to let you know I disagree with you," he tells me. "I think most of the stuff you said was bullshit. But I have a real problem at my institution. We have a growing number of Chicanos. They're asking for relevant classes in ethnic culture and studies." He asks if I know anybody who might be interested in going to Terminal Island to teach at his prison. "Do you know anyone?"

"I'll do it," I answer.

"Great. But I have a lot of blacks at Terminal Island too," he adds. "And, of course, if we do it for the Latinos, we also have to do it for the blacks. Do you have any ideas?"

I think about it and decide to ask Joe White, a psychologist and chairman of the School of Comparative Culture at UCI, who I know going back to my teaching days at Long Beach State when he is a full professor of psychology, very active in black studies and also helpful in working with Latino students on campus. He's a great professor. So I ask him and he agrees to handle the blacks at the prison. Then I deliver the package of both of us to the assistant warden. (I deal with the warden too once in a while, but mostly it's the assistant warden, Lee Jett, the operations guy at the facility.)

So in late 1969, I go to prison, where some of my high school teachers tell me I'll eventually end up. Officials at the institution set up an appointment for me to be interviewed for the teaching job by a panel of inmates, who have a say in the matter.

The facility sits on a point at Terminal Island, which at one time is home to a fishing fleet and packing sheds. Commerce from all over the world passes by. The prison is surrounded by water on two sides, with ongoing maritime industries on the other two sides. The buildings on the men's side of the prison are in a "U" shape, with housing and residential halls, an auditorium, library, kitchen, and classrooms, and a separate building for administration.

I always remember on my first visit when the first gate opens, walking into a reception area and then seeing the gate close behind me before the second gate in front of me opens up. Then you know you're in prison. If it is anybody but me, a visitor, coming in you know you're there for a while. There is this feeling of reality that sets in: you're incarcerated and there's no way out until you serve out your term. It is different for me, of course, since I'm arriving for a short, fixed period of time.

I head to the library, outside the main building. You turn to the right and there's a building with classrooms and then the library. I remember walking into one of the classrooms. I find five guys there. I meet them and know in my mind right away there's no way I'm not getting this job. The reason is simple: I grow up in the same neighborhood with four of them. One of them, the leader, is Chispas Sandoval. He lives around the block from our house. We lose track when he starts in the youth and later the adult penal system. Another of the inmates lives down the hill in El Hoyo. Two of the others I also know; one is from a rival gang about a mile away from where I live as a kid. We all go to the same junior high school; I remember going to school with them.

They sit there, handling the interview very professionally. It occurs to me the room may be bugged. The interview lasts maybe 15 minutes. They ask me to tell them about myself and what I have to offer. I tell them about Long Beach State and UCI. To them, I'm the professor.

After the interview and some brief deliberations by the panel when I'm not present, we are all outside in the hallway. Chispas walks up and says, "Ricardo, it's good to see you. It's good to see you, brother."

The only thing I ask is, "Was it a unanimous endorsement?"

"Everything we do is unanimous," he assures me.

The inmates get back to the warden and they agree with the assistant warden to hire me. I am processed and fingerprinted through the Federal Bureau of Prisons. I start teaching some weeks later. But before that begins, they ask if I am interested in doing something on the women's side of the prison. It's a coed institution, with separate wardens and staffs for men and women. The women's prison is considered a country club by comparison. The men's area is all asphalt and concrete on the outside. By contrast, the women's side of the institution has a lot of grass and some trees.

The female warden and the women inmates interview me too. They like me.

For me, no place is a good place when you're incarcerated. But Terminal Island isn't that bad. There's decent weather, sea breezes, and a mixture of different kinds of offenders, from organized crime figures to violators of various federal laws such as immigration, bank robbery, and narcotics.

Historically, the heavily minority inmate population is there primarily because of drugs. With few exceptions, the Chicano inmates I deal with in class are in for narcotics-related offenses. One day in class I'm talking about this phenomenon and how most everyone is present because they are drug addicts or dealers. "I bet you there's not a bank robber in the class," I say. One guy puts his hand up and says, "Well, I'm here for bank robbery." Everyone starts laughing. I make a joke out of it too, but I emphasize how it illustrates that it isn't the Mexicans who are making money off the drug trade. We're the "mules" who get caught transporting or stashing or, on occasion, Chicanos are the small-time dope dealers. It becomes a federal offense because it often involves interstate or international trafficking. One of the guys in my class is caught at the border with a ton of marijuana in the panels of his car, and in every other place they can hide it.

I teach classes one day a week with the men and another day a week with the women, all beginning at 7 p.m. and going until 9 p.m. Attendance is voluntary, although it's a smart move, a sign of their rehabilitation, for inmates to be involved in educational classes. There are probably 40 men and an equal number of women in each class.

The class structure is much the same as what I teach at UCI. It takes me a while to figure out how you teach students at a university; that's one thing. Those students are par for the University of California, considered home to the best and the brightest. The UCI students taking my classes are after a degree, have free movement to come and go as they like, and have the freedom to attend or not to attend my class. Then, three or four hours after I'm in the classrooms at Irvine, I drive north from the heart of Orange County to Terminal Island, which is a whole different world. The men and women at the prisons are very limited in their movements. They vary from some who will never leave the institution to others who probably think going to my classes is a good way to show they're trying to make something of themselves to others who have a genuine interest in the subject matter. For others it's just a great way to break the monotony of institutionalization. I think some are hungry for somebody from the outside to talk with them about what's going on in society during what many of them know is a tumultuous time for Latinos in the history of the country.

The curriculum is also pretty much the same. It's considered a history and government class. But you have to tailor and organize the material so it is relevant to the incarcerated life of the inmates and at the same time make it interest-

At the same time Richard is teaching ethnic studies at UC Irvine he is also conducting similar classes for both men and women Chicano inmates at the Federal Correctional Institution at Terminal Island near the entrance to L.A. harbor.

ing enough for them to keep coming back. There are times I walk out of a prison classroom and feel like I just hit it out of the park. Then there are times when I know I'm laying an egg. It takes me a while to adjust, but I do. One day it hits me that however the material is presented in class, it has to consider their reality, not my reality or the reality of the students I teach at UCI. The inmates' reality is that they sit in my class for two hours a week. Then they go back to their locked-down dorms. (Even though many of them are badass men and women, Terminal Island is still a minimum-security facility.)

Every time before I show up at Terminal Island, I do this little ritual: I stop by a nearby pub at the harbor, a combination hamburger joint and full bar. I eat and have a few beers, which prepare me for the reality inside the prison that is so different than the college environment I have just left. What I discover after a period of time is that all the best and the brightest aren't necessarily at the University of California.

Inmates dress in brown kakis or something similar with light green shirts. In terms of learning how to survive in life, many in prison already have their

Ph.Ds., even if an academic institution doesn't issue them. Unfortunately, they land in prison because of their antisocial behavior. Many of my students in prison are surprisingly well read—they have a lot of time on their hands to read—and profound thinkers in their own right. I learn a lot from teaching at the university. I learn a lot from teaching at the prison too.

The prison reality hits home when we're talking in class about the continuum of acculturation and assimilation, starting with Mexican values and how they conflict with American culture, which is predicated on assimilation. Then I observe that one of the cruelest experiences affecting Chicanos is what Octavio Paz writes about in his book, *Labyrinth of Solitude*. Paz describes the world of the Pachuco, young Chicanos who, in part as a method of rebellion, create their own culture, a unique way of dress and even language, called *Calo* or Pachuco, in the 1930s and '40s. Paz writes that the Pachuco is a person who is in a state of suspension in midair. He can't completely relate to traditional Mexican values but is also unable or unwilling to accept the values of Anglo America. Pachucos are totally confused, unable to relate very well to either world. So they develop a new reality unto themselves. This reality considers family important, but often Pachucos can't relate to blood relatives who reject their lifestyle. So they relate instead to an adopted family, the family of the gang.

This kind of perspective hits home with my incarcerated pupils. They can relate to it. It helps some inmates better understand what puts them behind bars. Before you know it, the two-hour class goes by quickly. "Ninety-eight percent of you will leave the institution at some point or another," I tell them. "The question will be, is this the last time you are here? The only way you don't come back is that you can't use any more excuses for your behavior. Remember what it's like to be institutionalized, away from family and loved ones, not even considered human—and being treated as less than human. If that's not the kind of life you want, you have to find a life outside that will keep you from doing what you know best, which is violating the law and eventually ending up back in prison.

"Every dope dealer at one time or another says to himself, 'I'm different. I'm never going to get caught and go back to prison.' Inevitably, they get caught and go back." In the year and a half I teach at Terminal Island there are guys who leave the place and before I finish my teaching stint are sent back for a new crime or for violating their parole.

I talk with them about institutionalization and how some inmates feel prison is their home. Some of the students react by saying, "Bullshit, no one likes to be in the joint." Others cop to it. I talk about the power of reading and knowledge, and about getting a GED, general education diploma or high school equivalency. During my time there, I see people who initially want nothing to do with such things turn themselves around, get involved with the program, and earn their GEDs.

I bring in outside speakers. I learn what the students like. They love boxing. So I bring in a couple of Mexican boxers who are champions of the world to talk about their lives. One of them is Ruben Navarro, lightweight champion of the world. Another is Mando Ramos, a world champion in two divisions who gets involved in drugs before finding religion. One is still an active fighter. The other is retired, but still revered in the Mexican community. The inmates find out they share common backgrounds with both boxers, who face many of the same challenges. It's just the boxers take their lives in a different direction.

I bring in live entertainment—*folklorico* dancers and live bands. While it is open to all inmates, these entertainers have a special social relevance to the Chicano inmates.

Chispas Sandoval, my friend from when we grow up together in East L.A. who heads the inmate panel endorsing me as their teacher, is a great *revote*, or handball, player. It's a sport Mexicans excel at. Once I'm at a Beverly Hills park and meet the actor Ryan O'Neal, who is a very good handball player. "I read you love handball," I say. "I got a group of guys I believe are better than you. Would you be interested in a tournament?" O'Neal puts together a group of players, including some other actors. They head over to Terminal Island and find out what it's like playing the really good handball players among the inmates. It's nice of O'Neal, who takes the competition seriously and discovers as good as he thinks he is, the guys in the joint are much better.

Chispas is a very worldly and sophisticated guy within the framework of his background. He's considered a sophisticated criminal, a very intelligent person who people in the administration of justice fear. He knows how to play the game, the politics of institutionalization. However, it doesn't manifest itself in anything positive in terms of behavior or working towards doing something productive so he can make it on the outside.

But he undergoes a kind of epiphany that I witness. It doesn't happen overnight. Maybe I help facilitate his desire for a better life. I recognize how bright he is and over a period of time he realizes there is something else for him outside of prison. His wife, who is also an inmate, helps him along to a great extent. He marries her in prison. She comes from a wealthy Jewish family. Through her he sees that other side of life and gets a taste for good food and music.

The subjects of my class fascinate Chispas. He reads Octavio Paz, understands him, and comes up with his own point of view. But he gets my point too. I try to instill in him that the best people to help our community advance are us, that the best people involved in penology who can help ex-cons are those who go through it and prepare and educate themselves. They'll be of the greatest use. If there is going to be a redirection in the lives of former inmates, it will come from having this kind of institutional support for them once they get out.

As tough as prison life is on the men, I think the women have it worse. What little in the way of programs and the provision of resources that are being supplied to the men, even less is being done for the women. There is a real sense of loneliness from the little contact they have with family or friends. They are frequently left feeling very isolated and in need.

The class subjects I teach are the same for both men and women. But I get the women to talking about women's issues. I make them laugh about how much power they have, but don't realize they have. They think the only thing they're good for is making babies and being on call for men. I tell them they're better and intuitively much more intelligent. But instead of realizing that, they let themselves take a backseat to whatever man they happen to be with. The women students look forward every week to me showing up. It may be the only contact they have with the outside that week.

On the men's side, all of my students are Chicanos. My women's classes are pretty much filled by Chicanas, with a couple of Native Americans.

The women are very protective of me. They usually meet me at the gate when I come in and escort me to the gate when I leave. They're also very territorial. They feel the only ones who should talk with me are other Mexican women from the class.

Early one evening on a beautiful sunny day, I spot all of my female students sitting in the shade under a tree. "What the shit are you guys doing?" I ask. "Why aren't you getting some sun?"

"We don't want to get dark," a woman inmate says.

That gives me an idea on how to talk about skin color and Latinos, and how many Mexicans don't want to be seen as too dark, a holdover from the Spanish Conquest of Mexico when dark-skinned indigenous people were thought inferior to the light-skinned Spaniards. It still holds true in Mexico and America, something I experience from the distance my uncle-in-law from Jalisco always keeps from the rest of the Alatorre family, which like me has a lot of dark complexions. There's a phobia among our people about the "*negros*," or dark ones, versus the light-skinned ones who are more acceptable in society.

I teach a whole class in the women's prison about it. "Think about the millions of white people who spend so much money to put stuff on their faces and bodies to get a nice tan—and many of us have that tan naturally," I tell the students. Then I once again ask them why they are huddled under the tree. None of them want to get dark because they look on it as a negative, they admit. "Look at me," I say. "I'm proud of how dark I am, but I don't have to spend the money others have to spend to get this color."

There's a very positive response. I never see any of the women underneath that tree again when I walk into the facility.

We also talk about current events and developments going on outside in the Chicano community that they're interested in and read about. They start reading more newspapers and magazines, and ask what I think about certain subjects. That can trigger an entire two-hour class discussion.

More than six months after I start teaching, I'm heading out of the women's side after class ends right around 9 p.m. I leave the classroom and turn onto the walkway. The students have to be back in their dorm. All of a sudden, this Native American inmate in her 30s, who isn't one of my students and obviously has some mental health issues, comes up behind me. She has a shank. It's a crude prison-made knife, but fully capable of killing or doing serious damage if you know how to use it. She sticks the shank right up against my back. I immediately know what it is. "I'm going out with you," she insists.

"You want to go in front of me?" I reply "Ladies first." She doesn't think it's funny. I know there's going to be a confrontation. The prison staff doesn't care about my ass, I know, and they aren't going to let her escape.

"They're not letting you out," I say. "You're just going to get in trouble."

My mind is working. I spot a sprinkler on the ground and deliberately trip over it together with the lady and the shank. The shank drops from her hand. She's moving to retrieve it but I get to it first. "Get out of here," I tell her. "I don't want you to get in trouble." But by this time a few inmates from my class spot her, see what's going on and are running towards us. A couple of guards come along too, see the knife and ask, "Where did this come from?"

"I didn't make it," I respond. The staff puts the lady in handcuffs and takes her away to lockup.

I'm fine because nothing happened. Sure, I'm scared. But I feel bad because I know what's going to happen to the woman with the shank. "Hey man, she doesn't know what she's doing," I tell the guards. "She needs help. Obviously, she's not all there."

The next day I call the warden and tell her, "Hey, there was an incident. I never feared for my life," which is sort of a lie. "I knew she wasn't getting out. But don't punish her. She's not all there mentally. She needs help. You're not going to help her by punishing her." Disciplining this woman would make it harder for me to relate to the other inmates, I add. The warden is decent. The inmate gets off with a write up, which I understand.

I find out later if the women in my class have their way, they will beat the shit out of her. We talk about it in the next class. "No one was harmed," I note.

"If we have a chance to get her, we'll get her," one of my students blurts out.

"No, what am I teaching you for?" That triggers a whole discussion. But from that point on, the students make sure they never let me walk to or from the building with the classrooms unless they're escorting me. I'm flattered and touched. "I can take care of myself," I laugh.

"No, this can't happen anymore," they say. "You're the teacher; we need you here."

While I'm still teaching the men at Terminal Island, I am also spending part time at the state Capitol in Sacramento with the Assembly Office of Majority Services, which provides adjunct staff to the Democratic members of the lower house. I'm drafting legislation for members. I get a call from a Chicano reporter who hears I'm still teaching at the prison. He gets word through the grapevine that a strike by inmates has stopped work in the prison industries and the strikers are locked down in their dorms. According to the reporter, a Native American woman is disciplined; staff put her in lockdown and in the process ruptures her spleen. The men hear about it, tell the women inmates not to go to work, and shut down the prison industries on their side, which earns money for the Federal Bureau of Prisons making license plates, clothing, and a variety of other things.

Then I get a call from the prison, saying they are canceling my class because of the lockdown.

A day or so later I get another call from the facility, this time from Lee Jett. He's been promoted from assistant warden to warden at Terminal Island. He tells me what's happening: the men have a negotiating team and the inmates want me to meet with them and help negotiate a settlement with the prison administration. "This is what they want," Jett says, "but we want to warn you that we have no control and can't provide you any protection. You have to do it on your own. Rest assured, I can't guarantee your safety."

"I'm more worried about what's going to happen to the guys than I'm worried about what they'll do to me," I reply. "I'll do it."

It's an eerie feeling once I'm inside the men's prison. The guards tell me where to go. With no staff in sight, I meet with the negotiating committee, a small number of guys, in the prison library. Chispas is one of them. The team is made up of blacks, Chicanos, a Native American, and this Anglo guy, who's Italian American. I go guy to guy, shaking hands. They acknowledge me, each of them saying his name. I put my hand out to the last guy, the Italian American. "My name is Salvatore Bonanno," he says.

Oh shit!, I say to myself. This is Salvatore "Bill" Bonanno, son of famed Mafia chieftain Joseph Bonanno, the main figure in Gay Talese's best-selling book, *Honor Thy Father*.

"You're Joe Bonanno's son," I tell him. "I just finished reading your book." Bonanno smiles. He's clearly the one in charge.

"I've heard about you," Bonanno says. "You have a good reputation. Thank you for coming."

"Okay, what am I here for?" is what I say. "Before we begin, are we sure..." And I point to my mouth and ears, asking whether the place is being bugged.

One of the inmates holds up microphones they disable and says, "Don't worry about it. Everything is fine here." We all laugh.

"So what do you want?" I begin.

"We don't know," someone answers.

"Well, wait a minute, man," I continue. "You can't just tell me you don't give a fuck. Obviously, you want something."

"But we don't know what to ask for," another one of them offers.

"Why don't you be ridiculous and ask for everything?" I suggest. "Then I'll tell you what I think is doable and what I think isn't."

They list everything, all of their grievances, from improving the food to more books for the library. They want to make sure that whoever does it to the Indian woman is taken care of, that she receives proper treatment, and that the brutality has to stop. I write everything down.

After they're finished listing things, I say, "Okay, man, why don't we start off with the fact that 60 percent of this shit is not going to happen. So let's start by you giving me an idea of what's really important to you." We start figuring it out. It takes a while.

I give them a quick course in how to negotiate with people: "I don't know what I'm going to be able to get, but there are some basics in how to negotiate with somebody that you guys have to learn. They aren't mind readers. You may think they know everything, but they don't know shit either.

"You always go for more than you think you can get," I go on. "Sometimes you can get everything, but more than likely that won't happen. So you make your asks sound ridiculous. But when you negotiate it all out, you make sure you get what you want."

Then I say, "This is what I'm going to do. I'm going to go back to them and say, 'This is the list.' I'm going to tell them I think you guys are crazy. But you're also serious that something has to be done or someone is going to get hurt. Then they're going to say, 'We can't do this' or 'We can't do that.' I'll tell them what your bottom line is and we'll see if they agree."

I tell the committee what I think I can get out of the administration. I assure them I'll never go below the bottom line they agree on. They say that sounds cool.

I meet with the warden. I make it sound worse than it is: "These guys are scary, clearly upset, not exactly rational. They gave me a laundry list. I think some of this is bullshit. I don't want you to get shocked. But there are some things that if you do them, I believe I can go and sell it to them." The warden is grateful I'm there and willing to help out.

"Shit, at least you know more than I do because they won't even talk to me," he admits.

I read him the list. It covers everything. "Oh, shit, I can't do that—it'll cost money," he says about more than one of the demands. Then I get to what I think he has to do at a minimum. I start with the outrageous stuff and then the things that are doable if they want to do them. Before I know it, they agree to more than I thought they would: improving food. More ethnic food. More books and current affairs newspapers and magazines for the library. Doing something about better medical care. Cleaning up the prison industry program, improving safety conditions. The bottom line is making sure the Native American woman's medical needs are attended to. She violates some rules, but Jett agrees to an investigation into why a 95-pound woman requires the intervention of four or five men, why no woman staff person is present during the process, and why the inmate ends up in the hospital.

There's more. Finally, Jett says, "Ah, shit, I can't do some of this stuff. Here's what I think the bottom line is." I've been through this so many times with school officials during the East L.A. battles. I sense there is an economic interest in getting the prison industries back on line. It's also bad for a warden when it looks like he can't keep his institution functioning. It's bad for the Federal Bureau of Prisons, which is losing money. And it's bad for the inmates who aren't receiving the minimum pay they get for working. The warden agrees.

"Okay, I'm going to go back inside," I announce.

"I can't guarantee your life," he informs me again.

"I already went in once and came out," I say. "Just make sure no one from your side makes it hard for me to get out by doing something stupid. I know my guys will take care of me."

"You got it," I announce to the inmate committee.

"What?" some of the inmates ask.

"Yes, this is what they agreed to," and I take them through it. "You guys have to work out the details. I already cut your deal. Now what you gotta do is work things out with them on your own time tables."

In the prison exercise area, inmates congregate in cliques. There are Mexicans, blacks, Anglos, white supremacists—and a good number of Italians. The Italians always fascinate me. Most of them have mob connections and are sophisticated criminals.

Bill Bonanno comes up to me at the end and remarks, "You're a man of your word."

I later convince Chispas he should get his high school diploma and go on to college. He spends a semester at El Camino Community College in Torrance. Then I get him into UC Irvine. He graduates *magna cum laude*. My relationship with Chispas becomes a matter of great concern among law enforcement. He is alleged to be a founder of the Mexican Mafia. A 1974 article in *Reader's Digest* tries to use my friendship with Chispas to tag *me* as part of the Mexican Mafia. I'm already a legislator and very active in my community, including aiding nonprofit organizations that believe in giving ex-cons like Chispas opportunities to turn themselves around.

At one point in the early 1970s a task force is formed that includes the FBI, U.S. Drug Enforcement Administration, state Department of Corrections, and local law enforcement agencies. They're very concerned about the number of people leaving prisons and whether alleged members of the Mexican Mafia are using self-help nonprofits to further their criminal enterprises. Among some police officials, this concern almost amounts to hysteria.

After I help him finish college, Chispas finds faith and abandons his criminal ways. There are people who get out of prison, go in a different direction, and never look back. Of course, there are others who revert back to their prior ways. I have no reason to believe Chispas is doing anything illegal. What he does do is work with young men and women who are trying to get out of the gang culture as part of a nonprofit group in Lincoln Heights called Community Concerned. But law enforcement never thinks he's genuine, right up until he dies. In the eyes of some cops, once a member of the Mexican Mafia, always a member. Friendship or not, I would not have had anything to do with Chispas if I thought he is still involved in criminal activity.

I help out a lot of people who are or have been incarcerated. I always tell them the same thing: "If you burn me once, I'll never have anything to do with you again." I believe people can be rehabilitated and if given the opportunity to lead a productive life they will choose it. I can't subscribe to the philosophy that once a criminal, always a criminal because of the community where I grow up.

If I believe in that view then anybody who is once a member of a gang, even at a young age, is of no use to anybody. We're not just talking about individuals who are once behind bars. We're talking about their mothers and fathers and other family members. All of them are constituents of mine. Once I'm elected to office, many of them come to my office asking my help for themselves or for a loved one who maybe needs a break. So long as I can see that the person in question is attempting to help him- or herself, I'm willing to try and help too. I view it as part of my responsibility as an elected official. For good or bad, I represent communities with lots of kids who end up involved with the administration of justice, the probation, parole, or prison systems. One of the first assembly committees I chair is a panel on prison reform.

Sometimes it means helping to get an inmate paroled. Sometimes it's relocating someone from an institution that's hundreds of miles away to somewhere closer so the inmate can maintain more regular contact with family members, which is paramount to the ability to stay out of prison upon release. I help get ex-inmates into school.

These are interesting times. Even though I never consider myself a professional academic—nor would anyone else mistake me for one—I probably receive higher ratings from my students than anybody in comparative culture. Students at UCI fill out evaluation forms at the end of each class. My scores are the best for course content, what students learn, and my classroom style, which is very unconventional, to say the least.

The first year at Irvine is great. It's up before I know it, probably one of the most rewarding times of my life. Towards the end of the academic year, UCI offers me a contract to teach for a second year. I have reservations, but I'm having a good time, enjoying the students, and the like. I teach two classes in the winter quarter of '71 and one class in the spring quarter. By December 1971, I know I am making a mistake; in the second year it starts to become more like a job. Besides, other things are happening I want to explore.

I have and maintain a great rapport with Dan Aldrich, who I grow to like and respect. After I'm elected to the legislature in 1972, the chancellor comes to see me at my office in the state Capitol. We talk about old times—well not really so old at that time—and he tells me how proud he is of me.

Then we get down to business. "This is my problem," he says, and goes on to lay it out: UCI has a fledgling medical school on campus but is having great difficulty trying to raise its reputation in order to attract top flight professors and medical specialists. One of their problems is they don't have a teaching hospital, like the Los Angeles County-USC Medical Center in Northeast L.A., which serves as the teaching hospital for the USC medical school, or UCLA, which also has its own teaching hospital, or UC Davis, which has a teaching hospital in nearby Sacramento. Aldrich explains that lack of a teaching hospital is a major impediment to growing his medical school.

It just so happens that this is the same time doctors are being allowed to be officers of private hospitals. Needless to say, anything that can compete with privately run, doctor-controlled hospitals—like a new university-operated teaching hospital for UCI—is being shunned by doctors in Orange County, which boasts some of the most politically powerful legislators in California. The chancellor turns to me, the newly elected Chicano from an East L.A. district, after getting nowhere talking with state lawmakers from Orange County.

I believe in the university because I work there, and in its medical school because it turns out one of the highest rates of practicing family physicians, neighborhood doctors. UCI's philosophy is turning out these kinds of docs because of the critical need for them in underserved communities like East L.A.

I see an opportunity. I'm appointed to the Assembly Ways and Means Committee, chaired by then-Assemblyman Willie Brown, during my first year in office, which is unusual. At the time, Ken Cory, one of the assemblymembers from Orange County Aldrich has a hard time convincing, is serving as chairman of the Democratic Caucus in the assembly under Speaker Bob Moretti, making Cory one of the most influential members of the house. One of Cory's biggest political benefactors and financial backers, and one of the biggest campaign contributors in Orange County along with developer and restaurant owner Dick O'Neil, is Dr. Lou Chella, a multimillionaire doctor who owns private hospitals.

I go see Willie. "In my mind, Aldrich is always controversial for the right reasons," I tell Willie. "Here's the problem—which I lay out—and here is my ask of you: to support my effort to put in the state budget an item establishing a teaching hospital in Anaheim, near UCI, with the idea of serving as Irvine's medical school—but also serving underserved communities. How about we also require that a fixed percentage of all incoming classes at the medical school be Mexicans and blacks?

"I know this guy," referring to Aldrich, I assure Willie. "I taught there."

"Fabulous," Willie replies. "Let's try for 25 percent."

"Fine," I agree. "But there's always been blacks and Chicanos in Orange County. How about we also require they set up 24-hour health clinics in both the local black and Chicano communities?"

"You're crazy," Willie laughs. "You got it."

"If I can get that," the university to support our conditions, I say, "will you support me and put [the teaching hospital] in the budget? I'm telling you, they're going to come at you, Cory and the other Orange County legislators. But I'm asking first."

Willie gives me his assurances. I call Aldrich right away, saying we need to meet. The chancellor flies up to Sacramento and brings with him a UCI vice chancellor I hate. This guy is always on the wrong side, an agitator against what I consider to be progress for the people, students and issues I care about. I end the meeting real quick. "Something came up," I say. "I got to leave. But Dan, can you let me talk with you alone for a minute?"

When it's just the two of us, I tell him, "I don't care what you do, but I don't ever want to see this guy again." Aldrich asks if we can have dinner, by ourselves. At the restaurant I start by laying out the deal I work out with Willie. But I add one more condition: that he fires the vice chancellor. To which the chancellor almost throws up. He says he can't do it. "Okay," I reply, "I guess this dinner is over with. Jesus, Dan, you're not helping me. It doesn't happen this way. It's a complete deal," including the last condition. "Take it or leave it." Within a day or two, he calls to ask when I want the vice chancellor gone. "It's up to you," I answer. I don't know what happens to him, but he goes somewhere else in the system, other than UCI.

"We got a deal," are my first words when I go back to Willie. "What do I do next?"

"Don't worry about it," he says. I'm serving on the Ways and Means subcommittee on higher education. Willie takes me through how to get it done through the subcommittee. He tells me who to get the language drafted by. I go to Steve Thompson, Willie's chief consultant to Ways and Means. I amend the language Steve writes into the appropriations section of the budget bill having to do with the University of California. I do it in such a way that no one is paying any attention. There are only three members of the subcommittee who do know. There's John Vasconcellos, a big lib from San Jose. There's Gene Duffy, a right-wing Republican who's also a doctor and thinks UC is producing too many medical specialists when there is a great need for practicing community doctors and respects the reputation of the Irvine medical school; he jumps at the idea of a UCI teaching hospital. And then there's me.

Before anyone knows it, the teaching hospital item is in the budget bill. I also quietly go to state Senator George Moscone of San Francisco to bury the exact same language in the budget on the senate side. (George is a really good guy and is later elected mayor of San Francisco before being assassinated along with Harvey Milk by Dan White in 1978.) Before the opposition can get organized, the UCI teaching hospital is a slam-dunk. Ken Cory goes to Willie. "How can you do this to me?" he complains. "It's my district."

"You know the rules," Brown replies. "You fell asleep while one of my committee members did his homework." Willie mentions how I come out of UCI and how much affinity I have for the university. He gives him all the bullshit, never letting on about his own complicity. "If you would have come to me first," Willie adds, "I would have told Alatorre 'No.' But he came to me and you know the rules, so try to fight it out. But I'm telling you this: it's staying and I'm going to make sure it stays in."

Chalk it all up to history. We get a teaching hospital in Orange County affiliated with the UCI medical school. Cory and I have this long talk about it. "You motherfucker," Cory tells me. "A punk Mexican outsmarted not only me but the hospital lobby and everyone else in Orange County." Later Cory admits the hospital is probably a good thing.

Dan Aldrich can't believe it. Getting the teaching hospital is the crowning moment of his career plus the development of the medical school and the university. Stanley van den Noort is the dean of the medical school at Irvine. He's given the responsibility for growing the school. In 1976, plans are set to build what's called the UC Irvine Medical Center about 12 miles from the campus in the city of Orange. It is completed in 1978, a four-story, multi-unit building with research laboratories, teaching facilities, and administrative offices. Under Dean van den Noort, the medical center really takes off and becomes a well-respected research and teaching hospital producing community docs. The two community clinics open in the barrio and ghetto of Santa Ana. The medical school turns out one of the highest percentages of ethnic and racial minority graduates and stays that way until Dean van den Noort's retirement. I come to know at least three Chicano doctors who are among the first wave of medical school students who follow the deal Willie Brown and I put together. One is still a community physician. One becomes a psychiatrist. The third is still practicing medicine in Orange County.

The 1960s and the dawn of a new decade, the 1970s, are a period of mass involvement in the streets by Chicano students and activists, beginning with the East L.A. walkouts. Adults are witnessing their children being beaten up by the police just because they're pushing for change in the schools, something most parents neglect to champion. In my eyes, it is the students who are embarrassing their parents. Few adults participate in political activism. Chicano adults of that generation don't seem to be joiners, despite their beliefs and opinions (that's how my father is); they aren't normally organizationally oriented. So the student movement is the first stride towards organizational participation. The movement manifests itself through groups like the string of teen posts that I work with; the high school students who walk out of their classes; the beginning of UMAS (United Mexican American Students, which later becomes MEChA); the Brown Berets; Catolicos por La Raza (Catholics for the Race), which takes on Cardinal James Francis McIntyre and criticize the Catholic Church for being insensitive to the needs of Chicanos; and the Mexican American Action Committee, my little group of political activists. Something is happening.

But one of the common fallacies people have about movements organizing for change is that such things are inevitable and continuing. In fact, they have a fleeting nature. They usually aren't long lasting. After engaging in the student uprisings over the Vietnam War and the conflicts over fighting to open up the doors for disenfranchised minorities, many people grow disenchanted or complacent. Once the war ends, or at least draws down, and the threat of being drafted is past, a lot of college students lose interest in protesting the war and other injustices. I guess it's just human nature.

Sure, MEChA chapters continue on college and university campuses, and there are still activists who are turned on and engaged over the years; I keep working with many of them. But too many people enter a phase where they admit to themselves, if not to each other, that "I made it and now everything's just fine. Now we're going to live happily ever after." Much of the '70s are pretty much a time of nonengagement. Students turn into themselves and do their own thing. Instead of moving forward, the movement stagnates for a while.

It's perfect timing for me because by this point, I'm entering a different arena. I continue my activism. Now it's just from the inside.

Chapter 4

Working from the Inside

I always believe real change doesn't happen by itself. It takes many forces to bring it about. You still need people agitating for change from the outside. Such agitation can create a reaction, but many times it is short-lived. So outside pressure isn't enough by itself. You need people on the inside who understand how to use the system to bring about change and who are willing to make it happen. By the late 1960s and early '70s, I recognize, as a result of my experiences up until then, that the political arena is the best place for me to bring about social change.

The Chicano movement, sparked by milestones like the student-led protests in East L.A., opens the door. While the students and others may believe the door will remain open, by the time I leave teaching at UCI in late 1971, the kind of progress envisioned just a few years earlier appears to be slowing down.

Within a few years, I come to see greater opportunities for advancing diversity in academia and elsewhere emerging at the state level, but it's going to be done through chucking and jiving by the likes of lawmakers like Willie Brown and me and a few others who make state policy and write budgets.

Not long after I'm elected to the state assembly in 1973, I remember meeting Frank Newman, former dean of the prestigious UC Berkeley Boalt Hall School of Law, distinguished professor of law and later California Supreme Court justice appointed by Governor Jerry Brown.

Boalt Hall then has the worst record on affirmative action. For example, the law school has just turned down the son of a prominent African-American newspaper publisher in the East Bay. Willie even tries to get the kid in and they tell him "no." Willie explains to me what it is that they've been doing and how resistant the administration is to blacks and Chicanos. He reminds me, "You know. You're on the [assembly budget] subcommittee on higher education. When this [Boalt Hall's funding] item comes up, I'd like you to be creative. Make 'em pay."

"Oh, no problem," I tell him.

Professor Newman comes into my subcommittee to present his budget. He razzles and dazzles members of the committee. I start asking him some questions about his affirmative action policy. He starts giving me every reason why it is intellectually bankrupt to have such a policy, that his law school is above it all, and that his law school is internationally renowned, and this other shit. He is telling me how, for academic or whatever reasons, the idea of affirmative action is fraught with problems and how his conscience does not allow for the creation of quotas at the law school.

So I make a call to Willie, who you remember is chairman of the Assembly Ways and Means Committee, which hammers out the budget on the assembly side; ways and means is the parent panel of the subcommittee I sit on. "I want to let you know I want to educate this elitist," I tell Brown, explaining what Newman says.

"Okay, this is how you get him," he replies. "Fund the law school in the budget but defund the administration," the line items in the UC budget that pay the salaries and expenses of the law school's deans and top administrators.

That's what we do. I put a call into Newman: "I might as well let you know, you don't have a job. We're not funding the administration" of Boalt Hall. "If you, in your wisdom, can come up with a suitable affirmative action policy—if it doesn't violate your principles and ethics and the like—then maybe we can talk," I tell Newman. It takes the good dean one week to come up with this very fashionable and progressive affirmative action program, and then we re-fund the administration of Boalt Hall.

About three years later, my *compadre*, my close friend, Luis Carrillo, graduates from Boalt Hall, after getting in through affirmative action. Willie and I are the keynote speakers at the ceremony, which is normally a pretty solemn occasion. We're marching in, everyone wearing their flowing academic regalia. The usual "Pomp and Circumstance" march is playing over the loudspeakers. Then, all of a sudden they pull the plug and *mariachis* start playing traditional Mexican music. You can imagine the scene. Newman's face drops. Man, I look at my *compadre* and he looks at me. Then they introduce Willie Brown and the *mariachis* start playing, "La Negra" ("The Dark One"), a song about a beautiful dark skinned young woman from the Mexican state of Nayarit who likes to drink. When I get up the *mariachi* band plays "Feria de las Flores" ("Flower Festival").

Willie and I, sitting on the stage, comment to each other about the law school graduates we see. There is a real diverse group of students coming up to get their diplomas: guys with long hair wearing painted overalls, white women, men and women who are Asian, black, and Chicano. I recall remarking to Dean

Newman, "Now this is what you said couldn't be done." He laughs, but Willie and I are never invited back to the law school.

The Ford Foundation Fellowship I get in 1969 affords me the opportunity to go to the University of Southern California, where I study and eventually earn a master's degree in public administration. At Ford, I become part of this 12-month internship program set up by state Senator Mervyn Dymally, an African American representing L.A. Merv and I are already friends through Phil Montes. Since the internship is for both blacks and Chicanos, Merv approaches me to see if I'm interested.

The internship is supposed to be focused on legislative activities. The first six months is to be spent with a state senator, the last half with an assemblymember. The senator I get is Al Song, a Korean-American Democrat representing Monterey Park. The assemblymember is Walter Karabian, an Armenian American representing a district centered in the Montebello area. Both Monterey Park and Montebello are just east of my home ground of East L.A.

Ford Foundation funds are not allowed to be used for getting involved in partisan political campaigns. But Song lets me out to work on Tom Bradley's first campaign that year for mayor of Los Angeles, which is a nonpartisan office. The internship is the first time I'm exposed to working full time in a political campaign. I volunteer for Governor Pat Brown's unsuccessful reelection in 1966, and Bobby Kennedy's ill-fated 1968 presidential campaign, but that's pretty much it.

Tom Bradley's story is of the emergence of a black former member of the LAPD who rises through the ranks and is then elected to the L.A. City Council from a basically middle-class district that goes from the African-American Baldwin Hills-Lemert Park neighborhoods, which are more stable, homeownership communities, north into parts of the Fairfax district. In 1969, Bradley takes on incumbent Mayor San Yorty.

Yorty is what you call the ultimate professional politician of his time. He recognizes the diversity of the city and has to do a little bit to acknowledge the existence of the Latinos, blacks, and Jews. To further his politics, he has a commission for the Spanish-speaking in the mayor's office, with his own Mexican running it. He has a similar outfit for the blacks with a black guy running it. These two communities have representation in the mayor's office, but it is mostly ceremonial, strictly designed to give cover for the mayor and quell any discontent among the minority populations. Yorty knows his base is with the predominantly white elements of the city, which at the time make up the majority of the electorate. He is, by definition, the establishment politician who wants to keep things as they are and doesn't want to do anything that will rock the boat.

Yorty's political approach contrasts sharply with Bradley. Here's a black councilmember who transcends the black community to seek coalition with other important groups in L.A. Bradley knows there is no way anyone who is from an ethnic or racial minority can get elected mayor with just the votes of his own people. So Bradley seeks to build a grand coalition that is ultimately named for him made up of blacks, Latinos, other minorities plus Westside Jews and liberals from across the city.

His candidacy is viewed as a rallying cry to take such a coalition, the idea has been around for a while, to a citywide level. Yorty understands what is going on. His only hope of prevailing is breaking up this new movement that is forming around the challenger and using what today we call wedge issues to scare enough nonminority voters into rejecting Tom Bradley. Yorty does that by trying to appeal to the fear among the nonethnics of electing a black man, a fear that goes back generations.

Yorty's racist strategy isn't successful in the primary, which results in a faceoff between the mayor and the councilman for the general election. But Yorty keeps painting a hysterical impression in the white community of the blacks taking over the city. He tells the Jews Bradley is anti-Semitic. He goes into the San Fernando Valley or wherever Anglos live and says a black revolution is threatening their existence. He plays this same divisive message in the Chicano community, which we work hard at trying to overcome with the troops we have at our disposal. Every conceivable fear tactic is used in the campaign. It's truly amazing the lengths to which the mayor goes, and how well they work even in late 1960s California. Yorty has some great operators, including Deputy Mayor Joe Quinn, father of Tom Quinn, chairman under Jerry Brown of the state Air Resources Board. But the one thing that helps cinch it for Yorty is the charge of Communist infiltration of the Bradley campaign. It's idiotic, but that doesn't matter.

The mayor's cause is aided by targeting a former top international union organizer with the United Auto Workers, brought in to run the Bradley campaign, who at one time years before has alleged affiliations with the Communist Party. Tom Bradley's experiment with coalition building proves unsuccessful that year, but it enables him to defeat Yorty during a rematch in 1973.

The 1969 race is a great campaign for me because it's consistent with my own developing politics, which are multiracial. I believe as Tom Bradley does that the only way Los Angeles will be a city for everybody is if we elect people regardless of race at the highest level. What he professes to be all about in my eyes ends up being the reason this city is where it is today: he paves the way for L.A. to come together and embrace the immense demographic changes that are just beginning to take place in the '60s and that continue to this day.

That changing demography, much of it spurred by birth rates and immigration, has the capacity to tear the city apart, pitting groups of people against each other ethnically, racially, religiously, geographically, and economically. That largely doesn't happen, and much of the credit goes to the election and long tenure in office of Tom Bradley. He is, in my view, what tips the scale towards progress and sets the stage years later for the ascendency of a Chicano mayor of L.A.

That doesn't mean major divisions don't remain. Nor does it mean racism isn't still a reality. The next great racial division affects the Latino community. Since its origins as a sleepy little Spanish village around present-day Olvera

Richard's introduction to politics is working on Tom Bradley's unsuccessful 1969 campaign for mayor against incumbent Sam Yorty, shown here at a joint campaign appearance. Bradley shares Richard's commitment to multiracial politics.

Street, L.A. is beset by waves of migrants and immigrants. Among the latest are Mexicans, Mexican Americans, then more immigrants from Mexico, and still more from Central and Latin America. The latest series of immigration once again spawns xenophobia. First there is Yorty's black scare. Now there's the brown scare.

But the capacity to work through it starts with Tom Bradley. He is a man driven by his belief that we can all work together, thrive, and accommodate diverse needs and desires into one decent society. We owe him a lot.

My internship with Assemblymember Wally Karabian comes later on, in 1971, after I teach at UCI and Terminal Island. It almost doesn't happen. He wants me to come up to Sacramento to work for him. "Jesus, I live in Huntington Beach," I tell him. "My kids and everything"—I relate how I'm juggling teaching chores, which are winding down, with seeing my two sons on weekends in L.A.

"Don't worry about it," he says. "I'll find a reason for you to fly down every weekend." So he offers me a job in Majority Services, which helps Democratic lawmakers.

I love Wally. He comes from Fresno but moves to L.A. to go to USC (where he gets his undergraduate and law school degrees). He graduates and becomes an assistant district attorney. He's part of a group of young guys who start in the legal profession or in business at the same time. Much of Wally's clout comes from this association.

When he decides to run for his assembly seat, Wally turns for help to his collection of guys, some judges and political operatives, including Joe Cerrell.

Richard's political mentor is Assemblyman Walter Karabian, who engineers Alatorre's first run for public office in 1971. This 1967 photo pictures (from left) state Senator Al Song, Richard, and Walter Karabian.

Cerrell understands politics. He puts guys together behind political candidates. He analyzes three area assembly districts Wally can run in and decides on the 45th because it is heavily Democratic and the balance of power consists of Chicanos. Wally is young, uses all the right buzzwords and learns how to project himself like a Kennedy. He runs against the well-established mayor of Alhambra, a white Republican woman. Without registering Chicanos and getting them out to vote, he can lose it.

Wally likes to joke that he discovers me stealing hubcaps in East L.A. and makes a "legitimate person" out of me. My sister, Cecelia Alatorre, is already working in Karabian's district office. I know Wally casually. Cecelia is the one who recommends her boss talk with me about being his administrative assistant, which he does—and he likes me. Wally becomes very close to the whole Alatorre family.

I work on his first assembly campaign in 1966, and end up running his reelection in 1968. I help organize a massive voter registration drive in Wally's district in '68, one of the most successful in the history of East L.A., working with the AFL-CIO Frontlash organization led by Jim Wood, who goes on to head up the Los Angeles County Federation of Labor. Wally and I become close friends. He's a smart, young guy. He knows Chicanos are the ones who ultimately tip the scales during any contested general election in his district skirting East L.A. But since he really knows little about Mexicans, he lets me do whatever I want. He never questions anything I recommend to him; he trusts me. When I decide to do my master's degree at USC, Wally says to do it out of his office. "I'll cover you," he tells me. That's part of how I get into the Ford Foundation internship program.

So at first I start out writing legislation in Sacramento, just learning about it. Lawyers with the Office of Legislative Counsel handle the actual drafting of bills. You come up with an idea for what you want to do and how it will work and turn it over to them. I also represent Wally at different places in the state, speaking on his behalf. I come down and take care of some problems he has in the district. All pretty standard stuff. Wally and I get along well.

All of a sudden there's a special election for the state senate in a district in East L.A. Then-Assemblymember David Roberti, who is a classmate of Wally Karabian's at USC law school, decides to move up and run for the seat. There's a meeting among political players at the Capitol to set the stage for Roberti's campaign. Afterwards, Wally tells me, "I'm going to loan you out full time to the [Roberti] campaign. I'm going to pay for you to work on this campaign. And your job is not only to do a good job on the campaign, but if he wins, there's going to be another special election for Roberti's open [48th] Assembly [District] seat. So why shouldn't it be you?" In other words, he's asking why I shouldn't run for the state assembly. I find out later that even before Roberti's victory, Wally is making plans to run me for the assembly seat.

"Wally [Karabian] surmises the following," Lou Moret, a longtime friend and political confident to both me and Wally, recalls. "When state Senator George Danielson runs and gets elected to Congress, the two local assemblymembers, Roberti and Alex Garcia, will run for Danielson's senate seat. Wally thinks Roberti will beat Garcia, creating a vacancy in Roberti's assembly seat. Richard Alatorre will run for it. Wally convinces Richard to leave his teaching posts to join [assembly] Majority Consultants in Sacramento. Richard goes there and works on Roberti's campaign, getting to meet everybody who is a supporter of Roberti plus the neighborhood leaders because it is the same territory Richard will run in.

"Wally is way ahead of his time," Lou reasons. "He knew reapportionment was coming up. They had to make a Latino seat. This could be it. He turns out to be correct. Everything he said did happen: Garcia loses to Roberti. Roberti's seat is empty."

It's not like I don't think about the idea of running before, going back to high school when my father talks about what a pity it is that Chicanos don't have their own legislative representatives. But now it happens so fast that I don't have much of a chance to think. I'm sent down to work for Roberti along with Jerry Zanelli, administrative assistant for Roberti, his political operative and alter ego. I do a very good job, handling the Mexican part of Roberti's operation, and he wins. I remember flying back to Sacramento, sitting next to Roberti, and him saying, "You might as well think about running. Deals are already being cut with [then-U.S. Representative Ed] Roybal" over a successor to Roberti in the assembly. Roberti mentions Ralph Ochoa, a guy I know from my '60s political activism, as a potential candidate who is backed by Roybal, among others.

There are meetings with Assembly Speaker Bob Moretti. Somewhere along the way a deal does get cut without even consulting Wally Karabian, who is the assembly majority leader. They leave him out, I assume, because everyone knows I'm Wally's choice. From Moretti's point of view, he's losing a member, Roberti, and the Speaker wants the special election to be a smooth transition. He wants whoever can win. Since it'll be the first time a Chicano is elected in this district, Moretti wants it to be *his* Chicano, Ralph Ochoa. It's also important because Moretti is already thinking of running for governor in 1974. Ochoa is a good deal for Moretti because he thinks supporting him will help win over Roybal's support of his gubernatorial candidacy. All these elements are coming into play.

Roybal, of course, is for Ochoa too. "Bobbie," Wally tells Moretti, "I know this guy Richard Alatorre well. He'll be a team player when he gets up here. Just don't go out of your way to raise money and so forth for Ochoa. Alatorre will be just as good for you. You can save the money and win either way."

Well, Moretti is not happy with all of that. It ultimately leads to Wally's removal from his leadership position in the assembly.

Just on the heels of the Speakership of Jesse "Big Daddy" Unruh, when the Speaker of the California assembly is arguably the second most powerful officeholder in the state next to the governor, Moretti exercises great power and near-total control in off-year special elections, especially in a safe Democratic seat where the outcome is usually decided in the primary. He can freeze most of the money that goes to other candidates, particularly when it comes from so-called Third House special interests that rely on the good graces of the Speaker for their lobbying. He can do whatever is necessary to ensure a smooth and uncontested election, including ample financial support, for his chosen candidate. Roybal is for Ochoa, and in Moretti's eyes and in the view of many others, Roybal is key to winning political support among Mexicans. If you really look at it, Roybal is a decent guy and an historical figure, but he can't draw on a political operation because he has none. The last time he puts any appreciable number of troops on the streets is more than 20 years before, in 1949, when he runs the first time for city council—and they aren't his troops; the Community Service Organization gets him elected.

Moretti makes the decision to support Ralph Ochoa. Some years before, I help Ralph get into law school. We are in the same ad hoc organization of professional Chicanos in the '60s I form, the Mexican American Action Committee. Moretti never thinks there will be a primary contest. I become the thorn in the side he doesn't need.

I go to see Moretti before things turn rough. "I have nothing against you and everything else," he tells me. "I know you work up here and the like." The

Ralph Ochoa (left) runs against Richard in the Democratic primary with strong support from Assembly Speaker Bob Moretti. U.S. Rep. Edward R. Roybal (right), a historic Eastside political figure, initially supports Richard's opponent in the 1971 Assembly special election.

Speaker informs me that it's not in my interest to get into this race. "I don't necessarily know this guy [Ochoa] and if I got to know you, I'd probably be for you. But I gotta do what I gotta do. If you get into this, I'm going to cut your nuts off."

"I'm real sorry you feel that way, but I don't give a shit." I reply. "I'm in it."

"Moretti backs Ralph Ochoa," Lou Moret notes. "Roberti comes on board for Richard because of Karabian. The only others supporting Richard are Merv Dymally, John Burton, [L.A. City Councilmember] John Ferraro, and the social workers union. The rest of the world is for Ochoa."

Wally likes to entertain national politicians. I remember Labor Day, in September 1970, when Henry "Scoop" Jackson, the U.S. senator from Washington state and a 1972 presidential aspirant, comes to California for an Independence Day celebration in Antioch, in the east San Francisco Bay Area. Wally flies Jackson down to Palm Springs in a private plane for another July 4 event. On the flight, Wally and I get into a conversation about me. "I'm going to tell you now if you decide you want to run for Roberti's seat, you'll have my unequivocal support and you don't have to worry about raising money; I'll raise the money for you. But I know if I do it, Moretti will strip me of everything. I'm prepared to lose my majority leader's job and everything else. I don't give a shit. You were there for me and I think it's time I have an independent political future that isn't tied to Bob Moretti." Wally can raise a lot of money on his own. That's why he is assembly majority leader. Even before Roberti's election takes place, we talk about what is going to happen with my subsequent campaign during the rest of the Labor Day plane trip down the length of the state.

Our game plan is to go after Roberti and get his endorsement. That's why Roberti doesn't have to pay me anything for working in his campaign. There will be a clear understanding. Roberti is always afraid of being challenged someday by a Latino candidate in a Democratic primary. That's why he wants me to run the part of his campaign appealing to Chicanos.

The Speaker brings together his leadership team at the state Capitol, which includes Wally. Moretti knows whatever chances I have are going to come from resources Wally Karabian can put together for me. In the leadership session, Moretti tells Wally, "Everyone here is supporting me for governor and supporting the things I do to enhance my efforts to be governor. I want you to get Alatorre out because it will cause problems for me. I made a commitment to Ed Roybal, who is important in my efforts to run for governor." The Speaker relates how he and Roybal believe electing Ochoa will be useful to show Latino voters there are other Latinos Moretti supports and can get elected.

"I can't do that," Wally responds. "He's been my guy. I'm majority leader. The district is in my back yard, not yours." Moretti essentially threatens Wally. Ironically, although Moretti assumes everyone in the room is supporting his gubernatorial ambitions, most of them end up double-crossing him and endorsing Jerry Brown for governor in 1974.

It turns into a great primary. Ralph Ochoa has all the endorsements and is well financed, thanks to the Speaker. I just beat the living crap out of him anyway.

First, Wally greases the politics for me. I get help from state Senator George Moscone, another Italian American like Roberti. State Senator Merv Dymally really helps me. L.A. City Councilmember John Ferarro is for me because of Wally. So is Roberti, who quietly passes the word he wants me every time anybody asks him. Assemblymember John Burton, also from San Francisco, comes out for me too. When nearly everyone else at the Capitol is supporting Ochoa because of Moretti, Roybal and state senate Pro Temp Jim Mills, Burton says he'll take Karabian, Moscone and Dymally any day because "those guys will do something where others will just lend their name to the campaign." Burton's words are prophetic.

I'm great on the issues in that district, from the left-center of the Democratic Party, something I share on most matters with Wally, Burton, and Willie Brown. Moretti is more in the center, which is still further to the left than Jesse Unruh and the assembly Democratic leadership from the previous generation during the 1960s.

Wally tells me that my job is to knock on doors. "I'll give you every dollar for your campaign from Friends of Karabian," Wally's campaign committee. He ends up giving me $97,000, a lot of money in those days. Compare that to the

Lou Moret, Richard's longtime confidant, plays a key role throughout his political career.

$14,000 Wally spends winning his first assembly race in 1966. Wally raises money for my campaign and channels it to me in the days when that is a legal way to help other candidates because there are no campaign fundraising limits.

I barely raise a dollar on my own, but I religiously knock on doors.

"Richard worked his ass off," confirms Lou Moret. "He was walking two precincts a day. He was nonstop. He lived it. He wanted it."

I also have some other smart and dedicated people around me. Most of them come from Wally. There's Michael Bowler III, nephew of the chief deputy district attorney of L.A. There's a guy named Kenny Katz, who comes out of USC Democratic politics and has run Wally's campaign before. Talk about cutthroat politics; USC is the height of it. It harkens back to the days when Jesse Unruh goes there, beginning with the Trojan Democratic Club. Kenny Katz graduates from USC and takes odd jobs. His father owns property he helps to manage. Later he is a public relations genius working for convention centers like the one at the city of Los Angeles.

Kenny just has a great mind and good organizational sense. He becomes very attuned to wherever he is. He knows how to put the pieces together and run all the elements of an effective political campaign. Kenny grows up in Alhambra and Monterey Park, so he knows parts of the district.

Then I have a guy by the name of Mike Navarro, who's a genius when it comes to doing campaign mailings, incorporating clever gimmicks into mail pieces. He works for Gray Advertising Company and is one of the most successful PR guys around. He does beautiful graphics and comes up with the idea of using the Happy Face, a brand new thing and big deal back then. The Happy Face he designs for me is in the color fuchsia. Where the smile is in the design, it spells out in stylized letters the name A L A T O R R E.

I also have Wally, who has great political sense too. Others, like Mike, may handle different elements of the campaign, but Wally and Kenny have total confidence in their ability to run the thing and make good decisions so the money is spent right—on getting our message out to voters. Wally proofs and corrects everything, all the drafts for the mail. He loves that stuff. Everything is high quality.

Kenny and Mike come up with the unique idea of producing a brief continuous running film about me showing on portable television monitors. Two-person teams, each with a man and a woman, walk door to door carting along the TV monitor. If a man answers the door, the woman makes the pitch. If a woman answers, the man makes the pitch. We have some very attractive women walkers. All walkers have to be articulate. There are 15 or 20 machines. The idea is for each team to try and reach, on any given evening, about 45 voters with the film. It opens with me saying, "Hi, my name is Richard Alatorre, and I know my people well." There are flashes of recognizable locales in the district plus pictures and buzzwords local residents can relate to. What you get at the end of seeing the movie is that, gee, he does come from the community and he's young and vibrant. The idea originates with Robert Kennedy, who uses it during coffee hours and at malls to attract people's attention when RFK defeats Kenneth Keating in the 1966 U.S. Senate race in New York.

Lou Moret has another version of where the idea comes from: "There was a little box that insurance agents who went door to door would use to sell new policies. It would show a continuous filmstrip of 35-millimeter film. Now we'd call it a PowerPoint. The policy would sell itself."

Kenny takes the idea to a guy he knows from USC, now teaching communications at a community college in Palm Springs. "That's interesting," the instructor says, and proceeds to explain the technology of how he can produce it and present it to voters. We develop the script and deliver it along with the still photographs to the guy from Palm Springs. He doesn't want it to last more than 60 seconds, which he says research shows is the limited attention span of most people. "If you get them to watch for 20 seconds, you got them for a minute," he argues. It turns out to be a minute and 20 seconds long. Of course, for my field volunteers who have to lug the big monitors around while they're walking precincts, it might not seem like such a great idea.

Art Torres's introduction to the political arena starts with him agreeing to come down and work on my campaign. Art, who is working with Merv Dymally at the Capitol in Sacramento, spends much of his time in East L.A. "carrying these stupid fucking televisions," he recalls. "People never saw a TV video for a candidate on their doorsteps. It was just cumbersome, with the big monitors. Very tiring for volunteers. So it lost its luster, not for the people we were visiting, but for the volunteers who had to carry around those damn things."

People have never seen such a thing before at their homes. Some don't know how to react. We have two versions. One is in both English and Spanish. The other is English only. Walkers quickly make a decision about which one to use at the door. The English/Spanish version for Chicanos shows me, from being with Bobby Kennedy at a rally to walking with Joan Kennedy, Ted Kennedy's wife. In English, it also starts, "Hi, I'm Richard Alatorre. I was born and raised in our community and I know my people well." The visuals are backdrops that include County USC Medical Center, Cal State L.A., a local high school, and more. The film proves to be very effective. It turns people around, those who are uncommitted and even some who start out supporting Ochoa.

Even though it's expensive, we also mail potholders to every household, which is not that common in 1971. Then we mail a scroll to Spanish-surname voters. They open it up and there's a picture of John and Robert Kennedy with a famous quote from RFK. We know in every Mexican home, next to Jesus there is an image of the Kennedys.

We also do some sophisticated personalized mailers to voters about issues. We divide up the mail using surname dictionaries that segment the electorate by ethnicity. For example, there are letters from Senator George Moscone and L.A. City Councilmember John Ferraro going to Italian Americans. Some voters think I'm Italian too; Alatorre sounds like it could be. I never say I am, but I never say I'm not. Roberti's support helps with these voters too.

But the campaign becomes a symbol for Chicanos. There isn't a hotly contested primary race for a long time where the victor, since the two leading candidates are both Latino, is going to be one of their own.

Then I discover gays. They are a silent block of voters in this and some other L.A.-area districts that political operatives have not discovered or concentrated on. I'm the first candidate to have an organized campaign geared to gays, even before Vince Bugliosi, the guy who prosecutes the Manson family. Bugliosi courts gays during his unsuccessful campaign for L.A. County district attorney in the early 1970s. But I discover gays before then.

It starts with Kenny Katz, my campaign manager. Kenny is very methodical and observant. Next door to my campaign headquarters on Sunset Boulevard is a flamingo joint, El Cid. Next door to that is a gay bar, which you can't tell from the outside. One day, Kenny walks in to have a drink. He looks around and says to himself, what the shit is this? He strikes up conversations with the guys in the bar and finds out they all live in the area and most of them are in households where there are two and two—two people of the same sex but with different last names living together in the same house or apartment.

My district starts on the west in East Hollywood, runs into Silverlake, Echo Park, and Mount Washington before heading east to take in parts of northeast and East L.A. These communities in the western part of my district have the greatest concentrations of gays in L.A.

"Kenny Katz surmises that the district has at least 10 percent gay voters," Lou Moret says.

Kenny strikes up conversations with this one guy at the bar. The next day Kenny comes into the headquarters and says, "I just met this guy and I think he'll be our entrée into the gay community." Most everyone in that era, including a lot of people in my campaign, is afraid of being associated with them.

"Jesus," Kenny asks me directly, "Do you have a problem?"

"I have no problem with that," I reply.

We set up a meeting with the gay leadership in the apartment of the guy Kenny meets in the bar, Troy Perry. He's founder of the Metropolitan Community Church. It is the first gay church in the country, at that time off of Alvarado Boulevard, right by USC. Troy is the man in L.A., the godfather of the gay community at the time. There are five guys in the apartment, all prominent gay leaders.

Troy Perry loves Mexicans. He has a running joke with me: "If you ever decide to change your colors, call me; you and I would make a great couple." Troy and his friends have never trusted politicians because they have never had good relationships with them. The politicians are usually overtly antigay or standoffish.

"I'm going to be perfectly honest with you," I tell them. "If I'm elected, and Willie Brown's consenting adults bill comes up [legalizing sexual relations between consenting adults] I'll vote for it."

At the time, the gay community is largely unorganized politically. They're fascinated a candidate will even come to them and ask about their community. Kenny is the kind of guy who can talk with them or with just about anyone. We get a lot of interesting and useful information about how to approach the gay community.

We take my campaign to the gays. I go to one of the services at the Metropolitan Community Church. There are probably about 300 gays there. I sit there and listen to the preaching. It's just a service. Then the congregation wants to help me. Troy introduces me to all the gay leaders. They agree to sponsor a candidates' debate that includes Ochoa.

"But we want to help you," Troy says. "You're the only one who has come to ask us, to get to know us and our issues."

There is an endorsing convention at the church. It's worked out so I'm going to be the last speaker. I know exactly what's on their minds in addition to the consenting adults measure. I blow them out of the water and become the darling of the gays.

Kenny does a lot of the follow up, going to meetings and talking with community members. We ask Troy where gays live. A lot live up in the hills, Silverlake and Mount Washington. There's a bunch in East Hollywood, where all the gay clubs are. Some are in Echo Park.

When officially filing papers to run in the 48th Assembly District, I get signatures on petitions in lieu of paying the filing fee. It's not because we can't afford the money. That's a good way to demonstrate broad-based grass roots support. I want to get signatures from all parts of the district. I remember walking in Mount Washington. I go to this house and knock on the door. A guy answers. The voter I ask for isn't around. So I ask for the other person on the voter sheet at that household, also a guy. The guy at the door panics. "Why are you asking?"

I introduce myself. He has never met anyone running for office before. We start talking. It turns out he's a teacher at Fairfax High School. The guy he's living with is a school administrator, also at Fairfax High. No one at their school knows they're living together or that they're gay.

"Look," I say, using some of the insights I pick up from Troy and others. "I'm not interested in your sexual orientation. I would never do anything to jeopardize you." The guy isn't going to sign my petition because he doesn't want his name on any document where people can find out where he lives. He tells me why. At the time, being gay is a no-no for people in public education. There is real fear of being fired if word gets out. We start talking about it. "Let me tell you something," I say. "I think this kind of discrimination is intolerable. I don't believe people should be persecuted because of who they are." I pledge to work to ban such bias if I'm elected.

The voter at the door is impressed with my knowledge and perspective. He finally offers to sign the petition. "No," I say. "I don't want you to sign it. I would never want something you're doing for me to later come back to haunt you. All I can ask you for is I would appreciate your vote in the special election."

"You have my vote," he pledges. "There are a lot of us up here and we feel very comfortable living up here because there are so many of us in this community."

I tell Kenny about this exchange, which becomes our rule of thumb. "I think it's safe to say if there are two or more men living together in the same household or two or more women living together, they're probably gays or lesbians," I conclude.

We send a mailer to voters in Mount Washington and Silverlake about gay issues without ever using the word. We talk in code, which gays understand. A gay PR guy tells us how to structure it. A lot of it is stressing individual rights and the like. Troy Perry of the Metropolitan Community Church signs the letter. It never mentions who he is or that it is a gay church. If you're gay, you know who Troy is. If you're not and you get the letter, the message is consistent with what all the liberals in the hills like to hear.

I court the gays, going two or three times to Troy's church for Sunday services. I get to know the parishioners, including some of the important ones. They contribute to my campaign.

Troy organizes big tours of the gay clubs in the district on weekends. We hit everything, from dyke bars to leather bars. One night we go to probably about eight or nine of them. Our appearances are advanced. While we're at one, somebody goes ahead to the next club. All the owners know who we are when I arrive with Troy. He introduces me at each place: "This is Richard Alatorre, candidate for the assembly and a friend of our community."

We're at one of them, on Hyperion Avenue in Silverlake. It's a very nice place, with a long bar that turns around the corner at the back of the room. There's really nothing to identify it as a gay bar. I start talking with this one guy. By the time I'm finished, he wants to send me some money for the campaign. I ask for the man's card. The guy to the side of him, his bodyguard, hears my request, reaches into his own pocket and hands me the first guy's card. He's a vice president of Occidental Petroleum Company. Then the VP takes the card away from me and asks instead for my address. He says I'll get a check in the mail on Monday. Sure enough, I get a $1,000 check.

We walk into another bar on Sunset Boulevard. For me, a Chicano raised in East L.A., it isn't shocking to be in an establishment where gays aren't afraid about how to behave around each other. I'm there to take care of business.

The last one we visit at the end of the evening is a lesbian bar, called Sur de Paris. After hitting bars with all-guy patrons, I have never been in one for women. A bunch of lesbians who are supporting me come up to us. I spot this one woman and think, oh, my God, I'm in love. I think I'll stay here the rest of the evening. I'm talking with this woman when all of a sudden, Troy grabs me by the arm and pulls me away. "What's wrong?" I ask.

"Don't you see this [other] woman about to come at you?" he warns. He knows the other woman is the lover of the lady I'm speaking with. "She'll kill you. Don't misinterpret the femininity of some of these women because when it comes to their girlfriends, they're worse than the men."

I stay another 20 minutes and then we leave. I'm totally dejected that all of these beautiful women are lesbians. But they are what they are.

I come away with the memory of all the well-dressed successful professionals or business people we meet at these clubs who are living a secret life. These are the only places they can be who they are. I talk to Troy Perry about that. "It's so sad people have to worry about their professional reputations," I say.

"We live in a society that is sick," Troy adds. "A lot of people have to be careful."

"Every Friday or Saturday night, Richard hits the gay bars," Lou Moret remembers. "He had an advance team that goes to the bars, distributes materials, and tells people Richard is going to be there to meet them. Art Torres heads up that group."

We also go to the gay newspaper, *The Advocate*, to ask for its endorsement. We run a full-blown mini campaign in the gay community.

I don't advertise to everyone else the stands I take for the gays, but I don't hide them either. The gay community never has to worry about its issues when they come up before the legislature because I always support them. I'm probably one of the very first politicians of any race in L.A. who seek out and openly embrace the gays and their concerns. I'm certainly the first Latino politician to do so.

"Richard was for them [the gay community] outright," Art Torres observes. "He had a comfort level because of what Willie [Brown] had been talking to him about because Willie had been doing it in San Francisco: reaching out to the gay community. You didn't advertise you were doing it other than within the community itself. But it sent out a powerful subliminal message throughout the gay and lesbian community that this guy was going to be for them and wasn't

Reverend Troy Perry, founder of the Metropolitan Community Church, helps Richard appeal for support among LGBT voters.

ashamed to be for them. Basically, Richard didn't give a shit" what anyone else thought.

The ultimate gesture is my first big fundraiser after taking office, a huge affair at the Century Plaza Hotel in 1973. I ask Troy Perry, as pastor of the Metropolitan Community Church, to deliver the benediction. Most people in that politically astute audience know who he is. He mentions who I am and what a great friend I've become to his community. Then he adds, "As I told my great brother, Richard Alatorre, if you ever change your mind, please give me a call because I think you're so good looking." Everyone breaks out laughing.

My opponent, Ralph Ochoa, is considered the front-runner. He has all the establishment money and Speaker Moretti's endorsement. I don't have a problem with money, thanks to Wally, and we spend our money intelligently. What I have going for me is a great campaign organization and a lot of people. There's a bunch of students from Long Beach State and UC Irvine who come to help out. And I just know a lot of people over the years who I help or who like me and what I stand for. Even though it's my first try at public office, I have a record to run on.

We have one thing Ochoa doesn't have: Dave Roberti. He's liked in the district; the farther west you go, the more he's liked. That is helpful. I also have

City Councilmember John Ferraro, another Italian American, which is helpful because there are a lot of Italian Americans in the district. I get Ferraro through my relationship with Wally. They go back to having gone to the same school. Ferraro is more Wally's relationship than mine, but I get to meet and know the councilmember, and he gets to like me; he becomes very important in my life when I get elected years later to the city council. Then we identify the one thing few people know about—kind of like our secret weapon—which are the gays.

It is a very multifaceted campaign. It has to be because my district is an early cross section of the diversity of what Los Angeles is today. The only exceptions are Alhambra and Atwater, the mostly white and more conservative parts of the district.

Now all we need to do is for me to get my piece of the Chicano vote since we are already going after everyone else. We don't need to get all of it, you know; we'll be satisfied with our share. It's like we kind of start outside and then come in. There are Chicanos in Echo Park, but primarily they are in the Lincoln Heights, El Sereno, and Boyle Heights neighborhoods.

Only 18 percent of the voters in the 48th are Chicano at the time. The district is a hodgepodge of different types of people; many of them are liberals and predisposed to vote for a minority. In my case, it is the chance for them to vote for a Mexican, which is not a big leap. Up until that time the only Chicano many elect is Ed Roybal, first to the city council in 1949, and then to Congress in 1962.

For me, the real issue is electing somebody who is educated, has experience in the social and political arena, and experience working on a variety of the issues of the day that are important to our community.

We wipe out Ralph Ochoa in the special election. Moretti spends half a million dollars of his money after being told Ralph will beat me three to one. I beat him two to one.

Paul Carpenter, later a state senator, comes in third and almost bests Ochoa. "He didn't even live in the district," Lou Moret says. "Carpenter did something in that election that was never done before: all he wanted was to go to any precinct and find one person who agreed to host a coffee hour. Carpenter takes three precincts and mails out a computerized letter saying, 'Dear neighbor, on Wednesday at 8 p.m. we have a coffee hour at your neighbor's home located at wherever to talk about important issues facing our community I hope you can join us. Sincerely, Paul Carpenter.'

"Nobody shows up. Carpenter takes the names of anyone who did show up out of the list and the next day sends another letter: 'Sorry you couldn't attend, but your neighbors and I discussed these issues. . . .'"

"That's all Carpenter did and he came in third, almost beating Ralph."

Lou has two jobs in my first campaign: directing all the volunteers to get out and walk. Then, "every night, usually around 9:30 or 10 p.m., we'd go out and have a beer to let Richard unwind and relax," Lou says. "Those were my jobs. I got to know him really well."

Actually, I know Lou going back to Belvedere elementary and junior high schools, and Garfield High School. "Richard was always one year ahead of me," Lou says. "Everybody knew him. He was student body everything in junior and senior high school, friendly to everybody, gregarious, outgoing." We became reacquainted again in 1969 or 1970, when Lou is running voter registration drives for Wally's reelection to the assembly while going to Whittier College.

Moretti and his people attribute my defeating his guy to the fact I work harder. There is no doubt about it. I kill myself for that campaign, in every geographic part of the district. Ralph is also sort of into the glamour of politics, less the hard work. He's convinced he is going to win because he has all the endorsements wrapped up. But I walk more precincts—and really walk them.

Part of it is we also find out Ralph has a sickness. He can only walk so long until he starts getting dizzy. I have my mother out walking for me. We out-walk, out-fight, out-organize, and out-everything the opposition.

Then in this heavily Democratic district, we look forward to what should be an easy time against the Republican candidate, a guy named Bill Brophy, in the off-year special election run-off set for November 16.

What should be a cake walk turns into a campaign that gets national attention because of the presence of a new phenomenon in East L.A. and nationwide Chicano politics: La Raza Unida Party.

Raza Unida is born in Texas, where it has some success, mostly in local elections. By the early 1970s, it's picking up momentum in California, mostly in Los Angeles. The party becomes home for a lot of disaffected students and others, mostly left-leaning activists who feel that neither of the two main political parties are relevant to their needs. They see La Raza Unida Party as a vehicle to bring about change. If it competes on the merits, what it says it is there for, it could be a positive force. Neither the Democratic nor Republican parties, as institutions, do the right thing for our people. The Republican philosophy is to help out big business and cut government, trying to reverse the legacy of Lyndon Johnson's Great Society. The Democrats are the party of my father and his generation. It's supposed to be the party of the workingman and woman and the downtrodden, delivering whatever social and economic goods that can come from Democratic administrations. When it comes down to doing the right thing for minority people, like allowing Chicanos to elect their own, that doesn't necessarily happen. I recognize all the shortcomings of the Democratic Party. It isn't the Republicans who gerrymander the Chicano community in such a way as to rarely allow it the right of self-determination. Reapportionment is done for the benefit of incumbent Democrats; very few of them are Chicanos. That accounts for the political predicament faced by communities like mine.

Yet, it's easy to criticize. It is harder to get to work and make change happen. With my background and philosophy, I'm not into just criticizing for the sake of criticism. I believe the Democratic Party is the party of ethnic and racial minorities, and the party has to better reflect the composition of the people of

California. Up until the 1970s, the Democrats have not taken into account the Chicano experience in their political behavior.

I learn change doesn't come about because the Democratic Party all at once decides doing so is a good thing. Blacks demand the Democrats endorse the civil rights movement's agenda during the '60s, and it does; change happens, including the 1964 Civil Rights Act and the 1965 Voting Rights Act, because the African-American community demands it. That change comes with a price: in the process the Democrats lose the once "solid South" they hold for generations, with southern whites forever abandoning the party to make Richard Nixon president in 1968. Legislative reapportionment in the '60s helps begin the political empowerment of blacks in California. But it does nothing for Chicanos because we aren't even in the mix advocating for our own interests. At least we are starting to become a force that has to be listened to at the dawn of the '70s.

I view my assembly race as an opportunity to create change for Chicanos. I know change can't happen just from agitation against political decision-makers by outside activists. It has to also come from Chicanos who leverage their skills and influence as inside players. I spend much of the '60s working at it from the outside; now it's my turn to try from the inside. What I learn from Merv Dymally and working on Tom Bradley's mayoral campaign is that for a Chicano to get elected requires somebody who is not just a candidate for the Chicano community, but for all communities. This is especially true in the 48th Assembly District, where the percentage of Chicano voters is only in the teens and where other people, mostly Anglos, who hail from a diversity of backgrounds and walks of life, will decide the election.

If La Raza Unida Party is sincere and truly committed to achieving political empowerment for Latinos, it would work to elect somebody from within its ranks. That is virtually impossible in this 1971 special election given the composition of the district electorate. Instead, Raza Unida is basically co-opted by people who are running another very cynical game, and Raza Unida leaders allow themselves to be used as a vehicle for the Republican Party to try to gain a foothold in places like the Eastside where the GOP can never hope to play using its own name. "The GOP sees Raza Unida as a vehicle to take a seat they wouldn't normally be able to get," Lou Moret says. The only role Raza Unida plays in this run-off election is obstructing the Democratic Party and, in the end, denying the seat to a Chicano—me. It is the first expression of a recently hatched Republican strategy that views the Chicano community as socially conservative with strong family and religious values. If the GOP can use organizations such as Raza Unida to exploit certain hot-button issues and legitimate resentment against Democrats who take Latinos for granted, then enough Chicano voters can be prevented from voting Democratic so that, maybe, Republican candidates can squeak through.

The Republicans find a perfect spoiler candidate in Raul Ruiz, a Raza Unida party leader along with Bert Corona of MAPA fame. Ruiz taps into all the unrest and political disillusionment that is common among Chicanos, especially students and younger activists. Ruiz becomes a symbol for them of political anarchy, *machismo*, a Latino form of male chauvinism, and *Chicanismo*, a type of Chicano nationalism aimed at recapturing Mexican and indigenous culture, and among some lefty—and fanciful—activists, "liberating" the territories taken from Mexico by the United States after the Mexican American War under the Treaty of Guadalupe Hidalgo. That gives the U.S. undisputed control of Texas and cedes to America what are the present-day states of California, Nevada, Arizona, Colorado, New Mexico, Utah, and Wyoming.

This odd alliance between lefty Raza Unida activists and right-wing Republicans is essentially a cruel hoax perpetrated against innocent students and other grass-roots activists who believe supporting Ruiz is the way to go—even though they aren't going anywhere. Ruiz knows exactly where he's getting the money to fund his campaign, which comes directly from the GOP or is laundered by the Republicans or the Nixon campaign. We don't really know exactly how much money they get. Obviously, it's not anything that is ever reported. The campaign finance disclosure laws aren't as strict back then, but you still have to report contributions and expenditures. "At the time there was not the campaign reporting like you have today," Art Torres notes, "especially for in-kind contributions." Mention is made in the transcripts of the U.S. Senate committee investigating the Watergate scandal that campaign money from Nixon or the Republican National Committee is going to a third party in an effort to divide the Chicano vote. Ruiz mounts a campaign with signs and mailers his very limited resources would never be able to cover except for the Republicans. We think he spends around $200,000 from the Committee to Reelect the President (Nixon) or the Republican Party. That's a lot of money in that period, especially for a small and previously little known third party.

Because of the ethnocentric nature of Raza Unida, the party is incapable of appealing to a broader electorate, much less winning in a multifaceted district like the 48th. What Ruiz and Raza Unida succeed in achieving is defeating a Chicano candidate. That makes them intellectually dishonest, in my eyes; instead of being serious about electing a Chicano, they take Republican money for the sole purpose of defeating a progressive Chicano Democrat. The real victims are the idealistic kids who dedicate a lot of time and energy working on the campaign because they are told it is possible to elect a Raza Unida candidate when Ruiz, and the Republicans, know it will never happen. A lot of people get involved with Raza Unida in the special election for the right reasons, seeing the party as a viable alternative to the status quo. They're just not told the whole story, about the money laundering and that the party is in bed with the Republicans. In the end, they are fed a bill of goods. That's a tragedy. It's hard enough as it is getting young people excited about being involved in civic and political affairs.

Ruiz and his camp call me a *vendito*, a sell-out. That doesn't bother me. Well, I guess it does. But they also threaten physical retaliation against me, people who work for me and my campaign volunteers, including students from Long Beach State and UCI who come up to work on my campaign. It is one of the most closely watched special elections in memory, by the press and law en-

Raul Ruiz and La Raza Unita Party, with Republican support, help defeat Richard in his first bid for elected office in the 1971 Assembly special election. Ruiz, right, is pictured with party founder Jose Angel Gutierrez of Texas.

forcement. The police get called; the cops try to deal with it because they don't like Raza Unida either, but not effectively. Monitors from the U.S. Justice Department get called in because of the threats to me and my campaign, and concerns over threats to voters.

"It was particularly galling to Richard," Art Torres says. "He was hurt by the attacks [from Ruiz and company]. He shrugged them off in public, but in private it hurt. You give your life to issues that they [La Raza Unida] were talking about and now they turn and say you're not entitled to their support because you're not for those issues. It was basic hypocrisy on La Raza Unida's part to say Richard was not there on their issues because he was there before many of them were. Its agenda was strategic: to embarrass the Democratic Party."

Meanwhile, a corollary form of Republican manipulation develops that we don't learn about until after the special election is over.

Donald Segretti is a young political operative who gets his start as a student at USC. He knows Kenny Katz, my campaign manager, from USC politics. Segretti all of a sudden shows up one Saturday morning at my campaign headquarters with a big smile. "Hey Kenny, what's happening? I heard you're running this campaign and I want to help out." Segretti ends up working in my campaign.

What we don't know until afterwards is that Don Segretti is working or will soon work for CREEP, the Committee to Reelect the President, Richard Nixon. At USC, Segretti gets to know top Nixon campaign and White House figures, including Donald Chapin, special assistant to the president, who recruits Segretti for the "dirty tricks" operation that falls under CREEP. Segretti comes to specialize in what he calls "ratfucking," sabotaging opponents' campaigns through false and underhanded tactics. One example, involving Segretti, is what comes to be called the "Canuck Letter," a semi-literate letter mailed from Florida to a conservative Manchester, New Hampshire newspaper publisher claiming a campaign aide to leading Democratic presidential candidate Edmond G. Muskie loves African Americans while condoning use of the term Canuck, a derogatory word for Americans who have French-Canadian roots. The letter produces a negative editorial in the paper. That, plus another editorial containing false and chickenshit accusations against Muskie's wife, causes the candidate to break down and cry in the snow during a New Hampshire appearance. Most experts blame the demise of Muskie's presidential campaign on that incident.

It turns out Segretti's involvement in my fall 1971 campaign is a trial run for the dirty tricks he is soon trying out the following year at the national level. We find out through the Watergate hearings that Segretti & Company use my race as a practice exercise, to see if they can discredit presidential aspirants like Muskie in 1972. So the Republican strategy in our special election is twofold: cause division among Chicanos through Raza Unida to neutralize support for a Democratic candidate and then disrupt the Democrat's campaign. They're successful with both of them.

I don't think it is an accident that eggs are thrown at Ed Muskie during a campaign stop with me in El Sereno or that disruptions take place when Hubert Humphrey comes to town. "Muskie goes to a Catholic church with Richard in El Sereno," according to Lou Moret. "There are Raza Unida people there, probably organized by Segretti. They throw tomatoes and eggs at Muskie's caravan. It gets covered in the press and the [Latinos] come off looking like thugs. They would stage demonstrations at events where unruly Mexican leftists were doing things and tried to paint Richard as a radical lefty.'

A week before the election "there's a mailer sent to voters signed by someone with an Italian surname name who's supposedly head of something called the 48th Democratic Council, with an address on Rowena Street in the district and a fake union bug," Lou recalls. "There is no such person or organization and when you go to the address, it's an empty lot. But it's nice letterhead with a donkey to make it look like a true Democratic club. There are more Italian-American voters than Mexican voters in the district and many of them assume Richard's Italian. We don't deny it. The mailer calls Richard an imposter and claims he burned an American flag on the steps of the state Capitol, portraying him as a left-wing Communist."

Actually, Kenny Katz is the one who later brings Segretti to my attention because I don't even know the guy. I don't find out that Segretti has worked in my campaign until after the election, when Segretti becomes infamous as a figure in the Watergate scandal. We also find out more about him from my friend, Ernie Camacho, the bail bonds agency owner who helps me get a lot of the L.A. Chicano activists out of jail. I guess Ernie and Segretti are in the National Guard together, serving in the same unit. Segretti later admits to Ernie that he is involved in dirty tricks during my campaign and that they use the race to try out different tactics to see which ones might work in preparation for the national campaign to re-elect Nixon.

Richard later learns that a volunteer in his 1971 campaign is Donald Segretti, who emerges as a dirty tricks operative for Richard Nixon's 1972 re-election committee. Segretti's role in Richard's race is seen as a trial run for his involvement in the Watergate scandal.

The assembly special election isn't the first time Republicans attempt to splinter Latino support for Democratic candidates. Capitalizing on issues such as abortion, gays, and moral decency, around 1968 the Republican National Committee recruits a Chicano Catholic cleric out of Texas to travel, on leave from his ecclesiastic duties, all over the country to areas that are marginal for Democrats and where Latinos make up important portions of the electorate. The cleric targets Latino voters and hammers away at Democratic candidates on social issues. It proves effective in states like Arizona and Texas. They hope to use it in key congressional districts in the Southwest. The Watergate hearings include references to the cleric and how he is part of a strategy organized by the Republican National Committee.

The same cleric goes after Wally Karabian during his 1968 reelection when I'm running his campaign, with political consultants sending out about three mailers. One has a picture of a black bag full of fetuses. Another is a letter from a Catholic cleric telling how he has taken a leave of absence from the church because he feels it is his duty to tell voters about candidates like Wally Karabian who are antilife. It's a perfect district for it. All the Republicans hope to do is to discourage people from voting for the Democrat. It scares the shit out of Wally, but doesn't work in his case because there really isn't a viable Republican opponent who can benefit. After Watergate is exposed, Kenny and I reflect on things that happen in my campaign and how they might be related to what happens later to some of the Democratic presidential candidates. That's when we put two and two together.

This is what we do know: there is intense publicity about my election and the chaos from Raza Unida's involvement. A line up of national Democratic politicians comes into the district to campaign for me: Senators Muskie, Humphrey, Ted Kennedy, and Alan Cranston.

It becomes a very charged, emotional campaign because on top of everything else, it will determine control of legislative reapportionment for the 1970s. Governor Ronald Reagan and the Democrats controlling both houses of the legislature can't come to terms on a redistricting deal in 1971, after results from the 1970 decennial census come out. Reagan vetoes a Democratic reapportionment bill that would set political boundaries—and therefore decide political realities—for the whole state over the next decade. But the governor makes it clear to the Democratic legislature that if a Democrat is elected in the 48th District special election, he will sign whatever plan comes to his desk. The stakes are very high, not only for the assembly, but for the state senate and California's entire congressional delegation since redistricting affects all of their political fates. That, and not just Chicano politics, accounts for the statewide and national interest in the outcome of the election. It's also what probably attracts Segretti's interest.

My Republican opponent, Bill Brophy, is allegedly into running dope. (Once he's elected, he makes noises about being a candidate for Congress against Ed Roybal in 1972. But his political career unexpectedly gets cut short after his young wife kills someone in an auto crash while driving under the influence. Shortly after serving very briefly in the assembly Brophy basically disappears—rumors put him in Central America—and we never hear from him again.)

But two days before the election, late on a Sunday, the front windows of Brophy's house are shot out. Brophy is in the back and isn't hurt. We later learn Brophy hires a *tecato*, a drug user, to fire the gun at his home.

Monday morning, I'm on my way to work the entry gates at the Pacific Telephone Company yards, listening to the radio news and hearing that they've shot into this man's house. It's all over the news that day. Brophy gets half a million dollars' worth of free—and sympathetic—publicity the day before the election.

"Shooting out the windows the Sunday before the election gives [Brophy] headlines he couldn't have bought," Art Torres says. "It had Donald Segretti's fingerprints all over it. That was Segretti's MO down the road during the Watergate scandal."

There are a variety of reasons why I lose the run-off. There are the threats from the La Raza Unida Party, the presence of federal monitors because of those threats and the last minute shooting add to the atmosphere of fear. The Republicans also claim their campaign workers are being intimidated, which isn't happening since I know we're not doing it and Raza Unida is only interested in bashing me and the Democratic Party with the money the GOP is giving it. Some voters are afraid to go out to the polls. However, there is higher than average turnout among voters in predominantly Anglo, middle-class areas such as Alhambra. Many of them, probably Democrats, are sick and tired of all the nationalistic, ethnocentric rhetoric of Raza Unida and vote for the Republican; the margin of my defeat, between 1,000 and 1,500 votes, is almost the same as the number I lose by in Alhambra alone. Other people think I'm going to win anyway, that it is a foregone conclusion—not a bad assumption under normal conditions in such a strongly Democratic district—so they say, Why go to the trouble of voting? When I run again six months later, many voters tell me that's why they don't vote in '71. The fact is a special election makes it difficult to get people out to vote on the natural.

Even though I lose, La Raza Unida Party also suffers as a result of the 1971 special election. All the emotion stirred up by Ruiz's candidacy against me, the resulting attention in the press and the community, and revelations of the truth behind the campaign's financing dampens interest and enthusiasm. The party's leadership, exposed as more interested in defeating a Chicano Democrat than furthering their stated goals, appears dishonest and self-serving in the eyes of many people. The party never has much legs after the '71 election.

Ruiz and his party keep on trying, but from that point on they cease to be relevant. One thing I learn from the Saul Alinsky school of community organizing is you have to give people victories, and that's something Raza Unida can't do. If you can't produce victories for people, then it becomes an academic exercise. But politics for me is a means to an end. By being successful, you can impact change and improve people's lives, both individually and collectively. By failing or leading people in the wrong direction, you can create disillusionment. Politics is not child's play. It has to be taken seriously. Ruiz and his crowd are playing recklessly with politics—and with people's lives.

It might be different if Raza Unida would go into a local city council or school board race where the voters are mostly Mexican. The party's victories come in Texas, in small rural Latino communities where it methodically organizes and chooses its fights.

Bert Corona, another Raza Unida leader, later says my '71 campaign is just a phase in his life. By the early '70s, his power in MAPA is waning—and so is its ability to shake down Anglo politicians in exchange for winning the support of the Chicano community. Bert is the kind of guy who latches onto different movements while they're popular. The one thing I give him credit for is the work he does in coming years for undocumented immigrants. Years later, Bert confidentially acknowledges opposing me in '71 is a mistake and although he respects me at the time, it is the "movement" that drives him to back Ruiz. He doesn't want me to take it personally because it isn't meant to be personal. "Bert, how do you want me to take it?" I reply. "If you are fucked by somebody, how do *you* take it?" Of course, "It's not personal" is a refrain I repeatedly use in my career when I'm doing it—or am about to do it—to someone else.

There is some comfort knowing I'm not the only one getting grief from Bert Corona and Raul Ruiz. They're giving plenty of it around the same time to Cesar Chavez and the United Farm Workers. It's over the union's support for a law authored by Assemblymember Dixon Arnett, a moderate Republican from the San Francisco Peninsula, which passes in 1970 making it illegal for employers to hire undocumented immigrants. This California version of the employer sanction is probably unconstitutional because of the federal preemption when it comes to immigration policy. Even though Cesar and the UFW organize all workers, regardless of immigration status, farmworker strikes are increasingly being broken by undocumented scabs, or strikebreakers, and the strikers and the union are becoming frustrated.

In 1972, Bill Brophy, the newly minted Republican assemblymember who beats me, introduces a bill to repeal what is becoming derisively referred to among Chicano activists as the Dixon Arnett law. Bert Corona and Raul Ruiz badmouth Cesar at every opportunity up and down the state. I agree with Cesar's position because, as the UFW founder says, "No one has the right to be a strikebreaker," regardless of ethnicity. Ironically, many of the strikers on UFW picket lines who are the loudest in calling on immigration authorities to raid struck fields where undocumented scabs are working are themselves undocumented. It's amazing how economics trump ethnicity any day. The Brophy bill, like his brief political career, doesn't go anywhere. In 1973, when he is serving as Cesar's legislative director, Art Torres engineers a change in position and the UFW becomes one of the first unions in the country to officially oppose the employer sanction, decades before other unions and the AFL-CIO act in the same way.

The whole issue of Raza Unida comes up as I'm running for the assembly the second time during the regular Democratic primary in June 1972, when I speak to a class taught by a friend of mine at my alma mater, Cal State L.A. I tell the students, many of them Chicanos, "You know, I think the cruelest thing anybody can do is to use their own people for their own selfish interests, getting them to work hard for a cause when you know you really have a very different agenda.

"I'll be honest with you," I tell the kids. "It could be said it's my fault because I'm a Democrat and my party hasn't always been very honest or forthright when it comes to serving the best interests of Chicanos. You can accuse me of a lot of things, but man, I don't believe in using people. I'm not one who's going to tell somebody something only for them to later find out it is a lie." I say this on the same Cal State campus where Ruiz is an instructor.

Ruiz, Corona, and that crowd know most Chicano kids have very little knowledge or understanding about politics or politicians. And as I say, it's not like the Democrats have a stellar record as it relates to Chicanos. It's one thing for Anglo politicians to screw Latinos. But for me it's the height of hypocrisy and deceitfulness when you do things knowing exactly what you're doing and claiming you're doing them for a higher purpose when you know damn well you're lying to people.

One of the most beautiful things I witness in the middle and late '60s is the growing politicization of the Chicano community. It starts with the young people, the high school kids who bravely walk out of classes in East L.A. and engage in a wave of protests all over the Southwest. Then many of them go on to college and try to make something of themselves with the idea of returning to the community to help it advance. Using the innocence and idealism of these kids as Raza Unida does makes the leaders who do it the lowest form of scum on the earth.

Legitimate political parties, like any other institution, are not going to give anything to anybody. Power is never given; it is taken. The idea too many Chicanos have, that "The Democratic Party owes us something," is based on a fundamentally false premise. You can yell and scream as much as you want from outside the political process, but that won't by itself make anything happen. You've got to go after what you want and force them to give it to you. What I learn about politics on the streets of East L.A. is change comes from a combination of things. The greater the pressure from the outside, the easier it is for inside players to interpret and leverage that pressure. But you have to have people working effectively on the inside too. There's no one correct way of political activism. The important thing to keep in mind is just because I direct my activism in a certain way doesn't mean everyone else has to act like me. The idea of unity without uniformity is the key to success. That's a line from Ron Karanga. It's one thing a lot of Chicano activists never really get. The mere fact Latinos are an important constituency of the Democratic Party doesn't, and shouldn't, mean it owes us a living. Nobody owes you a living. But that doesn't mean you can't make it accountable.

When you work so hard on something, overcome so much, and then lose the way I lose in 1971, not fully understanding all the reasons until later, it's devastating. It is the first, and last, time I ever lose an election. I don't win every battle I'm involved in from then on, but I never let the loss define or limit me either.

For a short time after the November election, I'm disengaged, wondering if this is what I truly want for myself. I kind of already know the answer, but I still ask the question. It's especially hard to accept that I've been done in by other Chicanos. How can people be fooled into believing this garbage? I ask, especially when you look at my body of work up until that time. All the doubts last for a moment. Then I come back and tell myself it won't happen again.

I'm not going to be a nice guy next time. And I'm not going to be the candidate *they* want me to be. You are expected to act a certain way in order to be a good politician. I sort of decide that some of it isn't me. If I'm going to do it again, as I do, I choose not to do it the same way. So in the campaign leading up to the June 1972 Democratic primary, I don't wear a white shirt and tie all the time, trying to appear least offensive to some people who may not be comfortable voting for a Latino. Instead of starting with the Anglo portions of the district, I first go to my strength, the Chicanos, although my mother and I walk precincts together in Alhambra. If she can't walk with me, she walks with another family member. It's hard to turn down a mother. I also don't equivocate on who I am, especially with white voters. While I never lie, some of them think I'm Italian the first time around. This time I run as Richard Alatorre.

Finally, I'm not going to let anyone push me around this time. During the special election the year before, when Ruiz and Raza Unida are threatening me, I'm approached by some of my friends who insist I should not tolerate such attacks. These are guys I grow up with or meet along the way during various causes I champion such as prison reform or labor rights. They offer to assist me in doing something about it. That could cause me more harm than good, I tell them; let the proper authorities handle it. Once I make up my mind to run in '72, I conclude this isn't going to happen again. Some of the same guys come up to me, citing the threats and everything else from the last campaign. "What happened was wrong," they say. They decide the word needs to get back to the ones who threaten us in '71, that this kind of activity will not be tolerated. They do, and there is no repeat in '72.

"This is late '71," Lou says. "Now Richard doesn't have a job or a place to stay because he has no income. He has to file for the 1972 regular Democratic primary by February of '72. My father has properties, including a small house on London Street in Echo Park in the district. I go to my dad and he lets Richard have the house rent free, until June."

We spend almost $300,000 on the '71 campaign. Three hundred thousand dollars spent six months before gives me a good foundation; people know who I am. I know there won't be an unlimited checkbook the next year, that I'll need to spend part of my time raising money, whatever I can, plus walking precincts. I think I spend $35,000 in the 1972 primary.

Lou Moret runs the second campaign that spring. This is his first time running a campaign, but he has worked for Karabian and knows the district inside and out. We run a much more aggressive campaign, with a full day-to-day field operation, get even more volunteers involved, and mount another big effort among the gays.

Lou tries some things that no one has seen before: lots of letters from local voters in the neighborhoods—specially targeted letters to ethnic groups. For example, we get a computerized Chinese dictionary and send out letters from Chinese-American supporters. "The last thing we did was I asked myself, 'Who's guaranteed to vote on Election Day?' Lou says. "The answer was poll workers. So we sent customized letters thanking them for working on this most precious thing we have, which is voting, and for donating their time, sending along a small American flag as a gift."

I seem to live for walking and talking. "All he did was go anywhere and everywhere there were at least 10 people," Lou recalls. "I would walk with him. We walked every gay community, every single street in Mt. Washington, East Hollywood, Silverlake, Echo Park. They were our biggest vote getters. We did okay in El Sereno and Lincoln Heights, where there were lots of Italians. We lost in Alhambra."

I run against Jerry Zanelli, Roberti's guy, in the Democratic primary, and win by a comfortable margin. There is no real contest against the Republican in the general election. This time there is also no third party to divert votes from me.

Chapter 5

Fulfilling a Childhood Dream at the Capitol

My life in the legislature can be divided into three parts. Each is associated with one of the three assembly Speakers I serve under over my 12-year tenure in Sacramento during the 1970s and '80s.

The first part is ever so short: just two years under the Speakership of Bob Moretti. I learn what you can have and the role you can play when you are closely allied with power. There are limits; you can never go beyond a certain line because you will get your wings plucked real fast. But those two years show me what happens when you're *in*. They turn out to be heady times for a freshman assemblymember.

Bob Moretti sees something in me that he wants as a friend and political ally. Latinos are an emerging minority, even in the early 1970s, and have to be part of the political ambitions of any assembly Speaker. I am an asset for Moretti's political aspirations, not just because of where I serve in my East L.A. district but increasingly because of the visibility I soon enjoy as head of the legislature's Chicano Caucus—in both urban and rural areas across the state.

This is not the term-limited legislature of today, where you can get elected Speaker of the assembly in your freshman term. This is an institution when I arrive in 1973, where many members are still considered rookies until they've been there for a number of years. You try to become something—build a reputation—because of your expertise in a subject matter or your relationships, including the ability to help out your colleagues in their home districts or your relations with ethnic groups that are more and more becoming influential in those members' districts. I find Mexicans to work with all over California. The decade of the 1980s is sometimes called the Decade of the Hispanic. The decade of the 1970s sets up that scenario.

Because of my developing contacts with Chicanos all over the state and due to my close relationship with Moretti, for two years I have all the benefits of being close to the seat of power at the Capitol. I always know in the back of my mind that it probably isn't going to last. I witness what it means to be on the outs soon enough. Just as fast as you find yourself on the inside, you can land on the outside—and learn what that means for your budding political career.

The second part of my legislative career is spent struggling in the wilderness. I call it my McCarthy Era—after the six-year Speakership of Leo T. McCarthy, a Democrat from San Francisco. I don't like Leo McCarthy, and he doesn't like me. You might say we hit it off on the wrong foot since late 1974, when I hold out until the bitter end on behalf of my close friend Willie Brown for Speaker against McCarthy—even when it's obvious Willie can't count to 41, the number of votes it takes to get elected leader of the house. My relationship, such as it is, with Leo goes downhill from there.

What I soon realize is McCarthy can influence how prestigious an office I get in the Capitol building, how big it is or not, and how much staff I get to hire. He controls the committees I serve on and to some extent the fate of my legislation. But what he can't take away from me is the seat I'm elected to represent and the fact I'm one vote out of a house with 80 members. And he can't take away my ability to champion the causes I believe in.

There are lawmakers who choose to have their legislative careers directed by the issues they become authorities on; many become genuine experts. That doesn't interest me for the most part. I guess I always view everything that happens at the Capitol as 95 percent bullshit and five percent what really matters. What matters to me is who you are and what you're about—to your colleagues and to the people you represent and care about. Also, unlike most members who primarily focus on their legislative districts, my boundaries come to embrace the entire state of California if it has to do with empowerment of a people who up until then have not really been part of the political process. It isn't common back in those days to use the words empowerment and Latinos in the same sentence; Latinos' potential to influence the political system is just barely emerging.

McCarthy doesn't matter to me because I still possess a forum not a lot of politicians have: my association with the empowerment of Chicanos is through my willingness to put in the time, money, and resources helping Mexicans in almost every corner of California. I decide early on that the cause of Chicanos, popular or not, is how I will be identified.

I decide not to be judged by what I'm doing in the legislative arena—how many bills I author and which ones they will be. I author bills around subjects I like and that make sense to me. As always, my interests are more to be found in the game of politics—and how I can use the political process to get things done on behalf of the people I commit myself to defending.

Part three of my career in Sacramento revolves around returning to power during the celebrated Speakership of Willie Brown and becoming an active participant in running state government. I find myself in the room when decisions are made—and help make those decisions—that impact people all over California.

That I return to power through someone who is one of my best friends since the beginning of my legislative tenure—and to this day—makes it even sweeter. I stick it out with Willie and suffer for it during six years under McCarthy. When he finally becomes Speaker in late 1980, I become one of four people in the lower house who during the last five years of my state Capitol service essentially get to run the state: Willie Brown, Mike Roos, Maxine Waters, and me.

Let's start at the beginning. I'm sworn into office for the first time in January 1973. The initial assembly district I represent, the old 48th, is made up of East Hollywood, Silverlake, Echo Park, Lincoln Heights, El Sereno, a little bit of Mount Washington, and a small part of Alhambra, up to the unincorporated line of East Los Angeles. One of the reasons I win even though the district is only about 18 percent Chicano is that it has all the right ingredients. It has every doper and every hippie; we have seniors, gays, blacks, Asians, Italians, and liberal Anglos.

The district has the kind of composition where a progressive Chicano obviously has a chance. And my image as a Mexican is the right one: a Chicano in a nice three-piece suit who is involved in the Chicano movement even before there is a movement.

Yet I also come from the old school that says you try to do what's good for people and be true to your core beliefs, which have to be maintained no matter what. I don't go up to Sacramento solely to be an ethnocentric assemblymember. But because it is basically a liberal district, you can do a lot of very creative things and people will still be happy with your performance in office. Yes, I clearly come to the Capitol to accomplish a dream from childhood, which is to win elected office and use it to make a difference. But I also have clearly defined values.

My objective is to take care of my district. That's the first rule to follow for staying in office. But since my district is so good, with plenty of progressives, I feel I can do more things and take stronger positions that other lawmakers don't want to or can't take, especially if those stands are good for Chicanos.

I am willing to take on issues that maybe aren't very popular in most other districts. It's not that they're unpopular in my district; most of them have little direct impact on the constituents who elect me. One of the biggest criticisms leveled at me is the amount of time and energy I spend championing Cesar Chavez and the farmworkers, people I don't even represent. The same thing can be said about supporting prison reform at a time when we are moving towards taking discretion in sentencing away from judges and mandating tougher sentences. Then there's my legislation on bilingual contracts, services, and education. Inevitably, I get a lot of hate mail over my work on these issues from all over the state—but rarely from inside my own district—with suggestions for me to "Go back to Mexico, wetback!" It doesn't matter to me. I don't give a shit.

I'm not intimidated. Of course, I don't really have to worry since my stands on these and other controversies are generally in sync with the great majority of the people who elect, and re-elect, me over the years.

Basically, when it's all said and done I'm a Chicano. What I do for Chicanos most of the white liberals in my district think is great. So I'm not really taking a risk since the district, by and large, applauds me and comes to expect me to do that. I'm also good for liberals on labor issues (in general), criminal justice issues, the right of choice for women, the delivery of health care and human services for the disadvantaged, and the emerging gay rights movement. All these things are consistent with my politics growing up. They are part of my politics when I get a college education, during my years as an activist with the Chicano movement, and as a university instructor in the 1960s and early '70s. For me, politics and activism are inseparable anyway. I'm never content as a '60s activist to sit back and let others take the lead or allow things to happen on their own when the major issues of the day are at stake. I jump in and want to help make change happen myself. Why should it be any different when I become an elected official?

My big advantage as a freshman member is I've spent time working in Sacramento before getting elected. I don't have to try to figure out where to find the bathrooms. I enjoy relationships that are developed before the election. I also like to view myself as being a quick learner. There are a handful of veteran colleagues I can rely on when I need advice or help getting something done. I also know which standing committees are good and bad, and which committees make sense for me to try to get on. The reality is that some committees you want to be on and some you don't.

I make good during my first term in office because the Speaker of the assembly, Bob Moretti, is dying to demonstrate to me that he is going to be my friend. That is certainly related to the fact he backs with all his money and power Ralph Ochoa, the guy I beat in my first Democratic primary. Now I'm going to be a member of the Democratic Caucus that will cast a vote for Speaker, which, after swearing in the members is the first order of business when the new legislative session meets for the first time at the beginning of 1973. I learn Moretti has a big thing about friendship. He's an *Italiano* in the best sense of the word from my vantage point. Family to him is important. Friendships are important. And loyalty, personal loyalty, is really important. That's what I believe in too, just on the natural.

But we don't hit it off all that well right away. We run into each other in Miami at the 1972 Democratic National Convention that nominates George McGovern for president. I'm in Miami as a delegate from California for presidential candidate Hubert Humphrey. McGovern and Humphrey compete against each other in the June Democratic presidential primary. McGovern wins the majority of the state's Democratic votes. The position of the Humphrey delegation is that the former vice president should have the number of delegates proportionate to his percentage of the vote in the primary election. McGovern's

Although originally an opponent, powerful Assembly Speaker Bob Moretti embraces Richard after his election in 1972, and aids his unprecedented albeit short-lived rise in influence as a freshman lawmaker in the era before term limits.

position is since he took the state, it is a winner-take-all result. The dispute goes to the party's credentials committee and eventually to a hard-fought debate on the floor of the convention. That's where Willie Brown, who co-chairs McGovern's California delegation along with then-Assemblymember John Burton and United Farm Workers First Vice President Dolores Huerta, delivers his impassioned speech concluding, "Give me back my delegation." The convention votes for the winner-take-all position.

Well, that means my role as a Humphrey delegate is over. But I get to stay at the convention in Miami because a friend of my political benefactor, Assemblymember Wally Karabian, is the U.S. Senator from Alaska, Mike Gravel, who is running for the vice presidential nomination. So even though I'm thrown out of the convention as a Humphrey delegate, Lou Moret, Lorenzo Patino, and I all sign onto the Mike Gravel campaign. By the second day of the convention, I have a floor pass as a political operative for Gravel.

I'm hanging out with the California delegation when Speaker Moretti comes up to me. The conversation starts off pleasant enough, until Moretti decides to get heavy handed. I guess he thinks I'm some young punk he can push around. Even though he backs the guy I beat in the 1971 special election, Moretti threatens me, laying out in precise detail exactly what he will do to me if I don't commit to support him for re-election as assembly Speaker when the legislature convenes for its new two-year session the following January. "I'm here working at the convention for Mike Gravel," I tell Moretti. "I'm not here to commit to you for Speaker. I haven't even been elected yet"—which won't happen until the General Election in November, four months away. That just pisses him off even more. Moretti insists on my commitment then and there, and says he'll cut my nuts off if I don't give it to him. I still refuse to commit to vote for him. He is so mad at me. His aides have to calm him down. I walk away, wondering what that exchange means for my legislative future.

Nevertheless, Moretti has raised a large sum of money for me. I have to go to his district office in North Hollywood to pick it up later in the summer. He introduces me to his wife Marilyn, who I later come to know as a wonderful woman, and he tells her, in front of me, that I'm a rising star and I will soon be the first Mexican in L.A. elected to the assembly in a while. Then, to his wife Moretti adds, "I'm giving him all this money and he still won't give me his commitment to vote for me for Speaker when everyone else has. Don't you think that's chickenshit, honey?" Then he tells her, "You don't have to answer that." Moretti starts laughing.

I smile at Marilyn Moretti. The three of us chat a bit more, just small talk, and I take off.

Moretti is working hard to shore up his majority and keep his Speakership in advance of the start of the new session. He and I talk some more at his invitation before I'm sworn in. It is a long, in-depth discussion and this time it's a whole different thing. He's not yelling at me now because I tell him, "Hey, I ain't gonna be intimidated. I don't give a shit if you're the Speaker. It doesn't bother me. I'm going to do what I'm going to do."

"I respect that," Moretti replies. Then he tells me—and this always sticks in my mind—"If you give me a chance, I will show you that I can be as loyal as Wally Karabian was to you because I'm that type of guy."

Ironically, I learn I have a lot in common with Bob Moretti. Moretti is a man's man. He is proud of being an Italian American; he likes to play at these little Mafioso roles. Like me, he is from a family of humble means. Nothing is ever handed to him. He goes to the University of Notre Dame. Just from the standpoint of where he comes from, how he is raised and his values, I have a great kinship with Bob.

Moretti always likes me—after our first meeting. He knows I'm not, you know, one of those prim, proper Mexicans—or anything else that's prim or proper. When things get tough and dirty, I can get down with the best of them. Nothing is ever given to Moretti and nothing is given to me either.

The Sunday before the 1973 session kicks off at the start of the New Year, Moretti calls me on the phone. "Would you do me the honor of seconding my nomination for Speaker on the assembly floor?" No freshman has ever done that. So my first act as a legislator is getting sworn in. My second act is seconding Moretti's nomination as leader of the house.

I later discover that is also the beginning of envy by other Democratic legislators, especially the handful of Latino members. Most of them have recently got elected too and here I am being asked to help nominate Moretti. They're probably asking themselves, "Why did he ask him and not me?"

There are other Chicanos at the Capitol: Assemblymembers Alex Garcia, Peter Chacon, Joseph Montoya, and Ray Gonzales (who only serves one two-year term). But I guess that doesn't matter in Moretti's eyes. I suppose he sees some things in me that end up being real: I'm fairly outspoken. I have already developed some significant relationships in and around the institution. I understand how the process works. I am loyal. I'm a team player. I can get things done.

When first starting out, you learn that if you're in the business long enough you appreciate that the most effective people at the Capitol are the ones who develop a mastery of institutional knowledge and procedure—how things get done in the place. There is a list of dos and don'ts. That freshmen legislators are expected to be seen but not heard is one of them. The assumption by more senior members is you've got nothing to contribute if you've just been elected for the first time. Their whole attitude is, "Why don't you stick around and learn a little about the body and processes of the legislature before you start opening your mouth and sounding uneducated and uninformed." By showing up, new members learn about the people who are important to their political and legislative careers. Eventually, if you are worth your salt, you rise when people in the leadership notice you, invest in you, and go to bat for you.

It's different with term limits. Now, everyone knows they have fixed and very limited periods of time to serve after getting elected. So they start opening their mouths before they can even find out where the bathrooms are located. That may sound like too cute a thing to say, but it speaks to the fact that all of the post term-limited lawmakers believe they must immediately make their mark. When you consider the current state of governmental affairs in Sacramento, you come to appreciate the problems term limits create in a legislature that at one time is rich with tradition and accomplishments.

None of the handful of my Chicano colleagues in the assembly (there are no Chicano state senators then) has a desire to chair the newly formed Chicano Caucus. It doesn't exist before 1973. All we have until then are Chacon and Garcia; Montoya and Gonzales are elected with me in '72. Now there are five of us. That's still insignificant in a chamber with 80 members, but significant because before there are only two Mexicans. Ironically, this is the beginning of something that ends up growing into the most influential—and numerically significant—caucus in the legislature today outside the two political parties.

My recollection is I'm the one behind creating the caucus. It also could be Lorenzo Patino or Lou Moret who come up with the idea since the discussion begins when the three of us are attending the Democratic convention in Miami the summer before.

I know none of the other four Chicano assemblymembers want the job because of who they are. They would never want to be seen as so outwardly ethnocentric.

Alex Garcia, also from East L.A., is happy to simply be a legislator. By temperament and because his district is similar to mine, he will support the things I support. But he doesn't want any added responsibility.

The claim to fame for Peter Chacon, from San Diego, is education. He has some blacks in his district and a high concentration of Chicanos, many of whom at the time are not registered to vote. Peter is a cautious guy. There is also a clear distinction among the generations between me and Garcia and Chacon, who are older.

Ray Gonzales is elected through the work of Chicano students at Bakersfield College, the community college where he teaches, plus black and Chicano community activists, and the United Farm Workers. The educational establishment is also for him. It's the kind of district you never expect would let a Mexican survive the Democratic primary. But Ray gets out of the primary, faces a weak Republican in the general election and wins. He comes to believe what he thinks the district is: conservative. One time he tells me he really can't openly advocate for a lot of Chicano issues, but he'll be with me on most of them. The one caveat is that Ray represents a Kern County district so he says (in so many words) that he won't be with me when it comes to the farmworkers.

Joe Montoya is a contemporary of mine, a former city councilmember from La Puente. He's a smart guy, but from the time he is elected to the time he leaves office Joe always deals in the negative, never the positive. He has a chip on his shoulder. Towards me, it's always, "How come they're prejudiced against me? Why do you [Alatorre] catch all the breaks? How come I [Joe Montoya] don't?" Joe also tells me that because he represents the San Gabriel Valley, he can't be the same kind of Mexican I am. "I wouldn't get re-elected if I was what you are," he observes.

Chairing the caucus also involves a lot of additional work beyond the duties of legislating and representing constituents. You'd have to take on many causes and serve as a spokesman for those causes, which some of my fellow Chicanos don't want to embrace. When we get together to formalize this caucus and decide who's going to head it, we all look at each other. Nothing happens. I volunteer to do it. "Great idea," they all say at the same time.

So at the same time I'm being sworn into office, I'm also elected to chair the Chicano Caucus.

All the new members—Chicano and otherwise—are in Sacramento with their families for the swearing in festivities at the Capitol. I organize a Chicano Caucus reception for the entire legislature at one of the old hotels on West Capitol Avenue in West Sacramento, and get the event paid for. We invite everybody. It's a big deal. No caucus like this has ever been established for Chicanos. For a Mexican and a freshman legislator, it's a great way to make a first splash on the opening day of session, particularly in an assembly freshman class filled with heavyweights, from Howard Berman in the West L.A. Jewish community to Julian Dixon from an African-American district in South Central L.A. Think about what it means for a Chicano, and a young one at that, dressed in a Levi suit with a red shirt and loud tie, all of which are very fashionable, which I al-

At the first reception Richard organizes for the just-created Legislative Chicano Caucus, in 1973 in West Sacramento, are (from left) Assemblymember Joe Montoya, Alatorre consultant Lorenzo Patino (in background), Assemblymember Alex Garcia, Richard, and Assemblymember Peter Chacon.

ways am, to get up on the assembly floor and second the nomination of Speaker Bob Moretti.

It sends a signal that the old adage of just sitting there quietly and learning the ropes doesn't apply to me. It earns me a lot of notice, but also a lot of envy and jealousy among my freshmen colleagues, including the Chicanos; most of them have to spend years slowly building up to doing something like that.

Between the election and swearing in, they give orientations for soon-to-be-freshmen assemblymembers. I don't go. I have already spent time at the Capitol working for Assembly Majority Consultants. I learn enough to know the process and, more importantly, befriend members who later come in handy. So shit, I say to myself, doing the orientation is a waste of my time. I mean I already know how to do that. I think some people resent me. As it ends up—and that comes two years later—there are ways to get back at me because I am seen as moving too fast and maybe because I become too much of a threat.

This is the dawn of a new day in Sacramento because the needs of Mexicans in the early 1970s are so great and there is hardly anybody else in California to whom Chicanos can turn for assistance. I have a safe district that allows me to take on issues important to the community that are consistent with my entire career of activism up to that point. I know the time is right. I know I have the energy. I know these are issues nobody else wants to talk about.

At first, I don't think the Chicano Caucus will turn into a big deal until, as things evolve, I'm being asked by Chicano activists and organizations to appear and speak, and to go to almost every part of the state to advocate. It means traveling to centers of activism outside my home turf of East L.A., to places such as Fresno and San Jose. Eventually it stretches from the Bay Area south to the Mexican border at Calexico and San Diego. But nobody else wants the caucus chores so I take them over. And I make the most out of them.

One of the Speaker's most important prerogatives is appointing committee members. I know I'm going to get my share of good assignments, but I don't know exactly what that means. Like every freshman legislator, I think I'll get one committee I really want—and the rest I'll just have to accept. The one I want is the Assembly Labor and Employment Committee because of my background and strong belief in the union movement. I know I'll be a good vote for working men and women. Growing up, my father and my uncle, Charlie Rico, who is with the local Teamsters Union, teach me if it isn't for trade unionism, as imperfect as it is, the state of our community would be much worse.

My committee assignments come out. I'm the first freshman in the history of the assembly to be assigned to the Committee on Ways and Means, the powerful panel that deals with all fiscal bills as well as the state budget. Moretti looks at me as having resources and influence not just in L.A., but throughout the state. He calls me into his office and says, "You know, it hasn't ever been done, but I want to let you know you're going on Ways and Means." When Moretti makes that announcement, everyone's jaw drops. "We need a Chicano in there," the Speaker explains to his colleagues. "He's a freshman, so he can't cause any problems." It feels great for me. Shit, it feels fabulous.

Willie Brown is chairman of Ways and Means, so he has to sign off on it. I know Willie since before I get elected. Willie and I have a ball. The guy is singularly the most brilliant man I have ever seen operate. While he runs Ways and Means, everyone on the committee understands that when Willie takes up a bill he wants to get out, in quick order the drill is that the chairman calls "Motion?" "Second?" "Unanimous roll." He finesses business before the committee like a good-fitting glove.

In the pre term-limited legislature where many members serve continuously for years, it can take a long time for newly arrived lawmakers to advance up the chain. I get every good committee I want. It is Bob Moretti's way of showing me he wants my friendship. Some of the other Chicanos in the legislature think, you know, that I just have this special relationship with the Speaker, which is why in their eyes I'm the one who gets everything, and they don't.

As a member of Assembly Ways and Means, you also get assigned to a subcommittee that governs a piece of the state budget. Because of my background in higher education, Willie puts me on that subcommittee, along with

Democrat John Vasconcellos of San Jose and Republican Gordon Duffy of Hanford.

From conversations with Willie, I learn every member of Ways and Means gets their one wish in connection with the budget; you get to ask for what you want first and if you make it happen, you get what you desire. Most members never take advantage of it. In my first year in office, I ask for state support of a new teaching hospital for the UC Irvine medical school, after UCI Chancellor Dan Aldrich comes to see me, and I end up getting it over the objections of the Orange County political establishment, including Democratic Assemblymember Ken Cory, who carry water for the county's doctor-owned hospitals that don't want the competition. Cory is real pissed because I make the "ask" first, but Willie reminds him that's how the system works.

"I want you to protect minorities in the CSU [California State University] and UC [University of California] systems," Moretti tells me when I get on Ways and Means. But it's from Willie Brown that I learn the finer points of chucking and jiving—using our power as legislators to get things done for the people we seek to help. It starts on the Ways and Means Committee when I threaten Frank Newman, former dean and professor emeritus at UC Berkeley's fabled Boalt Hall Law School, and later a Jerry Brown appointee to the California Supreme Court. When Newman appears before my higher education subcommittee and raises moral objections to accepting an affirmative action program to increase the number of minority law school students at Cal, I cut from the budget funding for all the deans and administrators at Boalt Hall. He quickly changes his mind and many more blacks, Chicanos, and other minorities are admitted.

What Willie and I do to the Boalt Hall administration is highly effective and pretty common for us, even after we're no longer in favor with the assembly leadership.

Brown agrees: "In those days, my experience in the world of politics is you don't have to debate whether or not to achieve lofty, worthwhile goals if you got the votes; you just use the power you have. We had it as legislators; we just had to use it. Richard was a great example of our using it for the greater good. We made herculean efforts and magnificent leaps all because we could. Sometimes it resulted in institutional changes.

"We also had so much fun doing it—first with Richard and later with Maxine [Waters] too. We were able to identify opportunities and execute solutions. And we became better at it as we went along because people like Richard did not seek or need the social acceptance of the status quo from people. He never felt obligated to be diplomatic. He just felt obligated to be effective for the people and causes he cared about. So that's what he did. There was never a personal benefit for him other than the satisfaction of knowing he was moving the agenda for equality forward."

Maxine Waters, also an L.A. legislator, is another of our co-conspirators in those days: "One of the best strategies I know Richard and Willie understood was that politics and leadership were about being smart, having knowledge, knowing how to execute and developing strategies and building alliances needed to implement them."

I'm beginning to learn, mostly from teachers like Willie, how to use my newfound power to accomplish things. That combined with growing activism by Chicanos and me being chairman of the Chicano Caucus starts generating a lot of attention—and publicity. I start introducing a bunch of ethno-centric legislation such as bilingual services and bilingual contracts. (I get the idea for a bilingual contracts bill from having worked for years in jewelry stores as a credit manager while putting myself through college. Back then, we negotiate sale terms with customers in Spanish and then give them an English-language contract they can't understand. If you think of the list of things most needed by people in our community, one of them isn't diamonds. But they're right up there among our people with cars, furniture, and other big-ticket retail goods.)

Lou Moret, who manages my campaigns and is my first administrative assistant, running the district office in Highland Park, is always the one who understands that money—and raising it—is where it's all at. Both Lou and I learn the art of political fundraising from Wally Karabian, who's the master. His style is you pre-sell everything. You invite your finance committee—people with the right means or connections—to a pre-fundraising "shake-down" event at a fancy place, like a nice restaurant. You feed them a great meal and let the booze flow. Understanding the dynamics in such a setting, inevitably ego overcomes everything else. Contributors want to one-up each other and outdo the next person on the committee by committing to how many tables they will sell.

In addition to the non-Latinos I have met who we target, Lou and I work hard identifying emerging Chicano business people and professionals, both those who have already established themselves and the ones who are aspiring to succeed. I also spend some of my time in 1973, going to a lot of organizational and professional functions. It gets to be generally known that if 15 or more Chicanos are meeting somewhere in California—from any business, occupation, profession, or organization—I'll manage to show up even if it means flying after legislative session in Sacramento and returning back late that night or early the next morning. (I rarely miss scheduled floor sessions or committee meetings.)

I begin to develop these younger up-and-coming Chicanos who really don't yet have a lot of conflicts in their political giving; they aren't invested in many other politicians, and certainly not Latino politicians. So I get them to invest in me. Many remain loyal supporters—and personal friends—over the decades.

Lou and I are working towards something specific. It emerges as a dinner held in October 1973, at L.A.'s spectacular Century Plaza Hotel, one of the premiere venues in the city. It takes a full year of work leading up to it, but we're committed to making it happen.

We carefully follow the game plan established by Wally Karabian. Our shakedown dinner is at Perino's Restaurant on Wilshire Boulevard in the Miracle Mile, a hangout for all the movie stars. I have heard about how the dynamics of such events work, but I have never seen them work for me. I have an informal finance committee of about 15 guys. They, in turn, have relationships with many, many others. They all get together and outdo each other in trying to see who will commit the most. We pre-sell the dinner for about $150,000, a huge sum in those days.

The biggest tribute dinner the Century Plaza has previously seen is for Ronald Reagan when he is governor of California. Our dinner matches it; there are more people at our fundraiser that anyone has witnessed up to that time. We are bigger than many dinners hosted at the hotel for presidents of the United States. It takes an hour for 1,600 people to navigate through the registration tables and into the grand ballroom. It blows everyone's mind. It blows the Speaker's mind. It blows Wally Karabian's mind. It blows the mind of anyone familiar with the customary fundraising draw for a freshman member of the California State Assembly. Those attending also represent a much more diverse crowd than they're used to seeing at the Century Plaza on the west side of L.A.: white, black, brown, yellow, pink, blue and everything else, including entertainers and movie stars such as Nancy Sinatra. Speaker Bob Moretti is there. So is Willie Brown, John Burton, Jerry Brown, and many of my Democratic colleagues in the legislature. It's a Who's Who of California politics.

What's even more impressive than the number of attendees is the fact that 75 percent of them are Mexicans. That is unprecedented. There is money out there in my community. If you go after it, you can get it. We go after Chicano money—educators, lawyers, doctors, all manner of professionals and business people and labor leaders. We're able to demonstrate that Chicanos can raise money, big money.

My star is rising. Everything seems to be falling my way in that first term. However, what starts to emerge is the crab syndrome in politics: you pull everyone down as you try to climb up. Jealousy sets in and everything else. I don't care. I'm doing my job. I keep my fellow Chicano Caucus members informed about what's happening. I give them credit because the one thing I understand is you need them to be with you. So I'm always talking about the other Chicanos who are in office and what they're doing. None of them is really doing very much—so they're also not getting the play within the institution and with the public that I'm getting.

You can say our plan is working perfectly. I'm doing everything I love to do; it's coming out the way I have always hoped. It is the realization of my belief about the political process being a vehicle to make change happen.

Mondays through Thursdays are taken up with committee meetings and session days at the Capitol. People in my district still regularly see me because I fly down every Thursday from Sacramento. I'm in town holding meetings with constituents and groups in my district office and attending outside functions across the district. When I'm not in my district outside of session days, I'm somewhere else in the state: making speeches to Chicano organizations, aiding Chicano causes, and campaigning or raising money on behalf of Chicano candidates for various elected offices.

I'm there at the formation of what becomes known as the Comisión Feminil Mexicana Nacional (National Mexican Women's Commission), spearheaded by a pioneering group of Latina activists. Their goal is to start a childcare program in the public housing projects of East L.A. and they want to meet with me. There are three women: Sandy Serrano Sewell (one of the group's first officers who runs the child care center once it is up and operating); Yolanda Nava, a well-known TV news journalist with one of the L.A. network affiliates; and Gloria Molina, a veteran activist who is subsequently elected to the state assembly, follows me to the L.A. City Council, and later is elected to Los Angeles County Board of Supervisors.

The comisión is "created as the natural outgrowth of a women's social organization that had traditional teas and fashion shows, and supported male political candidates because no one even thought of having female candidates," Sandy Sewell recalls. The coming of the women's movement in the late 1960s sows the seeds of the Comisión Feminil. "We should look at things in a different way because of the times," she says.

Latina activists attending a conference in Texas complain to a U.S. Department of Labor representative that there are no programs to train women for nontraditional jobs in the L.A. area. "Come up with a program proposal," the federal official says. By 1970, they shift their group from focusing on the social scene into a formal incorporated nonprofit, tax-exempt organization and start drafting proposals. One funded by the Labor Department is for the Chicana Service Action Center to train women in nontraditional occupations such as working for telephone companies, putting in wiring for phones and handling construction jobs.

While securing funding and putting women through training, the Chicana activists hit upon a problem, Sandy says: "Wait a minute," they realize, "these women have kids. What will they do with their children while they work?"

That's how the Comisión Feminil comes upon its second proposal, to the state, for a childcare center in East L.A. around 1972–73, Sandy recollects. They know I'm going to be elected in 1972, and the group approaches me after I'm in office.

We meet on a Saturday. The women want to give me an education about the oppression of Chicanas. "Let me stop you," I break in after a short time. "Why don't we stipulate to everything you say. What do you want from me?"

We need some money for this childcare program, they collectively answer. "I'll get back to you," I reply.

"Richard is on the Ways and Means Committee and uses his membership to push the proposal through the state funding process," according to Sandy. "He goes to Bob Moretti, the assembly Speaker, to get him on board too. Richard babies the proposal through.

"The result is it gets funded," she adds. The facility "is called Camino Real, but changes its name in 1974, to Centro de Ninos Inc., one of the first childcare centers on the Eastside to get state money." The center has two simultaneous impacts.

Richard helps encourage and support early development of Comisión Feminil Mexicana Nacional, a pioneering group of Chicana activists that starts in East L.A. Pictured are three key comisión leaders: (from left) future L.A. County Supervisor Gloria Molina, television newscaster Yolanda Nava, and Sandra Serrano Sewell, head of Centro de Ninos, a landmark childcare center on the East Side.

First, it further opens the door for the comisión. "The possibilities are endless," Sandy observes. "I don't think Richard Alatorre realizes he is the one who from the beginning helps plant the seeds for an eventual run [for public office] by Gloria Molina. Even though he was romantically involved with some comisión members, he was always giving women advice. They came to him with these problems. He says, 'I'll do this or do that.' Unwittingly, he doesn't realize he is training them and they are learning from him."

There are two types of women who belong to the comisión: college-educated women who should have unlimited horizons opening up to them and women who often lack formal education, who have chosen the marriage-mommy track. What surprises comisión leaders like Sandy Sewell is that both groups of members "are on the same track: they are limiting their possibilities. I recall they even wouldn't enter certain department stores like the old Broadway downtown L.A. store because it was a big department store and had an Anglo clientele and staff. That's just not where you would go if you were Latina."

As a transplant from the Midwest, Sandy brings a little different perspective. Plus, she comes from a union household; her dad is a steelworker. "My outlook was very much as a team player with a collective approach that benefits more people," she notes. So as these women are being challenged to change their views of themselves and of what is possible in 1970s L.A. by people like Sandy, "what Richard did through his interactions with the women was maybe inadvertently become somebody they could trust, which I thought was weird because he was dating two or three of them off and on during this time."

The new state-funded childcare center also has a direct impact by enabling the women in the program and the Eastside community itself to have a place to take their children and trust that the kids are going to be cared for in a healthy and safe environment. "As a community, we were not used to taking our children to childcare centers," Sandy says. "We'd take them to a grandmother or sister's home or find someone else in the family. So taking your child to virtual strangers was a big leap of faith for our community. Richard's role in securing the financing was known in the community, and knowing that this new guy on the block who had clout in Sacramento was behind the new center meant a lot to people. People knew who he was because he was just elected, young, smart, and good-looking. He had those attributes people like to see in an elected official. And he was part of them. For those of us in the comisión, he was like our Good Housekeeping seal of approval. I don't even think Richard knew about that."

Over the years, the center and the comisión develop their own reputation by doing a good job. They don't judge the families they serve, which is a big deal. The mothers who patronize the center are often "undereducated, with little experience outside their own circle of life," as Sandy puts it. "Some have had run-ins with the law or have boyfriends who belong to established gangs at the time. We never made any of those things an issue" in admitting children to the center.

"'How do you want your child cared for?' is all we ask them. 'If you could turn back the clock, what would you do differently about how you experienced life and do you want that for your child?' Their answers always include the closeness of family and tradition, and a high regard for showing respect. On the other side, they say over and over again that they wish their parents would have read to them, taken them to the beach, given them more experiences about the world around them when they were younger. Everything seemed to tie to a social education more than a formal education. We took that input from them and incorporated it into the program. Even today we're the only child development center in the whole country to have a partnership with NASA, with a whole space theme," adds Sandy, who still runs the center.

As a transplant from a Midwestern union family, Sandy says she has "no problems with a Dick Daley Chicago kind of mentality: you help those who helped you." She sells a whole table worth of tickets to my big 1973 fundraiser at the Century Plaza Hotel, for an even $500. "I can't believe I did that," Sandy exclaims.

She is married with two children of her own back then. "It seemed the women who were most taken with Richard beyond the fact he was an elected official, were the ones with college degrees. I tried to put that together. How does that work? Is there something I don't know because I don't have a B.A.? My first impression was he was sort of a gangster, because that's how he talked. Some women like bad boys. That was before I knew Richard. I was very intrigued and wanted to know him and figure out what he was all about."

So Sandy figures one way to know me better is to honor me. In late 1974, she gives me an award from the childcare center but spells my name wrong on the plaque. "How insulting," she recalls now. "Here he did everything for the center and I want to know him better and I don't notice his name is spelled wrong. But he's a real good sport about it. It really hit me that he was so un-politician about it."

Sandy and her colleagues also see me as "the farmworker guy." This is the early- and mid-1970s. "Richard would come to the organization with various issues that the farmworkers were involved with, soliciting our support as women. It was not a hard sell at all."

Then, in 1976, when the center and the comisión are opening a second childcare site on the outskirts of downtown L.A., they get targeted as part of an organizing drive by UTLA, United Teachers of Los Angeles, the local teachers union. Because she comes from a union background, it doesn't really bother Sandy, who by then is the center's director and administrator. The only problem is she operates on a shoestring budget and doesn't have money to meet any of the union's demands.

"One day I pull into work and the farmworkers are picketing outside my building," she remembers. "Somehow, UTLA got to the UFW, and they're all over my case with unsubstantiated allegations, including that I was serving boycotted table grapes and lettuce to the kids, which isn't true. I was shocked, totally unprepared. I called up Richard. 'What am I going to do?' I asked."

"'Don't worry about it,' Richard tells me. 'I'll take care of it.' Mysteriously, the farmworkers soon left and didn't come back. That was a big relief.

"I counsel with Richard about what to do about the union drive. He said, 'You have to let them hold an election. You have to have staff meetings and show the staff what the budget is and what it would mean to meet the union's demands. But you have to let them vote.' There was an election. Some third party conducted it. The union lost by two votes. At the time, I had 27 people on staff. One person voted 'no union' because it was against her religion. So the union really lost by one vote.

"I remember getting so sick over the whole thing. But Richard kept pounding away at me: 'You got to let them vote.'

"'What if I lose?' I asked him.

"'Then you got to deal with it.' He was right.

"Almost from the beginning, Richard was always a mentor and door opener for the comisión and its members," Sandy says. "He opened the door for the center. He helped the women with their chosen career paths. He helped people get jobs. He was also very instrumental in encouraging some of the women to continue their formal educations. He'd pull strings to get women into college programs. He encouraged the women who already had B.A. degrees to get graduate degrees. Also, whether they had a formal education or not, he treated the women equally within the organization as far as decision-making and having input. He took you for what you had to bring to the table and how you presented yourself. It was a big morale booster for many of us who didn't have the formal education."

First there is the national organization of the Comisión Feminil Mexicana Nacional. Then a year later, an L.A. chapter is founded. At one point there are

27 chapters spread throughout California, Arizona, Colorado, New Mexico, Illinois, and Ohio.

The legislative part of my legislative career starts with ideas growing out of late-night discussions during the 1972 Democratic National Convention in Miami between Art Torres, Lou Moret, Lorenzo Patino, and I. We're brainstorming over bills I can introduce after taking office the following January. We come to focus on bilingual services: how can a city or county—or the state of California—offer services it is supposed to provide people if it can't even properly communicate with the people needing the services? If the people being served can't communicate with the people providing the services, it's like two ships passing in the night, but never making contact. Agencies need to be required to make services available and publicize their availability so people know where they can go and see public servants who are able to speak their language.

We come up with the concept of setting a trigger that would force local government to hire bilingual personnel to provide those services. The requirement will kick in once 10 percent or a certain number of people in the jurisdiction speak a language other than English, be it Spanish, Vietnamese, Chinese, or another tongue. Then the entity also has to print and make available materials in addition to have people on staff to converse in that language.

The concept gets turned into Assembly Bill 86. Carrying it for me in the senate is state Sen. Mervyn M. Dymally, my friend in the upper house I know from the Urban Affairs Institute he runs in the late 1960s when I'm one of his protégés. Merv never has to be convinced of the importance of coalition politics or of providing basic services to minorities and the poor. I get AB 86 out of the assembly. Merv gets it out of the senate. It's signed into law by Governor Ronald Reagan and gets known by its tombstoned title as the Dymally-Alatorre Bilingual Services Act, Government Code Section 7290-7289.8.

The preamble of the new law couldn't be clearer if I wrote it myself. (The lawyers in the Office of Legislative Counsel draft it, based on input from my staff and I.)

> The Legislature hereby finds and declares that the effective maintenance and development of a free and democratic society depends on the right and ability of its citizens and residents to communicate with their government and the right and ability of the government to communicate with them. The Legislature further finds and declares that substantial numbers of persons who live, work and pay taxes in this state are unable, either because they do not speak or write English at all, or because their primary language is other than English, effectively to communicate with their government. The Legislature further finds and declares that state and local agency employees frequently are unable to communicate with persons requiring their services because of this language barrier. As a consequence, substantial numbers of persons presently are being denied rights and benefits to which they would otherwise be entitled.

No law I author has a more far-reaching impact on state and local government, from county welfare agencies to local hospital emergency rooms to state Department of Motor Vehicles field offices. If the agency or office reaches within its function or jurisdiction a certain percentage of people who are non-English speaking or who feel more comfortable communicating in a different language, then the entity is mandated to provide services in the beneficiaries' own language. The real target is Chicanos at the time, although it also applies to Asians.

Another pervasive effect of bilingual services is dramatically enhancing career opportunities for Chicanos and other public employees who speak languages other than English. All of a sudden, big public operations such as the Employment Development Department and DMV have to employ personnel fluent in languages commonly spoken by their customers. They also have to supply translated forms, materials, and publications. Agencies have to hire or promote Chicanos to accommodate Spanish speakers and offer them additional pay or other incentives to acknowledge their special skills and assumption of additional responsibilities. The law may not become a full employment act for Mexicans and other minorities, but it helps improve the employability and promotion of Latino and other civil servants and is one factor, along with considerations such as changing demographics, that boosts the ranks of Chicanos working for government in the coming decades.

More agencies get on board not necessarily by hiring staff with these skill sets from the outside, but by searching internally for employees who can fill those needs, offering them better pay and promotions for doing it. Many of these employees are lower-level blue-collar workers. All of a sudden, there are exams for better paying jobs in state agencies they are now qualified to fill. The end result is that tens of thousands of Chicanos get jobs and those who already have jobs get bumps for being able to provide these services. It means upward mobility and further opens the doors of government service to ethnic minorities.

AB 86 initially applies just to state agencies. Subsequent laws expand the provision of bilingual services to local government too.

Later, by the late 1970s and early '80s, legislation is enacted to provide bonus pay and spell out promotional opportunities for people with bilingual skills. Part of that is driven by the need to have more bilingual employees providing state and local government services in languages other than English for communities that have not previously been adequately served.

There is a priority list of certain agencies and departments that have to roll out programs implementing AB 86 by specific dates. Not everyone is required to implement bilingual services right away. Some entities are not initially covered. There are priorities for essential social and medical services that must immediately comply, including public hospitals. Later laws expand bilingual services to all state and local government agencies.

There is no mechanism for compliance at first, and no penalties. So it takes a long time, much longer than any of us think, to get from then to today. The state starts conducting audits of state and local agencies to see how many clients they serve, whether the 10 percent trigger is met and do they have qualified employees to implement the bilingual programs. If they don't, someone has to be given the responsibility for making it happen. The audits expose government's reluctance, mostly on the part of the state, to implement bilingual services. As non-English speaking populations continue growing and as minority groups become a more integral part of California, there is more pressure to implement AB 86. That's what keeps successor bills coming down the pike. A second generation of legislation imposes penalties because of the length of time it takes to make progress once AB 86 is on the books.

Opposition builds in the private sector on the assumption that if public agencies and facilities have to employ bilingual staff, it won't be long before the private sector will have to act similarly or be at a competitive disadvantage. If a major portion of the population can turn to public facilities to get bilingual services, people will be less likely to patronize private institutions. If people acquire an expectation of being served by someone at a public agency who speaks Spanish, why wouldn't they come to expect private providers to do the same?

Some private sector opposition to bilingual services reflects the discriminatory, noninclusive nature of trade groups and professional organizations of the day. Rather than do the right thing and in the process embrace new sources of business—more people who will pay more money for servicing them—it can be like pulling teeth. Power players in the Third House such as the realtors® and hospital association have to be persuaded to overcome their opposition.

"Richard faced substantial opposition in committees and on the assembly and senate floors," relates Toni Trigueiro, my very able and dedicated legislative assistant who serves with me throughout my legislative career. "But he succeeds through part perseverance and part realization by people that the time is right. There was increasing demand from minority communities that were just beginning to recognize they were entitled to equal access to quality services from public institutions.

"Richard had to work it very hard. He pulled out all the stops, did a lot of cajoling and hand holding. Remember, there weren't that many minorities in the [Capitol] building. At that time, when legislators had personal relationships with each other that crossed party lines, Richard could go to some of the older members like Bob Beverly and Paul Priolo, moderate Republicans, and have realistic conversations with them about the time being right for change and reassuring them that the flood gates [to political empowerment of Latinos] would not be opening up—whatever the message had to be. Richard could convey those messages to the less-than-enthusiastic members in ways that were very genuine. They had respect for each other."

Say that one of my moderate Republican colleagues has a bill and comes to me, for example, as a committee chair. The routine is, I tell him I don't like his bill, but offer amendments I'm recommending. If he agrees, we set the bill for a hearing and it probably gets out. If the GOP member doesn't agree, then he doesn't get a hearing date. It's as simple as that. Today, when members don't get hearings in committee, they will occasionally rise on the assembly floor and move to pull a bill out of committee. Committee chairs with subject matter expertise (or their staffs) have a lot more power back in my day.

I pick up some Republicans for that first bilingual services bill because that's in part why Ronald Reagan signs it into law. "Richard somehow convinced the governor to sign the bill," Toni says. Reagan as governor is a horse trader too: "You scratch my back, I'll scratch yours." He isn't particularly ideological, at least not when I deal with him at the state Capitol in the 1970s.

Separate bilingual services legislation I author requires translators for non-English speakers in hospital emergency rooms and medical clinics. Because it affects the private sector—unlike AB 86, which only applies to government facilities—this measure gives me a taste of the resistance that will later come from private businesses to my bilingual contracts bill.

Even though the emergency room bill is controversial, it still raises the fundamental issue of all Californians being treated equally and getting the same quality of services and protection. The hospitals and clinics have to know my proposal is coming, but they come unglued. Like everyone else in the business world, for hospitals it's all about the bottom line. You still have to make a profit even when you're in the business of saving and preserving lives. They don't like the fact they are being told that a specific kind of qualified employee—one who speaks Spanish or some other language—has to be available in the emergency room to aid non-English speaking patients. There is a sufficient number of deaths and other undesirable outcomes to absolutely warrant requiring bilingual services.

But mandating them faces a huge hurdle of opposition. Hospitals suggest they can't hire enough qualified people to provide the services. They claim it will take a number of years to work through. You can't just call in a janitor who might speak Spanish or Chinese and have that person translate in an emergency room. Also under the bill, personnel who are fluently bilingual and are knowledgeable about medical procedures and terminology have to be on call 24/7.

This is a logical place to start applying bilingual services outside the government realm because emergency rooms involve issues of life and death. I mean, having bilingual staff at DMV field offices is important, but if they aren't there it's not usually life threatening.

It's hard for hospital management to argue it isn't important for patients at risk of dying to communicate with caregivers. It is plain common sense. It isn't even an offensive idea for the Republicans. It is only offensive to anybody who is going to have to pay to provide the services. The funny thing is I argue that businesses wanting to make money know they have to effectively communicate with their customers. Businesses don't look at communicating with customers as burdensome; it's a basic premise that is essential to the bottom line. Many companies have no problem displaying signs proclaiming, "*Se Habla Espanol*" (We Speak Spanish). They have no problem advertising on Spanish-language television about what they have to offer. But when it comes to a life and death situation, the private hospitals have a problem.

Back then you don't have the drums banging about undocumented people receiving public services that you hear today—even if it's still inaccurate. It isn't fueling the opposition back then very much. The undocumented are always present, although not as many of them as there are today. But they are just as invisible. They don't then—and still don't—seek out government benefits or services. The last thing most of them want to do is show up at a government office and identify themselves. They only seek out emergency medical aid if they are hurt or very ill.

Because I know some Democrats will drop off, I need to make it up by getting Republican votes. I need to find some reasonable legislators who can look at the issue and forget about English being the language of the land; it's a basic right to be able to talk to the doctor or nurse in the emergency room so these professionals have the correct information and make the right diagnosis, and so the patient knows what's going on and can cooperate.

My quest succeeds. The bill becomes law. It doesn't seem a bit controversial today, but it is then.

As I point out, the bilingual services legislation involves the public sector. Another of my battles at the Capitol, enacting a bilingual contracts statute, turns out to be a tougher fight only because of strong and widespread opposition from some of the most powerful economic interests in the private sector. This bill is also pretty simple. It says if you advertise a product or service in one language you have to provide a contract in the same language.

It comes out of my experiences as a young guy with a wife and kids putting myself through college by working as a credit manager in East Los Angeles jewelry shops. I remember getting monolingual Spanish-speaking customers to sign contracts or finance agreements they can't even read because the documents are in English. Even today, when we rent a car and sign a two- or three-page small type agreement, we usually don't spend time reading the whole thing; we assume what the agency representative tells us is true. But at least we *can* read it. That isn't the case for many people before the bilingual contracts law.

Abuses are more common among sales people in other retail sectors, especially car dealerships. Deals are represented one way in Spanish over the radio and television airwaves, in newspaper ads, or when people get pitched in the showroom or sales office. Then the deal appears with very different terms on the contracts they're handed, which are only written in English. So customers are signing their names and obligating themselves financially and legally to terms and conditions they are completely unaware of. You're signing a contract to open a credit account. Is it 4 percent or 19 percent interest? Do you have a 30-day grace period to return the goods or 60 days?

Bait and switch schemes are clearly not divulged when advertising is conducted in Spanish and other languages. Terms and conditions are offered as an enticement to buy, but they are not included in the written contract that is in English only. Once you sign the contract, you're out of luck, even if you can't read it. You're still bound by those conditions whether you understand them or not—despite the fact you believe what the sales person explains to you orally in your own language. Poor and minority people get screwed. They end up losing cars or other purchased goods or they get charged higher interest rates they never agree to.

Like the fight to enact bilingual services, there are plenty of horror stories—incidents of people getting ripped off in southern California—making the case for bilingual contracts. People lose their life savings to pay for contract conditions they don't know they are committing themselves to. Of course, there's always an unsavory segment in the business community looking to make a quick buck at the expense of vulnerable people. While it's not just the real estate or car industries, there are enough examples of people whose livelihoods seem to depend on misrepresenting what's on a piece of paper. Even today

The bilingual contracts measure is a watershed in consumer rights. It acknowledges that language means something and just because people speak something other than the language of this country doesn't mean they shouldn't be afforded certain basic consumer protections such as knowing what they are signing. All the bill requires is an official facsimile or summary. The business doesn't have to translate a long legal document word for word.

Nevertheless, California retailers, and especially institutional advertisers, come out of the woodwork to oppose it. That's how it gets defeated the first time in 1973, when Governor Ronald Reagan vetoes my bill on October 1, 1973. The next day he signs my bilingual services bill. It seems like he does a trade, choosing bilingual services that only affect the public sector—plus at the time there is no enforcement mechanism—over bilingual contracts that primarily affects the private sector and the business community.

My thinking at the time is he won't sign either one of them. But I guess Reagan figures, since he's screwing me here (by vetoing bilingual contracts), then he'll give me a break there (by signing bilingual services).

I go to the Reagans' home in the upscale Fabulous Forties neighborhood of East Sacramento shortly after the veto. Nancy Reagan periodically hosts dinners for legislators and I'm often included. Maybe three or four freshmen legislators get asked. As a person, Reagan, like Bob Moretti, is a man's man. I remember him before he runs for governor when he's a movie star and later spokesman for General Electric and host of the "Death Valley Days" television program in the 1950s and early '60s. He loves horses, and riding them. At Reagan's home, I tell him how I remember he's always riding a horse in the 16th of September parade celebrating Mexican Independence Day in East L.A.

"I was really very impressed by the fact that even before it was popular to be with Chicanos, you'd ride in the 16th of September parade," I say. "On the first 16th of September after you became governor, you rode on that same horse without any banners or hoop-la proclaiming you're the governor. No special publicity. And people on the sidewalks clapped for you. Up to that time, there were no Republicans who ever showed up. They wouldn't waste their time."

Reagan kind of smiles. He asks me to tell him a little about myself. I do: born and raised in East L.A., my father a repairman at a stove manufacturing company. The governor asks who my father works for. I tell him.

"Yea, I know where it was," the governor says of the plant. We talk some more.

"I could tell [from the parade] you had a great command of the horse," I say.

"Yeah, that's my horse. I love to ride. As a kid I rode horses." I tell him as a kid I sometimes rent horses to ride down at a stable in Pico Rivera.

"If anyone would understand the need for bilingual contracts, I thought you would," I finally say to the governor. I relate why I introduce the bill, about my experiences as a young credit manager in local jewelry stores and how people get messed over.

Nancy Reagan is listening too. "Ronnie, I think he's right," she injects.

"Yeah," Reagan responds. "The only reason I vetoed it was I got a phone call from Danny Villanueva, who's a good friend of mine, saying what a bad idea it was." He knows Danny, who is also a Republican, from Danny's days as a star field goal kicker for the Dallas Cowboys and later the Los Angeles Rams.

I'm trying to figure out the best shot I have with this guy.

"I know Danny," I reply. "He's a friend of mine too," which is true from the days since the late 1960s when I hang out with Chicano journalism pioneer Ruben Salazar while Danny is general manager at the Spanish-language television station KMEX-TV, before Ruben is killed by a Los Angeles County deputy sheriff during the 1970 Chicano Moratorium. "But you need to separate the need for the bill from why Danny wants it vetoed," I continue. "I think it's chickenshit that the big institutional advertisers are putting heat on Danny."

"If you get Danny off my back, I'll sign it," Ronald Reagan says, and we shake hands on it.

Danny is struggling to get more institutional advertising for Channel 34. This is before it becomes the most popular L.A. television station in either language. So the advertisers, anxious to kill bilingual contracts, get to Danny. "If this thing passes," they claim, "we're going to be fucked; we won't have any money to advertise with you." The advertisers tell Danny in so many words that if he calls his friend the governor and gets him to veto my bill, they will take care of him.

I have to decide how to approach Danny, who really is one of my heroes, after the conversation with the Reagans. Some time passes after the veto. I have to wait for the next legislative session, at the beginning of 1974, to reintroduce the measure. During the interim, Danny and I have our come-to-Jesus moment. "In case you don't know, I know why bilingual contracts got vetoed," I finally tell Danny. "I know why it was done." He's flabbergasted—more than a little nervous.

"Danny, I understand what you did. But it was wrong and inconsistent with what I'm trying to do and what you already know."

"You're right," Danny says. "These fucking institutional advertisers. They promised the station [KMEX] they would look favorably on getting the large car producers and dealers to advertise with us," which can make a big difference for a fledgling station like Channel 34 that he is struggling to build up.

"I'll help you," Danny promises, by making a phone call to Governor Reagan at the right time.

The bill is reintroduced in 1974, as AB 2797, and once again faces vigorous push back from every conceivable business and trade group that would be subject to providing bilingual contracts if it is enacted. When the chairs of the policy and fiscal committees in both legislative houses call for opposition, the hearing rooms seem to stand up en masse and step forward to testify. It's the usual cast of characters—saying the usual stuff: the sky is going to fall; it will cost business too much money. Then there are questions about what the translation will be like. Who will translate? What kind of Spanish will it be, Castilian Spanish versus everyday East L.A. Spanish? There are lots of claims about how difficult translating will be.

The only ones for my bill are groups like the ACLU, California Rural Legal Assistance, and Latino organizations. None of them have any clout in the legislature.

What I do have going for me is making sure the bill gets to the right assembly policy committee, Judiciary. This committee's composition is pretty good, with enough libs, civil libertarians, and trial lawyers. The only reason Bob Moretti doesn't fuck me is the Speaker is running for governor in a crowded and tough Democratic field. If anything, he wants to be seen as a champion of Mexicans and progressives. Then again, he is also my friend and knows how important the bill is to me.

It's tougher when the bill gets to the senate. There, I have my friend and mentor, Merv Dymally.

Still, the senate has more of a reputation of being owned by this industry or that one. So I go to George Moscone, chairman of the Senate Judiciary Committee, and he agrees to be the floor jockey. (The floor jockey is slang for the member who brings up your bill on the floor of the other house when it makes its way there. The author of an assembly bill needs to find a state senator who will serve as a floor jockey when his or her bill gets taken up before the entire upper house.) When a bill is important and I want it passed, I go to Moscone. He's one of the few legislators who endorses me during my first run in the 1971 primary election when I'm being opposed by Bob Moretti even though they're both Italian Americans. George is a true progressive, a decent guy, and a man of his word who's highly respected by his colleagues. We become the best of friends. (It is such a tragedy, and a great personal loss for me and so many others, when George, as mayor of San Francisco, is shot to death along with Harvey Milk by Dan White in 1978.)

The senator who gives me the hardest time on this bill is Dennis Carpenter, a Republican from conservative Orange County who is close to Reagan. He's a former FBI agent who spends a lot of time in Mexico during his bureau days. He

Essential in getting Governor Ronald Reagan to sign Richard's bilingual contracts law is Danny Villanueva, general manager of Spanish-language television station KMEX—even though Villanueva asks the governor to veto an earlier bill.

thinks welfare is a give-away. But he speaks Spanish and we become friends. I just keep beating him down over time. "You're a good guy," I say to Carpenter. "But you're fucking all these Mexicans" who are victimized by English-only contracts.

"They're my friends and my people," he answers. "I got a phone call [in 1973] from my good friend Danny Villanueva and he said it's a fucked up idea," Carpenter argues.

"That was before," I reply. "I'll have him call you."

"If my friend Danny, who's also a Republican, is for you, then I'll be there too."

Sure enough, that takes the argument away from him—and Carpenter reinforces what Reagan tells me. I finally get to Carpenter, both on my own and with Danny's help. He turns around and becomes the jockey for the measure on the senate floor, which makes it easier for the governor. And with help from senators like Dymally, Moscone, and Carpenter, I get the measure to Ronald Reagan's desk. Danny calls him at the right moment. The governor signs it on September 26, 1974, during a signing ceremony in the governor's office I attend along with Lorenzo Patino and Marc Grossman. The bilingual contracts bill becomes law in California.

You can't say Reagan is a deep thinker. He is kind of detached. But he is a basic guy, a nice guy. Even though he screws me on bilingual contracts the first time, I get him to sign it the second time around. What I learn from dealing with him is you have to paint the right picture. He'll listen and sometimes sign off if he sees merit in the issue.

"It's tough sledding, but Richard gets the bill out through persistence and hard work," Toni Trigueiro says. "He's well liked even as a freshman, trustworthy and politically astute. The learning curve is pretty short for him. He doesn't take long to figure out how the game is played. Whatever it is, his nature brought him that ability to be a politician. You either have those skills or you

Richard has a good relationship with Ronald Reagan, convincing the Republican governor to sign landmark legislation on bilingual services and bilingual contracts. At the signing ceremony for Richard's bilingual contracts law are (from left): Richard; his consultant, Lorenzo Patino; and his legislative aide, Marc Grossman. (Governor's Office photo)

don't. If you don't, you don't turn out to be a particularly successful legislator in terms of the number of bills you get through the process and signed into law by the governor of the opposite party. It was easier then than now. There was not so much importance attached to who the author was or how many Republican votes it got, what did the focus groups say.

"It was no small feat to get three bills into law on bilingual issues."

I also tackle changes to bilingual education, with fewer immediate results and just as much controversy, including opposition from many professional educators who are Chicanos. Even in the early 1970s, bilingual education is starting to become a full employment program for a cadre of Chicano teachers and administrators who are making a good living out of keeping disadvantaged brown kids in bilingual classrooms. That's the problem as I see it: for many bilingual education advocates, it becomes more important that they have classes to teach kids in Spanish than making sure they learn English so they can succeed in school—and in life where in the majority society mastering English is the key to success.

Bilingualism is a pillar of the Chicano movement in the 1960s. Lack of bilingual and multicultural education is a grievance voiced by the kids walking out of East L.A. high schools in 1968, and they are issues when I'm teaching some of the same kids at UC Irvine and Cal State Long Beach, and during my time in the classrooms at Terminal Island federal prison. So I'm a bilingual education proponent.

What opens my eyes are meetings I attend with parents of bilingual students at public schools in my Eastside assembly district. These parents, many of them immigrants from Mexico, are unequivocal: bilingualism as a principle of the Chicano movement means little or nothing to them. They just want their children to learn and conquer English. So I'm all for helping out bilingual teachers, but what's more important is doing what's right for the kids.

My colleague Peter Chacon, the Chicano assemblymember from San Diego, is always the designated author when it comes to bilingual education bills. He considers it his bailiwick. Peter tackles several related issues in small ways, but isn't particularly effective. His proposals don't go anywhere.

"It was easier for Richard," says Toni Trigueiro. "He had a bigger platform he could stand on. He was more engaged in Latino politics than Peter was. And all things being equal, Richard was more liked as a legislator.

"Also, when he first took office, he was close to Speaker Moretti, which paved the way for a real young kid who wanted to see things change more quickly than they had up until then use all the connections he had at his disposal to keep the ball moving forward.

"The other difference between Richard and Peter was Richard didn't need to have his name on a bill to get credit for it. If it happened, it happened. Peter had to have his name on everything, to get credit and recognition." Remember, in those days they have tomb stoning, where the principal authors of a major law have their names "tomb stoned," or inserted, in the first sentence of the bill.

"Richard only cared about the end result, and he did as much behind the scenes as in front of the curtain," Tony says. "He was also more effective behind the scenes than he was on stage—during debates in committee or on the assembly floor. He wasn't the most articulate debater, but he knew how to play the system; as long as he could get the system to work, that was enough for him if he got the right result."

It's not that I don't have the same ego needs as anyone else. But there are times when my interest in producing a result means it's not wise to have my fingerprints on things because it will just spark unnecessary opposition. I recognize my ability to arouse that kind of reaction. So for me, the issue can sometimes be better served by me not being formally associated with a bill even though I have everything to do with getting the thing through. This principle comes somewhat into play, positively or negatively, when I take up bilingual education.

Bilingualism is increasingly under attack. It is hard enough fending off challenges from Republicans and those who don't like doing anything for Mexicans. But Democrats, members of my own party, are starting to question bilingual education. Peter Chacon reacts irately. I begin the process by articulating in my own head the importance of the program and what should be its ultimate objective.

I meet two women who get their doctorates in education from Stanford University by doing research on bilingual education, Heidi Dulay and Marina Burt. They come up with three categories of Chicano students: English speakers, those who are monolingual in Spanish, and a third category of students who are not primary language dominant—in other words they aren't fully proficient in either English or Spanish, kind of like me growing up. Research by the two women determines that this last category is the largest percentage of kids in California schools with language needs.

Different people have different ideas on the best way to teach these kids. Some advocate total English immersion: slam everyone into English classes and let them sink or swim. Of course, there's the model defended by bilingual educators, which too often sees kids staying in bilingual classes longer than they need to be and sometimes never leaving them. As far as I'm concerned, it doesn't really matter what language you use to teach them; they need to be brought up to proficiency in English. It's not about denigrating their first language. English is the language of the land, whether I like it or not. My thinking evolves to the conviction that bilingual education is supposed to be a means to an end and not an end in itself. It isn't a maintenance program where you see how many students you can get into it and keep them there; once you get kids in the program and they become comfortable in English, you move them out into the general student population.

It's disturbing to see how tone deaf some bilingual advocates are about the reality of what parents want. That reality hits home again more than a decade later after I get elected to the Los Angeles City Council, and go to talk with parents whose kids attend public schools in my council district. "We'll deal with preserving our culture and language," the parents tell me in response to some of the arguments for bilingual education. "That's our job at home. The job of educators is to teach our kids to be literate in English," they insist, realizing that is the key to success in life in this country. They want their kids in mainstream classes as quickly as possible. Some parents of students who really need to be in bilingual classes in order to eventually transition out oppose the idea because they feel so strongly that their children should learn English now.

The idea these Stanford researchers come up with is to let the parents of students decide by giving them choices: if the kids speak English, put them in English-language classes. If they are monolingual Spanish, have them attend bilingual classes—but with the goal of transitioning into mainstream English classrooms. But for the great majority of students whose tests show they fall into the last classification of kids who are in-between English and Spanish, parents should decide whether the best thing for their children is English-only or classes taught in both languages.

In the face of growing attacks against bilingual education, I craft a well-reasoned bill. It is fundamentally about parental choice. It says if a child is Spanish-language dominant or at least not dominant in the primary language (English), then the parents get to decide whether or not their offspring should be in a bilingual program. Research shows the largest group of kids who are in the middle—not dominant in either language—do just as well in English-language classes as in bilingual classes in terms of making progress towards developing their English-language capacity.

My bill becomes very controversial. Leaders and activists in the bilingual education establishment hate it. Many of them also hate me despite my credibility from years of fighting in the education trenches for Chicanos going back to my days in the '60s with Phil Montes helping to form the Association of Mexican American Educators. CABE, the California Association of Bilingual Educators, which wants the middle group of kids required to be in bilingual classes, pickets me. I want kids to be in whatever classroom setting where they will learn English most quickly. In any case, with parental choice, if one program (bilingual or English) isn't working, the parents can switch the kid to the other one where he or she might do better. CABE even bad-mouths me to Cesar Chavez when he speaks at its convention.

By now we're talking about having a large number of bilingual teachers around. It is clear to me that for groups like CABE, maintaining lots of kids in bilingual classrooms is about maintaining a lot of jobs for bilingual teachers. At that point the debate ceases to be about helping kids; it becomes about protecting jobs for adults. In a way, it is like today where it seems some teachers want the union to make sure it protects the jobs of all teachers, whether or not the teachers are worth a shit. Then it becomes an ugly battle.

It gets ugly with my bilingual reform proposal. Peter Chacon has a heart attack over my bill and ends up in opposition.

The bill gets out of the assembly and at the end of the two-year legislative cycle makes it all the way to the Senate Finance Committee—further than Pete Chacon's earlier efforts. It's June or July 1974, just before the legislature's summer break after which lawmakers return to finish out the session during August. Al Rodda, an older Democrat from Sacramento who at one time also chairs the Education Committee, is now chairman of Senate Finance. He decides to hold a hearing on the bill during the recess.

The hearing goes well, I think. CABE is always against it because it only wants bilingual teachers teaching bilingual students—more work for the teachers, who receive special compensation because of their literacy in both languages.

The legislature returns after the break in August. Only 30 days remain before adjournment. We need to get my bill through the Senate Finance Committee, off the senate floor, and back to the assembly floor for concurrence in senate amendments. I'm waiting for a hearing date to be set for my bill before Al Rodda's committee. My legislative assistant, Toni Trigueiro, calls the Finance Committee consultants and secretary. They're not answering questions or returning phone calls. Rumors are swirling around. Toni turns to me, very nervous.

She sees me sit in my office over much of three days with the door closed, not wanting to talk with my staff about the bilingual bill. I know why they aren't making any headway, but don't have the heart to tell them.

After all the hard work we put into the bill, there will be no hearing date. Rodda is intimately familiar with education in California. He authors the law granting collective bargaining rights for teachers. But Rodda is not going to allow a bill, even with a Democratic author—and a Chicano at that—to get out of his committee with the kind of opposition CABE is mounting. The opposition cows him. "He's an older white man," Toni says. "Maybe his upcoming re-election scared him. He couldn't stand his ground against CABE, which had no political influence but was very vocal and had an extraordinary visible presence in the Capitol. They could deliver busloads of CABE teachers to lobby, people who had a vested interest in making sure they had more classrooms to teach in. And, of course, they got higher pay for being bilingual teachers."

The disappointing part is how it demonstrates how CABE is no different than other teacher groups; sometimes all they want to do is protect their own instead of protecting the interests of children. Rodda thinks he needs teachers on his side. He's eventually defeated for re-election in a political upset by Republican John Doolittle in 1980.

Rodda and the senate leadership see the reform bill as too controversial. They don't want to put upper-house Democrats in a difficult position, risking political fallout from Chicano bilingual education groups like CABE. Also, there is no indication from Governor Jerry Brown whether or not he will sign it. So I agree to be a good soldier and pull the bill. It's a huge disappointment. I never bring it up again.

It is obviously a bill that should pass because it is really consistent with the needs of the times. There is no way to justify the continuation of bilingual education without some reform. Nobody in the legislature, especially those tied to the education establishment, wants to touch it for fear of being called anti-Mexican.

The Stanford researchers, Heidi Dulay and Marina Burt, are extremely articulate, dynamic, young experts. Marina is Latina. My bill, based on their efforts, takes a middle ground that I believe will at least preserve bilingual education where it makes sense and where the kids' welfare is being taken into consideration—not just because teachers and administrators say students need it.

I don't know how many other bills get introduced to change or reform bilingual education that don't go anywhere because of the kind of opposition I encounter. I warn bilingual education advocates that if nothing is done, they'll wake up one day and find out they don't have anything left. As time passes and bilingual education grows, opponents get handed new and more effective ammunition, continuing to bolster the case that bilingualism is about furthering the interests of bureaucrats instead of helping children learn English. I get that argument early on, realizing bilingual education won't last unless success can be demonstrated in getting kids to learn English and then mainstreaming them into regular classrooms.

The battle for me is always acknowledging that bilingual education is a legitimate education methodology with the clear objective of eventually mainstreaming the kids without undermining or discriminating against their first language. On the other side are the critics who see it as a permanent maintenance program, whether or not the students become proficient in English. Starting with the 1990s, bilingual education also becomes a target of the anti-immigrant, anti-Latino bigots, chiefly from the GOP and now from the Republican Tea Party.

By 1998, in the wake of the anti-immigrant backlash begun by Governor Pete Wilson during passage of Proposition 187 in 1994, a new initiative, Proposition 227, is approved by the voters. Put on the statewide ballot by Silicon Valley software businessman Ron Unz, it effectively ends bilingual education in California. The results in how non-English speaking kids are learning more than a decade later are mixed depending on which side does the talking. Would enactment of my unsuccessful reform bill in the 1970s prevent the divisiveness that leads to the success of Proposition 227, some 20 years later? I don't know.

At the Capitol I earn a reputation that sticks as a master of back-room politics. When they give it that term, it sounds corrupt. I learn during the early part of my political career that's the only way deals happen and things get accomplished. Contrast this view of me with other politicians who come to the legislature at about the same time as me such as Howard Berman. There's a big newspaper spread in the early 1980s reporting mostly favorably about Howard, a Jewish lawmaker who is the other half of the Berman-Waxman machine that comes to dominate Democratic politics on L.A.'s Westside and parts of the west San Fernando Valley. The other leader of the machine is Henry Waxman, who like Howard ends up in Congress. But Berman and Waxman are Westside libs. When I use the same strategies and tactics that make Berman and Waxman successful, I'm viewed negatively—and I do a poor job of emulating the cutthroat politics Howard and Henry sometime practice. So the pundits see Howard as a brilliant public servant who can get things done. When it comes to me, I'm just seen as seedy, beset by blind ambition, and only in politics for myself. I let such views roll off of me, but they stick nonetheless in the eyes of many.

It comes down to this about minority politicians: there are good Mexicans and bad Mexicans. The same can be said of blacks. It is often a surface distinction. The good Mexicans are well spoken and presentable in majority society, adept at making a favorable impression in any crowd. My longtime *compadre* and ally Art Torres is a great example. Art is the good Mexican. He is articulate, well educated, and able to relate well in any social or political environment. I'm always the bad Mexican. A lot of it is my fault, coming out with my flashy style of dress, my bravado and colorful language. I hold a master's degree in public administration from the University of Southern California, but you don't know it from how I act and talk.

I only serve in two public institutions during a political career that stretches over three decades. I don't spend my time, energy, or political capital constantly searching for another job in elected office, as do many of my colleagues. I certainly don't retire from public life a wealthy man.

I don't make the rules. I learn them and how to apply them on behalf of the people who are important to me. If you look at who gets things done and who doesn't, if you judge me by that standard and forget about appearance and style, then I think I come off looking better than most.

Achieving something meaningful depends on a politician's abilities and reputation. At one time, political parties stand for and mean something. Today, parties as influential political institutions in California, for all intents and purposes, stand for very little. In the absence of strong political figures who don't come along that often, the political process breeds mediocrity because too many of those who get elected are mediocre-thinking people who get dazzled by bullshit as opposed to caring about substance. How many times do I meet guys or gals who dress well, wear nice shoes, and give good meeting? But then you find out that's all there is to them. They can't actually get much accomplished. Of course, it's also a hard, cruel reality that many times the quality of legislators is no better than what the people demand or deserve.

The legislature is a great cross-section of society. You have some brilliant minds in Sacramento, and you have some real dumb-asses there too—who, if I would ever leave them at night in an ally in East L.A. would never survive; they wouldn't know what to do.

After the election is over, friendship counts for a lot in politics. It is everything to me. It's easier to get a vote from a Democrat than a Republican, but I will sometimes get votes from Republicans too after they become social friends. Sometimes when I get a Republican to vote for one of my Mexican bills, some of my fellow Democrats will ask, "How'd you get that vote?" I never ask a friend, regardless of party, for a vote I know he or she can't give. You never put a person in a situation that can come back to haunt that individual. Since I don't meet a whole lot of people like that, it's not a big hindrance to my career.

At least with the Republicans, you know where they're coming from and that they rarely waver; they're usually against me on my base stuff concerning Chicanos. I can occasionally get some votes out of them on my issues by making good arguments or tapping personal relationships. On the other hand, the liberal Democrats are great at rhetoric—saying all the right things. But they too frequently fail to internalize the rhetoric, to match it with action. When they deviate from their liberalism—when they whore out as nearly all politicians do from time to time, for good or bad reasons—liberals are great at coming up with intellectual arguments and excuses to justify their whoring out. Liberals can even be enemies of minorities and poor people. Really?

One thing I always feel good about is my ability to figure out people real fast and draw conclusions about them. I quickly size up men and women, deciding whom to trust and not trust. And you know what? I'm not wrong very often. After a very short period of time in Sacramento, I start questioning who a lot of the liberals really are. I start wondering about people, liberals, who should naturally be on the side of my issues without equivocation, but who when the chips are down sometimes can't be trusted to do the right thing.

A classic example is Democratic Assemblymember John Vasconcellos of San Jose. Vasco is as pie-in-the-sky and touchy-feely as they come. He's a pillar of liberalism, very progressive and everything else. When Willie Brown has me head up reapportionment as chairman of the Assembly Elections and Reapportionment Committee in 1981, Vasco doesn't want to have anything to do with the reapportionment process because he says it doesn't have anything to do with representing the people. He sees it as crude partisan politics—until it comes to his own political survival. Towards the end of the redistricting process, he wants me to make some changes in his district lines that are inconsistent with my interests, which involve maximizing political representation for Chicanos who have long seen their electoral strength dissipated by jerrymandering in San Jose. Vasco just expects me to come down on his side, and he is indignant when I don't.

There are exceptions to the rule about liberals such as John Burton in the assembly and George Moscone in the state senate. They're die-hard liberals. Yet, they not only verbalize their strong-held beliefs, but feel them deep down inside. I rely upon and become good friends with both of them. Burton in particular grows up the hard way, like me. He's a former bartender. I see him cry about issues affecting Chicanos and poor people and the like.

Others I see in action have absolutely no sense of loyalty, except to themselves. Before he goes to Congress in 1975, Henry Waxman is part of the top leadership team under Speaker Bob Moretti. He participates in all of the key political meetings and strategy sessions conducted by Moretti's inner circle of top lieutenants. He lambastes Wally Karabian for supporting me over Moretti's favored candidate during my 1971 special election, and helps depose Wally as assembly majority leader in retaliation. As with all members of his leadership team, Moretti—for whom loyalty is probably the most important quality—assumes Waxman is endorsing him for governor in the 1974 Democratic primary. What Bob Moretti fails to do is ever ask Henry Waxman for his endorsement. When the gubernatorial campaign gets into gear, Boom!, Waxman double-crosses Moretti and supports Jerry Brown, the eventual winner.

See, the only thing you have in politics that matters is your word. When your word isn't worth anything, then in my eyes you cease to be. I don't have anything against Henry Waxman. He was a stalwart liberal all these years in Congress. I'm just saying it is disappointing when you dissect what he says he's about and then discover it turns out not to be true at all.

Bob Moretti is an awesome mother-fucker, excuse my language. I grow to love the guy—and I have every reason to dislike him at first. Yes, he is ruthless, and tough, and everything else. But everything he talks about he believes in.

In the June primary balloting, Moretti loses and Brown wins in a heavyweight gubernatorial field that also includes Brown, George Moscone, and San

Francisco Mayor Joe Alioto. Moretti's stock as Speaker immediately evaporates, and he's unceremoniously ousted in what turns into a heated contest for his successor between Leo McCarthy and Willie Brown, both Democrats from San Francisco. It starts a few days after the primary when McCarthy makes his move for Speaker. Moretti is for Willie Brown. Earlier, Moretti promises Willie he'll have enough guys to make him Speaker, which Moretti can promise when he still has the clout of his Speakership behind him. All that changes when he comes up short in the race for governor and discovers his power has disappeared.

I'm committed to Willie that spring. Others of my colleagues, no longer subject to the risk of crossing Speaker Moretti, begin jumping ship to McCarthy, including most of Moretti's so-called leadership team. The rest of my Chicano brethren—Ray Gonzalez, Joe Montoya, Alex Garcia, and Peter Chacon—jump ship too. (I later learn that the Chicano Caucus goes en masse, minus me of course, to see Leo and pledges to be for McCarthy "on the condition you screw Alatorre." It's get-even time.) March Fong, the Chinese-American assemblymember from Oakland, throws her purse at Peter Chacon on the assembly floor after he votes against Willie. I'm the only Mexican who sticks with Brown. Ironically, a few of the black members, Leon Ralph and John Miller, double cross Willie too. He gets chided for not being able to count votes, and Leo wins.

Foreshadowing a much more bitter and drawn-out 1979–80 Speakership battle, the fight between Willie and Leo continues into the November General Election. Both men try to elect Democrats pledged to cast votes for them when the Democratic Caucus meets after the election to nominate their candidate for Speaker. Since the Democrats enjoy a comfortable majority, whomever the Democratic Caucus nominates will become leader of the lower house. I dump my entire campaign account into Willie's candidates. Anyway, more McCarthy Democrats get elected than Brown Democrats. Until late the night before the first day of session, I'm holding out in Jack Fenton's state Capitol office with Willie and a few other die-hards, trying to put together a last-ditch scheme to turn back Leo. It doesn't work.

Now my political fortunes take a nosedive. As soon as McCarthy becomes Speaker, I go from great committees to all the shit committees everyone hates. I get stuck on every lousy panel in the world, including Human Resources (which does welfare) and Elections and Reapportionment, also the end of the world except once every 10 years when it does reapportionment following the decennial U.S. Census at the beginning of each new decade (which is not in 1974). I'm also on the Criminal Justice Committee, which is fine with me since I can always vote to stop the bad bills and help pass out bills that will force embarrassing votes by McCarthy Democrats in the Ways and Means Committee and on the assembly floor.

We figure out how to turn lemons into lemonade. For me it's like having a free rein. Jack Fenton and I conspire to put bills out of Elections and Reapportionment that nobody wants to vote on, like public financing of political campaigns and other good-government measures. The Republicans vote for them in committee to put the Democrats on the spot. I'm being the super-bad Mexican. Fenton knows the ins and outs of the E&R committee and where all the bodies are buried. We see to it that bills get out that wouldn't normally even get a motion—and if they did would fall off the "I" Street Bridge into the Sacramento River.

"We were free, totally and completely," Willie Brown recalls. "So, on every issue we could take a nonpolitician position. We didn't have to worry about the fate of other colleagues or of the [Democratic] caucus. We only had to concern ourselves with our own districts. We could pick and choose when we would be soldiers [cleaving to the interests of assembly Democrats] and when we would be critics. Even though we were Democrats, we were operating like independents. The nonpredictability of our conduct terrorized those who were running the place [the assembly], both Republicans and Democrats."

It becomes an embarrassment to Leo, who is forced to make his people kill the bills we put out of policy committee. Some are stopped in the Ways and Means Committee. Others have to be killed on the assembly floor, which means awkward votes for Democrats, some from marginal districts. I don't necessarily believe in the bills we pass out of committee. It's shit disturbing aimed at making life harder on Leo. Chairing the Chicano Caucus, which I continue to do because my fellow Chicanos still don't want the job, also gives me a forum through which to speak out, sometimes in ways that make the Speaker uncomfortable, although I'm careful to only use the Chicano Caucus to promote issues I genuinely care about.

"Richard was the victim of his loyalty to me and to what we collectively believed in," Willie says. "Whatever the treatment was, from Leo McCarthy and Howard Berman and that whole crowd, it really didn't matter. Although the comforts of a [Capitol] office with a window and a view, and good committee assignments meant something, it was never our collective goal to be comfortable with the status quo. Therefore, we enjoyed being outsiders more than being insiders, I think, because once you're an insider you had to be responsible. An outsider had zero responsibilities so you could hold people accountable on principle. That embarrassed them even more.

"So being on the outs was not a place of dishonor, shame, or humiliation. And it wasn't a place of impotence either. Since Richard and I never had had anything to start out with in life, it really didn't matter. Anyway, title and acceptability from the establishment wasn't something Richard Alatorre craved or needed. And those things didn't play much of a role in his movement up the political ladder. Being outside the reins of power meant we played a lesser role in the minds of many people. But we knew it was only a matter of time before some day we would be in charge of everything."

This is still a difficult period for me in many ways. In addition to losing my good committee assignments, I lose the staff that goes along with being one of Moretti's chosen. Toni Trigueiro staffs all of my legislative work. In fact, other than secretaries, Toni, who is always fiercely loyal to me, is the only staff person I have left. (Marc Grossman, who I teach at UC Irvine and later goes back to

Toni Trigueiro is Richard's devoted legislative assistant through his entire tenure in Sacramento. (Photo: Larry Sheingold)

work for Cesar Chavez, works for me at the Capitol for about a year in 1974–75, when we pass the farm labor law I coauthor, but I pay him (very little) out of my campaign account.)

I'm very fortunate to have a good staff person in Toni who I trust and who knows my interests, knows what I don't give a damn about, and definitely knows what I do give a damn about. When I later chair standing committees, they usually come with slots for consultants with expertise in the subject matter who also assist me in analyzing legislation and preparing for hearings. But Toni is the only one who is with me throughout my entire legislative tenure in Sacramento, handling the bills I author myself and always making sure I'm properly briefed and prepared, especially on the measures or issues she knows concern me.

"Richard didn't read a lot," Toni says, referring to what can often be complex and lengthy bill and budget analyses, and correspondence from factions and parties with interest in bills before committees or on the assembly floor. "So we'd go through the committee or floor agendas, the budget items or bills. Richard and I had a simple system, whether it was a bill agenda or budget review. We'd give each item a plus or minus, meaning if it was a good idea or something we think he would be interested in, we'd give it a plus. If it was something that wasn't reasonable or it didn't sell, we'd give it a minus, meaning he wouldn't support it. On the day of a committee hearing or a floor vote, he walked in the office, and we'd review what was on the agenda. You didn't have to draw him a picture. It was pretty clear from identifying the author or what the subject matter was—or from his experience with the issue—how he was going to go.

"In that regard, Richard was probably different than many other legislators," Toni observes. Other members, at least the ones who try to be more conscientious, "looked at all things from both sides or from eight different angles, carefully examining the measure and wanting to know what all the consequences were. Richard never got that deep. With him, if it felt right and it was consistent with what he knew to be true, that was as simple as it got."

During most of my tenure in the legislature I'm sitting on two budget subcommittees, dealing with different parts of the state budget. You have to be a member of the powerful Assembly Ways and Means Committee, the fiscal committee in the lower house, to sit on a budget subcommittee. After a time, Leo McCarthy finally lets me back on Ways and Means. Most Ways and Means members are on one subcommittee at a time. I'm usually on two at a time.

Hearings by the two subcommittees don't overlap. Typically, one subcommittee meets on a Monday afternoon and the other on a Thursday upon adjournment of floor session. "Hardly any other member sat on two budget subcommittees," Toni says. "Richard was one of the few."

One of them is the assembly budget subcommittee on governmental organization, which oversees all the state agencies. It is chaired by Maxine Waters, and she wants me there with her. At other times I'm also either on the health and human services subcommittee or the higher education subcommittee; both of them deal with big pieces of the budget—and lots of thorny and complex controversies.

It's the higher education subcommittee I like the best. Before getting to Sacramento, I teach at UC Irvine and Cal State Long Beach. I have direct experience working inside both the University of California and California State University systems. Issues like access and financial aide at UC; the state universities and community colleges are important because they are the tickets for Latinos to become whatever they choose through a college education.

What I enjoy the most is having UC officials come begging before my subcommittee. UC is the outfit you hate because back then they're so resistant to equal access for ethnic and racial minorities. The university offers all these excuses why more can't be done for minorities. But with help from Willie Brown and others, I understand their dirty little secret: there is one thing the barons of UC really do care about, which is taking care of their own pet projects. Early on, I learn the most important thing to institutions are themselves. So to bring an institution to the table willing to deal with you, all you need to do is threaten that institution over something it really wants.

I already relate when Willie shows me how to persuade UC Berkeley's prestigious law school to accept more minority applicants—by eliminating the budget line item for all the law school administrators. A great place to find out where a big institution like UC is vulnerable is by looking at their construction programs. Then you play like it's time for revenge and get them to do whatever you want them to do. UC San Diego wants a new library. It is a very lily white campus at the time. We threaten the library financing. We get them to provide more money for minority recruitment and open up more access to attend the medical school for ethnic and racial minority students. UC Davis is home to a lot of development of mechanization and pesticide research for agribusiness and the chemical industry. We threaten that funding to get more minorities into the law and medical schools. UC officials always have sanctimonious reasons why they can't do anything for the people who are important to me, mostly Mexicans and blacks. Ultimately, they quickly make concessions when you threaten the stuff that's important to them.

The Legislative Analyst Office puts out a budget review. Even in those days it is as thick as a fancy Bible, thoroughly analyzing all the state agencies and proposed expenditures, often going over concerns and issues identified by the legislative analyst versus what the governor is recommending in the annual budget plan he offers. "Since Richard was sitting on two subcommittees, that means he had to cover at least three quarters of that book," Toni says. She has to brief me on each issue that will come up so I can figure out the side I will end up on.

"Literally, you had to read the legislative analyst's current recommendations," Toni recounts, "but Richard also had to know where we came from to get there—the last few years of analyses on the same issue. For example, when a categorical program was created in the education budget—specific funding going to help specifically targeted students—the reason the legislature created the program in the first place was because those children were not being properly served at their school sites." School district principals and superintendents are always demanding flexibility in how they spend their money. But their priorities are often different than the needs of certain categories of needy students, such as poor, non-English-speaking and special ed kids. That's why categorical programs, which are frequently criticized, are created in the first place. Even today, class size reduction programs in grades one through three are categorical programs.

"The reason the legislature identifies these programs is to make sure funds are actually going to meet particular needs" that might otherwise get ignored or short-shrifted, Toni points out. "So when the legislative analyst comes up and says there are too many categorical programs or we could use our money more efficiently if we didn't have so many categoricals, you have to have the historical perspective to know that some populations of underserved students were not being served and that's why the legislature created that categorical program to begin with. Analyzing the budget to see where cost savings might occur or considering something different to do with that money is something an analyst or accountant can do without considering the human wants and needs of the students a categorical program serves.

"Richard had a penchant for taking on those kinds of budget issues where agencies from local school districts to the state were failing to serve certain residents of California, from English-language learners to the deaf," Toni says. "He came from an era, from his college days to his early political life, where he wanted to give a voice to those who hadn't been equally served."

I think that core belief pretty much guides everything I do in the legislature. It also gets back to the question of specialization. Some legislators make their mark in a field like health or education. They really learn everything there is to know about one area. In the decades before term limits, lawmakers have that luxury, to spend years of their time developing an area of expertise. Their entire legislative career can be concentrated in one area they're interested in. To some extent, I serve in a specialty legislature.

I'm more of a generalist because for me what's important is trying to fill a void for people who aren't represented. In education, it can be brown kids in K-12 classrooms or higher education or the blind, deaf, and disabled or migrant or special ed students or even gifted students. They're the ones I want to represent. That's why for me, the categorical programs, properly administered, are the most important part of the education budget.

Take the gifted program, as an example, at campuses as different as Palisades High School in the affluent Pacific Palisades section of the Westside and Lincoln High School in the Lincoln Heights neighborhood of East L.A. If you reduce or remove the gifted program at Palisades High School, those kids will probably be okay in the end because they go to a good school; if the kids need resources over and above what the school can offer, most have parents who will make sure they get what they need.

Not so at Lincoln High School or any other public school in my assembly district. If those kids don't get special resources and services on campus, they likely won't get them, period. So why jeopardize or sacrifice the kids who are blessed with the intellect to be successful? Because the legislative analyst wants to transfer away funds from the gifted programs to meet some other priority, thinking that gifted programs are expendable, especially in tough fiscal times? Maybe they're expendable on the Westside, but not on the Eastside. You have to balance the realities.

The same thing applies to programs for the mentally or developmentally challenged or disabled kids or students with reading or language problems. I always try to keep in mind the diversity of the students I represent who often have very limited options outside of the opportunities they get in public schools. I don't represent many rich kids. That's why, in my work on multiple budget subcommittees, I champion any resources we can give children in my district so they can have the chance to succeed.

Because of my interest in labor, I sit on both the standing committee, Assembly Labor and Employment, and on the budget subcommittee dealing with the state agencies that cover labor issues. Overall, I take my cue from watching how Maxine Waters chairs this subcommittee dealing with the state administration, all the bureaucracies, the different agencies and departments. This subcommittee is often overlooked.

Maxine has Exposition Park in her district, which includes the L.A. Coliseum, the Museum of Science and Industry, and the Natural History Museum, among other things. She gets a black history museum located there too. The Exposition Park facilities have an ample number of older African-American employees working there and Max is their champion. When she red flags an issue in the subcommittee, we call a time out—meaning we stay quiet while Max takes over. If administrators want to do something that's bad for the mostly African-American employees, they never get anywhere.

"They tried to do away with the security guards at Exposition Park who were mostly minority, particularly when the Olympics was coming to town in 1984, and replace them with state police," Max says. "They thought the minority guards weren't good enough to be out front and center during high profile events such as the Olympics. This was the kind of battle where the workers didn't have any power and someone needed to be looking out for them. I wouldn't let it happen."

We just lay back in the subcommittee and watch Max do her thing. When she's done, she gives us the high sign and we get back to the regular business.

Max ensures the agencies important to her and her constituencies get the attention they deserve. She also gives the other committee members the freedom to address the things we care about. Everybody has a particular interest in something. When it comes your turn, she indicates, "All right, you have an interest in this item; the floor is yours."

The Agricultural Labor Relations Board, created by the farm labor act I co-author in 1975, is constantly under fire from the mid-1970s to the early 1980s, during the administration of Jerry Brown, who makes ALRB appointments. Republicans and rural Anglo Democrats who carry the growers' water for them are behind the attacks. Their often-repeated bogus complaint is that the farm labor board is biased towards farmworkers and the United Farm Workers. Of course, the preamble of the law I help write says its purpose is "to encourage and protect" the right of farmworkers to organize. These critics target the ALRB for budget cuts so it can't conduct union representation elections where farmworkers vote for the UFW and so the farm labor board can't go after growers for breaking the law. Opponents of the ALRB succeed in shutting down the agency in early 1976, six months after it gets started, by cutting off the funding. They can do that because between all the Republicans and the rural Democrats, the growers can round up a majority of members in the assembly and senate.

But the growers and their allies are powerless within the confines of the budget subcommittee on state administration when Maxine turns the floor over to me and supports me along with Mike Roos, who also serves on the panel.

"On Latino issues, I will follow a good Latino leader and whatever he or she says needs to be done," Max says. "One thing I understand is that good leaders in any of these ethnic communities know their history, know the players, and know what is needed to advance their cause. I was absolutely thrilled with Cesar Chavez. Cesar and Dolores Huerta would come to the legislature advocating and fighting when I was in Sacramento. So I never asked any questions when Richard took the [subcommittee] floor. If it was good for Chicanos, Cesar, and Richard, it was good for me."

All in all, I take under my wing five or six state agencies with subject matter that interests me. I learn what's important to them, what they need and don't need. I arrange to put something more for them in the budget or take something out, depending on what I believe in.

There are no bill limits back then. Today, each assemblymember is limited to introducing only 40 bills during each two-year session. "Richard couldn't say 'no,'" Toni reminds me. "Someone comes to him, anybody with a bill idea. If he likes the bill idea—if there are people whose lives would be improved or there's a better way to do business—Richard would agree to carry the bill even if there was no expectation of being successful." This is especially true during my dark McCarthy Era years.

"A lot of social services and good government people knew Richard would be there for them," Toni continues. "He never viewed himself as just the assemblyperson from the 55th District. "There was always a statewide constituency of people who needed help, who didn't have a voice. Richard gave them an opportunity to be heard.

"One group that came to him on a regular basis was an L.A. group for the blind. Richard was one of the first legislators who took up the cause of the disabled, tried to find employment opportunities for them in state buildings, and paved the way to have services provided to them that they were entitled to but weren't getting."

Over a period of years, my Sacramento office becomes the secondary office for UTLA, United Teachers of Los Angeles. It is where all the lobbyists for the teachers union hang out when they're at the Capitol. It is one of many offices they use, but mine is central because of the relationship I have with them. But I am also friendly towards their district, the L.A. Unified School District, because of the close relationship I have with its lobbyists, especially later during my assembly tenure with Santiago Jackson.

There's Bill Lambert, who serves during my entire time in Sacramento as lobbyist for the union. Then you have guys like Ted Kimbrough and Ron Prescott, lobbyists for L.A. Unified, who in my mind are geniuses when it comes to understanding the importance of education, knowing where the emphasis needs to be placed, and working with the Big Five school districts in the state to make it happen. It so happens that the Big Five are heavily composed of ethnic and minority populations that have special needs when I'm in the legislature—needs that because of all of our efforts are finally getting some recognition by the state of California. Many of the programs for disadvantaged students, including many of the categorical programs, are created thanks to the genius of Willie Brown, who recognizes early the particular problems in his San Francisco school district are part of common problems in other districts like L.A. Unified. That's when we start creating categorical programs with money for specially impacted student populations. They become an accepted part of the line item budget for K-12 education.

Willie Brown has a history of taking care of his local school district in San Francisco. That's when I develop a relationship with representatives of my district. Am I championing the school board or the district administrators or the teachers union? No. My thing is always the kids. If either the union or the district is working in the interest of helping the kids I represent, I am interested in helping them.

You can walk into my office nearly 400 miles north of Los Angeles and it is either UTLA central or LAUSD central because during those years you don't see the rancor you do now between teachers unions, school administrators, and school boards. It isn't such an adversarial relationship. There are times when they're on different sides, but when it comes down to what I see as 95 percent of the debate over education funding and policy, there is respect among the lobbyists—if not the leadership of the groups they represent—because they're all there to do the same job in Sacramento. In those heydays, you probably have the best collection of lobbyists you can ever find whose sole objective is not internal bickering between competing labor and management factions, but how we can work together to advance the cause of students. Obviously, that changes later. In the 1990s, L.A. Unified Superintendent Ray Cortines thinks the Sacramento lobbying operation is a waste of money during a period of limited resources. Actually, after the passage of Proposition 98, the landmark school funding initiative in 1988, Sacramento becomes even more important. But by that time, I'm gone from the Capitol.

When I'm there, my reputation is for delivering hundreds of millions of dollars for my school district, whether it involves defending categorical programs or courting the chairs of the policy committees and key members of the budget subcommittees from both houses. As a member of Ways and Means, I use people like John Vasconcellos, who chairs the assembly fiscal committee after Willie Brown, to champion one or another categorical program important to L.A. Unified. Another reason for building those relationships is to overcome the fact that I am on the outs with the assembly leadership during most of McCarthy's Speakership.

Yes, it helps if you're part of the assembly Democratic leadership. But when you aren't—and I'm not for about six years—you can still exert influence through the relationships you build with your colleagues. I don't get anything done because I'm such a recognized public policy expert on education.

At first, I start with what's important for kids in my district. That soon gets expanded to include disadvantaged kids around the state—and also other minority kids such as blacks. That's how I develop credibility among African-American elected officials. They know, yes, I care about Chicanos. But what I really care about are poor and minority students, who become more and more predominant in California public schools in the 1970s and '80s.

My instincts on the job are pretty good, starting off with the fact I don't have a great love for most of the other 79 members of the assembly. It is real clear to me: if a member is a Democrat—depending on the kind of Democrat—I can either tune in or tune out. If the person is a Republican, well, I have respect for some of them during a time when there are still moderate Republicans. A few care about things that make sense. They might get my attention, at least at first. If they prove me wrong, it's easy; I just shit can their ideas if I'm in power—as in chairing a committee—or I just vote "no." Or sometimes, if their measures get enough of my attention, I ask questions, using their answers to derail their items.

I can't say my Republican colleagues are on the top 10 list of my best friends. But there are a few exceptions. One is Dr. Duffy, Gordon Duffy, who later marries Jean Moorhead, a Democratic assemblymember from suburban Sacramento. The one thing I know about Duffy is he cares passionately about what you call local docs, meaning general practitioners. I believe he is one himself, from Hanford in the Central Valley, and very respected.

When Duffy speaks about local docs, people listen because they know he has knowledge. He is one of the biggest advocates for what I am trying to do to create greater diversity in medical schools, to train and graduate more family practitioners, improve doctor-patient ratios, get more doctors to practice in underserved communities, and open up UC Extension facilities for people other than agricultural interests. Gordon Duffy gives legitimacy to what I'm championing, which is extremely important for me.

Duffy is also a key ally when I wage a successful battle on behalf of UC Irvine Chancellor Dan Aldrich to get a teaching hospital located in Orange County over the opposition of local doctors who own nearby private hospitals, the California Medical Association, and local Democratic legislators like Ken Cory. Duffy recognizes, as I do, that the reason UCI medical school is having problems recruiting quality professors and students is because it has no teaching hospital. But UCI's medical school is invested in turning out more family doctors, which both Duffy and I like. Once I get his support, it's amazing the other support I'm able to line up.

Other Republicans end up being my friends too. There's Bill Campbell, Paul Priolo, Bob Beverly, and Ken Maddy. Sometimes, I even end up getting votes from them on my agendas.

When I'm short of staff while being on the bad side of Leo McCarthy in the mid-1970s, help comes from other people who bring me causes I believe in and volunteer to staff me to help move things forward. One of them is crazy Dr. Bob Montoya, a former medical doctor who gets bored practicing medicine and begins championing the admission of more Chicanos in medical schools and the graduation of more Mexicans as doctors. He forms an association that provides assistance to college students thinking of entering medical schools. I am very fortunate to have support like that.

Whatever success I have—and most legislators enjoy—is a result of whom you're surrounded by. I'm blessed to have people who care about the same issues I care about—and who are very good at either learning about them or teaching them to me. They all make up my very loyal staff or quasi staff. They are why I am able to be as substantive as I am. They also know that with a few exceptions, my attention span is limited because I'm balancing so many bills or issues in the air at any one time.

Serving on multiple budget subcommittees and carrying so many bills "was Richard's way to stretch himself and expose himself to different issues," Toni observes. "It was a way for him to touch as many things as he could to make improvements, which is what he wanted to do. You have to remember there were only four other Latinos in the assembly when Richard arrived (Ray Gonzales had only one term) and before Art Torres was elected in 1974. There were not many black members either. So you had only a handful of legislators maybe looking out for people who haven't yet had a place in line. That's how Richard approached it."

It's very common for lobbyists to go to freshmen members with bills, especially problematic ones. Freshmen are looking for chances to carve out a niche and make names for themselves, learn about a subject, and gain expertise. Say you're lobbying, representing an interest. You have a bill that interests want you to introduce or reintroduce until it gets passed even though you know it's a dog. You can't get any veteran legislator to carry it. You'll go to anybody in the house who will put his or her name on the measure. Who's that anybody going to be? Most likely it will be a member of the freshmen class who doesn't know any better. Much of the time the freshmen member won't bother to find out that this bill has been introduced four or five times before, all unsuccessfully.

It only takes me half a year to find out about the bills I'm introducing that are put forward before. A lobbyist will pull that trick on me once, but not again. I don't carry bills to bail out lobbyists who have nowhere else to turn. There are a few I really like, and I'll sometimes tell them, "If you can't find anybody else, come back to me and I'll introduce it."

Contrary to popular belief, even the best legislator doesn't always know everything about the legislation or budget items they're proposing, and there are nearly always staff members or lobbyists who are happy to make you aware of any deficiencies. You quickly learn what makes each legislator tick, their strengths and weaknesses, the ones who do their homework and the ones who don't. I have the added advantage of traveling all over the state representing the Chicano Caucus. I gather a lot of useful intelligence about individual members from friends and contacts I make in their home districts, mostly Chicanos but others too. Many of these constituents of other members turn to me over bills or budget matters or problems that bother them. I also draw on contacts collected prior to my public tenure, during my work with the Chicano civil rights and student movements, from teaching at universities and working with the farmworkers. So I have independent sources of information on many other lawmakers.

There isn't the time or space to cover all—or even a significant number—of my bills over a 12-year legislative tenure. Here are just a few examples. (Please accept my sincere apologies for the many deserving measures that are left out.)

• I get passed and signed into law a bill changing the mandatory retirement age of people working in the public and private sectors so workers don't have to automatically retire when they reach a certain age. Service Employees International Union Local 660 in L.A. and the California State Employees Association sponsor it. This law means workers, especially in state or local government, don't have to be arbitrarily forced into unwanted retirement at a relatively early age if they decide to keep working without suffering hits to their pension benefits. The measure is important today because many people are still vital and productive into their 60s and 70s.

• When I first run for office, a friend connected with the Church of Scientology introduces me to the issue of medical experimentation and people who bring to light pharmaceutical houses that use prisoners throughout the world as guinea pigs to test drugs, many of them antipsychotics. Sometimes inmates are supposed to be paid money they don't receive. Safeguards are supposedly in place, but not really. People die from getting the drugs. Sometimes experimental medications are given to prisoners who are perfectly healthy. Some convicts who want to get out of the trials are not permitted to do so and are forcibly medicated so as not to compromise the experiments.

A lot of drug testing is being done in California state prisons without notice or compensation for the inmates who are serving as the guinea pigs. Inmates comprise a classic captive audience—excuse the pun—that is very vulnerable to being abused during the process. Even when prisoners are offered some compensation but don't want to participate in the trials, they have trouble refusing since there is no other way to earn money to send home to loved ones while they are incarcerated.

I introduce legislation reforming human medical experimentation in state correctional institutions. We're talking about a multibillion dollar growth industry so it is difficult to move the bill. The pharmaceutical industry and it seems the rest of the world is opposed. There aren't many people waiting in line to come to the defense of prison inmates.

We get wind prisoners are being forcibly medicated in certain penal institutions. My Scientology friends identify specific institutions where the practice is happening based on letters they receive. Two of them are the California Medical Facility at Vacaville in northern California and the state prison just north of San Luis Obispo on the Central Coast. Both have large medical wings. We try to expose what's going on. The state Department of Corrections denies it is forcibly medicating anyone.

One day I get the news department at KABC-TV Channel 7, the ABC affiliate in Los Angeles, interested in doing a story. A crew from KABC, including an investigative reporter and cameraman, agrees to meet me at the San Luis Obispo prison. We show up at the same time and enter the reception area. I identify myself as a California state legislator, chairman of the Assembly Select Committee on Prison Reform and Rehabilitation. I tell the staff I want to take a tour of one of the medical quads. This is where I have information people are being medicated against their will. Inmates have told me they are put on heavy antipsychotic drugs as a means of controlling the population. Prison officials conclude it is easier to medicate inmates than discipline them or keep them under control in some other way.

I ask someone in reception to take me to this unit. The TV camera is on, even though my claim is I know nothing about KABC being there. Confronted by the reporter, the camera and me, the officials don't know what to do at first.

"We don't have the authority to let you in," they say. I ask to speak with the warden of the prison.

"He's not available," I'm told. "He's off the facility and isn't working today." I know he lives close by.

"I'm not leaving here until I get in," I reply. "If not, heads will roll." I act like an asshole.

The warden shows up half an hour later. His name is Dan McCarthy. He later ends up being director of the Department of Corrections under Jerry Brown. McCarthy shows up, citing the part of state law that says they don't have to let me in.

"I don't know who you think you're dealing with," I tell him, and give him all this shit. He refers to the KABC TV news crew, accusing me of staging some kind of publicity stunt.

"I'm here separate and apart from them," I lie. "I don't know why they're here."

The investigative reporter says it's a coincidence that the news crew is there at the same time I arrive. "I'm going live this afternoon on Channel 7," the reporter informs the warden, "and the network is interested in the story too. What do you have to hide?"

Finally, McCarthy agrees to lead us into the medical quad, a substantial section of the prison where they house inmates with disciplinary problems. He claims they don't forcibly medicate prisoners: "We don't do that at this institution. We have protocols on what we do"—and everything else.

"Prove it," I demand.

The news crew and I are taken inside the institution.

In the medical quad we come across this poor Filipino American staff guy who dispenses medicine to the inmates. I ask to talk with him.

"Tell me what you do," I say. He tells me.

"Okay, so if I'm an inmate and I'm supposed to take certain medications during the day, it's your job to make sure I get them?"

The guy explains they have pill lines. Inmates have to show up and get watched while they take the pills.

"How do you know what pills to give them?" I ask.

All of a sudden, the staff guy pulls out an envelope he chooses at random for one of the inmates to show me. Right there on the front of the envelope, in clear red letters, it instructs staff that if the prisoner refuses to take the pills, he will be forcibly made to do so.

"What is this?" I demand. The guy looks at me and then looks at his warden—all with the TV camera shooting the whole thing. He says, "Oh, that's a mistake," and he hastily puts the envelope away.

"This interview is over with," the warden announces. "I'm going to escort you out of the institution."

The camera records the dialogue between the warden and me, which is not pleasant for the warden or the Department of Corrections because they have been caught in a lie.

It is a great exclusive for KABC and substantiates what we know is going on.

As a result, we get the Department of Corrections to stop forcibly medicating inmates by making them set up new protocols. That's when we find out it is cheaper for the department to medicate prisoners than assign extra staff to discipline or control them. The department also stops the drug trials on behalf of the pharmaceutical companies, which is a blow both to the industry and to the department, which is making money off of them.

My bill still dies because it is such a hard sell at the Capitol. How do you argue against the pharmaceutical industry when no one gives a shit about inmates' welfare? But the bad publicity forces prison officials to clean up their act. Later, I do get my law enacted.

- "If you look at other legislators serving at the same time, I doubt few of them have the breath and width reflected in Richard's legislation," Toni says. "He couldn't say 'no' is the simple explanation. But everyone deserved a voice in his view. While many members only carried legislation reflective of their districts' needs or bills that came from their districts or helped their districts, Richard saw his district not only as representative of all of L.A., but all of California. He may not have had a serious depth of knowledge about developmental disabilities, but he wanted those individuals to get the services they deserved and that the state provides to other classes of people."

Many of the disabled are invisible at that time. I meet Marcella Meyers, founder of the Greater Los Angeles Council for the Deaf, a civil rights and advocacy organization for the hearing impaired. She is a very sophisticated lady who always has an interpreter with her. The interpreter ends up as a teacher in one of the high schools in my district. GLAD is never able to get anyone to pay attention to its issues in Sacramento, either in the legislature or the governor's administration.

Call me a softie, whatever you want. Marcella gets my attention one day. I meet a couple of other advocates for GLAD. We start working together. I carry bills year after year on behalf of the deaf community, to broaden services available to them. There are two schools in California for children who are deaf and blind. They receive less in average daily attendance funds—the money they get for each day a student spends in the classroom—than public schools for other kids. If we're giving some kid at a public school in Sherman Oaks or Palo Alto a certain level of ADA funding, why not give the same amount to kids in public schools for the deaf and blind?

Pushing their bills is a constant battle at first. We have to fight for their money every year. It isn't a group or a service very high on the priority list for legislators.

Mostly, I work with GLAD on the budget subcommittee to keep the admittedly limited funding for their services in the state budget and eventually make it a regular line item in the budget, where it remains today. What we do for the developmentally disabled is get them MediCal reimbursement for services rendered to the hearing impaired. Until then, MediCal isn't covering services and treatments for those who are blind or those with impaired hearing.

• A perennial conflict at the state Capitol is over what they call scope of practice. It often pits the medical establishment dominated by physicians against an onslaught of other medical-related interests trying to win recognition and broaden the ability to practice their professions. It comes down to the established status quo trying to protect its turf at all costs against any changes, no matter how beneficial to the public. Major campaign contributions are associated with these fights.

For me the podiatrists, who supply medical and surgical care for patients suffering from foot, ankle and lower leg problems, are well respected. Before, medical doctors tell people with leg or foot problems to just go and see orthopedic surgeons. Podiatrists are qualified professionals in just one specialty. They undertake the same studies that doctors go through and then they go into their specialty. They just aren't recognized by the state as medical doctors because their degree says Doctor of Podiatric Medicine and they don't have an M.D. after their names. The medical doctors don't want them to practice unless they go to medical schools.

This period is the beginning of the end of this exclusive fraternity of M.D.s who are resistant to any ancillary practice being handled by people who specialize in the offshoots of medicine. If you're not a member of this exclusive M.D. fraternity, you're out of luck. During this time you see medicine begin to go in different directions. You start seeing a variety of offshoots. There are licensed vocational nurses, nurse practitioners (who get advanced degrees to handle minor ailments or injuries), and others wanting to be recognized for the expertise and additional training they earn.

Podiatrists are another one. Their legislative strategy is to keep their campaign for change of practice reform on the front burner. They want to keep introducing bills on their issues, even if they initially don't go anywhere, while they organize podiatrists throughout California and eventually make progress. I carry their original bills.

I might be the wrong author because of my poor relationship with the Speaker, Leo McCarthy. But I'm the only one willing to champion their cause and Bob Walters, the podiatrists' able lobbyist, has a sense of loyalty to me.

Part of their strategy is using this time to turn podiatrists into a political force in the state. They form their own political action committee and get involved in politics.

When all these fights begin, the state of California is exactly where the powerful California Medical Association wants it to stay. The traditional argument against allowing podiatrists and other specialists to practice their professions is, "If you want to engage in that scope of practice, then become a medical doctor." Except these are practices most medical doctors don't want to do or aren't doing.

The onslaught of bills is amazing. I remember for just a few years when I'm serving on the health committee, whenever an idea surfaces allowing someone other than a medical doctor to do a medical procedure, the CMA lobbyists stand up and object. Once, when the lobbyist for CMA comes before the committee to testify, I stop him and say, "Before you proceed, let me try to save some time by telling the committee what you're going to say: 'If these people want to do this thing, they should go to medical school and become medical doctors like the members of the CMA. And any change in the law will have an adverse impact on the quality of medical care.'" I say it in a funny way and at first the CMA lobbyist kind of starts to laugh. Then he figures it out and gets mad because he thinks I'm mimicking him, which I am.

For me, it is a justice issue. I'm not in the legislature just to listen to the same old arguments the docs make over and over again. For me they are the height of arrogance, blindly protecting their jurisdiction regardless of the need for reform. It doesn't matter what the specific subject matter is or what minor offshoot of medicine it involves, but when it comes to bills expanding scope of practice, the CMA has the same standard line. The power of the docs is enough to kill most bills during at least the first half of my legislative service; they have a stranglehold at the Capitol. It takes years for many of these bills expanding scope of practice to pass. Each time one of the bills is taken up, you always see me voting "aye"; the CMA doesn't like me much. Unfortunately, the bills I introduce on scope of practice early in my tenure don't go anywhere.

Then the legislature gets sick and tired of it because of tireless efforts by groups like podiatrists and nurses. Plus the docs don't keep wielding the same kind of unchallenged influence. Some of my bills eventually become law—or they pass later when carried by other authors. If the CMA's power is not checked, today we would not have podiatrists, acupuncturists, nurse practitioners, doctors of osteopathic medicine, and many other professionals practicing as they do today, and improving the quality of medicine and the quality of people's lives.

• I meet Ann Getty, married to the son of tycoon J. Paul Getty. Ann is wearing emeralds from her earlobes down to her shoulders when she first comes traipsing into my Capitol office wanting more state funding for the California Arts Council. It's set up in 1975, under Jerry Brown to encourage public participation in the arts.

She comes to see me because I'm a member of the Ways and Means budget subcommittee on government organization that handles the arts council. When its budget is cut, Ann is the face of the arts council they send to the legislature to beg for more money because of the importance of the arts in schools, the community, blah, blah, blah.

I become a voice for the arts when the council is reorganized and under siege. We expand it to become more diverse and reflective of the different elements that make up the arts community in the state. I join others in minority communities who don't want the arts council to just be controlled by wealthy benefactors. We want grants issued by the council to go to community arts groups that are more diverse than those that up until that time are receiving funding for arts programs.

I carry water for the California Arts Council throughout my years at the Capitol and continue on the Los Angeles City Council by championing the city's Cultural Affairs Department. At City Hall, I expand the definition of public safety to include more than funding for police officers and firefighters. Public safety also comes to embrace more support for parks and recreation and senior citizens activities, youth and gang intervention, and arts and cultural programs.

• As technology progresses, all of the judges and lawyers want to record trial proceedings on videotape to remove the need for court reporters and the costs of transcribing. Somebody is always claiming that the judiciary will save money in the trial system if we don't have to pay court reporters. All you have to do is rely on the videotapes as the trial record. But the technology doesn't exist to deal with glitches or when witnesses or other participants in trials aren't speaking loudly enough. A court reporter can stop the proceedings and ask someone to repeat something. But a videotape might not catch it.

"Richard always carried the bills to say, 'no,' to protect the court reporters so trials will be more representative of what actually takes place," according to Toni. "You can't take the chance of losing something because of the quality of the tape, which was a problem in those days. This was before digital technology and the televising of court proceedings."

Local government and the courts want to save money by not having to pay for another public employee, who can be pretty costly, to take down and transcribe the proceedings—or to hire a private stenographic firm to do it. These are good middle-class jobs, an important pathway to a decent life for a lot of young men and women, although initially most of them are women. Then the men get into it too. There are also a lot of minority court reporters. I get even more motivated to take on this issue because stenographers who are bilingual qualify for extra pay when parties or witnesses are monolingual, mostly in Spanish, and the record has to be translated. For me it's about preserving the positions and the jobs, and later about helping the bilingual court stenographers.

It's also about preserving due process, making sure you have a proper trial record, especially when criminal cases go up on appeal. You can always find errors when proceedings are recorded and the like. Who knows the kinds of things that can be manipulated if we only rely on videotaping. That's why these state-certified stenographers are so important.

Every time video technology improves, there is a new move to eliminate the court reporters. Every time it is tried, my bills stop it. Even today, with the televising of some cases, court reporters are still required. I carry bills, working with a lobbyist friend, Frank Murphy. If banning court reporters is such a great idea in the 1970s, when these legislative battles take place, how come it still hasn't happened? The proponents of banning the stenographers get beaten down each time and finally move on to other things.

• Lorenzo Patino is the bright young Chicano activist from Sacramento who helps piece together my bilingual services bill in 1972, before I first take office, during late-night sessions we have with Lou Moret at the Democratic National

Convention in Miami. He goes on to work for me as a consultant at the Capitol. Later, Lorenzo passes the bar exam after I send him away for two or three weeks to study at a cabin in Lake Arrowhead near L.A. He fails the test the first time. I get the idea of the cabin from Wally Karabian, who after graduating from USC law school checks himself into a hotel with a friend for two weeks and spends morning, noon, and night studying for the bar. I tell Lorenzo this is the only way he is going to pass because if he stays in Sacramento he will always find one excuse or another to do something more exciting than studying for the bar. Lorenzo always wants to be in the middle of everything. "You do me no good doing that," I tell him. "You do me a lot of good if you pass the bar."

Lorenzo becomes a successful civil, criminal, personal injury, and civil rights lawyer in Sacramento, building up a good practice and doing well financially. Governor Jerry Brown names him to the Sacramento Municipal Court in 1980, the youngest judge ever appointed. Lorenzo does a lot of innovative stuff like sentencing youthful drunk driving offenders to visit the county morgue. He comes up with innovative ideas that only a socially conscious person would think of doing.

But Lorenzo's life is tragically cut short about a decade later when he comes down with leukemia. He becomes very weak as the disease progresses. Shortly before Lorenzo dies in 1984, Willie Brown calls me down to the Speaker's office. Dave Roberti, president pro temp of the state senate (and a key supporter of mine when I initially run for the assembly in 1971) is a passionate champion of animal rights. Roberti has a bill that clamps down against the use of animals in medical research experiments, which he finds cruel. At the time, the early- to mid-1980s, I'm chairing the Assembly Governmental Organization Committee.

"The UC medical research world, which is located in San Francisco, was apoplectic over the prospect that all of those animals they were utilizing for experiments would be off limits to them," Willie says. "They had all that money from international research operations.

"This bill should never have gotten here [in the assembly], but it's here," Brown tells me. "I can't find anybody who is willing to commit to making sure this bill doesn't get out of committee." Roberti, as leader of the senate is very powerful, can be very vindictive and makes it clear to everybody who can hear him that a vote against his animal research bill is tantamount to declaring war against him personally. Members of the assembly are leery of incurring Roberti's anger because they all have bills in the senate that are at his mercy.

"I can't find anybody who'll guarantee me this bill doesn't come out of committee," Willie states.

"What are you asking of me?" I say.

"Would you be willing to take the [Roberti] bill [in my committee] with the clear recognition that whatever [bills] you may have in the senate side may be dead?"

"I don't give a fuck," I reply. "You want me to do it, I'll do it."

"You sure you can control your committee?" Brown asks.

"I can control my committee."

I'm thinking of Lorenzo during this conversation. Later I get a call from him once he hears it's been set for a hearing before my committee. Lorenzo tells me how important killing the bill is for medical research. "I'm too far along in my illness for it to help me," he explains, "but it will help people like me in the years to come if we don't let this bill take effect."

"You're in your mother's arms," I tell him, repeating a refrain I hear from Phil Burton.

Lorenzo says he wants to testify against the bill at the upcoming hearing but he isn't feeling very well.

"If you make the decision you want to testify, you have my word that whenever you come, I'll put you on so you can testify and leave," I assure him.

"That's not the way it works," Lorenzo says. He's right. There is a set order and procedure for taking the testimony of proponents and opponents of any bill.

"That's the way it's going to work for you in my committee," I insist.

On the day of the hearing I make sure it is totally understood by the Democratic members that they are going to come and show up so the committee has a quorum. They can stay and listen to the testimony. But if they aren't going to vote my way—against the Roberti bill—they will leave before a vote on the bill is called. I also explain to my Republican counterpart, Vice Chairman Frank Hill, who is my friend, why the bill needs to be killed, including the story about Lorenzo, who Frank also knows too. "I'll stay through the end and vote with my chairman," Frank says. "And you have my commitment that my people will never vote for this bill."

Roberti makes it clear to Willie Brown that this measure is his whole legislative agenda. If the bill doesn't get out, he will retaliate, and he explains to Willie how inevitable the retaliation will be. "Oh, I understand," Willie tells him. Brown never says "yes" or "no." In his own way, but without really specifically committing to anything, Brown makes Roberti feel everything is going to be fine.

Traditional protocol is for the leader of the senate to talk with the leader of the assembly. Once that happens, if the conversation is satisfactory, there is no reason to talk with anyone else. Roberti also feels he is my friend, which he is since he provides important support when I first run for office. We have a good relationship. Roberti knows I know how important it is for him to get this bill through. I also know the consequences if it doesn't get out. He doesn't have to explain them to me.

We find out the hearing is on a day history will be made. A week before we learn that the television news program "60 Minutes," which is doing a segment on the Roberti bill, is going to film the hearing. Morley Safer, the famous CBS News correspondent, is doing the story.

Safer is there in the hearing room. It's my time for stardom. Finally, I'm going to be a great American.

On the day of the hearing, at about 1 p.m., Lorenzo calls me from his chambers some blocks away at the county courthouse. He's too weak to leave.

"Lorenzo, you're in your mother's arms," I assure him again. "I'll call you when it's over with."

"Are you sure?" he asks.

"I'll call you."

Roberti comes into the hearing room and makes his statement as author of the bill. The Democratic and Republican members agree with me ahead of time that as is the custom we're going to listen to the proponents, and there are a lot of them, and then the opponents. It is also agreed there will be no questions from the committee and that I will then call for a motion on the bill.

There's a wonderful presentation by the proponents, led by Roberti. All the animal rights groups testify, feeling they're on the cusp of victory and about to make history. The opponents do their thing.

When it's all over, I ask for a motion. I turn to look at both sides of the dais where the committee members are seated. No one says anything. After a moment passes, I declare the bill is dead for lack of a motion and immediately adjourn the hearing.

Dave Roberti is livid. He runs up to me and starts yelling: "How could you do this to me? I'm the leader. You embarrassed me." He yells a few profanities.

"I guess it's not your day today," is all I say. And I walk out. Whatever bills I have left over in the senate are killed. Fortunately, I have few bills in Roberti's house. But those that are still there stay there.

It's safe to say during the rest of the legislative session, Roberti tries to retaliate against the entire assembly, slowing up all lower-house bills that are within his control. Willie Brown answers with an appropriate reaction. With members of Roberti's house not getting their bills heard in the assembly, eventually a truce is called and business goes back to normal. It isn't normal for me; my bills are still dead, but I accept the consequences. Willie Brown asks, "You didn't even let him get a motion?"

"If I had done that it might have gone out," I answer.

"I couldn't trust anybody else but Richard," Willie says later. "He did a great job. You go to the guy you can trust for most of the key things. Maxine [Waters] was not chair of any committee then. [Mike] Roos was not chair of any committee. I had a limited number of real quality people who had finesse and skills, brains and loyalty. You don't have many of those people—people who would ultimately be willing to sacrifice whatever [bills] they had on the line in the other house [the senate]. I don't think Roberti ever forgave us."

Roberti's animosity may come back to haunt us nearly a decade later when Proposition 140, imposing term limits on the legislature—it really targets Willie Brown—is put on the statewide ballot in 1990. Former President Ronald Reagan writes a letter that opposes Prop. 140, aimed at his Republican constituency. It goes something like this: but for term limits I would still be your president. I'm personally voting "no" on term limits.

"We never get that letter out," Willie reveals. State lawmakers raise most of the money to oppose the initiative. "We [assembly Democrats] had the media responsibility, [paying for] radio and TV [ads]. It was about four times more expensive" than the rest of the campaign. "We raised that money from our membership and bought all the TV time. We did all that. What we did not know until the Saturday before the election when it was too late to do anything was that the bulk-rate letter from Reagan wasn't going to be mailed because Roberti held onto his $400,000 [to pay for the postage]. It was clear in his mind that his tenure [as senate leader] was the very first to be affected" if term limits passes. "He wanted to hold onto that money to run for some other office. All though his career, Roberti played that game with us.

"Plus, this was a chance for him to even the score" for us killing the animal-research bill.

Right after my exchange with Roberti in the committee room, I make a bee-line to my office and call Lorenzo: "You can watch it on the news. It's safe to say the bill is dead and as long as I'm in the legislature it will never pass."

Lorenzo dies about a week later at the age of 35. In my eulogy at his funeral service, I tell the story of the Roberti bill and everyone laughs.

He could have become anything: a superior or appellate court judge, even a justice of the state Supreme Court. I still miss him.

It can be troubling since everything a member of the assembly does that involves spending money, from hiring staff to producing newsletters for constituents in the district, has to go through the Assembly Rules Committee, which is tightly controlled by the Speaker, who is then Leo McCarthy. Toni's salary comes out of an assembly select committee covering admissions policies at the University of California and California State University systems, which are the subjects of interim hearings I hold. My office gets a call one day from the Rules Committee saying Toni's salary has been eliminated and she should clean out her desk and leave the Capitol that very day. No 30-day notice. No nothing.

Toni talks with one of McCarthy's top aides, who she knows socially, asking him what to do. "Richard will have to talk to Leo," the aide says. So I call McCarthy, get an appointment with him and walk down to see the Speaker in his office.

"This is inappropriate," I tell him about Toni getting the ax. "People's lives are involved here. You can't just eliminate someone's job on a whim. What do I need to do to resolve this?"

Toni gets her job back. Resolving it involves Leo having me come into his office and making me ask him for a favor. It's not anything that will benefit or profit me personally. Leo knows I care about Toni and that I will do it. It is all about showing me he is in charge.

The funny thing is that on the Republican side, they always take care of their staff. No one who I remember is ever left high and dry, not secretaries or consultants. But it's different on the Democratic side in the assembly, maybe because of the bitter and bloody Speakership fights that break out twice in the 1970s. If there's an interparty split and you're on the losing end of a leadership vote, your staff can be gone. The victorious new leadership sometimes doesn't see the value in retaining the institutional memory the staff can represent.

They're mostly interested in taking revenge out on the members who lose. So the loyalties of their staff members are also questioned.

In 1979–80, Howard Berman challenges Leo McCarthy for Speaker, sparking the most bruising and protected Speakership fight in legislative history. "For Richard, who was not the most touchy-feely kind of guy," Toni Trigueiro recalls, "one of the hardest things was when he called staff at home on a weekend to let them know he and Art [Torres] had switched sides [jumping from Berman to Willie Brown], and that we could likely lose our jobs and be unemployed the next week, depending on what happened."

I stay in legislative purgatory until the mid- to late-1970s. Leo finally gives me chairmanship of the Human Resources Committee around 1977, the first standing committee I get to lead. It's only because there's a vacancy and maybe he wants to discourage me from stirring up so much trouble for him. The only good committee I get to stay on as a member is Labor and Employment. That's because Jack Henning, head of the California Labor Federation, the state AFL-CIO, goes to Leo to have me appointed because I'm a reliable labor vote.

But I'm really in purgatory until Willie Brown becomes Speaker at the end of 1980. Being on the outs doesn't stop me from being outspoken on the things I believe in.

On top of my troubles with Leo McCarthy you have to add my difficulties around the same time with Jerry Brown. Art Torres, who gets elected to the assembly in 1974, and I go after Jerry on January 6, 1975, his first full day in office after being sworn in as governor. He gives us the opening by appointing Mario Obledo as secretary of the mammoth Health and Human Services Agency. Our objections have nothing to do with Mario, who has a long and distinguished career as a Latino civil rights advocate, including setting up the Mexican American Legal Defense and Education Fund, which I work with him on in the '60s. But Mario is from Texas and by appointing him without consultation we argue the governor is disrespecting California Chicanos.

Okay, it's not exactly a cardinal sin, but it seems enough of an excuse for Art and me to schedule a news conference in the governor's press room, a theater-style chamber with a raised stage especially built to accommodate TV news crews on the first floor of the Capitol building. I have an apartment in midtown Sacramento while working for Assembly Majority Consultants before getting elected in 1972. During my first term I stay in flea bag motels like the Sandman on Richard's Boulevard, next to the Sacramento River just off the I-5 freeway coming in from the airport. At 3 the morning of our news conference, I'm at the Sandman when these severe abdominal pains come on. The week before, Assemblymember Julian Dixon gets an appendicitis attack that requires emergency surgery. I think that's what I have too. Art takes me to the hospital emergency room. It turns out it's only a kidney stone attack, which is still very painful. They keep me in the hospital for two days.

So there's poor Art, a newly minted freshman assemblymember whose first official act in the legislature is trying to take on a new governor from the same party, facing the Capitol Press Corps, which packs the room for the opening controversy of the new gubernatorial term, alone. Not a very positive experience, especially given the fact that our case questioning Obledo's appointment is sort of a stretch. With the entire press corps arrayed in front of him, Art starts out trying to elicit some sympathy from the reporters by describing my medical emergency as a way to explain why I'm not there. That doesn't work so well. The press corps fries him. It is horrible.

Since I know and have worked with Mario through MALDEF, I talk with him after the news conference. "Look, don't take it personally," I say. "It has nothing to do with you. It has to do with your boss"—the governor. Although Mario is an attorney, a veteran political activist, and dresses like a lawyer in conservative dark suits, he acts and speaks like some of the stoic *vatos* I know growing up in East L.A. Mario has been beaten up socially and politically in Texas, survives to lead MALDEF, and serves through most of Jerry's first governorship as head of the state's biggest agency. I really think it's a great appointment.

Mario says the little stunt Art and I pull off is "nothing to worry about."

"But if you want to disrespect us, fine," I joke. "We'll disrespect you too." We always have a good relationship after that.

I don't care about the fallout from the news conference—easy for me to say since I don't have to be there—since we're just trying to get Jerry and Leo's attention, and let the governor know we're not going to be pushovers.

That's a good thing because straight off, I'm in a big fight with Jerry early during his first year in office when he tries fucking the farmworkers. He ends up in the right place by working with Cesar Chavez, Jerry Cohen, and the United Farm Workers to forge the landmark farm labor law. But that doesn't happen until later in the spring. On the first day of session I introduce AB 1, my own farm labor bill staking out left field for the UFW. Together with Cesar we relentlessly attack the governor by traveling all over California through the late winter and early spring months until Jerry Brown and Leo McCarthy come around to the bill Cesar and the union need, and then Jerry convinces most of the agricultural lobby to get on board too.

Even though Jerry Brown is at the height of his influence and popularity—becoming a novel phenomenon in front of the national news media—unlike others who just meet him I have my own relationship with him going back to before he runs for public office. My history with Jerry dates from 1966 or '67, when he wants to meet with a group of young, upwardly mobile professional Democrats. I'm included in the group because I am already socially active and they want a Mexican in the room. I know Jerry Brown then as a lefty lawyer who represents pot dealers from the Silverlake District after they get busted. He's not living far from me in the same area. I remember going to Jerry's house for a function he hosts to help student activists. I next see Jerry a short time later at a session in downtown L.A. Wally Karabian puts together when Jerry wants to run for the Los Angeles Community College District Board of Trustees.

Although he comes to like him, Richard has a mixed relationship with Jerry Brown during his first tenure as governor in the 1970s, but they reach an accommodation.

The purpose of the get-together is so Jerry can ask for input on whether he should be a candidate. They're mostly young attorneys like Wally, who is already serving his first term in the assembly. Jerry gets up and says, "Everyone knows me as the son of the governor, Edmund G. "Pat" Brown, one of the greatest governors in the history of California. But I think I'm going to run as Jerry Brown."

One guy at the meeting, an Armenian-American attorney like Karabian, whispers to Wally, "The next time you want to invite me to a meeting for this guy, don't invite me. Anyone who is wondering what name he should use to get elected, especially when he has the name Edmund G. Brown Jr., is a fool and shouldn't be in public life." Then he gets up and walks out. Jerry later appoints the same guy to the Superior Court and later to the state Court of Appeals. Meantime, Edmund G. Brown Jr. is what appears on the ballot when Jerry runs.

Deep down, I think Jerry is crazy, the Governor Moonbeam nickname being well deserved. I know he will end up going the right way on most important issues—he certainly does later on in helping Cesar Chavez push through the Agricultural Labor Relations Act of 1975. He's also the most unconventional politician in modern American politics. At first he has no respect for the legislature. Eventually he figures out that if he wants to be successful and accomplish anything meaningful it will require negotiations and some accommodation with lawmakers. His second four-year term in office is probably more productive.

After the space shuttle first lands at Edwards Air Force Base in the Mojave Desert—Jerry is big into space—the governor asks to meet about space exploration with the Assembly Democratic Caucus. We meet in the Caucus Room off the assembly floor. It's not a big space, and it's packed with Democratic legislators. Everyone talks like they want to tear his ass apart; he's that unpopular among members. But when he walks in the room everyone is kissing his ass because he's the governor. I'm lying down, sprawled on a couch in the Caucus Room. Jerry asks if he can sit down on the couch.

"Fuck you," I reply. "You know what, I don't give a shit about space. I only care about poor people. That's the trouble with you liberals"—referring to their misplaced priorities.

Once the meeting begins, Bill Lockyer, a young assemblymember from the East Bay (and later state senate leader, state attorney general, and treasurer), starts talking. Bill is extremely bright and well read. He decides to use this caucus meeting to get into a philosophical debate with Jerry Brown over the space program. A big fucking mistake. I learn about such things early from Phil Montes, who tells me about how he challenges Wilson Riles when Riles is state superintendent of public instruction, over textbook reform, which Riles knows a lot about. "When you deal with a guy like that, someone who is an intellectual, never try to compete with him in *his* comfort zone," Phil tells me. "You make him compete in *your* comfort zone," which for me is using a lot of four-letter words and talking to the governor in a manner you know he will never stoop to. That's how you automatically win the fight, Phil Montes advises me.

Because he's very smart and well versed, Lockyer will normally win an argument against almost anybody—but not with Jerry Brown. The governor proceeds to beat him up, swallow him, spit him out, and stomp on him. The episode reinforces for me how futile it is to argue with the governor at his level. Jerry has this sagacity with words. He is so well read and can quote the Bible, philosophers, everything. No, the best tact to take with Jerry is to just tell him to fuck off. When I say that, Jerry walks away from me. I know he will. That's kind of the way we talk to each other back then.

One evening in the mid-'70s I walk into Lucy's El Adobe Restaurant on Melrose Boulevard in Hollywood, very popular among L.A. politicians and one of Jerry Brown's favorite hangouts since he lives in the Hollywood Hills not far away. At the time I'm chairing the Assembly Select Committee on Prison Reform and Rehabilitation and I'm taking on the state Department of Corrections and local sheriffs who run county jails over widespread abuses of inmates and prisoners, especially Chicanos who are being beaten up in places like the Orange County Jail. I spot Jerry having dinner with Linda Ronstadt, who he's been seeing—the subject of much national and international publicity since he's considered the most eligible bachelor in America. I stop over in front of their booth.

The governor greets me, "Hey Alatorre, How're you doing?"

I ignore him and tell Linda Ronstadt how much I like her, what a wonderful singer she is and what a great fan I am. "But what are you doing with this guy?" I ask. She laughs. All this time while I'm chatting with Linda, Jerry is drawing something on a paper napkin. He shows it to her and she shows it to me. Using stick figures, Jerry depicts a man behind prison bars with no expression on his face. Jerry does away with the word "Rehabilitation," as in the old California

Richard confronts Jerry Brown when the governor and Linda Ronstadt are dining at a prominent Hollywood eatery.

Department of Corrections and Rehabilitation. Jerry doesn't believe in rehabilitation. He believes people should go to prison, serve their time and get out without any programs or services to help them change their lives.

"What is this?" I ask dismissively.

"See this?" the governor says. "These are the kind of prisoners I want in our prison system."

I look at Jerry. I look at Linda. I just say to her, "This is what I mean. This is the most fucked up guy I have ever met in my life." She laughs.

"You're nuts," I tell the governor. Then I turn around and walk away.

But deep down, I recognize how brilliant Jerry is. And you know what? I get to like him. I'm just not going to roll over for him.

He is fascinating even if throughout most of his first eight years in the governor's office we never have a real relationship. I'm not interested in one. He isn't exactly my kind of guy. Jerry ultimately befriends Art Torres and ends up liking him because Art is very good at building those types of relationships.

Jerry Brown and I do kind of reach an accommodation, even if we're never close. I can't say he is ever vindictive towards me, whatever I do politically to him. He signs most of my important bills. His appointments to the administration and the judiciary do more to open up the governmental process at the highest levels for ethnic and racial minorities and women than any governor before or since—even if he occasionally appoints minorities in the wrong jurisdictions so they can't win when they have to run for election. Like he'll appoint a Mexican or a black to a judicial seat in a conservative community like parts of Orange County. Or he'll put in people who are too liberal to blend into the territory where they have to face the voters. That can lead to polarization and political backlash against the appointees. The judges he names are good, but he doesn't always think about matching them to places where they can get elected and re-elected. A local deputy district attorney or a law-and-order candidate frequently beat them. The same thing applies with his appointments to the state Supreme Court. I respect Rose Bird's loyalty to the governor, but she has tremendous political flaws that later become her undoing.

To show you how fucked up Rose Bird is, consider what she does in the case of *Maggio Inc. v. United Farm Workers*. Carl Maggio, a big grower, sues the UFW out of the bitter 1979 Imperial Valley vegetable strike, claiming strikers engage in violence and demanding the union pay the grower for all the damages the company suffers as a result of the workers going out on strike in what is a very effective walkout. In the middle of the trial in El Centro, it is revealed that the wife of Imperial County Superior Court Judge William B. Lehnhardt, who is trying the case, has been working as a scab or strikebreaker for the very same grower during the very same strike involved in the lawsuit. (This is the same Judge William Lehnhardt who, after Rufino Contreras, a young striker, is shot to death on a nearby picket line, lets the three grower foremen who fire on the dead man out of jail on the lowest bail for murder in the history of the county and later dismisses the criminal charges.) After Mrs. Lehnhardt's scabbing is revealed, UFW lawyers demand Judge Lehnhardt recuse himself from the case because of bias. He refuses. The union appeals, trying to get the judge removed, first to the state Court of Appeals and when that doesn't work to the California Supreme Court.

When the appeal comes before the state high court, Chief Justice Bird does recuse herself, withdrawing from ruling on the case. She explains it is because the chief justice "wrote" the Agricultural Labor Relations Act, the state farm labor law. Well, first, the farm labor law has nothing to do with the lawsuit for civil damages Maggio, the grower, brings against the union. Also, she does not write the farm labor law. I know because I'm in the room when it gets "written," with Rose Bird, who is then Jerry's secretary of the Department of Food and Agriculture, the governor, UFW General Counsel Jerry Cohen, and then-Assemblymember Howard Berman. Progress only gets made late at night when Rose Bird falls asleep.

After the UFW loses the appeal against Judge Lehnhardt before the Supreme Court by just one vote (Rose Bird's), the trial resumes and the judge hands the grower the verdict and $1.7 million of the farmworkers' money. Cesar has to borrow funds to pay the judgment from the Franciscan order in order to be able to appeal the verdict, which the UFW ends up losing too. It takes Cesar years to pay off the loan, but he does. Thank you, Chief Justice Bird.

This just shows how sometimes, instead of helping you, liberals end up hurting the very causes they're supposed to be championing.

Tragically, Rose Bird's political shortcomings also undo two other good Brown appointees to the Supreme Court who are recalled along with her in 1986, Justices Joseph Grodin and Cruz Reynoso. Cruz is a great civil rights lawyer who leads California Rural Legal Assistance in the '60s, and is the first Chicano ever named to the high court.

Jerry Brown and I philosophically agree for the most part. I just hate his politics and the seemingly self-righteous attitude he displays. For me, the monastic lifestyle is not befitting a governor.

I think his time out of elected office and his return to politics as mayor of Oakland change him tremendously. He decides to take up residence in northern California, which surprises me. The time out he spends since being governor teaches him how to govern, which he really doesn't completely master as governor the first time around. He develops a solid reputation for accomplishment in Oakland, where he makes a difference as mayor. Not many people are given a second chance in politics or in life; Jerry gets one.

In 2009, I'm invited by a friend, the head of security for a casino in the city of Commerce, to a fundraiser at Jerry Brown's home for one of his favorite charities, the Oakland School for the Arts, a performing arts charter school in Oakland that Jerry starts. We drive up into the Oakland Hills where Jerry, who by then is state attorney general, lives in a very contemporary multifloor house with lots of Buddhist artifacts and paintings. We're one of the first guests to arrive for the event. Jerry is very welcoming, which strikes me as so unlike him because he is just so weird during the '70s.

Jerry is well dressed, also unlike what he is before since he never makes a fashion play for anybody in the '70s. He isn't in a suit but has on a pair of what I consider expensive slacks and a great tailored shirt. He proceeds to take us on a tour of the home. I'm surprised because he is never one for small talk when he's governor the first time. He introduces us to his wife, Anne Gust Brown, explaining to her how Jerry and I go back a long way, how I endorse and work for his father in the 1966 governor's race (when Reagan beats Pat Brown), and how I support Jerry when he first runs for the community college board in 1969.

"You've done an amazing job with Jerry," I tell her. "First of all, your home is beautiful, a far cry from his rather humble '70s housing accommodations" in Sacramento, when he lives in a sparsely furnished penthouse apartment with mattresses on the floor in a state-owned building at N and 15th streets across from Capitol Park.

"Thank you very much," she replies. "He's really a good man."

"Absolutely," I said. "Hopefully, he'll make a decision to run for governor as rumored."

"Does that mean you're endorsing me, Alatorre?" Jerry asks.

I'm praying that L.A.'s mayor, Antonio Villaraigosa, doesn't run so I tell him, "If Antonio's not in the race, clearly you're the best man for the job."

"See, Anne," Jerry says, "remember this: he's one of my first endorsements in the Chicano community."

"God bless you, Jerry," I offer a little sarcastically.

We see him welcome a small group of people who contribute a lot of money, displaying the fruits of his labors with students from the arts academy, including a cellist, pianist and other musicians performing on different levels of the residence. You can tell he's justifiably proud of his charter school undertaking.

"How did this start?" I ask Jerry. In his inimitable style, Jerry answers without missing a beat: as part of the effort to fix Oakland's public schools during his tenure as mayor, "I set up the first boot camp [through the Oakland Military Institute], a highly militaristic program for at-risk kids. I couldn't do something just on the right. I had to do something for the left at the same time. So I came up with this idea for an arts academy charter school. That took care of the left." The explanation just flows seamlessly right out of him. That's Jerry Brown. Always slick and quick-thinking.

Now I love the guy. No matter what is said about Jerry Brown, it's good that voters finally elect somebody who knows what he is doing. He's not throwing bombs at anything anymore. If anything, he's very thoughtful, but still unorthodox. Yet, he has a philosophy; he believes in something.

Before Jerry, we have the George Deukmejians and Pete Wilsons of the world who create so many divisions for purposes of advancing their cynical politics. We have Gray Davis who unfortunately stations himself at the most exclusive restaurants where the rich and powerful dine, being there to set up his next hit for a fundraiser or getting somebody to raise money for him. With his zeal in trying to appease the public employees and safety officers, he helps create economic dilemmas for state government that come back to haunt us. Then the irony of it all is when the people recall Gray and elect this asshole actor, Arnold Schwarzenegger, who promises the world and delivers nothing except burrowing us into the fiscal hole even more.

That's why we need somebody like Jerry, who at least is practical in his unorthodox liberal ways.

Oh, despite the disdain for liberals, my overall voting record consistently ends up comparing pretty favorably to other progressive Democrats in the assembly.

Meantime, my record of introducing—and passing—bills is also pretty good. In my first term as a legislator, during the 1973–74 legislative session, I introduce 65 bills; 40 are held in committee, three are vetoed during Ronald Reagan's last two years in office and 22 are signed into law.

"If you introduce 65 bills and 22 get signed, that's a better percentage than most," Toni Trigueiro observes. "If any member in today's legislature got 22 bills off the governor's desk during a six-year career under term limits, he or she would be happy. But there were no bill limits then."

The '73–'74 session doesn't set the record. In the 1978–79 session, I introduce 100 bills; 64 are held in committee, 26 are signed into law by Jerry Brown and he vetoes 10 others.

Finally, another reputation I get, somewhat undeservedly I think, on the weekdays is as a partier and carouser in a state Capitol and capital city that during the '70s becomes a culture unto itself. You live there. You work there. You play there. It is a 24/7 type of lifestyle. Especially during my first two years in office before Proposition 9 puts limits on campaign contributions and accepting food, booze, and gifts from lobbyists, a lot of things are going on.

There are always card games happening in Capitol offices and in the back rooms of some of the bars. Frank Fats Restaurant, Sacramento's most celebrated legislative hang out down L Street from the Capitol, hosts card games in an upstairs room overlooking the street. Some members are big gamblers.

When legislative deadlines approach—dates by which bills need to be out of the house of origin or at the end of session—committee hearings and floor sessions go late into the evening and sometimes into the early hours of the morning of the next day. The Ways and Means Committee I serve on can sit *ad nauseum* going through item by item on an interminable agenda. If the hearing starts at 2 p.m., you're easily still there at 6 or 7 p.m.—we don't break for dinner as they do now. So sometimes I have a few beers brought down in manila envelopes and keep a glass under the dais to help tide me over. During long night sessions, lawmakers host get-togethers in their offices near the floor, popping open bottles.

My thing is unless hearings or sessions go on until late at night, I wait until I leave the building and drink my life away at home or sometimes have dinner and drinks with colleagues and friends at the capital bars—or I drink, often alone, at home in the district on weekends.

"In the office, regardless of the length of the day, Richard is always there and always present, both physically and mentally," affirms my aide, Toni Trigueiro. "As a staff person who was with him day and night, unlike some members I never saw alcohol infringe on Richard's ability to do his job." It's true. As much as I already have a pretty serious drinking problem by then, I never let myself be compromised during working hours.

Chapter 6

Dedicating Myself to Cesar's Cause

In his now landmark 1984 address to the Commonwealth Club of California in San Francisco, Cesar Chavez reflects on the historical role of his movement.

> All Hispanics—urban and rural, young and old—are connected to the farmworkers' experience. We had all lived through the fields—or our parents had. We shared that common humiliation.
>
> How could we progress as a people, even if we lived in the cities, while the farmworkers—men and women of our color—were condemned to a life without pride?
>
> How could we progress as a people while the farmworkers—who symbolized our history in this land—were denied self-respect?
>
> How could our people believe that their children could become lawyers and doctors and judges and business people while this shame, this injustice was permitted to continue?

Cesar articulates an experience that is so common among Latinos. And no one appreciates his words more than me. The fields are places many Chicanos where I come from on the streets of East L.A. have never been to in their lives. I remember one summer growing up as a kid when I find out a way to make some extra money by working in the fields. There is this aunt or someone outside of

Bakersfield with a connection to agriculture. I remember going with my father to visit her family. I work one day in the fields. That's enough.

The first time I meet Cesar Chavez is in 1966, at a meeting sponsored by the Social Action Training Center on Florence Avenue in South Central Los Angeles. It has programs so black and Mexican kids who are gang leaders can learn about community activism and social change. It is funded by one of the War on Poverty agencies I am working with and modeled on Saul Alinsky's community organizing principles. We have racial issues between blacks and Chicanos. The kids are together in this small meeting area in the back of a storefront. They have already listened to Ron Karanga, a brilliant black educator-turned-preacher who is also a Black Panther-type militant and a fiery speaker.

Then Cesar walks in a little late. He may be the first Mexican the blacks have ever met—other than me. He's this little guy, shorter than me and looking younger than I do, although he's not. He sits down and starts talking in a very measured, soft-spoken voice and with none of the oratorical embellishments I'm used to seeing or hearing from the prominent black or Latino public figures I've met before. He speaks in a vocabulary that can't compare to Karanga. Most of the kids don't understand Karanga. But they do understand Cesar. One of the things I come to love about Cesar is his ability to communicate in simple, clear ideas that are really profound. He talks about community, sacrifice, and what it means to be a man. He talks about his days working in East L.A. with the Community Service Organization. He talks about recommitting your life to social justice.

For me, I can still visualize in my mind Cesar walking into that room. The only thing I can compare it to is the feeling of seeing Pope John Paul II walking into St. Vibiana Cathedral during his visit to L.A. after waiting for three hours—with everybody getting restless. But when the Pope makes his appearance there is this power of his presence. You know you are in the company of a simple man of God. I have the same feeling that first time with Cesar.

I'm involved with the farmworkers again a short time later, when the U.S. Commission on Civil Rights conducts a hearing in San Antonio on how the Texas Rangers have broken United Farm Workers-led melon strikes in South Texas's Rio Grande Valley in 1966, including the physical abuse of Latino strikers by Anglo rangers. In one incident during the strike, a group led by Protestant Reverend Jim Drake, Cesar's assistant in California, and Gilbert Padilla, another leader of the Delano Grape Strike who is sent to Texas to help farmworkers there, are kneeling and praying outside the Rio Grande City courthouse. Strikers are in jail and being denied bail. Drake and Padilla are arrested and charged with interfering with a janitor in the performance of his duties. Many people are arrested in an effort to break the strike but there are no convictions.

Phil Montes is western regional director of the commission and I am helping out with the hearing work as a consultant. By then I am also working full time as western regional director of the NAACP Legal Defense and Education Fund. Staff show up in Texas a week before the hearing is set to begin.

We hear that Rangers Captain A. Y. Allee Jr., responsible for much of the abuse endured by the striking farmworkers, is going to refuse to come to the hearing. He doesn't want to dignify the thing. A lawyer for the rangers claims the captain fears for his life, making it sound like the farmworkers are the ones using violence or threatening it, instead of the rangers. It's a Sunday. The hearing starts the next day. A meeting is set up that Sunday between Allee and the Reverend Theodore Hesburgh, chairman of the civil rights commission and president of the University of Notre Dame. Reverend Hesburgh laughs at Allee's claim that he fears for his life. "If you're not there [at the hearing] at 9 a.m., we're sending federal marshals to arrest you and force your appearance," Reverend Hesburgh warns. Allee shows up.

Reverend Hesburgh, who's chairing the hearing, grills Allee on the conduct of his rangers during the farmworker strike. The captain sometimes responds by mumbling. The final report issued by the civil rights commission royally screws the Texas Rangers.

Later, while teaching at UC Irvine, I get active with students volunteering in Orange County for the UFW's grape boycott, which is seriously underway across the nation by 1969. We picket in front of supermarkets and join pro-boycott marches in the barrio of Santa Ana. Not long after that I start to get involved with the farmworkers legislatively as a consultant working in Sacramento with the Assembly Office of Majority Consultants, which provides adjunct staffing for Democratic lawmakers at the state Capitol.

In summer 1971, Assemblymen Ken Cory, a Democrat from Orange County, and Robert Wood, a Republican from Salinas, introduce what becomes known as the Cory-Wood bill. Introduced on behalf of the agricultural industry, the measure would severely limit the farmworkers' rights to strike and boycott. Most strikes are eventually broken by scabs, or strikebreakers, increasingly undocumented workers imported from outside the country by grower foremen, farm labor contractors or *coyotes*, smugglers, working with the industry. But in the 1970s, the walkouts are initially pretty effective and still costly to the growers. They are also demonstrations of defiance by farmworkers resisting the paternalism of the growers who by then are increasingly attempting to make the decision about union representation for the workers by unilaterally choosing another union, the Teamsters, which at that time is primarily run by Anglos. The growers just the year before experience a big strike in the lettuce and vegetable fields of the Central Coast.

In 1970, the farmworkers walk out on strike in the Salinas Valley because they "were very angry and because they didn't want to be treated like chattel," says Jerry Cohen, the UFW's brilliant and irreverent general counsel whose disheveled appearance covers up a first class mind. I can't remember the first time I meet Jerry, but I'm immediately taken by his smarts and conniving ability, something I admire. His legal mind is second to none. But he's also a great organizer in addition to being a great lawyer. That's why I love him and why he becomes an invaluable asset to Cesar and the union.

The ultimate "disgrace" that causes the 1970 Salinas strike "was that the Teamsters only obtained a paltry half-cent increase in the piece rate" for the lettuce and vegetable pickers who are now Teamster members because of the union contracts the Teamsters have signed with their employers, Jerry recalls. "So naturally the workers were angry." But the giant strike that year is "not simply a demonstration of defiance. People thought they could win and there was enough economic pressure at a few companies" that the UFW, with help from the boycott, pressures a few large farms to abandon their Teamsters contracts and sign with the UFW.

The power of the boycott is also getting to the agricultural industry. Remember, by 1970 it is a national and international boycott that forces most California table grape growers to sign their first union contracts with the UFW.

The 1971 Cory-Wood bill is scheduled for a hearing that summer before the Assembly Labor Relations Committee. It would sharply limit the right of farmworkers to strike and boycott. Shortly before the hearing, I pick up word that Assemblyman Alex Garcia, a Democrat from East L.A., is about to stab Cesar and the UFW in the back by voting for the growers. Garcia is first elected in the same June 1968 California Democratic primary that hands an ill-fated victory to the presidential campaign of Senator Robert Kennedy, largely because of intense door-to-door campaigning in Eastside barrios by Cesar and the farmworkers. I'm busy running for the assembly in the 1971 special election, but pass this news about Garcia along to Cesar through Marc Grossman, my former student who's serving as an aide at the UFW president's office in Delano during a summer break from Irvine.

To the dismay of Chicanos all over the state, Garcia helps vote the Cory-Wood bill out of the labor committee, allegedly because he is "rented" for the day, probably by the Teamsters. Cesar organizes a rally in Sacramento by thousands of farmworkers on the Capitol's west steps. Chairman Willie Brown soon kills the bill in the Assembly Ways and Means Committee, although it forms the basis for similar proposals backed by the Farm Bureau that do pass the next year in three other states (Idaho, Kansas, and Arizona).

However, what the growers can't get done legislatively in California, they try to do through an initiative they put on the statewide ballot, Proposition 22, that the UFW mobilizes against and defeats in the fall of 1972. Also, Cesar encourages and supports Art Torres's state assembly run against Alex Garcia in the 1972 Democratic primary. Art, who insists on only taking campaign contributions from "the people," as opposed to Third House special interests, loses his first try for public office by a slim margin.

But stopping state legislation and defeating the California ballot measure are all defensive battles by the farmworkers.

After I get elected to the assembly in 1972, the very next year I'm named to a select committee on pesticides chaired by March Fong, a Democratic assemblywoman from Oakland who is helping the agricultural and pesticide industries. By then I'm chairing the Chicano Caucus of the legislature. (None of the other Latino legislators wants the job.) The select committee holds hearings on pesticides in the Coachella and Central valleys, where Cesar and the UFW testify.

Many of my closest friends and political advisors, Anglos and even some Chicanos, warn me against getting too active with the farmworkers. Lou Moret, who is Chicano, one of my best friends to this day and is then serving as my administrative assistant in the district office, doesn't think helping the UFW will lead towards anything constructive for me. "Okay, you can vote for them and I would do the same thing," Lou says. "But why spend so much of your time and energy when you could use that time and energy to cultivate people with more financial means without offending the big interest groups you offend by taking up the cause of the farmworkers?" In those days, in addition to going up against the state's wealthy agricultural industry, Cesar is of course in a fierce battle with the powerful Teamsters Union, which has allied itself with the growers, and the industry itself is still at that time a major donor to Democratic candidates.

"We were merely saying you don't represent the area," Lou says years later. "Your district is in an urban area. [The farmworkers] ain't important there. We were on the same page philosophically," with Cesar, Lou emphasizes. "But there was more potential damage that could be done to Richard's political career than there was being an upside. But we also agreed, shit, it's your career. So that ended that."

It isn't just that I am voting for the UFW; I am starting to dedicate a considerable amount of my time, energy, and political capital in support of Cesar's cause. A number of people on my campaign finance committee, the core group responsible for most of the money I raise, tell me the same thing. "Hey, we all support Cesar and his efforts," one member observes. "But in the long run it's not in your interests to get too involved. If you ever go for statewide office, you're going to be viewed as an enemy of certain powerful segments."

"The Democrats were divided," then-Assemblymember Wally Karabian recalls. "A lot of Democrats wanted to be with the Teamsters. I always looked for ways to be with the Teamsters. Cesar was an annoyance at the beginning. Later he became a great national hero. But I never held it against Richard or thought he was doing something to harm himself by being with Cesar because I knew everybody understood why Richard was there: these were his people."

"If you were a political consultant with a different set of interests than the farmworkers, the UFW was in a relatively weak political position then," Jerry Cohen acknowledges, describing Cesar's farm labor movement as "a sleeping giant. Growers and business interests knew they had to react" to the union's newfound demonstrations of power, "and they reacted with strength. It was by no means clear the UFW could take the victory in the table grapes in 1970 and translate it into permanent political power."

I have a different take anyway. Even before the East L.A. student walkouts in 1968, which is sometimes cited as the beginning of the Chicano movement, the only real organized movement that all Latinos can claim as their own is the farmworkers. Chicanos, even those in urban areas, gravitate to the grape boycott in the 1960s although they may never have had any experiences in the fields. Championing Cesar and the UFW allows me to continue the ethnocentric part of me, the part that is still movement-oriented, even after I "sell out," as my lefty friends complain, by seeking a career in elected office.

Other liberal legislators, like my buddy then-Assemblyman John Burton, also unequivocally support the UFW. But they aren't willing to put in the same kind of time I am. And not many legislators are willing to jeopardize their political capital. They'll vote, sometimes reluctantly, for the UFW when the occasional issue comes in front of them. There are some automatic votes that members have to take because of their political ideology or where their districts are located.

Of course, the pure political logic of that argument doesn't impress people like Cesar Chavez or Jerry Cohen. "We always dealt at arm's length with Republicans and Democrats," Jerry notes. "When you're in a fight you want allies you can count on. I didn't see a lot of difference between Republicans and Democrats, especially rural Democrats who were beholden to the same set of interests—not only the growers, but the Teamsters as well."

For others among my Democratic colleagues, especially the rural Democrats, Cesar and his union are the kiss of death. These are guys like Rick Lehman, John Thurman, Norm Waters, Jim Costa, Ray Gonzales for a short time, and later Bruce Bronzan, Gary Condit, Rusty Areias, Steve Peace, and Steve Clute. Some are my friends, like Lehman, since we start in the assembly around the same time. They make speeches against the UFW and take—and earn—the growers' political contributions. Most of them vote pro-labor when it comes to issues concerning other unions or even on pro-ethnic legislation. Many of them represent Mexicans in their districts, although because of reapportionment there are not enough Latinos to threaten their political existence. But when it comes to farm labor or anything to do with fights between the UFW and agriculture, these rural Democrats go south.

I come to figure out some of them, like Thurman and Waters, are themselves growers or ranchers. I remember talking to John Thurman one day and spending a day going with him around his Modesto-area district. He's a real redneck and has this 1950s-period flattop haircut. "I used to hate you because if anybody, you as an Oakie during the Depression should understand what the farmworkers are trying to do," I tell Thurman. But I get that he's the real thing, and I can respect him.

To be honest, back then I don't understand why some of my fellow Democratic politicians can't see the magnitude of the injustices facing the farmworkers. But that just shows my own naïveté, something that doesn't often happen to me. When these Democrats have to choose between the plight of the farmworkers and their perception of political reality in districts where they think the growers hold the balance of power, it's not a hard choice. But it's funny how perceptions of reality dramatically change over time along with changing demographics. Nearly all of those rural Anglo Democrats from the 1970s and '80s are no longer in public office. It's mostly because of term limits. But Latino lawmakers who are farmworker supporters later replace most of my former Anglo Democratic colleagues in places like the Central Valley and Central Coast.

I guess I don't listen to some of my advisors counseling me against standing too close to the UFW because when the second grape strike begins in spring 1973, I join the picket lines in the Coachella Valley near Palm Springs. The first grape strike, beginning in the Central Valley around Delano in 1965, and the grape boycott that starts in 1967, result in victory for the UFW when most California table grape growers sign union contracts in 1970. But when those contracts expire in 1973, instead of renegotiating them with the farmworkers union, all but one of the table grape growers join up with the Teamsters. They do so by signing "sweetheart" contracts, pacts that benefit the employers more than the workers. International Brotherhood of Teamsters President Frank Fitzsimmons, who succeeds Jimmy Hoffa, kicks off this infamous alliance with the growers by addressing the American Farm Bureau Federation national convention at the Los Angeles Convention Center in December 1972, while farmworkers protest outside.

Once growers sign with the Teamsters in 1973, workers at the affected vineyards have no choice but to walk out on strike, which they do when the nation's first table grape harvest starts up in the Coachella Valley of southern California in April. The strikers are immediately subjected to systematic violence, mostly at the hands of "goons," burly men recruited from local unions of the Teamsters who are paid $67.50 a day to threaten, intimidate, and often physically attack striking farmworkers, their families, and supporters. Strikers are accosted on the picket lines. They are assaulted on rural roads. Some of their homes are burned down. One especially brazen group of Teamster goons throws boulders from the back of a flatbed truck at a car carrying Cesar Chavez. As spring turns into summer, the strike and the violence spread north along with the table grape harvest into the Central Valley. When these brutal tactics don't stop the strikers, growers turn to court injunctions issued by rural judges, basically banning the freedom of association and the right to strike by strictly limiting picketing in the vineyards.

Strikers are shot, beaten, many of them savagely, and arrested for violating court orders. Many of the injunctions are later overturned as unconstitutional. At one point that year in the Central Valley, every jail and county honor farm from Mettler near the grapevine to north of Fresno is filled to overflowing with defiant strikers. (An honor farm is a minimum-security facility maintained by many county sheriffs where prisoners are held—and sometimes made to work, especially in the South. They are also sometimes called industrial farms (for some reason).) It is a testament to Cesar and the strikers' dedication to nonviolence that despite all these provocations and many more, there are no significant acts of violence by strikers in retaliation.

I take my two young sons with me to a couple of UFW rallies during the strikes in Coachella and Delano. I also propose to Assembly Speaker Bob Moretti that he appoint a select committee chaired by me to investigate the violence in the vineyards. I'm sure I tell Moretti that I will be balanced and objective, that I'll get both sides of the story. You have to give both sides a chance to be heard anyway, so I'm telling him the truth about that. I tell the Speaker how it's better that I run the committee rather than somebody else he can't trust and who might let things get out of control. I also argue with him to set up the committee and make me the chairman because I need it for my own district since it's such an important issue for Chicanos. Well, sorta. "I'm not going to embarrass you," I assure Moretti. "I'll always sing your praises"—or whatever I need to tell him at the time.

Moretti collects a lot of his political money through the Assembly Insurance and Governmental Organization committees. The GO committee covers sin, including booze. Moretti has been big into the wine and alcoholic spirits industries, and close to the Gallo wine family, fellow Italians, as chairman of GO. (The Gallos, whose contract with the UFW goes back to 1967, also sign with the Teamsters in 1973, fostering another bitter strike and boycott by the workers.) Then, too, the ag boys continue to be big players with the Democrats.

The Speaker is also not on the best of terms with the UFW, which thinks he's in the pocket of the Teamsters. Later, in 1974, at an assembly committee hearing in Los Angeles over the use of the pesticide Monitor 4 on lettuce, the UFW lines up a consumer advocate, Ida Honorof, to testify and wants her to go on first while the TV news cameras are still rolling. The chair, Assemblywoman Fong, has other plans and tells the Teamsters to "go first with their stooge witnesses," as Jerry Cohen puts it. The UFW tells Honorof to go up and testify first anyway. Bob Moretti and Jerry Cohen get in this big argument, with Moretti shaking his finger at Cohen after Jerry tells him, "What's the matter, Bob, the Teamsters got to you?"

"Cohen, I'm going to rip your balls off and stuff them down your throat," the Speaker replies.

"You're never going to be governor, Bob," Jerry says calmly.

Luckily, by 1973 Moretti and I are close so he gives in and names me chairman of the newly created Assembly Select Committee on Farm Labor Violence. He doesn't like me pushing him. But one thing about Moretti is he allows you to do your thing unless you become a big pain in the ass for him. Then he mows you down. I can't remember a time when he tells me, "You're embarrassing me and making it bad for the others [assembly Democrats]." I know he doesn't have a problem just telling me "fuck you" if it comes to that. Still, he knows and respects my temperament too, even if he doesn't always agree with me.

Mexicans are not exactly on the top of Moretti's list, even though he does learn to speak Spanish by the time he is gearing up to run for governor in 1974.

United Farm Workers General Counsel Jerry Cohen (seated) in verbal combat with Assembly Speaker Bob Moretti during a Los Angeles legislative hearing in February 1973. "Cohen, I'm going to rip your balls off and stuff them down your throat," the Speaker vows.

Despite what I assure Moretti, I have a different agenda, developed in coordination with Cesar and Jerry. It is part of an overall strategy to expose the need for a comprehensive legislative solution to the farm labor problem.

Farmworkers are excluded from the National Labor Relations Act, the Wagner Act passed in 1935, giving organizing and collective bargaining rights to industrial workers. Not covering farmworkers is the price President Roosevelt has to pay to win the votes of southern Democrats; in those days, 85 percent of southern blacks are farmworkers.

Cesar avoids the question of including farmworkers under the national labor laws proposed by some of his supporters throughout the five-year Delano grape strike and boycott. (As early as 1972, Assemblyman Howard Berman travels to the union's La Paz headquarters at Keene "to propose secret ballot elections in return for giving up harvest-time strikes," Jerry recalls. "Even our friends were thinking of a legislative solution early on that would inhibit farmworker economic power. They were being 'realistic' and said we needed to be realistic too. We told them we were not going to give up our economic power. But the outcome was by no means clear.")

Unlike other unions, the UFW can't use the federal labor laws to get growers to recognize the union and negotiate with the farmworkers. It does that by using a novel weapon, the boycott, which before Cesar comes along has never before applied to a big-time labor-management dispute. But the UFW also benefits in some important ways from not being covered by the federal labor laws. Amendments to the law, called the Taft-Hartley Act, passed in 1947, outlaw secondary boycotts.

A primary boycott is when you ask somebody not to buy a certain product that results from a primary labor dispute, such as boycotting grapes produced by growers who are being struck by farmworkers. A secondary boycott is when you ask people not to do business with a particular company because the firm does business with another company that is involved in a strike. Secondary boycotts become a very successful tactic used by Cesar and the farmworkers when they ask consumers to boycott supermarkets selling boycotted grapes that come from struck vineyards. That is illegal under the Taft-Hartley amendments to the National Labor Relations Act. But since farmworkers are excluded from federal law, it's not illegal for them.

By 1973, Cesar is organizing a three-pronged boycott—of grapes, lettuce, and Gallo wines—all resulting from growers bringing in the competing union, the Teamsters, to try to defeat the UFW. The grape growers wipe out nearly all the gains from the tough five-year struggle in the table grapes from 1965 to 1970 within three months in 1973. The lettuce boycott is from the huge lettuce and vegetable strike that begins in the Salinas Valley in 1970, after growers there, fearing they're next on Cesar's list, preemptively sign sweetheart deals with the Teamsters. The Gallo boycott comes out of the 1973 strike in the Livingston and Modesto area after the winery signs with the Teamsters.

The UFW loses most of its contracts and nearly all of its members to the Teamsters in 1973. It is nearly wiped out on paper. Any other union is considered destroyed if its dues income is cut off. But since most everyone in the UFW, from Cesar on down, is "paid" $5 a week plus room and board, no one quits because they aren't getting a paycheck. And the UFW manages to raise money to keep going from other unions plus small donations from hundreds of thousands of supporters among the general public.

Then there are the beatings and killings of strikers, which Cesar, who bases his commitment to nonviolence on the teachings of Mahatma Gandhi, Dr. Martin Luther King Jr., and his own devout Catholicism, cannot accept. In a significant shift in thinking, by 1973 Cesar and the UFW leadership are considering setting up some kind of legal framework to avoid violence and give farmworkers the same, or better, organizing rights that nearly all other American workers have had for nearly 40 years.

What's galling to the UFW is not just the violence, but the fact it is unable to protect the union contracts it had painstakingly won. "If growers can cut sweetheart deals with the Teamsters and take the grape industry away from the farmworkers union, then we need a mechanism to protect our victories," Jerry concludes. "We had two strikers dead from violence [in 1973]. Other strikers were seriously injured. It wasn't just the economic stakes; people's lives were at risk. We needed an orderly procedure to protect our membership and union contracts. That's the conclusion we came to."

Jerry recounts taking a ride with Cesar in the Coachella Valley in the spring of 1973, in the midst of the bitter and bloody strike that begins there. "Cesar said we had to get serious in preparing a legislative solution for two reasons: without one we'll never have any stability in the contracts we win. And we needed strike benefits [during the '73 walkouts] and we knew the AFL-CIO's price for getting those benefits was some kind of legislative solution." AFL-CIO President George Meany is under other kinds of pressure: unions in supermarkets and packinghouses don't like farmworkers picketing facilities outside the fields. Those pressures from other unions "translate to us," Jerry admits.

Jerry and Cesar meet with Meany in April 1973 over the UFW's desperate need to provide some modest benefits for grape workers and their families who are or are going out on strike. Meany sends a delegation of top AFL-CIO leaders to the Coachella Valley to talk with the UFW. "We met at some restaurant in Coachella," Jerry remembers. "It was clear" they wanted the UFW to be for legislation. The UFW has already decided that "with the Teamsters lurking on our flank we needed legislation. But Cesar was a very good negotiator. So he played hard to get" with the AFL-CIO big shots. "Cesar used the commitment to pursue legislation as leverage to get strike benefits." The AFL-CIO comes through with a $1 million strike fund, a lot of money in those days.

"By this time, Cesar has a good enough feel for Richard [Alatorre] to understand he is an ally we can rely on," Jerry says. The farm labor violence select committee hearings I'm going to chair are "part of an overall strategy to expose the need for a comprehensive legislative solution to the farm labor problem," Cohen adds.

By this time I've spent enough time in Sacramento to learn the power of the committee chair. The chairman creates the agenda and controls the gavel. You know you have to let each side in an issue participate. It's not rocket science. As chairman, you start with the questions, those you are going to pose to the witnesses plus the ground you want to cover and the points you want to end up making. You also have to start by recruiting good staff who do the research and preparation, and feed me the questions. To handle this job for my select committee I hire Lorenzo Patino, a former student activist in Sacramento with lots of experience among all the lefties, but a young man who truly understands politics and the legislative process.

I meet Lorenzo while I'm teaching at UC Irvine. He is a student at UC Davis, with a long history of activism in the finest sense of the word in Sacramento, where he is involved to the hilt with the farmworkers, the anti-Vietnam War movement, and within the Chicano community. We maintain our friendship through Art Torres, who Lorenzo knows since they both attend law school together at Davis. By the time I come up to Sacramento to work for majority services at the Capitol, Lorenzo is an intern with state Senator Merv Dymally. We reconnect and become very close. Lorenzo is among the political operatives from Sacramento who come down to L.A. and help out in my first assembly election, which I lose. Six months later, in the spring 1972 Democratic primary, he's down again for my second campaign when we win.

Lorenzo, without a doubt, is one of the most brilliant kids I have met in my life. He combines a great intellect with a streetwise mentality. Lorenzo grows up in Mendota, in rural west Fresno County, the son of a farmworker. He sees all the discrimination that people living in urban areas are not exposed to. He moves to Sacramento, completes college and becomes a protégé of Joe Serna Jr., later the dynamic mayor of Sacramento, the first Latino to be elected to lead a major California city before his untimely death in office in 1999. Lorenzo is also incredibly focused and has an uncanny public relations sense, almost a sense of smell about how you can turn something that is nothing into a big deal. He knows how to present any issue in a public forum and manage to get publicity out of it. When I see how his mind operates, it's clear to me Lorenzo is the guy I want as consultant for my farm labor violence select committee. I have implicit trust in him. By then he's like a member of my family.

Lorenzo plays a big role during that fall of 1973 in setting up the hearings by my farm labor violence panel and attracting publicity that achieves our goals. After much preparation, we hold three daylong hearings. The first one is in Bakersfield on October 1, followed by Fresno on October 2, and Palm Springs, near the Coachella Valley, on November 26.

For me from the outset it is not a question of laying guilt on the growers or Teamsters or anyone else. That doesn't matter. I'm taking my cues from the farmworkers. What I am trying to accomplish with the hearings is getting publicity about the strike violence. To me it is black and white. You have innocent people getting the fuck beaten out of them for exercising their fundamental rights. Law enforcement not only frequently stands by and allows the violence to take place, the cops sometimes inflict their own violence on innocent farmworkers and also enforce unconstitutional orders from rural judges, arresting thousands of peaceful strikers whose only crime is freely assembling. My aim with the hearings is to expose these injustices.

By having me conduct the hearings in the wake of the strike, the UFW legal department is "forced to focus resources on collecting declarations on violence that were presented" to my select committee, Jerry Cohen says. That extensive documentation the UFW assembles "not only showed violence by Teamster goons but also the bias of the whole Kern County legal administrative network, from District Attorney Al Lady on down. So having the Alatorre hearings was an anecdote to people like Lady. Richard gave people some faith that their grievances would be heard. And that's crucial if you're maintaining a nonviolent movement because if people lose faith, how do they stay nonviolent?"

Two farmworker strikers are killed only two months earlier. One dies at the hands of an Anglo Kern County sheriff's deputy who brutally clubs to death a slightly built and shy striker, Nagy Daifallah, 24, a Muslim from Yemen. Two days later and not far away, Juan de la Cruz, 60, a gentle dedicated family man and original member of the farmworkers union, is shot to death by a scab passing in a pick-up truck.

My subcommittee hearings help expose the human toll of the grape strike during that spring and summer of 1973: approximately 2,500 farmworker strikers are arrested for violating what are often unconstitutional antipicketing injunctions. Hundreds of strikers are beaten. Dozens are shot. Two are killed.

The beating death of Nagi Daifallah, followed a few days later by the shooting of Juan de la Cruz, are too much for Cesar. Following Juan's murder, Cesar, fearing more violence and deaths, orders a halt to all strike activities. He appeals to strikers who are willing to pick up their families and belongings, and travel to cities across the U.S. and Canada to organize a second boycott of California table grapes. Hundreds volunteer, joining UFW boycott organizers already in place throughout North America.

By October, as Lorenzo and I are conducting my select committee hearings, grape strikers and supporters are once again fanning out to distant cities organizing the boycott, "going throughout the country [and] letting everybody know what [growers] did here in California," Cesar says in his testimony to the committee.

I make it publicly clear at the outset of the hearings that they are not being held to debate the merits of the farm labor dispute. However, I know the hearings and the light they shine on the brutal events that have just taken place in the fields are setting the stage for the UFW's first attempt at sponsoring a legislative solution to the dilemma farmworkers have faced for 100 years trying to organize without any legal protections.

The select committee hearings in fall of 1973 are followed by introduction in early 1974 of Assembly Bill 3370, by John Burton and me. After John gets elected to Congress later that year, I carry the bill by myself. Sponsored by the UFW, it simply provides farmworkers with the right to hold secret-ballot elections to decide whether or not they wish to be represented by a union.

"We wanted a bill and wanted somebody we trusted to carry it for us because it was a risky calculation," Jerry Cohen, the UFW's chief lawyer, recalls. He and the union seek to use the bill to "establish in people's minds the notions of the industrial unit, holding quick elections for union representation within seven days and that if there are objections to the elections," having them dealt with after workers cast their ballots. These are crucial issues that have never been debated at the Capitol and, even though AB 3370 only deals with union elections, it is very important that the issues be decided in the UFW's favor before a more comprehensive farm labor law is introduced later.

Richard chairs a series of hearings by his Assembly Select Committee on Farm Labor Violence across central California in the wake of the bloody 1973 grape strike. As Cesar Chavez testifies at the hearing in Fresno, seated in front of him are committee consultant Lorenzo Patino, Richard, and Fresno Republican Assemblymembers Ken Maddy and Ernest Mobley. (Photo: Fresno Bee)

The industrial or single unit bargaining concept is really about race and discrimination. Under it, all farmworkers at a company, no matter what jobs they do, are part of the same bargaining unit that votes together on whether they want to be represented by a union and then, if the union wins, negotiates together for a union contract. The other system, called craft units, would see workers at a farm divided up among different bargaining units depending on what job, or craft, they do. In mandating the industrial unit, AB 3370 takes in the long history of ethnic and racial discrimination in California agriculture, including pitting one ethnic or racial group against another to compete for jobs or to break strikes. In those days, one unit, say irrigators or mechanics, can be reserved for higher-paid, more skilled workers, often Anglos or whomever the grower favors. Other units are for lower-paid stoop laborers who are often blacks or Chicanos. We call the craft concept a system of legally mandated ghettos in the fields. The industrial unit is actually also in the best interest of growers, who only have to deal with one union representing their field workers instead of several as is the case in industries where bargaining units are divided up on the basis of crafts.

So my AB 3370 seeks to end racism in the fields by requiring that all farmworkers bargain together with their employers in one industry-wide unit.

Holding elections quickly is essential in a highly seasonal industry such as agriculture. Under the National Labor Relations Act, it can be months before a union election is held at a company. That might be all right when workers go to their jobs every day, 52 weeks out of the year, at a factory. But since most farmworkers are migrant or seasonal, and the majority of them are employed during the relatively brief peak harvest period, delaying the election for months would disenfranchise most of the workers who will be long gone by the time the voting takes place.

Two parts of AB 3370 aim to ensure timely elections. The peak-season requirement says that a union petition can only be filed when a majority of the work force at a ranch is employed. Without it, a petition can be filed during the off-season when a tiny fraction of the farm work force, usually "steadies" who are more likely to favor the employer, are present and voting on behalf of the great majority who are absent.

The seven-day rule says elections also must be held within seven days after the filing of a valid petition signed by the majority of the workers saying they want the union.

The other key part of AB 3370 has to do with election objections. Under national labor law, objections from any of the parties can be decided before workers cast their ballots. Under AB 3370, any hearings on issues or objections are held after workers vote. The idea is not to delay voting and risk disenfranchising most of the farmworkers who are seasonal.

AB 3370 is an attempt to play out these critical issues and win the arguments over them before the union introduces a full-blown farm labor bill. What is missing from this 1974 bill are unfair labor practices, a detailed set of standards outlawing practices employers use to intimidate or fire workers and defeat unionization.

So there is a risk associated with moving AB 3370 forward. It is 1974, and Ronald Reagan's last year as governor. We don't think there is any chance the UFW can get the bill signed into law even if it passes the legislature that year. But if AB 3370 passes without unfair labor practices, growers can just fire or threaten farmworkers with impunity during union election campaigns and there is nothing anybody can do about it. We also believe that if the secret-ballot election measure passes the assembly, the Teamsters, thinking they will lose most elections at companies where they have contracts, will kill it in the state senate, a more conservative body.

Cesar is hospitalized in San Jose because of his chronic back condition when Jerry Cohen calls him to report that AB 3370 has passed the assembly in the summer of 1974. "Jerry, I think I'm going to throw up," Cesar responds, concerned it might become law. But, just as we think, the bill dies in the senate during the final days of the '74 legislative session after Governor Reagan comes out against it.

"The headline in the *San Francisco Examiner* is, "Teamsters kill election bill,"' Jerry says. "It worked out just right.

"So we had the best of all worlds," Jerry concludes. "We are able to establish the industrial unit, seven-day elections, the peak-season requirement, and postelection objections. It's all because Richard did the heavy lifting in getting AB 3370 as far as it went." The bill "set things up for the next year," when the historic Agricultural Labor Relations Act of 1975 is enacted. In 1975, "we didn't have to spend any capital arguing for seven-day elections, industrial units, or postelection hearings. By then they were a given. For me, those things are the essence of what made the farm labor act work. There was other nice stuff, but if we didn't have those three things, we would not have had a workable law.

"Farmworkers may not know it, but they owe Richard Alatorre a debt of thanks for that," Jerry says.

Help for the bill comes reluctantly from another place. "The other element of what Richard did was help in dealing with the rural Democrats," who in those days are all Anglos and close to or courting the growers, Jerry adds. "The question was can we get the votes" to move AB 3370 out of the assembly.

The bill comes up during the general election of 1974, and "Jerry Brown is running for governor" Jerry Cohen notes. "I put a call into him," asking him to call reluctant Democrats and urge them to vote for the bill. "As the Democratic nominee he is the titular head of the party in California. He isn't responding."

The UFW endorses then-U.S. Representative Jerry Waldie, from the eastern San Francisco Bay Area, for governor during the Democratic gubernatorial primary in spring 1974. "It may have been a negotiating tactic by Cesar to make the point with Brown that he had to pay attention to us," relates Jerry. "Remember, when I put in a call to Brown [for help on AB 3370 that summer], I didn't get a call back. It was not until we did some guerilla warfare that he responded. So Cesar was no dummy."

The UFW sends a delegation of farmworkers to Brown's campaign headquarters in San Francisco. I let Jerry coordinate the union's campaign for AB 3370 and against Jerry Brown out of my state Capitol office. "Finally, because of that pressure we got the candidate for governor to make some calls that enabled us to get the votes for AB 3370 on the assembly floor," Jerry says.

Of course, enactment of the farm labor law becomes Jerry Brown's first big achievement as governor. Like me, his relationship with Cesar and the farmworkers goes back to the 1960s. Jerry Cohen recalls Brown, as an elected community college trustee, comes to Delano in the late '60s, "wanting to know what we were doing legally with farmworkers." As California secretary of state in 1972, he goes to court to try and knock off the statewide ballot Proposition 22, the growers' antifarmworker initiative, because of massive fraud in collecting signatures to qualify it.

Still, the UFW thinks the union will hear from Jerry Brown after he is elected in early November. No such luck. "The only thing I can remember is hearing from someone who ran into Brown at the supermarket and the governor-elect

Among more than 10,000 people in Modesto for the end of the UFW March on Gallo on March 1, 1975, are (seated from left) John Maher, head of Delancey Street Foundation; Manuel Chavez, Cesar Chavez's cousin; Juana Chavez, Cesar's mother; Cesar Chavez; Richard; and Father Eugene Boyle.

saying, 'Well, Cesar blew it, didn't he'—referring to all the grape contracts the UFW lost in 1973."

Meanwhile, I introduce Assembly Bill 1, the UFW's comprehensive farm labor bill, as soon as the 1975–76 legislative session opens at the start of 1975. (They go in alphabetical order in introducing bills. As Alatorre, I get to introduce the first bill of the new session.) "AB 1 is our stalking horse," Jerry Cohen admits. "We loaded it up with stuff we knew would represent an extreme position," very pro-union provisions that the UFW doesn't think it can get. "It had to be stuff we could lose. It was our extreme negotiating position, where we start. But still no call from Brown."

Finally, after tens of thousands turn out in April to demonstrate against Gallo in a UFW-organized march from San Francisco to Modesto that I join, Cesar gets a call from the governor. "Brown tells Cesar, 'I have something I want to show you,'" Jerry Cohen remembers. They meet at the governor's home in the hills above Los Angeles. At the meeting are Cesar Chavez; Jerry Cohen; Rose Bird, the new secretary of food and agriculture; Herman Levy, a labor law professor who is working under Bird; and LeRoy Chatfield, a former Christian

Brother and top aide to Cesar who leaves the farmworkers to work for Jerry Brown in 1974, and is now part of his administration.

The governor presents Cesar and Jerry with a proposed bill, which the UFW finds unacceptable. "But while everyone is arguing about it, Jerry and Cesar take a walk outside," Jerry says. "When we were together driving back, Cesar said, 'I think things might work out, but we don't know yet.'

"Cesar and Brown were playing it very tight," Jerry continues. "LeRoy and I were shocked because Cesar never allowed himself to be alone with a politician. He didn't trust what the politician would represent later without witnesses. But Cesar told me, 'I think Jerry [Brown] is a good egg.' That was high praise for a politician from Cesar."

Nevertheless, the bill from the administration is still unacceptable.

Then the theater starts. Jerry Cohen holds a news conference in Sacramento where the UFW attacks the governor's bill. "Cesar tells me, 'You do that stuff in Sacramento. I'll float around the state.' He was going to state and community colleges, speaking with students [in front of reporters] and saying the governor doesn't know the difference between a tomato and a potato."

This guerilla theater causes a sit-down meeting in Sacramento. It's just Jerry Brown and Jerry Cohen at the governor's modest residence on the top floor of a state-owned apartment building at the corner of N Street and 14th Street across from Capitol Park—sparsely furnished with mattresses on the floor. "I had a short written list of what we needed and showed it to him," Jerry Cohen recounts. "There was stuff in there like circumventing rural courts" that had been so eager to issue grower-sought antipicketing injunctions during strikes. "There was a three-man, instead of a five-man, farm labor board. Then we wanted access [the right of union organizers to speak with workers in the fields during nonworking hours], complete lists of employed workers at each company, continued use of the secondary boycott, a make-whole remedy [making workers 'whole' for economic losses they suffer when growers break the law] and recognitional strikes [workers walking off their jobs to show their desire for union representation]. Jerry [Brown] didn't commit."

But all the turmoil leads to a series of weekend meetings in the governor's office where real negotiations start. The governor keeps the parties (the growers, Teamsters, and UFW) in different rooms inside the horseshoe, the suite of his offices on the first floor of the state Capitol annex surrounding an atrium. "Brown would go from the room where we were to the room where the growers were to the room where the Teamsters were," Jerry Cohen says.

At one point, "things weren't going well so we left and took our team out to a movie," Jerry recalls. "Brown sent the state police out looking for us. We went back for an evening meeting in the governor's office that lasted all night.

"A crucial point came when we were arguing about the confines of the boycott in the legislation and came to an impasse," Jerry says.

Rose Bird and her lawyers say Jerry Cohen is misconstruing the law. Jerry remembers that "Brown left and went to read the case law and returned to the

Cesar Chavez and Richard Alatorre confer in the mid-1970s. (Photo: Cathy Murphy)

meeting. 'Jerry's right,' he announced, 'let's keep on moving,'" Jerry Cohen continues. "Rose and her gaggle of attorneys left. That's when progress started to be made" in the negotiations. "That's when Howard Berman came in with Stephen Reinhardt, a great lawyer [and later U.S. circuit court judge], and we were able to resolve the boycott in the bill."

The new Brown administration measure, presented as a compromise between the parties, wins the support of the Teamsters and most of the state grower organizations. The compromise is announced by the governor before a gathering of farmworkers and supporters on the Capitol's west steps. It sails through both houses of the legislature with the two-thirds margin needed for an "urgency" statute that takes effect 90 days after enactment. The UFW wants the new law in place in time for the late summer and fall 1975 harvest seasons in California. Passed in early June, it takes effect in early September.

The UFW asks me to take a secondary public role in the unveiling, partly to reinforce the compromise nature of the final bill and partly because I'm not exactly very popular with the governor or the assembly Speaker, Leo McCarthy. I guess I'm a little disappointed at the time, but it's not a big deal. When the compromise agreement is reached that permits the farm labor law to move forward, a special meeting of the entire assembly is called to take up the measure. By then, the issue is drawing national attention. The assembly leadership calls the special session for 5 p.m. so it can be covered live by the local and national news media. It's a well-orchestrated event, with a limited number of members designated to speak on the bill. Jerry Cohen comes to me: Leo McCarthy doesn't want me to

Governor Jerry Brown gives a pat on the back to Richard after signing the Agricultural Labor Relations Act into law on June 6, 1975. From left are state Senate leader James Mills, Lieutenant Governor Mervyn Dymally, Jerry Brown, Richard, and state Senator George Zenovich. (Photo: Associated Press)

be one of the speakers. "But I want to let you know Cesar said that was unacceptable to him," Jerry quickly adds. McCarthy and his leadership team ultimately back down and allow me to speak on the bill for which I am a principal author.

McCarthy also doesn't want my name to get included in the "tomb stoning" of the bill, in which an important piece of legislation is named for its main authors—even though I play a big role in offering the UFW's bill and in the behind-the-scenes negotiations. It is considered common courtesy up to that point that whenever the subject matter is deemed historic, the people who have something to do with the bill get the recognition they deserve. Jess Unruh does it when he's Speaker. So does Bob Moretti. Willie Brown carries on the tradition later, even if a member is not much in favor with him.

Cesar also insists I be included. So the law becomes officially known as the Alatorre-Berman-Dunlap-Zenovich Agricultural Labor Relations Act of 1975, named to honor its four principal authors, all Democrats: Assemblymember Howard Berman of West Los Angeles, state Senators John Dunlap from Napa and George Zenovich of Fresno, and me.

"Cesar's posture was we were going to go in and do this law ourselves," Jerry says. "I went back to the main elements of Alatorre's 1974 bill. Without AB 3370, we would not have gotten the industrial unit, seven-day elections at peak season, or postelection objections."

In anticipation of large-scale organizing, elections, and later negotiations, Cesar dismantles the UFW's extensive and well-staffed boycott organization throughout the U.S. and Canada, bringing back the most talented organizers for election duty in California.

The agricultural industry agrees to the law, believing that the growers working hand in hand with the Teamsters means the UFW will be defeated in the elections that follow. It is a reasonable belief. When the employer is supporting and working for an incumbent union, it is very hard for an upstart, outside union to win. That conventional thinking is turned upside down in the early months of balloting under the farm labor law.

After more than 36,410 ballots are cast during the first two months of elections, the UFW wins 154 elections representing 22,278 farmworkers, or more than 48 percent of the total, according to election statistics kept by the UFW. The Teamsters win 91 elections and represent 10,994 of the workers, or 24 percent of the total. The vote to keep the UFW at the companies where the farmworkers union holds the contracts is overwhelming. At companies such as Interharvest, Pik'd Rite, and Christian Brothers, the vote for the UFW ranges from 96 to 100 percent.

However, at the 159 ranches where the Teamsters hold the union contracts, a majority of workers at 54 of them vote for the UFW; a majority at six other companies vote for no union. The Teamsters win at 85 other farms, but the alliance between the growers and the Teamsters, which is illegal under the law, plus massive unfair labor practices and election violations by the growers and Teamsters result in the filing of numerous objections to the Teamster victories. Many of them are later thrown out by the Agricultural Labor Relations Board, which oversees elections and enforcement of the law. Election results at another 14 ranches are contested and those elections are undecided.

During the first two months of the law's life, a survey by the UFW of its 11 election offices in California shows that 1,165 farmworkers have been fired for exercising their rights under the law.

The Teamsters Union, out of embarrassment from its poor showing in the elections, damage to its reputation from years of fighting the farmworkers and trying to avoid damages from a major lawsuit filed by the UFW, negotiates a jurisdictional agreement with Jerry Cohen and leaves the fields for good in 1977. As indicated, the UFW does very well in its elections, wins a number of union contracts, and sees its membership rise once again through the 1970s and into the early '80s. But in-the-field enforcement of the pioneering law, even under a governor like Jerry Brown, never matches what is promised. Within a short time after Republican George Deukmejian takes office as governor in early 1983, his political appointees basically shut down enforcement of the ALRA. As a result, UFW membership plummets once more. Towards the end of his life, Cesar bitterly regrets having shut down the boycott and placing so much faith in a legal process that in the end doesn't adequately protect farmworkers.

But for me those several years in the early and mid-'70s—including the grape strike, my select committee hearings and the following legislative battles in Sacramento—are the best times of my life.

Years later, in the late-'80s, after I'm elected to the city council, Cesar attends a political function for me at a supporter's home in Los Angeles. I guess there's a lot of prominent Latino elected officials and political players present. But after a while, Cesar finds my mother, who is sitting off by herself in the corner of a room. A couple of times I spot them talking together, just the two of them, for the longest time. Later, I ask her what they talk about. Me, she says. "Cesar said you're the only Chicano politician he met who has balls." My mother says it was the greatest compliment anyone ever said about me.

Chapter 7

The Speakership War

It is pretty much a foregone conclusion that once Bob Moretti relinquishes his position as Speaker of the assembly in 1974, he will be replaced by his choice as successor, then-Ways and Means Committee Chairman Willie Brown. Everyone believes—beginning with me—that Willie, one of the most intelligent members of the legislature, will become Speaker.

So the biggest surprise of the year inside the state Capitol is the ascension to the Speakership instead of Leo McCarthy, something no one in my circle believes will happen. Leo is someone I am never close to. It's probably because he is not an endearing, friendly, or outgoing type of person. He is very proper. He is very family oriented, a devoted husband and father. He's guided by his religious faith; Leo's a devout Catholic, which I can respect. He isn't one of the boys who hang out after hours around the Capitol at bars and restaurants, partaking in social activities.

Moretti is running in a formidable Democratic field in the June California gubernatorial primary election. It includes Secretary of State Jerry Brown; San Francisco Mayor Joseph Alioto; another San Francisco Democrat, state Senator George Moscone; and East San Francisco Bay U.S. Rep. Jerry Waldie, a member of the House Judiciary Committee who will vote the following July to impeach President Richard Nixon. Willie is Moretti's candidate. Brown will always be my choice as Speaker. We become close friends since I enter the legislature.

But in the months leading up to the June 1974 California gubernatorial primary, Moretti makes it clear to Brown that he wants to stay on as Speaker for as long as possible, using the position to raise money for his governor's race. We try telling Moretti there is nothing worse than someone running for some other office while he's occupying the Speakership. Moretti is confident he has enough control of his cadre of leadership and over the Democratic Caucus in the lower house to hold onto power and then turn it over to Willie after the election.

Well, Moretti is wrong. The June primary is held. Moretti loses to Jerry Brown. Unbeknownst to us, there is a move afoot by some of Moretti's closest lieutenants in the assembly. It becomes known when they call a Democratic Caucus for the purpose of electing a new Speaker right after the primary. We know McCarthy is behind it. What we don't know is that the *putsch* involves a double cross by the four other Latino legislators—Joe Montoya, Peter Chacon, Alex Garcia, and Ray Gonzalez—who are all supposed to be Moretti loyalists. We also don't know that some black members of the assembly who are committed to Willie—namely Leon Ralph, chair of the Rules Committee, and John Miller—are also in on the double cross.

The plot organizers all hold key leadership positions under Moretti, including the duel heads of the fabled Berman-Waxman machine in West L.A.: Henry Waxman, who is chair of the Health Committee, and Howard Berman, later rewarded by McCarthy who names him the youngest assembly majority leader in the institution's history. It is understood that as Westside liberals, Berman and Waxman will go for Willie both because he's Moretti's choice and because he will be the first black Speaker. The caucus is held. We assume certain things that should never be assumed. To our amazement, the caucus elects Leo McCarthy as Speaker. He takes office right away.

Assemblymember Jack Fenton and I tell Willie: "The problem with the black kid is he's living proof that blacks can't count because they all went to segregated schools."

What's still left is the November general election. A bunch of Willie Brown adherents decide we will seek out targeted Democratic candidates, try to get them to commit to vote for Brown for Speaker and then spend the summer and early fall months raising money and campaigning for them. We think some other Democrats might be convinced to switch over from McCarthy. We think this strategy really has a shot.

Since I never again face a contested election in my Northeast L.A. assembly district, all the money I raise during my two-year legislative tenure—including all the money from my huge Century Plaza Hotel fundraiser—goes to helping other Democrats or allies of mine get elected. Most of those political dollars get handed over to Willie for his candidates who he feels have a shot at getting into office.

The November election comes and goes. More new or re-elected assembly Democrats survive who are committed to McCarthy than to Brown. After every even-year election, the first order of business by the state assembly right after the beginning of the new year is convening to elect the Speaker. A small group of us diehards are still holding out for Willie to make one last-ditch effort. We even turn to some of our personal friends in the Assembly Republican Caucus such as Ken Maddy and Bob Beverly who we think might be convinced to vote for Brown. I remember meeting until late into the night with Willie and a handful of holdouts in Jack Fenton's Capitol office, desperately struggling to come up with any scheme, no matter how farfetched, to avoid McCarthy's victory the following day. It's not meant to be.

Now it's payback time. Willie and I end up on McCarthy's shit list. We both get moved up to modest offices on the sixth floor of the Capitol annex outside the elevators and next to the cafeteria. I stay in Siberia longer than Willie.

You can never hold Willie Brown down for long. He's just too savvy about the process and how the system works. Both Brown and McCarthy are from San Francisco. As I recall, around this time Dan Boatwright leaves the assembly to run for the state senate. That leaves the chairmanship of his standing committee, Revenue and Taxation, vacant. What better person to fill the opening than Willie. He makes his peace with McCarthy and Brown gets moved off the sixth floor and becomes Rev & Tax chairman. One by one, just about everyone else makes an accommodation with Leo as he settles into the Speakership for a while.

Everyone except me. I'm never interested in being Leo's friend. I don't like him. I respect him for what he stands for, but he will never be my Speaker. My attitude is if McCarthy keeps me on the outside, that's fine with me; it'll give me a lot of time to do my work on behalf of the Chicano Caucus, which I still chair because my fellow Chicanos in the assembly still don't want the job. And it gives me time to involve myself in mischief. Jack Fenton and I report crime or good government reform bills out of the Criminal Justice and Elections and Reapportionment committees that embarrass other Democrats—especially those from marginal districts. As Speaker, Leo is forced to kill them in fiscal committee or on the floor. It's during this period that I get heavily involved in a lot of farmworker stuff—going around the state to campaign for a legislative solution to farm labor strife and carrying the 1974 bill sponsored by Cesar Chavez and the United Farm Workers that is the predecessor of the Agricultural Labor Relations Act enacted the following year.

I don't get chairmanship of a standing committee until the later 1970s, and then it's not exactly a juice committee; Human Resources deals with welfare recipients, whom nobody thinks is a powerful force in California politics then or now. The only reason I get on the Labor Committee in 1979 is because Jack Henning, head of the state AFL-CIO, goes to McCarthy and insists on me because all the unions see me as a reliable advocate.

Remember that line from George Santana: "Those who choose to ignore history are destined to relive it." Bob Moretti makes the fatal mistake of using the Speaker's office as a platform to run for something else: governor in 1974. The bug of personal ambition for higher statewide office also bites Leo McCarthy nearly six years later. He wants to become a United States senator. He uses his Speakership as a platform from which to raise money and lift his profile among the electorate. By doing so he commits a classic political mistake.

Members, especially those in potentially tough races, rely on the Speaker to help them raise money and run their campaigns. It's one of the Speaker's most important duties every two years when all 80 members of the lower house are up for reelection. During the 1970s, there are always some contested campaigns in each election cycle. But it's safe to say that most members have relatively safe districts. The upcoming 1980 elections threaten to upset that balance. First, Jimmy Carter's presidency at the top of the ticket is seen as weak; Ronald Reagan ends up trouncing Carter that year. But the 1980 elections are also going to determine control of the legislature going into the all-important decennial reapportionment, the once-every-decade process by which state politicians re-draw legislative and congressional boundary lines. So it is even more important that as Speaker of the assembly, Leo McCarthy guarantees the electoral fate of his caucus members. It's not a good time for Leo to be distracted by his own run for a different office.

There are the beginnings of grumbling among assembly Democrats as soon as Leo surfaces his interest in running for statewide office. It's not like such dissatisfaction is unprecedented when people perceive that the interest of the Speaker is something other than making sure his members are taken care of. Initially it isn't much of a problem; few legislators are paying attention.

Not unlike Moretti before him, Leo feels he will be different because his base among assembly Democrats is loyal to him, including the assembly Minority Leader, Leo's top lieutenant, Howard Berman. The only problem is that Howard is a first class political strategist with his own crew of close allies and a veteran and highly effective political machine based in West L.A., with a reach in its own right across the state.

Just as the mutiny from within confronts Moretti without warning in 1974, the same elements of destruction take McCarthy by surprise. Leo thinks he's doing a good job as Speaker. He's raising money for his people; he relies on Berman and Berman's allies to raise a lot of it.

It all comes to a head at this big 1979 unity dinner for assembly Democrats at the Los Angeles Convention Center. There must be 2,000 to 3,000 people there. It is done very nicely, very glamorous—with an impressive showing of California's Democratic political elite because Leo has a big money raising operation in L.A. as he does in other places. It raises an exorbitant amount of money for McCarthy from Third House lobbyists and their clients, other interest groups, and traditional Democratic givers.

However, at the dinner a number of assembly Democrats start asking where all this money is going? People aren't sure whether the funds are going into the campaigns of the assembly Democratic team or for McCarthy's efforts to get himself elected to the U.S. Senate. The questions start turning into concerns and the concerns start turning into discontent. "What's happening?" is the question from many inside the Democratic Caucus. "I thought this is *our* money."

It doesn't help his cause that the only thing Leo talks about in his speech at the dinner is his senate bid. That just provokes talk about how too much of his time is being taken away from preparing for the 1980 election and reelection of Democrats in the assembly.

Not long after that, Howard Berman jumps into action. Leo's top lieutenant goes to his Speaker and tells him, "I think it's time for you to set a date when you're going to be leaving [the Speakership to run for the senate]. If you're unwilling to do it, then I'm going to call for a Democratic Caucus" to consider electing a new leader of the house.

Howard is a very analytical and methodical guy. He is concerned about who will control reapportionment in 1981. Remember, his brother, political consultant Michael Berman, is widely respected for his skills in taking apart and figuring out legislative districts, waging hard-nosed election campaigns, and mastering the intricacies of redistricting. Howard is also good at fanning concerns and doubts—some of them legitimate—about his erstwhile leader.

Howard is nothing but an operational guy. After the face-off with Leo, Howard starts hitting up his fellow Democratic lawmakers—except for the ones who remain loyal to McCarthy. Howard co-ops many of the L.A.-area members and some of the blacks; some have stood before with Willie Brown, who remains with McCarthy. None of this happens overnight; I'm sure the planning and spadework behind the Berman coup has been going on for a while. Howard has to be lining up his guys before he makes his move.

Now it is clear that the war is on. The end result is a classic Speakership struggle that begins in late 1979, and only builds in ferocity through the primary and general elections of 1980. The history of the California legislature has never before or since seen a battle to match the Berman-McCarthy Speakership fight.

Howard calls a meeting of the Assembly Democratic Caucus. He wins a majority, defeating Leo. The tradition is that the person who wins the support of the majority of the sitting members of the Democratic Caucus is the unanimous choice of the entire caucus. Howard mistakenly believes his caucus victory is tantamount to becoming Speaker. Then Willie Brown informs Howard and his crew: "Hey folks, I don't know if you've read the rules, but it takes 41 votes on the floor of the assembly to elect the Speaker."

Leo's people aren't going to vote for Howard. And the Republicans in the assembly won't help him because they are deathly afraid of Berman since they know he will be a formidable opponent when it comes to sticking it to them on reapportionment—and a fierce foe in organizing campaigns against Republican candidates.

Sides are taken. Everything at the Capitol becomes chaotic. The chaos jeopardizes everything, including everyone's legislative agendas, which become secondary to the mammoth internal political conflict that consumes assembly Democrats for a year. Both Leo and Howard start recruiting, fielding, financing, and running campaigns for competing candidates in the relatively few seats where there are no incumbents. Both men even recruit candidates to run against sitting incumbents committed to the other guy. That happens during the general election of 1974, when Willie wages a drive to unseat Leo from the Speakership.

But it happens on a much wider scale in 1980, beginning with the June primary legislative elections.

The level of personal bitterness is also unprecedented. McCarthy's faithful say, "You can't trust him [Howard]." It gets to the point where McCarthy acts like he's shell-shocked. He's Mr. Self-Righteous. "How could somebody who has been like a brother to me do this to me?" Leo asks. He becomes inept at first: "Poor me," and everything else. But the McCarthyites just say, "fuck this shit" and the blood bath begins. Millions of dollars are spent on political campaigns by both sides. That creates more divisiveness and hatred. Enemies are made. Friendships break apart. People play hardball. Dirty tricks in political campaigns set new records. Some members or staff people run keys along the sides of vehicles in the Capitol's basement garage belonging to partisans from the other side, leaving long ugly scratches.

I'm not with either one of them. I don't really care that much for Leo or Howard. Leo has finally done something for me: putting me on some decent committees and giving me a few committee chairmanships. My sidekick in the assembly from East L.A., Art Torres, and I are at some Democratic County Central Committee function in Los Angeles when Art tells me he's going to be the next majority leader of the assembly once Leo's re-elected Speaker. Art asks me to support Leo, saying what a prince of a guy Leo is and how Art Torres and Art Agnos—a former McCarthy aide, recently elected assemblymember from San Francisco (he defeats Harvey Milk) and one of Leo's chief lieutenants—are like brothers.

So I tell Art, "fine, I'm for Leo." After that, I say to myself, "Oh, well, that's good and everything else." I don't really care that much one way or the other. For me, the Speakership is a matter to be decided among the members of the Democratic Caucus. It's not anyone else's business; it's our business. That belief doesn't change—to this day. But how it works out for me does change soon enough.

Willie Brown's take is that people like him and me are in demand. "The minute the Speakership fight started every applicant for the Speakership, Berman or McCarthy, desperately wanted the warriors," Willie says later on. "We were the warriors. We became invaluable because their supporters [most of those who backed one or the other candidate for Speaker] were incapable of adding anything to their agenda and their support base. We were the people who possessed the skills and the ability to make a difference."

I always remember Christmas Eve 1979. It is 10 p.m. I'm at the house of my sister, Cecelia, in Pasadena. The phone rings. Cecelia answers and says, "Cesar Chavez is on the phone."

Most of the agricultural lobby supports passage of the Agricultural Labor Relations Act in 1975, because in those days most growers have signed contracts with the old Teamsters Union in efforts to keep Cesar's United Farm Workers out of their fields. The unqualified success of the second international grape boycott from 1973 to 1975, forces the growers to accept the farm labor

Cesar Chavez sits on the ground with Richard during a 1976 UFW political rally in East Los Angeles. Behind them is Father Luis Olivares.

law. But conventional wisdom in the labor movement says it is almost impossible for an outside union (the UFW) to prevail when employers are allied with and aggressively supporting an incumbent union (the Teamsters). So the growers are confident their chosen union, the Teamsters, will win most of the union representation elections held when the law takes effect as an urgency statute in September 1975.

The industry and the Teamsters seriously underestimate the loyalty and support Cesar and the UFW enjoy among farmworkers once they are able for the first time to choose a union for themselves. The UFW wins most of the elections it participates in. The Teamsters perform very poorly once farmworkers have the right to vote. International Brotherhood of Teamsters President Frank Fitzsimmons and Cesar Chavez sign a jurisdictional agreement in 1977, under which the Teamsters formally pull out of organizing farmworkers.

As soon as they see how farmworkers are voting, growers react by falsely claiming the Agricultural Labor Relations Board that enforces the law is biased towards the UFW. They spend the next several years trying to weaken or repeal the farm labor act. Most industry bills are killed in the legislature. But two make it to the governor's desk and Jerry Brown has to veto them. Worried that crippling amendments to the law will eventually be enacted, in 1978 Cesar is searching for the best way to stop that from happening. Many unions and the state AFL-CIO under Jack Henning hand out campaign contributions to lawmakers in Sacramento, nearly all of them Democrats, one politician at a time, usually in fairly modest amounts since there are so many of them.

Cesar turns for advice to the United Auto Workers and me (through Marc Grossman, my former student at UC Irvine who is now Cesar's spokesman and personal aide). Both the UAW and I say the same thing: cut a deal with the legislative leadership at the Capitol; have them stack the labor committees of one or both houses so antifarmworker bills never make it to the floors of the assembly or senate. By giving all the money directly to the Speaker, you hold him accountable for your legislative agenda.

Taking our advice, during the fall 1978 general election campaign Cesar goes to see Leo McCarthy at the Speaker's office in the state office building in downtown L.A. By this time, the UFW has money coming in from tens of thousands of farmworkers under union contract who contribute one day's pay a year to the UFW Citizenship Participation Day Fund, its PAC. Cesar says he and Leo exchange pleasantries and discuss the farmworkers' concerns. There is an understanding about what the workers' interests are; they are consistent at the time with Leo's solid history of supporting labor. At the end of the meeting, Cesar says the UFW wants to be as helpful as possible to Leo's political cause and hands him a union check for $38,000, adding, "There's more where that comes from."

Jump ahead to 1979. Lettuce and vegetable workers trying to renegotiate their UFW contracts walk out on strike against big growers in the Salad Bowls of the Imperial and Salinas valleys. Growers respond by fighting the union. Three foremen shoot to death Rufino Contreras, a 27-year-old union member and father of two young children, after he enters a struck lettuce field owned by the Mario Saikon ranch. Ku Klux Klan crosses are placed in struck fields. Growers go on public high school campuses, recruiting Anglo kids to break the strikes of the Chicano kids' parents. White townspeople show up in the fields outside El Centro to work as strikebreakers during a "Harvest Day." The spectacle is laughable since the scabs don't last more than a few hours attempting the backbreaking work of harvesting struck crops. Racial tensions are rising. The strike is turning ugly.

When violence is escalating during the 1973 grape strike, the UFW has me convince then-Assembly Speaker Bob Moretti to make me head of a Select Committee on Farm Labor Violence. We hold hearings to investigate strike brutality and discrimination by law enforcement agencies enforcing antipicketing injunctions.

In 1979, Cesar Chavez appeals to Leo McCarthy for help.

Something happens when you become Speaker. Now all of a sudden you can't just consider your own politics; you have to reflect the politics of everybody else who is part of your caucus. That's what comes with the leadership.

Leo turns to Assemblymember Floyd Mori, a Democrat from Pleasanton in the East Bay, appointing him to chair a Joint Committee to Oversee the Agricultural Labor Relations Board. A Japanese American, Mori is very close to the ag industry. Instead of looking into abuses of farmworkers during the '79 vegetable industry strike, Mori uses his committee to make life miserable for the ALRB and the UFW, sometimes intervening on behalf of individual growers in cases where they are accused by the state of breaking the law. A Mori committee consultant shows up at the ALRB's offices in Sacramento for a settlement conference involving charges against a grower arm in arm with the employer's attorney. Cesar feels betrayed by McCarthy.

So when Howard Berman, a longtime farmworker friend who coauthors the 1975 farm labor law along with me, comes to Cesar asking the union to support him for Speaker, it's not a hard sell. Dolores Huerta, the UFW's first vice president, also loves Howard and hates Leo.

As my sister hands me the phone, I wonder how Cesar knows where I can be reached.

"Hi, Cesar, how are you doing?" I ask.

"Hi, Richard," he replies. It's like he's suffering.

"How did you find me?" I ask.

Cesar laughs. He doesn't really answer and I don't know to this day how he finds me. Finally, he gets around to what he's calling about.

"You know about my relationship with Leo McCarthy?"

"Absolutely, I understand," I say. "He's an asshole. In my eyes they're both the same—Leo *and* Howard. The difference is that one already screwed you and the other one hasn't done it yet."

"Well, you know, you may have a point," Cesar says. Then he goes off on what a wonderful guy Howard Berman is. It's like listening to a speech I've already heard Dolores Huerta make about Howard.

"We're going to get heavily involved for Howard," Cesar tells me.

"Yeah. What are you asking me to do?"

"I don't want to talk about it now. I'd really like for you and Art [Torres] to come and meet with me."

"It's Christmas, Cesar."

"I was thinking right after Christmas Day. I'd really like to get together with you guys. Meet me in San Jose."

"What are you asking?" I repeat.

"I want you both to support Howard Berman."

"I don't need a meeting. If that's what you want, I'm there."

"Well, I want to get together with you *and* Art."

"Cesar, I'm going to tell you something: I think you're going to have a real hard sell with Art. I was just with him and I think Leo agreed to make him majority leader of the assembly. You know how Art is; he gets heavily involved in all this stuff. He's going to tell you Leo's like a brother to him."

"You think you can get him to go [to the meeting]," Cesar says.

"Yeah, I think I can get him to the meeting."

Even though I'm doing what he wants, I also tell Cesar about my belief that the Speakership is an in-house play; members of the assembly are the ones who elect the Speaker.

I call Art the next day. He's in Sacramento, I think.

"What's happening, brother?" Art starts out.

"Cesar just called and he wants to have a meeting with you and me in San Jose." Remember, Art works for Cesar as the UFW legislative director for the year or two before his first successful run for the assembly in 1974.

"What do you mean?" Art replies, all concerned.

"He just called."

"This is Christmas."

"Look, Art, I'm flying back today [to Sacramento] and I thought we'd go tomorrow over to San Jose."

"But what does he want?"

"Art, he didn't tell me. But he asked if you and I would do him the favor of meeting with him."

"But what do you think he wants?" Art keeps coming back to it.

I convince him to do it. I don't have a good feeling about all of this. We drive from my house in Sacramento to San Jose, to the law offices of Cesar's oldest son, Fernando, on The Alameda, a historic street near downtown. All the way during the drive Art lets his thoughts roam. He is very nervous. I ain't telling him I already told Cesar I'm with him.

At one point Art says, "Cesar better not ask me to be for Howard because I'm not going to do it because this is a legislative function and shouldn't be determined by outside interests"—and all that stuff. I actually agree with Art's position, but it's Cesar and the farmworkers asking, so that settles it for me.

"Yeah, fine," is all I say to Art.

We arrive. Art and Fernando Chavez, who works in Art's '74 assembly race and is a friend to both of us, bullshit for a while. Cesar arrives and embraces Art and me. "Hi brother, how are you?" he says to Art.

Art is not real happy. Cesar proceeds to talk about history and about what a rotten mother fucker Leo McCarthy is. And how Cesar doesn't like politicians, but both Art and I are different.

He tells Art, "You grew up with us" and blah, blah, blah. He tells me, "And Richard, you've been an ally" and dah, dah, dah. I turn and look at Art.

"Leo's like a brother to me," Art explains. "He's eaten at my house" and blah, blah, blah.

Cesar just sits there, listens and nods. Finally, he says to us, "The union is going all out for Howard. Are you with us?"

Standing behind Cesar Chavez in the mid-1970s are Assemblymembers Art Torres and Richard Alatorre.

I turn to Art again: "I have different reasons for going for Howard. From the time I got elected, Leo's screwed me. I know you have a relationship with him. He made you chairman of [the assembly] Health [Committee]. But he also screwed the farmworkers and me." I announce my support for Howard.

That just puts Art up against the wall. He has no choice. Art meekly says, "Yeah, okay. But I don't know how I'm going to do this"—meaning how he's going to tell Leo.

Cesar must be telepathic. "I think you ought to call him right now. Might as well do it."

Cesar makes Art call Leo right there from Fernando's law office. It is probably one of the more unpleasant conversations Art Torres ever has with anybody.

Leo's never good at hearing bad news. But an even worse conversation is the one Art has with his (former) good friend, Art Agnos, Leo's chief guy in the assembly.

One thing about Art Torres: whenever he involves himself in something he puts his heart and soul into it. First he becomes a key lieutenant for Leo. Then, after Art and I switch to Howard, Art becomes a key lieutenant for Howard. Later, when we both switch from Howard to Willie Brown, Art becomes a key lieutenant for Willie.

I switch my vote from Leo to Howard (and later, of course, to my friend, Willie), but never try to convince any other member of the assembly to do the same. The only thing I offer by way of explanation to Cesar in December 1979 is, "I gave my word to Leo, but I never liked Leo." I never buy the line from Cesar and Dolores that Howard is this righteous guy.

"Cesar," I say, "I'm doing this because of my love and commitment to you and because Leo screwed me for years." And then I reiterate that the difference between them is that Leo screwed the farmworkers and Howard hasn't—yet. "But remember, he's fully capable of doing it." (Howard turns out to be a true friend to the UFW over the decades. He becomes the union's chief champion on Capitol Hill after going to Congress in 1982, getting the union to negotiate with the agricultural industry to create the landmark bipartisan AgJobs immigration reform bill for farmworkers beginning in 1999. It lays the groundwork for the bipartisan comprehensive immigration reform bill negotiated by Cesar's successor, UFW President Arturo Rodriguez, and the nation's growers that the U.S. senate passes in 2013.)

This frenzy of activity occurs between Christmas Day and New Year's Eve. Art immediately becomes immersed in Howard's Speakership campaign operation. Meanwhile, for me it's vacation time.

From January through the June 1980 primary, Leo and Howard put up candidates to run against each other in assembly districts across California. They fund the races and send in political consultants to manage the campaigns. It's an all-out war. Multimillions of dollars are spent doing battle among Democrats.

The war continues from after the primaries through to the November general election. Each side does everything it can to make sure its candidates beat their Republican opponents in the fall. Art is in all the strategy meetings with Howard and has negotiated with him to become assembly majority leader when Howard wins. My attitude in the midst of the political carnage is that it's not my problem. I'm for Howard, but except for the fact I give a little money to some of Howard's candidates, I don't go out of my way to help or hurt anyone.

Michael Berman, Howard's political consultant brother, and Carl D'Agostino, Michael's partner and also a political genius, periodically call me for advice. I've known both of them for a long time and try to be helpful.

Howard Berman emerges from the primary and general elections more or less victorious. More of his candidates get elected than Leo's. Howard's position within the Democratic Caucus is strengthened. But that doesn't change the reality that you still need 41 votes on the assembly floor. So Howard needs the votes of at least some McCarthy supporters to become Speaker.

Berman can't seek to cut a deal with the Republicans. They don't trust him because he's such a good political operator and so highly partisan the GOP knows he will screw them during reapportionment, which is the real end game.

I don't think Howard can win over many McCarthy members. Things have become too bitter. There is so much ill will at the end of the yearlong election cycle. For example, during the June primary campaign, Jack Fenton goes to the Bermans, who give him their word they will not campaign against him in his Montebello-based district. Jack is gruff but well-respected, a good labor guy; for several years he carries the bill extending unemployment insurance benefits to farmworkers that Ronald Reagan vetoes and Jerry Brown signs in 1975. Jack takes Howard at his word and doesn't mount much of a campaign. Just days before the election, the Bermans dump a bunch of mailers for Marty Martinez, their handpicked candidate, who is Chicano but viewed by many as being weak. By the time the Bermans' mail program hits voters' homes it is too late for Jack, who is totally unprepared, to respond, and he loses the election. Fenton's defeat is unprecedented; it comes to symbolize the collateral damage of the Speakership battle.

There are also indications that the Bermanites have helped some Republicans against Democrats committed to McCarthy. To make matters worse, instead of being conciliatory, Michael Berman, thinking his brother has won the Speakership, treats McCarthy backers as vanquished foes. By the end of 1980, McCarthy loyalists are even more determined not to support Howard. They see him as too Machiavellian to ever be trusted.

By now, Leo is so wounded he can never get reelected Speaker. Some in his camp start talking about an alternative candidate. At that point Leo, recognizing reality, has no problem with it; he just wants to make sure Howard doesn't get the Speakership. The name of Frank Vicencia, a well-liked Portuguese American from Bellflower in L.A. County, is thrown about. It becomes clear he isn't going to make it. Then people focus on Willie Brown.

While still in the assembly, Willie is making a lot of money with his very lucrative law practice. At that time the Speakership still counts for a lot. Considered the second most powerful position in state government after the governorship, it holds a great deal of power. So I guess somebody like Willie never dismisses the idea of becoming Speaker. He is initially a casual observer of the Berman-McCarthy fight. As the campaign wears on, he is never a McCarthy confidant, but becomes operationally involved against Howard.

"In the Speakership fight, I was for McCarthy and Richard Alatorre was for Berman," Willie confirms. "But that was not a true assessment of where we really were. We didn't want either of them. But the hand that was dealt was the hand we played. That whole year there was never a separation of Alatorre from his natural base even though he supported Berman. When it became very clear that Berman was not viable, Richard became the key to establishing my candidacy."

Willie calls me in mid- or late-November. Through a combination of McCarthy supporters and assembly Republicans, he feels he can get to 41 votes. Obviously, Willie has most of McCarthy's people, especially the diehards who stick with Leo through thick and thin. For them, there is no way Howard will ever become Speaker. Others are just tired of the warfare and looking for a compromise candidate. Willie has a relationship with some Republicans. When he runs the Ways and Means Committee, he can always count on Frank Lanterman and a few other Republicans in a pinch to get out key legislation. That is a different era, when the Lantermans and Paul Priolos and other members of the moderate wing of the GOP (when it has one) know they can deal with Willie Brown. It isn't until the birth of the so-called Proposition 13 babies—conservative Republican ideologues elected in the wake of passage of the 1978 tax-cutting ballot measure—that GOP legislators begin setting as their goal the destruction of government. In 1980, there are still GOP moderates left standing.

Willie goes to see Carol Hallett, the assembly minority leader. Along with her colleagues, she is dead set against Howard becoming Speaker. Willie negotiates a deal with Hallett to get a sufficient number of Republicans to vote for him for Speaker. Hallett and the GOP later dispute the specifics of the deal. Nobody is smart enough to negotiate with Willie. What the Republicans think they get and what they actually get are two different things. Willie promises they will get more staff and the perks of power at the Capitol. He keeps that promise, which is when the staff and budget of the legislature begin to significantly increase.

The Republicans are afraid of Berman because of their fears over what will happen to them in reapportionment. So Willie promises he will be fair in how the Republicans are treated when redistricting happens the following year. There has to be clarity when you're dealing with Willie. To him, being fair means giving assembly Republicans staff and resources to come up with their own reapportionment proposals, which he does. That doesn't mean Brown promises they get to have their way on the assembly and congressional redistricting plans that eventually get approved. Ironically, by avoiding having Howard Berman do reapportionment in 1981, they end up getting me—and I treat the Republicans as bad or worse than Howard would.

Since holding out for Willie for Speaker until the bitter end in 1974, I tell him, "Hey brother, if the time ever comes—and it's serious and I can make a difference and I can see you've learned how to count to 41—I'll always be there for you."

During that phone call to me in November 1980, Willie says, "Okay, brother, I told you I'd never bother you again if you weren't going to make a difference. If you and Art go with me, I got the Speakership."

"The farmworkers are important to me," I respond. "They're with Howard. I need a commitment from you that I don't need to worry about their interests not being protected. And I need to know Chicanos' interests will be protected in reapportionment."

"You don't even have to ask me," he replies. "I'm there."

I know Willie enough to know he will never double cross me.

Now handling Art Torres is another thing.

Brown tells me Wally Karabian, my mentor and assembly majority leader when Bob Moretti is Speaker, is setting up a meeting Art and I will attend in Wally's law office at the Wilshire Grand Hotel in downtown L.A. "I'll be phoning into the meeting at a certain time to ask both of you to support me," Willie says. "But I wanted to talk with you first."

"Count me in," I say.

I'm at the meeting with Wally and Art. Wally is talking about the fact Willie is now in the Speaker's race. Willie calls. Wally puts him on the squawk box. Willie talks to both of us like he doesn't already have me on board—kind of the same drill Cesar did with Art and me nearly a year earlier in San Jose.

"I'm a candidate," Willie announces to us. "I think with you two on my side, you're talking to the next Speaker of the assembly."

Also just like the meeting with Cesar, I chime in: "Yep, you've got my commitment," blindsiding Art.

"How about you, Art?" Willie asks.

I don't recall if it happens by the end of this conversation or whether we call Willie back. But before we leave Wally's office, Art is in too.

"Richard played a much greater role in making me Speaker than most people know," Willie explains much later. "Richard had one obligation: when he let the world know he was a Willie Brown vote, he really brought two votes—his and Art's." In addition to the Republicans rounded up by Carol Hallett, "I had to have the two guys who ought to be core with me. Richard had to be part of the first 10 Democrats who would come over to me. And Richard had to bring Art with him. That was a tough decision to make because they were going to vote against the Democratic Party's alleged control" of the assembly.

Art's conversation with Howard might be even worse than the similar one he has a year before with Leo, only because Michael Berman, Howard's brother, is less forgiving than McCarthy. Michael holds a grudge against Art for a long time after that because of what Art does to Howard. The Bermanites never forgive Art for jumping ship to Willie because he is so operational in their campaign, attending the meetings and assuring himself a leadership position under a Berman Speakership. Howard and Michael get mad at me too, but I find out through somebody else that they're more understanding with me because of the relationship Willie and I have. Michael later tells me that as soon as Willie Brown gets into the Speakership race after Leo and Howard deadlock following the November elections, Michael knows I'm gone from Howard's camp because of my friendship with Willie. However, it is a double whammy for Art because he ends up being hated by both Howard and Cesar—but especially by Dolores Huerta, who holds grudges better and longer than anyone I've ever met.

Right away I put a call into Cesar: "Brother, Howard will never be Speaker. It's over for him. Willie Brown is my friend. You know that. You have my word that your interests will always be protected under a Brown Speakership. You've got a liberal black guy who has committed to me that your interests will be protected. I would never allow Willie or anyone else to do something against your interests."

I also remind him that electing the leadership is up to the members of the legislature. He doesn't want to hear any of my explanations.

Willie Brown and Richard at the UFW's 1982 political convention in Salinas. Willie Brown is one of two dominant figures in Richard's political life. The other is Cesar Chavez.

"Willie can't be trusted," replies Cesar, who is very unhappy with me. "He's making book with the Republicans. You betrayed me. How could you do this to the farmworkers"—and everything else.

There isn't much for me to say, except to repeat that Cesar will never have to worry about either Willie or me. "You need someone close enough to Willie to make sure nothing bad happens," I add.

I never regret switching over to Willie, even though it costs me my relationship with Cesar—at least for a while. Willie and I share more than personal friendship. He gets hit a lot for caving into special interests, the price you pay for political leadership. But deep down we share a common commitment to poor people of color. It comes from how we grow up, me in the barrios of East L.A. and Willie in segregated East Texas. "I don't think Richard Alatorre's experience is dramatically different from those of us who were part of the efforts to make democracy a reality for people of color and for disadvantaged and underprivileged people," Willie says. "Before he ran for office, Richard didn't just sit around and think, 'I can do more for the world of Latino liberation if I stop teaching and start acting [by running for the assembly].' The opportunity presented itself [in 1971]. His motivation like the rest of us was he wanted to do everything possible to make life better for the people he cared about."

Despite what he says, I don't think Cesar is much into the whole fight. But Dolores is since she does most of the stuff on behalf of the UFW with Howard, who she greatly admires. I start getting calls, starting from Dolores: "You betrayed Cesar." The censures and the threats go downhill from there. I never respond in kind—or hardly at all.

The UFW isn't finished with Art and me. The union, I think with input from Howard and Michael Berman, go after Art Torres in his district, trying to pressure both of us to return to Howard's camp. Both of our Eastside assembly districts are logical targets since they're heavily Chicano with lots of farmworker supporters. I believe they especially target Art for a couple of reasons.

Cesar always views Art as being a son who goes wayward on his father. So the union's leadership feels more betrayed by Art—not to lessen the betrayal they feel against me. But Howard and Cesar—and the people close to them—also know of the depth of my friendship with Willie; Art doesn't have the same relationship. That doesn't make it all right in their eyes, but I don't give a shit. I'm going with a person who is my friend and everybody knows it—and many expect me to do it.

Then there's the fact that other than switching my vote twice (from Leo to Howard and then from Howard to Willie) I'm never involved in the strategic or operational sides of the protracted Speakership war. Art is deeply involved with McCarthy, Berman, and Brown.

I also think a political decision is made by the Bermans and the UFW that they have a shot of possibly turning Art around if they put enough pressure on him, which they try doing. The UFW pickets Art's district office and his house, which outrages him. "How could they do that?" he tells me. "My own house, in front of my children" and all that. Art's wife at the time, L.A. television news anchor Yolanda Nava, inflames things even more.

"It's horrible," I say.

"Why aren't they doing that to you?" Art asks

"I guess they're more mad at you than they are at me."

The UFW sends organizers into Art's district. They go door-to-door convincing people to sign cards or petitions trying to get him to change his mind. It doesn't work. Even when facing vitriolic opposition—like when the Chicano bilingual teachers and administrators from CABE, the California Association of Bilingual Educators, picket me over my bilingual reform bill—I always try not taking it personally. Of course, it's easy for me to say that since I'm not being targeted by the union beginning right after Thanksgiving in 1980. But not taking things personally isn't in Art's make up.

The pickets outside his home call Art a "sell out." "How could you sell out Cesar?" they ask. "Willie Brown is going to make a deal with the devil. The Republican Party will take control." Those things aren't true, but it doesn't matter. You don't always have to tell the truth when you accuse somebody of something. The UFW is doing what it does best: using pressure to accomplish its political agenda, in this case trying to salvage all the hard work and resources the union spends over a year's time to advance Berman's chances at becoming Speaker, even though Cesar apparently doesn't understand Howard's time has already passed. Art feels personally betrayed too because he believes he is a loyal soldier for Cesar.

"Richard Alatorre brought himself and Art [Torres] in the third week of November over into my camp and away from Berman, to the great displeasure of Berman and to the farmworkers who marched on Art's house," Willie observes. "None of which fazed Alatorre at all."

There's nothing I can do for or about Art. When things heat up against him, I have another conversation with Willie. I make it clear to him: "Look, brother, whatever happens I have to have an assurance from you that the farmworkers will be protected. They're out there doing what they think is right."

"Brother, you never have to worry about that," Willie assures me. "I'll never sell out the farmworkers no matter what they do."

"My reputation is at stake," I tell him. "I've fought too hard to see everything given away to the Republican assholes who want to destroy the union."

"Those aren't my politics anyway," Willie affirms. "I would never do anything to betray Cesar or his movement."

"Fine, I'm there to guarantee that," I add.

"You have my word," Willie says.

From that time forward I make it my job to make sure Cesar and the UFW are protected against the Republicans and rural Democrats (all of whom are then Anglos) who wish to wipe out all the union's gains of more than a decade. I feel confidant things are going to be fine if I do my work.

Are there moments of apprehension? I never believe Willie Brown will double cross me over the farmworkers. But there are other forces at work that hope to see that happen. I learn during my time in Sacramento that California is a strange state. The interests and commitments of the community in my L.A. district where the UFW is very much admired and respected aren't the same everywhere, especially among the Anglo community in places like Fresno and Riverside that may elect Democrats but where the agricultural industry is very strong. (The reality even in those places changes with demographic trends and the mushrooming political influence of Latinos during the last few decades.) I realize the coming together of different interests at the Capitol can spell problems for causes—like the UFW—that are so simple for me. It just means I have to be vigilant in order to keep my promise to Cesar.

I'm sure it is a very uncomfortable time for Art Torres. I feel bad for him and tell him, "Art, don't worry, you'll be fine." He reminds me: "It's easy for you to say. They're not picketing your house."

I too still get comments about how I'm a sell out from people, some friends or supporters of mine, who are just doing the UFW's business. But it's not the first time I've been on the receiving end. I've been Bogarted by the best; remember La Raza Unida Party causing me to lose my first assembly race in 1971. What is hurtful is anybody questioning my commitment to my principles and things that drive me and are part of my activist and political history: the rights of Chicanos and farmworkers and working men and women. All of them are strongly embedded in my philosophy of government and my life. When they're questioned, it hurts. But you have to move on.

I finally feel very comfortable about the person I'm supporting for Speaker. Much of his history in public policy is all about working for civil rights and representing the oppressed. It is not outmatched by anybody in the legislature. Yeah, I know, we all whore out to this or that special interest at one time or another. That's the price of getting and holding power—and we usually don't hurt anybody who matters to us. I can honestly say Willie never disappoints me in terms of the issues I hold as important.

There is a sense of relief within the institution when the whole Speakership fight is over. People are tired of a fight that goes on over two damn years—all the divisiveness and the money flowing down the toilet. It's like we forget the real issue that should be front and center in elections: electing Democrats and defeating Republicans. That becomes secondary to the political agenda of who is going to be Speaker. At a time when we should be concentrating on not cannibalizing each other and instead going after Republicans, it is not healthy. (An unintended consequence of the fight is probably electing more Democrats than might otherwise have been the case since both the Berman and McCarthy sides pour unparalleled resources into getting their respective candidates elected in the 1980 general election.) The Speakership contest dramatically changes directions at different times. It lasts much longer than anyone expects. There is never a nastier or more prolonged fight for Speaker with more far-reaching impacts on members, political financing, and California politics. It is something we hope will never happen again—and it doesn't.

Fortunately, the following year reapportionment heals the wounds (among most) within the Democratic Caucus and guarantees the election of Democrats and the longevity and the history-making tenure of Willie Brown's Speakership.

It is fabulous when Willie becomes Speaker. I've been waiting for that day since 1974, when it is (incorrectly) understood he is the heir apparent to succeed Moretti. When the day finally comes, I tell Willie, "Well, the black guy finally overcame the segregated schools in Texas and learned how to count."

I don't think Brown, in his mind, ever questions his credentials or political principles as a Democrat. But early on in his Speakership, there are some who either don't want to see the battle come to an end or support other candidates—and Willie Brown does not overwhelm them. Then the conspiracy theories come into play since it takes assistance from the Republicans to make Willie Speaker even though historically the ruling party solely gets to elect the Speaker.

That's one issue Willie faces. There is a much more important one he tries to figure out: what does he really owe these people, the Republicans? He tells me, "They stuck their necks out to elect me Speaker. What is it we should do for them? I'm going to have a little more democracy [in the assembly], but every committee will be controlled by a majority of Democrats and by somebody [a chair] who is ultimately loyal to me as Speaker and leader of the Democrats." Once that reality takes shape, there are still discussions and commentary, mostly by local yokels that Willie has sold out to the Republicans. But it's mostly outside the Democratic Caucus.

There are still rumors circulating around the Capitol and outside it. The ones who lose—the Bermanites—might not expect to get anything good initially from a Brown Speakership; you expect to get shit committee assignments, reduced staff, and fewer accoutrements of power that any Speaker hands out as rewards to friends and punishments to enemies. That's what happens to the losing side of previous Speakership contests; it's what happens to me in 1974.

Willie is smart enough to know he needs to heal the house. One thing about Brown is he understands talent; he likes smart people. He knows all of the talent certainly doesn't reside with the people on your side. So he carefully begins the process of bringing the house back together. When you think about it, no intelligent person in his right mind who gets into that office at that moment can afford to continue the fight—and Willie is nothing but intelligent and perceptive.

The real proof of the pudding is what is going to happen about reapportionment. There is rampant speculation about the "deal" Willie cuts with the Republicans over redistricting. One of his first appointments is making me chair of the Elections and Reapportionment Committee, which does redistricting once a decade—but is a backwater committee the other nine years. It's not an assignment I'm going after. But Willie knows he can trust me, that I will never do anything to hurt him, and that I will make preserving his interests—and his Speakership—my first and foremost priority.

The first thing I ask him is, "I know reapportionment starts with the Speaker. Tell me if there are things I need to worry about and be aware of—any deals you have made I should know about—because I don't want to hear about them later on."

"No, don't worry," Brown responds.

"Good," I say, "because I ain't. If you promised something then I have total deniability. I'll just do what I'm going to do in spite of you."

"No, you don't have to worry about that," Willie adds. "I'm going to give them [the GOP] staff and money so they can do their own work on reapportionment. But we clearly need to keep our majority" at the end of the process.

There are a few times while I'm heading up reapportionment during 1981 when Willie thinks I should be helpful—or at least deferential—to Republican leaders like Carol Hallett, Bob Naylor, or Ross Johnson. But I don't listen to Brown about that; it is never going to be part of my job. Once he turns over reapportionment to me, I have four goals: fuck the Republicans, do everything I can to take care of Chicanos, come up with a redistricting plan that will pass legal muster, and eventually get rid of the potential for another Democratic mutiny in the assembly by sending Howard Berman and his key cohorts away to Congress. I use pressure to comply with the federal Voting Rights Act as the excuse to achieve what I ultimately end up doing in righting the longtime wrongs Chicanos have suffered in redistricting. And, as Willie puts it, "when we won the Speakership, one of the first things we did was get rid of all the opposition [from the Berman camp]: we put them in positions where they had to cooperate with our administration. The most important of those positions was reapportionment"—which means getting Phil Burton to create congressional seats for Howard and his friends.

Rural Democrats give Willie a lot of support when he becomes Speaker. There are former McCarthy backers like John Thurman and Norm Waters. Other rural Democrats are Bermanites like Jim Costa and Rick Lehman. All of them either introduce, co-author, or support grower legislation to stop Cesar and the UFW from making any further progress by weakening or even repealing the farm labor law. All those bills go to the Assembly Labor and Employment Committee.

New committee chairs and members are selected by the Speaker at the beginning of each new two-year legislative term—and especially with the start of a new Speakership. Committee chairs and memberships can pretty much stay the same if there are no changes in the party and Speaker making the appointment decisions. But it is very common for committees to be reshuffled and reconstituted at the start of a fresh legislative term. I know Willie's going to do it in early 1981.

To keep the pledge I make to Cesar, I ask Willie to put me on the Labor Committee. I tell him, "I want to make sure labor has a solid lock on what does or does not come out of that committee."

Brown agrees: "I'm putting you on the committee to protect Cesar's interests and show him what I've stated is in fact the truth—I'm not in it to destroy the farmworkers. That's not my politics."

"Okay, now let's talk about who else is on [the] Labor [committee]," I say. We add reliable Democrats so the farmworkers' interests will be taken care of, enough of them to kill anything we don't want. That's critical because if antifarmworker legislation does get out of Labor, we will likely have to kill it on the assembly floor, which makes it much more difficult because rural Democrats will vote with the Republicans—and because it puts Democrats from marginal districts on the spot.

While all this is going on, the UFW's Dolores Huerta is still in charge of lobbying for the union in Sacramento. She has her person, Sal Alvarez, who I like, doing a lot of the day-to-day work at the Capitol. It doesn't matter what I've arranged with Willie—or my protests that things will be taken care of for the farmworkers. Dolores dislikes me for betraying her hero, Howard Berman. She and Sal engage in constant shit disturbing, rumor-mongering, and trying to stir up the pot inside and outside the building, among Chicanos and with anyone who will listen to them.

It's not like it turns out there is anything to worry about. I don't think killing the grower bills in the Labor Committee will take a lot of rocket science given how Willie and I have set things up, packing it with a lot of urban liberal Democrats. It's almost a bulletproof committee—not just for the UFW but for the rest of the California labor movement that also benefits. Nothing antilabor is getting out of that place no matter what the issue is. Every time an antifarmworker bill is set for a hearing, I don't take anything for granted: I go to the Democrats I'm counting on and make sure they're voting "no"—even though after a while I can see there is no chance the bills will be anything but dead.

It seems my two major issues then are making damn sure my promise to Cesar comes true and trying to navigate my way through the bigger issue of the day: making the right moves on reapportionment so whatever questions people have about my ability to get the job accomplished—and there are many—are being answered.

Unlike my *compadre*, Art Torres, who is still smarting from the UFW campaign against him late the year before, I never say a bad word to anyone about Cesar or the union—even when Dolores is going around bad mouthing me. Art's reaction is one of personal outrage. He vows to get even for what he thinks he and his family go through, the indignities he feels he suffers. He lashes out at Cesar and the UFW a lot, even if much of the time he thinks he's talking to people, especially Chicanos, in confidence. In my experience, there is no such thing. I just assume everything Art or I say to people will get back to Cesar. I'm right.

I try to tell Art: "To me, that's a page out of history. You got to get over it. You can't take your anger out on innocent people"—meaning the farmworkers. "You worked for CRLA [California Rural Legal Assistance] and the UFW," I remind Art. "The needs of those people haven't gone away. What happened was in the heat of battle. Now it's over. We got to move on. Don't do anything that will hurt you later on because of the anger you feel now."

But I keep hearing from other people that Art is still openly expressing his bitterness over actions that took place during the Speakership struggle.

For my part, I never say anything about Cesar in public or private. I know he isn't happy; he doesn't like to lose. But I tell him when my vote switches to Willie that regardless of the outcome [of the fight for Speaker], I will never betray the things I believe in even if there are some hard times between us. For me, it is bigger than Dolores Huerta, who seems to be spending full time shitting all over me. (Cesar doesn't seem to be saying much about me to other people, at least that I hear about.)

Around this time, my former student Marc Grossman, who is serving as Cesar's aide and press secretary for a number of years, comes back to work for me at the Capitol. Making $10 a week (up from $5 a week in the late 1970s) with a wife and three small sons to support becomes sort of tough. I make it clear to Marc right away what my hope is: "This Speakership fight is over with. It's very important to me that this thing between Cesar and myself end. I'm perfectly content to grovel if I have to in order to make it happen."

I keep killing the grower bills in the Labor Committee. And I get immersed in the grueling, frustrating, and thankless reapportionment process. We end up creating 16 assembly districts where Chicanos make up more than 30 percent of the population. That's the threshold required for Chicanos to have real influence in a district—and potentially elect one of their own either now or in the future.

Even the Chicano activists who have complained up until now about me selling out my community are favorably shocked at the achievement.

One of those 16 Latino seats is in the 58th Assembly District in Montebello, Monterey Park, Pico Rivera, and Alhambra, the area east of East L.A. This is one of the districts I make sure is reconstituted in the 1981 reapportionment so it is possible for a Latino candidate to win election. Several candidates from the district vie in the June 1982 Democratic primary. Among them is someone backed by Assemblymember Joe Montoya, whose district is next door; Monty Manibog, the mayor of Monterey Park and a Filipino American; and Chuck Calderon, an attorney and school board member in Montebello.

After the 58th District is redrawn in reapportionment, I give Chuck Calderon the idea of running for it. He toys with it. It all comes down to a meeting I set up with Chuck at Barragan's Restaurant on Sunset Boulevard in Echo Park. It's just the two of us. We have a long discussion. "It's important we elect a Chicano to this seat," I tell him. Monty Manibog is a popular guy in Monterey Park. He tries to get my endorsement. I would naturally go with him except this is a chance to elect a Chicano.

Chuck is a lawyer. He's been a deputy city attorney. He now works for a law firm doing municipal law. He is already a local elected official—and a moderate, which is perfect for that district. He reminds me of the story about how he and I cross paths, sort of, in 1971. We laugh over it. Then I get to it: "I want you to run for the assembly." I give him every reason: "I will raise the money for your campaign. I will get you the endorsements you need, get you the Third House support and—most importantly—get you the Speaker's support" and have his campaign run by Willie's crack political organization headed up by Richie Ross, which is running campaigns that year in 16 open seats across the state.

By the early 1980s, as a result of the tremendous sums spent on internal battles during the Speakership war, we have to come back to some sense of reality, knowing our first job is to fight Republicans. That's when Willie learns he has to build a political machine from scratch. It's not something he has had to be concerned with in San Francisco, where his election is always guaranteed.

The operation begins with talent from the old Assembly Office of Majority Consultants, where I work as a staffer during my first time at the Capitol in 1971. It's kind of a holding pen for political operatives who help members with legislative or constituent services during legislative session and get sent out to work on campaigns during the political season. Majority Consultants is under the control of the assembly majority leader. Brown wants to centralize the operation under himself. Under the direction of Richie Ross, who begins Willie's tenure as chief administrative officer of the assembly, the name gets changed to the Speaker's Office of Majority Services. Richie also upgrades its services for members during session, specifically targeting vulnerable assemblymembers with help on their legislation, presswork, and official direct mail to constituents. When the election comes around, he flips the operatives to be the Speaker's agents running each of the campaigns in the 16 open seats Willie needs to defend. (He wins all 16 races in November.)

"Ross runs a great 1982 political operation," Brown agrees. "It was the first time any assembly operation had really been unified with all the resources where they are needed. The selfishness of members completing an election cycle with huge surpluses in their campaign accounts is nonexistent. We collectively apply all the resources available to handsomely fund the operation. Sixteen open seats. We won them all. We also instituted a protection act against accusations of undue influence by special interests because we centralized the fundraising operation. That shielded members from criticism" that they are beholden to special interests. "However, it tagged me forever."

"But my goal in life was to be Speaker until death. Term limits [voter passage of Proposition 140 in 1990] took me out. I'd be Speaker today if it hadn't been for that. I was never ambitious beyond wanting to be Speaker. I was incredibly supportive of any member who wanted to do something else, whether it was Richard Alatorre going to the city council or Maxine Waters going to Congress. I made it possible for individual goals to be achieved. The interesting thing about my tenure [as Speaker] was that almost no [assembly]member wanted to go to the [state] senate—until I left [the Speakership]."

Chuck Calderon will benefit from all of that political organization we set up. All he has to do is work in the campaign, walking precincts and going to events. Well, sitting there in the restaurant in Echo Park, Chuck is all pumped up. He now sees himself getting elected.

I never think through the whole conversation, until I'm getting to my car in the parking lot, about asking him the most important question. "Chuck, come over here," I say. "I forgot to ask. I've made certain assumptions. What is it you're all about? What do you stand for?"

"Whatever you want me to stand for?" he replies. I start laughing. But back in my car pulling out of the lot, I ask myself, "Oh, shit, what did I do?" It later comes back to bite me—and Willie—in the ass when Chuck joins the "Gang of Five" conservative Democratic assemblymembers who unsuccessfully try to topple Willie's Speakership in 1988. But that doesn't happen until later.

Meantime, I get the Speaker's blessings. "This is my side of town," I tell Willie. "It's a Latino district." He pretty much gives me *carte blanche* to find the candidate who can win. I make it clear to him: "I'm going to get the candidate, but I need your support and money to go to my guy." We identify Chuck as that guy and close the deal. "He's a Montebello school board member, a lawyer, and he'll be loyal to you," I tell Willie. Oh, well.

I go to Willie's political allies that work with voters in Chuck's district, including labor unions like the cops, firefighters, and teachers. I hit up influential local elected officials. I make it clear to all of them that Chuck is Mr. Brown's candidate and get most of their endorsements and support for his candidacy.

I put Lou Moret in to run the day-to-day campaign for Chuck and to help raise local money. It's the Speaker's job to raise money, pile it into one pot and disseminate it to candidates supported by his operation so they have the resources necessary to get elected. Chuck becomes one of the recipients. Typically, the way it works is Willie goes to various Third House interests, gives them the names of candidates he is supporting and they take care of putting contributions into the right campaigns. Or they just give the money directly to Willie, who distributes it to his guys himself. A lot of Chuck's money is also money I raise and direct to his campaign by making transfers from my own campaign account.

That year, each of Willie's freshmen candidates get assigned "Godfathers," veteran assemblymembers who serve as sponsors or patrons to their charges. I serve as Godfather for two candidates in that primary: Chuck Calderon and Jack O'Connell, who I also get Willie to support for an open assembly seat in a Santa Barbara-Ventura-Oxnard district. (Jack turns into a consummate politician and a standup guy through distinguished service in the assembly and state senate, and later during two terms as California schools superintendent.)

Richie Ross creates the strategy for Chuck's campaign. Richie and Marc Grossman, who although he works for me at the Capitol is now on loan to the Speaker's political organization, write the mail. It is produced by Richie's operation that centrally gang prints mailers out of Sacramento for all the campaigns to leverage volume and save money with vendors. I also send Marc down to Montebello the last three or so weeks before the primary to make sure the mail program gets properly sent out to voters' homes and to organize get-out-the-vote precinct activities.

The district is safely Democratic, so by winning the primary Chuck is all but certain to win in the fall general election.

There's just one problem. Dolores Huerta gets wind of the fact Chuck is the candidate backed by Willie and me. Howard Berman and a number of his allies from the Speakership fight cut deals the year before with Willie, Phil Burton, and me to jump ship from the assembly and run in congressional districts Phil and I carve out for them. It doesn't take long for good politicians to bury the hatchet when their political futures are being guaranteed. Dolores is still smarting from Howard's loss to Willie in late 1980, and is still very much looking to get even, especially with me. So she gets the UFW to endorse Manibog, the Monterey Park mayor, even though he isn't a Chicano running in a seat that can elect one. She also gets the union to commit $10,000 to his campaign.

But whether Cesar has other ideas or whether it's just a coincidence, events unfold to change the UFW's direction. Cesar calls up Marc Grossman out of the blue in May while he's working for me on Chuck's campaign in Montebello, and suggests they get together. The UFW founder is in East L.A., since he pledges to attend a fundraiser for Alex Garcia, whose state senate reelection is being seriously challenged by Assemblymember Art Torres. This gets complicated, and awkward, for everyone concerned.

Remember, Cesar hands Leo a big check in 1978, Leo betrays the farmworkers in 1979, and Howard fails to become Speaker in 1980, despite heavy support from the UFW orchestrated by Dolores. Cesar is left without a relationship with Willie Brown. But he is still heeding the advice he gets from the UAW and me in 1978. I can't remember how many times Cesar tells me that he hates politicians—before he cuts me off after I abandon Howard for Willie in 1980. "They're with you one day and gone tomorrow," he bemoans. My pitch to him goes something like this: "So long as you need the legislature and you have a need—a need to protect the farm labor law from being gutted by the growers—you have to get involved in the political process. How do you do that?"

Of course, the one thing the farmworkers have early is bodies. Going back to Bobby Kennedy's 1968 presidential race, the UFW uses the weeks before an election to saturate legislative districts where there are lots of Chicanos with ground troops going door to door. They can often make a difference in the election outcome. This scenario gets repeated many times.

"That's one thing," I tell Cesar. "Bodies are important. But the other thing all politicians understand is getting another kind of assistance. 'Money,' as Jesse Unruh once said, 'is the mother's milk of politics.'" The UFW doesn't have money to give until the late 1970s, after it signs union contracts with growers following passage of the Agricultural Labor Relations Act. Then its PAC gets created and the union starts to get contributions from its members. By 1982, after seven years under the law giving farmworkers the right to organize, workers' contributions build up a sizeable fund. The UFW keeps putting lots of bodies into political campaigns, but all of a sudden for a short time it also becomes a major political player in contributing political cash. (That lasts until Republican Governor George Deukmejian takes office in January 1983, and quickly stops enforcing the law, causing the union to lose most of its contracts within several years.)

The mistake too many groups make is that they want to control the money they give in politics, I tell Cesar. They dribble it out among dozens of legislative candidates, with not much going to any one of them. It is important for labor leaders like state AFL-CIO head Jack Henning to have personal relationships with everybody. The other alternative, I explain, is giving all your money to the Speaker so he can divvy it up among his favorites or he can direct you to give it to candidates identified by him.

One thing anybody who's ever been Speaker understands is getting money, especially when he gets to decide where it goes. That's how big business and agriculture do it, I say to Cesar; they give big chunks to the leadership and get maximum credit because when the leadership hands out the money the Speaker or the senate leader tells the recipient where the money comes from.

There is also the lesson from Operating Engineers Local 3 in San Francisco. It operates a pretty modest printing press. But it's perfect for producing two-color brochures, a mainstay of political direct mail in that day. Local 3 gives politicians' campaigns use of its press at cost, which makes the San Francisco union a big-time political player far beyond its membership numbers and financial clout. Cesar gets that example. He expands an existing printing plant at the UFW's La Paz headquarters near the Tehachapi mountain town of Keene near

Bakersfield and turns it into a sophisticated printing operation that is run by his middle son, Paul Chavez.

In fact, Cesar has already carried out our advice about making book with the legislative leadership on the senate side. Earlier in 1982, Cesar makes a deal with the senate president pro temp, Dave Roberti, who recently offs his predecessor, Jim Mills, over Mills's weakness in protecting senate Democrats from Republican assaults. Roberti's first test as senate leader is defending Alex Garcia from a challenge by Art Torres in the Democratic primary. Alex is usually a decent vote on labor or Chicano issues. But in my eyes he represents another generation that views politics in a different way; he isn't a risk taker and doesn't want to make waves. Interestingly, in 1971, Garcia is the deciding vote getting a bill out of the Assembly Labor and Employment Committee that would ban strikes and boycotts by farmworkers, at the behest of either the growers or their then-allies, the Teamsters. The UFW has to later kill the bill.

I too have the opportunity to run for the senate against Garcia in 1982, but opt to stay where I am. Why should I leave the assembly just after Willie Brown becomes Speaker? I also don't want to go to the senate or take on a Democratic incumbent. Art, who makes his first, unsuccessful, run for the assembly against Garcia in 1972, with UFW backing after Alex betrays the farmworkers, decides to take him on. I support Art and believe he will by far be the more effective representative.

It's not a pleasant campaign. Art gets hit hard in the East L.A. district by Roberti's political operatives who are working for Garcia over abortion (Art is pro-choice), the fact that Art is a Protestant and not a Catholic, and a multitude of hot button issues that are very hurtful to Art, further open up wounds. Cesar supports Garcia, despite Garcia's checkered past with the UFW. Art thinks Cesar's motivation is getting even with him because he helps make Willie Brown Speaker. That may be a small part of it. What is lost on Art is the commitment Cesar has just given to support Roberti's leadership in exchange for Roberti's commitment to bottle up antifarmworker legislation in the Senate Industrial Relations Committee, which is exactly what I have been doing in the assembly on my own with Willie's help.

Art beats Garcia in the primary, but his bitterness towards Cesar remains. He takes his senate seat at the beginning of December 1982, the last month of Jerry Brown's first tenure as governor. The UFW, with Roberti's help, is working to get the senate to confirm some 11th hour gubernatorial appointments to the Agricultural Labor Relations Board. The most critical is the all-important position of farm labor board general counsel, which controls enforcement of farmworker rights under the law. The governor appoints Nancy Kirk, an ALRB attorney. Art, as a brand new state senator, becomes the deciding vote to confirm her. He doesn't vote for her and the nomination fails. In fairness to Art, there is an alternative candidate for general counsel, a veteran consultant to the Senate Judiciary Committee. Jerry Brown appoints him at the last minute, but then Roberti and the governor get into a pissing contest over something else and time runs out before the guy can be confirmed.

One of George Deukmejian's first appointments after becoming governor in January 1983, is David Stirling, a former Republican assemblymember, as ALRB general counsel. Stirling immediately starts to systematically shut down enforcement of the law. Growers illegally refuse to renegotiate their UFW agreements and Stirling does nothing. That causes the union, over the next several years, to lose most of its contracts—and tens of thousands of farmworkers lose the protections they once enjoy. Hundreds of workers are fired or blacklisted. One 19-year-old farmworker, Rene Lopez, is shot to death just after voting in a union election conducted by the board at a dairy in Fresno County—after Stirling ignores pleas from the UFW to move against foremen brandishing weapons. Deukmejian serves two four-year terms. Another Republican governor, Pete Wilson, who is also in office for eight years, follows him. So it is inevitable that the Republicans will dismantle enforcement of the law. But it happens several years sooner because Jerry Brown's late appointments for ALRB general counsel don't make it. Cesar blames Art and never forgives him. They never talk again.

Cesar does his last, and longest, public fast, going for 36 days, in summer 1988, over the pesticide poisoning of farmworkers and their children. He's in bed in Delano, clearly suffering the effects of the fast. His eyes are closed when an aide says Art wants to come and see him. Cesar opens his eyes. "Fuck him," he says softly.

After they speak on the phone, Marc Grossman picks up Cesar, who is alone in East L.A. Cesar asks Marc to drive him to the Garcia fundraiser. "Wait for me in the car, I won't be long," Cesar says. In other words, Cesar is going to hold his nose and make a quick appearance at the Garcia event. He isn't gone for more than 20 minutes. That evening Marc drives Cesar back home to La Paz in Keene, 28 miles southeast of Bakersfield.

They talk during the two-hour drive. Cesar lays out his legislative predicament: Jerry Brown is leaving the governorship after two four-year terms. In recent years he has vetoed at least two grower-sponsored bills to weaken the farm labor law that is his first big accomplishment as governor. But Jerry won't be there much longer. The likely Democratic candidate to succeed him is Los Angeles Mayor Tom Bradley. The UFW is one of the first unions to support Bradley when he initially runs for mayor of L.A. against Sam Yorty in 1969. But by 1982, Bradley gets this idea in his head that he can convince the growers to support his candidacy. (Yeah, the growers are going to support a black Democrat against a white-guy Republican, Deukmejian, to whom they eventually hand over $1 million in political cash.) So Bradley is echoing the phony grower line that the Agricultural Labor Relations Board, which administers the law, is "biased" against the industry. Cesar knows he can't rely on Bradley to protect the law, even if he is elected governor.

"What do you think we can do to protect the law?" Cesar asks Marc.

"Why don't you do what you did with Dave Roberti and jump into bed with Willie Brown," Marc answers. The UFW can cut the same deal with Brown: stack the assembly labor committee so bad bills never make it out.

"But I don't have a relationship with Willie Brown anymore," Cesar replies.

"Yeah, but Richard Alatorre does."

"But I don't have a relationship with Richard Alatorre."

"That can be fixed."

It's one of those cases where a good lawyer never asks a question when he doesn't know the answer.

After dropping Cesar off in Keene, Marc travels back to L.A. and calls Richie Ross and me. With help from Marc and Fernando Chavez, Cesar's oldest son who practices law in San Jose, a meeting is set up between Cesar and me at a local steakhouse in the town of Tehachapi, about 10 miles from Keene along Highway 58. Marc and I drive up to Tehachapi from L.A. before the June primary election. There for the UFW is Cesar, his brother, Richard Chavez, and another union officer. It's the first time I've actually spoken with Cesar since the break up over the Speakership. The get together is friendly, even if it isn't that comfortable. Cesar understands the importance of getting back together for the good of the membership he represents. There really isn't much to hammer out when we meet; we all know what needs to happen.

After the Tehachapi session, I tell Brown: "It's time for you and Cesar to have a meeting of the minds. It's in both Cesar's interest and yours. Cesar understands Jerry Brown is leaving. He needs to protect the interests of the farmworkers from future legislation that would weaken or kill the ALRA. Cesar understands the importance of the political process and wants to play." Oh, and I mention the union has money and printing presses, which Willie already knows.

As Speaker, Willie is building his political operation—and influence. He recognizes there has to be reconciliation with an important leader like Cesar Chavez. It is something he wants to do anyway. And he knows I can be the vehicle to make it come about.

Brown is a little apprehensive, but I convince him it's the right thing to do. Marc and I are concerned how it will play out exactly. I want it to play out positively for Cesar and Willie. I now have vested interests on both sides. These are the two most important people in my public life. It's important for me that the reconciliation takes place and that past misunderstandings don't interfere.

In the meantime, right before the primary, we decide to take a chance. With permission from Richie Ross and me, Marc takes Cesar into his confidence, briefing him about our campaign strategy for Chuck Calderon in the 58th Assembly District, sharing the mail program with him and letting him know Calderon, and not Manibog, is going to win the election. It works. Cesar can't withdraw the UFW endorsement for Manibog that Dolores Huerta engineers. But he stops the $10,000 check for Manibog's campaign. Cesar sees we are right: Chuck wins by a good margin.

A number of weeks pass after the primary. All I remember is that we meet in the spartan conference room at the motel next door to Meadows Field, Bakersfield's modest airport in Oildale, on the north side of town. Cesar comes down from La Paz with another UFW leader. Willie arrives on a twin-engine chartered plane with this young black guy who is his aide. Marc and I get there too.

The meeting lasts for less than an hour. Right away, things go well. Cesar and Willie start out agreeing with each other about what a son-of-a-bitch Leo McCarthy is: Cesar because Leo screws the farmworkers during the 1979 vegetable strike after the UFW tries to play with him; Willie because Leo stops him from becoming Speaker for six years. They begin with the commonality of mutual dislike.

Willie talks about the last time he is in the Bakersfield area for some occasion. Cesar recalls being there too. They reminisce about old times when they are allies. Cesar discusses the farmworkers' legislative agenda. Willie agrees that is his agenda too. That's it. Not a word about money or campaigns or political support.

Cesar heads back up to La Paz in the Tehachapi Mountains. Marc and I hop into the chartered plane with Willie and his aide. We fly from Bakersfield to Modesto. Willie gets off the plane and is picked up on the tarmac by smiling local Farm Bureau officials. They whisk him off to a big grower fundraiser for Gary Condit, who is making his first run for the assembly in one of the 16 open seats up that year. When Willie gets off the plane, Marc and I laugh: he has come fresh from jumping into bed with Cesar Chavez. We fly on to Sacramento's Executive Airport.

Willie and Cesar get together again a short time later at a Chinese restaurant in San Jose. Also there is Paul Chavez, Cesar's son who replaces Dolores Huerta as the UFW's chief lobbyist in Sacramento. "Cesar was so saintly and well informed that it was a joy to exchange views with him and to listen to him," Willie recalls. "He asked for nothing. We talked about issues and how to deal with them, even beyond those concerning the farmworkers.

"At the end of lunch, Cesar said, 'I know you really need help and the farmworkers want to help you. So here's a little something.' Then Paul Chavez handed me a check."

Paul says just about then that Willie makes an excuse of having to use the rest room.

"I don't normally pay much attention to checks" when they're presented on occasions like this, Brown says years later. "But I look at this one and see the number 25—and then I look more closely to count the zeros after the 25; there are four of them. That is the single biggest check I have ever received as Speaker of the assembly. Still, to this day, I have never been given financial support in one check equal to what the farmworkers did. It was huge for me. It took me back to my marching with Cesar during his 1966 march from Delano to Sacramento. It brought me back to my bucket collection around the same time at the CDC [California Democratic Council] convention in Fresno where I ordered the doors locked and we wouldn't let anybody out until they put something green in the collection buckets for the farmworkers on strike. I repeatedly did the same thing over the years at other Democratic Party or UFW events. It became a labor of love."

For me, the reconciliations I'm able to make happen between me and Cesar and Cesar and Willie produce a great feeling of relief. It goes exactly as we want. I'm glad it is over. It signals the resumption of a relationship I always prize.

Closer to the November election, Cesar invites Willie to bring a delegation of Democratic assemblymembers to the union's political convention with hundreds of farmworker delegates held in Salinas at the Hartnell Community College auditorium. Six or eight assemblymembers and candidates fly with Willie and me to Salinas, including Art Agnos and Chuck Calderon. Cesar's father recently passes away at age 100 (or 101, they aren't sure). So I bring with me to present at the convention a framed copy of an ornate Assembly Joint Resolution I author and get passed by the house honoring the life of Librado Chavez.

I present the resolution to Cesar from the podium in front of the convention, but before I can get off stage, delegates all of a sudden are lining up behind several mikes placed on the floor. They take me to task in Spanish over my vote reversal during the Speakership fight nearly two years before. There's talk of betrayal and double-cross. It isn't fun.

But what am I supposed to do? Nothing. I just stand there and listen to it, along with Willie Brown and my fellow assembly colleagues. (Since the denouncements are in Spanish, most of them don't know what's going on, or so I think.) After a short period of time—that seems to drag on forever—Cesar, who is presiding, says in Spanish, "That's enough, he got the message," or something like that.

I'm a big boy. It's a small price to pay for getting what I want.

Willie is going to try to deliver his speech to the delegates in Spanish, which he doesn't speak. His lady friend, Wendy Linka, is from Central America. They fit him with a small earpiece. Wendy, who is back stage, phonetically says the words slowly in Spanish into a microphone using short phrases or sentences. Brown tries to repeat them in Spanish, but it just isn't coming out right. He abandons Spanish and speaks to Cesar and the farmworkers in English. It goes fine.

As Willie and our delegation are walking outside of the auditorium to be driven back to the airport, Brown says to me in front of the others, "And why did I need you here?"

Chapter 8

Righting a Wrong

One of my proudest legacies as a lawmaker comes during the early 1980s when I oversee legislative and congressional reapportionment in California. It helps pave the way for the mushrooming growth in political participation and influence among Latinos in the years that follow. (I do the same thing as a freshmen city councilmember in Los Angeles later in the same decade.)

There are often similarities between fathers and sons, and my father and I share some things in common. One has to do with how we deal with the whole thing of discrimination. My dad gets taken to jail as a young man because he refuses to leave a restaurant after being informed they don't serve Mexicans. It comes up again when my parents want to move out of East L.A. for a nicer neighborhood with better schools, only to discover no one is selling to Chicanos at the time. Plus there's the fact of my father's dark skin, like mine, and the prejudice, even among Latinos, against those who are darker. I grow up seeing the fear and resentment over race bias that deeply engrains itself in my father.
He rarely, if ever, speaks about his experiences with racism and they don't come up when we sit around the dinner table and talk about what's happening during the day or in the community. What he does mention from time to time is the sad commentary that Chicanos can't get our people elected to public office in our own community. My dad, although he has a limited formal education, reads several English- and Spanish-language newspapers, and is very well informed and politically sophisticated for his generation. He understands the reason for the lack of representation. The territory between Boyle Heights and East

L.A. could have several Anglo politicians sharing pieces of it, he points out. No wonder we can't elect our own.

My father's observations about politics stay with me and have a profound effect. The political predicament for Chicanos where we live is absolute bullshit, I conclude. I know there have to be people who come from us and can represent us in public office. I remember thinking in school that if I ever run for office, the ultimate accomplishment will be representing the community where I'm growing up and where later, after my dad's death, my mother still lives.

The first, and until the 1960s the only, Chicano politician to represent parts of our community is Ed Roybal. He's elected to the city council from East L.A. in 1949. I'm too young to remember, but I recall growing up thinking it is a great accomplishment. Whatever you hear about Ed Roybal in the daily news has to come from the local throwaway papers like the Belvedere Citizen because you seldom if ever catch much about him in the major daily newspapers, unless it is negative. I read about him and know he's a liberal. He takes on the right causes.

I learn for myself from leaving the legislature for the city council in 1985 that even though I like to think the work I do in Sacramento is important, it's really an abstraction in the daily lives of most people living in the communities I represent. Sacramento or Washington, D.C. are far removed from the realities of their existence. Given the difficulty of commuting from coast to coast in those days and the kind of guy Ed Roybal is, it's no wonder he isn't around a lot, and when he is it is usually for short periods of time.

It takes a long time to get yourself into a position of power, to get on committees of influence where you can make things happen, because of the seniority system in Congress. But Roybal is the real deal. He gets on the House Appropriations Committee later in his career, does some important stuff, and begins to make his mark. One of his contributions is in the delivery of health care for senior citizens through the funding of geriatric centers.

Ed Roybal becomes sort of the political godfather of our community. Even though he is an establishment politician, I believe he sets the stage for a lot of other Chicanos to break into politics. Once I get involved with the student and Chicano movements, while I always respect him—anybody has to respect the years in elected office he gives to the community—his methodology and approach to change leave a little to be desired in my eyes. I am younger and take a more militant approach about making systemic change happen.

So I have a lot of respect for Roybal even though we are never close. We know each other. He endorses me when I run—after I beat his guy, Ralph Ochoa. But I'm never his favorite. You know how sometimes veteran politicians listen for the footsteps of those coming up behind them and get a little distrustful and insecure about potential competitors, like me. The irony of it is that I come from the old school, which says you never run against someone like Ed Roybal, although at one time I consider a congressional race to someday fulfill my career objectives in politics.

Every 10 years lawmakers at California's state Capitol redraw legislative districts to reflect changes from the decennial U.S. Census. What is at stake with the 1981 redistricting is Willie Brown's future as Assembly Speaker and increased political empowerment for Chicanos.

By the '60s, other Chicano politicians in East L.A. are beginning to follow in Roybal's footsteps. John Moreno is a bright guy who gets elected to the state assembly. So does Phil Soto, who comes out of the CIO unions and early activist movements. They only serve one or two terms. Neither leaves much of a mark.

I believe 90 percent of the problem in electing more Chicanos is reapportionment. There are other factors too. Even back then, many non-Latinos have no reason to feel comfortable voting for anybody who is Latino—or anybody who is not them. Mexicans also have an inherent mistrust of government. Most of the contacts we have with government are negative, whether it's social service program providers, law enforcement and the administration of justice, public schools, or political entities. Most Chicanos are nonjoiners and consequently lack the sophistication to fully understand the importance of participating in the political process to affect the daily lives of ordinary people. The Community Service Organization tries changing that attitude during the 1940s and '50s, in part with the election of Ed Roybal, but by the time I'm maturing politically in the mid-'60s, CSO is no longer a major influence.

Even if there are good people willing to run, it's almost impossible to put together a winning campaign without sufficient resources. For a Chicano to get elected it takes money, institutional political support, and campaign professionals suitably versed in running races. But even if you have all of those things, the big issue is: how can you get elected when Latino political power is severely diluted because of discriminatory redistricting? As a result everybody's vote is not counted equally.

Democrats, under leaders such as Assembly Speaker Jesse Unruh, control reapportionment during the '60s. Democrats are set to control it again for the '70s, but the Republican governor, Ronald Reagan, vetoes their plan that is passed by the legislature in 1971. Reagan makes a commitment to legislative leaders that if Democrats are successful in the 48th Assembly District special election that fall, the governor will sign whatever measure is voted out of the two houses. Democrats hold a supermajority in the senate with the ability to override Reagan's veto of a reapportionment bill. But in the assembly, although there is a healthy Democratic majority, it is just shy of the two-thirds margin needed to override the governor.

When I lose my special election to Republican Bill Brophy in the 48th, the deal with the governor falls through. An impasse results and the courts take over redistricting because of the federal requirement that reapportionment for congressional districts be in place in time for the regular elections in 1972, the following year.

The U.S. Constitution's one-person, one-vote requirement is strengthened by Supreme Court decisions in the '60s. It is the federal Constitution that requires every decade, after completion of the U.S. Census, congressional districts be redrawn so that in the following even-numbered year, elections can be held according to the one-person, one-vote mandate. The California Constitution also requires that new boundaries for the assembly, state senate, and state board of equalization be in place for the first regular election cycle of the decade. In practice, legislative reapportionment is done at the same time as congressional redistricting and the assembly traditionally handles redrawing congressional lines. The law also says districts have to be geographically contiguous.

The California Supreme Court appoints a panel of judges who design district maps. But they handle it in a totally different way than if the legislature would do it. That suits me just fine. The end result is that the 48th District in East L.A. where I lose in 1971 is 80 percent different than the one I win in 1972. When the judges get through with my new 55th Assembly District, it is about 55 percent Chicano as opposed to 18 percent Chicano in the old 48th. I would win in the old district anyway even though there aren't as many Latinos because it is still very progressive and heavily Democratic, with voters who share my political convictions. By 1972, I'm very well known and the obvious frontrunner. By the early '70s, my ethnic identity isn't as a big factor. Voters in my district care much more about my political ideology.

For decades, local, state, and congressional districts in the Chicano community have been aligned, mostly by Democrats who control the legislature, in order to benefit sitting politicians, of whom we have few, and incumbent Democrats, of which we have few. This is not only true in East L.A., but in other major population centers in the state where there are appreciable numbers of Latinos.

It is no accident that in the '60s and '70s there is the beginning of a movement towards more accountability among the Democratic and Republican par-

Assembly Minority Leader Carol Hallett supplies Republican votes to elect Willie Brown Speaker of the Assembly in late 1980. She also believes Brown promises to treat the GOP "fairly" on reapportionment.

ties in addressing the needs of ethnic and racial minorities. By the dawn of the 1980s, there is growing insistence among Chicano political activists for more equity and a greater voice in legislative reapportionment.

Willie Brown becomes assembly Speaker in December 1980, finally winning the job that eludes him since 1974. The scene he inherits is a divided Democratic Party in the legislature because of the chaos and turmoil of an unprecedented lengthy and bitter Speakership fight. Republican lawmakers in recent memory play little or no role in electing the Speaker since they don't have the numbers to elect one of their own people. But they play a big role in electing Willie Brown Speaker in 1980. Carol Hallett, then Republican minority leader in the assembly, convinces her caucus to support Willie after the Democratic caucus is divided, with neither Howard Berman nor Leo McCarthy mustering the votes needed to get elected. Most of McCarthy's partisans line up behind Brown, and both Howard and Willie try to woo the Republicans. Brown wins with a minority of the Democrats and all of the Republicans voting for him.

To get the Republicans, Willie Brown makes two promises to Hallett: he will be more generous in giving Republican members bigger staffs, better offices and committee assignments, a promise he keeps. And he will be "fair" to the GOP in reapportionment and allow minority members and staff to participate in redistricting, which is on top of the legislative agenda beginning in 1981, to prepare for the regular 1982 elections. In Carol Hallett's eyes, that means Republicans will have a voice and will play a much bigger role in the process. (Willie sees things differently: he gives her and the Republicans money for staff and resources so they can come up with their own reapportionment plan. Period.)

At first, I don't want anything to do with reapportionment. Initially, as the Speakership fight begins, I support Leo McCarthy for Speaker. Then, because of Cesar Chavez, I switch to Howard Berman. Everybody knows I'm not really for either one of them because I don't like either one of them. Once my friend Willie becomes Speaker, all I want is chairmanship of a good "juice" committee, one involving lots of special interests that lets you raise a lot of campaign money. I prefer the Governmental Organization Committee, but Frankie Vicencia has it. I figure maybe I can have the Health Committee.

Then Willie calls me and says, "This is what I'm thinking about: I need you. You're one of the few people I can trust. I know you'll take care of me. I don't have the same trust with a lot of other people. I want you to do reapportionment."

Willie later says, "I've been a reapportionment person from the day I was first elected" to the assembly. U.S. Representative Phil Burton "was responsible for creating the district [in San Francisco] I ultimately represented." Initially, in the 1961 reapportionment, three districts are planned for San Francisco. Burton, the quintessential master of redistricting, "had a separate map he kept in his pocket showing four districts" in the city. "At the 11th hour, he presented the map showing where we picked up an additional seat in San Francisco, a seat available for me or someone of my ilk.

"So I understood from day one how important reapportionment was to the exercise of power on the political scene and [redistricting] became a cornerstone of my involvement in politics. You have to make sure you control reapportionment because where the lines are drawn produces who will win" elections, Willie says.

"There was truly only one really talented person who could do [reapportionment] without apology. That was Richard. You could hand the ball to Richard Alatorre on reapportionment and you wouldn't have to tell him what was needed to be done or how to do it. And you would never have to second-guess him. Although there is a reapportionment committee, you only have one person doing reapportionment. You also had to make sure you had somebody who people wouldn't think is lying. Almost every other potential reapportionment chairperson had credibility issues. Richard did not. My Speakership would be blessed because if during the process we agreed on a set of lines, that would be it. You wouldn't have to worry about watching the process 24 hours a day to make sure the lines didn't move. The other advantage would be that one thing every member knew was Richard had the power; he would be the only power in reapportionment. Members would not have a place to go to appeal because they would know I would not second-guess Alatorre."

I think it's a great idea to be part of reapportionment, but I don't want to do it myself. I know what a huge pain in the ass it is and all the egos and petty requests from politicians I'd have to deal with. I've heard all the stories about how selfish lawmakers become in reapportionment and the stupid headaches you have to put up with. It's not a pleasant job.

After he lets me know he wants me for reapportionment, I tell Willie I'll think about it. Then I get a call from Phil Burton. Willie and Phil have a long relationship; they're both from San Francisco and Willie is part of the Burton machine there. I too have a relationship with both Philip and John L. Burton, but mostly John L, who is still my buddy, even after he leaves the assembly for Congress in 1974. So it's no accident that Phil is on the phone. "This is a great opportunity for you," he's telling me. "I commit to you, if you want a congressional district, I'll create one for you. I want you in Congress."

Democratic U.S. Rep. Phillip Burton, a legendary powerhouse in the U.S. House of Representatives, works with Richard on congressional reapportionment in 1981.

Phil Burton at the time is the political powerhouse in the U.S. House of Representatives. He's probably the most astute political operative they have, responsible for passage of more progressive, labor, and environmental legislation than anyone else in Congress. He's viewed as the successor someday to Tip O'Neill as Speaker of the House, which he would become if Phil doesn't suddenly die in 1983. I know Phil is delivering the message for Willie, saying how important it is for him and the Democrats in Congress to have my help. I also see it as an opportunity. I would like to go to Congress, but later decide for my own reasons not to do it.

So I tell Willie I'll take the job.

"Phil Burton, in his initial conversation with me about organization of the house [the assembly] was pleased to know I was asking Richard to do the job of reapportionment because Richard and John [Burton] were more than tight," Willie offers. "I didn't have to urge Phil Burton to call Richard; he would have done it on his own.

"Also, taking a look at the rest of the membership [of assembly Democrats], no one else was there you could trust to do the job. If Richard had turned me down, I would have had to take Maxine [Waters] out of [being chair of the] Ways and Means [Committee]; she would have been the next natural candidate" to head up redistricting.

The only time the Assembly Elections and Reapportionment Committee isn't the worst committee in the legislature is following the year of the census when legislative district boundaries are redrawn. It's an irrelevant committee most of the time because few people or interest groups care very much about election law. The average citizen also never understands the importance of reapportionment to the social and political fabric of our society. Several statewide ballot measures go before the voters over the years seeking to take reapportionment out of the hands of legislators and place it with the courts or an impartial citizens' panel. They all fail until 2008, when Governor Arnold Schwarzenegger succeeds by a slim margin because the governor paints it as a bipartisan proposal with language about diversity, the legislature is so unpopular, and voters are distracted by other races and measures.

So I make it clear to Willie that once reapportionment is over, I ain't staying with the elections committee because I want more than that. He agrees.

After he talks me into it, I know what I have to do. I know I can look somebody in the eyes and say, fuck you, and not worry about it. You know what, I can tell members, this is it. Take it or leave it. No sweat off me.

I'm not at the Capitol to make friends with the Republicans anyway. Some of the Democrats I don't like much better—and I can tell them the same thing.

That's why Brown puts me there. A lot of my colleagues, other Democratic members, put it to him: "Why Alatorre?" It's not like I have a stellar career as a heavy hitter legislator. I'm on the wrong side of the Speakership fight through most of the '70s when Leo McCarthy is Speaker. I'm elected to office in 1972, but I don't chair a standing committee until the late '70s, and when I do get one it's Human Resources, which is welfare, not exactly a juice committee. I do a good job as chairman and so they give me the Labor and Employment committee because the unions want me. During most of that decade I also have an ongoing battle with the governor, Jerry Brown. I have a safe district they can't take away from me. I have an office at the state Capitol they can. They can also cut my staff, but I'm entitled to a certain number of them.

Another strike against me in the eyes of many members is I'm not known as a detail guy. Bruce Cain, who I recruit to be a main consultant to the Elections and Reapportionment committee when I take over as chairman, remembers, "People wondered how Richard would handle the technical and legal details, and deliver this very complicated piece of legislation on time and without a lot of mistakes. In those days there are no computers to catch mistakes."

I have a pretty good reputation as a political strategist, but not as "a policy wonk," as Bruce puts it. "So, to many people there was the question of how Richard could get interested in the minutia of the census data," which is at the heart of the reapportionment process. But "in retrospect, Willie scoped out the job much more accurately than the critics did. Willie was exactly right in concluding that the technical work of redistricting is absolutely secondary to the negotiations that have to take place. And having tough negotiators like Richard Alatorre and Phil Burton are key to getting anything done." Even though my constituency as chairman of assembly redistricting is every Democratic member in the lower house, they all have interests that sometimes conflict with the interests of other incumbents. Members are also prone to backstab on deals they agree on to try to get a better deal right up until the last minute. Redrawing dis-

Bruce Cain (center with folded arms) is a political science professor at the California Institute of Technology in Pasadena when Richard recruits him to oversee the intricacies of Assembly and congressional reapportionment. It is the first time computers are used to redraw legislative boundaries.

trict boundary lines that "create something inherently better for Democrats means some people with comfortable, cushy seats have to sacrifice," Bruce Cain notes. "Those who don't have to work hard to get reelected are going to have to accept some changes in their districts" they may not like.

If the person heading up redistricting backs down every time somebody complains or whines, "you'd get nowhere; there wouldn't be a resolution," according to Bruce. "You needed someone in the middle of the negotiations who was strong enough to make it happen, particularly since there were a lot of changes: seats were added to Congress from California. There was major population growth that required big shifts in the districts of Democratic and Republican incumbents. Then you had heat from the Latino and black communities to make sure they got fair representation" in whatever plan that comes out. "When he asked, 'Who can I trust not to fold in that situation?' the only person Willie could have turned to was Richard, and that's what he did."

Willie concurs: "The reason why we were better at reapportionment [in 1981] than anybody else was because mastery of all of the little zip codes and census tracks and other things that went with it weren't nearly as important as the negotiating skills people like Phil Burton and Richard Alatorre brought to the table."

"Surprisingly, the people Richard was able to have some of the best negotiations with were moderate and conservative Democrats and some Republicans because Richard understood the importance of keeping Willie in office," Bruce continues. "So he was willing to help these people even if he didn't agree with them on everything. Plus Richard's a pragmatist all the way."

You have to remember my only real constituency is 41, the number of assemblymembers it takes to elect a Speaker. No one else. My job is to keep Willie Brown Speaker and keep the Democrats in power. So making me chairman of reapportionment is an appointment Willie can justify because of the relationship he and I have. It's well known we have both a political and a personal relationship. I am one of the few members who hang with Willie in 1974, when he gets his ass kicked the first time he tries to become Speaker, even after it's clear Leo McCarthy will win. And I pay for it for years. So Brown can hide behind the fact he needs to put somebody doing redistricting he can blood-ass trust and who has the ability to get the job done.

Putting me out front also insulates Brown from having to get into the nitty-gritty of deciding all the petty, and not so petty, fights between members of his caucus over who gets what line drawn where. Willie is "interested in the overall picture, but he didn't want to get dragged into trench warfare," Bruce points out. "He wanted as many of the tough decisions as he could made by Richard. It gave him cover. So appointing Richard was partly based on friendship but partly because Willie didn't want to get dragged into things he knew Richard could do. The trust in Richard was also built on Willie trying to keep himself above the fray."

There is no question about my loyalties. There *is* a question about whether I have the ability to do the job because of the inherent political nature and difficulty of the process. In the eyes of many Democratic incumbents, the only people who can do reapportionment in 1981 are Michael Berman, brother of Assemblymember Howard Berman, and Carl D'Agostino, partner with Michael in a very successful consulting firm in West L.A. that runs political campaigns. Berman and D'Agostino are considered the most sophisticated in campaign techniques and the most bare-knuckled in political brawls. They allegedly have a statewide database and, to top it off, they are very close to Phil Burton, the congressman overseeing congressional reapportionment who has used Michael and Carl to do number crunching.

In contrast, I have no experience with reapportionment other than being an advocate of fairer representation for Chicanos. Some people want Carl and Michael to be put in charge of assembly reapportionment, but Willie Brown can't have that. He can't trust them. They are closely associated with Howard Berman, the guy Willie has just beaten for the Speakership. It isn't clear what Howard's political agenda will be since losing in 1980. It's soon apparent that Howard and some of his allies have decided to skip to Congress, and that takes the heat off. But in the meantime, there's still lots of distrust between the Brownies and the Bermanites.

"Every time there is a reapportionment in my history [in the legislature], Berman and D'Agostino have always been viewed as the best brains available for Democratic [Party] purposes," Willie Brown explains. "For some of us, however, that brainpower has always been tainted because it was skewed towards protecting and enhancing certain members [starting with Michael's brother, Howard], sometimes even to the detriment of expanding influence for minorities that have previously not been full participants in the process—and to punish those who had not sufficiently followed the party line. I selected Richard because I knew he could and would do the job and that at the end of the day and the end of the decade the Democratic Party and racial minorities would have gotten their best shot at participating in the political process. And Richard proved me to be right."

That distrust adds to worries about who will actually do the work of redistricting. The GOP members in the assembly are already gearing up for reapportionment by turning to the Rose Institute of State and Local Government at Claremont McKenna College, a big-time Republican-oriented think tank that has a lot of expertise. The Rose Institute is also effectively playing the minority card with a lot of talk about how they're going to be fair to ethnic and racial minorities, especially Latinos. That's easy for Republicans to do since they make progress for Chicanos by taking it out of the hides of Anglo incumbents who are Democrats. "White Democrats, particularly in the Berman faction, suspect since Willie got his power from a deal with the Republicans, he will turn everything over to the Rose Institute," Bruce says. What the Bermans and other doubters don't think of is that we, the assembly Democrats, "will develop our own capacity, a critical decision made by Willie and Richard that took courage," Bruce adds.

I take the reapportionment job at the end of 1980, shortly after Willie gets elected Speaker. I have to become operational pretty quickly in 1981. Immediately after getting appointed chairman, I have to find someone who will be in charge of the nuts and bolts of getting all of the information together from the census and developing a set of indicators of voter loyalty we can use to identify the types of people who live in each legislative district.

In prior times, all the work of reapportionment is done in Sacramento. Now the Republicans have the Rose Institute, which is a lot more sophisticated than Michael Berman or Carl D'Agostino. We need to set up from scratch a sophisticated computer-driven operation with the capacity to digest all the reels of information the Census Bureau is able to deliver about the state of California, download the information, and segregate it so it is functional for our needs.

The first order of business is hiring a staff. The second order of business is beginning the process of coming up with a computer program that helps us decide what is important to know and what is not important to know. Then we can come up with indicators of predictable Democratic loyalty and voting patterns and everything else. Eventually we have to translate all this data, reducing it down to the smallest level possible to form an overall picture.

I don't have the foggiest notion of how this is going to be done. I have a meeting with Daniel Keveles, who at the time is a full professor of political science at California Institute of Technology in Pasadena. I first meet him in 1966, during the first assembly campaign for Wally Karabian. Dan is a friend of Wally's. The guy is a genius when it comes to numbers and politics. He is the guy I feel can do it. We meet for lunch at the Statler Hilton Hotel in downtown L.A. Dan Keveles brings with him this baby-faced guy who looks to be in his 20s and who turns out to be Bruce Cain, a Rhodes Scholar who's also a professor of government at Cal Tech.

We're laughing about my appointment to run reapportionment and what I have to do. "I don't know what the shit I'm doing," I tell Dan. "I know what I got to do. I got to put together a staff that will help me accomplish my goal and convince Willie I know what I'm doing. And my staff has to be credible enough to make it happen."

Dan says he has just signed a book deal, he's in the middle of a sabbatical writing it and he can't take time off. "That's why I brought Bruce Cain with me," he says. He tells me about Bruce.

"Bruce can help you, but I need you," I insist. "I know you and know you have the capacity to do it."

"Whatever you need, Bruce can do it," Dan reassures me. "To give you relief, I'll work with him to make sure it's done."

Then Bruce starts talking. He knows enough about reapportionment and what has to happen. "It's clear to me you know politics," he tells me. "You take care of the politics and I'll take care of the creation of a program that will surpass anything Michael and Carl are doing. What they do one of my freshmen students can do."

I say to myself, "I got to hear about this." But I don't have a choice. I don't have anyone who can come up with a second team. If Bruce is going to be it, it is all I have.

"Richard didn't have a lot of other options at that point," Bruce later says. "He hedges his bets. At the same time he hires me he hires Jim Tucker, an ACLU guy, to be principal consultant to the Elections and Reapportionment committee. Richard sets the division of labor: Jim handles the work in Sacramento and I handle the technical operation, with the prestige of the Cal Tech name and the computer geniuses I'm bringing on board. I understood Richard doesn't have complete confidence in me, but I know what my job is and I'm in it to get the inside view of politics.

"My colleagues at Cal Tech are horrified because they're on the straight and narrow academic path, continuing their teaching and writing," Bruce remembers. "They predict I'd never return to being an academic again. I see this job as an opportunity, but there is a risk I could get fired by Cal Tech and that I might not do a good job. I still want to try."

Even though I don't have the slightest idea of what is going to be done, I begin to develop this relationship with Bruce Cain and it is constantly reinforced to me that I don't have anything to worry about; he will take care of it.

I also meet this other guy, Jim Wisely, who works for California Secretary of State March Fong Eu. For four years prior to this, Jim has gone all over the state looking closely at communities in flux. One of the things we have to look out for is growth. Growth, especially suburban growth, is bad for Democrats. We discover if we don't take it into consideration, it will only be a period of years after new housing subdivisions are built before Democratic officeholders we think are safe will be defeated. Jim Wisely becomes familiar with where growth is taking place in regions like the Inland Empire and Santa Clara County.

After our first meeting with Jim, Bruce says to me, "I can do the quantitative stuff and look at the state through census tracks and [voter] returns. But it's not a bad idea to have somebody who has actually gone out and visited these neighborhoods and studied housing tracts. It's a useful addition to have somebody who really knows these things like a political operative. That knowledge sometimes improves on the data." Wisely ends up becoming a very important ally. We rely on him heavily. He also has close contacts with the Census Bureau staff and acts as a liaison with them.

Working together, Jim and Bruce became familiar with areas where growth is happening and take steps to account for it. For instance, if we know a piece of land is planned for new housing in a marginal Democratic district, with the simple draw of the line that parcel can be shifted to a more Republican-leaning district next door so as to safeguard the Democrat, at least for a decade.

We explain where this phenomenon is occurring in their districts when we meet with Democratic legislators. They are often oblivious to it. They have not watched out for areas slated for growth or what that growth means to their political viability and survival. But Bruce, Jim, and I are considering it and as a result over the rest of the decade our plan becomes even more beneficial to Democrats. Explaining these nuances that we are factoring in eventually reinforces to most members that we know what we're talking about and that our operation is the real thing.

"Richard Alatorre's choice of his professional assistants, with Bruce Cain at the head of them, created a whole new generation of respected genius technicians in reapportionment," Willie Brown says. "Cal Tech provided the hardware and software, and Bruce Cain provided the brainpower. Because of Bruce's participation, our plans became more defensible in court than any plans Berman and D'Agostino would ever have created. I'm the one who put the legislature into the computer business. There were no computers until I came aboard. That was my pioneering."

"The '81 reapportionment helped keep the Democrats in power during the Reagan years," Bruce says. "At the time, [Assembly Republican Caucus Chairman Robert] Naylor was predicting ascendency of the Republicans in the state. It was not an unfounded theory. California had Republican governors throughout the '80s and '90s, George Deukmejian and Pete Wilson, during a period when Democrats consistently controlled the legislature."

"Naylor's prophecy—his prediction that Republicans in reapportionment would gain seats and power—was clearly not realized," according to Willie. "The Republicans were lucky to hold onto what they had. The only test that matters is what happens after reapportionment is over, during the rest of the decade. We held the house [the assembly]. There was never a threat that the Republicans would take over. The assembly and congressional—and the senate plan [that relied on the same data we created for the assembly and Congress]—survived court challenges."

Right around this time Willie starts getting nervous. He says he trusts me and everything else. But a lot of people in the assembly are telling him he should hire Carl and Michael. I'm sure he has second thoughts. Of course, it's coming from people who have selfish interests because they have ties to Carl and Michael, and to Howard Berman. Then there are others who come out of political operations and have relationships with them. They're all telling Willie that Carl and Michael are the only guys who should do it.

"It's your ass, just like mine," I tell Bruce. He keeps repeating, real calm, "Don't worry about it. You just take care of the politics and I'll create what you need.

"Willie was hard, there's no question," Bruce says. "Both of us were under the gun. Now, in retrospect, we see why: Michael and Carl wanted the business. The Bermanites wanted to control redistricting. People had doubts about Richard's priorities and whether he could do the details. I didn't have ties to anyone politically. So there were big question marks about both of us.

"This is where Richard's attributes figure in, especially the loyalty component," says Bruce. "Fairly early on he came to like me. After the first couple of months he became comfortable with me. We had good conversations. He understood what I was trying to do. I could explain things fairly clearly. So he was loyal. When people, Willie and others, had doubts, Richard stood up for me. By late spring we had pulled together an operation that was working 24 hours a day. By May or June, the state senate reapportionment people and others were using our data and relying on us. We had gone from being a big question mark to being the dominant operation."

Up until then everything involving the computing of voter behavior and trying to reduce it to the smallest unit has come down to the census tract level. That is the smallest unit. Bruce believes he has the capacity through development of computer programs to reduce the universe to an even smaller level, ultimately reducing it down to the city block, which is unheard of at the time.

Michael Berman and Carl D'Agostino have collected census and voter registration data too, of course, because they do direct mail as part of their political consulting services for candidates. But they have also only reduced it down to the census tract. Computerization, putting all the data on computers, opens up a new "age of negotiation" in reapportionment, Bruce argues: when district lines were all drawn by hand, "you couldn't make changes very easily. That worked perfectly if you were just going to tell people what the lines were and you weren't interested in their feedback. If you were and wanted to be able to make changes, it was very cumbersome to try and do that by hand. By having everything on computers, we were able to make last-minute accommodations" to take care of members' requests or objections. "Plus we had data going back in time so we could look at the historical evolution" of voter behavior and factor it into the consideration of changes in boundary lines. It is called GIS, for Geographic Information System, "and the level of sophistication was unheard of at the time," Bruce notes.

Computerization made for more flexibility in negotiations. We could make changes in a district—adding or removing this or that piece of land—and by the next morning we could go in and show the changes to the legislator in terms of how it impacted potential voter behavior and how it would affect this particular politician. Then I could immediately ask, "Do we have a deal?" and push for an answer. "In the end, the ability to make changes diminished the number of incredibly unhappy people" who might end up voting against the plan, Bruce observes.

Getting the data down to the city block level is a priority because "we were primarily interested in it for the purposes of evaluating Latino voting rates and polarization of whites," Bruce says. "So if you had a census tract and half of it was white and half Latino, you could more precisely carve it up both for partisan purposes and to enhance ethnic representation. It gave more precision to the whole process. Now, of course, that's how all systems work in every state, down to the block level."

I tell Bruce we should find a place for the operation to work out of in Sacramento. "I got a problem," he replies. "All the people I'll hire are students of mine at Cal Tech. They don't have the luxury of picking up and moving to Sacramento." That doesn't go over very well in the eyes of some assemblymembers.

"I also knew Richard didn't want members involved in the process," Bruce says. "The advantage of being in L.A. as opposed to Sacramento was that members couldn't drift into the office and make changes in the plan. In the end, that was a big plus. Nobody other than Willie ever came down and tried to come into our office," which was in Pasadena.

No members even know where the office is because I don't tell them. There is no need to set up in Sacramento because there is nothing we need there.

The office in Pasadena is within walking distance of Cal Tech. It is in a large retail space in an office building. It has a front office and a big open space with lots of desks. There is a receptionist and inside, everyone else is working on the mapping, programming, and line drawing processes.

The staff is made up 100 percent of students from Cal Tech. At the height, there are probably 150 kids paid by the hour. Over a year and a half, I am maybe the largest employer of Cal Tech students, maybe one of the largest employers of people in Pasadena.

"We had people working both day and night shifts, 24 hours a day," Bruce recounts. "Once the census data arrived, we had to merge the data. There was both precinct data and census block data. We had to draw the precincts by hand onto the census maps and then enter into the computer the correspondence between the precincts and the census tracts. It was very tedious and time consuming, with a lot of double checking."

The raw census data and precinct information has to be downloaded and made compatible with the programs we set up. It is very complicated. It takes months to set up. I learn the jargon as well as I can but it isn't my job.

The state senate operation that is supposed to be doing the same work is at Sonoma State University in Santa Rosa. "They were a bunch of pot heads," Bruce says. "We didn't think they would get the work done. Early on, in January or February, I told Richard we had to build our operation from scratch."

Most of the time Bruce is working out of the Pasadena office. He comes up to Sacramento when I need him. He is in on every meeting we have with the legislators, which is our first order of business. We don't have a lot of information to show members in those sessions. We show them a map of their district—it might have been a census tract map—which we lay out on a table or on the floor and provide basic voter registration and population information. Bruce recalls, "We'd usually tell them about neighboring districts so they understood the situation they were in."

Then I ask the members to tell me what is important, what do they want to keep and what do they want to gain. If they need to lose some residents, I ask who they want to get rid of. I do this especially for the Democrats so they can never say I didn't do something they wanted done. We do the same thing with the Republicans, but this part is an absolute exercise. It is okay for some of the Republicans I like; I sometimes try to accommodate them. Often what a Republican is asking for is personal.

"It's rarely partisan," Bruce says about requests from members. "It's about keeping neighborhoods that raised money for you. Or amusement parks or restaurants where you could do fundraisers or get tickets comped. Or genuinely eccentric things like having your mother in your district.

"Richard himself pulled a fast one on me. In an early version of the plan, I'm living in Altadena, in the assembly seat next to Richard's, just across the street from his district but not in it. He wants to move me. I believe it was Richard who changes the lines to go down Topeka, my street, to take in my house so Richard can invite me to all his fundraisers. I spend the next decade buying tickets to them."

I also arrange to have the little mountain hamlet of Keene, in the Tehachapi Mountains where Cesar Chavez lives at the UFW headquarters northeast of Bakersfield, moved into an assembly district covering the Central Valley instead of leaving it in the adjoining district that goes into the Mojave Desert.

"What's happening?" Willie always asks me. Every time I give him the same answer: "Everything is going fine."

"I don't have a good feeling," he says. "Maybe I made a mistake appointing you. I don't have any assurance progress is taking place." I always blow him off and don't pay attention to him.

One day sometime in July Bruce and I are talking. "I'm getting too much pressure," I tell him. "I got to see for myself and be able to report back that we do have an operation and it's working. I want to go down there" to Pasadena where Bruce has set up shop.

"Why do you want to come down?" Bruce asks. "You won't know what you're seeing."

Okay, I say to myself. I trust Bruce. But Willie isn't as trustful.

I decide to take off for a few days, driving from Sacramento and stopping in San Francisco to have dinner with Willie. It's a hundred degrees in L.A., but like winter up on the North Coast. I drive up Highway 1 for a few days in Mendocino. While up there I get a frantic phone call. It's Bruce. Willie L. Brown Jr. has shown up unannounced at the reapportionment headquarters in Pasadena.

Willie starts insulting the staff, the workers, Bruce is saying. These are college kids. Every one of them is off the charts in intelligence. They're computer programmers, scientists, computer wizards. Most of them know nothing about politics; it's just a job for them. What they know is they're working hard and being paid by one of their professors.

What Willie doesn't like is that everybody isn't kissing his ass. The dress code is very informal. Some of the kids you wouldn't allow out in public during the day. Some aren't very socially functional. They don't have the social graces Willie has.

One of the workers is this bald-headed guy, a brilliant programmer who designs programs, but he has great difficulty communicating with the average person. Whatever he eats last is on his shirt. He hasn't slept for two or three days. He probably smells.

Here comes walking in the Speaker of the California state assembly, elegantly dressed as always. His immediate conclusion is that everything is in shambles. I can just hear him saying, "Oh my God, these people. . . ." He starts using some of the jargon he hears me periodically throwing around to deflect him. Willie's trying to show that he knows what he's talking about. He's the kind who has to be an expert at everything.

Many of the workers don't know who Willie is. Before he leaves, he's going to make it clear he is the boss. He's offended they aren't presentable and that everyone doesn't know who he is. "You're representing me and the state of California," he declares. But they're college students.

Bruce calls me: "Willie Brown is here and things are going horrible. He's demeaning the kids who are busting their asses, saying they don't know what they're doing."

"Put Willie on the phone," I tell Bruce. "Put him on the fucking phone."

"Willie," I tell him, "I don't ever want you to do this again. If you wanted to go down, I would go with you. These guys are busting their asses. We've made a lot of progress. I told you I'm going to deliver the product that is being done by these people. If we have to start all over again, you are fucked because we're getting down to the wire. Just get the fuck out of there and never come back. You're just messing everything up and I can't have that. You gave me the responsibility, so stay the fuck away." He leaves and never returns.

"We did a lot of briefings for Willie" in Sacramento, Bruce recalls. "He would typically stay for the first 15 minutes and walk out. We would write things up for him, not realizing he couldn't see [because of his limited vision]. Somehow in the end the only reason Willie stayed the course was that even Willie couldn't tell Richard what to do. He was going to listen to Richard. If Richard hadn't been there, possibly Willie would have caved in to the pressure and given it over to Carl and Michael."

After the Democratic coalition is united, with the Brownies and Bermanites cooperating, Bruce starts dealing with Michael Berman on a regular basis. Bruce works with Michael on the seats the Bermans care about, especially in the San Fernando Valley where many of their people are. "In the end, Michael got to know me better and came to like and trust me," Bruce says. "That took some of the heat off things, which was important because we didn't yet have the whole state on the computer. So sections of the state had to be done by hand. There were some trivial mistakes, involving a few thousand voters here and there." After the reapportionment plan was enacted, "we had to go back with a clean-up bill. To do that meant opening up negotiations again. So the fact that Michael developed confidence in our operation was a good thing."

Willie knows my first priority is protecting him and his caucus. "I want you to know," I tell him, "since you've given me reapportionment that I make the commitment I'll do a good job. I'll take care of your interests and make sure we elect a Democratic majority. I'll make sure the blacks are not screwed" in the process. But I also say, "I want something else; I've earned it and you should understand. My job is also making sure Chicanos are taken care of." He agrees. That's important because when my name is first floated around as chairman of Elections and Reapportionment, everybody is concerned that members who have Mexicans in their districts should worry. They all know what they've done in past reapportionments to minimize Latino political clout. You know, the John Vasconcelloses of the world who represents San Jose. Or the Rick Lehmans of the world in the Central Valley. There is a great deal of concern.

Because of that I put it to Willie, "Reapportionment starts with the Speaker, with his district. Tell me who are the members who have to be taken care of under any circumstances—Democrats who are special to you or have special needs." He says he wants to make sure the ethnics are dealt with. "And I know you're going to take care of the Chicanos," Brown adds.

Taking care of Mexicans is my goal right from the start. "It was something Willie might not have put much priority on had he not done this deal convincing Richard to head up redistricting," as Bruce puts it. "He might have put the [Democratic] party and the coalition [with Republicans] that got him into power first. So Richard's concern [for the interests of Latinos] brought a new constraint to the table that might not have been there certainly if the Bermans had done [reapportionment]. As soon as I was hired as consultant to the committee, I was made aware by Richard that this was a priority, and one that I shared. When I looked at the [census] data, I agreed with Richard [on the need to make progress for Chicanos]." Jim Wisely, the reapportionment consultant who works under Bruce, shares that strong commitment. "It was a convergence of forces," Bruce says.

It pisses Willie off because I won't tell him anything about what's going on with reapportionment. On the one hand, it pisses him off because he wants to know. It also pisses him off because redistricting is the most important political function of his young Speakership and it will decide whether or not he stays Speaker. On the other hand, my refusal to give him any information is a great excuse. Other assemblymembers are constantly bugging him to tell them what's happening. "I don't know," he replies, "ask Alatorre." It gives him the cover he wants. Either way, I don't care. I'm going to do it my way. I don't give a shit what Brown wants.

"Willie and Richard had quite the routine," Bruce says. "The Speaker got to say, 'I can't control this guy. He's going to do what he's going to do.' So the Speaker never got as much blame as he might have otherwise received. Meantime, Richard was able to control things."

What I relearn during reapportionment is that it is the most selfish, self-serving process there is, where everybody is looking out only for himself or herself. Political survival is number one, two, three, and four. With very few exceptions, no one is willing to take "one for the team." Some legislators lead people to believe they think redistricting is corrupt and distasteful, and they want no part of it in order to preserve the purity of their progressive credentials. These liberals say they can win anywhere regardless of where the lines come down. But when they're in the room with just me or other members and it comes down to *their* districts, they want to make sure their mother's in the district; they want this or that major contributor in the district; they want this or that campus or institution in the district; or they want this or that existing or potential political competitor in the next district over.

Bruce adds, "There's no question that when Democratic incumbents came in to talk with Richard about their districts, they rarely asked about the big picture: how many Democratic seats can we create? How can I help the Democrat in the more marginal seat next door? No one comes in to deal with that construction. It was, 'How can I strengthen my seat?' or 'There are these neighborhoods I've always wanted to have in my district.' Members get very uptight and emotional" when it comes to themselves.

Even members of the Democratic leadership who are in safe districts get all worked up in reapportionment. According to Bruce, one of them said to Richard in a meeting, "Richard, I want to help you in any way I can. I'm safe no matter what direction you put me in. Make whatever changes you want and I'm a vote [for the reapportionment bill]." So Richard puts him onto the "I-don't-have-to-consult-with-you" list and makes some changes to his district. Two days to go before the bill is voted on, [this member] sends his chief aide to my office with a whole list of changes requiring opening up negotiations with a whole bunch of other legislators at the last minute. I told him we couldn't do that and get the bill out on time. The aide gets all upset. I say, "I'll have you talk to Richard." I could tell the aide didn't want to do that. I put him on the phone with Richard anyway. Richard absolutely rips another asshole in the guy. He is literally reduced to almost a tearful wreck by the whole experience. To this day, this ex-aide hates my guts and badmouths me.

"Another example was the beloved Speaker himself, who essentially asked the same thing of Richard, sending his assistant to ask for all of these changes at the last minute, none of which had any bearing on the Speaker's chances of holding his seat," Bruce says. "One change involved alterations to the assemblymember to the south of Willie, Lou Papan. Papan was a pretty intimidating guy and not easy to negotiate with. I don't know if Richard was involved with Willie's changes to Papan's district or not, but he may have signed off on them. Papan found out about them the day of the vote. He called the Speaker and wanted to talk about them with both of us. I had to meet with Papan in back of the assembly podium. Richard wasn't around. 'How dare you do this to me?' Papan said.

"'But Willie's staff asked me to do it.' I replied.

Then Willie saunters in. "'What's the problem?' the Speaker asked. Papan described what went on. 'Who signed off on it?' Willie asked, even though he knew all about it. 'You're kidding,' Willie said, commiserating with Papan. 'Bruce did that to you. That's outrageous.' I kept my mouth shut.

"'You know what else,' Papan continued, 'Bruce not only made those changes on my border, but he made these other changes,' which he went on to recount."

"'These bastards are always doing it and we just have to accept it,' Willie said. Then the two of them went out arm in arm onto the assembly floor, with Papan imagining I did this to him as if I was responsible for it. I thought to myself, 'You've got to be kidding me.'"

Since Willie gets elected Speaker in a coalition with Republicans, speculation runs rampant about what the Republicans get in exchange for supporting a black liberal Democrat from San Francisco. Rumors are still running when I take over the reapportionment committee. "Hey brother, what is it you want me to do *vis-à-vis* the Republicans?" I ask Brown.

"I promised them nothing," he responds. "I just said I would be fair and I want you to be fair."

"Fair is in the eye of the beholder," I say. "I'll be fair. I give you my commitment I'll be fair." He knows not to believe me.

Then he simply says, "Protect me."

I say, "No problem."

I never trust the Republicans. Personally, I've made some friendships with a few of them: Ken Maddy, Paul Priolo, Bill Campbell, Bruce Nestande, Frank Hill. I drink with them and we sometimes go fishing together. But I don't like their politics.

Willie insists "The promises I made to Carol Hallett and the Republican Caucus were the same promises anyone else would have made: you will get resources as needed to conduct your own reapportionment. You will have membership on the [reapportionment] committee proportionate to your membership among the 80 assemblymembers. Those were the only commitments and I totally keep them. That's just how I am. There wasn't any give-away to anyone. That's just good organizational structure."

"Things were more complicated for Richard," Bruce Cain says. "It wasn't clear how to get to the 41 votes we needed" to pass a plan. We aren't sure we will be able to satisfy the Democrats who support Berman and there's the chance they won't vote for our reapportionment bill. "Because that was a real and present danger, we went into negotiations with the possibility we might have to get some Republican votes by giving them some things they wanted and pass the bill without the Berman votes," Bruce adds. "We opened up lines of communication with the Republicans, interviewing Republicans" along with Democratic members to get their concerns and input about their districts.

One of the first things I do is meet with every single assemblymember, first the Democrats and then the Republicans. It takes a month. They come in one at a time. I have basic information about each district for them.

When individual members come in for our personal meetings, what is important for me is asking about what's important to them, what do they want. I remember bringing in this white racist Republican, Bud Collier, one of their senior guys representing a district from South Pasadena into San Marino. He's old school, a good old southern boy, not well educated, and conservative to the max. "Let's just say hypothetically," I tell him, "I present you with something [a reapportionment plan] that meets every one of your needs. Are you predisposed to voting for that plan?"

He looks at me: "Son, when it comes to nut cutting, it's every man for himself and everyone has to understand it because that's the way it's done."

Democrat or Republican, it doesn't matter. If Collier gets what he wants, he'll screw his own caucus. He ends up voting for the plan because I give him what he wants. When it comes to reapportionment, he isn't caught up in Republican ideology.

"Those were the olden days," Bruce says. "In those days you could peel some people off, get some defections on the budget or other important party-line votes. It wouldn't happen today because the caucus would discipline renegades, members who weren't obeying the party line."

That was then. Yet as time goes on, Bruce says, "it became pretty clear as we went through talks with individual [GOP] members and with [assembly Republican Caucus Chairman] Naylor and their staff that they believed the Republican Party was on the cusp of a renaissance. [President] Reagan had just been elected. Their idea was they were expecting growth in Republican voter registration—expecting to be the dominant political party in California. So they were not going to just take their current share of [assembly] seats. They wanted more Republican seats. If they had come to Willie with a bipartisan [reapportionment] plan and said, 'Just give us the seats we have right now and let us tell you how we want those seats drawn up,' quite possibly Willie would have gone in that direction."

But in early 1981, the Republican Party in the assembly sees itself as the party of the future in California that needs to gain some more seats. So the Republicans are not in a negotiating mood, and neither am I.

It takes a while for all of us to get to that point. One day in early 1981, just as I'm getting into reapportionment, Willie says, "We're having a meeting with the Republicans."

"Why do you want to meet with them?" I ask.

"Because I promised them, I got to keep them happy and they're getting leery and want to know what's happening with redistricting," he says. "I told them the process is just starting. They want a status report."

We meet in Willie's small office in the temporary quarters housing the assembly floor built on the east lawn of the Capitol that is being used while the original, historic building is being renovated. There is just enough room for his desk, a couch and a few chairs. I arrive first. I spread myself out on the coach, complaining of a headache. Brown is there. Hallett, the assembly minority leader, walks in with Bob Naylor, the caucus chair, and Assemblymember Ross Johnson—I forget his exact title, but he's the Republican bulldog. I like Carol Hallett. So I'm lying down as they walk in. That leaves them standing there since there isn't much room to sit down.

"Hey Alatorre," Willie says, "make room for them."

"I've got a headache," is all I say. I just don't move. Hallett doesn't know what to do. Here's this crazy Mexican. It's kind of like with my body language I'm communicating the fact I'm being disrespectful to Willie, but more importantly I'm being disrespectful to the Republican leadership. I'm making it clear I don't want to be there, I'm not interested in what they have to say and I'm there only because the Speaker asked me to be there.

The meeting starts. "This is the problem we have," Hallett starts explaining to Brown: "We're not getting information" about reapportionment. "You promised us a role. We don't know what's happening."

Fifteen or 20 minutes into the meeting, I suddenly announce, "I've got another meeting," and I get up.

"The meeting isn't over yet," Brown says.

"It's over as far as I'm concerned," and I walk out.

Twenty minutes later, Willie marches into my office. "What the fuck are you doing?" He's irate.

"Didn't I accomplish my and your objective?" I reply.

"What are you talking about?" Willie asks.

"That the meeting would end," I answer. "How long did you want the meeting to last? Did you want me to give them any of the information they wanted?"

"Not necessarily."

"Well, they didn't get any did they?"

"No."

"Willie, use me," I tell him. "I'll go to any meetings you want me to. But at the point you want the meeting to end, give me the high sign and I'll act like an asshole and walk out."

He starts laughing. I make a big joke of it too. Then he says, "I don't want you to be disrespectful like that to me. That's not good for people to see."

"Okay, Willie, whatever. Fine."

When asked later about his recollection of that meeting with the Republicans and me, Willie says, "Richard was more than contemptuous. He was downright hostile. Richard's diplomatic skills for people he disliked and didn't trust were never concealed. That's one of the delightful things about him."

You know me. Sometimes when someone I know, even a fellow Democrat, a member of my own caucus, asks me a question about reapportionment, they don't know what I'm telling them. Think about what it's like when it's someone I don't want to give information to. And even if I did give them information, they don't understand it because it is all high tech talk I don't even understand.

"Because people misunderstand reapportionment, there is really nothing to discuss until there is a proposed plan," Brown states. "The war games played in all the various configurations that could be envisioned [in drawing district boundaries] don't lend themselves to discussions with anybody. Before [a plan is put forward] it's really an information gathering activity. Richard was unusually good at handling that."

Since "partial interim reports" are not possible during reapportionment, Willie says, "it was my job to try to convey to everybody else that the process was moving forward." What's more, "because there's not much changing you can do at the 11th hour, just before the final plan is presented [to the legislature], that's why the Republicans were so eager to gain information—so they could have input. And that's why Richard was so resistant; he wanted to make sure they got minimal information, if any. Plus, they could not raise too much hell because we'd been providing them with adequate resources to do their own reapportionment plan. And we never asked them to show us their maps."

If the Republicans had been smart, Willie Brown says, "they would have had open season on their maps, exposing them to public view. In many cases, their maps would have better reflected individual Democratic members' selfish desires than anything Alatorre could have done. That kind of political pressure could have been formidable. But they didn't do that; they never thought of it. Like everyone doing reapportionment, they were only looking out for their interests."

"All of this is why you have to have a profound amount of confidence in your architect on reapportionment," Bruce notes. "And a profound amount of trust that on judgment day [when the plan is unveiled], it's going to magically appear, get the required votes, and be court-defendable."

Not long after the meeting with Hallett and company in Willie's office I get a visit from Judith Briggs, a fundraiser from the East Bay who is very close to Willie and Assemblymember Bill Lockyer, as well as Richie Ross, then chief administrative officer of the assembly and a top political strategist. They come to see me to say Willie is thinking about giving the Republicans what they want. "You've got to stop it," Judy says. "We're afraid he may ask you to do things and he's got to understand that this is about [protecting] the Democrats. The Democrats don't trust him. If he makes concessions to the Republicans that he doesn't have to, it will jeopardize his Speakership."

I make a beeline to Willie's office in the Capitol's temporary annex. It's just the two of us. He's sitting behind his desk. I jump up on top of it. He's looking up all wide-eyed at this crazy guy standing on his desk. I put on this great show. I'm yelling at him: "What the fuck is wrong with you? I don't care what you committed to them [the Republicans]. You can't do it. You're a Democrat. You're a Democratic Speaker. We have the majority. We don't need them. Whatever commitment you made to them, say it's out of my hands and that this guy, Alatorre, is crazy. I'm going to do the best I can. . . ."

We're interrupted when the phone rings. "I got to take this call," he says.

"Answer it," I say. He's only on for a few seconds.

I go back to yelling at him: "What I'm doing with reapportionment is important to you. What I'm doing will guarantee your Speakership for as long as you want it. The Democrats expect this," I insist. "You can't give in to the Republicans because you're a Democrat and you represent the Democratic majority. If the Republicans could, they'd slit your throat. They don't care about you anyway. And if you expect me to do what you're thinking of doing [giving in to the Republicans] I'm just not going to do it." I stalk out.

Not much later, Judy Briggs and Richie Ross come in to see me. "I think you got him," one of them says. "I think he heard you and I think you convinced him that the only way to go is to come up with a solid Democratic plan and then things will be fine."

"I'll quit before I do something with the Republicans," I tell them.

Later, Willie says, "If you want to be a good leader, you have to be prepared to farm out the work to be done. And Richard's conduct in that regard was no different from that of Maxine Waters on the Ways and Means Committee. It was why Maxine and Vasco [John Vasconcellos] were forever the two members of the [two-house] conference committee I relied upon to do budget work. I only wanted to be called on by my chairpersons in key spots at the end of the rainbow on the issues they didn't want to handle. That served me well and eliminated the need to be worried about whether someone was organizing against me."

At about the same time Phil Burton is recruiting Howard Berman and others from his camp to run for Congress. So my relationship with the Berman faction is solidifying and it is becoming easier to draw up a plan accommodating what all Democrats want without help from the Republicans.

"We encouraged folks to go to Congress who we didn't want in the assembly," Willie Brown explains. "Howard Berman owes his career in Congress to us. Richard could very easily have done the line drawing to reflect the shrinking of the influence of [Howard] and our friends in those parts of [West L.A. and the San Fernando Valley] where their population wasn't growing. The population was growing elsewhere in L.A. [among Latinos, for example]. But we carefully drew the lines in such a way that [the Bermans] ended up with great representation reflected in numbers they would not ordinarily have been entitled to. And Howard was the chief beneficiary of that."

"At a certain point in the process, in late May or June, before the bill was written but as we were moving along drawing the lines, I was in negotiations with Republican consultants when I got a phone call from Richard," Bruce remembers. "He said we're pulling the plug on negotiations and for me to get out of there. That was the moment in which the whole emphasis switched from bipartisan to partisan. The decision was made that we were doing a partisan Democratic redistricting plan."

My job is to create a Democratic majority for a decade, not just an election. I understand the process well enough to know that so long as you have the support of the Speaker, you can do anything within reason. Within that context, to the extent I can, I also want to develop districts throughout the state so what historically takes place hurting Chicanos does not take place again. I want to bring together communities that are separated strictly because of the belief by white Democrats that they can keep themselves in power by preventing Mexicans or other ethnic or racial minorities from electing their own. My agenda is not anti-Democratic. I don't see any inconsistency in helping out the Democrats and Chicanos at the same time, even though I know it will create problems for a lot of individual members who will feel threatened. When some members respond to Willie's announcement of my appointment, there are comments questioning whether I can do it. They don't say they don't want a Mexican doing it. Instead, they say Chicanos in the state will place a lot of pressure on Alatorre and that might end up hurting the party, meaning hurting individual Anglo Democrats who depend for years on dispersing Latinos into different districts in order to stay in office.

"There were layers of concern" among Democratic members, as Bruce says. "One layer was the concern Richard would pursue a Latinos-only agenda. This view was amplified by rhetoric coming from the Rose Institute and from Latino activists who worked with the Rose Institute."

In the eyes of these Democrats, preserving a Democratic majority would be secondary to me.

"It's fair to say right from the start, Richard was looking at making the two concerns [maintaining Democratic control and making progress for Latinos] duel priorities and finding compromises," according to Bruce. "We could have pursued maximizing a Latino agenda to the detriment of all things Democratic, but we didn't. Instead, we created these 'influence' seats, chiefly relying on Latino populations in Republican areas."

The difficulty in 1981, when we actually look at where we can create new seats with significant numbers of Latinos, is the political reality that many of them would have relatively small numbers of actual Latino voters. "You would have had large numbers of unregistered Latinos or noncitizens who couldn't be voters," Bruce points out. "So you clearly would not get seats that elected Latinos. It wasn't until the 1990s, when you had the trio of Propositions 187 [denying public services to undocumented immigrants], 209 [against bilingual education], and 227 [all school instruction in English] that the Latino community really got energized, with those measures bringing about a big change in Latino political registration and participation. But that hadn't yet happened in the early 1980s; there was nothing to motivate Latino voters at that point."

I know in my head what I want to do. But I have to walk a fine line so it doesn't appear overtly clear. My philosophy is if you keep them dumb, both Democrats and Republicans, you can do anything. Don't give out numbers or any information about how the plan is developing, including to members of my own caucus, so they have no ammunition to complain to the Speaker or begin a movement to resist my plan.

I think it's safe to say even the Democrats don't know what I am up to. I never tell one member what I am doing in his or her district and how it impacts another member's district. That way no member can ever compare notes on anything I am up to—until we are ready to unveil the plan itself. All I do is assure them, "You're in your mother's arms."

Some are unhappy with what we do. But I end up with 41 Democrats who are happy.

Not sharing much information is also very much the attitude on congressional redistricting taken by Phil Burton, who spends a lot of time at the state Capitol during the reapportionment process. "Burton was very much a mentor to Richard," Bruce remembers. "He would come to Richard's office regularly, usually late in the afternoon, and talk with Richard and the rest of us about redistricting and anything else on his mind."

That was unusual. "Not many members of Congress, particularly from San Francisco, made their way to Sacramento and hung out in offices at the Capitol," Bruce says. "That's because Phil was very much hands-on, in person during reapportionment. The first time I met him was in Richard's office. He was a hero of my dad's. I thought: this will be a lot of fun. I made the mistake of sitting away from the door in the office when Phil came. What I didn't know was Phil started drinking in the late afternoon and by early evening could become abusive and not much fun to be around. Most who knew Phil would sit next to the door so they could more easily slip out."

Phil is a brilliant guy. He comes into my office all the time, drinking and everything else. One day at three or four in the afternoon, Phil Burton walks into my "bunker" office on the second floor of the Capitol (so-called because it's without windows), unscheduled to see me. He goes into my personal office and we don't come out until 6:30 p.m. By then, only my legislative assistant, Toni Trigueiro, is still around; she usually waits around until I'm ready to leave for the day. I introduce her to Phil. "This is the woman you will talk to if you ever have to convey information to me quickly," I tell the barrel-chested congressman from San Francisco.

Phil turns to me: "Who buys the booze?" I look at Toni. Toni looks at me. "I guess that would be me," Toni says.

"Richard wasn't a big drinker, but did have a bar inside a cupboard in his private office," Toni recalls. "Since none of us were really drinkers, I'd buy those big gallon containers of Scotch, bourbon, or vodka.

"You need a better brand of vodka," Phil declares.

"Yes sir, I'll take care of that," Toni replies.

Later, after Phil and I leave, Toni goes into my office and discovers this huge bottle of vodka with a big handle that has never been opened is about a quarter gone. There is no ice in the office, and no mixer either; only paper cups. Phil sat there and drank down a quarter of that jug and then walks away perfectly sober, with no slurring of words. Toni is flabbergasted. She never realizes a human being can drink that much alcohol and remain standing—all in the middle and late afternoon.

Phil can be heavy-handed in dealing with members and others. He "was the brain, if we needed one beyond us, on reapportionment," according to Willie. "He was more experienced, older—plus Phil's temperament was worse than Alatorre's. He was less tolerant of fools than Richard. And for both assembly and congressional reapportionment, Burton never trusted the senate to do anything." Still, his presence begins to be counterproductive. Towards the end of the redistricting process, I send him back to Washington.

"Richard's right, he didn't show his hand [details of the assembly plan] too early and allow coalitions to be built [in opposition to it]," according to Bruce. "But he was more transparent by far than Phil Burton. We at least gave a version of our first set of assembly lines to members several weeks, maybe six weeks, out. Phil didn't give [Democrats in Congress] maps until after the [reapportionment] bill was passed [at the state Capitol]. Phil would keep everything on a hand calculator, not on a computer. We had things on a computer so people [assemblymembers] could come over to this office we rented in Sacramento and we would go over the data with them."

By the time we get towards the end of the process and present the initial plan to Democratic members, a hell of a lot of negotiating is going on. "Everyone who was our critic got pulled into the process," Bruce says. "By then we pulled in Michael Berman and Bill Cavala, an aide to the Speaker who increasingly in the last few weeks sat in the offices of members who had problems and worked with Richard in negotiating. Within the Capitol staff there were factions and people who wanted to control things. Cavala didn't know me and wanted some control of the process. So he was sticking knives in our backs."

Assembly redistricting in 1981 "is a case where being loyal was very helpful with Richard," Bruce notes. "With me, if he hadn't been loyal despite the pressure from members and if he hadn't been the tough person he was, Willie would have folded, given over to Michael and Carl, and we would have gotten a very different redistricting plan that would have done much less for Latinos and been more partisan, a plan looking more like the Burton [congressional] plan."

It isn't until the day we have the news conference where we introduce the plan, within a half an hour of our presentation of it, that Willie Brown figures out I accomplish what needs to be done. He can tell by the number of Republicans who come to him and are outraged that he screws them the way he does.

That's when Willie tells me, "Fuck, you must have done something right."

At the end Willie is fine. Right up until then, he is very nervous. But he leaves me alone. He disavows me when I'm not communicating with the Democrats or Republicans. "I'm not getting information either," he tells them. "Alatorre's crazy. He refuses to give me anything either." At least the Republicans feel they are being treated equally.

Some "good-government" Democratic members complain about the plan being too political and how they're only there to do the business of the people. Some of the Democrats who care more about themselves than government, good or bad, are outraged by what I've done to them, thinking I stabbed them in the back. One of the best things anybody heard during the reapportionment process in the '80s was the line I get to frequently repeat: "Then was then and now is now." I promise certain things, and I might be serious at the time. But time passes and new realities present themselves. That is my explanation for them getting fucked.

Like any plan, ours produces some odd-looking assembly districts. One in Ventura County is only linked by a mountain range that is impossible to traverse. Our theory is this district meets the contiguous requirement because the famed California Condors that nest in the area are able to fly over it. Therefore, we have succeeded in unifying this Condor habitat, an important achievement.

Phil Burton draws a congressional district in San Francisco in such a way so as to protect his brother, John. It is only contiguous when it is connected by land during low tide. When confronted by reporters at the news conference revealing his congressional plan, Phil is asked to explain how the district is connected because two separate pieces seem to end up in the Pacific Ocean without a land link. "Oh shit, what did I do?" he responds. It is later explained to him that the district meets the legal requirement since it is connected during times of low tide.

There are some other bizarrely shaped congressional seats because at the end of the process, Michael Berman comes in and, to get the votes of Bermanites in the assembly, insists on redoing some seats for West L.A. Jewish politicians for the sake of picking up a few additional Democratic voter registration points. "Michael argues a couple of registration points are worth several hundred thousand dollars in campaign money," Bruce notes.

"It's a miracle we pull it off," Bruce says. "If I'd known all the problems, I wouldn't have taken the job. But Richard dealt with them all. If it had been anybody but Richard, we would not have pulled it off."

Nevertheless, we do manage to line up the minimum 41 votes needed to approve the plan in the assembly. With one or two exceptions, there isn't support from Republicans. Some of the negative reaction is a "change to a more partisan orientation," as Bruce explains it. "Part is the ripple effect." When a change is made in a district in the northern part of the state, it "affects how districts are drawn in the south. The change cascades throughout the process. That creates problems when you're trying to put together any plan." Members in central or southern California "don't expect to see their district changed because of something that happened far away up north."

The results of reapportionment, as viewed from the reactions in the press, are interesting. "If you look at the press clippings, the assembly was criticized for some of the districts, but there was far less criticism of the assembly plan than the state senate and congressional plans," Bruce recalls. "At least Richard was trying to create more minority-influence seats, which most people thought was a good thing. And we didn't have the same wildly noncompact, partisan gerrymanders that were in the congressional or senate plans."

Gerrymandering is one of those terms that mean different things to different people, depending on who's doing it and who's getting it done to them. All redistricting is a "conscious manipulation of lines," as Bruce puts it. "Some purposes are good. Some are bad, and some are trivial. So we have a tendency to use the term gerrymandering for things we don't like and we use the term line drawing for things we do like."

I do my duty to protect Willie. "The foundation for Willie Brown's record-breaking Speakership was 1981 reapportionment," Bruce says. "He had other qualities that gave him longevity. We gave him the architecture that made it possible."

"There is no question that the re-electability of Willie Brown was in the reapportionment plan," Willie affirms. "Also keep in mind how that plan got rid of a number of Willie Brown's natural enemies by sending Berman and his crew to Congress. They literally owe their careers to me. Berman was ranking Democratic member of the House Foreign Relations Committee. He has to remember he got to Congress because we gave him a district. We found a way to help each and every solitary one of our folk who were potentially disloyal because they were on the losing side [of the Speakership fight] to move on to Congress. They did. And their replacements were never from the same gene pool."

But what really gives me pride to this day is what we also accomplish for Chicanos.

Very few people really know about my parallel agenda. From the start it is setting in motion a plan to produce immediate gains by creating seats where Latinos can get elected and producing long-term gains by creating minority influence districts where Mexicans can be elected down the road, including two new congressional seats in southern California. I also want to unify communities that are historically divided. I seek to end the practice of Chicanos finding out that the extent of their influence is solely helping to elect non-Latino candidates to the exclusion of electing some of our own. My aim is to create political opportunities for Chicanos that would, over the decade and into the future, see the election of more Latinos.

"Richard was probably the first Latino in the country to take control of the redistricting process," Bruce observes.

I think that's true. I also had to take a lot of heat from advocates of increased ethnic representation. "He had his critics in the Latino community when the process began," Bruce says. "Californios for Fair Representation, an advocacy group that was heavily involved with the [Republican-leaning] Rose Institute, were in Richard's office giving him a hard time. There did exist more aggressive plans than ours," he adds, that might have created more seats for Chicanos, although whether Chicanos would have been elected from such districts is another question given the reality of citizenship and voter registration rates at the time. Another question is whether such a plan will pass muster in either house of the legislature.

"In the end, we compromised between Democratic and Latino goals," Bruce says. "This is the tension that persists to this day between the way Democrats think of redistricting and activists think of it."

Since I'm not telling anyone, including Mexicans, what is up with our plan, the groups with an interest in creating districts that would elect more Latinos are questioning my commitment to their agenda. Californios for Fair Representation pickets and sits in at my district office on Figueroa Blvd. in Highland Park in L.A. My assistant down there, Dan Arguello, wants to close shop and have the state police arrest the demonstrators. "You don't need to do that," I tell Dan. "Don't let anybody abuse anyone, but I don't need problems." The protesters get tired around midnight and leave. One of the participating activists I know is Leticia Quezada, who is later elected to the Los Angeles Unified School District Board of Education. I have to straighten her out. "You're picketing your friends," I tell her.

"But you won't tell us anything," she responds.

"I won't tell my fellow members [of the assembly] anything either, so at least you're in good company."

Because they have unsuccessfully tried to get information from me, one day before the assembly plan is even out, the same group pickets Willie Brown at the state Capitol. They just figure the plan will adversely impact Chicanos. Brown is pissed off. "Relax," I tell him, "I don't like it any more than you do."

There are also leaders within the African-American community "who were worried because the intermingling of their communities with Latinos would result in losses for African-American elected officials," Bruce adds. "Richard was the first politician to deal with all these issues in reapportionment from a position of power."

During the process of developing the plan, we hold hearings in San Jose, Fresno, Stockton, Sacramento, Los Angeles, and San Diego to get people's input on what they think is important. You have people who are nuts about maintaining communities of interest that are not ethnic. Don't divide cities or counties wherever possible, they argue. I talk to Chicano groups, urging them to participate and testify, and put on pressure. I already know what I'm going to do, but I need to have some cover. Any time Latino activists speak out in public about righting wrongs it is helpful for me when I have to listen in private to legislators talking about their selfish interests.

Whenever useful, I shove the 1965 federal Voting Rights Act down the throats of Democrats and Republicans. Ever since the '60s, minority activists have been more aggressively asserting their rights. There are also some federal and state court rulings that say politicians can't use the reapportionment process to disenfranchise ethnic and racial minorities.

In the following year, the '65 federal voting rights law is up for a crucial renewal by Congress. In 1982, the law is significantly strengthened to "require that in all situations of severe underrepresentation of a protected minority group, a jurisdiction had the obligation to create a majority minority seat," Bruce says. After 1982, the U.S. Justice Department is required to be an ally in making that happen. But "when Richard and I worked on redistricting in 1981, the Voting Rights Act had not yet been renewed. We didn't have an aggressive Justice Department [under President Reagan] or an amended Voting Rights Act."

So our '81 reapportionment plan is put together under a lower legal standard: before 1982, for a Latino group to successfully sue a jurisdiction, it has to prove redistricting is intentionally dividing Chicano communities for political reasons. In reality, what happens is a political body—a city council or board of supervisors—draws lines a decade before, and in the intervening years the Latino population grows and happens to randomly divide itself over several districts. Of course, there are also examples of a city council or legislature deliberately gerrymandering to protect incumbents. But there are also many cases where you can't argue the jurisdiction is intentionally discriminating. (The tougher '82 amendments come in very handy when Bruce Cain and I do redistricting for the Los Angeles City Council in 1986.)

So in reality, "we had a much weaker legal framework" to work in, Bruce says. "If Richard had the legal framework that existed in 1982, he would have wielded it like a sledge hammer." We use the possibility of violations of the Voting Rights Act and the threat of the courts taking over anyway.

We argue that the danger of the legislature ignoring minority interests in redistricting, especially those of Mexicans, is losing control of the process—having it taken out of the legislative arena and handed over to the courts, which has happened before. At least there are controls, I tell my colleagues, if we're allowed to do it. If you allow the courts to find us in violation of the Voting Rights Act, it would take reapportionment out of the hands of the legislature and give it to the courts or a citizens' panel that nobody can control. Then no member's preferences will be considered.

I use this argument with each individual member when I meet with him or her in my office. I reassure them that I'm going to do everything possible to accomplish their objectives subject to making sure the Voting Rights Act is not violated. I say the same thing to both Democrats and Republicans, but primarily to the Democrats since they're the biggest violators anyway. Republicans do not do past reapportionment plans that compromise Latino political influence.

The capability of our operation, with people like Bruce Cain, Jim Wisely, and all the Cal Tech kids, is also a big advantage in advancing a Chicano agenda on reapportionment. Before, when state lawmakers meet every tenth year after the U.S. Census to draw legislative and congressional boundaries, there is little or no accurate measurement of Latinos. The Census Bureau doesn't even try to gauge the Latino community. Also, until the 1950s and '60s, Chicanos lack the political sophistication and organization to press their agenda. So gerrymandering continues into the '70s.

By then, President Carter initiates reforms, resulting in a much clearer recognition of Latinos across the country. My Assembly Elections and Reapportionment Committee staff uses computers to build a database with better identification of Mexicans than ever before. By uniting political and computer science in each big city and small town in California, we are able to locate Latinos neighborhood by neighborhood and even block by block.

"This was a growth period for California and a period of Latino growth too," Bruce notes. "It was helpful to know where Latinos are now and five years from now. If you knew a white, upper-middle class subdivision was going up in an area, you don't want to create a Latino or Latino-influence seat there. You give the areas of white, middle-class growth, which is much more conservative and Republican, to the Republicans. Anticipating changes was where Wisely was coming from."

It doesn't hurt that Latinos, through groups such as Californios for Fair Representation, are by far the best-organized interest group lobbying in the 1981 redistricting process. Ultimately, though, the lesson I learn in the 1960s is that it takes pressure from both activists on the outside and leaders working from the inside to bring about genuine change. The fact reapportionment for the assembly and Congress is headed up by a Chicano and a former activist doesn't hurt either.

To remedy decades of discrimination and unfairness, our goal for Latinos in redistricting is attacking the two gerrymandering techniques that have historically been used to dilute minorities' voting strength: overdispersion and overconcentration. The Eastside barrios of Los Angeles and San Jose are prime examples of the effect of overdispersion. Latinos in both communities are divided over legislative districts so their numbers are too few to elect a Spanish-surnamed candidate or exert much influence with incumbent politicians. Overconcentration can be just as damaging to minority political aspirations. By forcing too many Chicanos into one district, more than is needed to elect a Latino candidate, the number of districts where Mexicans can have clout is significantly reduced.

These kinds of practices have a two-fold impact: they reduce the chances of Latinos winning multiple seats, especially in heavily populated Latino areas like L.A. And when they are planted in "safe" seats, with few non-Chicano opponents, Latinos are denied the incentive to develop political organization and skills that only arise in response to competition.

The reapportionment plan proposed that year by assembly Republicans opts for the overconcentration strategy. By forcing Chicano populations into as few districts as possible, the GOP hopes Latino voters will not form the cornerstone of Democratic strength in adjoining districts. When it suits their needs, Republicans also adopt the overdispersion mode of gerrymandering. For example, in the Central Valley, the Republicans bitterly fight creation of a Latino seat by uniting Chicano communities in Kern and Tulare counties. The assembly minority leader, Carol Hallett, from the Central Coast city of Atascadero, stridently resists uniting a large Latino community in the Salinas Valley with Latinos in nearby Santa Clara County. She does so both because the resulting district will be more Democratic and because she will lose big-grower constituents who are a potent source of campaign contributions.

The assembly plan we put together is unique because we force Democrats to create Chicano seats out of their own political hides as well as out of the Republicans' territory. Previously, Anglo Democrats have practiced the dispersal of ethnic and racial minorities: you can never put too many minorities in one district because that can adversely impact the electability of the sitting white incumbent. The practical impact of dispersal is to dilute the vote so Latinos can't elect a Latino in the Democratic primary. This is the principal reason why there is an outcry, primarily by blacks and Latinos, for fair representation. "Dispersal is a strategy used by Democrats, particularly incumbents, who wanted Latinos in their districts because Latinos were a loyal Democratic constituency," valuable in a general election against Republican candidates, Bruce agrees. "But they didn't want so many Latinos that they would pose a primary challenge."

The assembly plan is based in part on what we call the Goldilocks theory of ethnic balance. Goldilocks, you recall from the children's story, doesn't want her porridge too hot or too cold; she wants it just right. Our assembly plan doesn't want to disperse too few Latinos in too many seats so they will have little leverage in any one district. We also don't want to concentrate too many Latinos together in too few districts so their strength will be inefficiently utilized.

By contrast, the Republican strategy is to make the porridge either too hot or too cold, depending on their needs. They try to reduce the number of seats where Latinos can have clout by concentrating them in a few districts that are already heavily Latino. In other places, they oppose uniting Latino communities in adjoining areas if it will boost Latino voting power. All the Latino seats in the GOP plan of 1981 are carved out of Democratic strongholds.

The Rose Institute and legislative Republicans see a real chance to weaken some white Democrats by sucking the Latino neighborhoods out of their districts to create an overwhelmingly loyal Democratic seat nearby. Let's say you have two seats next to each other. In each of them Democrats have a 60–40 percent lead. If you take 20 percent of the electorate who are Latinos out of one of the seats and stick them in the other district, it turns into an 80–20 percent Democratic seat. That turns the remaining district into a Republican seat. So you go from having two districts represented by Democrats to having one Democrat and one Republican.

That is the Republican strategy, Bruce concurs, "hoping to drive the imperative of helping Latinos down the throats of the Democrats. They were able to pick off some advocates in the Latino community who were more interested in minority representation than strengthening the Democratic coalition. Richard obviously was in the middle: on the one hand he didn't want Latinos to be divided and discriminated against. On the other hand, he wanted to make sure the Democratic Party wasn't unduly penalized in the effort."

That's why our assembly reapportionment plan is historic. For the first time under our plan, incumbent legislators, Democrats, agree to accept larger numbers of Chicano residents, realizing they must pay more attention to Latino interests and, perhaps, face primary opposition from Latino candidates. Democratic assemblymembers like Mike Roos of L.A. and John Vasconcellos of San Jose deserve credit for this landmark achievement.

The first question is what makes up a Latino-interest district or one that can or can someday elect a Chicano? Up until that time, the early 1980s, the conventional wisdom is that Chicanos can only get elected in places like East Los Angeles, where there are heavy concentrations of Latino voters. A Latino is not elected to the assembly north of the Tehachapi Mountains until 1993, when Cruz Bustamante wins a special election in Fresno.

When I first run for the assembly in 1971, it is from an Eastside L.A. district that is about 18 percent Latino. Because the courts do redistricting that decade, the reconfigured and renamed 55th Assembly District has a little over 50 percent Chicano residents, although voting wise it is about 40 percent Latino. Other factors to take into consideration in deciding whether a Chicano can get elected are the way people vote and their political ideology. I can win in a district where there are fewer Latinos because the voters see me as being consistent with their progressive political views.

So my philosophy is you don't have to create seats that are 70 percent Latino. Back then, the Republicans favor overconcentration—using overwhelmingly Chicano numbers to define a safe Latino district—because fewer Latinos will be elected. Such strategies, where almost everyone in the district has to be Mexican, are designed to minimize the election of Latino candidates, which is as discriminatory as the Democrats' favorite strategy of overdispersion, dividing Chicano communities into separate districts to bolster the chances of Anglo candidates.

Even in newly created districts of influence that might not be able to immediately elect Latinos, we look at other factors such as how public policy can be affected by Latinos being a large potential voting block that helps decide who gets elected, thereby asserting their influence over the issues successful candidates have to address.

Willie Brown's San Francisco assembly district is never even close to 50 percent African American. But he learns how to work in coalition politics with people of different races and ethnicities. I do the same thing in East L.A.

By the 1970s, between high Latino birth rates and new immigration into California, Chicanos are not just seeing their numbers grow in traditional urban areas such as L.A. or San Jose. They start moving into places they have not lived in in larger numbers such as the San Fernando Valley and the Central Valley.

Also, more and more Latinos aren't just following the crops and working seasonal industries such as agriculture and construction, and then leaving for their home countries during off-seasons. They are increasingly putting down roots in the communities where they live. The emergence of political influence by Latinos begins locally, with Chicanos getting elected to school boards and city councils. Eventually, Latinoization catches up to the legislature. Latinos get elected in the last decade of the 20th century and the first decade of the 21st from places you would never think possible just a short time before: the Central Valley, parts of Santa Clara County, the Central Coast, Inland Empire, and East Bay.

During my service in the assembly in the 1970s and '80s, my rural Democratic colleagues are just about all white men with names like Bronzan, Condit, and Costa. Ten and 20 years later those same districts are being represented by legislators with names like Florez, Reyes, and Salinas. In 2002, I'm on the assembly floor witnessing the debate over a landmark law sponsored by the United Farm Workers allowing farmworkers to bring in neutral state mediators to hammer out union contracts when growers won't negotiate. When I serve at the Capitol, the rural Democratic legislators can be counted on, almost to a person, to stand up and oppose such a pro-UFW bill. When the 2002 legislation backed by the union is debated, most of the rural Democrats in the house rise to speak on the measure's behalf—and all of them are Latino.

The actual purpose of that trip to the Capitol is to use some of my old connections to push for immigrant rights.

The first of many attempts by then-Assemblymember Gil Cedillo at granting drivers' licenses to undocumented immigrants is stuck in the state senate. My old friend state senate leader John Burton won't let it off the floor. Gil goes to veteran political activist George Pla, my good friend, to get to me to fly to Sacramento to directly appeal to Burton.

George and I sit in the front row of the visitor section immediately behind the senate floor, in full view of John Burton.

Burton spots me in the rear of the chamber. He raises his arms above his shoulders, asking what's going on, and emphatically gestures towards the hallway behind the Senate Chamber, indicating that I should go out there so the two of us can talk. George follows me. Gilbert follows George.

Once the four of us are in the hall, Burton blurts out to me, "What the fuck?"

"Shit!" I reply.

"What are you doing here?" Johnny wants to know.

"You gotta support this bill," I answer him.

"It's a piece of shit."

"Yeah, but it's for Mexicans."

"Ah, shit!" Burton declares, and angrily stalks off.

After John storms away, George, Gilbert, and I look at each other. "Well, that was eloquent," George remarks.

The bill gets out of the senate and the legislature, but is vetoed by Governor Gray Davis. Governor Jerry Brown finally signs another version of the bill into law 10 years later.

The final results of our work are also seen in how the Republicans react in criticizing the redistricting plan and how Chicanos respond in praising it.

Latino activist leaders are "favorably shocked" when our plan is unveiled, according to Bruce Cain. It creates 16 Latino seats with more than 30 percent Latino residents, the level necessary to have political clout in a district, up from 10 districts under the 1973 court-ordered reapportionment plan. Seven of those seats are 40 percent or more Chicano.

Miguel Garcia, chairman of Californios for Fair Representation, says the assembly plan is "the first major victory in the quest for Latino representation." Richard Santillan, also with Californios, says we "went beyond what Californios proposed."

"I gave Richard total space" to come up with plans that make improvements for Chicanos, Brown says. "He had to make progress. That only inured ultimately to the benefit of the Democratic Party and to us [the assembly Democrats] specifically. The more people of color we elect, the more women we elect, the better off our present and future will be. We knew that if we did nothing else but increase the number [of Chicanos in the legislature] and left the day after that, we would have made a positive impact for generations to come."

The 1981 assembly redistricting law "preserved a high level of participation in the electoral process for the African-American community with its dwindling numbers in the total population," Willie continues. "But more importantly, the Latino representation grew dramatically" in the years to come. "The Richard Alatorre reapportionment is the seeds of that. Bruce Cain's line drawing reflected the potential geographic growth of [Chicanos] throughout the population. The impacts from that line drawing are still with us today." Chicano candidates who come along afterwards "would not even have been viable candidates without the '81 plan," Brown adds. "In their quest to expand opportunities for Latino representation, Richard and Bruce closely looked at places such as San Diego and Imperial counties, places not traditionally Democratic but where they were looking for Latinos to register as Democrats. Their work was even more reflected in the growth of Latinos in the state's congressional delegation," whose reapportionment plan is also drawn up by us along with Phil Burton. By contrast, Republicans don't want more political participation by Chicanos "because the Republican policy agenda was so adverse to Latinos' interests that if they ever got organized and registered to vote, they would not vote Republican," Willie notes. "Take the farmworker issue, which Republicans opposed. There was no separation among Latinos on the farmworker issue. They were all 100 percent behind Cesar."

Our assembly plan benefits in contrast to what senate and congressional redistricting does, or doesn't do, for Latinos. State Senator Dan Boatwright, who runs reapportionment in the senate, can't put together an independent staff operation and program, and ends up using the information we generate. The senate is a different reality. It's still a good old boys' network. They take care of those who are there. There is no movement towards recognizing ethnic realities. Take a look at the Chicanos who are there then: Alex Garcia, Joe Montoya, and Ruben Ayala. None of them is very interested in the redistricting agenda of Latino activists. So the assembly is where the whole game plays out.

Since the assembly also redraws congressional district boundaries, we work closely with Phil Burton. Phil comes in and in his typical way takes no prisoners. He isn't interested in helping anyone he doesn't have to help. There are a small number of assemblymembers on his list—including Howard Berman, Mel Levine, Rick Lehman, and Maxine Waters—who are positioning themselves for congressional races. In our plan we create two new seats for Latinos in L.A., both east of Ed Roybal's district. Marty Martinez and Esteban Torres later take them over.

Phil Burton understands reality. The reality in L.A. is he has to create a new Eastside Latino seat. In the process, we discover it's possible to create a second seat, which Phil does. There are opportunities to set up some chances for Latinos in the Inland Empire, which ends up sending former Assemblymember Joe Baca to Congress. In other parts of the state, especially suburban areas, it is difficult to draw seats that would immediately elect Chicanos, but you begin by making it possible for Latinos to have greater influence in the public policies of candidates and later elect our own.

Phil keeps his promise and makes sure the Roybal district has me living in it so I can run if Roybal decides to retire. It becomes clear Roybal is not going anywhere. I contemplate running in one of the two adjoining congressional seats, eventually taken by Martinez and Torres. I believe I would do well. But neither district has the communities where I grow up. Before Roybal makes a decision to leave Congress, my time has passed. I go to the city council in 1985. Later, I support Ed Roybal's daughter, Lucille Roybal-Allard, to replace him. I never consider running for Congress again.

The Republicans' reaction to my assembly plan is best characterized by the meeting I have with Ross Johnson, the GOP caucus chair in the assembly. Every member from both parties is called into my office one at a time so we can show them their draft map and the initial proposed look of their district in our plan. Ross is so furious. In the course of screaming, his dentures fly out of his mouth. I'm not kidding. He's a worthy advocate for his side, but he's the kind of volatile guy that it doesn't take much to get him upset anyway. But then he starts spitting and yelling, and the fucking thing just rolls out. He puts the dentures back in without missing a beat and keeps on screaming.

The Republicans are so pissed off with assembly reapportionment that they put a successful referendum on the 1982 statewide primary ballot repealing all the redistricting plans. By that time, I move on and Assemblymember Maxine Waters is running the redistricting show as chair of the elections and reapportionment committee. "The Democratic leadership cuts a deal with the Republicans," Bruce recalls. As part of that agreement, the Democrats essentially "give the Republicans their territory and tell them to draw the lines any way they see fit. And we'll keep our Democratic seats and draw the lines the way we see fit." But this deal doesn't negate or compromise any of the gains we accomplish for Latinos.

"The complex data and computer operation we set in motion also became state of the art by 1982," Bruce notes, when redistricting has to be done over again. "By that time the whole state is on computer. By the next reapportionment process in 1991, it has become routine. We put California on the cutting edge" of using the latest in technology to handle redrawing of the lines.

The potential for increased Latino representation we encourage comes to pass in the decades that follow through a combination of dramatic demographic and population changes from migration patterns and people becoming permanent residents that are overtaking the state. There is also heightened political awareness by Chicanos, provoked in no small way by anti-immigrant scapegoating from politicians like Governor Pete Wilson and a series of anti-immigrant ballot measures beginning in 1994 with Proposition 187. When you think about immigration, it starts in places like East Los Angeles, but later waves of immigrants move elsewhere because there isn't enough room there. They move to wherever they can blend in or where there are economic opportunities, jobs in need of being filled that other Americans won't take, scattering people across the West and later into other regions of the country. Immigration and migration take us from being a regional minority, centered in the Southwest, to a national minority. Latinos are moving into unconventional locations, places where they don't use to live in significant numbers. They are mostly drawn by the attraction of low paying, no-benefit jobs in agriculture, processing, manufacturing, and the service sector that non-Latino workers don't want.

Increasingly there is intermarrying. Before you know what's happening, it's guess who's coming to dinner? Businesses, stores, and restaurants serving Latinos are popping up in many communities in the South and Midwest. There are Hispanic chambers of commerce in places like North Carolina. Mexicans play a decisive role in handing Barack Obama states such as Colorado, New Mexico, Nevada, and Florida.

The pervasive presence of Latinos in many places—with their unique food, language, and cultural traditions—triggers fear and resentment among some people, even if they welcome the Latinos' cheap labor to keep their economies going.

But by the 1980s, the community is growing even more militant, sophisticated, and demanding, the result, at least in part, of Cesar's example. With greater access to higher education, there is the emergence of more and more Mexicans entering business and the professions, and more Latinos becoming activists and leaders in the labor movement. I show Chicano political candidates and elected officials how they can raise money in order to be competitive. The amnesty provisions of the federal Immigration Reform and Control Act of 1986, allowing large numbers of undocumented immigrants to adjust their status and later become citizens, is a big help too.

You don't have to worry whether Latinos who become citizens during this period will realize the importance of taking part in the political process. Pete Wilson and other Republican politicians help awaken them to the necessity.

I remember the first election after the 1986 federal immigration reform law takes effect. I walk into a Mexican *panaderilla*, or bakery, on Ford Boulevard that I know from when I am a kid in East L.A. I'm standing in line next to a lady wearing a little tag on her coat saying, "I Voted." We talk. She tells me, "I registered and this is the first time I'm voting to teach that miserable governor we have as many rights as anyone else."

There are always citizenship classes and organizations encouraging people to register and vote. Now you no longer have to educate our people; they understand who the enemy is and want to get them out of office. The campaign ads for Wilson's reelection and Proposition 187 do more to politicize and teach Latinos the importance of participating and electing our own than all the advocacy by activists over the decades put together. When people think they're being scapegoated, it makes them angry. Mexicans are taken for granted by the political establishment for decades. Even though there are a lot of us, we are largely dismissed by the powers that be because so many of us can't vote, haven't registered, or don't take part. Then, beginning in the mid-1990s, the sleeping giant wakes up.

So progress in reapportionment together with other advances lay the groundwork for election of the Cruz Bustamantes, the Dean Florezes, the Sarah Reyeses, and the Martha Escutias. Today, the largest caucus at the state Capitol, outside the two political parties, is the Latino Legislative Caucus.

"If Richard hadn't done his work on reapportionment," political activist George Pla says, "it would have been another 20 years or more for there to be Assembly Speakers Cruz Bustamante and Antonio Villaraigosa—before Latinos would be so prominent in politics or the Latino Caucus in Sacramento."

"It was a synergy," Bruce Cain agrees, "partly enabled by redistricting. But it was also demographic, stemming from the continued growth of the Latino community from immigration and higher birth rates. Even when immigration slowed down, there was still growth occurring. A key consideration is the fact that when the courts did redistricting it was based on population and not registered voters."

Latino representation would only be a third to a half of what it is now if district lines were drawn strictly based on registered voters, Bruce believes. But with Latinos, angry at the anti-immigrant fervor of the '90s, incited to become U.S. citizens, to register and vote, many more residents get turned into citizens and voters.

I remember Cesar once saying back in the '80s that what Chicanos lack in influence at the voting booths they are making up for in the maternity wards.

It would be up to others to turn the gains of reapportionment into victories at the polls for Latino candidates. Richard Polanco, who follows me into the assembly from the 55th District, takes reapportionment and runs with it. He is very operational, understanding what it takes to run winning campaigns. He raises money, develops databases and organization. He travels around, recruiting good candidates and innovative political consultants like Richie Ross, who elects a lot of them. He creates nonprofit groups and independent expenditure committees as vehicles to elect Chicanos. Polanco takes it to another level. But it would not happen without the districts created in 1981 redistricting. Chicano communities that are once divided are united where it makes sense.

Chapter 9

Giving It All Up to Come Home

I'm at a fundraiser Mike Roos and I help set up for the reelection of U.S. Representative Maxine Waters of Los Angeles in September 2010, at the home of an African-American businessman in Sacramento. In the eyes of the people who are there, 95 percent of whom are black, Max is a hero, and rightfully so. She's a great role model and an elected official who is committed to all the right causes. The people in the room are mostly younger than Max and me. They are the next generation of black leaders—lawyers, business people, doctors, and the heads of nonprofit organizations.

Max is talking about leadership. "You're probably wondering why I'm here with my buddy over there, Richard Alatorre," she says. "He's been a very important part of my life and he's been important to the man I love and respect, Willie Brown, my leader when I was up here" at the state Capitol before leaving to run for Congress in 1991. "I decided to run for Congress after Richard ran for the L.A. City Council. I was the next one out," leaving the legislature because of the opportunity redistricting gives her to win the Los Angeles congressional seat held by longtime U.S. Representative Gus Hawkins.
"In the early 1980s there were four people who really ran the state from the Democratic Party's standpoint," Max continues. During that decade, the Republicans control the White House, under Ronald Reagan, and the governor's office, under George Deukmejian and later Pete Wilson. "But we Democrats still held onto power in the legislature," she continues. "And as a result of redistricting we got even greater control of the legislature and the state congressional delegation." Max names the four people from the state assembly who really run Cali-

fornia back then: Willie Brown; Mike Roos, then assembly majority leader; Max; and me. "Two blacks, a Mexican, and a white guy," she adds.

In the '80s, when the legislature moves back into its original quarters in the state Capitol building after a $68 million restoration, Willie Brown has this beautifully ornate high-ceiling office, furnished with antiques and historic paintings. The beautiful thing is that Maxine and I can walk right into his office at any time of the day or night. On almost every major, and minor, issue coming before the legislature that affects the state, we can get involved as much or as little as we want and help control the decision. It is the fulfillment of a dream that few people ever believe they will have. It is an especially heady time for me because, to a greater extent than Willie, I have been on the outs with the leadership in the legislature—and with the governor, Jerry Brown—most of the time since first getting elected to the assembly in 1972.

It is obviously sweet for me because the reason I have been on the outs all that time is the same reason I have recently become a power in the legislature: my friendship and loyalty to Willie Brown. I pay a steep price for that loyalty until 1981, when Willie becomes Speaker. Then I go through the pain in the ass of reapportionment that year, not because I want the job but because he asks me to do it, although it ends up being the best decision that is made for me by Willie Brown.

I'm finally in a place where I always want to be, that I have ever dreamed of being in. And the best part of it is that I'm there with and for a person I have nothing but admiration and affection for.

Maxine's point that day at her event in 2010, is to ask why would she and I give up that kind of influence to leave Sacramento when we could hold onto such power for as long as we want into the foreseeable future? Remember, both of our L.A.-area assembly districts are very safe Democratic seats. This is some years before legislative term limits, which aren't even a threat at the time. Plus, Willie's Speakership has been cemented by reapportionment in 1981, which my then-consultant, Bruce Cain, correctly says is the architecture of his longevity as Speaker of the assembly. In a decade of Republican political ascendency in California, Democrats still firmly hold onto power in the legislature largely because of reapportionment.

What also cements Willie's Speakership is his innate ability to command loyalty. He lets people develop their own levels of expertise in areas they want and he lets them pursue their agendas. He is what anybody—at least any legislator—would want in a Speaker, what is aptly described on many occasions as a members' Speaker. Whatever members want, within reason, Willie is there to help them obtain, whether it's helping them with their legislation, with raising money, or getting reelected. By operating the way he does, Willie L. Brown Jr. is able to get everything he ever wants.

Also, whenever a particularly difficult issue comes up, most people cannot even begin to comprehend how Willie can engage himself and become an expert, whether it's taxation and budgets or education and governmental organization—anything. He is truly, I believe, the most intelligent and intellectual guy I have ever met, without losing the folksiness people remember him for.

So why do I consider giving up all of this to run for the city council in Los Angeles in 1985?

The answer lies with developments about 400 miles south of the Capitol.

Arthur K. Snyder is born and raised in Highland Park. He's from a working-class family. Nothing is ever given to him. He fights for everything he ever gets. He fights to get an education, graduating from Franklin High School in Eagle Rock and finally earning a law degree from the University of Southern California. He speaks Spanish and genuinely likes the Mexican people and culture. Somewhere along the way he gets involved in public service as an aide to the local Los Angeles city councilman, John Holland. Art works for Holland for a decade or more. Then the opportunity comes to run for his seat after the councilman's death in 1967.

Art knows the 14th Council District better than anyone. What I don't learn from Art until I run for it myself is that he makes the district sound like it is a Mexican district; population wise it's 70 percent or more Latino. All of the deputies or field representatives Art hires are Latino, and they're good. Art is the consummate councilmember who pays close attention to his district and its residents, going to every event, especially in the Latino community. But it isn't until later that he tells me about the role Eagle Rock plays in municipal electoral politics. Eagle Rock, on the northern side of the 14th District, is back then and remains pretty much today a middle-class, largely white, blue-collar community comprised mostly of modest but well-kept suburban-style single-family homes and small businesses.

What Eagle Rock affords you, Art explains to me, is the opportunity to have a buffer between the left and the right. If a candidate challenges you from the left, all you do is develop a base, a strong relationship, in largely white Eagle Rock and tell the voters there that the Communists are after you. Art becomes good at doing that. He says, "Because I'm not a Mexican, that's why they're running against me," and the Eagle Rockers get pissed off. If a candidate or activists run after you from the right, there are not enough white voters in Eagle Rock—and not all the Eagle Rockers are right-wingers—to defeat you given that the rest of the district has lots of Mexicans and white progressives.

So while Art Snyder convinces the world that the 14th is a Mexican district, he knows that, at least in his time, this isn't so. So many of the votes are actually in Eagle Rock, and they're white, although as the years go on, the Chicano vote becomes much more significant. Still, Eagle Rock serves as a buffer to guarantee his, and my, reelections.

I bring this point home in 1987, the first time I run for reelection to the city council. I only have one guy go after me, Jim Becham, a white guy from Eagle Rock. He's a businessman, an old-line Chamber of Commerce type, coming after me from the right. Art Snyder says he will talk with Becham, but advises me to talk to him first, right away, before he falls in love with his candidacy. So we get together over a couple of drinks at Columbo's Steak House in Eagle Rock. He tells me why he's running.

"I just got elected," I say. Then he proceeds to tell me how he thinks he's going to get elected.

"I really don't want to disabuse you of your belief of why you think you have a chance," I tell him. "I just want to give you my analysis and then you should meet with Art Snyder and see what he thinks." So I tell him: "You think Eagle Rock is here [in the district] for no reason at all? That there wasn't a grand design, aside from the fact I live here now and love this neighborhood? The idea, contrary to popular belief, that you can win the election here in Eagle Rock is mathematically impossible.

"I know you're a great leader in Eagle Rock," I acknowledge to Becham, "and you'll get your share of the votes here. But as you move south [into the Latino portions of the district], I'm going to kill you. I'm going to go over there and tell the Mexicans that you're running against me because I'm not Anglo, because I'm a Mexican.

"If you think I'm wrong, go talk with Art Snyder," I say. "You're going to find out the problems in Eagle Rock have nothing to do with daily reality in other parts of the district. Let me give you that reality. You're concerned about the trees not being pruned the way you believe they should be pruned [in Eagle Rock]. That's one reality. The other reality is parents in the Mexican parts of the district who are worried about their kids' ability to get to and from school without being shot in drive-bys." That kind of shocks him.

By this time I debunk Jim's reasoning and tell him I'd like to have him as my supporter. "You criticized me for not having moved fast enough to satisfy you," I say. "I just got here." Two days later he calls me back: "I've changed my mind." Jim ends up being a great supporter of mine until his death. His wife later tells me she is glad he changed his mind and didn't run.

At the time I run for city council, Eagle Rock is beginning to change, with more Chicanos moving into the community and many white voters becoming more anti-Mexican and anti-immigrant. Some white people believe the influx of Mexicans is the reason crime is going up in Eagle Rock.

One day I walk into one of the local Chamber of Commerce meetings in Eagle Rock as this guy is finishing a speech all about the cause of community deterioration being the influx of so many more Mexicans. He cites graffiti, gangs, problems in the schools, and the increase in crime. Then he spots me in the room and adds, "Oh, I didn't mean you. I mean those other people."

"Oh, thank you," I respond.

Still, I work hard to earn the support of voters in Eagle Rock, and I do pretty well there over the years. One of the reasons is my decision right after getting elected in 1985, to rehire Shirley Minser as a field deputy. She also graduates from Franklin High School in Highland Park and never leaves the community where she grows up. She's white, a die-hard Republican who wears her hair in an old-fashioned bun behind her head, like something out of the 1950s. Shirley is worried she won't have a job as Art is leaving office because she hasn't

Veteran Los Angeles City Councilmember Art Snyder eventually endorses Richard to succeed him and offers sound advice on how to get elected in the 14th District that includes Eagle Rock.

reached retirement age. "You have nothing to worry about," I reassure her. Some people on the left can't understand why I have this woman working for me. She is even too far to the right for the younger generation of conservatives. But she knows where people live and work in Eagle Rock, and she knows how to get votes. Shirley makes it very clear to everyone she helps—and she helps a lot of constituents every day—that "If I help you, you better help my boss (that's me) because he makes it possible for me to have a job and allows me to do things for everybody."

Still Republican to the hilt, Shirley kiddingly (I guess) refers to me as a "Communist" and refers to my "Communist beliefs." But she remains totally loyal for the 15 years she works for me while I serve on the council. She will take a bullet for me. Shirley remains a friend after she finally retires, well into her 70s and 80s, and to this day.

Art Snyder maintains good working relations with other elected officials. He does with me when I'm in the assembly and he does the same thing with Art Torres after he gets elected to the legislature since our districts share much of the same territory. Art Snyder makes sure his deputies respond to our requests and take care of our business. Our constituent issues and concerns are the same. Art is very congenial; he wants us to work as a team. He may be a conservative Republican, but not on social issues. He's pro-farmworker, for example, and can be very liberal, particularly on things that concern Latinos.

In 1974, Art Torres goes to Sacramento in an assembly campaign Lou Moret and I help orchestrate. I'm also reelected that year. We've now been through two election cycles where we've proven our ability to raise large sums of campaign cash and mobilize all the ground troops we need. Some of my core group of supporters feel we're pretty invincible. There's even talk about a new Latino political machine we're building on the Eastside.

It's true that I've learned how to raise a lot of money in politics and Lou Moret, my administrative assistant and chief political operative, has mastered the mechanics of collecting the money and running effective campaigns. I have an army of former college students and everyone else who will turn out to walk precincts, make phone calls, and do whatever is needed in a campaign. Of course, without the ability to raise money, the grass-roots operation, which costs money to run, means nothing. We are building what no one else does up to that time. Ed Roybal never does it; he never needs to. Roybal is a *cause celeb* unto himself: first Latino city councilmember, first Latino member of Congress—a trailblazer for his generation. But he never builds a functioning political organization that can put troops on the street, even though his first council election in 1949 owes much to the activism and grass-roots organizing principles of the Community Service Organization founded by Saul Alinsky and run by Fred Ross.

We are also successful because we can make what we are doing into a cause for Mexicans to rally around, and we figure out how to turn out a lot of political participation among Chicanos, who because of upward mobility are increasingly becoming more of a force in business, the professions, labor, and government.

But I am coming to understand that there is a dramatic difference between working four or five days a week as a lawmaker in Sacramento and being in L.A. on a full-time basis. The differing perspectives about people's needs are night and day. It isn't until I run for the council after serving for 14 years in Sacramento that I learn how little I know about my district—and the everyday concerns of my constituents.

The way Art Snyder stays reelected is focusing his attention and his staff, more than any other politician, out in the field instead of inside City Hall doing legislation or city business, which he knows is bullshit. Art can handle City Hall himself. So he puts his staff out in the field—maybe 70 percent of them—taking care of people's needs. He knows that alone is worth a good percentage of the vote in each area of the district. Art writes the Bible, actually a little booklet, on what to do and not do as a member of the city council and hands it out to all incoming councilmembers.

Despite all of that, in 1975, Art Torres, Lou Moret, and I, along with our political allies, run Ed Avila, an aide to Ed Roybal, against Art Snyder. We spend all the money we want on the campaign, walk door-to-door in the district three times and send an impressive direct mail program to voters. On Election Day, we have breakfast, which is our tradition—Art Torres, Lou Moret, the candidate, and I—and make predictions on who will win and by how much. Everybody in the room feels we're going to win, but not by much. After all, there is nothing we hadn't done.

That night, early on, by 9 p.m., Lou Moret calls Art, Eddie, and me into a back room at our campaign headquarters. "Eddie, get ready for your concession speech," Lou tells him.

"It's too early," I say.

"It's over, guys, Snyder kicked our ass big time," Lou responds. We can't overcome the pro-Snyder vote from Eagle Rock. Snyder gets more than 60 percent of the vote, easily beating Eddie.

Art Snyder knows he needs to get people to vote, and vote for him, as he comes into the northern part of the 14th District, especially in Eagle Rock. I'm spending most of my time in Sacramento. It's the same with Art Torres. We think we're on a good roll politically. But we still don't get the reality that Art Snyder knows, which is this is a tough district for a challenger because Snyder has a lock on Eagle Rock and because many people are still loyal to him in Lincoln Heights, El Sereno, and Boyle Heights. Eddie Avila grows up in Boyle Heights, but Art Snyder still beats him there.

At some point we let Snyder know he shouldn't worry about us putting up another candidate against him and that we should keep working together. There is no animosity since we have not run a dirty campaign, hitting on Snyder. The councilmember is subsequently reelected two more times, in 1979 and 1983, mostly without significant opposition.

But things start to change. Running against Snyder in 1983 is Steve Rodriguez. His main claim to fame is when President Jimmy Carter spends a night at his house in El Sereno. Rodriguez runs as a "Lone Ranger," without any major endorsements or support. He loses, but does surprisingly well, collecting more than 40 percent of the vote.

By this time, Art Snyder is facing more serious legal and personal problems and is being targeted by the press. Art has always been accused of corruption, but now his image is getting seriously beaten up. Steve Rodriguez feels a movement is building out there to get rid of the guy.

The next year, Rodriguez is behind an attempt to recall Snyder, collecting signatures to put the issue on the ballot. The recall takes place during the 1984 Olympics, which are being held in L.A. As the date for the special election is being set, we commission a poll that shows support for Snyder is slipping and there is great potential he can lose the election because of all the bad press he is getting.

Lou Moret, who at the time is an L.A. city commissioner of public works appointed by Mayor Tom Bradley, gets in the race at our urging and with our support, his first and only bid for public office. Lou raises all the money he can use and walks two precincts a day himself. We get Richie Ross, the Sacramento political consultant I know when he runs Willie Brown's political organization for three election cycles in the '80s, to do the mail program. Everyone does a good job.

Snyder, as smart as he is, runs a more effective campaign, including a special program directed at getting voters to vote by absentee ballot. George

Deukmejian, another Republican, gets elected California governor two years before because of his absentee ballot drive even though he loses in the Election Day polling to Tom Bradley. The recall of Snyder wins among Election Day voters, but he still pulls it out when absentee votes are counted. He stays in office.

Once again, we run a high-road campaign, refraining from attacking Snyder because we don't need to; Steve Rodriguez does all the attacking anyone would want.

Very soon after the election, word starts going around that Art Snyder is talking about resigning. He sees the writing on the wall. He knows his time is limited. He doesn't want to wait until the next election. Moreover, he's getting tired and knows it will be harder and harder to stay in office.

One day I get a call from Angie Vasquez, a professional fundraiser and event planner who does all of my political fundraising. (We get married in 1991.) "You hear about the word being out that Art Snyder is resigning?" she asks. "What will happen is Steve Rodriguez will end up running and he could end up winning it? This [council district] is your home. What do you think?"

"Why the fuck do I want to run for City Council?" I reply, to Angie as well as to myself. It's the furthermost thing from my mind. I'm helping to run the state of California in the state assembly. Why do I want to go back to Los Angeles and deal with potholes and zoning issues? I kind of like the idea of being away from L.A. and flying in for three days over long weekends. I am in Sacramento for four days a week.

I have started to spend even more time in Sacramento lately. I ask myself: is this what I really want to do? I'm just finished with my 1984 reelection. None of my races have been bruising but I hate them. I start looking at it this way: I'm born and raised in L.A. Mexicans are becoming a bigger and bigger player in L.A. politically and in every other way. I have already given up any ambitions of running for Congress; I want it when I'm doing reapportionment in 1981 with U.S. Representative Phil Burton. I can probably go to Congress and eventually retire from there if Ed Roybal leaves office when he tells me he is. He is retiring at the end of every term after 1980. He finally does so in 1993.

"Richard was looking to run," Angie remembers. "There was no reason he couldn't come home to L.A. Mainly, what I set out in my little speech to him was L.A. is a bigger market. Richard's not going to D.C.; it's too far. But L.A. is it—it's the city. Since Art Snyder is not going to run, the 14th District could be a Latino seat. There had not been anyone on the city council with brown skin since Roybal went to Congress in the early '60s. Richard could help make history. 'If you're elected in L.A.,' I told him, 'you're known nationally.'"

Also, especially with the Olympics, the focus of the nation and the world is on L.A. in 1984.

We know if I run, we can knock anybody off. We make the decision to do it. But we know we have to get Snyder on our side. I'm the only one who can do that.

I have people who go talk with Art, just to feel him out about whether he will get involved in the election of his successor. He's playing coy: "Maybe I will or maybe I won't." He and I are at the point where I have developed a relationship with him. I am tolerable to Art Snyder. He likes me because at least I'm not a Johnny-come-lately. He is probably more inclined to support me than anyone else. It only becomes a question of when. I make sure to be respectful, to not step on his toes. Art Snyder endorses me early. It's over after that, even though I still have to face a campaign. Of course, Steve Rodriguez is outraged. He sees himself as the "community" candidate and me as overly ambitious. I don't give a shit about that.

As chairman of the Assembly Governmental Organization Committee, which is my only ask of Willie Brown after running reapportionment, I raise a lot of money. It comes with the territory. All I ever do is give it all away, mostly to fellow incumbent legislators or candidates the Speaker tells me to support. The city of L.A. has just passed campaign contribution limits: $500 maximum for individuals and $1,000 for a husband and wife. But I now have $400,000 sitting there in my assembly campaign account that I plan on using for the council race.

We start tapping the assembly money for the council campaign even before I officially declare. The city hasn't yet adopted regulations that govern how its campaign reform ordinance will be enforced. I ask the city ethics commission what we can and cannot do with my assembly campaign funds. They usually reply, "We haven't developed the regulations." I figure until they do, I can use the assembly money. Later on the commission develops regulations and makes them apply retroactively. That's when I get snared, later having to pay back my assembly campaign fund close to $300,000 plus a fine.

That probably just reinforces my image, especially with the press, as a wheeler-dealer who plays fast and loose with ethical matters. But I know the truth and it doesn't bother me that some people, including some reporters, think that way. I never like, trust, or rely on them anyway. The press is never there to be my friends, I believe, and often they aren't.

The council campaign itself is a blast. We do some innovative stuff and I actually have a lot of fun. Richie Ross manages it, and we field what Richie describes as the Hoover vacuum cleaner salesmen technique. We hire clean-cut, well-dressed young college graduate types, primarily guys, but some women too. They are all carefully interviewed and screened. We educate them about me. They get incentives for what they produce: so much money for getting a voter to endorse me so we can use the name; so much if they get a commitment to put up a lawn sign at the house. If there are multiple voters in the household, they make more money.

There's competition among the door-to-door workers at first. They try to screw each other, get to the good places before their competitors. As time goes on, they become a tight knit group and help out one another. Instead of traditional precinct walking, they sprint from door to door, working seven days a week.

My Hooverites carry a big binder talking all about my career, accomplishments, and endorsements. They take voters through the binder while standing on the front porch, just like Jehovah's Witnesses. Richard Polanco, my administrative assistant who later takes my assembly seat, runs the day-to-day, door-to-door operation. As a result of their work, we put up almost 10,000 lawn signs on one day, fulfilling commitments the Hooverites collect while walking. We know the signs won't last because opponents steal many of them, a time-honored practice in the district. Nevertheless, seeing all those lawn signs go up at once is mind-boggling.

Also coming down to help out from Sacramento are many Capitol volunteers—legislative staff, Willie Brown political operatives, especially Sandi Polka, and even some of my colleagues like assemblymember (later state schools superintendent) Jack O'Connell from Santa Barbara/Oxnard—who help implement the overall campaign in L.A.

Richie Ross is at his best with the mail. We mail pictures of the Kennedys. And Richie has the campaign deliver small potted plants to voters' homes.

My main opponents in a big field are Steve Rodriguez and Gil Avila, who is put up to run by the Republicans. I win it all outright in the primary.

The world shows up for my swearing in at City Hall. At least many of the people I care about most are there. Sitting in the front row are Cesar Chavez, Willie Brown, Maxine Waters, Merv Dymally, and Tom Bradley. It is history, I guess. And it is an exciting time, not just because it follows a hard-fought campaign—although the outcome is pretty certain as far as I'm concerned—but also because it represents a big change in my life. I actually don't realize all it means at the moment.

The spectacle of that front row of heavy-hitter minority figures—I'm also serenaded by a Mariachi band from the rear of the chambers—"was a harbinger of things to come," observes Latino political activist and entrepreneur George Pla.

"The city of L.A. bureaucracy is conservative and redneck then," George continues. "There are no Latinos of any power either on the council or staff at the time. Richard is really the first Chicano elected who is a big guy who can raise a ton of money, is very popular in his district—he won outright in the primary with 62 percent of the vote in a field with eight candidates. The news stories said that was mathematically impossible in such a large field."

The council campaign does serve an important purpose: it teaches me how little I know about the people I have represented for the last 14 years in Sacramento. That's when the realization sets in that government closest to the people is the government that is most important to them.

I also remember my first year in city office as being fraught with investigations, largely over my use of the assembly campaign account and mostly egged on by politicians at City Hall who see me as a threat to run for the mayor's office when Tom Bradley decides to retire.

"The world shows up" at Los Angeles City Hall for Richard's 1985 swearing in as only the second Latino elected to the city council in the 20th century. Among them are U.S. Rep. Ed Roybal, who once holds the same seat, and Cesar Chavez.

Interestingly, I begin a significant trend that takes off only in the following years. The normal political ascendency is always viewed, not just in L.A. but all over the state and country, as beginning your career by getting elected to local office—school board, city council, or county board of supervisors—and then using those positions as springboards to move up to the legislature and eventually to Congress and maybe statewide office. That is the case until I do something totally different.

So speculation immediately begins, as early as the campaign, that the council isn't my real agenda. It is commonly assumed that Tom Bradley will retire. So you have members of the city council who have been there for long periods of time and are rumored to be candidates for mayor—Pat Russell, council president; David Cunningham, a black guy; Zev Yaroslavsky, another councilmember from the Westside; and Joel Wachs, the openly gay councilmember. Because of my seemingly counterintuitive move "down" from the assembly to city council and since I'm the first and only Latino member of the council in more than two decades in a city where the population and political participation of Chicanos is rapidly expanding, I'm quickly viewed as a mayoral contender.

In this game, I learn you never say never. I toy in my mind how great it would be to be mayor of Los Angeles; look at what I could do. But I don't like to kiss babies and perform at ceremonial events. I'm not especially articulate in public, I don't enjoy jumping in front of TV news cameras, and I haven't mastered the art of the sound bite. (I work with media trainers who my chief deputy, Robin Kramer, finds for two or three months after taking office at City Hall and notice I'm getting better. They help you learn how to condense your thoughts into short sound bites and credibly deliver speeches. I'm never very good at these things and usually try to avoid them when I can, but they're all skills that can be acquired. And I work on improving my Spanish; I understand it fluently but like English, I never quite conquer speaking that language either. So I don't enjoy my Spanish studies. What really improves my Spanish on the council is going out to speak at district events all the time, much more often than when I'm in the assembly.)

By this point in my life I know it's the legislative process I most like. I'm really content to finish out my career representing the 14th District where I have grown up.

In L.A., the nation's second largest media market, the press spends more time covering the city council than any other level of government. The local press corps hangs out at City Hall and closely follows developments there every day.

Being a legislator in Fresno or Bakersfield may be a big deal, but not in L.A. There are as many as 40 assemblymembers within the range of the L.A. media market, which also covers neighboring counties beyond Los Angeles. There are only 15 members of the L.A. City Council, and at first I'm the only Mexican, until Gloria Molina follows my example by jumping to the council from the state assembly in 1987.

Early on I make a calculated decision that works to my advantage: I pay special attention to the Spanish-language media, especially the electronic outlets and the respected daily newspaper *La Opinión*, something most Anglo politicians rarely, if ever, do. I make sure they have easy access to me and to my office. See, the English press corps prizes its balance and objectivity, even if it doesn't really achieve it. In English, editors and reporters view their relationship with government and elected officials as adversarial. In Spanish, the press is different, with journalists seeing their role as much more about advocacy of issues affecting their people that they care about. For Spanish-language reporters, it's not a sin to take a position or advocate a point of view, particularly if it's the point of view of the community I represent on the council.

So the Spanish-language press is always much more sympathetic with me than the English, and I make a deliberate decision to solicit it and be available to it. By this time, KMEX-TV Channel 34, the Univision affiliate, is the number one television station for news in Los Angeles—in either language. I have a relationship with Danny Villanueva, an early general manager of KMEX, going back to the East L.A. high school walkouts in 1968, even before I'm elected to the assembly. And I'm a friend of Ruben Salazar, the KMEX news director killed by an L.A. County sheriff's deputy during the Chicano Moratorium in 1970. I maintain those kinds of relationships with Spanish-language journalists all the years I'm serving at the state Capitol.)

When I hold news conferences in L.A. about anything as a legislator or councilmember, I don't care who else shows up. I know I'm guaranteed that Channel 34 will be there, and later Channel 52, the local Telemundo affiliate when it emerges in that market. They're always interested in what I have to say, and the influence of the Spanish-language press is growing in direct proportion to the growth of the Latino population.

One of the things I learn from Willie Brown is how to use my clout as a lawmaker at the Capitol to make change happen for the people I care about, chiefly Chicanos and other minorities. I find out there are similar, and even better opportunities, to do the same thing at City Hall.

One day Paul Kim, the LAPD's first Korean-American lieutenant, approaches Lou Moret. "I'm not political and don't understand politics," Paul admits. "But I'm getting screwed and I think it's racially motivated. I've been number one on the promotion list to captain for three years. People are being promoted who are below me. The list is about to expire," meaning he will have to take the captain's exam all over again. Paul asks if Lou has any advice for him.

Lou checks out Paul Kim with Bernard Parks, then assistant chief of the LAPD (and later police chief), who Lou knows. Parks vouches for Kim as a standup guy and a good officer. "He deserves to be promoted," Parks affirms to Lou, "but like all firsts of anything, the LAPD is reluctant because he's a minority." Blacks and Latinos share the same experience over the years; now it's happening to Asians.

Lou calls me. "I checked out the guy with Parks," he tells me. "Even Bernie Parks thinks he's getting shafted. Will you meet with him and see if you can help?"

"Bring him over," I say.

Lou and Paul Kim arrive at my City Hall office for a 10-minute meeting. I size him up and ask some questions, just to see if he's real. I'm satisfied. "Let me see what I can do," I say as they're leaving.

I learn enough about the LPAD in the last 20 years to know how it functions. And I understand one thing Asians and Mexicans have in common is they're very proud people, the kind who think they'll get promoted on their own, that the world is fair, that if you get an education, if you learn how to talk good, you'll be promoted and be white just like everyone else. If Paul Kim stays in that mode of thinking, he will continue to be a lieutenant for the rest of his life.

I don't like Willie Williams, then chief of the LAPD. I think he's kind of afraid of me because I have my own constituencies. I prefer someone from within the department. Williams is eventually canned and I help the mayor move the process along to get someone else.

I'm thinking that Willie Williams won't do anything for me about Paul Kim. But his chief of staff, Ronald Banks, another black guy, is a friend. Banks has moved up the ladder inside the department to become the LAPD's second in command. He ends up chief of the Inglewood Police Department after Williams is gone.

I call Banks. "Hey, brother, what's happening?" Banks says. "What can I do for you?"

"It's not what you can do for me, Ronnie," I tell him. "I'm going to warn you of something that's coming up. I just had a conversation with a group of 50 Korean-American ministers." I just make it all up. The longer I talk with Banks, the more I make up. I can't think of anything better to tell him. I know there's a Korean church in my district. There has to be at least 10 members there. So I make up 50.

"I'm calling to warn you, they're ready to come over to City Hall and raise nothing but crap against the chief," I keep going. "They're ready to file a lawsuit with the Asian American Legal Defense Fund, to sue the LAPD for discrimination."

"What are you talking about?" Ronald Banks asks.

"You know this guy named Kim?" I reply.

"Paul Kim, a great guy," Banks says.

"Well, he can't be that great because he's been on the promotion list for captain and you keep passing him up," I explain. "I'm just telling you they've asked me what should they do—and you better get ready. One thing about Koreans is they can deliver bodies. They're all men of God and they all have big constituencies. I have this Korean church in my district with 1,000 members. They and the other churches are going to come to City Hall and ream Willie Williams's ass. They may not know what to do from there, but I do. I'm going to be leading the charge and this is what I'll start off with: the chief of police is a racist. He doesn't care about the growing Asian-American constituency in L.A."

"Don't do it," Banks begs. "He [Williams] can't take that kind of heat. The guy, to begin with, has his own problems. What is it that will make him [Kim] happy?"

"What do you think it is?" I answer. "You think I'm here for my health. He's been number one on the captain's list for three years. Thing's ready to expire. It's a three-year list, and it's expiring. How many people have you promoted during those three years Kim's been on the list?"

"Ahhhh," is all he replies.

"Precisely," I say.

Two days later I get a call back from Banks. "I got good news for you. The chief would like to come by your office."

"I'd love to see him," I say. "Have him come over."

The chief is a big dude, 6'4" tall. He walks in my office and I am totally disrespectful. He knows I don't like him. He doesn't like me either.

"I have some good news for you," he announces.

"You do? Good news for me," I respond. "I'm not a member of the police department. It's not for me."

He ignores me: "This matter has come to my attention. I'm very happy to let you know if you want to take credit for it."

"Credit for what?" I ask. I'm being an asshole.

"We're going to appoint him [Paul Kim] captain by the end of the week. He'll have his letter notifying him of his promotion."

"I don't think I should tell him," I say. "You should tell him. It's only right that you tell him you're promoting him. You need all the good publicity you can get. I don't."

Williams leaves. I call Lou Moret, who calls Kim.

There's a big ceremony in Korea Town with 500 people in attendance when they "pin" the captain's bars on Paul Kim.

I get to know Kim. He is very proud that he doesn't have to kiss anybody's ass to get promoted. That's the problem, I tell him. He has to learn how to play the game. Koreans are like Mexicans: proud; it should happen on the merits. But life and politics don't work like that. I later help him get promoted to commander, shortly before Bernard Parks leaves as chief.

It feels good using my influence to help people like Paul Kim. I work to do that stuff all the time when I'm on the city council for lots of people, but especially if they're Chicanos. That's part of why I decide to give up everything I work so hard to get in Sacramento and come home to L.A.

After getting elected to the city council and taking office in 1985, one of the first things I have to do is look for whom to hire as chief deputy, the title for the person who serves as chief of staff. I ask a bunch of people, including Kathy Moret, Lou Moret's wife and a longtime staff person for Councilmember Gil Lindsay. Kathy is an establishment lefty, part of Tom Bradley's brain trust, has strong ties to the downtown business community and is very political. She and Maureen Kindel, chair of the board for the city Public Works Commission, are called the Gold Dust Twins because they raise so much political money for the mayor.

"You need someone like a Robin Kramer, head of the Coro Foundation," Kathy tells me. "But of course, she would never come to work for you. She's out of your league."

I tell Kathy, "Fuck it, why don't you set up a meeting with her for me?" My idea is obviously to see if she will work for me, but at least I get to pick her brain, let her know about me and understand what I'm looking to do so she can give me some good leads.

"As executive director of the Coro Foundation, you get lots of requests from all kinds of people—from labor, business, government, and philanthropy—looking for someone who knows how to navigate," Robin recalls. "Here was a person, Richard Alatorre, who had been newly elected. I didn't know him. He called me up: 'Can I talk with you? I want to find the right chief deputy. Let me buy you lunch.'"

We have a long lunch at the Pacific Dinning Car on West Sixth Street, a restaurant near downtown L.A. I make it real clear to Robin that I'd love to have a Mexican as chief of staff, but fuck it, we can train somebody later to take over the job. What I really need right now is a person of stature who will give me

Robin Kramer is Richard's first chief deputy, or chief of staff, at City Hall. He needs her extensive knowledge about the city beyond the Eastside.

instant credibility. She knows I'm just elected and Kathy probably tells her I'm thinking of hiring somebody who makes sense.

Robin comes to the meeting with one expectation. There is enough already written about me painting me as a back room politician who knows how to get things done. If such things are said about someone like U.S. Representative Howard Berman, they simply say he's a real effective and intelligent politician. But when I get tagged with the same label, it comes off making me look shady and the like. And, of course, that's not how things are done in Los Angeles politics. Shit, it's all done the same way everywhere, just with different players.

"There's the expectation Richard is going to run for mayor," Robin remembers going into our first meeting. "Richard was just like Antonio Villaraigosa before he became mayor: Richard came from spending time in Sacramento. He was close to Willie Brown, a big player at the Capitol, close to labor, canny and politically adept. He's the first Latino since Roybal, which is an historic quality. That he would run for mayor was being reported on."

"Let me just ask you some questions about what you're trying to achieve and the kind of person you're looking for," she says to me. I know Robin has extensive knowledge about the city. She knows and understands the movers and shakers. She has Westside and Jewish connections. She knows nothing about Mexicans, which is a consideration for me, but a minor one. I need someone good. I know I can take care of the Mexicans myself, and she can learn.

We hit it off. At one point in the conversation, she says she comes there prejudging me to be A, B, and C. I laugh. It doesn't offend me. I make a joke out of it. She feels good I don't get upset. I tell Robin I want to hire her.

"What?" she says. "I have a job."

"So what does that mean?" I reply. "It would be good. Your politics are like my politics. You care about certain issues like I do. I represent a part of the city nobody really knows anything about, including you. But you bring a sense of history in Los Angeles, an understanding of how things are done at City Hall—something I can use even though I know I'll learn it myself. But why should I reinvent the wheel and learn it all by myself?"

Robin tells me her own ideas about the job. "I tell you what," I say to her, "You know how to organize what is needed in a City Hall office. I want you to do that. I want to bring on some people to work in different areas, people who worked in my campaign. They're young and energetic." I explain how I'll introduce her to the part of the city that's east of the Los Angeles River. She already knows the history of Boyle Heights because of the Jews. I break out and explain the other parts of the district that she doesn't know.

I'm aware that Robin doesn't know much of anything about L.A. east of Western Avenue. But I figure she brings to the table other things I need.

That turns out to be true. But first, I get immersed in the kind of thankless challenge I think I've left the state Capitol to avoid.

Chapter 10

Laying a Foundation for Decades

There's an old Mexican saying that goes, "That which you don't like, you get at home." Here I make the decision to give up the fast life in the halls of power at the state Capitol—along with the big-ticket pain-in-the-ass chores such as legislative reapportionment—and go home where I've always lived in favor of the more mundane, closer-to-the-people concerns of local government. Yet the first big challenge I get to tackle—and lead—at City Hall is reapportionment of city councilmembers' districts.

Of course, doing council redistricting confirms what all the pundits are saying about me—that my real ambition and the reason I run for the council is to eventually get elected mayor of Los Angeles. But that reinforcement doesn't lessen the mess the city council already creates for itself.

Before I get elected, the council does a quickie reapportionment based on results from the 1980 U.S. Census. But in typical fashion, all it does is take care of itself. The redistricting plan that is enacted doesn't address the startling growth of Latinos in South Central L.A. and the San Fernando Valley. The plan butchers up Chicano communities in Boyle Heights, Lincoln Heights, Elysian Park, and all of the northeastern parts of L.A. Those and other Latino neighborhoods are divided up in much the same historical manner that partisan state and congressional legislative reapportionment schemes victimize Mexicans in the same places for generations. These highly concentrated Chicano areas are separated into multiple councilmanic districts to guarantee sitting incumbents that Latinos will not threaten their reelections because there won't be enough of them in a single district to elect one of their own. However, there are still enough Mexicans to provide safe margins of victory for mostly Democratic and progressive non-Latino incumbents against more Republican or conservative opponents. It isn't a new story for me.

So it is surprising to many that the federal government, under the Reagan administration, intervenes against Los Angeles based on violations of the U.S. Voting Rights Act. That is historic.

"There was a civil rights lawsuit filed against the city of L.A. by the U.S. Department of Justice over gerrymandering of Latinos in the council's reapportionment plan in the early '80s," affirms Bruce Cain, who I bring in to engineer reapportionment for assembly and congressional districts when I do it for Willie Brown a few years earlier. "The city of L.A. had to respond." If they fight the lawsuit, they will almost surely lose.

That's because the Justice Department has a solid Section 2 violation of the act, according to Bruce: the council's redistricting plan is illegal because as "an institutional arrangement, it has the effect of denying equal opportunity to elect an individual of their own for a protected group, Latinos. Coincidentally, 1982 was a pivotal year in which the Voting Rights Act changed to an *effect* standard: you didn't have to show discriminatory intent, just that whatever their motive, the council's action had a discriminatory effect.

"So the Justice Department became aggressive looking for Section 2 violations," Bruce continues. "They were looking at the case of L.A. city where there was only one elected Latino councilmember, Richard, who had just been elected, despite a municipality that was close to 30 percent Latino."

I get to City Hall when the federal lawsuit is pending.

I also get the council president, Pat Russell, to have Bruce Cain do an independent evaluation and advise the council on its liability under Section 2 of the law.

"The presumption at the time by the city council and even reporters was how could L.A. possibly be violating the Voting Rights Act when it is a largely liberal Democratic city that has minority representation?" Bruce says. "How could it possibly be discriminating against Latinos? That was my assumption going in too.

"I was teaching at Cal Tech, got the data and analyzed the lines," he goes on. "I saw what the Justice Department saw: the council divided the Latino community into several pieces and there's only one majority Latino seat when there could easily be at least two or three.

"I said to myself, Pat Russell won't be happy with these findings," Bruce notes. "In fact, she wanted to kill me. I have never seen anyone so angry with me—well, sometimes in Sacramento during state reapportionment. She didn't believe it and thought there had been a betrayal. She probably assumed Richard put me up to it she was so mad—assuming if Richard hired or referred the consultant, the consultant would say whatever Richard wanted.

"But I said to her, 'you have a real problem. You will lose [the lawsuit].' They soon hired Jonathan Steinberg as an outside attorney. He came to the same

Los Angeles City Council President Pat Russell hands Richard his first big task at City Hall by putting him in charge of reapportioning council districts, the same job he has recently handled at the state Capitol.

conclusion I did, and he knew the legal arguments better than me. So Pat Russell was stuck between Steinberg and me telling her they might lose."

A backdrop to the story is dramatically changing demographics in the city involving blacks and Latinos. Blacks in L.A. are beginning to become a fading minority. More and more are moving from South Central with all its related crime and drug problems into the Antelope Valley and the Inland Empire. Old blacks are dying and younger blacks are moving out. Meantime, the influx of Mexicans has already started. Many blacks hate or fear Mexicans because they see them starting to move into their neighborhoods. African Americans aren't going to let Chicanos take away the hard-won political gains blacks have made over the decades. So there is a lot of concern at City Hall about how blacks will be impacted by the reapportionment process that a Mexican is going to be leading.

"By the 1980s, the demographic shift, especially in South Central, has serious implications for electoral politics and specifically reapportionment," Bruce confirms. There were two pieces of the puzzle, he explains. "One, there would be fewer African-American representatives. And two, more importantly, African Americans had represented the downtown-area development areas and development in downtown was a big issue in the '80s."

But most of the African-American community resides in areas that doesn't have much development. That means they have less control over the economic future of the city, less control of donations to political campaigns and all the other things that come with economic development.

"The big divide in the '80s was between slow-growthers on the Westside who already had a lot of development and money, against Eastsiders and people from South Central who didn't want to lose what they had," Bruce says. "A lot of the fight was about African Americans maintaining their influence over downtown. There was an old distinguished councilmember, Gil Lindsay, who represented downtown." Fashioning a redistrict plan that would see "a Latino taking control of downtown would mean challenging this icon of city politics."

Pat Russell's council district is on the Westside, and it has many African Americans in it. These include a lot of affluent middle-class blacks she wants to keep. "I realized part of Pat Russell's horror was that if you moved the African-American council seats westward to keep the existing number of African-American seats, it could squeeze out Pat Russell and push her north into areas that were not hospitable to her," Bruce observes. "Pat had reason to be worried about this, and the African-American community was uptight about it too. It helped that Richard Alatorre had a close relationship with Willie Brown and a reputation of working well with African Americans. It may have been one reason he got the job" of overseeing city redistricting.

It turns out that a key ally of mine on the council, who is the point person for Pat Russell with the African-American community, is Councilmember David Cunningham. Dave and I know each other from our War on Poverty days in the 1960s. He serves as vice chairman of the reapportionment committee and is probably put there by Russell to block me—or at least keep a close eye on me. Russell thinks that because of all the publicity touting me as a possible mayoral candidate—in a political body with at least several members with mayoral ambitions—I will never be able to convince my colleagues to be with me on a redistricting plan and come up with one that will answer the Justice Department lawsuit against the council. At some point I lay out to Dave that he has nothing to worry about; I'm going to do everything to protect what he—and the blacks—got.

(Blacks aren't the only problem. There is also Asian-American Councilmember Michael Woo, who wants to represent sites where future development can take place in the Hollywood Hills and the San Fernando Valley.)

Pat Russell, the council president, has a great relationship with the black community, much of it because of her friendship with Mayor Tom Bradley. The next thing you know, the city has to respond to the federal lawsuit and she offers me chairmanship of the council's Elections and Reapportionment Committee. There isn't anyone on the council who can do it. They can't come up with the answer because, as at the state Capitol, reapportionment is about everybody who is already in power protecting their asses.

"Richard had done reapportionment for the state, had a good relationship with African Americans and then there was the fact that having a Latino chair would help the defense against lawsuits down the road because they couldn't accuse white councilmembers of drawing the lines to their own benefit," Bruce adds. "Then there were the same traits that helped Richard do the job in Sacramento: you cut your own throat when you make enemies, particularly in a small body like the city council where things tend to be done by logrolling and unanimous consent. The norm is to roll with the punches and not create enemies or piss people off if you can avoid it. Walking in and taking a job that is guaranteed to annoy at least a third of the members if not more is not a good way to collect favors. Richard was not afraid to make enemies."

For me it is a challenge, but not a big deal. I know I can get it done if I get Bruce Cain and others involved. I take over reapportionment quickly after getting elected. I assume office at the end of 1985. In January 1986, the reapportionment committee chairmanship is offered to me.

Bruce and I know how to work with each other because we have already done it successfully just a few years before. "Once Richard became chair of council reapportionment, it's just like the olden days," Bruce says. "When I first met Richard he didn't know me from Adam. By the time this [council redistricting] happens, he's been working with me for a while. He knew I'm experienced." Bruce is technically consultant to the city attorney, but he works with me because I'm chair of the committee and responsible for the politics.

"The first thing Richard does is convince everyone to hire Bruce Cain and his team," notes Robin Kramer, who is my new chief deputy. "That's a big step for the city because in the past such staff work had been in the hands of the city's legislative analyst. Computers were just coming into use for reapportionment [which Bruce innovated for state redistricting]. That was amazing."

Bruce's operation at Cal Tech is right up the Pasadena Freeway from City Hall. He already has the same infrastructure, using the innovative model he makes up for 1981 legislative redistricting, the first time computers are used to draw lines. Willie Brown decides not to dismantle the infrastructure only to have to start it up all over again from scratch at the beginning of each decade. "At the time, I was keeping the data base updated, maintaining the computers and perfecting the software design," Bruce says. "Now there are commercial companies that produce it, but then we had to do it on our own."

Somebody is going to get had in this reapportionment plan. There is no justification for the manner in which Chicanos are reapportioned by the city council in the early 1980s. We have to undo what was done.

"It was all about incumbent protection," Bruce concludes. "Art Snyder had represented Richard's district. He could represent the Latino neighborhoods pretty well; he knew how to work their politics and had good office staff. So he could survive in that district. But Latino growth was creeping up on other councilmembers who had been there for a while. They were using redistricting to protect themselves. They weren't anti-Latino, just pro-themselves."

As a result of failing to elect more Latinos to the council, "there were no Latinos to speak up for Latino causes," Bruce adds. "That's what Section 2 of the Voting Rights Act was designed for. Prior to 1982, you had to prove malice in the hearts of incumbents and people drawing the lines. You could determine that based on intent with the L.A. County Board of Supervisors in a subsequent case in the late '80s, where the evidence was on the record that the supervisors went out of their way to intentionally dilute Latino" voting power.

When Bruce presents the result of the evaluation, the council decides it can't afford the black eye of violating the Voting Rights Act. It decides we will try to fix the lines and avoid the expense and embarrassment of the lawsuit.

That being said, there are plenty of contentious issues a new reapportionment plan has to address.

We have to do something about the San Fernando Valley. There is a growing population of Chicanos who previous plans have split all over the place. We have to try to bring them together and not divide them up among different districts so every councilmember in the valley has a piece of them.

"A lot of growth among Latinos occurred in the '70s and '80s just south of and around the city of San Fernando," Bruce says. "It looked like you could create a 40 percent or 50 percent Latino seat based on that growth if you united Latinos into one district. Creating a Latino district in the valley was unheard of. Historically, the valley was a white, middle-class region. Also, the valley had a strained relationship and was traditionally very suspicious of the inner city. Valley residents didn't want any contamination from inner city politics in their area. That tension persisted into the 1990s' fight over charter reform in L.A."

We have to do something about the 13th District, whose member is recently reelected Mike Woo. It is north, west, and slightly east of downtown and covers parts of Lincoln Heights, Silverlake, and Echo Park—plus the southeastern San Fernando Valley with Latinos in it. If reshaped, it can become a seat for Latinos. But Mike Woo doesn't give a shit about anything outside of the yuppies in Hollywood. His residence is there, and it's that group he will ultimately battle over.

"There were neighborhoods Michael Woo represented where his family or associates were involved in development projects," Bruce points out. "He didn't want to lose control of those areas. We tried moving him into Chinatown, to make the district more Asian American, and taking out more heavily Latino areas. But some of the Latino areas also involved development projects he was interested in.

"Michael made a big deal about charges we were causing a race war. The Justice Department even sent representatives to interview people; they interviewed me. They wanted to know what we were doing and why we were doing it. I responded that we needed more consolidated Latino seats and it made more sense to give Michael more Asians. His concerns weren't just that he liked yuppies; he had financial stakes in development projects there."

Then there is what to do with the 9th District, which is Gilbert Lindsay. There isn't much to do from a Latino perspective because what you have there are a lot of "dead" voters: Mexicans who are not yet registered to vote in any significant numbers. You can try to figure out where Chicanos eventually might end up. But we're talking about the 1980s. Latinos don't shake the hell out of electoral politics in the state of California until the late '80s and '90s when Mexicans are able to become legal residents, eventually become citizens and then vote in greater numbers in part through the amnesty provisions of the 1986 federal immigration reform law and after the Republicans, beginning with Pete Wilson, begin scapegoating immigrants for short-term political gains. (If we ever get another federal immigration law allowing undocumented immigrants to become legal, the politics of California will be transformed even more. Latinos would wipe out blacks in terms of South Central L.A. political participation if the undocumented become legalized, citizens and registered voters.)

But that isn't yet the case in the mid-'80s. "In those days, voting rates among African Americans were much higher than the voting rates of Latinos," according to Bruce Cain. "It's not clear what the potential is to create a real Latino seat in some places of L.A. You can create them on paper, but if there aren't enough Latino voters who vote, the districts could still be won by non-Latino candidates. This was the first time we spent a lot of time worrying about non-citizenship and the age distribution of the population. If there were a lot of under-18-year-olds or noncitizens, you could create a seat that looked Latino, but in reality you'd just be setting yourself up for defeat on the short run. The 9th District was a good example."

Just like Sacramento reapportionment in 1981, Bruce and I go around and meet with councilmembers one on one at City Hall to learn what they want and incorporate their desires. The open meeting law governing the state is much weaker than the Brown Act covering the city council. So we have to be careful. This time we work much more closely with the lawyers, because the threats of both federal litigation and possible technical violations of the Brown Act are hanging over our heads. "That's why I did a lot of work with the council offices [staff]," Bruce says. "There was no question Richard made the big calls. I did the hand holding, making some neighborhood adjustments here and there. Then the attorneys would weigh in with their opinions."

"There was a tremendous back and forth using maps with individual members of the council, lawyers, and MALDEF," the Mexican American Legal Defense and Education Fund, Robin Kramer recalls.

We hold hearings around the city over what to propose. The blacks attend in mass. We have hearings in the San Fernando Valley where it seems like the Klan has turned out. They are ugly people.

"They had reapportionment hearings all over," Robin adds. "I remember one of those hearings was in the valley. Person after person stood up and talked about 'those damn Mexicans' and how they're ruining the public schools and changing the faces of neighborhoods. Richard just sat there. I said to him a few days later, 'How do you hear all that? What do you do with it?' He just said, 'they weren't even talking to me. They're people with a lot of anger and ignorance and we have a huge road ahead.' I came away thinking that here's a guy who really did feel each of those dagger words in a deep way. He heard them, remembered them, and personally buried them. A reapportionment plan that would create new Latino seats was his ultimate response. It's all about the old saying, 'Don't get mad, get even.'"

Bruce has this point guy named David Ely, a student of Bruce's at Cal Tech. (Now he does this kind of work full time with MALDEF and other groups.) David Ely is Bruce's assistant; they draw lines together in this little office, a broom closet really, at Cal Tech's Social Sciences building in Pasadena. It's a small office with no windows that Bruce gets permission to use. By that time it is pretty much handled on computers. There is no more hand inputting of stuff.

"What Richard brought as the leader of reapportionment," Robin says, "was he knew what he was doing, he trusted Bruce Cain on the technical front, he knew the law [involving the Voting Rights Act], and he had a very keen understanding of politics and what made his colleagues on the council go—a human understanding. He also brought with him the art of the long view. He realized this is the beginning of laying the political foundation for Latinos in our city, not just today but for a long time into the future.

"People think of reapportionment as a moment in time," Robin continues. "Richard Alatorre, from his experience, saw it as laying a foundation for decades. In legislative redistricting, Richard created a dozen or more seats where Latinos could someday get elected. It often didn't happen right away. Others would come and make it happen. But it would have never been possible without Richard's [state] reapportionment plan. He did a similar thing with reapportionment for the city of Los Angeles. It all started happening in the '90s, but '86 redistricting opened the doors."

"The idea was to create two Latino seats, one in the San Fernando Valley and one in the central city area to satisfy the Justice Department," Bruce states, "and do it with as little disruption elsewhere as possible."

I know one thing: I will not fuck around with the blacks. I am going to eventually give them their territory. I tell them, "You cut it up how you want. But in exchange for that, you need to help me on what I need," which is taking care of Latinos, which is eventually what the plan does. The blacks have no bitch with me at all. "I would say most of our attention was focused on the creation of these Latino seats," Bruce says.

There is little difference between legislative and council reapportionment, except maybe it's a little less partisan with the city. What councilmembers want "is a little less connected to party registration and a little more parochial," Bruce adds. "One member was absolutely adamant about having his mother's grave in his district. Others wanted a particular restaurant or development project. There was a lot more of that kind of nonsense—less of 'I need more Democrats.'"

There was also no Willie Brown I had to be responsible to and reply to his demands for reports about progress. "My sense is that [council president] Pat Russell did not lean on Richard as much as Willie did" a few years before, Bruce agrees. "The purpose of reapportionment in Sacramento was keeping the Speaker in power over the next decade"; it was Willie's first big test as Speaker of the assembly. What was at stake with council reapportionment "was not keeping the presidency of the council," Bruce says. "It was avoiding litigation."

As fate—and the political double-cross—would have it, we have to do reapportionment twice that year.

Our initial strategy is to dump as many Mexicans as we can into the 13th District, the seat held by Mike Woo. In the process we unify the Asian community into an adjoining district, putting all of Chinatown and Korea Town—or as much of it as we can—into one seat. After our plan gets unveiled, there's a Paul Conrad political cartoon in the *Los Angeles Times* showing a falling apart Hollywood sign with the caption underneath, "Taking the Woo out of Hollywood." The idea we propose is moving Woo out of these key neighborhoods in Hollywood that he wants. "Under this first plan, Woo would have lost a lot of the Hollywood Hills territory he coveted," Bruce says.

Mike Woo hates me. We put him in a district where he immediately has to learn Spanish and where he may not survive if it goes to an election. "Woo was a pretty good politician who might have survived in the seat we created for him," according to Bruce.

Of course, Woo goes ballistic and organizes the Asians, and he has a lot of big moneyed interests behind him. The Asians get together with all the liberals. (Remember, the district we create next door unites Asian communities into one seat. Woo's grievances with my reapportionment plan have nothing to do with advancing Asian political empowerment; they're about keeping territory he wants because it is rich in business and development potential.) I remember being at a meeting and listening to Antonio Villaraigosa, who is then with the ACLU, siding with Woo and talking about his poor Asian brothers. I'm saying to myself, "You stupid motherfucker. The 13th is a seat that a Chicano can get elected in, but because Michael Woo has all this money behind him, he's threatening to sink the whole redistricting plan."

"Woo is not much different than anyone else," Bruce concedes. "If somebody did that to Richard Alatorre, he wouldn't react much differently."

I have nothing against Mike Woo. He just gets elected in the wrong district. When I go after him, I say, "Don't take it personally." But he hates me anyway. We have a strained relationship afterwards, even though I am invited to his wedding. His father, Wilber Woo, who I really like, supports me in past campaigns. He is just trying to protect his kid.

"Woo is very cerebral," Robin Kramer observes, "but without Richard Alatorre's political acumen or legislative wherewithal. He was the first Asian-American councilmember so there were a lot of celebratory observances. Woo moved into a set of offices in the old historic City Hall and was redoing the space. He chose beautiful colors of mauve and gray. There were cubicles just like all members' offices. But Woo had this ragged etched glass put on top of the cubicles to give them a more decorative affect. 'Come see my new office,' Woo tells Richard, who drags me along to see too. Richard looks around. 'It's really, really beautiful,' Richard tells his colleague. 'When's it going to be finished?' Of course, it was finished. That incident was one window into how differently the two of them saw the world.'"

Meantime, we get royally double-crossed by Councilmember Joel Wachs. In crafting his seat, we give him everything he conceivably wants. He's gay and the darling of rent control. He passes a major city rent control ordinance. His is an ideal district. We pack in as many gays and as many renters as we can fit. It's a great district for Joel Wachs, one that is a perfect fit for him to get reelected in.

Councilmember Michael Woo convinces Mayor Tom Bradley to veto Richard's reapportionment plan.

As a result, Joel commits to me that he is a vote for the reapportionment plan. I know how to collect—and count—votes. I give gays the district they want.

Well, Joel fucks us. He gives this heart-rending speech about how he has to vote his conscience—against my plan—after we treat him with kid gloves and after he lets us steal every square block of gay and renter territory we can possibly find for him. His problem is basic: no guts.

"When the reapportionment measure was up for debate, Wachs was trying to lecture Richard in an open council meeting on propriety and process," recalls Gerard Orozco from my staff. "After a long diatribe by Wachs, Richard got up and grabbed his mike. I was standing next to him. Richard said, 'Mr. Wachs, you are no political virgin.' Then he swung the mike and I had to duck to avoid getting hit by it. Everyone in the council chambers gave up a gasp at Richard's use of language. Wachs uncharacteristically remained speechless."

Although Wachs goes back on his promise, that's not what kills the plan. I get the full city council to vote for it anyway, never thinking that Tom Bradley will fuck with the goddamn thing since I know I've worked hard to keep the blacks on my side.

What I don't count on is what Michael Woo brings to bear on the mayor: big Asian money. Mayor Bradley vetoes it.

A new plan has to be quickly pieced together. "People are not terribly happy with it," Bruce says. "I go off on vacation on July 1. Then I get a phone call. They say, 'Bruce, you got to come back.' 'Why?' I ask. '[San Fernando Valley Councilman] Howard Finn died of a heart attack and we have to redo the lines.' I was told the decision to redraw the lines was made at his funeral."

We get to take advantage of the fact that all of a sudden there is a vacant council district in the valley we can collapse and reconfigure. "This was one of those wonderful cases where in musical chairs it's a lot easier when not everyone is in a chair," Bruce explains. "Now we had 14 instead of 15 incumbents to take care of."

After the guy drops dead, it's a lot easier. We collapse Finn's district like it was never there, which helps us take care of a lot of other problems.

In the end, we create a new Chicano district in the San Fernando Valley where it is only a question of time before a Mexican gets elected. And we draw another Chicano district in the central city area too. These districts result in the elections of Richard Alarcon and Gloria Molina, respectively. Another redrawn valley district creates the opportunity of sending another Latino to the council, who later turns out to be Tony Cardenas.

To make it all work, I give up some higher-participation Chicano areas in my district, the 14th, so the new neighboring seat—that later elects Gloria—has enough voters to actually send a Mexican to City Hall. "The important thing is not everyone was like Richard, who was willing to weaken his own seat or give up his voters for the sake of creating a new district that was winnable for Latinos," Bruce says. "Richard deserves a lot of credit for that."

In addition to giving up voting Chicanos, which I do, in retrospect I make the mistake of giving up Dodger Stadium at Chavez Ravine, which I love. We would have a professional football team there today if I kept the territory in my district. I could be a pig, but reapportionment isn't going to be done any other way even though at the time I bitch and moan.

The second reapportionment plan that year goes through the council and is signed by the mayor. The stakes are high in needing to overcome the Justice Department lawsuit over Voting Rights Act violations. But we accomplish it with the help of a deceased councilmember.

The initial legacy of 1986 council reapportionment is beginning the unification of Latinos in the San Fernando Valley that eventually enables the election of Alarcon and Cardenas, and creating a new Chicano central city district, all by putting together the numbers of Mexican voters that guarantees Latinos should always hold those seats. Today, you have two Latino councilmembers from the valley and four Chicanos on the council altogether. As the demographics keep shifting and with federal legalization of undocumented immigrants possible some day, you can easily get an additional three more Latinos on the L.A. City Council.

The stakes are high back in 1986. I don't know what would have happened if I didn't do reapportionment. But nobody on the council is going to give a shit then. What the council doesn't want to see happen is having it all end up in court. My thing is I'm putting the Mexicans together one way or the other.

"The really significant thing was the interethnic tensions," Bruce concludes. "It turns out to be Asian-Latino tensions drummed up by Michael Woo" that sideline redistricting at first. "But you were acutely aware there was a ticking time bomb of African-American representatives in power in majority Latino seats and that couldn't last forever given the demographic trends.

"Richard's legacy is he did reapportionment at two levels—the state and city—within a few years of each other and he did it successfully when it could easily have blown up. More broadly, the city and the people living in Los Angeles became much more aware of the Voting Rights Act and the importance of minority representation. I vividly remember early meetings with councilmembers who insisted, 'I would never intentionally do anything to hurt minorities, so why is the Justice Department picking on us?' We did a lot of education about voting rights and the history of representation in L.A. that many people never looked at before because they assumed this was a liberal Democratic area and therefore had no problems with minority representation." The federal lawsuit and resulting 1986 city redistricting "blew the cover off of that. It made the Democratic Party aware it could be an obstacle to minority representation, which became a major theme across the country in the 1990s."

Chapter 11

I'm There to Do More Than Just Take Up Space

Just as the Assembly Speakers I serve under—Bob Moretti, Leo McCarthy, and Willie Brown—heavily influence my 13-and-a-half-year legislative tenure in Sacramento, my service during 14 years on the Los Angeles City Council is significantly shaped by three larger-than-life public figures who play key roles. They are two mayors of L.A.—Tom Bradley and Richard Riordan—and the long-serving council president who becomes like a father to me, John Ferraro.

I first get involved with Tom Bradley through the Urban Affairs Institute, set up around 1967 by Mervyn Dymally, then a state senator from Los Angeles born in Trinidad and Tobago, for the purpose of training and exposing young Latinos, blacks, Asians, and women to the political process. It is part of a Ford Foundation fellowship. One piece of it gives people like me the opportunity to get a master's degree, which I do, through the University of Southern California. The other part of the fellowship is Merv wanting us to learn the ins and outs of practical politics by getting involved in election campaigns. By the time I'm into the fellowship, the biggest campaign around is the 1969 mayoral contest pitting Tom Bradley, an L.A. city councilmember and former LAPD cop, against the city's incumbent mayor, Sam Yorty.

My first contact with Bradley is when I meet him and other local politicians between 1966 and 1968, but especially during the '68 presidential campaign of Robert Kennedy that Bradley supports as a councilmember. In the years leading up to the '69 mayor's race, Bradley becomes a vehicle of the liberal Westside of town, which is anxious to form a coalition with minorities in other parts of L.A.

For Richard, Tom Bradley becomes proof of what Los Angeles can become. The mayor is shown here at City Hall after Richard is elected to the city council.

to win citywide elections. Tom Bradley is not Merv Dymally's favorite politician, but Merv is deeply committed to coalition politics, and the simple reality is that Bradley becomes the standard bearer. The tall and imposing former police captain embodies the possibilities of what can happen when people from the east, west, and south sides of town coalesce to get something meaningful accomplished. Just as Ed Roybal is a darling of the lefty community, primarily liberal Jews, Tom Bradley becomes the symbol among the same people of a changing Los Angeles, given the clear trend of transforming demographics in the city and the changing complexion and color of its people.

I'm beginning my political internship when Bradley starts running for mayor. I want to work on his campaign. Merv says that's fine. I become the other face of the Viva Bradley campaign, the drive among Chicanos on the Eastside. It's officially run by Bert Corona, then one of the Chicano political establishment figures as head of the Mexican American Political Association. Bert is clearly the leader of Viva Bradley, but I weasel my way into the campaign. Bert likes the idea of having younger faces around. But Bert represents the old while in my view I represent the new.

The fact is I also care about Tom Bradley and work hard for him. To me Bradley, when he first runs for mayor, is living proof of what the city can become. Chicanos are very important in that election because Yorty is a notorious race baiter. He goes to the Chicanos and tells them, "Vote for me because I've set up this Committee for the Spanish Speaking in the mayor's office. I've hired Mexicans. All Bradley will do is take care of the blacks at your expense."

There is a long history of racial antipathy that still exists between blacks and Chicanos. They constantly fight each other over scarce resources all throughout Lyndon Johnson's War on Poverty beginning in the mid-1960s. They fight each other over jobs. They fight each other in prisons for control of the institutions. There is a long tradition of not getting along.

My idea—honed under Merv Dymally—is that the only way Chicanos, blacks, and other minorities will ever make progress for their own communities is by coming together. I always remember a comment describing the state of minority politics by Ron Karanga, a militant professor of black studies at California State University, Long Beach who I get to know while I'm teaching there. He later becomes a minister and founder of Kwanzaa, the first uniquely African-American holiday. Ron believes "unity without uniformity" is the way minorities can learn how to peacefully co-exist and advance by working with one another.

I always get along with blacks. So for me it's easy to work with and for Bradley. I work in the Boyle Heights headquarters of the Viva Bradley effort. We do everything from setting up the office to licking envelopes to organizing precinct walking and phone banking to putting on fundraisers. We are pretty self-contained and supplied with the resources we need from the overall Bradley campaign.

That's when I also get exposed to some of the lefties in Democratic Party politics, mostly the unions after the United Auto Workers gets heavily involved. The UAW has a long record of underwriting and setting up community organizations in the black and Chicano communities.

Tom Bradley has all the right instincts about the role of government. He is a very compassionate guy. He dedicates his political life to becoming more than a black elected official. He wants to be a servant for all people, but with a clear understanding he is black.

None of that bothers me. I understand what Tom has to do. I once tell him in those days, "You have to understand what I have to do too"—for Chicanos. Such notions of diversity are very consistent with the principles and tenor of his election campaign.

Bradley emerges from the primary election as the top vote getter and goes into a runoff against Yorty in the general election, where he gets killed. Yorty successfully tags Bradley, a former cop and mainstream establishment politician who happens to be black, as a tool of the Communist Party. Bradley comes back four years later and beats Yorty in 1973. Tom serves as mayor for 20 years.

My friendship with Richard Riordan, who succeeds Bradley as mayor in 1993, also goes back a number of years. Riordan is a close ally of Tom Bradley; Riordan chairs the city Parks and Recreation Commission under Bradley. But I come to know him as a very generous benefactor to many good causes across L.A. He's the guy you always go to whenever there is the need for significant contributions to worthy Eastside charitable or community organizations or programs. There's also the Catholic Dick Riordan, who is a prominent figure within the archdiocese as a donor and contributor to Catholic charities, including the church's extensive education programs throughout the L.A. area. The Catholic schools in my district are probably about 80 percent Latino.

In the eastern part of L.A., especially in my council district, Dick is often Mr. Anonymous because of his benevolence in contributing computers and other equipment to many of the public elementary, middle, and secondary schools. It's anonymous because that's the way he wants it. He isn't somebody who needs adulation, at least then. Nor is he into publicity and the like. He helps because he genuinely believes in the literacy of children.

I also work with him on one of his favorite projects in Boyle Heights. Puente Learning Center, a literacy program that teaches people in need of basic survival skills and learning English, receives national acclaim and is a model for adult education. Its funding at the time comes through the Los Angeles Unified School District. But when Dick and I begin working on the center's behalf, it is struggling financially and also because it has outgrown its facility, an old beat-up site it is being forced to abandon because of seismic worries. Puente needs another place. Dick's solution is simple: Let's find them one.

He puts his real estate people to work on it. I get a phone call from Dick. He's found this property, not initially telling me exactly where it is located in Boyle Heights. At first, Dick doesn't realize I, too, do a lot of work with Sr. Jennie Lechtenberg, SNJM, founder of the center.

Dick tells me the location of the property, with a picturesque view of all of downtown L.A. He asks me what I think about it. I stop him: "Let me ask you a question. Is it owned by this [developer]?"

"Yes, how did you know?"

I shake my head and start laughing because after six months I've just obtained city entitlements on behalf of the same developer for the same piece of property to build badly needed multifamily housing. All of a sudden the developer falls out of the deal because of financial difficulties. "You better watch this guy," I tell Dick. "He's less than honorable."

"Richard, don't worry about it," he replies, "I wasn't born yesterday. I'll get a fair price out of him because I'm going to pay for it in cash. But let's get back to the topic. Can you help me get the property" as the new state-of-the-art home for Sr. Jennie's Puente Learning Center?

"Yeah, sure I can."

About a week later, Dick gets back to me: "The property is going to be mine. I really need to get this projected started."

Entitling a sizeable piece of land like that—navigating through the city's laborious bureaucracy—usually takes six to nine months if you're lucky. I have to change the land designation from multifamily to a public facility use specifically for an educational purpose. A lot of hoops have to be jumped through. A lot of waivers have to be made. I get it done in 30 days. Dick can't believe it. He thinks I'm the greatest living city councilmember in all of mankind, marveling at what I am able to do because he does real estate and buys and sells properties. I get it done by pulling every string imaginable because I believe in what Sr. Jennie is doing.

I help the property survive a lengthy struggle for entitlements when it is going to be multifamily housing. Because I have doubts about the veracity of the developer who is supposed to build a multifamily community on the site, I extract many concessions to add amenities in order to make it more livable and functional for the families that will move into it. So I have some influence over this property. That's good because now I go back to the same city entitlement officials and sell them on the fact this developer is less than trustworthy and we finally have found another buyer for the property who will produce an equally beneficial use for the community. Instead of affordable housing, it will now be a place for adult education under the new sponsor, Puente Learning Center, which is more than reputable. The name of Sr. Jennie, the beneficiary, is gold in L.A., and city officials understand that.

Within a month's time, the project is fully entitled. Puente Learning Center continues operating today out of that site in a beautiful, modern building. The Prince of Wales comes to visit. Presidents of the United States go there. Presidential candidates tour the center. It's a marvelous program, one of the best adult education operations in the country and a credit to Boyle Heights.

Another proposed project Dick and I work on together is building a center on a piece of property up on a hill overlooking El Sereno and Boyle Heights. The Department of Water & Power owns it for many years with a limited-use designation by the public utility. Because it's the only land suitable for a park in El Sereno, I have this vision of constructing a multipurpose recreation center. The city Parks and Recreation Department owns the adjacent property; chair of its commission is Dick Riordan. Because of the stellar work I do with him on Puente Learning Center, I go to Dick with my idea for building a state-of-the-art recreation center using both parcels of land.

Riordan suggests turning the two properties into a regional park where many more city resources can be brought to bear. "I'm chairman of the Parks and Recreation Commission and I'll be the one who can make it happen," he says. "And if there is privately owned property nearby, I'll purchase it and donate it to the department to make the park even more attractive."

Once the architectural renderings and feasibility study are done, we come up with a proposal for a full-sized gym, Olympic-size swimming pool, Olympic-size track and field facility plus places for passive recreation—where people can use and enjoy well-landscaped grounds without participating in sports and the like. We propose walking trails for senior citizens. Since the regional park would attract so many people, we are also going to build an area police station so the police presence will deter people from using the place in the wrong way.

The regional park never happens because the neighbors in Hillside Village, an area of El Sereno, protest. Instead of supporting something that would be a net addition to the entire community, the neighbors are more concerned about attracting negative outside elements. In the end, because I get the land from Water & Power transferred to Parks and Recreation, what gets built are little walking trails and some passive recreation—but nothing on the scale originally envisioned by Dick and me. The local residents are the ones who lose out.

That is the kind of relationship Dick and I have based on mutual respect going back to before he becomes mayor.

When Tom Bradley decides to retire in 1993, there's some talk about me running for mayor. I get a phone call one day from Dick Riordan asking for a meeting at his place in a big office building on Bunker Hill. He speaks of his interest in running for mayor. Dick says he's prepared to spend a lot of money, much of it his own; the rest he will raise. Then he pays me a high compliment: "I want to tell you if you decide you want to run for mayor, I will withdraw and support your candidacy."

"Look, I reply, I'm not prepared to tell you right now that I'm going to run and make it public. That's not the way politics works. But just between you and me, at the end of the day if you're going to run, run." I tell Dick early on that I've toyed with the idea of campaigning for mayor of L.A. But I also recognize what I'm good at and what I don't believe I have an interest in doing: Kissing babies and getting in front of TV news cameras. I'm good at bringing people together and finding resolutions to problems. That's all I'm going to say on the subject. Dick says okay.

What I'm really telling him without saying it is I'm not going to run.

Tom Bradley will go down in history as one of the city's great mayors. But unfortunately, partly because of a mutual distain for the chief of police, Daryl Gates, both men stay around too long and their true potentials are never fully realized. I always personally like Dick Riordan, finding him to be a man of his word who cares about Los Angeles. He also knows somebody has to provide renewed hope for L.A. during a very difficult time.

The city is in recovery. Someone needs to envision ourselves coming back from the brink of twin disasters—the 1992 civil disturbances following the verdict in the Rodney King criminal trial on April 29, and not long afterwards the devastating Northridge earthquake on January 17, 1994. Both events come in the midst of a serious economic downturn. They all hit L.A. hard. So there is a lot on the city's plate.

"At a time when the city is facing multiple consecutive disasters—the earthquake and civil unrest that underscored the poverty that already existed—L.A. needed champions, people who thought big," says my last chief of staff, Hillary Norton. "Sometimes Richard used to say, 'It's time for a Profile in

Courage moment.' It was all about telling his staff that it's time to think bigger. We need to set the city on the right course in the wake of these twin disasters."

Both of those disasters can't come at a worst time. Aside from the economic downturn you have a disaster that hits across much of L.A. after the King verdict is announced. The long-ago riots of the summer of 1965 hit a community that is mostly African-American. South Central is an entirely different place in 1992, when it is well on its way to having a nonblack majority—meaning a lot of Latinos. Additionally, by 1992, there is a lot more mobility in terms of where people live, work, and get around. The civil unrest of '92 isn't just concentrated in Watts, as is the case in '65. It spreads out over a much larger geographic area and even threatens to come into East Los Angeles. The local gangs in Boyle Heights get together, institute a truce, and threaten that anyone trying to come into their community will be met with violence. If the rioters cross Soto Street, the gang members say it's going to be all over; they will make their stand and beat the fuck out of the invaders.

The looting in 1992—destroying markets, stores, businesses, and community institutions—spills over as far as the Westside and into the San Fernando Valley. This frightens the LAPD and everybody else because it has never happened before. It hits and spreads so fast and is so widespread that the cops don't know what to do. They don't know where to plug the holes because there are so many of them popping up so fast and across such a great distance.

The destruction from a man-made disaster is followed by havoc from a natural disaster, the earthquake that especially devastates parts of the valley. Apartments come down. Buildings become unusable.

Both afflictions speak to deeper issues: The volatility of communities and the frustration of powerless people in L.A., issues that need to be addressed. The response from some people is, "We can't allow this lawlessness (in the case of the civil unrest) to go on." Others like myself agree that you can't permit lawlessness and there is no excuse for savaging your own community that has so little already. On the other hand, you must acknowledge the powerlessness of people who feel rioting is the only way to gain attention. It all shows the potential for such an incendiary reaction by people. It is amazing how quickly the riots spread. They aren't planned, but it looks like it because they are all over the place, you can't predict where they will show up next and they aren't being contained by law enforcement. I take a helicopter tour over L.A. in the midst of the unrest with Mayor Riordan and Councilmember Zev Yaroslavsky. It gives you an eye-opening perspective to see the community's economic institutions—the providers of goods and services and employment—burning. Sure, the majority of the pillage is in South Central, but it also seems to be everywhere.

What is disturbing is the aggressive targeting of Asian Americans who own and operate many of the markets and liquor stores that are gutted. They are hardworking, industrious people who know how to make money. But many are perceived as insensitive to other ethnic minorities, much as Jewish-owned businesses are resented during the Watts Riots of 1965. Many Asian shop owners arm themselves and run their own security patrols trying to protect their businesses, which you can understand but can't condone.

Luckily, you have some of the smartest minds at City Hall. Among them is Zev Yaroslavsky, who is still on the city council before getting elected to the county board of supervisors. There is Joel Wachs and the council president, John Ferraro.

I realize Dick Riordan is the kind of person who can move the city forward—not because of his wealth but at least partly because of the circles he runs in and his access to the resources of business and industry. I feel he can get things done once he makes up his mind in ways I witness myself while we work together on projects in my district. What amazes me once he becomes mayor is the access he has—and leverage—not just because he is mayor of L.A., but because of the personal relationships he has built. Much of it comes from his generosity in charitable and political giving. And it isn't just among Republicans; I think Dick has more clout among Democrats at the local, state, and federal levels. He has impressive access inside the top echelons of the Clinton administration, on Capitol Hill among leaders of both parties, within the federal bureaucracy, the governor's office (held by Republican Pete Wilson during my remaining years on the council), and within the Democratic-controlled legislature. He also has phenomenal access to the corporate world, in L.A. and across the nation. I'm in the mayor's office when an issue comes up and Dick needs to raise a million dollars for some worthwhile cause. I see him pick up the phone and call the presidents or CEOs of major corporations. After two or three calls he has raised the million dollars—or more—needed to resolve that particular situation. This is just one insight into one of Dick's great strengths.

The mayoral campaign begins. The main candidates are Riordan and Mike Woo, a councilmember with whom I have less than a good relationship going back to when I run municipal reapportionment in the mid-1980s; I don't think he has the qualities it takes to be mayor.

I end up endorsing and working for Dick early in his campaign. It's a risk. First, he's a Republican running against a Democrat. But since this is a non-partisan office in municipal government, I don't feel that matters. Second, Jim Wood, then head of the Los Angeles County Federation of Labor, the county AFL-CIO or County Fed as it is known, is an old friend of mine. Organized labor in L.A. doesn't see Dick as a friend, which it finds out later is not altogether true. It is true that Dick doesn't start out with the greatest opinion of public employee unions. But we help educate him that unions and public employees are a fact of life in city government and he needs to recognize that fact. Eventually he does with a lot of help from me behind the scenes and in front of the public. Later, when Miguel Contreras becomes the leader of labor in L.A., I help him get together with Dick Riordan and they hit it off well. Mayor Riordan appoints Miguel to the prestigious and powerful city Airport Commission, where he serves until his death.

I get criticism from some of my friends who object to my endorsement of a non-Democrat for the city's top job. I tell them (sometimes politely, sometimes not) that it's not any of their fucking business and that I know what I'm doing. During the campaign and once he's elected mayor I become an intimate in Dick's inner circle. Council President John Ferraro and I carry out the Riordan agenda on the council—as well as inform Dick when his ideas are not going to fly.

From the time before Dick first gets elected mayor to the time I leave office—and since—we remain the best of friends. I don't apologize for my relationship with him. He is very good for the city. The theme of his campaign—and his theme while governing—is very simple: Instilling pride and turning the city around. That central message is his focus throughout the campaign. It doesn't matter who he is speaking to, some form of that message of hope and affirmation gets communicated: "This is a great city that can be turned around. I firmly believe that." Yes, he has a great deal of money bankrolling him. But the ultimate success of his campaign comes from putting together some of the best political minds. One is his campaign manager, Bill Wardlaw, a seasoned local and national political operative with ties to the Clinton White House who works for a venture capital firm. Wardlaw puts together a great campaign with resources enough to set up very effective local operations in all parts of the city.

I sit in on all the strategy meetings and go out and make speeches for Dick. He has these young Latinos who are running part of the campaign and think they know what they're doing. I'm not interested in running the operations, but know how to position myself in the right place. At major functions for Latinos, I'm the one who introduces Dick. His hierarchy recognizes the work I do in the contest.

My wife, Angie, becomes part of his transition team once it is established after the election. We influence the transition, including who is hired for important city positions. And we influence Dick's public policies once he takes office.

I'm pretty much the mayor's point person on the council on his major initiatives. It's like you see in the movies or on television shows like the "West Wing"—the players are all arrayed in the Oval Office, making decisions affecting the major issues of the day. Except these meetings take place in the mayor's office at City Hall. You have these illusions from the TV shows, about how decisions are made by these brilliant people who are able to thoughtfully come to agreement on solutions. It isn't until you get in the middle of it all with elected officials and close intimates of the mayor, his so-called kitchen cabinet, that you come to see these geniuses first hand and say to yourself, "Oh, my God, we're in trouble."

Many of the intimates may be very intelligent and successful in the private sector, but too often they lack common sense and the capacity to make decisions based on clear thinking and understanding of political reality. I may not be all that brilliant, but those qualities are what bring me to the table and allow me to contribute to the discussions in my own inimitable style. Dick once says I'm the only person he knows who can repeatedly say fuck and use it as multiple parts of speech. It's flattering. But I am grateful for the good fortune of learning how to function under the best and worst of circumstances—and being able to survive.

In those days—before changes in the city charter beef up the mayor's prerogatives and alter the balance of power—the executive branch has limited authority, even though the mayor always enjoys a bully pulpit. The real power rests with the city council. In those days, you don't see as much of the political rancor—either dictated by partisan or personal politics—that plagues legislative bodies today. L.A. benefits from a political environment that for the most part works during the 1990s. Much of the credit goes to the knowledge and experience of some veteran members of the council and its president who are able to craft policies making the city as livable as it can be. Dick Riordan deserves his fair share. But many of the ideas he advances are refined and turned into reality by the council. L.A. benefits from some great warhorses on the city council. My colleagues Zev Yaroslavsky and Joel Wachs are two of them. But the man who stabilizes it all is John Ferraro, president of the council during most of my service at City Hall.

Pat Russell is council president when I arrive in 1985. There is much speculation—and no small amount of anxiety among fellow councilmembers who harbor ambitions to replace Tom Bradley when he retires—about me as a potential candidate for mayor. At that time, going from a state lawmaker to a city councilmember is seen as a step down the political ladder. Setting up a run for mayor is the only reason an ambitious politician would entertain such a move, according to common reasoning. Russell and others on the council hand me the job of council redistricting shortly after I take office because they see it as a thankless and impossible task. They're sure I'll screw it up, which doesn't happen. John Ferraro succeeds Pat Russell as council president in 1987.

I meet John Ferraro, who is already on the city council, through veteran political consultant Joe Cerrell during my unsuccessful 1971 assembly special election campaign. John is one of the first to endorse me along with George Moscone and Dave Roberti in a district that still has a sizeable Italian-American constituency. What I know about John is he is Italian American, a one-time All American college football star, and a former city commissioner. Even though he's a Republican and I'm a Democrat, we are political allies throughout my service in the legislature. I reciprocate his support when John makes a failed run for the board of supervisors against Ed Edelman. John is one of my first and strongest supporters when I run and get elected to the city council. We become closer as I serve with him. When he runs to become council president, I convince other councilmembers to support him, helping him line up the votes he needs. My feeling is that since I'm one of those closest to John, after I help him get elected president I'll be appropriately rewarded.

My reward, in my way of thinking—what I feel I'm owed because of what I've done for John and because I have already served on the Budget and Finance Committee, then chaired by Zev Yaroslavsky—is John appointing me chair of the powerful panel.

I always remember driving to LAX to fly out to Washington, D.C. for something to do with the Metropolitan Transportation Authority. John calls me, catching me right when I'm getting on the Santa Monica Freeway.

"Hey baby, how you doing, sweetheart," he starts out. Those are terms of endearment I know preface something I don't want to hear. I'm waiting impatiently for him to get to the subject I know he's calling me about.

Finally, I just ask him outright: "Am I getting it or not?"

"Hey baby, you know you're my *hermano*," and all this shit. Then he tells me he's thinking of giving chair of Budget and Finance to Zev Yaroslavsky, who is on the other side during the contest for council president. I call John every swear word under the sun as I continue driving down the Santa Monica Freeway, up until I pull into the parking lot at LAX reserved for councilmembers.

He keeps on trying to tell me, "You don't got it right," and how he has something else for me that will make it all fine, which is chairman of the Public Safety Committee.

I run out of swear words. "Do whatever the fuck you want," I say, hang up and go on my way.

About three weeks later, I walk into the council president's office at City Hall and say, "John, I never thought I would tell you this, but you were right. Getting the Public Safety Committee is the best thing that could have ever happened to me at the time because I wasn't ready [for chair of Budget and Finance]. I haven't been on the council long enough and there are things I need to learn."

I stay on as a member of Budget and Finance. When Yaroslavsky leaves after getting elected to the board of supervisors in 1994, John names me to replace him as committee chair—without me even asking him.

Not getting the chairmanship I want is the beginning of my greater appreciation and understanding of the greatness of John Ferraro. He understands I'm not ready and need some seasoning. Once I get beyond my own ego, I see everything that goes into John's analysis and decision is absolutely correct. It takes me three weeks to get over my anger and figure out John is right.

John and I develop a strong bond and trust over time. It comes from our approach to working within the institution we serve and from our view of the role and purpose of government.

"Lawmakers always have needs," observes Robin Kramer, my first City Hall chief of staff. "They want this or that, which puts pressures on you. Richard, despite his public persona as being tough, was really pretty mellow. But he could also display spine and backbone. When there was a disagreement or problem, he wouldn't pick up the phone and yell. He would go talk respectfully with John Ferraro. That sounds like common sense, but it wasn't how things were

John Ferraro serves as president of the Los Angeles City Council during most of Richard's council tenure and becomes his hero and mentor at City Hall.

always done. He was also relentless. When he got the answer, 'no,' it wasn't always no. He'd work to save the core of his argument and compromise where needed—all the time thinking creatively about how to get where he wanted to go. How refreshing for a council president to have someone with those kinds of skills."

I come from the same school as John that believes government has a role to play in making people's lives a little better. We may sometimes differ on means and emphasis, but in the end the result is always the most important thing for both of us. Over a period of time John and I are involved with the major issues and accomplishments of our time in Los Angeles, including municipal reapportionment, redevelopment of downtown L.A., and establishment of L.A. Live, the Staples Center, and other important venues.

If another councilmember needs credit for something good that takes place, John and I are the first ones to let them claim it. That's one thing I learn to respect about John. He allows for the individual growth of his colleagues who want to grow. He allows people to learn, to accomplish things that are mutually agreed upon and then he doesn't interfere while they're doing them. He thinks people do a better job that way.

John Ferraro is a genuinely unselfish guy. He is amazing as a man and as a public servant. He becomes my hero, and one of my best friends. He is a true giant on the council. I don't believe there is ever another leader like him in city government. He runs for higher office and doesn't make it. But he's completely comfortable in his own skin, especially when it comes to what he does and whom he does it for.

I also become close with Margaret Ferraro, John's wife. He is unfailingly attentive to her even though she suffers a stroke and becomes elderly and frail. She still enjoys the limelight and John brings her with him to public events and everywhere, whether or not she is in a wheelchair. I always sit and talk with her. Most elected officials and other big wigs ignore Margaret; they're only interested in networking and rubbing shoulders with people they think can help them—or those who are famous. Few pay any attention to Margaret. It's a small thing, but I really like her and I know how important she is to John and about the fierce loyalty she has for her husband. That's good enough for me. She is a beautiful woman, loud, foul-mouthed and she loves to drink—the very opposite of John Ferraro. She calls him, "My big Teddy Bear." He is wonderful towards her.

Thinking about Margaret reminds me of how Cesar Chavez treats my mother at a political event he attends in my honor at a nice home in the Hollywood Hills. Of all the important people in the room, Cesar seeks out my mom where she is sitting out of the way in the corner of a room and spends the longest time just with her. At first she is intimidated by all the attention from this iconic figure. But after a while I notice off and on over the next two or three hours the two of them just talking and laughing.

"The first time I met Margaret Ferraro was at a luncheon in Union Station," my wife, Angie, recalls. "Richard and I were seated next to John and Margaret. It was one of the first occasions when we went anywhere in public as a couple. Richard introduced me to Margaret. I was nervous. She was great. She was always glammed up with jewelry, low-cut dresses—a sexy look regardless of whether she was using a cane or in a wheelchair."

"After a few pleasantries, Margaret asks me, 'What is your sign?'

"'I'm an Aquarian,' I answer.

"'I am too,' she replied. 'That's good. I love this man [meaning me] and you're for real. You're going to be good for this man. And don't give a shit about what other people tell you. Don't listen to the fray; don't listen to other people out there. What matters is what you and he have.'

"Margaret probably says those things because it's the same between her and John," Angie continues. "He was an All-American football hero at USC, a very successful businessman who went into politics. And she was a former famous burlesque dancer. When they were first together the social mores frowned on such relationships. When you first saw them together, it seemed like an odd couple. When you came to know them, you could see it was a perfect match."

No one is allowed to smoke in the council chambers at City Hall. But Margaret sits there and smokes. No one dares say anything to her because she will tell him or her off. She knows who all the hypocrites are.

Margaret knows how much I love John and how we always look out for each other. It doesn't matter where it is, but whenever she sees me, she yells out, "Ricardo."

One thing I'm very traditional about is respecting the institution I serve. That's true during my service in the state assembly. (Even though I unhesitatingly support Howard Berman for assembly speaker when Cesar Chavez asks me to in 1979, I tell Cesar it isn't a good idea for him or any other outsider to be involved in the internal politics of the house; that is something for members of the assembly to hash out.) I have respect for the people who are elected to serve, whether I agree or disagree with them. The longer I'm in the assembly, the greater respect and understanding I gain for the differences of its members and their philosophies. Many times they are dictated by region or ethnicity or ideology. Over time, I even learn to temper my own ideology. I respect the institutions of governor and speaker of the Assembly, even when I don't like the particular occupant of the office.

I bring the same respect for the institution to the city council and the mayor, which is something John Ferraro and I share. The council is a body made up of 15 people. Not long after I get there, a former councilmember describes for me what you can or cannot become: You can become an activist and be a change agent for the betterment of the people you represent. Or you can just be happy you got elected and do little or nothing, and still probably get reelected. You see people in office today who are happy they are there, don't want to make waves and are happy collecting their paycheck. You make the decision about the kind of councilmember you want to become.

Over time, I choose the former definition. I'm there to do more than just take up space. John feels the same way. "Richard Alatorre and John Ferraro both had a sense of humor and a temper," Robin Kramer says. "Richard always said, 'Here's what's going on and here's where I'm at. I want you to know first.' And then he would not waiver or change his mind. His word was golden. If you're the council president, you say, 'Thank you. Here's somebody I can rely on and trust.' Ferraro had a lot of experience with colleagues as fellow legislators and as people. He learned you can't trust most of them in a consistent way all the time. Richard he could always trust all the time."

I respect and support John. He is a great council president because he believes in accountability and reward and punishment.

Willie Brown becomes known as a members' speaker in the state assembly. John is known as a members' president on the Los Angeles City Council. In the end, John has no enemies, not because he doesn't do anything but because his character endears him so much to so many people. He dies in office in 2001, not long after I leave the council.

Public safety becomes the theme song for local government in L.A. from the late 1980s to the present because of recognition of the need for more police and more modern ways of tracking and tackling crime.

The relationship between the cops and the Latino community has an uneven history. Serving in the legislature during the 1970s and '80s, I'm in Sacramento four or five days a week. Growing up in East L.A. and my activism in the Chicano movement in the 1960s forms one impression of the police. In this view, the cops are often seen as more of an occupying force that can sometimes violate the civil rights of people. That impression is a holdover from my earlier experiences such as with the East L.A. high school walkouts in 1968 and the "police riot" during the 1970 Chicano Moratorium.

One of my old friends is Luis Carrillo, who handles a lot of police abuse cases in East L.A. Luis is a former member of the Brown Berets. I bail David Sanchez, one of the founders of the Brown Berets, and his friends out of jail on more than one occasion when they get into scrapes with the cops in the '60s. My generation still remembers the old LAPD Red Squad under the infamous Chief of Police William Parker. I recall my friend Sol Monroy, who I find out later is personally recruited by Parker to spy for years, posing as a communist instigator beginning in the 1950s against the Community Service Organization and a string of Chicano civil rights groups. So I understand people's passions when it involves the police.

Still, coming back home permanently after getting elected to the city council in 1985, is an eye-opening experience when it comes to the cops.

As much as people want and need the police, and as much as residents in places like Boyle Heights are grateful for their presence, every time I attend a meeting in El Sereno where there are LAPD representatives present, you have to listen to every horror story about what the cops do or don't do that upsets people.

There is a 100 percent dichotomy. The best example is in Boyle Heights. Real people who live there respect and appreciate the police. They need to be safe from gangs and drugs and drive-bys. Parents worry whether their kids will make it safely back home from school without getting shot at. All those things happen every day, generation after generation. The strongest support for the LAPD comes from the Hollenbeck Police Council, composed of community members, residents, and small businesses that want more protection. I'm with them. I long ago decide that cops are people too, and the people I represent need them. That doesn't mean I necessarily like the LAPD hierarchy or its history of racism up and down the ranks, of which Tom Bradley is just one example; he suffers discrimination within the department years before when he is a cop.

Chicanos have a history of similar grievances with the LAPD. A classic example of the impermeable wall blocking access to Latinos for decades in the department is Hank Hernandez. Hank is part of the first wave of Chicanos who want to join the LAPD after service in the Korean War. He is born and raised in Boyle Heights before joining the military and ending up in the military police.

Walking around downtown L.A. one day with the woman who becomes his wife, Hank comes across a big billboard urging residents to "Come and be part of our department"—the LAPD. "That's where I'm going to go to work," he tells her.

He takes the written exam to become a cop and is number one on the list. He takes the oral exam and is number one again. A background check and medical exam are next. They flunk him on the medical, claiming one leg is shorter than the other one. Hank is in his early 20s, and is in the best of shape. He works out. But the LAPD refuses to let him in.

Hank is no dummy. He goes to this medical office in Boyle Heights. The guy in charge is named Dr. Francisco Bravo, a member of the L.A. Police Commission. Hank asks to see Dr. Bravo, knowing he's the only shot to plead his case. Dr. Bravo sees Hank.

"Why are you here?"

"I'd like you to give me a physical. I need it for a job I'm applying for."

"You're in perfect health," Dr. Bravo concludes after the exam is over.

"I'd like you to measure my legs," Hank says. "I'm told one is shorter than the other."

"Absolutely incorrect," Dr. Bravo says after looking at them. "Both legs are the same length. Why are you asking me these questions?"

"I applied to the LAPD," Hank explains. "I came out number one on both the written and oral exams. They couldn't get me any other way so they got me on a medical [issue]."

Dr. Bravo is a conservative Republican, but very respected. He's also ethno-centric. He calls someone high up in the LAPD: "I have a young man here who you god-damned people have turned down. I hope before I get to the next meeting of the [police] commission in two days that this matter will be resolved."

Hank gets admitted to the police academy in Elysian Park. He is number one graduating in his academy class. They only tolerate him because of Dr. Bravo's intervention; otherwise, he would not even be a cop. Hank knows the department is not very friendly to Mexicans. There are very few officers who are Mexican American then. There is no one above the bottom rank of police officer. Hank sees all the discrimination going on. But he's from a generation that says, fuck you, I'm going to show them. He is number one on the promotion list for sergeant. Hank is number one in everything he tries. He gets promoted to sergeant and goes as far as the rank of lieutenant, but knows he will never make it higher than that.

He survives under Chief Parker and the administrations of Mayors Fletcher Brown and Sam Yorty. He doesn't play the game in a department beset by racism. In the late 1960s, Hank becomes an expert interrogator and polygraph operator. He periodically disappears, spending months at a time on special duty with other law enforcement or intelligence agencies all over the world. When Robert

Kennedy is assassinated at the Ambassador Hotel in 1968, Hank conducts lie detector tests on many of the people who are involved in the investigation.

Hank and I get to know each other in the '60s when I'm working for the Teen Post antipoverty program right out of college. By then his job in community relations is to know what's happening before it happens. We run into each other at different places during the civil rights struggles such as the East L.A walkouts and the Chicano Moratorium. Even though he is an active Republican, we always have a good relationship. I also become friends with his wife and sons, who both graduate from Harvard.

Hank retires from the LAPD in the late-'60s to set up his own private security company. His son, Rick, or Enrique, Hernandez takes it over. It's now a huge global outfit handling protective services for diplomats and high-ranking government officials.

Hank is a proud guy as a cop, refusing to kiss anyone's ass. At the time, in the '60s, he is bitter. He's certainly no lefty. He understands the police department up until that time is not a very inclusive organization. Hank makes no secret of the fact that he gets as far as he can in the department and then retires and makes millions of dollars.

Other Chicanos who come after Hank are inspired by his example. He ends up hiring a number of deputy chiefs and other high-ranking LAPD officers, mostly Latinos, for his security business after they retire from the force.

"Just as Tom Bradley was a door opener for equal opportunity for African Americans in the city of L.A., Richard Alatorre becomes the go-to guy to open doors for Latinos," notes Robin Kramer. At one time not long ago, the LAPD is pretty much a good ol' boy network led by and largely composed of Anglos. With the emergence of Tom Bradley as mayor, more and more blacks are getting into the department. As Chief Daryl Gates once tells me, "they [the blacks] know how to play the game." African Americans in particular learn how to get promoted and by getting themselves into coveted positions move up the ladder in a more rapid way. These are positions within the LAPD where higher-ups can see you prominently on a daily basis. So when these slots open up, you're more visible and more likely to get promoted.

I have an interesting relationship with Chief Gates. My close political ally, fundraiser, and good friend George Pla, CEO of the civil engineering firm Cordoba Corporation, one of the largest Latino-owned independent businesses in the country, recalls, in George's words, "how the LAPD got integrated."

Quickly after I become chairman of the city council's Police and Fire Committee, in comes Chief Gates with his command staff from the LAPD with all their regalia to present themselves. George is rarely at City Hall, but he is there that day. "I'm going to meet Daryl Gates," I tell George. "Why don't you stay for the meeting?"

Gates enters my office with his command staff in tow. I have my feet up on the desk in front of the police chief and his commanders. ("I used to hate this about Richard," George says.) My body language is communicating complete contempt. "Gates is a powerful guy in the city of Los Angeles," George recalls. "He's like the local J. Edgar Hoover."

The chief is clearly disturbed by my conduct and doesn't know what to do. "Mr. Chairman, I want to introduce our command staff and make sure you meet our senior managers," he offers. "Please know we're available to answer any questions for...."

"Where are the greasers?" I interrupt, with my feet still on the desk.

Daryl Gates gives me a look of disbelief about what I've just said and how I said it.

"Excuse me?" the chief manages to get out.

I move my feet down to the floor and lean forward: "Where are the greasers on your staff?"

"I'm sorry, I don't quite understand."

"Let me explain it to you. I represent Mexicans. My district is the Eastside. And you have no one who reflects my community on your staff. So you come back and see me when you do. This meeting is over."

You can see the thermometer rising inside Gates. His face is turning beet red: "Okay, very well, Mr. Chairman." He gets up and walks out. His commanders are horrified, not knowing what to do or say. They get up and leave too.

"Richard, why do you have to do that?" George asks me. "I hate it when you behave that way."

"George, let me tell you something," I reply. "If I don't do that, they'll bullshit me with statistics and numbers, and nothing will ever change. Let me tell you something else: He will come back with a plan to integrate the LAPD with Latinos. You'll see."

A few decades later, George Pla is attending an event in Washington, D.C. where he meets this lady he doesn't know who is introduced to him as the assistant director of personnel for the city of Los Angeles, which handles all personnel matters for every city department, including the LAPD. George asks her, "I heard a rumor that Richard Alatorre singlehandedly integrated the LAPD for Latinos. Is that true?"

"'Absolutely true,' she responded. 'We heard about this meeting Councilman Alatorre had with the chief. The chief came straight to the personnel department. 'Find me every Mexican in the LAPD,' he instructed; 'I want to know where they are, what their rank is, and how can we advance them.' Years later, she verified the story."

Chief Gates is not the most popular guy with African Americans or the mayor. But one day, I tell him, "Whatever the blacks and Tom Bradley say about you, during your administration as chief you've opened up opportunities for blacks to be promoted and move ahead. You haven't done that for Chicanos. I don't want to get in a full-blown battle with you over this because then I know you won't give it up easily and I won't back down from whatever it will take to begin to get you to look more favorably on Chicanos."

"Let me tell you why Chicanos or Latinos aren't more integrated into the police department," Gates replies. "It's because they don't like to do what it takes to move up the ladder, which means getting college degrees and learning how to play the game—like identifying the people who make decisions about the assignment of coveted positions that are almost automatic roads to promotion and then making inroads with those people. That's why. Latinos are great, fabulous cops. But a lot of them, all they want to do is be cops; they don't want to go out of their way to get promoted. They like being out on the street and being good cops, but that's certainly not a formula for getting ahead."

By the late 1980s and early '90s, what Gates talks about concerning Latinos is pretty much taking place. The promotions and upward mobility of Chicanos within the LAPD begins to happen once more and more younger police officers start at the department who are better educated, because of increases in the Latino population, and because of a consent decree imposed on the LAPD by the U.S. Department of Justice setting standards that have to be met to improve the integration of the force. The first logical candidate for promotion is Rudy DeLeon out of the Hollenbeck Station in Boyle Heights. He's the first Latino to make captain and ultimately commander.

My role is to work with Gates and his successors through the subtle tactic of exerting pressure inside the department and sometimes bringing public pressure through political means. I seek out individual officers eligible for promotion. Others come to my office or call me. We meet individually and I sit down with representatives of the Latino Police Officers Association, which covers the LAPD (where the organization starts) as well as the L.A. County Sheriff's Department. They become a lobbying force that boosts the numbers of Chicanos in coveted positions and as detectives, sergeants, lieutenants, captains, commanders, and deputy chiefs.

When good candidates come to me, I start off by going to the chief. He's the one who makes appointments and recommends who is going to be elevated. A lot of what I'm able to accomplish is just based on relationships, first with Chief Gates and then with his successors, Willie Williams and then Bernie Parks. Starting with Gates, they know I'm a friend. The chiefs know if their department gets out of line I will try and resolve it behind closed doors and only if that doesn't work take my case to the general public. Gates in particular appreciates that I give him a chance to fix things in private. He knows the leverage I will have if it goes beyond that. As head of the council's Public Safety Committee I can use my chairmanship as a bully pulpit and have hearings on the numbers of minorities in the department. I'm not a trickster. I don't try to embarrass him. If the chief gets it, then that's well and good. If not, I don't care about going after him. And he knows it.

That original conversation with Chief Gates about why Chicanos aren't moving up fast enough happens early during my tenure as a councilmember.

Ironically, my very good relationship with Gates continues to the point that I'm one of the last people on good terms with him after he burns too many bridges at City Hall. We talk periodically. He leaves when Dick Riordan becomes mayor. By that time the L.A. riots break out after the Rodney King verdict. The chief is attending a political function at the time and he doesn't have the right administrative command structure ready to quickly respond. So there is a period of inaction that leads to greater riots and financial losses in many parts of the city during civil unrest that is a lot more mobile and fast moving than the Watts Riots of 1965.

Daryl Gates lives by my residence in the Monterey Hills neighborhood, between Highland Park and El Sereno. I can walk to his house, which I do a couple of times just to bullshit. I'm probably the last person to see him alive before he passes away.

Because Hank Hernandez is the perfect example of what Daryl Gates says about Chicanos and the LAPD, what the chief tells me resonates as true. More importantly, I know why. A lot of people surrounding Gates are born-again Christians, which makes me nervous. But he and I work together to change the department.

My relationship with the next chief, Willie Williams, is probably based on his fear about the things I can do to him. I make no bones about the fact I believe he should never be appointed chief in the first place. I want a chief to be named from within the department and Williams comes from out of state. He also makes a lot of mistakes and becomes a perfect target for anybody who wants to criticize his tenure. He doesn't have peace officer status, meaning he doesn't have the right to carry a gun, which is a big deal with the rank and file. The Police Protective League, the LAPD cops union, vocally expresses its discontent. Williams and I don't exactly have a friendly relationship.

Art Lopez is a pioneer in the department. Daryl Gates talks to me about him. He is very book smart, with a master's degree in the administration of justice. "Watch this guy," Gates says; "he's one of the smartest guys I've seen—he could be chief of the LAPD one day." That resonates with me. I help Art Lopez get a promotion under Willie Williams.

Then I negotiate the retirement package for Bernie Parks, who has risen up the ranks to become deputy chief of operations, meaning he oversees all of the divisions and the 80 percent of the department that is composed of operational police officers. The smartest, book wise, of anyone I meet who is a police officer, Bernie applies to succeed Daryl Gates as the first black chief of police. Bernie is my candidate. But Mayor Riordan decides that instead of hiring from within the department, he wants to get someone from outside to clean up the corrupt Rampart Division and some of the other stations with corruption problems. So Williams, who is also black, gets the nod. Bernie is insulted and decides to retire.

Now Williams has to decide what to do with Parks. Williams wants him out because it's pretty hard to keep a guy who is one of your top lieutenants if he

I'm There to Do More Than Just Take Up Space 323

Richard uses his relationship with Los Angeles Police Chief Daryl Gates, a conservative born-again Christian, to integrate Chicanos into the upper ranks of the LAPD. They become good friends.

Richard does not have a friendly relationship with the next chief of the LAPD, Willie Williams (seated to the right of Richard).

also wants your job. I end up calling Williams into my office to try to get him to come up with a retirement package that lets Bernie retire at his highest rank, which is second in command of the department. Bernie is knocked down a notch after Williams becomes chief.

"Absolutely not," Williams insists at first.

"Don't be stupid," I reply. I want to try to resolve the situation. Williams knows of my relationship with the mayor. So he figures why not get Bernie Parks off his back. He agrees to rehire him at the higher level. Bernie wants a few extra years tacked onto his retirement eligibility. Williams agrees to everything.

Three days later, Bernie comes back to my office to tell me he's changed his mind. Now he wants to stay with the department. So I go back to Williams to negotiate a position for Parks in the LAPD. The catch is he will have to drop down to commander, which represents a significant reduction in pay and, more importantly, in retirement eligibility. It also comes with a major reduction in responsibility, which for cops is humiliating. That's why so many who are confronted with such reductions in the higher echelons of the LAPD end up applying for retirement or chief of police jobs in other cities across the country.

I give Williams the bad news about Bernie's change of mind. "I can't do this," he says.

"Fine, if you don't want to do it, get ready," I respond. Some of my threats that follow are real; others are created out of whole cloth. But I prevail. Williams keeps Parks and makes him a deputy chief. I arrange it so Bernie keeps the pay he makes before as assistant chief, which Williams hates. Bernie Parks stays in that position until Dick Riordan fires Willie Williams and makes Bernie chief of police. Bernie's wife acknowledges to this day that I'm the one who helps her husband during his worst days as a police officer under Williams and helps him become chief. Bernie is later elected to the city council. With Bernie Parks as chief, my leverage at the top doesn't really change.

There are limits to what I can do. A young kid who works for me as a deputy in my council office has a brother who's an LAPD cop, 10 years on the force out of the Hollenbeck Division. All the brother ever wants is to be is a police officer. One Halloween night he gets into trouble in nearby Monterey Park, a separate jurisdiction. Off duty, he leaves a restaurant following another vehicle driven by two girls and a buddy, another cop. The women are pulled over at an intersection for drunk driving by the Monterey Park police. My guy gets out of the car and shows his badge. A report is made of the incident.

About three weeks later the Internal Affairs Division in the Monterey Park Police Department looks into the incident. They try to interview my guy. He's a cop's cop and keeps his mouth shut. The Monterey Park department files a grievance. This officer doesn't break any laws. He doesn't ask for any special treatment during the encounter in Monterey Park. But he's accused of trying to use his influence to try to get the girls off the hook.

There is a board of rights hearing of my guy by a panel of captains and above convened by the chief of the LAPD, Bernie Parks. I call the chief: "Look, man, the guy's a great cop, been there 10 years. He'll have supervisors and everyone else testifying that he's a good cop. This charge is bullshit. He didn't do anything wrong." But the LAPD and Monterey Park Internal Affairs Division feel he's been less than honest. So the hearing goes on.

I've never testified before a board of rights panel. I walk in, facing three guys on the panel. Every one of them has at one time or another worked in one or more of the LAPD divisions in my district. I know them before they are promoted and always enjoy a warm and cordial relationship with each of them. I help bring the kind of recognition to the work they do that puts them in the position to become captains and commanders. I figure this hearing will go perfectly. I make my pitch for the officer.

Instead, the panel issues a decision to fire him from the LAPD. I later learn that the panel members are acting on word from above. I go to Parks: "Bernie, I've never come to you like this before on someone's behalf. But this is wrong. This is a promising young man with a great family and a great record. Give him a suspension, days off without pay. But this doesn't rise to the level of the punishment you guys are issuing."

Parks fires him anyway. That's just the way he is: Rigid. The rank and file end up hating him. He is probably the most despised chief of police mostly because he doesn't like the police union. With Bernie it's his way or the highway. You don't disagree with the chief.

Luckily, over my years on the council there are dozens and dozens of other officers, mostly Chicanos, who I help advance within the department one way or the other—through personal intervention or word of mouth in the right place. I counsel or advise many of them on what they have to do to get themselves in a position to be promoted. There is a promotion list for everything: Sergeants, lieutenants, and captains. They have to pass rigorous oral and written exams or I can't help them. Once they get on the promotion list, where they can remain for three or five years, the appointing officer can name anybody on the list. One of the greatest feelings I get is being able to advance somebody who I feel is a good officer and will be an asset to the department. My interest is in helping whomever I can, but obviously Latinos are a priority.

I have a very different take on the conventional approach to public safety. Even before John Ferraro appoints me chair of the Public Safety Committee, I'm trying to expand the conventional definition of public safety itself. I want to add a new dimension that includes the greater need for libraries, parks, and recreation, gang prevention, and other programs to prevent kids from becoming entangled in the administration of justice. I make all of these things part of the jurisdiction of the Public Safety Committee.

Libraries offer safe havens for children to read and study so they don't have to be out roaming the streets. Parks and recreation centers are where kids can recreate in safe environments. Cultural and arts programs offer young people enrichment opportunities. Here's how I explain it: Having more LAPD officers is well and good. But what does it matter if we have 20,000 officers in the department? How does that translate into creating safe environments for children, places where they can learn and study and play—and avoid the carnage associated with gangs? I later redefine what comprises public safety as chairman of the council's Budget and Finance Committee, which deals with the central question of how city government gets funded. If we're going to take care of the cops and put more police officers on the streets, we also need to apply the same commitment to other pressing public safety needs. Making that happen becomes the imprimatur of the rest of my years in public office.

An offshoot of redefining public safety to embrace a broader agenda than placing more cops on the street is how my office takes the lead in developing the first children's policies for the city, which I start working on shortly after getting elected to the council. The city of L.A. is not in the business of delivering services to kids through the public schools, which are run by the Los Angeles Unified School District, or supplying health and welfare services that are provided through county government acting as an agent of the state.

But the city does serve children through its budget allocations in support of parks, recreation, childcare, cultural and artistic enrichment, and safe streets. "Richard had this idea that there should be mindfulness about" prioritizing children's services in city budgeting," Robin Kramer observes. "He started that work and it was later picked up by Mayor Riordan. The result was a children's budget policy. A children's budget was produced. Child advocates began to see that the city had a role in the well being of kids and families that was indirect but still huge."

It starts when I work on council redistricting. You ask questions: What's the population? What are the natural communities? Where do people live? How old are they? The data is all there. It turns out that just under a third of the city's population is 18 or younger. It's 25 percent in most urban centers. L.A. is a growing, young city. And Latinos make up the leading engine of youth creation.

About a decade before its time, I suggest there has to be a way to focus on children's needs because they're the future. Now the National League of Cities has a concentration on children and youth. It's the same principle. What is L.A.'s role? The city doesn't provide educational or social services; those are the jobs of the schools and the county—and ultimately the state. But people on the street don't differentiate between governmental jurisdictions. And city government is closest to home.

Government in general always neglects children. They have no constituency of a political nature per se because they don't vote. The parents of the kids who need help the most—poor and minority children—are not participating in politics in any great numbers up until then. Although the decision-making and budgetary processes at City Hall are developed to meet the specific needs of all the people, up until the time I decide to venture into this subject, there is no focus on the needs of children by the city of Los Angeles, one of the largest cities in the country. Meanwhile, the consequences of ignoring problems facing our youth are beginning to be seen through increasing negative behavior such as the growth of gangs and the influx of guns. Human life—the lives of our most precious commodity, our children—is not seen as very important. Kids are dying, and the city of L.A. is not paying much attention.

We spend such a big portion of city resources on hiring more police officers to go after bad kids. Government devotes so much time and money to the 10 percent of children who are creating havoc and chaos, who are involved in deviant behavior such as gangs and attacks on people and property. Towards the end of my state legislative tenure I start seeing this tremendous negative reaction to the increase in crime, especially among young people. The reaction is nearly entirely negative: Put them away when they're younger and younger for longer and longer periods of time. You've been in trouble with the law before and you spit on the street—that's six months in lock up. That may be an exaggeration, but not much of one. The irony of it all is when all we do is put them away, we're just turning more young kids into hardened, sophisticated criminals.

You have to acknowledge the roles drugs and guns in the hands of young people play in the destruction of human life—theirs and others. You can't turn your back on that. But we're still talking about a small percentage of kids.

What are we doing for the 90 percent of kids who also have real unmet needs but have not yet become problems, to keep them from going down the wrong path? Many of them are struggling to survive in a very difficult environment. It's a priority for me because in the Latino neighborhoods I represent a disproportionate percentage of the community is young. It's higher than the third of L.A.'s overall population that is 18 years or less. When you look further into who comprises that third of the citywide population, they are disproportionately black and Latino.

That is why the redirecting of city entities and resources to have a positive impact on children's lives becomes a very important part of my council career. I believe in the human potential of children. I believe if kids are given opportunities they will take the right path. I even believe if we invest in kids who have committed offenses and show them there is a better way, many of them can be saved too. That's the genesis for the creation of the Feliz Navidad celebrations that we organize. It only takes place once a year, but it creates a festive and happy time for the poorest and most disadvantaged kids in my district living in public housing projects. That's why I help raise several million dollars to create the El Sereno Youth Center to serve as a safe haven in a community on the brink—a community that can go either way; it isn't so heavily under gang control, but at the time is moving in the wrong direction.

So I come up with the idea of developing a policy for all city agencies that asks each of them: What percentage of your budget is spent on helping children? What is your agency specifically doing towards meeting that need?

Richard spearheads a far-reaching Children's Policy at City Hall, making the welfare of children a responsibility of all municipal agencies and calling for a coordinated approach for delivering services to them. A broad array of activities and programs follows.

The first step in developing a children's policy in the late 1980s is requiring a study of all municipal agencies through the budget process. The report, showing how much of each agency's budget is spent on children-related services, goes to the Budget and Finance Committee. To compile the data and oversee the study and report, I hire Bonnie Brody, who applies for the job. She comes out of Louisiana, where she works on the staff of Governor Edwin Edwards. A very politically savvy attorney and public policy wonk, Bonnie's report shows that with few exceptions city agencies are doing very little for kids. There is no coordinated approach to providing them with services. Very few people in these agencies are really giving any thought to delivering services for children. The two exceptions that stand out are the Parks and Recreation Department and the Cultural Affairs Department, which handles all the arts and cultural programs, from music and visual arts to murals and cultural festivals.

What is clearly needed is for city government to be advocating for children. My aim is to get city agencies more attuned to reaching out to children and providing for them using a coordinated approach. That way everyone knows what everybody else is doing, whether the agency's main job is helping kids or whether that is only part of its agenda.

With the report from the study in hand, my staff develops a citywide policy that the city council adopts. It affirms the responsibility for the welfare of children by the city of L.A. and calls for a more coordinated approach to delivering services to them. Agencies need to look at better ways to accomplish these objectives under the auspices of the new commission on children, Youth and Their Families, which is created as an offshoot of the new policy. Each agency must annually report back to the council on the progress it is making to develop and enhance services for families and children.

Out of the new policy comes a wide array of activities and programs. Since the policy is tied to public safety, one program is preventing kids from getting involved with gangs, encouraging them instead to participate in alternative activities. We improve parks and expand their hours, extend library hours and increase organized activities there, establish programs for summer youth employment, and stage children's and cultural festivals in communities that bring people together and enhance the city's pluralism and multi-ethnic flavor.

From the time I become budget committee chair until I retire from public office, every yearly budget process asks agencies what they're doing for kids and evaluates their responses. Instead of just investing at the back end—spending money to arrest and incarcerate young people—we also invest on the front end, trying to work with kids so they don't end up as wards of the county or state.

"In putting together a children's policy for the city that creates a new focus on how dollars are used to affect the lives of kids who have had no voice at City Hall, Richard galvanized a lot of people he knew from Sacramento who were involved in education, early childhood education, social work, social welfare, and health," notes Robin Kramer, who gets heavily involved herself.

Because of the years I serve in the legislature, I have more resources at my disposal and people I know who are involved in one aspect or another of dealing with kids. I recruit them and apply their expertise to helping the city in what it's trying to do.

Our efforts also foster the L.A. Best program that begins small at a handful of primary schools across the city towards the end of the Bradley administration, using Department of Water & Power funds to organize after-school programs. The first beneficiaries are campuses in heavily minority and crime-plagued neighborhoods. After classes are finished, kids engage in organized activities and cultural enrichment programs. Tutoring is offered in academic subjects, and students also take field trips to museums and other places.

L.A. Best grows into a program spending tens of millions of dollars a year in nearly 200 schools throughout the Los Angeles Unified School District. The schools supply the facilities and some funding. Other monies are privately raised or come from state and federal sources. The program is considered a model of after-school programs in the world, studied by states across the country and by other nations as well. It all begins with our movement to establish a children's policy and focus municipal agencies on meeting their needs.

Dick Riordan plays an important part. Even before he becomes mayor, he is a champion of children's interests and a big giver to programs for young people, especially in minority communities. Although his philanthropy starts with Catholic schools and grows through his foundation, he becomes one of the biggest contributors to computers and computer labs in both Catholic and public schools in L.A. Once he gets elected mayor, it becomes easier to advocate for children under his administration than during Tom Bradley's tenure. Dick, because of his love for children, is an easy sell.

The children's policy "gained traction under Riordan because Richard Alatorre shared with the mayor the belief that the city needed to do something," Robin says. "If you shine a light on something, people will go there."

The Commission on Children, Youth and Their Families dies in 2010, the victim of draconian city budget cuts. That is so foolish, probably the result of the lack of vision that makes these programs so dispensable when I am convinced they are indispensable.

Kids on the Westside or in other more affluent parts of L.A. have options. Most of them have parents who will make sure they are involved in productive activities such as after-school recreation and organized sports. Resources exist in local community centers or through private clubs. The government doesn't need to offer them as much help.

However, a local park or YMCA or youth center, if it is available and safe, is usually the only option after school for too many of the children in my district or elsewhere in East or South Central L.A. or in parts of the San Fernando Valley who live in poverty or have particular needs. Kids in these less affluent areas are totally dependent on what, if anything, government provides in their communities. A park or library or recreation center can be the only safe bastion where children and their parents don't have to worry about becoming the victim of gangs or random crime or violence.

This is why it is important for city government to look at more than the amount of money it spends overall on caring for children; it must also examine how money is divvied up around L.A. so communities with the greatest needs receive more of the resources to provide things for kids that are taken for granted in wealthier parts of town.

One of the deficiencies I identify during my council years is the "Rule of 15." Let's say $1 million is earmarked for a particular program or project in L.A. Every council district theoretically has the right to 1/15th of those resources, irrespective of the need in each district. I argue along with others that there are greater needs in some communities than others. Instead of the Rule of 15, the Rule of Need should dictate how we apportion out resources. I encounter varying degree of success in convincing my colleagues of this position. We prevail on some things; on others we don't.

I'm afraid the emphasis on children and other services for people as an important part of public safety fades away after I leave office. Just focusing on more cops and a bigger LAPD misses additional important priorities that are needed to help rebuild the city. Improving infrastructure, services for youth and the aged, parks and cultural affairs take a big hit in the wake of the recession and resulting huge hits on the city budget. If you hold harmless 60 or 70 percent of the budget—police and fire—all you have left to reduce are the crumbs, relatively speaking, that are left for services covering everything else. Many of those services should also be part and parcel of how you define public safety. My priorities suffer because of this commitment by city leaders to an almost mystical number of cops and firefighters. Even fire safety is adversely impacted, but not to the extent that human services are slashed. Once I come to genuinely understand the role of local government, my emphasis always becomes geared towards working to improve the human potential of people. That's what I fight for in public office; I still believe in it. If all you're fighting for is to stop the spread of the cancer of crime by saving one city department, the LAPD, then by the time you realize it the cancer will have spread throughout the body politic and just adding more cops won't excise it.

I come into my own on the city council as chairman of the Budget and Finance Committee after Zev Yaroslavsky leaves the council. Anything that requires the appropriation of funds goes to Budget and Finance in addition to the appropriate city council policy committee. This includes all lawsuits against the city and proposed settlements, and any amount of money over $100,000. If it is below that amount, I can sign off on it as long as there is agreement by the appropriate city staff.

When I'm serving before the city charter is changed, it's a weak mayor system. The mayor's only authority then is to present a budget, appoint but not really dismiss the city general manager, and appoint citizen commissioners who are confirmed by the council.

Cities have to have balanced budgets, unlike the state. Everything for purposes of balancing the budget is based on assumptions. You project the revenue that will come in during the fiscal year that begins on July 1. The revenue isn't always there. Christmas sales may not bring in the money you expect. Or you don't see the money anticipated from receipt of property tax payments. If you're in the hole, how do you make up for it? An easy one is raising fees for recording documents. But it has limitations. Because of Proposition 13, which strictly limits increases in property tax that is passed by the voters in 1978, you can't raise property taxes. If your city needs to bring in extra revenue, do you put something on the ballot, asking the voters' permission? If so, what?

In some ways, my work as budget committee chair is kind of like what I do overseeing reapportionment of council district boundaries because both involve creating "the overarching policy framework for that year and the years ahead," as Robin Kramer puts it. "It's a statement of values," she says. "The whole council doesn't have the depth of experience to be budget wise. Members think of what's important to their district. But the [budget] committee chair, like the mayor, has to be mindful of the overall budget needs of the entire city as well as be responsive to neighborhood needs expressed by colleagues. It is also the case that the mayor speaks to members of the council in constructing the budget, but councilmembers don't get everything they want from the mayor. There's never enough money."

The structure of the city financing process begins with the annual budget introduced by the mayor around March. This is the council's first consideration of the mayor's proposal. Oftentimes, the budget committee makes major changes to the proposed budget, presenting its recommendations to the full council for its consideration and approval. All the mayor does is propose. If I disagree with the mayor on his budget, it doesn't matter how good a friend he is. I have a responsibility to my body, the city council, to express objections in public—and I do it, if necessary. First, I tell him to his face in private when I think he's wrong and make my case for why I think I'm right. More often, I use the budget process to bring the mayor along to my way of thinking. I'll use friendly argument or sometimes I just tell him, "Fuck you, this is what we're going to do and if you don't want to go along with us and veto it we'll override your veto and embarrass you publicly." My advice to him is why it is more important for the mayor to get along with the council on the budget so as to preserve his political capital to use for agendas he feels are more important. More often than not, I'm successful. The thing about Dick Riordan is he recognizes he can't fight and win every battle. He picks and chooses his fights.

About two weeks after receiving the mayor's budget proposal, my committee begins calling in all the department heads for hearings so they can give us their take on their piece of the mayor's proposed budget and how it will impact them. After the hearings, we wait for a couple of weeks for the May revise—a revision of expected revenues that are coming in from payment of property and sales taxes plus what we can anticipate to collect in state and federal funding. At that point, my committee staff works with the city's chief legislative analyst to draft the council's version of the budget.

The mayor sets out his agenda but the council makes the changes that we want and also makes the ultimate decision. Since the Budget and Finance Committee takes the first whack at the council budget, for me there is one simple reality to keep in mind: Three votes. As long as I can count on three votes out of five members on the committee, that's what the budget will be.

First, I make sure my priorities are taken care of in the budget: Funding for cops and firefighters, of course; parks and recreation; other senior and youth activities through the Department of Aging and youth diversion programs; the Cultural Affairs Department (all of the arts programs, festivals, and special events). Then I do whatever needs to be done to take care of the needs of the two other committee votes I need—whoever my allies are going to be—to pass the budget. Finally, I do whatever needs to happen with the budget to get the majority of the 15-member city council to vote for it. You have to make sure you have those eight votes too.

So what really counts is "the rule of three"—three votes on the budget committee—and "the rule of eight" for the simple majority on the council floor to pass the final budget.

There are some other concerns. For example, when the budget is being taken up before the entire council I don't want the police chief going behind my back to councilmembers to get all the "Christmas trees" he wants. These are budget items that take care of the top brass at the LAPD, which the chief cares a lot about. My concern is the Los Angeles Police Protective League, the police union, and first making sure the rank-and-file cops get taken care of. I want to guarantee that the guys on the street have the resources they need to protect us. That can include having enough money for patrol cars, overtime pay, and special units such as those working on gang intervention. I'm confident the chief's needs—benefiting command officers of lieutenants and above—will be looked after. They always are. There's usually enough for assistant and deputy chiefs to take care of their little fiefdoms. The rank and file—sergeants and below, the men and women patrolling the streets and staffing the special units—are the ones who make the difference in ensuring we live in a civilized society. They keep the department functioning. So I work to make sure they have enough people and resources.

After the police come the firefighters. My approach with the Los Angeles Fire Department is the same: Make sure the rank-and-file firefighters have the resources to do their jobs. That means ensuring there are enough paramedics plus all the equipment the LAFD needs to serve the city and keep us safe.

The same thing goes for the sanitation workers. Altogether, police, fire, and sanitation are the great majority of the city budget.

Every city department head or general manager comes before the committee complaining that the budget proposal is taking away this thing or that thing that they absolutely must have. I make it clear to them: "Here is what the mayor has proposed. Do you agree or disagree? Tell me what it is you really want that is not there and let's see if there is a way to get it."

When I first get to the council, before becoming chair of Budget and Finance, we devote a whole week just to hearing from the departments, one by one. Once the committee recommends its budget and it goes to the council floor for debate, you hear motion after motion from individual councilmembers asking for special augmentations to the budget on behalf of particular departments—or somebody who wants to spend $10,000 more for this project or festival or more money to hire two more building and safety inspectors. The individual motions are frustrating because it's all stuff you've heard before from the department heads during the budget committee hearings. Sometimes there are as many as 200 individual motions. It can take up to 10 days to go through the budget and all of the motions.

When I become budget committee chair, that practice ends. We require that if a councilmember makes a motion to spend more money than is included in the budget committee version, he or she has to come up with the way to fund it. I make it clear to the department heads, in public and private, that they are not to go back to individual councilmembers when the budget hits the full council, asking them to make individual motions. At the end of the committee hearings, the department heads know what the Budget and Finance Committee is going to recommend. That's it.

By the second year I'm budget committee chairman, we hear all the budget items from each of the departments and funds; that takes three or four hours. Then we deal with individual motions from councilmembers by consolidating them all and sending them to the budget committee after the budget is passed. That's a sure way to kill all of them. If a motion is a good idea, we figure out a way to pay for it and add it to the budget or subtract the amount of the item from someplace else.

Another practice during the budget process is that I always go to John Ferraro first. When I run municipal reapportionment, I start with John's district and ask him what I ask Willie Brown when doing legislative reapportionment in 1981: "What do you need to protect yourself? Who else do you want to protect on the council?" Our intent is to keep eight councilmembers happy; without eight votes we don't have anything. The same thing happens when it comes to the budget. I always want to find out what's important to John and what he thinks is important to the city—to make sure those things are protected at all times.

I also believe members of the budget committee have a right to something special they want that isn't already in the budget. I take care of arranging to grant their request—so long as they give me their commitment to vote for the budget. If they can't commit their vote, they don't get what they want. I discover everybody has selfish interests. Most members don't care enough about their interests to take the time and effort required to master the ins and outs of the budget process. If I take care of them, there's no reason to believe they won't take care of me, which means voting for the budget. My job is to construct the budget, round up the votes for it and get it out on time. I always manage to do that.

I'm used to breezing through the budget when it hits the committee or the floor. I don't make speeches. I just get to it. If I call for a vote, I always make sure I have a second. If people have questions, they get answered quickly and we move on to the next item—fast. One time as chair of the Budget and Finance Committee, I present the budget to the full council and get it passed in an hour, including consideration of all the motions from individual members, which become fewer and fewer every year. Some councilmembers want to make long-winded speeches on behalf of their motions. I'm presenting the budget in the chambers so I have the floor—and don't let them. It's the same thing on the occasions I preside over the council. Those meetings go by real quick. The advent of televised proceedings and cable TV leads to meetings having to go on longer than necessary to accomplish the work of the city. Everybody believes they're an expert about everything; consequently nobody really becomes an expert on anything. They just love to hear themselves talk.

Unlike the federal government and even state government, which survive on a lot of fancy accounting tricks, the city cannot deficit finance. You have to produce a budget that is actually balanced when it is passed. Do we do some smoke and mirrors? Yeah. We can pick up a $50 million windfall because the city sells something. You can take that money and use it for something else.

What gets the state in trouble—and the city too—is hiring more people than government can afford to cover. It's often not the hiring itself. The problem comes from the second year of people's employment when all the benefits start to be counted such as health and pension contributions and the like. Dealing with such issues long ago would make things a lot less painful today. Now reality is setting in.

As chair of the budget committee, I'm also a member of the city's Executive Employee Relations Committee (EERC). It represents management for the city in contract negotiations with the city's public employee unions. The five members include the budget committee chair, city council president and vice president, chair of the council's personnel committee, and the mayor. They help bargain union contracts and then bring contracts back to the council for review and approval. The unions include AFL-CIO affiliates and the independent Police Protective League, representing the rank-and-file officers of the LAPD.

"Richard played the same critical role with the EERC that he played in overseeing reapportionment for the council," Robin Kramer notes. "He understood empathetically where the workers were. He understood the resource constraints and opportunities facing the city. He was a good negotiator, not a yapper or a gossiper. He didn't talk out of school. He could broker deals because of relationships of trust he built up and his reputation for tough-mindedness. He could say to the Police Protective League on an issue, 'Now you're being greedy' or 'That's a tough one; let's try to do it.'"

International Brotherhood of Electrical Workers Local 18 can be a most disciplined and singularly most powerful union when there is a breakdown in communications with local government because it has the ability to shut down the city. Local 18 represents the Department of Water & Power employees who bring water and power to L.A. and attend to its infrastructure. The union's business manager is Brian D'Arcy, who is a formidable figure himself. This reality comes into sharp focus—along with the role the EERC can play—when negotiations break down between Local 18 and Dick Riordan after he first gets elected mayor.

Riordan is not a union friendly guy. He's not really pro-union or anti-union. But if given the choice, he won't be with the union. From what I know about him, he's also ends-oriented, and that's how he wants to govern. His ego is not such that he always has to be right as much as he doesn't want to be embarrassed. But he sometimes arbitrarily makes decisions without understanding the city and how it actually works. He wants a five percent reduction in labor contract costs. When Local 18 doesn't want to give it to him, he tells the union, "You know what? You haven't met a tougher guy than me." Dick is trying to play the big dog, proving he won't be pushed around by big labor and the like.

All of a sudden one day there is a small little power outage in a part of the city—to jar the city and its residents into recognizing the reality that municipal officials aren't interested in seriously negotiating. The power gets turned off in the San Fernando Valley, and nobody is working. No lights, no gas, no utilities, no nothing. Local 18 threatens to go on strike. There is the prospect that maybe the power is not getting turned back on any time soon. The question for those residents is how long they will have to live with it. It becomes a macho game between the union and the mayor. The union isn't in a hurry. They're sending a message to the mayor: You've got to come and talk with us. The mayor insists he will not be intimidated.

I meet with Brian D'Arcy and ask him, "What's the problem?"

"That son of a bitch doesn't know what he's doing," he tells me. "Who does he think he is to push us around? I got these crazy redneck linemen, KKK guys, gun toting, rifle-carrying guys—you name it. And the mayor refuses to negotiate with them." I ask Brian what it will take for the union to settle. He tells me. He doesn't trust the city negotiators or the city administrative officer who they report to. He thinks they're a bunch of assholes. "The only way it will be settled is if the mayor gets involved," he insists.

"I'm going to tell you what I'm going to do," I tell Brian. "I'm going to tell the mayor what the union is prepared to do. I just want to know you won't say anything and keep management wondering if what I tell the mayor is true or not. Then I'm going to tell him what it will take to settle. If I'm successful, I'm going to get the mayor to sit down to negotiate with you some time later this evening. So I want to know you will sit down and talk with him and it won't be about bullshit."

Brian agrees. He gives me his bottom line. "No one can afford more power outages," I state. "You got my attention with the 'accidental' blackout. I know you got the mayor's attention."

I tell the mayor one of my stories that I make up: "You think this [the power outage] is bad? What you saw in that outage will not go away. Let me tell you what I hear. [I don't say who I hear it from.] What I hear is there's going to be roaming outages across the city. Some are easily repairable. Others are not. Dick, you are going to be the laughing stock of the city of Los Angeles. There's nothing worse than a pissed off resident who doesn't have power, light, or fresh water. And it's just going to get worse because they [Local 18 members] are prepared to stop the city from operating for as long as it takes. Can you afford to have that happen? The employees don't want to strike. You're the only one who can resolve it."

"I can't afford to have that," the mayor replies. "But they're not willing to talk. So how are we going to get this resolved?"

It's 3 or 4 in the afternoon. "I'll have them in your office at City Hall at 9 o'clock tonight," I say. "But if you're not willing to sit down and negotiate I'm not going to waste my time and you can clean up the resulting mess. I don't have any credibility to try to avert this thing if you're not willing to negotiate in good faith."

I get the union there and the two sides meet that evening. Within three hours after the session starts there's an amicable settlement. We bring the deal to the council and the Department of Water & Power board of directors, and it is approved and quickly ratified by union members.

I do the same thing with the cops.

Contract talks between the city and the cops are always the hardest negotiations because there are so many more of them and more money is involved—in terms of wages but especially benefits. The Police Protective League always has a big ask. What usually ends up happening is if the cops' union contract is among the union agreements up that year it is taken up last since there never seems to be much early movement towards resolution of issues.

Keith Comrie is the legendary city administrative officer for L.A., one of the smartest, toughest, most ruthless guys you ever want to meet. He oversees a negotiating team, giving them instructions to meet and confer with the LAPD cops union. This goes on over four or five months. Every time the EERC, the committee representing management, gets a report from city negotiators it's always the same message: They've met with the cops and there is no progress to report.

Unbeknownst to Keith Comrie, I have direct contacts with the union. This is what I'm being told by its leaders: Meaningless sessions are taking place over a long period of time. If the city is unwilling to see the cops' problems, things will turn to shit pretty soon. Then where are us guys [city officials] going to be? The cops hate the negotiating team, Keith Comrie, and everybody else. That's the cops.

"You've got a friend," I tell the union. "I want to see this thing resolved." I inform the union that the committee on which I serve has given the city administrative officer instructions to offer A, B, and C to the union at the next negotiating session. "These are the parameters we've instructed him to offer."

A week or so later Keith Comrie comes back to me and the other committee members. We ask about the status of the bargaining.

"We met and they're hard-headed," Comrie answers. He gives us a long report that in essence says nothing has happened.

I check back with the cops union. "Yeah, we met—for 10 or 15 minutes," they tell me. "We had good donuts. We asked if the city had anything to offer. The city negotiators said 'no' and the meeting ended."

Then I know we're being lied to. At the next EERC meeting I say, "I got a real problem. I don't know who's telling whom a story. But from what I'm hearing, nothing is being talked about at these meetings. Now, either we're going to get serious about negotiating because we the committee members are elected officials and are the ones who will take the heat if something bad happens or we're not getting the right information from our own negotiators, I'll be damned if I'm going to take the fall for our ineptness and unwillingness to bend." Then, addressing the city administrative officer, I add, "I know you're trying to impress the mayor and city council that you're being tough and you're not a patsy to the whims the cops have. But this has got to stop."

Comrie insists it's the cops who are being unwilling.

I go back to the cops: "I'm not going to tell you what to do, but I think it would be a good idea to fill the council chambers with officers to talk about all the great bargaining sessions you've had with the negotiators and to tell the city council that it is being lied to and everything else. Blame the city negotiators for everything that is going to happen. Tell the council that the cops will hold the councilmembers responsible and go to the public with mailers and protests and publicity. Then introduce the union's new negotiating team. Tell them you're changing negotiators."

Then I stand up on the table in this conference room at the union offices: "When you introduce the new union negotiating team, I want it led by the rottenest cocksucker and the biggest asshole you got. The council will die when it sees who it is." I make it clear to the cops' leadership that the new bargaining team members are going to be there just to scare the council and that as soon as the mayor gives in and is directly negotiating with the union, then the biggest asshole's job is over and he is gone from the scene.

One of the leaders of the union nominates the meanest, most ornery irrational member of the Police Protective League as the new chairman of the negotiating team. Then the union communicates that it's a new day in Dodge.

The cops show up in mass at the council chambers. By law, the cops can't strike because there are laws against it and they can get enjoined, but they threaten roaming sick-ins and sickouts and everything else they can think of. Then they present the new negotiating team to the council. The new chair of the team introduces himself. He's this biker who hates government and hates the city council and hates everyone. The stunt gets all this publicity.

I ask the union leadership what they are willing to give up and what they need to get for it in return. "I want to make it clear to you that this is what I'm going to say. If what I'm going to say is inappropriate, you tell me now. I don't want to go into meetings with the city administrative officer, the mayor or discussions with council colleagues in executive session, get some concession and find out you don't want it."

I meet with Dick Riordan. "This will turn to shit," I tell the mayor. "You want to increase the force [adding more LAPD officers is the top priority of his mayoral campaign and administration] and you can't even keep these guys from threatening to leave [work]? Dick, you don't want to piss off the cops."

Dick tells me he doesn't like the cops' union. "Mayor, you can't negotiate with individuals," I tell him. "You got to deal with the union. This is the rank and file and these are the people you're supposed to be championing." I kind of exaggerate what will happen and how bad the mayor will look if the cops decide not to show up for work or have roving sick outs.

"I don't know what they want," Dick says. "They don't want to talk."

"I don't think that's true," I reply.

I get an okay from Dick Riordan on certain issues and arrange to get the mayor's office and the union together. The mayor offers a deal in six hours.

Earlier, I tell John Ferraro, president of the council, that I can come in and get the contract resolved. I never tell the rest of the council, which has to vote on approving negotiated union contracts, what I'm doing. No one wants to be seen as anticop and some of them might want to be involved in the talks even though the union can't bargain with 15 councilmembers. But John knows about my role.

I meet with the cops again. The new union negotiating chair—the antigovernment biker—gets the idea that his role isn't such a bad thing. He falls in love with the TV news cameras. When the deal from the city is brought up, he gets up to protest. I interrupt him: "Hey, man, time to sit down. You did a great job. Take all the credit for it you want. Now we need someone to go in and finalize the deal." The union forces him to step aside, although he later runs for president of the Police Protective League and loses.

Later, I pull aside Keith Comrie: "I'm not going to embarrass you or make it public, but you guys lied to us about this entire negotiating process. You're reporting to us that at every meeting you have the union is unwilling to give in or discuss resolving the contract when in fact it's not happening the way you're telling us. The fact of the matter is our negotiators are not seeking any meaningful resolution. This can't continue because the next time it happens I won't be as gentle. As long as you and I are on the same wave length, just consider it something that happened and is over and will never be discussed again." He says he understands and it doesn't get repeated.

I personally intercede on many occasions when city unions face difficult contract battles in L.A., from AFSCME (the American Federation of State, County and Municipal Employees) to SEIU (the Service Employees International Union), staying true to my commitment to helping the workers while also looking out for the fiscal interests of the city. (It isn't as hard in the 1980s and '90s as it is in later decades with the chronic budget crunches brought on by a much worse economy.) Unions often come to me and tell me what's really happening in negotiations—or what isn't taking place.

My role is clear: I'm there to help take care of the unions and make sure the men and women of the city work force are respected. That's why I always have the respect of the rank-and-file cops, firefighters, secretaries, clerks, everyone. If the city has the capacity, we work together for the best deal we can get. "Richard had access to everybody," says Hillary Norton, my last chief of staff. "All the unions went to Richard for his help as it related to both the budget and negotiations because their ability to win progress in contract negotiations was related to what the city budget looked like."

Because of these kinds of relationships with the city worker unions, I get help and cooperation for my district from on-the-job public employees in ways other councilmembers don't. I earn labor's confidence and support because I don't give into the traditional attitude of too many elected officials and pundits—it is becoming even more popular today—that public employees are lazy and the dregs of the earth. The one thing I insist city employees understand about me is as long as the needs of people in my district are being taken care of, they will always have me as a friend. Of course, my support for organized labor never waivers during my history in public office. During my years in the assembly, there aren't that many state employees who really have a direct impact on the day-to-day lives of the constituents in my district. It's different on the city council. I figure out not long after getting to the council that the only way I will get what I want for my district is to demonstrate to the rank-and-file union members who work for the city that I will be their champion so long as they help the people I represent. If I treat city employees well, they will take care of my constituents. That's just elementary to me.

Frequently, requests from me or my staff for help on behalf of my constituents or to push along projects in my district go to city departments and get very favorably received. When these requests go to management and then to supervisors or rank-and-file workers in the field, they act quickly and affirmatively because they see me as an ally and friend.

A lot is done via the city budget. The numbers of employees in the city departments are determined by the budget. Everything is. If a department gets its budget cut, where will it cut back? The great majority of any department's budget is taken up with paying for employees—and that includes benefits and retirement costs as well as salaries. During the great majority of my service on the council I'm either a member of the Budget and Finance Committee or its chairman. During discussions before the committee or in the council chambers you hear people shitting all over public employees. I always speak up and talk about the good work they do. If I have criticisms or disagreements with a city workers' union or with the conduct of city employees, I never voice them in public. I take them up with the union leadership or the relevant department head. I never make public employees scapegoats, which they too often become. What goes around comes around.

That philosophy also applies when I'm chair of the Metropolitan Transportation Authority that oversees the region's huge bus and mass transit systems with its thousands of employees providing crucial services for so many people in my district who are transit dependent. Even today, as seldom as I go to the MTA headquarters building near Union Station, when I do show up rank-and-file office workers or visiting bus drivers come up to me to say how much they miss me and how much I helped them when I was MTA chairman or a member of its board.

The 14th Council District is unique in that City Hall is such a short distance away from my constituents. In any case, I'm constantly out in the district. It's where I live, shop, and go out to eat. I attend a lot of events and meetings in the district. I do the same thing while representing the same territory for 13 years in the state assembly, even though I'm usually home in L.A. around three days a week back then. This is where I am born and brought up. You can't help but develop an incredible network of people. I know many of them for years, some since childhood. After all this time I'm pretty recognizable. Many people know who I am and feel free to come up to me if there's a problem with tree trimming, street signs, traffic signals, potholes, or street repair. I hear about it—directly.

Art Snyder, my predecessor, probably understands from working both as a councilmember's field deputy and as a City Hall deputy before getting elected in his own right that he needs to place his staff in every community. Preferably they are from those same communities and their entire responsibility is making sure everybody's needs are looked after, everyone's call is returned, and everyone's letter is answered. Art discovers what I learn for myself soon after returning to L.A.: You're not elected or reelected by what you do at City Hall. You're ultimately elected and reelected by what you do in every respective part of the district. Art Snyder becomes famous as the master of retail politics. He has no conscience about showing up at any event and trying to co-opt it and make it his event. He has a loyal staff that does all of his bidding. But the competency of his staff only takes him so far; his own effectiveness is what helps give him longevity. I watch Art operating for years, including while I serve in the legislature, and know how effective he is.

That's why I carefully assemble a staff of energetic and dedicated field deputies and make sure they concentrate on the communities where they are assigned. There's a certain level of natural superiority felt by council staff that work at City Hall as opposed to those working in district offices. City Hall staffers come to believe they're the ones who elect the members they work for. They go to work in nice suits and ties, hob knob with councilmembers all day, and see the mayor all the time. This falsely leads them to believe they're more important than the council staff members who get their hands dirty by laboring in what the City Hall staff calls Siberia.

I know it's the other way around. Every day I constantly reinforce the importance of what my staff does in the district. What I or anyone else accomplishes at City Hall is an abstraction to most people. So I make sure people's calls and letters get responses and that we're helpful to them. Maybe my office can't answer every complaint or request, but we make a genuine effort to respond to concerns and solve problems. People appreciate the effort. It's safe to say that when you're successful in taking care of a problem, when election time comes around, people remember what you do for them and reciprocate by telling their family and friends what a good person you are.

Because of this network, the great staff I assemble, the focus I give them, and the relationships I establish with the city bureaucracy—from management to employees on the streets—I instantly know the right connections to make, who to call, or who to get into my office, if necessary, to implement the solution.

"All the staff learned how to do it themselves by watching Richard," says Gerard Orozco, who starts out as a high school junior working as an intern in my assembly district office at 52nd and York in Highland Park, and later when I'm on the council comes on staff in my Boyle Heights field office in 1987. "He encourages his staff to develop alliances with department heads so we could directly go to the people in charge to get things done for constituents when problems came in the door. Since he was already Budget and Finance Committee chair—which I staffed him on—it was a very simple approach. During the budget process, he'd bring in the department heads, listen to their priorities for their departments and how much money they needed for the coming year. Then he would graphically point out to them the way it would work: 'This is Gerard. He's my deputy. You take care of him in terms of what he needs—which is going to be services requested from my constituents—and I'll take care of you at budget time.' It was an easy deal for the department heads to agree to. Then Richard made sure they had the resources from the city they needed as they were available."

A lot of elected officials I know over the years—state and city lawmakers—are selfish about access, about empowering people other than themselves. I'm not. I empower my staff and teach them what they need to know and how to go about getting things done for people.

"Whereas some other electeds chased newspaper articles or TV news coverage, Richard chased results—using city government to get things accomplished," Gerard says. "I never saw him waste his time hounding a reporter to solicit coverage. He had a press deputy, but most of his or her work was responding to inquiries. If you were looking for someone to make a good speech, you'd call somebody else. If you wanted votes or consensus on a tricky issue—if you wanted your project funded or your budget approved—you'd go to Richard. Budgets were balanced and passed when Richard was budget chairman. And we went through tough economic times, including the early '90s recession when money was tight. Richard made sure there was a prudent reserve in the general fund. And he very consistently made sure cops, libraries, parks, and programs for kids were funded first."

I also didn't care much for the ceremonial role the council plays. The late Caroline Leonetti Ahmanson is a wealthy philanthropist who backs a lot of foundations and causes, including support for the arts. She's speaking one day during the ceremonial part of the council agenda, when commemorations and proclamations are issued. "Richard had little patience for these sessions because he thought they were a waste of time. He was anxious to get down to business," Gerard says. "Mrs. Ahmanson was talking about China, its relationship with the United States and fostering better ties between these two great nations. I noticed Richard sitting intently on the dais, watching her speak with his hand on his chin in a very pensive pose. I thought to myself, 'This guy is brilliant. I wonder what he's thinking about.' I had ambitions of being an ambassador down the road. Diplomacy and foreign affairs were longtime interests of mine. I thought maybe Richard would have some special insight and knowledge since he was looking on so contemplatively.

"'I went up to the horseshoe where the councilmembers sit. Richard spotted me, summoned me over to where he is sitting and tells me, 'Ask me if I give a fuck about China? When are we going to start the real meeting? Let's get it done.'

"Richard was about the business of governing, making sure everyone did their job, that the services that were supposed to be delivered were delivered," Gerard points out. "In his view, Mrs. Goldstein in Brentwood was entitled to her services from the city. Mrs. Gonzales on North Fickett Street in Boyle Heights was just as entitled. Richard leveled the playing field by never being satisfied with being told it can't be done. He'd tell them to find a way. In Richard Alatorre, the 14th District had a very committed, connected, and powerful problem solver. The fact that he didn't chase headlines freed up a lot of time for making real things happen. He put me along with others from his staff on the right course. He taught me and still teaches a lot."

Many parts of L.A. like the 14th District can go either way. You're not living in West L.A. or in areas of the city where property values will always appreciate and be valuable no matter what happens or who represents them. Places like Boyle Heights, Lincoln Heights, Highland Park, and even Silverlake, Mt. Washington, and Eagle Rock need a councilmember who fights for constituents and values the history, cultural heritage, and uniqueness of these communities.

The focus for Art Snyder is keeping people happy, especially the established property-owning residents who can be counted on to vote. That's why Eagle Rock, in the northern part of the district where I live today, is his stronghold. That's where elections are won and lost for years. Art Snyder successfully plays the electoral political game: Doing what he can in the southern part of the district that is poorer and most needy, but really paying attention to the voter-rich part of the district farther north by catering to Eagle Rock where there are more people like him—historically white, Republican, and more conservative.

Representing the poorer communities of East and Northeast L.A. is much more challenging than representing communities like Eagle Rock, Echo Park, East Hollywood, and downtown. The reason is that in the minds of most people in many of these more affluent communities the greatest challenges are whether the esthetics are correct or how much density should or should not be allowed. Are they going to let multifamily housing in what is mostly a single-family neighborhood? That's not to say these places don't face challenges. But they're not nearly on a par with the challenges in neighborhoods farther south in my district such as Lincoln Heights and Boyle Heights. El Sereno, Eagle Rock is very similar to Silverlake or parts of Los Feliz. Farther south you get into Highland Park, which is changing over the years from a single- to a multifamily community, maybe with a 60–40 split. El Sereno is considered affluent for Mexicans even as it is undergoing changes. Echo Park has some real challenges by the time I get to the council. There are factors of changing immigration patterns, increases in housing density even though there is not a lot of room for new construction; it's built out. But there are conversions from single-family to multi-family residences.

If as an elected official you go strictly by who elects you—where the people who really vote are located—it leads you to focus on the northern part of the 14th Council District, which is Eagle Rock, Highland Park, Mount Washington, and the like. They are the communities with the luxury of being concerned about stuff like making sure the trees are properly trimmed and the streets are kept clean. Then you have the other extreme: Boyle Heights, where esthetics is the last thing people are concerned about. There, people face life and death questions every day. There are immense health, safety, and sanitation issues. Those are the two realities.

Then you have variations in between in the district. It is very symptomatic of the cross section and diversity of Los Angeles itself, running the gamut from middle-class neighborhoods in the north to the south, where conditions run mostly downhill. The challenge gets greater the farther south you go. To be effective for people in places like Boyle Heights it takes a councilmember who cares about making a difference and making change happen, even if doesn't come as fast as you and many others want.

The oldest and most densely populated area of Los Angeles is Boyle Heights. Along with El Sereno and downtown, this area has the greatest number of the oldest public housing projects run by the city. There are gangs dating back to well before my time that are still active plus newer gangs that I see created in the 30 years I'm in public life.

The crying needs of these communities create the dilemma for a councilmember of where you concentrate your efforts and spend your time. You always have to take care of the entire district. But because of who I am and where I grow up, it seems to me that the greater emphasis has to be where the greatest need exists. That's pretty much what I do. That's why I start my Feliz Navidad project, bringing holiday presents, food, and cheer—and even snow that many kids have never seen—into public housing projects in my district. That's why there is a special emphasis working with and empowering neighborhood organizations to help resolve their own problems. That's why I work so hard bringing in and expanding multimodal modes of transportation—from better bus service to light rail—in these dense and transit-dependent neighborhoods. That's why I work for more recreation and cultural programs, park resources, and extended library hours in the district. That's why I relentlessly work at improving infrastructure and street improvements—anything that improves the quality of life. That's why I push city departments to provide more services to my constituents by championing their budgets and resources so when my staff or I contact them, they respond promptly and completely.

Historically an immigrant community, Boyle Heights is the port of entry for people coming to the L.A. area to begin new lives from other parts of the U.S. and from many foreign nations. It begins as a single-family neighborhood with large old, historic homes. It is often beautiful housing stock with great architectural features. Many are craftsmen homes. They are built during a time when people pay attention to style and details. Yet over time, these homes get subdivided, legally and illegally. Today the area is saddled with some of the most highly dense housing stock in L.A.

That creates multiple problems when it comes to infrastructure. There is greater demand and more wear and tear on streets, sewers, and utilities. The need for public services intensifies. That puts pressure on all the respective city departments. Because of the age and overuse of public facilities such as parks, schools, and the like, there is a greater need for upgrading, renovations, and improvements. Yet Boyle Heights tends to get less attention from government in the district because the communities to its north are more educated, better organized, and more vocal in demanding their due share. With the increased density and socio-economic make up comes more crime.

This places disproportionate pressure on elected officials to respond to legitimate demands from constituents for public services. That pressure is especially felt when the elected official is born and raised in that community and really cares about improving its people's quality of life so they are treated as well as people in any other part of the city.

It is a pressure I personally feel. You don't stay in local government unless you happen to love what you're doing. As opposed to being a state legislator, as a city councilmember you're in the district 24 hours a day, seven days a week. There is no place to hide from the real problems residents face. If you care, as I do, the pressure to perform and accomplish things is that much greater.

It's great to drive around the district, stopping and talking to people at stores and restaurants I patronize. Constituents know me. The people I represent are the salt of the earth. Sure, they complain a lot—and justifiably so in many instances. Some take you for granted. But it's amazing that even today, years after leaving City Hall, I still meet people who know who I am and know that I still live where they live. They approach me and say, "Gee, I wish you were back. We took a good thing for granted." It's very flattering and everything else. Sometimes they think I'm still in office. When I am in office, everywhere I go people bring me their problems. I take the responsibility seriously.

I regularly bring in the general managers of the city departments and ask them to give me a list of the infrastructure in my district by age and state of repair. They keep that data for the whole city; maintaining it is their responsibility. I especially catch managers during budget time when their spending proposal is before my committee. That's a good time to draw their attention to the needs of my district. Other councilmembers may do the same thing. I do it because of the tremendous needs of so many of my constituents.

Some people say politics is a frustrating and thankless pursuit, and ask why I want to get into it—or stay in it. My answer is simple: "I came from a generation where there is virtue in public service, in helping people. Helping people is the only way you can really succeed in politics."

In Eagle Rock, Highland Park, El Sereno, Boyle Heights, and even parts of downtown long-neglected giant sewer lines are decaying. It costs hundreds of millions of dollars to replace them. In a quiet moment during the budgetary process we prevail on the city Sanitation Department over the urgency of replacing the sewer system in my district because of the tremendous decay and wear and tear. The heads of the department agree in principle and eventually agree in reality. It all gets down to knowing what can and cannot be done and then knowing how and when to ask. They are willing because they know I'm a great ally for their interests when it comes to departmental needs and worker issues.

A lot of tearing up of streets for sewer and street repair plus construction involving the upgrading of public facilities is going on all the time in my district. Some residents see it as an inconvenience. I see it as a healthy sign of a councilmember who cares about his district. If you are invested in owning a home or other property, all that construction and tearing up tells you the city facilities, infrastructure, and services you depend on are being taken care of. In the poorer areas of the 14th District, all those activities show we are not letting them get overrun by crime, become dilapidated, and turn into blighted neighborhoods.

It also happens on much smaller matters. There can be a tall stack of requests piling up at a city department. It's amazing how your request can go from the bottom to the top of the pile very quickly if there's a will. I don't just limit my relationships to the top managers either; I keep up with the middle managers, the people who actually do the work in the fields and their unions. So when my staff or I have requests, these departments respond in a timely manner.

One stand we take in Boyle Heights is over absentee landlords. When it is the entry point for Jews, Russians, Armenians, Chinese, and Japanese earlier in the 20th century they build and live in large houses. As they assimilate and improve their economic standing, there is an exodus by these ethnic groups as they move to other parts of the city. As new immigrant groups move in and encounter a severe lack of housing stock for large families, many of the original owners, now absentee landlords, subdivide the homes, often illegally. One single-family home can get turned into housing for 10 families living in overcrowded and substandard conditions. The unwillingness of the landlords to improve the properties creates a breeding ground for crime, poor sanitation, and health problems. I don't object to the idea of converting housing stock from single- to multifamily homes. But it has to be done legally and safely.

One day a lady, clearly undocumented, turns to my district office in Boyle Heights with an all-too common grievance. She lives under deplorable circumstances in a house in Boyle Heights that has been subdivided into 10 cramped and overcrowded units. It takes some courage for the woman to come forward at all given her immigration status. She also recognizes that by reporting the problem and my sticking various city departments on the landlord, many of the residents will probably be thrown out of their homes because the illegal conversion violates maximum occupancy rates. The lady says she is not speaking just for herself, but on behalf of all the other residents too. That's how bad conditions have become. There are problems with inadequate trash disposal, sewage back-up, lack of storage, and general overcrowding.

The hardest thing for me is that the absentee landlord is a Latino now living in the San Gabriel Valley. He grows up in the same community as me and has gone on to become one of the worst examples of a slum landlord, sticking it to his own people. You expect that these guys are after the almighty dollar. But they think they can get away with anything because the tenants don't have options.

I get the owner on the phone. "We can resolve this issue the nice way or the hard way," I declare. I give him 48 hours to start cleaning up the property to my satisfaction based on all the complaints from the residents and the multiplicity of code violations he is committing. He has to begin the process of properly subdividing the units and providing adequate plumbing and electricity, and bringing the house up to a livable condition. If he doesn't do it I pledge to send in inspectors from every appropriate city department he knows about and some he doesn't to go after him. Whatever rent money he is collecting each month will disappear into the fines and payments for mandatory corrections he will be made to pay, I add. (The rent money he's collecting every month from these poor people is incredible; they are paying him premium prices for shitty housing.)

I go down to the house and meet with a number of the residents. I'm not sure what the landlord is going to do, but once I start the process, there's no turning back I tell them. There may not be enough room for some people once the changes and improvements are made. I promise to bring in city and nonprofit agencies to help relocate those who are going to be forced to move. The residents all agree. They know the laws on the books say if you have X number of square feet only so many people can live here and no more. The city can either choose to enforce the law or look the other way. Most of the time city officials do the latter. With my encouragement, the city departments get on the ball.

The landlord finds religion very quickly. He begins the process, meets with the appropriate building and safety agencies that instruct him on what to do to bring the house up to code and create decent living standards. Some residents have to relocate with help from the city.

The same absentee landlord owns other dubiously subdivided properties. I just look them up on the city roll and find out where they're located. They also get inspected and required improvements are made. The guy gets to hate me. I don't care.

This is just one example of what elected officials can do if they want to. I do it because habitability is important. A decent place to live is critical to enjoying a good quality of life.

A related issue is coming up with a new approach to the changing complexion of homelessness in the city. We always have a skid row on the eastern edge of downtown, a place where people end up as a result of mental conditions or addiction, or economic circumstances. The skid row street population historically is composed of adults. But the demography changes over the years. You start seeing an influx of people who have lost their homes and landed on the streets. The problem starts in L.A. but becomes a national dilemma. When I get back home to L.A. in the mid-1980s, you start to see the homeless in places they haven't been seen before—living under bridges and on empty lots. There is the advent of AIDS and violence. More homeless people are dying on the streets during inclement weather. Most disconcerting to me is the growing impact on children since now families—mothers, fathers, and children—are among the ranks of the homeless.

Tom Bradley advocates using redevelopment money to set up single-room hotels to relieve homelessness. Hundreds of millions of dollars get put into them. But it doesn't seem to solve the problem, and we don't understand why people are not availing themselves of these sources of shelter.

City officials really have no solution. We want to do something, but what? There is no coordinated approach because we don't understand the problem of homelessness—what causes it and how you combat it. More importantly, there's the question of who is responsible for dealing with homelessness in the city.

We start learning more about the complexity of the problem. It isn't just people who have all of a sudden lost their housing. It's about veterans coming home from the Vietnam War or other conflicts addicted and suffering from post-traumatic stress syndrome, unable to function back in the city where they used to live. There are still the lingering impacts from then-Governor Ronald Reagan's decision to close down the state mental hospitals, shipping people to urban areas but without the promised funding for community mental services so patients can function outside of the institutions. Then there are those who can't or don't want to live inside shelters or other programs for the homeless, people who prefer the lifestyle of the street. There is a hodgepodge of various causes and multiple solutions for the different kinds of problems that cause people to be homeless.

Urgency builds for taking action when homelessness, at one time more or less limited to downtown's skid row, begins to move out into Hollywood, Santa Monica, the beach cities, and the valley to the west and north as well as into poorer communities to the south and east. Those communities start to rebel.

My deputy, Bonnie Brody, works with me on developing a coherent homeless policy for the city. I'm the first to admit our initial reaction and the immediate response from the progressives and lefties—let's open up armories, buildings and city facilities to the homeless—is not very effective. It does some good, but people are still dying on the streets. Besides, opening City Hall and other facilities for people to have a warm place to stay between the hours of 5 p.m. and 6 a.m. doesn't work for a certain faction of the homeless population that just wants a place to drink, deal drugs, and destroy property. This isn't the answer for a lot of people who don't want to be inside places where they have to obey certain rules. Others are mentally ill and need different kinds of help. Some who are homeless for economic reasons just need help coming up with the first and last month's rent to get a new place.

After studying what is happening in other cities and the county, what becomes clear is the need for a more unified and comprehensive set of services dealing with issues such as medical and mental treatment, counseling on employment, and providing transitional housing leading to permanent housing. Our ultimate homeless policy that is passed by the city council calls for attacking the problem on a much more coordinated, collegial basis. Many city agencies and departments deal with the homeless. Each one that has anything to do with homelessness has to work together on a coordinated basis with all the other agencies so each does what it is good at doing. The city starts doing a better job of providing appropriate shelter during periods of cold weather. We set up a physical facility, a kind of one-stop homeless advocacy office, on skid row.

There is what we can do and what we need to do, which is still up for debate because homelessness only gets worse in the following years. There are open questions. Do you concentrate the homeless in one part of the city or allow them to disperse into different communities with services that follow them? I argue at one time for concentration along with making sure all the necessary services are available in one area, which is downtown. I probably have a different attitude today. But unless it is addressed, homelessness leads to the decay of communities and a degrading quality of life for everyone involved.

Investing in resolving grievances over substandard housing, improving and modernizing infrastructure, and preserving historical sites show that you value these communities and the people who live there. They deserve the best attention the city can offer. This approach can make the difference between neighborhoods prospering and improving or degrading. It stands to reason that residents living in decent conditions will keep them up. Making change happen also encourages entrepreneurship among residents and gives them a greater stake in the community. What makes places like Boyle Heights and the rest of Northeast L.A. so interesting is that the people who live there are opening up restaurants and shops. They are living out the character and diversity of their community.

This is a long tradition that doesn't start with Mexicans. When Boyle Heights is heavily Jewish, people set up small businesses that flourish. Latinos too have a great entrepreneurial spirit. They may start with a little barbecue pit or taco stand and then move on to open up a small Mexican restaurant. The next generation grows and expands the enterprise and continues the vitality. One guy starts a little Mexican fish eatery called El Pescador (the fisherman). Now there are seven of them, including one in Whittier after one of the sons moves there.

Northeast L.A. communities see a lot of this: People who live there starting up businesses, working hard to make them work, and often succeeding because they know what the community wants better than anyone.

All of a sudden taco trucks are the latest trend. Now they're not just Mexican taco trucks, but Korean taco trucks—taco trucks serving Dim Sung. And they're all over L.A. A big line of them can be seen parked on Wilshire Boulevard outside the Los Angeles County Museum of Art. It's amazing. Sometimes they have to scatter when the city turns out to cite them; local restaurants see them as mobile competition. I can understand why the restaurants are worried, but it's free enterprise. I also like the taco trucks, not just because they're cheaper but also because they're tastier. It's part of that great American entrepreneurial spirit you have to encourage, not discourage. Where did the taco trucks start? They start with Mexicans on the Eastside. It's also about a sense of identity. People don't labor these long hours, whether at a restaurant or inside a taco truck, unless there's a market for their product among the people they live among.

There's a recent film, "Meet me at the corner of Brooklyn and Soto," a documentary about Boyle Heights. It describes the area as having this Pilgrim pluralism, a sense that East and Northeast L.A. is a place where everybody fits in somehow. It doesn't matter if you're old or young. Your sexual proclivity or religious faith don't matter. You can be Jewish, Catholic, Japanese, or Latino. It's an incredible melting pot.

Changing the name of Brooklyn Avenue to Cesar Chavez Avenue, especially the part of the main east-west artery running through Boyle Heights, is a big challenge. Some people feel the gesture of honoring the farm labor and civil rights leader takes away from recognizing the Jewish heritage of the community. Just because few, if any, Jews still live in Boyle Heights doesn't mean strong feelings for the area in the Jewish community have gone away. That's why I champion preserving the Breed Street Shul in Boyle Heights.

Is it naïveté that I decide on using Brooklyn Avenue? We try to think of a major street to rename for Cesar. Since Brooklyn starts in the city of L.A. and goes through my district I can control the agenda at City Hall. Eventually, we get the county involved too since Brooklyn continues east of the city limits. County Supervisor Gloria Molina helps out with the county piece.

But we soon realize the obstacles. This is the first time I ever push to change a street name. You don't anticipate the economic issues that get raised. Businesses and individual property owners have to get new stationary, business cards, signage, and advertising. All legal papers have to be changed. Then there are Jews—and some Mexicans—who think it's disrespectful. Most of them have nothing against Cesar. They just want to honor him somewhere else, not there. It's because of the long and colorful history of Brooklyn Avenue. At one time it's the heart of commerce on the Eastside. Cantor's Restaurant. Currie's Ice Cream Parlor (with the neon sign of the little kid licking his ice cream cone). Zellman's Haberdashery; the owner just about shits all over me. Everyone grows up there. I do. East Los Angeles College has to see the name of the main thoroughfare it faces being changed; they about die. Everybody knows it as Brooklyn Avenue. There are as many moving personal stories involved with the avenue as there are people who can tell them. Among critics, the older the generation the more insulted they feel. I learn you're better off not changing the names of streets. It causes a lot of grief among some people. You get people really blaming you.

We respectfully listen to all of their concerns and then move on with what we are going to do. People get over it. They don't have a choice.

Then there's the question of what happens once we get into downtown L.A., past Alameda Avenue. Where does it end heading west? Some people are even more up in arms over the prospect of changing the name of Sunset Boulevard, which is an even more famous street as it runs west to the Pacific Ocean through Hollywood and Beverly Hills. So we end Cesar Chavez Avenue at Grant Street.

As a young boy growing up in East L.A., downtown Los Angeles becomes the center of my life one day a week, particularly during the summer months when I'm not in school. Every Monday I take my grandmother on the yellow car train line into downtown to go see her doctor. After that, we eat at Clifton's Cafeteria, one of the oldest continually operating restaurants downtown (it is now closed) and then hit one or the other theaters on Broadway, like the Mayan or Million Dollar, that show only Mexican pictures. Broadway is also the center of retail business life back then. There are J. C. Penney's and Bullock's department stores. At Christmastime, the whole place is all decorated in bright lights. When I get older, I take streetcars to Broadway on Saturdays and Sundays to go to the movies. There are English-language theaters too. Many of them are takeoffs of theaters in France, with beautiful architecture. Altogether, the Broadway of my youth is a place where commerce thrives and where all kinds of people gather to go to films, eat, and recreate. It has attractions, especially the fancy theaters and department stores, that don't exist in East L.A.

By the time I get elected to the council, downtown L.A. is going downhill. (Interestingly, downtown still commands per square foot rents that favorably compare with what is being paid along Rodeo Drive in Beverly Hills because of the vibrant commerce and the heavy traffic of people who continue to be drawn there.) By then, the movie theaters that I patronize as a kid are gone, all shut down. They are sold off largely to Persian investors who during economic downturns start buying up a lot of buildings as they become empty. All they care about is renting out the bottom floors that face Broadway and holding on to the properties until they can resell them for bigger profits later on, which many do.

No theaters and little retail life are left. There is no hope of attracting back the large department stores. Yet it is still the focal point for commerce among new generations of immigrants, primarily Mexicans, who are attracted on weekends to do their shopping in the many little *puestos*, or small stores, selling gadgets and knickknacks. Some people criticize the appearance of Broadway, feeling it looks kind of tacky.

A visionary property owner and champion of the historic downtown core when I get on the council is the late Ira Yellin. He owns the landmark Grand

Central Market, with lots of stalls hosting small vendors selling fresh fruits and vegetables, meats and fish. Above it are the former first offices of the L.A. Department of Water & Power during the 1920s. He also has the old Bradbury Building at the intersection of Third and Broadway. Both are architecturally significant structures that fall into disrepair by the time he acquires them and that he restores to their original beauty. I help Ira push his projects through and get Community Redevelopment Agency funds—state and federal monies used for redevelopment of blighted neighborhoods—invested in them.

Ira and I began talking. We know we can't get large retail stores to return to downtown. So what should the vision be? He feels downtown L.A. needs to become a 24-hour city, especially for a resurgence of Broadway to happen. We talk about downtown, from First to Third streets, remaining the center of government. We eventually see Third Street down to probably Olympic Boulevard as heavily residential with the conversions of old buildings and properties into apartments, lofts, or townhouses. This will require sizeable economic investments.

A friend of mine, Reverend Gene Scott, once owns the famous sign proclaiming "Jesus Saves," on the old Philharmonic Theater at Fifth Street, between Hill and Olive. It's an empty lot now. When all the churches abandon downtown, at first he too holds his services in Glendale. But Gene is a lover of old movie theaters and wants to return to downtown in order to preserve the spirituality that has flourished there in the past. He buys the historic United Artist Theater at Ninth and Broadway and moves his congregation there. He spends about $1 million restoring the structure, returning it to its old glory. It is now one of the crown jewels of downtown. He also installs in the theater one of the most extensive Bible collections in the region.

Gil Lindsay, a veteran African-American councilmember who comes from the mostly black district to the south, represents the majority of downtown. An area has to be in my district in order for me to have influence and a say about what happens there. When I oversee city reapportionment again in 1990, I get the idea of trying to put a bigger piece of downtown L.A. into my district. It's a fight. Rita Walters, a council colleague, initially fights me on the first rendition of redistricting. But downtown and Broadway don't hold the same sentimental importance and potential as a shopping area for Mexicans for Rita Walters that they do for me. We finally cut a deal. I take Broadway on both sides of the street from Hill Street all the way down to Olympic, including the Farmers Market. Then I balloon out into parts of Skid Row and get connected east into Boyle Heights and the rest of the 14th District.

We start an organization called Fiesta Broadway, committed to bringing life back on Broadway. While chairing the Metropolitan Transportation Authority in the early 1990s, I propose bringing the streetcars back to downtown so they can serve as connections from different parts of the city. The old yellow car streetcars of my childhood, which are still mothballed somewhere, start out in East L.A. at Rowan Avenue and run west along First Street to Broadway. They once go down Broadway south to Pico Boulevard, then west to Rimpau Boulevard and back to Broadway. My idea is to renovate the old streetcars, which are the forerunners of light rail, and use them as electric-powered vehicles. My proposal doesn't go anywhere.

However, as MTA chair, I help expand the red line heavy rail from Union Station out west towards Vermont, Hollywood, Universal Studios, and ultimately to North Hollywood. We build the blue line from Long Beach ending at Ninth and Flower streets. Then there's the gold line from downtown out to Pasadena and ultimately Claremont. And finally we expand the red line from Union Station east through Boyle Heights and eventually out to Atlantic Boulevard. In addition to enhancing the environment and reducing pollution by providing options to get people out of their autos, all these major transit projects help economically rejuvenate downtown L.A. by making it easier for people to get into and out of the city core.

I work with Ira Yellin and the Central City Association downtown. We invest money in renovating and improving the Grand Central Market, creating housing units on top of it—a forerunner of the loft and apartment housing movement that spreads throughout downtown. We put money into renovating a couple of old theaters, including the Los Angeles Theater and the venerable Orpheum Theater, helping the owners bring them back to their historic beauty. Some show films, including many of the old movies that are restored and brought back to life.

New state buildings go up downtown. I'm a big supporter of the new Staples Center, helping round up the votes on the council that will build the new stadium to house the Lakers professional basketball team—and eventually the Clippers basketball team and the L.A. Galaxy hockey team. The Los Angeles Convention Center is just outside my council district, but working with Gil Lindsay I help get financing and collect votes for approval of its major expansions.

Downtown's St. Viviana's Catholic Cathedral, the main church for the archdiocese and the residence of then-Cardinal Archbishop Roger Mahony, is in danger of being demolished following the 1994 quake. Needing a bigger facility, the archdiocese gets $120 million in gifts on the condition it builds a new cathedral. Eventually, property is acquired from L.A. County for a new cathedral downtown next to the I-10 freeway. Developers want to buy and raze the old cathedral to build something else. This is where Angie and I are married. St. Viviana's is also where Pope John Paul II holds a special mass when he visits L.A. My interest is maintaining the building as an historic landmark and as a symbol of the spiritual presence of the archdiocese in downtown. I believe the history of buildings is important even though I'm not always considered a devout preservationist. It just happens that I believe strongly in preserving historical structures in downtown L.A.

I broker a deal with the L.A. Conservancy, the local historical society, the Catholic archdiocese, and the developer. The physical integrity of the structure will be maintained and appropriate uses will be found. The old church becomes a cultural venue for performances, receptions, and educational purposes. New housing and a library are also planned on the property.

The most ambitious renovation project downtown becomes an epic struggle I lead to preserve and rebuild L.A.'s iconic 32-floor City Hall. After the '94 earthquake, an analysis is done and the news is horrific. They can't guarantee the safety of the building or people's lives in the event of another big quake. Parts of City Hall have to be closed off. Among them are the historic upper two floors that offer major reception areas and spectacular views of the city. We ask for an analysis of what it will take to do a restoration, seismically reinforce the building against new quakes, and do upgrades necessary to meet current building and safety standards. It needs extensive work, including reinforcing the suspension underneath the massive structure completed in 1928.

Many people say it will cost too much money. It is suggested that we build a new city hall at a different place—or just make changes to the old building in the cheapest possible manner. The *Los Angeles Times* runs an editorial saying maybe it's not such a good idea to invest more money in the existing City Hall—that this may not be an effective strategy.

Mayor Riordan brings in Stuart Ketchum, a well-known developer in the city, to do an analysis of costs involved in rehabilitating City Hall. He comes back with a plan saying the rehab can be had for a lot less, but his analysis doesn't include air conditioning and a lot of other things that are needed to do the job right.

Albert C. Martin Sr. is one of the chief architects who designs and builds the original structure in the 1920s. His grandson is Chris Martin, also an architect—and CEO—with AC Martin Partners, his family business. Chris still has the original drawings and plans from his grandfather's day; he knows what it will take to do the restoration and restore it back to the beautiful building it is. Chris Martin's plan calls for some important changes, including locating all the city council offices on the same floor.

I love City Hall. It is a world-recognized place, an enduring symbol of the city. To me it represents what L.A. is all about. I have already gone through one remodeling of a gem, the historic west wing that comprises the original state Capitol building in Sacramento during the late 1970s and early '80s, also because of earthquake concerns. We restore the Capitol to its turn-of-the-century glory. That is one of the biggest public works restoration projects of its day in America. We hear the same arguments against spending the money when the Sacramento renovation is debated. Even the naysayers change their tune when the Capitol building is reopened to critical acclaim.

Ron Deaton, city legislative analyst, and I work to make sure enough money and effort goes into preserving and rebuilding this vital historic prize. I successfully argue with John Ferraro and others on the council that we need to invest the money in restoring our City Hall. We all have to temporarily move out during the construction, setting up offices in the City Hall East annex. It takes a

I'm There to Do More Than Just Take Up Space 355

Richard leads the fight that preserves and restores Los Angeles' iconic City Hall building after it sustains damage during the 1994 Northridge earthquake.

long time and much expense. For a number of years I sit on the council committee dealing with the expenditures while the renovation and upgrade is underway to ensure we are getting the biggest bang for our dollars—and that we end up with a building that is safe for employees and citizens.

Like the state Capitol renovation, when City Hall is finished and reopened the consensus from nearly everyone is that this is the right thing to do and a wise investment after all—despite the pain in the ass of moving over to City Hall East while the rebuilding is underway. There's only one drawback: Before the renovation, I have one of the great council offices of all time, a spacious suite with plenty of room for my staff on the third floor. After the renovation, I end up with half the space. But that's progress, I guess.

The San Antonio Winery, located in another historic building off North Main Street going towards Lincoln Heights, is the city's only functioning winery where they make wine and have tours, retail sales, and a restaurant. The Raboli family owns it; the founder is still around but now the kids pretty much run it.

Meantime, the United Parcel Service regional distribution center operates on Washington Boulevard in Boyle Heights since I am a kid growing up there. UPS is historically a great employer of young people who are just starting out or needing part time employment while they go to school. These are good Teamsters Union jobs that pay well and provide great benefits. The property housing UPS is being sold, and the company has to look for another location. UPS is attracted to a suitable site nearby on North Main Street, an abandoned Pabst Blue Ribbon brewery next door to the San Antonio Winery, where UPS can have a bigger and more modern facility. UPS takes over part of the building. We work with the developer to create artist lofts in the rest of the structure, which is totally renovated on the inside. It becomes a place where artists can have live/work spaces with galleries long before it becomes trendy.

At first, it looks like the move by UPS to North Main may threaten the space needed for the winery to survive. At one time a developer wants to knock down the winery. But it is too important to the history of L.A. I convince UPS that it needs to be more understanding and respectful of its neighbors. We help the winery minimize any negative impacts—such as limiting egress and ingress—from locating the UPS regional center nearby. San Antonio Winery and UPS end up working out an arrangement that meets the needs of both firms, each of which are a credit to the community. Later, the winery undergoes a renovation itself using its own resources.

Now we have an artist community, a UPS distribution center, and an historic winery, all getting along next door to each other.

The Northridge and later the Whittier earthquakes cause ripple affect damages on a lot of government buildings and bridges in the city. Many need to be seismically reinforced.

I use some seismic funding coming from the federal government and other sources designed for older structures affected by the 1994 Northridge quake. To allow us to use the earthquake money to restore buildings we put a citywide bond measure before the voters in the 1990s. (The Hollenbeck Police Station near First and Chicago streets in Boyle Heights is also old and unsafe in a quake and needs to be rebuilt with space to encourage more opportunities for community meetings and involvement. The station has to be seen by area residents as a haven for this largely immigrant community, a place where all people can gather. We rebuild Hollenbeck too.)

Then we take care of the city's cops in a big way by building a new headquarters for the LAPD at First and Spring streets across from City Hall. Parker Center, which is built in the 1950s, is seriously out of date. Many police officers who should be at the central headquarters are spread out at other locations across downtown. The cops need a bigger and better facility. They get it.

More than two decades before Arizona's anti-immigrant law, SB 1070, is passed in 2010, the LAPD, its police chief, Daryl Gates, and the city council implement a mandate instructing L.A. police officers not to check on the immigration status of residents, witnesses, or crime victims. Called Special Order 40, it says, "Officers shall not initiate police action with the objective of discovering the alien status of a person. Officers shall not arrest nor book persons for violation of [federal immigration laws]."

L.A. has a long, colorful, and sometimes not very pretty history in modern times when it comes to how we treat immigrants. There is a time not long ago when the LAPD feels it has a duty to cooperate with—and sometimes act as—immigration officers rather than police officers. In the 1930s, the LAPD aids and abets in the unlawful mass deportation to Mexico of hundreds of thousands of brown-skinned residents, including many who are later found to be legal residents and even American citizens. The state of California issues a formal apology in 2005.

The city and state go back and forth on how to address the issue of cooperation with federal authorities when it comes to immigration enforcement. More recently, the LAPD, to its credit, is usually on the right side of the issue, which conforms to my way of thinking. I have conversations with Deputy Chief Bill Rathburn, head of the LAPD's South Bureau, covering all the divisions in the southern part of the city. He deals with the problem first hand and gives me the best arguments why it's so damn important that the department has some credibility during a period when so many crimes of color against color are occurring in South Central L.A. Mexicans and other Spanish-speaking groups are being ripped off and having their money and possessions stolen going to and from the store. Rapes are taking place and not being reported. Gang crime and violence is a plague in too many parts of my district. Imagine if people become victims or witnesses to crimes and every one of them who is undocumented is afraid to cooperate with the police. How can police officers serve in a gang enforcement unit in Boyle Heights when residents are too scared to help them or even be seen speaking with them because they are undocumented? Having police officers do the work of immigration officers sends a message to criminals that they can victimize immigrants with impunity without fear of the consequences. Suppressing crime in those areas helps keep everyone safer, regardless of their immigration status. The police are there to serve and protect immigrants too. The deputy chief says the LAPD can't be sending double signals to immigrants. They have to feel secure that if they report crimes, they don't have to worry about being deported.

The issue surfaces when we start to get information that one LAPD division, Rampart (just west of downtown), is allegedly taking it upon itself to provide space in the precinct building for the immigration service to detain people who are arrested and who the feds think are here illegally. The word is that there's a line on the floor of the station. Immigrants are told to follow this line that leads to immigration officers who are hanging out at the other end. This part of town is now a port of entry for many immigrants from Central and South America, especially Cubans, Salvadorans, Guatemalans, and Nicaraguans. Crime, both the organized and street variety, is running rampant there. There is also a push at the time by anti-immigrant ideologues demanding that the city of

L.A. more closely cooperate with immigration officials to deport more of our residents.

This comes at a moment when L.A. is at a threshold. There are growing social pressures and tensions because immigrants are fast moving into neighborhoods inhabited by other minorities, including African Americans and Asian Americans. There are different philosophies within the LAPD about enacting Special Order 40. Some are for cooperating with immigration; others are not.

So as chairman of the Public Safety Committee, I conduct hearings in the mid- to late-1980s to reaffirm the principle stated in Special Order 40. Before Bill Rathburn makes his presentation, he tells me, "Given what I'm going to say I need you to give me some cover."

"You got it," I reply. I ask him questions knowing how he'll answer. He testifies about the need for a strengthened Special Order 40 so the LAPD will be able to reduce crime in certain areas of L.A. and so all residents see the cops as their friends and not as some repressive instrument threatening their very existence in the city.

The council makes it stronger so the cops have a clear understanding that their job isn't immigration enforcement. Deputy Chief Rathburn is in charge of all the security during the 1984 L.A. Olympics. He is a very progressive guy and is one of my favorites to become chief of police to succeed Daryl Gates before Rathburn leaves to take another top police post in another city.

Progressive immigration policy and the labor movement historically don't always come together very well in California or the nation. Going back to the 19th century, predecessors of today's unions are often virulently anti-immigrant, from resistance to recent arrivals from countries like Ireland and Italy to passage of the Chinese Exclusion Act that is heavily backed by the Knights of Labor, which sees big business using Chinese immigrants to keep wages depressed for white workers. All that begins to change in a big way in Los Angeles during the 1990s.

It starts with Miguel Contreras, probably one of the most significant labor leaders and civic figures in L.A. history. I meet Miguel during my time in Sacramento and my work with Cesar Chavez and the United Farm Workers, in which Miguel is involved first as a 1973 grape striker and later as a negotiator trained by Cesar. Another person I meet the same way and who also ends up becoming a major L.A. labor leader is Maria Elena Durazo, who later marries Miguel. She too comes out of the farmworker movement. I lose track of Miguel after he leaves the UFW to become an instrumental force and trusted lieutenant of Herman "Blackie" Levitt, head of the hotel and restaurant workers Local 11 in L.A.

Since before I'm elected to the assembly, when I'm getting involved in local Democratic politics during the late 1960s and early '70s, the L.A. labor movement is controlled by Sigmund Arywitz, executive secretary-treasurer of the Los Angeles County Federation of Labor (AFL-CIO), the central labor body in which most local unions in L.A. are affiliated. He's an old-line lefty Jewish labor leader, very progressive. When he retires, power shifts to Bill Robertson, who comes out of the building trades. During Arywitz's tenure there is a younger component of the movement called Frontlash, which does a lot of voter registration and is funded by the A. Phillip Randolf Institute, mostly composed of African Americans.

Arywitz and Robertson are into traditional Democratic politics. If you're a political candidate, you can rely on labor in those days for a county AFL-CIO endorsement from its Committee on Political Education, or COPE, and be assured of always getting a little bit of money for your campaign. Then you have the ability to go after further endorsements, funding, and ground troops from affiliated unions. But those locals—and the labor federation itself—have a very limited ability to turn out their own members, much less other working-class voters. They often have trouble convincing their own rank-and-file union members to vote for endorsed candidates.

The one consistency for the county federation is always advocating for working men and women, and advocating for progressive causes. It is always on the right side of issues like civil rights, to a point; for example, it supports the farmworkers' struggle. But the federation is primarily concerned with the established public and private sector unions that make up most of its membership.

One of the leaders of Frontlash who I run into in 1968 is Jim Wood. Jim is a nice, progressive southern boy. We become the best of friends, organizing through Frontlash one of the largest voter-registration drives ever held in the city, during Bobby Kennedy's presidential campaign that year. Frontlash becomes the biggest vehicle to register Latinos to vote through the 1970s and into the '80s. Jim, a trusted soldier under Arywitz and Robertson, later becomes the county labor federation's political director and succeeds Robertson when he steps down.

Jim is into building labor's political organization through greater activism and working to raise more money so L.A. Labor can educate union members, get them registered to vote, get them out to vote, and eventually get them to participate in political campaigns. Instead of listening to union members complain about paying dues and contributing to political action committees, Jim begins trying to politicize the rank and file, especially the younger members, and bring them into the fold. As head of the county federation, Jim emphasizes city politics and becomes a trusted ally and lieutenant of Mayor Tom Bradley, as Bill Robertson is before him, while still struggling to increase labor's influence in city politics and political institutions. Jim uses his tenure as a mayoral appointee to the Los Angeles Redevelopment Agency to push through project labor agreements, or PLAs, requiring that major public construction projects pay union scale and benefits and often use union labor. PLAs become a part of all big development programs where public funds are expended in the city of L.A. It is attributable to the great work begun by Bill Robertson and carried out by Jim Wood.

One of Richard's closest allies is Miguel Contreras, head of the Los Angeles County Federation of Labor, AFL-CIO. Miguel turns the L.A. labor movement into a political powerhouse and revolutionizes labor in L.A. and across the country by closely linking together the causes of unions and immigrants.

Jim Wood's ultimate effectiveness is never realized because of his untimely death from leukemia in 1996, at too young an age. We change the name of West 9th Street from Alvarado Street west, which runs by the labor federation headquarters, to James M. Wood Boulevard.

Right around this time, hotel and restaurant union Local 11 is placed under receivership by its international union. Blackie Levitt, who heads the local for years, is succeeded by inept Anglos who won't even allow membership meetings to be translated into or conducted in Spanish even though the union membership is fast becoming heavily Latino and immigrant, with many workers who don't speak English. Many Local 11 members labor in the big hotels and restaurants that are booming in L.A. But the wealth those properties are generating isn't really being shared very well by the majority of the workers even though they are union members. Local 11's leadership gives little priority in its contract bargaining to the numerous workers, mostly Latinos, who fill the ranks of the lower-paid job classifications.

Maria Elena Durazo is pressing for basic reforms and a greater voice for Latino union members against an entrenched Local 11 Anglo leadership that is insensitive and out of touch with most of its members. She unsuccessfully runs for head of the local. Miguel comes in as the international union's trustee, having worked earlier for the hotel workers union in San Francisco. At first Maria Elena suspects Miguel's motives, but he quickly moves to reform Local 11, eventually leading to her election as local president. They get married afterwards. Miguel also catches the attention of Jim Wood at the county federation of labor. Jim and Miguel share a common vision for increasing the political influence of L.A. Labor. When Local 11 comes out of receivership with Maria Elena as its president, Jim hires Miguel to be his political director at the county AFL-CIO. After Jim's death, Miguel is elected as the first Latino to head the venerable labor federation in its more than 100-year history.

Miguel and I hit it off as soon as he arrives in L.A., first because of our shared experiences with the farmworkers and later because of our common backgrounds and philosophies about the need for organized labor to play a greater role in city political affairs. Miguel, along with Maria Elena, recognizes the growing importance of Latinos emerging out of the changing demographics of the city. He also recognizes the importance of raising money—big money—for lobbying and political campaigns. But he takes it a few steps further. First, Miguel expands political participation far beyond labor's traditional boundaries, which concentrates on making relatively modest contributions to individual elected officials and political candidates. In Miguel's words, he "changes the way unions do politics in L.A." "Instead of becoming an ATM machines for politicians," Miguel says, the labor federation dedicates its resources to educating union members, getting them registered to vote, and turning them out to the polls in unprecedented numbers. L.A. Labor, under Miguel and continuing under his successor, Maria Elena, is transformed into a powerhouse for progressive political activism in L.A. County. Unions, under the county federation's leadership, can put thousands of labor activists on the streets going door-to-door or operating phone banks in any given political contest. The federation's political resurgence becomes a model for the national labor movement of what a central labor body can accomplish.

Miguel also demands more of the politicians he elects. Many local, state, or federal elected officials, almost all of them Democrats, are good votes; they vote right when issues of concern to working people and their unions come before them. But many don't distinguish themselves by going out of their way to champion labor's causes in their everyday public service. Miguel demands that the candidates L.A. Labor endorses and supports be "warriors for working people," that they put their careers, and sometimes their livelihoods, on the line to advance the unions' agenda.

He also places the federation's considerable influence and resources behind affiliated local unions as they face tough organizing campaigns or drives to negotiate or renegotiate their union contracts. Sometimes Miguel personally intervenes to force settlements of contentious labor disputes. What also amazes me about Miguel is that he acknowledges early in his tenure as head of the county federation that service employees, many of them Latinos and immigrants, are the future for organized labor in the years to come. So he begins educating them, getting them involved in civic and political affairs, and making them a force in labor and city politics on a scale that has never been seen before.

Meantime, in 1994, just before Miguel becomes the leader of L.A. Labor, then-Republican Governor Pete Wilson hands a huge break to Latinos across

California and the nation, and to Miguel in L.A. That year, Wilson makes a statewide ballot initiative to deny undocumented immigrants nearly all public services—including public education—the centerpiece of his difficult reelection campaign against Democrat Kathleen Brown, Jerry's sister and the state treasurer. Proposition 187 becomes seen by most Latinos simply as the anti-immigrant—and anti-Latino—initiative. Wilson's political strategy to appeal to the prejudices of Anglo voters succeeds. I know Pete Wilson; as a U.S. senator in the 1980s he helps me get federal transportation funding when I chair the Metropolitan Transportation Authority as well as obtain other benefits for L.A. He's not a racist. But by capitalizing on Prop. 187, Wilson does more to politicize and motivate Latinos to become citizens, register, and vote than all the combined efforts by Latino activists over the decades.

Prop. 187 kicks off a national trend in the 1990s, mostly by cynical Republican politicians, to score political points among white voters who fear the mushrooming presence and influence of Latinos; many of us are popping up in places we haven't been seen in large numbers before such as the South and Midwest. Up through and including the 2012 presidential primaries, GOP candidates try to outdo each other in seeing who can do a better job of scapegoating Latinos and immigrants and blaming them for all of society's problems, especially in down economies when there's a lot of anxiety by working people. Of course, Donald Trump takes appeals to bigotry against Mexicans and immigrants to new heights during his 2016 presidential campaign. At a time when immigrants are increasingly feeling threatened, only two institutions in L.A. welcome them and champion their rights: The Catholic Church, largely through the efforts of Cardinal Roger Mahony, and the labor movement through Miguel Contreras's leadership.

People become very angry when they believe they're being discriminated against because of who they are. After the Republicans elect Herbert Hoover by running a virulent anti-Catholic campaign against Al Smith, the first Catholic presidential candidate from a major party, in 1928, generations of white ethnic Europeans—including Polish Americans, Italian Americans, and Irish Americans—vote Democratic. That phenomenon doesn't start changing until Ronald Reagan's election as president in 1980, with support from many blue-collar white Democrats. Pete Wilson begins the same kind of trend among Latino voters in the mid-1990s.

Miguel carefully selects the best pro-labor candidates in strategically targeted L.A. County congressional, legislative, and councilmanic districts. He directs millions of dollars into L.A. Labor-run campaigns for those candidates, mobilizes thousands of campaign volunteers, and turns out hundreds of thousands of voters; many of them have never participated in the political process before. As a result, the political organization he puts together is instrumental in electing city councilmembers, state legislators, members of Congress, mayors of Los Angeles, Speakers of the assembly (including the first two Latinos, Cruz Bustamante and Antonio Villaraigosa), and governors of California. He does all of this in large part by energizing and involving hotel workers, janitors, and other

Latino immigrant union members, some of whom aren't even citizens—and some of whom aren't even legal residents.

Miguel is still careful about minding the store at the labor federation by mastering the intricacies of per capita politics inside organized labor. Delegates to the county federation selected by affiliated local unions elect Miguel. Each local sends delegates to the labor federation based on the number of members for whom it pays per capita, essentially membership dues that go to operate the organization.

One morning I show up at 7 a.m. at the county federation's office near MacArthur Park. It's the day after municipal elections and I'm taking part in a seminar for the federation's political action committee. I walk upstairs to Miguel's second-floor office. Despite his late hours the night before, Miguel is there bright and early sitting behind his paper-strewn desk. "What the hell are you doing here so early?" I ask.

"Well, you gotta stay on top of per capita politics," he responds. In other words, he is busy analyzing which local unions send how many people to work on which election campaigns and how much money each one contributes to the county federation's political pot—all based on the commitments they make before the election. "I gotta stay on top of the enemy," he adds. Some unions are not happy with Miguel's focus on increasing organizational efforts and political activism among Latinos. "But fuck them. I gotta strengthen my base."

To that end, when the Metropolitan Transportation Authority bus drivers and mechanics—many of them are black—go out on strike, Miguel is with them and puts L.A. Labor's power squarely behind their cause. He sits in on and participates in day-and-night negotiations and engineers a settlement of their union contract. From that point on, those workers and their unions are among his biggest allies.

The kind of political clout Miguel builds during his nine years heading the federation translates into genuine influence at City Hall. It's considered a coup for a city councilmember who is carrying an issue with a direct or indirect impact on labor to get Miguel to show up in the city council chambers when it comes up for a vote. Sometimes he doesn't even get up to testify. He just sits in the first or second row of the ornate chambers and crosses his arms. Over a short period of time, every member of the council leaves the dais and comes up to Miguel to shake his hand and pay his or her respects. Lobbyists for the Chamber of Commerce and other business interests who are frequently on the other side of the matter watch and shake their heads in frustration knowing they are going to lose. Miguel is one of a kind because he understands politics—labor and otherwise—and sees the big picture.

After his untimely death from a heart attack at the young age of 51 in 2005, Miguel's wife, Maria Elena Durazo, who maintains the same kind of proactive and progressive leadership for the county federation, eventually follows him into the office.

The genesis of L.A.'s pioneering living wage ordinance is the struggle by hotel workers belonging to Local 11. Prior to Miguel and Maria Elena taking over that union, the Latino and immigrant hotel workers who fill most of the lower-paying jobs lag behind in pay and benefits and are often subjected to abusive working conditions by management. The old guard Anglo union leadership is too cozy with the hotel and restaurant industry, which is a key reason Maria Elena gets elected. I'm close to her because I show up at most of the strikes and demonstrations to picket and support the workers.

Poor and immigrant workers, mostly Latinos and blacks, are coming to dominate the private sector, mostly service workforce in L.A. Our city is considered one of the most diverse and progressive places in the country. So how can we expect the city to prosper and continue moving forward when we leave behind large sections of the workforce that make up the working poor? This dilemma will only worsen given the changing demographics that are reshaping L.A. Some remedy is needed.

By the 1990s, a coalition is formed, led by Local 11 and its leader, Maria Elena Durazo, of labor, clergy, civil rights, and community groups. A study is conducted to determine how much a hotel worker needs to earn per hour to have a relatively good chance of enjoying a decent standard of living in L.A. The coalition dedicates itself to enacting a city ordinance establishing this living wage covering hotel and service workers. At the time, a living wage is pegged several dollars above the state minimum wage if the employees get health benefits. If they don't, the living wage is higher to help workers pay for their own coverage.

Author of the ordinance is Councilmember Jackie Goldberg, a former teacher, school board member, and assemblymember who comes out of United Teachers of Los Angeles, the local teachers union. Her 13th Council District is just west of my district. Jackie's entire education and political history is one of progressive activism, and she is viewed as a very liberal person. She takes up the living wage ordinance early. Her problem is some of her colleagues on the council see her as a lightning rod for antibusiness sentiment. That's a dilemma confronting labor as it tries to pass the ordinance. It takes several years for it to become viable because of stiff opposition from large, wealthy, and well-organized groups that include the hotel and food service industries and the Chamber of Commerce.

Jackie and I always get along. I admire and respect her. There are some councilmembers I have relationships with who are not initially supporting the proposal. Some are captives of business interests. Overcoming the opposition involves changing how we sell the measure and how we go after votes on the council. Jackie, Maria Elena, and I develop strategies to get at individual members, to pick up the votes necessary for the ordinance to become law. It is a long, drawn-out fight. We get certain groups to lobby specific councilmembers. I pigeonhole and cajole members myself. The expanding influence of L.A. Labor under Miguel's stewardship also widens the sphere of influence unions can exert.

One big roadblock remains: The new mayor needs to sign the ordinance in order for it to go into effect. Dick Riordan campaigns for election on a platform of bringing back business to L.A. He is not perceived as naturally friendly to labor, and especially to something called a living wage ordinance. I use what I know of the mayor's own predilections to our advantage. I know he cares deeply about kids, particularly poor and Latino kids. After the ordinance passes the council, my job is selling the mayor on signing the measure. I do it through guilt and Dick Riordan's natural inclination to be sympathetic to the working poor. I get the mayor to sign it.

A short time later another living wage ordinance is proposed covering hotel workers around LAX. I also help push it through the council. When the time comes to figure out how to get the mayor to approve it, Local 11, which Maria Elena heads, is having a big event for the LAX Living Wage plan. She asks for my help in getting Riordan to attend. After thinking about it, I tell Maria Elena to turn the union meeting into a family affair and to make it clear that this is not just a union issue. Whenever the mayor is going to meet with union members about the ordinance, I tell Maria Elena to make sure he sees lots of kids whose lives will be improved because their parents get paid a living wage. I propose that she have the kids greet the mayor when he arrives, tell him their mothers need to make a little bit more money to buy them food, and then have the children escort him into the Local 11 union hall. That way, when Dick begins to deliberate on the question he won't be looking at the ordinance as just involving workers and union members; he will translate it into children and families. I know Dick Riordan will never turn against kids and their needs. By the time the mayor walks into the meeting, he will already be on the union's side, I argue.

Maria Elena sets up the meeting so there are lots of kids front and center. The mayor shows up and spends some time talking and playing with the kids before they escort him into the actual session with their parents. There, he meets with union members and leaders, and then announces his support for the LAX Living Wage ordinance. Maria Elena later tells me she can't believe how well it works.

That's the kind of relationship—and access—I have with the mayor while he and I are in office together. Dick knows I will never embarrass him. But that doesn't mean I will always support him either. There are times when we have different ideas, such as when it comes to budget matters and other things. But usually I can ultimately win him over to support what I believe in.

Before I decide not to run for reelection in 1999, for a final four years under the city-enacted term limits law, Miguel Contreras comes by my office at City Hall. He describes me as L.A. Labor's go-to guy when they really need help and sees me as his biggest ally. "I believe in staying true to my friends," he says. "If you decide to run for reelection, you'll be our number one priority. That means money, troops, everything. You are number one for us."

Although Mayor Richard Riordan is a Republican, he and Richard Alatorre develop a strong personal bond and Richard becomes part of the mayor's inner circle.

Richard works with Los Angeles hotel workers union leader Maria Elena Durazo to convince Mayor Riordan to support a living wage ordinance benefiting LAX-area hotel workers by appealing to the mayor's love for children.

"The biggest thing I can say about Richard is he ended up leaving city service after having done a great deal for it," Hillary Norton says. "L.A. lost a real champion for workers and poor people everywhere."

Mayor Riordan and I also get together to enact fundamental reform of the city's business taxes. Dick Riordan is convinced that during Tom Bradley's two-decade tenure at City Hall, L.A. loses its competitive edge in business. We are viewed as too costly a place to do business. Dick runs for mayor on the platform of a businessman and venture capitalist who is going to make L.A. more business friendly. Once in office he establishes a business and economic development team and a city office to expedite the processing of permits for new businesses wanting to locate or expand in the city. One thing that makes it difficult to attract new businesses is the business tax structure we have.

With the existing tax structure, the amount of city taxes that companies pay is based on their gross receipts of volume sales. If you make a product and it sells for $50, you pay city taxes based on the $50, even if it cost you $46 to produce the product. Even if you only make a profit of $4, you still pay city taxes on the full $50. There are lots of nearby cities, including those in L.A. County, with tax structures more favorable to local businesses. They are starting to lure companies away from the city of L.A. Dick and I realize this unfair tax system is why a large number of operations are not locating or expanding operations in L.A. The proposal to change the system comes out of the mayor's office of economic development. I champion it on the council with support from the Chamber of Commerce and the Valley Industry and Commerce Association.

You'd think everyone would be for the tax reforms. But it takes setting up a council advisory committee that comes up with recommendations. Lengthy hearings are held on a package of business reforms that are designed as inducements to get more businesses into the city. The centerpiece, my measure, is passed by the council and signed by the mayor.

The reforms reduce some categories of business taxes. They also offer some incentives such as no business taxes on new businesses. There is a business tax amnesty program for companies that owe back taxes. They can come forward and pay the taxes owed without having to fork over penalties. This brings in much-needed new revenue.

Overall, these changes attract a significant number of businesses to the city. Some are new. Others are companies returning to L.A. because of the more favorable tax structure and improved business climate.

I champion economic development strategies to revitalize neighborhood commercial strips in Boyle Heights, Highland Park, and Eagle Rock. In the case of the last two areas, economic development helps strengthen communities where businesses coexist next to lots of single-family residences.

The major commercial and retail core of Eagle Rock runs along Colorado Boulevard. When I first come into office, many people complain about the lack of local places to go out to shop and eat, and about the proliferation of body and fender shops and other less desirable businesses that don't compliment what at one time is seen by long-time residents as a nice middle-class single-family, homeowner-based community.

How do you revitalize it? Bring in more businesses that can satisfy the needs and desires of the residents? It's more difficult than most people think. First, you have to identify what the community wants and needs—and the residents' tolerance level for the businesses you're going to try to recruit. Businesses will not come in if there is no market for what they are selling. I discover there is sometimes a gap between what people say they need and what they are willing to patronize.

The reality of what is feasible sometimes frustrates community desires. Everybody in Eagle Rock says they want to attract an upscale Nordstrom's department store, which is a big retailer requiring a lot of space. The fact remains that there is no appropriate parcel to build a Nordstrom's store, which usually requires a mall or a very large piece of property—as well as market surveys justifying that or any other big retail chain. What we do have on Colorado Boulevard is a small mall with limited offerings near the California State Route 2 freeway. We don't have a location with a big enough footprint or enough space for parking and other amenities to support a full-sized mall. That's because of a lack of space and because many of the mostly single-family houses are built right up to Colorado Boulevard, which is a secondary highway with three lanes going in either direction. The only place to put in a new or expanded mall is to build it up to the north or south sides of the street. You'd have to take out a lot of homes to make room, which no one supports.

There's also the concern by residents to keep the boulevard pedestrian friendly. Communities like Eagle Rock and Highland Park have one thing in common: There is never enough parking. If you take out a permit to build a new restaurant that's expected to handle a certain number of patrons, it's supposed to also accommodate a set number of parking spaces. There is rarely room to be found, which is still a problem.

What we come up with in the mid-1980s is an interim control ordinance for Eagle Rock prohibiting the siting of certain types of businesses that are viewed as inconsistent with the neighborhood plan. They include more gas stations, body and fender repair shops—anything that doesn't accommodate the type of community people want to see. We also want to make Colorado Boulevard pedestrian friendly. That limits the scope of the type of businesses we can recruit.

I get a Target department store to move into Eagle Rock at the shopping center near the 2 freeway after a theater and another enterprise go out of business, freeing up room for the popular and reasonably priced retail chain. It is not as prestigious as Nordstrom's, but the Target is a godsend because it meets the everyday needs of the people who live around it and in outlying communities that act as feeders to the shopping center.

We don't end up getting any other big time retailers or department stores. Instead, independent boutique shops and restaurants crop up along the boulevard. They draw in nearby residents and people from adjoining communities who are attracted to Eagle Rock because of its unique nature. Eagle Rock boasts a lot of period Craftsmen homes and California Bungalows as well as other single-family residences and some apartment complexes. This is not suburban-style tract housing.

The community is changing, along with the demographics of L.A. itself, as new generations of successful and professional young people are either moving back to where they grow up or are moving in because the neighborhood is attractive, a nice place to raise a family and because it offers good shopping and dining amenities.

We begin that revitalization of Eagle Rock in 1986 and '87, and it continues today.

Part of that revitalization involves a small shut down public library on Colorado Boulevard, built in the early 1900s. Starting during Art Snyder's reign as councilmember and continuing into my tenure, there is discussion in the community as to what should be done with the building. It could reopen as a library, but a newer and bigger library has been built not far away. Many ideas are put forward. It seems every organization in Eagle Rock wants a piece of it, but none can afford the upkeep that is required. Using friendly persuasion and moving people away from their own provincial interests, I help create consensus for a cultural center using monies I obtain for seismic reinforcement of city-owned structures after the '94 earthquake. I get some of those funds earmarked for what becomes the Eagle Rock Cultural Center. The concept starts out as a community center and ends up being a cultural center in a beautifully restored building reflecting the character of Eagle Rock run by a nonprofit organization that is responsible for keeping the building up, maintaining it, and the like. The renovations are paid for entirely out of funds from a citywide bond act I get passed. Everything happens there, from performing plays to music, art, exhibits, and dance. The local Eagle Rock Historical Society has offices there. There's also multipurpose space. The place is active and vibrant.

A similar transformation of an historic building takes place in nearby Highland Park. It's an old two-story brick police jail that for years serves as the Northeast substation of the LAPD. Built in the 1920s, it is famous, having been featured in numerous films and television series, and is given an historical landmark designation by the city of L.A. When a new police station opens in Northeast L.A., I inherit what is now an abandoned eyesore. The outside is occasionally used as a filming location, but there is considerable debate over what to do with it now. We can't demolish it because it is an historical landmark. We have to work with the existing structure. There are limited options.

The Highland Park Historical Society wants to use it. There is a developer's proposal for a multi-use facility—housing above and commercial and retail downstairs on the street level. Other people have different ideas. During tough economic times we look at selling the property to raise money for the city. Everyone is interested in doing something, but no one can put up the money to seismically reinforce it so it can be occupied for public use.

After working with and getting mixed signals from the community one thing stands out: It is an old police station. Around this time the Los Angeles Police Historical Society is formed. Its leaders get the idea of making the old station their home. That's a great idea, but the society doesn't have any money. It just wants to move into the place. That can't happen because it is declared unsafe in the event of an earthquake.

As chair of the council's Public Safety Committee and a member of the Budget and Finance Committee, I work to draft a motion and ordinance to put before the citywide electorate a measure for the seismic reinforcement of city-owned facilities. The measure includes two facilities that are important to me: the Eagle Rock Cultural Center and the old police station in Highland Park that will become headquarters for the L.A. Police Historical Society. The voters pass it, and more than $1 million goes to reinforce and renovate the former police station.

We don't put out a request for proposal, or RFP, allowing anyone to submit a bid to take over the building once the renovation is completed. If we do an RFP, it'll go to the highest bidder; the police historical society can't effectively compete and won't get the place. So I carry another motion before the city council to give the historical society a 50-year lease of the facility that becomes known as the L.A. Police Historical Society Building.

It is now a museum for the LAPD. There are period police cars, old police uniforms, badges, and guns. Still remaining is a replica of the old jail holding suspects arrested in Northeast L.A. It houses books and manuscripts describing the history of the department. Visitors and scholars visit. It is still used as a site for TV shows and major motion pictures, including parts of the inside that are restored to look as they did when the station was first built, including the reception and booking areas, and detective offices. Area residents use the community rooms. The building is still controlled by the historical society, which holds annual fundraisers to support upkeep.

When he is on the council, Art Snyder is an old-fashioned, very pro-development guy—at least for that part of the city outside of Eagle Rock. Most Eagle Rockers are slow-growthers. The rest of my district is less so.

Eagle Rock is still mostly single family. As you move south in the 14th District, more apartments are built, placing pressure on single-family housing. Monterey Hills, a little to the east of Highland Park, is a redevelopment community with condos and town houses and a lot of white-collar workers. Next door is El Sereno, once a lower middle-class single-family neighborhood with blue-collar Anglo and Latino workers that is impacted by growth and apartment units. Now gangs and poverty beset it. Then there is Boyle Heights at the far southern end of the district, bursting from the seams with single-family residences chopped up into four-plexes and five-plexes and more—whatever the market will bear—and a spattering of apartment houses. Finally, there is downtown L.A., once marked by skid-row hotels and now turning into a 24-hour city with lofts and apartments for lovers of what is called the New Urbanism.

Everyone in Eagle Rock resists the growth they think threatens their lifestyle. For almost everyone else in the 14th District change represents an improvement because they genuinely need new development. El Sereno, for example, could greatly benefit from new housing stock because so much of what exists is old and in need of upgrading.

"Because the district is an amalgam, very dense in the south and almost semi-rural in the north, Richard encourages multifamily, market rate, and workforce housing in his district," Robin Kramer says. "Multifamily housing is not seen at the time as an attractive thing. There is a push in other parts of the city to disallow multifamily rental projects in favor of ownership housing. Richard thought multifamily was an important part of the housing mix, especially for working people."

I believe if there are no jobs, there is no future. If there is no affordable place for working people to live in a community, where do they go? Decent workforce housing for the working-class people who populate much of my district is a necessity. On the other hand, developers can't just have a free hand. Land use is the bread and butter of city government. The perception of overdevelopment is a huge problem in some parts of the city like the valley and the Westside. I understand those who have the luxury of being able to say, "We don't want any more in our community because it's going to reduce the quality of life as we know it." God bless people who have that problem. My problem, and the problem in so many other parts of L.A. during that time, is there isn't enough economic investment to replace substandard housing people are forced to live in. Proposition U is a citywide slow-growth measure proposed by Zev Yaroslavsky and Westside interests to cut allowable development in half. I oppose it. It's a fight I have with Zev. How can he and people from his side of town impose their will on others who live under very different circumstances?

(Another measure where I differ from Zev and Westside residents in the 1980s is over offshore oil drilling. Backed by business tycoon Armand Hammer, who is represented by prominent attorney and Democratic activist Mickey Kantor, it would allow drilling off Santa Monica. I'm one of the few who support it. I am sensitive to the concerns of environmentalists about potential pollution of the ocean and the shoreline. I vote against allowing oil drilling off California's Central Coast when I'm in the legislature. But these wells are already there. And there is a need for exploration at the time. It's also a matter of basic economics: There is a need for more jobs that come from drilling, and it can be a source of employment for people in my community. I'm offended by the sensational ads aired against the proposal, which claim the mountains will fall down and houses will be lost. It is a cleverly run campaign that promotes mass hysteria insulting Hammer, a great citizen and philanthropist.)

Much of the Eastside is neglected; much too little economic development and a scarcity of affordable housing takes place in recent years. Still, there's even resistance to good quality affordable housing in the southern parts of the 14th District where residents ask, "Why do you want to dump more poor people into communities that are overpopulated and already full of poor people?" It's a difficult balance.

When developers of affordable housing ask me to support their projects in my district, I make them go out into the community and organize indigenous support. "You get that support and I'll give you support from my office with the city," I promise. Sometimes it works. In some areas where I know there is nothing but opposition to affordable housing proposals and I know the only chance is reaching accommodation with existing residents, I get the developers to provide extra amenities to make their projects more attractive. There are times when I just have to steam-roll over the objections of some residents because the affordable housing is so desperately needed and those neighborhoods are plagued by substandard conditions. Any time you provide more good housing stock, you relieve some of the pressures that come from overpopulation and blight. That's my philosophy.

New multifamily housing is important because of the pressing need for it. In certain parts of my district, the strain of high density on the housing stock is such that something has to give. Immigrants are moving into anything they can find and afford in Boyle Heights. A new influx of Central and South American immigrants are coming into the Westlake area, creating a strain on scarce housing there.

With permission from the residents, I hold a news conference in Boyle Heights at the house owned by an absentee Latino landlord that is illegally subdivided too many times. We let the press see the substandard and miserable conditions—with deplorable plumbing, lack of sanitation, and infestation by rats. We want to get people in L.A. to understand the need to invest in housing stock and build more quality housing to relieve these overcrowded conditions. And it is an effort to stem the anti-multifamily sentiment that is increasingly popular in better off parts of the city.

I'm not antigrowth in places like Boyle Heights and Lincoln Heights where overcrowding and substandard housing are realities. Given the state of the contemporary housing market, a good developer can make affordable housing look like market-rate housing. You can demand the developer include specific amenities and architectural features that make the multifamily communities much more attractive and livable, which is my big thing. They can also make sure the development meets the needs of large families, which means larger units and higher bedroom counts. It also means places where kids can breathe and enjoy open spaces and safe areas to play. It can be more profitable for developers to build more one-bedroom apartments than three-bedroom apartments. Many of them don't care who rents them as long as they collect rents. All these are issues a councilmember has a duty to address through zoning and when project proposals in his or her district move through the city entitlement process. Ignoring these concerns is how barrios and ghettos and blight are eventually created.

I work to get the city to recognize the urgent need for affordable housing and to balance growth with the pressure on communities that growth creates. For example, you don't want to concentrate all the apartment complexes in one area, even though many neighborhood residents sternly resist any additional multi-family rental housing going up anywhere near them.

My district, especially Boyle Heights, has more than its share of large public housing projects, seven in all, including the oldest in the city. One, Wyvern Wood, is privately owned but the equivalent of public housing. Too many people think the only people who live there want to live there. They are all seen as welfare cheats and the like.

"As a councilmember, Richard is attentive to the residents of those projects," Robin says. "He knew what they grew up with, the generations who lived there." Most of the people who reside in these projects aren't there out of choice. That's the only housing they can afford. But many times they have to live under the worst conditions such as overcrowding, crime, and inattention on the part of the owners. The public projects are subsidized by the federal government, but the city housing authority manages them, and too often does not do an adequate job of repairing and keeping up the premises. Once on the council, I appreciate how the people who live in the projects are misunderstood. They don't live there for free, even if they pay less in rent than residents of nonpublic housing. I also marvel how so many people I know who come out of the projects go on to become good, productive citizens—successful lawyers, doctors, educators, government employees, and even athletic directors for major universities.

These residents have to struggle. How many people because of economic circumstances lose their homes to foreclosure and end up in public housing? How many other people can't appreciate how difficult it is to find an affordable place to live that is fitting for their children? Public housing residents ask very little of their government that owns and manages where they live. They want what any other family wants: A decent and safe place they can afford to call home to raise their loved ones. As with any circle of people, there are those in public housing who violate the law. But most residents I meet are very humble, caring people who want nothing more than for their government to do its job. I can do very little over the grievances of a resident who pays rent to a private landlord. But I can do something when city government is doing a piss poor job of keeping our public housing stock viable—a job that we the taxpayers pay it to do.

I decide at the beginning of my council service to do something about improving the physical rehabilitation and providing additional human services to all the public housing projects in my district. It all starts during Christmas 1985, my first year as a councilmember. The year after the 1984 Olympics in Los Angeles, Paul Gonzales, the Olympic champion from Boyle Heights, decides to do a Christmas party in one of the parks in my district, Costello Park, named for half of the Abbot and Costello comedy team. It's located between two big housing projects, Estrada Court and Wyven Wood.

I'm invited to the party. There is always such a focus on Christmas in poor Latino communities, even though many parents have so little to give their kids during the holiday season. I'm not at Costello Park for more than half an hour when, because so many kids show up, the organizers run out of toys. It's heartbreaking when the kids are told there are no more toys. I never want to see that happen as long as I'm in public life and can do something about it.

That's when I establish the Feliz Navidad project. We stage our first party in Ramona Gardens, one of the largest public housing projects in Northeast L.A., and among the oldest. It's also one of the most crime-ridden, controlled by a particular gang and known as a spawning ground for the Mexican Mafia. I raise all the money, making sure there are enough presents for every kid who is registered and shows up to the event that is held in the project gym. We transform the gym into a winter wonderland. We spread real snow outside—something many of the children have never seen before. There are plenty of Christmas trees with bright lights; the whole place is festively decorated. There are plenty of toys and food, and games for the kids to play. We give away Christmas baskets with food to the parents. It is all privately financed from money I raise. We spend $30,000 to $40,000 for this first Christmas celebration.

Word about the success of the Feliz Navidad project spreads. The second week of January I am at a different housing project in my district and the parents there want to know why I'm not organizing the same kind of affair for their kids. By now, I plan to arrange for a similar party in a different housing project each year until they are all covered. So I promise these parents to do the party the following Christmas in their project. Rather than just do one party in one project annually, I decide to stage the events in each of the housing projects every year. We do that from 1987, until I leave office in 1999. We raise $150,000, sometimes more, to organize all of the projects each year. Altogether, 30,000 kids are taking part each December, sometimes more, sometimes less. Every resident from one of the housing projects who registers is assured of receiving toys and food or whatever we are giving away. We're fortunate to raise the money from good sponsors I recruit, including Mattel Toys, large construction companies, public utilities, and local businesses. We encourage the givers to come and see where their money is going. Once they show up to one of them, they are contributors from that point on. Organizing the parties is a big undertaking that takes place over a period of many weeks and months. I hire Eventfully Yours, an event planning company run by Angie Vasquez, whom I later marry, to both raise the money and put on the events together with help from my council staff.

The kids are grateful, as are most of their parents. Everybody who is part of putting on the events feels good too. Feliz Navidad becomes a model for other public housing projects. Other councilmembers try to replicate them in their districts.

I'm There to Do More Than Just Take Up Space 375

Big annual "Feliz Navidad" Christmas parties Richard organizes for children in his district's public housing projects become a model across the city.

"I went to the first one Richard put on during Christmas, and I'm Jewish," says Robin Kramer. "It's worth all the energy and effort that takes place over the whole year when you see people start to line up at 5 a.m. because they're worried they won't get in or there won't be enough stuff. [The parties] are a gesture of caring and respect."

The Adelante Eastside Area, a community redevelopment area and enterprise zone, is established in the south of my district through the city's Community Redevelopment Agency (CRA) as a result of a campaign my office and I lead. It covers a large part of Boyle Heights, especially the old Sears site at Eighth and Soto streets. It also includes Lincoln Heights and goes up to the borders of El Sereno and the city of Alhambra. I know the designation will create new economic opportunity for investing in the light industrial base of these communities and make additional funds available for affordable housing over a long period of time. My office does the study that leads to the formation of the redevelopment area.

CRA is the city redevelopment agency set up under state law. After Jerry Brown becomes governor for the second time in 2011, he abolishes local redevelopment agencies and uses their funding to help him fix the state budget mess.

But at that time, instead of sending property and other locally collected taxes to local government, the money goes into a pot of funds that is used to invest in communities by promoting affordable housing and economic development in disadvantaged neighborhoods. The tax increment financing is used for infrastructure improvements such as fixing sidewalks and streets, and beginning to extend the garment district from downtown into Boyle Heights, with its easy access to transportation from adjacent freeways and railroad yards.

Three major clothing manufacturing companies move in there. The University of Southern California invests tens of millions of dollars in a biotech center near the County-USC hospital in Lincoln Heights. New markets open up in small- and medium-sized strip malls. The light rail line, the gold line, connects Boyle Heights with downtown and is being built into East L.A. Over time, you will see development of mixed-use—housing, commercial, and retail—around the light rail stations.

"The amount of affordable housing built or upgraded in Richard's district during his tenure was huge," says Hillary Norton. "It happened because he was good at helping to get federal money for low-income communities. He also went back to work his old contacts at the legislature in Sacramento. And he had talented staff. Robin Kramer, his first chief of staff, is a guru of public policy to this day. Richard attracted people who really know how to get things done beyond Richard himself. He put together a very hard working staff that was constantly looking for avenues to improve the community. It was also important that a lot of his staff members lived in the district they served."

I carefully create the Adelante Eastside Area in a way that residents don't have to worry about eminent domain being imposed on them. Many of my constituents hate eminent domain because of their experience with Chavez Ravine, which at one time is made up of three historic Chicano communities—La Loma, Palo Verde, and Bishop. The area consists of small single-family homes built up on hillsides just northwest of downtown. The city uses eminent domain to buy the properties from the owners in the early 1950s, promising to use the land for a big affordable public housing project in addition to playgrounds and schools. The city later hands over the land to the O'Malley family, owners of the recently arrived Los Angeles Dodgers baseball team, as the home for the brand-new Dodger Stadium.

Some residents hold out in protest against the deal during a 10-year fight to stay in their homes. It becomes known as the Battle of Chavez Ravine. The Community Service Organization, the main Latino civil rights group in L.A. in the 1950s and '60s under the leadership of Cesar Chavez, helps lead the battle. The residents end up losing. Cesar refuses for the rest of his life to attend baseball games at Dodger Stadium because of the bitterness that lingers even years after the dispute. Typical of those with long memories who are thrown out of Chavez Ravine is Lou Santillan Sr. When asked where he is born, Lou always says, "On third base." Dodger Stadium forever lives as one of the low points of the Chicano experience in L.A. because of the forced mass removal of people in

Elysian Park who purchase, invest, and live in a beautiful community they call home. An entire community is cleaned out with evicted residents largely left to fend for themselves. They move to different parts of L.A., including Lincoln Heights or the San Gabriel Valley, but the words eminent domain are two of the dirtiest words in the vocabulary of a certain generation of Chicanos when it comes to the promised construction of multifamily housing.

That's why many Latinos look so askance at eminent domain. What happens to Chavez Ravine is why when anybody hears the words eminent domain, they think one thing: They're trying to take something away from us.

So I assure the existing residents in and around the Adelante Eastside Area that we aren't interested in taking their homes from them. From the beginning, I take the threat of eminent domain off the table by exempting residential areas from the possibility. We draw the boundary lines for the area so it almost only includes places that can benefit from the infusion of tax increment, enterprise zone, and other government financing for business improvements and economic development—including light industrial and biotechnical development and improvements to retail and commercial enterprises—as well as affordable housing.

It is a long and involved process. First, a study is done on the viability of the area. The results are analyzed to see if the area qualifies as "blighted." The study and the CRA determine it to be a good candidate for redevelopment. Then the council approves the Adelante Eastside Area in the late 1990s.

The tragedy since I leave office is we don't see anyone there long enough to do anything more of note with the Adelante Eastside Area. At one point my dream is to develop a regional shopping center at the site of the old Sears and Roebuck retail store, the oldest Sears site and at one time its largest grossing location. It can include property from the L.A. River coming east to about a block east of Soto Street and covering two or three blocks on the north and south sides of Soto. I seek to overcome the conventional wisdom among developers that poor areas such as Boyle Heights are not worth investing in. The study my office does to set up the Adelante Eastside Area proves that Mexicans who live there spend a disproportionate amount of their incomes on goods and services. I start working on this dream in 1985, until I leave office in the late 1990s. It can happen, but it needs someone to make it a reality.

More effective use of the redevelopment area can easily be made in the future. But it's there nevertheless and a viable tool to encourage economic growth and new affordable housing.

Mariachi Plaza is another project contributing to economic development in Boyle Heights. I remember it as a kid being raised in Boyle Heights as an historical gathering place in the community for mariachi musicians. These are the day laborers of the Mexican music world. Many immigrants from Mexico live in the neighborhood. The open plaza with a bandstand in the middle of it is where musicians wait around all day in the hopes of being hired, often for bargain prices, to play as a band or trio at *quincenerias*, christenings, birthdays, anniversaries, weddings, parties, or any social gathering. It becomes known as the mariachi

Remembering Mariachi Plaza in Boyle Heights as a kid growing up, Richard fosters a campaign to restore and improve the L.A. landmark that inspires an annual mariachi festival.

hub of the Eastside. But it's rundown and in need of renovation and upgrading. Across the street are little stands selling tacos and other ethnic food.

The plaza is selected as a stop on the gold line light rail system heading east from downtown through Boyle Heights that I am overseeing as chair of the Metropolitan Transportation Authority.

The idea for remodeling the plaza comes from one of my deputies who is responsible for cultural events. Henry Gonzales attends Catholic high school in Glassell Park and then USC before working for the Olympic Organizing Committee than puts on the '84 L.A. Olympics. He campaigns for me during my city council race the following year as a Hoover Vacuum Cleaner salesman, a term my political consultant, Richie Ross, coins for the team of young people whose full-time job is going door to door with big binders, like Jehovah Witnesses. Except instead of converting people to God, they use the binders, which are all about me, to convert voters to the second best: Making Richard Alatorre a city councilmember. Henry has an extremely creative mind for media opportunities and other things. As a result of his Olympics involvement, he has connections with a wide variety of contacts in Mexico and Central America.

Henry's family is from the state of Jalisco, Mexico, known for its culture and music. He proposes getting a kiosk built in Mexico and bringing it here. Henry gets the government of the state of Jalisco involved in building this elaborate structure with stairs using Mexican marble. It's big enough for good-sized mariachi bands to play before large audiences in the plaza. It is suitable as the centerpiece of the new gold line station going up besides the plaza and is modeled after Plaza Garibaldi in Mexico City and other plazas across Mexico where mariachi and other musicians perform and the community gathers to listen to them. The kiosk is built in Mexico and assembled here by skilled Mexican artisans who travel to Mariachi Plaza to finish their work. Other transportation-related improvements are made in the plaza and it attracts additional investments into the area.

The improvements spark a mariachi festival that is still staged annually. All this is testimony to the cultural and musical tradition known as mariachis.

Unfortunately, those responsible for maintaining the plaza do not have quite the same interest, and it experiences some problems with disrepair. It's still an L.A. landmark and residents come to hear performances.

Preserving the Breed Street Shul and preventing it from being demolished is a testament to the rich historic heritage of the Jewish community that once flourishes on the Eastside. Like synagogues in Europe, this one is named for the street in Boyle Heights it is on. The massive 1,100-seat Byzantine Revival-style structure is built in the 1920s when there are 60,000 or 70,000 Jews living in Boyle Heights, then predominantly Jewish but already with a strong mix of Latinos, white Russians, Japanese, other Asians, and some blacks. At one time 40 or 50 synagogues serve the Jewish population of Boyle Heights—along with bakeries, delicatessens, and a lot of other Jewish businesses.

Helen Chavez, Cesar's widow, remembers Jewish neighbors when they live from 1959 to 1962, at the corner of Folsom Street and North Fickett Street, near what is now the intersection of North Soto Street and Cesar Chavez Avenue. (Cesar moves from there to Delano in 1962, to begin what becomes the United Farm Workers of America.) An elderly Jewish lady who lives next door brings Jewish bread she bakes for the Chavez's eight small children. Helen, in turn, helps out the woman, who can't write, by penning letters to her son.

Over the decades, the Jewish community moves out, first to the Fairfax district and then to points west. By the time I get to City Hall, the Breed Street Shul is pretty much abandoned. There aren't enough Jews in the neighborhood to make up a *minyan*, the quorum of 10 Jewish men needed for religious services. The worst sin is for a synagogue to be converted into a church, which happens to many of them in that area. The rabbi who owns the synagogue pulls a permit to demolish it in the late 1980s. My council office gets a copy of the request for demolition. The Jewish Historical Society of Southern California also hears about it. It conducts bus tours of historic sites in L.A., of which this is one of the most important.

The historical society calls me, saying I can't let this happen. You can't believe how much attention and time we put into this project, first under Robin Kramer and later with Hillary Norton, to save that building. "Richard wasn't

Jewish and didn't understand the Orthodox rules, but he engaged other councilmembers, including Zev Yaroslavsky and Hal Bernson, who was bar mitzvahed there," Robin recalls.

It's a beautiful building. The inside is still beautiful even if it needs work. This is where they film Barbara Streisand in the movie "Yentl," about a young Jewish girl who falls in love with the son of a rabbi. Robin Kramer gets all the Jewish organizations involved. We call the rabbi who owns the building and tell him it's not going to be demolished. As a result of all this renewed interest, it is decided that the shul shouldn't just survive as a tourist bus stop. It should be kept alive and be used to continue to serve the needs of the current neighbors.

The bottom line is that the city takes over the property. It is fenced in. Ultimately, I lead an initiative that quit claims the city's ownership of the property to the Jewish Historical Society. Heavily damaged by the '94 Northridge earthquake, the building is in the process of being restored.

It is also nominated for the Save America's Treasures project that then-First Lady Hillary Clinton sets up to bring attention to preservation and restoration of some of the most important historical sites in the nation. The First Lady later comes out and appears at an event in front of the shul. It is being restored for use as a community center and is run by a nonprofit group, designed as a gathering place for people that will also preserve the Jewish history of the area. "There are a lot of Latinos who value that Jewish 'church,'" Robin says. "Because L.A. is so divided in many ways by race and class, here's a place that actualizes the idea of building bridges of understanding by preserving history and serving the current community, all at the same time."

It is real simple for me. I always say Boyle Heights serves as the true melting pot. It is the forerunner for communities of different ethnic origins that can peacefully coexist, learn from one another and be friends with one another.

I suppose word of our drive to save the Breed Street Shul gets around. I forever remember the invitation I get from this rabbi to address one of the biggest temples in the San Fernando Valley. I think this is a great opportunity, but what will I say? I figure some of the older members of the congregation may have been born and raised in Boyle Heights. My whole pitch is addressing the xenophobia that is taking place in the valley because of the tremendous demographic changes it is going through. Traditionally the valley is mostly white with some Mexicans. But now, in the eyes of many Anglos, Mexicans are overrunning the valley, and they are being blamed for every social ill—from crime to graffiti. I never expect to go to a synagogue in the valley, but they are inviting me; I'm not pushing myself on them.

I show up for Saturday services. The rabbi is a transplant recruited from Brooklyn, New York, a real lefty although he doesn't look it. They introduce me. I start out talking about diversity being the strength of this city, and all that crap. I ask a question of the audience: "How many of you grew up in Boyle

Richard champions the campaign that saves and restores the historic Breed Street Shul, an abandoned Jewish synagogue in Boyle Heights. First Lady Hillary Rodham Clinton later speaks at a ceremony in front of the shul.

Heights as I did?" A lot of older Jews raise their hands. This is my cue to talk about how we serve as the best example of how people—whether they are Russian Jews, Japanese, or Mexicans—can learn from one another, share our goods and services, and converse with each other. I ask for questions when I'm finished.

They start with the taco trucks and "Why do you people sell goods out on the street?"—and then it goes downhill from there to things like, "Why do you people all live like you do? Why is it that the young Mexican kids join gangs? Why is it when you have parties, they last until all hours of the night?"

It is the biggest awakening for me. I know honkies; they just want to send us back to Mexico. I know blacks; it's always a question of the haves versus the have-nots—with the have-nots fighting among each other. But I never expect to hear Jews spewing this shit. No sooner when one person finishes than another stands up. There are questions about graffiti and crime. "Those things never happened before [all the immigrants or Mexicans moved in] because we were a law-abiding community. You could walk around and play and not worry about our kids getting raped."

The rabbi listens to these questions, but doesn't allow me to answer. Finally, he speaks to his congregation: "I want you to know I didn't come here all the way from Brooklyn to oversee a bunch of bigots and racists like the ones I see in this room right now. I am embarrassed and insulted." The meeting is adjourned. He escorts me out.

The next Monday he calls to invite me back, this time to the services on the following Friday night. "I don't blame you if you refuse," he says. "But I guess I gave my congregation more credit than they deserve. I'm outraged. I'm insulted. I'm embarrassed. There aren't words to describe how I feel."

The place is full Friday night. The rabbi proceeds to shit all over the congregants: "Haven't you learned anything from history? Haven't your families that immigrated here told you what it was like when they came to this country? I don't know much about Boyle Heights. But why was it all right for us to open our little businesses, use the sidewalks to sell our goods and services there? Why was it okay for us to do it then and not for *'them'* to do it now? If anybody should understand, we should. We have been subjected to the Holocaust and we still live amongst bigots and anti-Semites. If this continues, I'm leaving. I will not stay here and oversee a congregation that is made up of this. I thought I taught you better."

He turns around to me: "Would you like to say something?"

I stand up and come to the podium: "To say I was surprised is probably an understatement. I really came here with a warm feeling because I always said the beauty of Boyle Heights was the experience of people who grew up in that area and who lived, congregated, went to school and played together, and learned from one another what it was like to be from another country or an oppressed ethnic or racial group and still be welcomed in that community. Yes, there were conflicts. But we were always big enough as a people to overcome them and never let them separate and divide us in the community of Boyle Heights. I learned a lot from the Jews and the Japanese. The city learned a lot from our common experiences. We are part of the fabric of this city.

"I grew up in the '40s and now we're in the '90s. But my God, just because you moved to the San Fernando Valley, do you who shared the same experience I did have no historical memory of what it was like to grow up in a city that was not initially yours but where eventually everyone welcomed you and where you have flourished? God bless all of you, the professionals, the lawyers, the doctors, and the entertainment figures. Why not give someone else the same chance you had?"

I get a standing ovation.

No wonder we still have problems with intolerance in this city, I think to myself. Because of that experience, I tell Robin Kramer, "I don't want this building [the restored Breed Street Shul] to just be a place where people come on tours during the weekends—to see how people once lived a long time ago. There's not a lot of Jews left in Boyle Heights. But this marvelous facility needs to be a place that is alive today and still services people." It takes a lot of money. It isn't a small undertaking. Work still remains to be done on it, but it is progressing.

Still another battle over preserving a community institution important to my district is rebuilding County-USC Hospital after it sustains extensive earthquake damage. The old hospital is still standing then, but it is no longer in use as a hospital because of seismic safety concerns and the high costs of renovation and upkeep. The county board of supervisors considers various options. One of them is no longer having the hospital in Lincoln Heights and dispersing the care it provides among other medical facilities around the county such as the Martin Luther King Jr. Hospital in South L.A., the Olive View-UCLA Medical Center in the San Fernando Valley, and perhaps building a satellite facility in Baldwin Park. People in my community want to build a new hospital at the County-USC site in Lincoln Heights with enough beds to meet the current and future health needs in that part of the county. So I work with the board of supervisors, including friends or former colleagues from the council and legislature: Gloria Molina, Zev Yaroslavsky, Yvonne Braithwaite Burke, and Mike Antonovich (who is a Republican, a former legislative colleague, and a fellow student when we both attend Cal State L.A.).

The fight goes on for a couple of years. Our initial goal is to have 950 beds, which we can justify. The issue is put out to study by the county and a new figure emerges due to the economic pinch local government is facing: 750 beds. I feel we can find the votes on the board to support it.

We pack the board of supervisors' chambers with supporters of the 750-bed proposal during a climatic and contentious board meeting. They range from representatives of the public and private sectors and the health community. Many step forward to testify, including me. I'm also working behind the scenes, speaking privately with Yaroslavsky, Burke, Antonovich, and Don Knabe, another Republican supervisor. I believe I've lined up a sufficient number of votes.

But internal political rancor wins the day. The board eventually approves a new hospital next to the old one in Lincoln Heights, but with less than 600 beds. The new hospital is at over capacity on the day it opens. Everyone now acknowledges that less than 600 beds is not sufficient and there are those working to add more capacity. But at least the new hospital stays in Lincoln Heights.

I tap my contacts in Sacramento for help on issues such as affordable housing, but I come to use my influence more and more at the state and national capitals on behalf of other city needs too. "Richard Alatorre was a formidable voice in those days in Sacramento," Robin Kramer says. "In those days under the old city charter, the responsibility for governmental relations was in the hands of the city council, not the mayor. So lobbyists representing L.A. in Sacramento and Washington, D.C. reported to John Ferraro, the council president, and the city legislative analyst. Under a new city charter enacted in 1998, these powers moved to the mayor's office. Richard had extensive legislative experience. He knew how policy worked. He knew the players at both the state and national levels. And he knew how to get things done. John Ferraro would turn to Richard to plan strategy. Richard could quickly figure out what was going on and how to proceed. He often went to Sacramento or made calls himself on behalf of the city. That was huge."

In order to function, city government is heavily dependent on both state and federal funding. L.A. needs Sacramento to understand its plight on issues like public safety and the local impact of state legislation. I learn while at the Capitol that the California League of Cities is frequently not the best advocate for the particular needs of Los Angeles. L.A. often has difficulty in moving its agenda forward because we're so large, which dictates the amount of resources we're entitled to. Smaller cities, both urban and rural, are very jealous of L.A.

I spend 14 years in the state assembly. When I arrive on the city council the Speaker happens to be Willie Brown, and he remains Speaker during most of my tenure on the council. The evolving leadership in both houses of the legislature is made up of people I serve with in Sacramento. I know them. The same thing applies in the nation's capital. I come to know many key members of Congress through my shepherding of assembly and congressional reapportionment in 1981, and because of my activism with the Democratic National Committee. I know and have relationships with many of the lawmakers who control decision-making affecting city issues.

Many times when there is a state concern or issue impacting the city of L.A. while I'm on the council, I simply call Willie Brown. "Willie, here's my problem," I begin. "It would help us if you could do A, B, or C." Very seldom does he turn me down if the request is at all possible, reasonable, and timely. Of course, on some occasions he checks it out, gets backs to me, and says, "The train has already left. I can't do anything about it."

I have great relationships in Washington with California U.S. Senators Alan Cranston, Pete Wilson, Dianne Feinstein, and Barbara Boxer. I know Wilson when he is an assemblymember and mayor of San Diego. He knows of my relationship with Willie. Pete Wilson is a moderate Republican next door to the U.S.-Mexico border. Back then he's decent on immigration. When the *migra*—the U.S. Immigration and Naturalization Service—raids businesses with lots of Latino employees, I call on him as a U.S. senator and he puts pressure on them.

We get along and he likes me, less so after 1994, when he decides to go the anti-immigrant route. But I call on him as a councilmember after he becomes governor in 1990.

One day out of the blue, then-U.S. Senator Wilson gives me a call at City Hall. "Do you have any needs?" he asks.

Well, it turns out that around this time tens of millions of federal dollars are being held by the U.S. Department of Housing and Urban Development's regional office in San Francisco, earmarked for Jordan Downs, an old housing project in the Watts section of South L.A. The money is supposed to be used to tear down Jordan Downs and rebuild it as low-income housing along with some for-sale units. But the city can't get a consensus on spending the funds because the community doesn't want to tear down the old project, being very suspect of government and fearing what will emerge will no longer be available for poor people.

The director of the city housing authority says L.A. is going to lose the federal funding. He asks if I know anyone within the Clinton administration or U.S. Senator Pete Wilson, to see if we can keep the money in L.A. and use it for public housing in Boyle Heights. I call Art Agnos, the former mayor of San Francisco and a one-time colleague of mine in the assembly; he's now western regional director for HUD, appointed by President Clinton. I also put a call into Pete Wilson. Wilson calls back first.

"Do you know Art Agnos?" Wilson asks.

"Yeah, I served with him in the assembly," I reply.

"Let Agnos know I support your efforts to keep the money in L.A., and not have it redirected somewhere else." I talk with Art and he says okay.

That's how we get the first installment of funding to tear down the aging Pico Gardens public housing project in Boyle Heights and replace it with affordable new rental housing and for-sale town houses for first-time homebuyers.

I do a lot of work in Washington, D.C. while serving as chairman of the MTA. Sometimes I'm able to do work for the MTA as well as get something done for the city of L.A. when I'm in at the capital. L.A. has in-house lobbyists through the legislative analyst's office and MTA has its own contract lobbyists. But my D.C. trips work out well for me in getting money for transportation and other projects from the federal government. Just like I hit up Willie for state resources in Sacramento, I draw on my nearly decade and a half of service at the state Capitol where I develop relationships with future members of Congress like Maxine Waters, John Burton, Rick Lehman, Howard Berman, and Mel Levine. Most of them get their safe congressional districts when I head up legislative reapportionment in 1981. (In the case of Berman and his allies that's also the way Willie Brown gets rid of potential challenges to his speakership.) L.A. benefits from the relationships I build with them over the years.

What you discover about politics is so much of it is based on relationships. That's how it functions. Why does a Republican U.S. senator call me, a partisan Democrat from his state? I once have a reception for Pete Wilson over something he is doing for L.A. I arrange with a friend, a big business Republican, to get business people—all Republicans—to show up. Shit, it's perfect for me. My friend gets the crowd together at the function I sponsor at another friend's restaurant on Olvera Street. All I have to do is show up and introduce Wilson at the reception and he's forever grateful.

The state Capitol in Sacramento is a partisan environment. You understand where you can go and where you cannot go when it comes to certain issues and measures. Democrats vote one way and Republicans another. But only about 10 percent of the issues are partisan back then; the great majority of them are up for grabs. Individual commitments come into play at that point. I come from a place where all you have in life is your word as a man or a woman. It stems from my youth. My father ingrains it in me as a young man. You ask anyone who ever works with me or serves with me. If I give you my word, you can take it to the bank. I even learn that if you give your word and later find out you have made a mistake you can't undo it. If I can't get out of a commitment, then I have to live with it good, bad or indifferent. I can think of a number of examples of when that happens.

To me nothing is more sacred in the political arena than honoring your commitments. When people in Sacramento give their word on how they will vote, they usually keep it. There is some honor among lawmakers. Sometimes you have to remind them about their commitments, but with few exceptions, they will honor them.

When I arrive at the city council, a person's word doesn't seem as sacrosanct as it is where I come from. Some councilmembers laugh when you remind them about their commitments to vote in a certain way. They turn around and double cross you, saying something like, "Gee, I'm sorry, but commitments are made to be broken." I can never understand or respect that. A classic example is when Councilmember Joel Wachs gives me his word to vote for the mid-1980s reapportionment plan I piece together after bending over backwards to give him everything he can ever want in his district. That is the beginning of a rude awakening for me on the council. But they're not all like that.

Art Snyder, my predecessor in the 14th District, has a reputation for being a solid guy; he gives his word and you can take it to the bank. Another one is Hal Bernson, a Jewish councilmember and former clothier from the San Fernando Valley. I get along with Hal, a Republican, better than I do with many Democrats on the council. Hal prizes his days growing up in Boyle Heights. If he says "yes" on a vote, it means "yes"—even if I may have to remind him from time to time towards the end of his life because he is starting to forget things.

Relationships come into play in the late '80s, when I play a key role in passage of the city's landmark ethics law—a subject many people don't associate with me. Mayor Bradley has some ethics problems towards the end of his tenure. There arises in the community an effort spearheaded by Councilmember Mike Woo to create a vigorous city ethics ordinance. Geoff Cowan, then a UCLA law professor and later dean of the prestigious Annenberg School of Communications at USC, chairs it. A proposal is presented to the council so it can place the measure on the ballot since it would change the city charter to create a city ethics commission dealing with campaign contributions disclosure and transparency on conflicts of interest for elected and appointed city officials. It is meant to be tougher than the state Fair Political Practices Commission's rules and standards.

Hearings are held by this community group of good-government leaders to look at best practices. Then Mike Woo brings the proposal before the council.

I'm always a great believer in full disclosure and the like—let's disclose anything having to do with political money, contributions, and special interest involvement. You think special interest control of lawmakers and bodies like the legislature and city councils is bad? Lawmakers should only be concerned about representing the best interests of the people? Then so be it. Why not have public financing of election campaigns, which I support?

Woo, who in my eyes is Mr. Self-righteous, is carrying the proposal. He wants the ethics ordinance so badly because he plans to use it to run for mayor as Mr. Ethics. But the proposal is going nowhere fast because of the approach taken by the proponents. They characterize anyone who isn't supporting it as a crook. So if you're going to be accused of being a crook anyway, the hell with trying to work with the proposal. Enough members of the council find different reasons for opposing it. It doesn't have the votes.

I'm half listening to the debate on the proposed ethics law, reading the newspaper at my seat on the dais. People don't associate me with ethics laws and rules anyway, so what the heck. The proposal is destined to fail because its advocates, starting with Woo, don't do their work talking with councilmembers, trying to convince them to support it or working with them to come up with something that might get eight votes. Some members get tired of feeling beat up by other members over the ethics proposal in order to make the proponents look virtuous. That's why I'm reading the newspaper during the presentation by Woo.

Geoff Cowan comes up to Robin Kramer while Woo is presenting and says, "This is going to fail, isn't it?"

"Yep," she replies.

"We put so much effort into this and there's so much about it that's good," he adds. "Do you think Richard could be of help?"

"I don't know, let me ask him," she answers.

Geoff and I have a conversation. The council just finishes going through the drill of increasing our pay. It's not a pleasant experience for the body. What happens is everyone charges we're just lining our own pockets. There are newspaper editorials making us look bad. It's ugly. It will keep being a problem unless something is done.

"I have an idea for you," I tell Geoff: "Up until this time the city council has set its own salary on an annual basis. It's a terrible policy—bad for the council. It doesn't make sense. We get beat up over it. Why don't you make it part of the ethics package that salary setting for councilmembers just tracks that of whatever superior court judges receive—so when a judge gets a pay raise, so do city councilmembers? That way we're not voting for our own pay raises all the time. You never hear about it every time judges get a pay increase. People know there is a process for making that happen that is objective."

I tell Geoff that there are other people like me on the council who have no sources of independent wealth, no additional forms of income. Whatever I'm paid by the city is all the money I make. I choose to live that way. My kids are growing up. I have responsibilities. The cost of living is going up. While my council salary is higher than what the state legislature pays, I also don't have the tax-free per diem I get while working at the Capitol. Mike Woo is the son of a wealthy Chinese-American banker, a multimillionaire. It's nice for a kid who has everything growing up and no financial worries now to talk about the need for ethics. But I know there are enough councilmembers looking for a resolution of the salary-setting dilemma because we've just gone through it.

Geoff confesses to me that he and his group have never thought about my idea during the year of conversation they've had putting together their ethics plan. But after conferring with his colleagues, he comes back and says it makes sense. I know the ethics proponents want the other ethics provisions more than the salary tie. But we work out a deal.

So I go around, talk to my colleagues on the council and line up the votes to pass the amended ethnics proposal still being sponsored by Mike Woo. I pretty much scare Woo into supporting it too. To show you how spineless Mike Woo is, the next day he comes up to me and says he is under a lot of pressure because of the compromise deal I work out to save his ethics proposal. Therefore, he has to amend the ethics ordinance so councilmembers' salary hikes are tied to those of municipal court judges instead of superior court judges; municipal court judges get paid a little less. It passes anyway, imposing strict new ethics rules and assuring pay hikes for members of the council on a more regular basis—and with a lot less grief.

Later, the state decides to do away altogether with the distinction between superior and municipal court judges. So now councilmembers get paid the same as superior court judges.

The ethics law lets me exercise my strength. I'm at my best coming up with solutions that move things forward. Sometimes you can even solve two problems by combining them together.

"Richard had what I call the pain of knowing," as Hillary Norton puts it. "He'd say, 'In six months this will happen concerning this particular thing. In eight months this will happen.' He was almost always right. It was an advantage that comes with institutional knowledge and a lot of experience.

"That institutional knowledge was missing from the rookies who got elected to the city council when the first term-limited class arrived. Riordan put a term-limits measure on the citywide ballot. Members got new seats. The rookies came in knowing they only had eight years in office. 'I need to make a name for myself right away,' many of them felt. A lot of the other councilmembers who had been there for 16 or 20 years were recommending the rookies create broad-based consensus and work with their colleagues. A lot of the newbies said, 'No, I'll do it my way.' They'd run against the rest of the council to prove they were mavericks."

"Richard was the go-to guy for advice and strategy," says Robin Kramer. "People did it all the time. People Richard ran into at a restaurant or a grandma with a problem would hit him up on the street in his district."

I never think much about it at the time. People—and issues—come up to me inside and outside of City Hall. Some are constituents. Others aren't. When you're the only Mexican on the council—or later there are just two of us—people from all over come up to you to ask for advice and help. I never turn anyone down. Someone's having a hard time figuring out a resolution of a problem. "How can we move this forward?" they ask. I give it some thought and can usually come up with a resolution—or solve a problem someone's having with a city agency. It is similar to the experience I have when first serving at the state Capitol, as first chair of the Chicano (now Latino) Legislative Caucus, and throughout my tenure in the assembly. Chicanos from all over the state come to me with their grievances and problems. It so happens that a lot of these issues deal in the early days with access to employment or higher education.

"A lot of the men and women he taught at Terminal Island federal prison got out and came by to see him, asking for advice or help," Robin adds. "He would see them or take a phone call or if they wrote a letter, he would respond. And he'd do whatever he could to help." It dates back to the time I work in the federal correctional setting or when I go to speak at prisons throughout the state. A lot of constituents of mine are incarcerated; heck, half the kids I go to middle and high school with are in the joint at one time, it seems. Parents come to see me with requests involving their sons or daughters who are inside institutions. It doesn't matter if they're convicts or ex-cons. They deserve someone to care about them too.

Most of these people aren't from the district I represent in L.A. It's like everyone in California is a constituent. But if I have ideas, I freely give them. If they bring me grievances against a state or city agency, I go to bat for them. I thrive on it. Today, now that I'm out of office for well over a decade and a half, people still stop me and ask, "What do you think we can do?"

I good-naturedly tease Hillary for being a do-gooder who graduates from Wesleyan College and then the Kennedy School of Government at Harvard. I rib her that she has a master's degree in public policy. I have a postgraduate degree too, in public administration, from USC. "But Richard's master degree is in what it really takes to get things done. It's one thing to say, 'Here's what I want to achieve.' It's another thing to put it into practice. Richard had a sense that people don't just agree with you on things or give you anything. You have to look at what it's going to take to get things done in this world. I thought it very interesting that he actually took the time to try to make it clear to his staff what it takes to get things accomplished."

Hillary is still pretty young when she starts working for me. I can't expect her to be somebody who knows everything. But she has this incredible ability to catch on; she's quick on the uptake—and I like her. I spend a lot of time helping her to understand how I make decisions and when problems come up how I try resolving them and how I want her to resolve them. (I do the same thing with other people who work for me at City Hall and in my district.) Most of what I do in public life is trying to help people who don't have a voice or don't have anywhere to turn to get a resolution of their grievances. That's consistent with Hillary's do-gooder mentality.

She never fathoms why many people have this negative attitude about me when in her eyes I'm this wonderful human being. She gets what many others don't get about me. That's why she stays around as long as she does. That's why she never quits at the right time later on—when I'm facing a lot of controversy and serious distractions from a multitude of sources, including some of my own making. Someone tells Hillary her future is in jeopardy by staying with me then. She remains a loyal friend to this day. And I've been a loyal friend to her as well.

"It was very interesting to have this crusty, funny Latino guy who had seen it all working with me, when I'm this squirt young idealistic white woman," Hillary says. "That was also how Richard worked with Robin Kramer, his first chief of staff. But it was a great relationship because we the staff would be working hard on the policy but it was Richard who was the one who actually knew how to make it stick. To genuinely try to solve the ills of the city you had to have muscle behind what you were doing—not muscle as in being a thug; Richard wasn't like that even if he talked that way. He was really a pussycat in real life. It wasn't enough to have a good idea. You had to have the political will. Most importantly, Richard knew the Xs and the Os—he knew that in order to win you needed to have a game plan. He'd figure out what everyone needed and then made sure everyone got a little of what they wanted.

"Add to that the fact he is a good student of human nature."

"An example of how Richard judged human beings was when a top city official, brand new on the job, came into our office to introduce himself," Robin Kramer remembers. "Richard told me to come in with him for the 10-minute meeting. The guy was polished, wore a beautiful Armani suit, and had a winning manner about him. It was a quick, respectful meeting. The guy left. Richard asked me what I thought about him. It was only 10 minutes and it was hard to tell. 'Oh,' I said, 'he seems really nice and smart.'

"'Are you kidding?' Richard said. 'This guy is a cold-blooded motherfucker. He has ice water in his veins. Just wait. You'll see.' Richard was 100 percent correct. It turned out that the guy came out of the whatever-it-takes, no-matter-who-gets-hurt school. He later ended up in Washington, D.C. and was a big success."

The picture this guy paints in my office is too good to be true. Time passes and sure enough, this guy is treacherous; he will do anything it takes, stepping all over you if necessary. But somehow, along the way we end up becoming good friends. You want him on your side when you have to get into a fight. He has big balls.

One of the things I have a knack for is sizing somebody up. Ninety-five percent of the time I'm correct. I can sit and talk to someone for a short time and then tell you a lot about the person—whether he or she is going to be an asshole, good, bad, or indifferent. I can usually spot users, abusers, everybody. It often works to my advantage. I use it in hiring my own staff and in my working relationships with all kinds of people.

"Richard also really liked flawed characters because they were real characters—kind of like him. He couldn't take these holier-than-thou types because they weren't his reality," Hillary says.

Chapter 12

The Godfather of the MTA

Mayor Tom Bradley's longtime dream is creating a mass transit subway system accessible to the people who need it the most.

There are two transportation-related agencies in Los Angeles County back then. The oldest is the Southern California Rapid Transit District, or the RTD, which runs the Southland's bus system. In the mid-1980s, county voters pass a half-cent sales tax initiative to fund a rapid transit system, which at the time means rail. Legendary L.A. County Supervisor Kenny Hahn is among those championing the sales tax measure. The Los Angeles County Transportation Commission, or LACTC, is formed and put in charge of planning and ultimately implementing a mass transit system in southern California. Most of the money from the sales tax hike goes to the LACTC.

The state of California charters the Metropolitan Transportation Authority (MTA) through legislation authored in 1993 by Assemblymember Richard Katz, consolidating the RTD and LACTC into a single regional transit agency. As a member of both the RTD and the LACTC boards of directors representing the mayor—and later as first chairman of the MTA, appointed by Mayor Bradley and reappointed by Mayor Richard Riordan—I get put in charge of turning Tom Bradley's dream into a reality by making this very hard thing happen.

It's not hard to understand why this is such a hard thing to do when you look at a map of the greater L.A. area. Both L.A. city and county are extremely horizontal and geographically dispersed. There are very few pockets of high density in the '80s, although that is less so now. Given the geography and Angelenos' historic love affair with the automobile, the idea of installing a subway system is considered pretty radical. Subways are very expensive. There is much skepticism about whether the taxpayers will pay to build such a thing and whether very many people will pay to ride it. Meanwhile, the buses, which make up the city's only mass transit system for decades, suck.

Tom Bradley aggressively moves forward with a heavy and light rail mass transit system—and improvements of the old bus system—to help fix L.A.'s traffic congestion and pollution dilemma and because he cares about the working people who can't afford their own vehicles and are most dependent on public transit. I join in the fight shortly after joining the city council. Many of these transit-dependent residents live in my council district. The irony is that more freeways blanket Eastside communities like Boyle Heights than any other part of the city. Yet many residents from these neighborhoods can't use them because they don't have cars. So many of my constituents rely on public transportation to go to work, shop, and take care of personal needs. That is why the communities east of downtown L.A. are important to the solution of the gridlock we see in the city.

A decision is made at one point in the history of L.A. that the only way to move people around is through freeways. So we build a lot of them, which causes this horrendous problem with traffic congestion—followed by polluted air. The bus system does nothing to relieve the congestion because the great majority of the people who depend on their automobiles to get around will never ride the bus as an alternative way of going to and from work. Other great cities address these issues and continue to grow by adopting alternative transportation systems. They all still have bus systems that continue carrying the great majority of the population that uses public transportation—and will always have them. This is not a competition to decide what's more important, buses or rail. We don't need to debate that.

When I'm first appointed to the RTD and then become a member of the LACTC, everyone on the city council (you have to be a councilmember to be a mayoral appointee) is for all intents and purposes asleep. Nobody much cares about RTD bus service. And other councilmembers don't really share much of a vision about the importance of the LACTC to the future of transportation in the Southland. That changes later on and members of the council wake up and see the relevance of these two bodies when they merge into the MTA.

L.A. learns some important lessons from putting on the games of the XXIII Olympiad in 1984. Many worry it will be an absolute nightmare trying to get hundreds of thousands of athletes, participants, spectators, and journalists from one place to the other in a hopelessly gridlocked city. It is decided to do something about commerce and trucks. Officials limit the hours trucks can be on the roads to either early in the morning or late at night. They work with the private sector to stagger working hours so not everybody is getting on the freeways at the same time. Altogether, these and other steps probably only affect maybe 10 percent of the riding public. But it's enough to avoid gridlock during the Olympics.

We know buses will continue carrying 90 to 95 percent of the people who use public transportation. We know we will never get 40 or 50 percent of those who drive cars to abandon them. So all we need to do is convince five to 10 percent of the motorists to trade their private cars for light and heavy rail cars. That would significantly reduce pollution and gridlock in L.A. and make for an economically viable rapid transit system. It would also avoid the gridlock that experts predict will paralyze the greater L.A. area unless something changes. We recognize that most middle-class people will never get on a bus. But they might possibly ride on something like light rail or a subway system—if there is connectivity; it has to start and end someplace, or multiple places, offering people real options.

The cost of living in the central and western parts of L.A. become so expensive with higher and higher real estate values that many of the working and middle-class people who make our economy function are forced to seek more affordable shelter to the east or south of the central city. That is where you find the greatest concentration of housing for people outside of the San Fernando Valley—going towards the Inland Empire and Orange County. Much of our pollution comes from vehicles struggling to drive from or to those bedroom communities during morning and evening rush hours. It is estimated that without alternatives, eventually people living to the east and south of L.A. will become immobilized, unable to get into the central and western parts of the city. This is the genesis of Tom Bradley's vision and it's why I get involved in transportation.

Tom Bradley talks about rapid mass transit when he first runs for mayor in 1969, but nothing comes of it mostly because the funding sources aren't there. That changes with approval of the half-cent local sales tax and federal funding through the U.S. Department of Transportation. The merger of the two separate transit agencies into a regional joint powers authority created by the state makes it a reality.

I'm on a cruise to Cabo San Lucas with L.A. County Supervisor Yvonne Braithwaite Burke and her husband, Bill Burke, a doctor and one of my oldest friends, when the boards of the RTD and the LACTC meet to comply with the merger law by picking the first chairman of the steering committee that will implement the merger into the MTA. Representing me as a member of the RTD board is Gerard Orozco, one of my council deputies. We first meet when I'm handing out awards at a dinner in 1984, at Franklin High School in Highland Park, where he is a sophomore. "Richard spoke about giving back," Gerard says. "He says it's not good enough to just talk about it. He showed everybody you can be anything you want to be if you work hard, but you also have to remember how you got there.

"Before, we had a lot of slick politicians come by the school in flashy clothes. They'd say, 'Look at what I did. Look at me. I'm a success.' Richard spoke directly to the students about the potential in each one of us. That's what struck me."

Gerard interns in my assembly district office during his junior year, in 1985. After finishing up at UCLA, he is a field representative out of my Boyle Heights field office. Then he comes downtown to City Hall and handles legislative work for me, including the council agenda, the rules and budget committees, and transportation issues.

Gerard comes up with the brilliant idea of me heading up the MTA steering committee. He's very good at developing relationships with people. Although Gerard is not a sitting member of the RTD board, he gets someone else on the board to nominate me as the first chairman. "I made the case [to the RTD board] how this new entity will have a major economic impact on Richard's council district and around the entire county, and with Richard as chairman the new MTA would finally be able to deliver rail service to the Eastside, which several elected officials had talked about but never been able to do. I argued that Richard was a doer and that I would staff him." Somehow, Gerard's arguments hit home and I'm elected. I remind him when I return from the cruise that he never asks my permission.

My first challenge as chair of the consolidated MTA is dealing with big conflicts the merger instantly creates between bus advocates from the old RTD—whose clientele will always comprise 80 or 90 percent of the riding public, mostly minorities—and advocates for the rail system, which is still under construction.

Bus advocates always focus on buses and bus routes, and they're against cuts in funding for buses. I believe then and now in spending more money on buses and improving bus service. But where the future lies—and where the funding is available—is in rail, both heavy and light rail systems. All the hotshot visionary transportation gurus are rail advocates from the former LACTC.

When I first get into transportation, I tend to lean towards the bus advocates. My perception is that the most important thing is improving the bus system in the city and county. The district I represent is one of the most transit-dependent in L.A., with a large resident work force that needs to travel to downtown L.A. but also into the San Fernando Valley, South, and West L.A. Their only means of getting there are buses. So that automatically becomes the focus of much of my initial interest and time. The heavy rivalry at first between bus and rail supporters is unavoidable. Some of the unions have an organization called the Bus Riders Union, funded by the L.A. County Federation of Labor. Together with the bus industry and everyone who makes buses and parts and provides upkeep and maintenance, they want more buses for working people and believe everything being spent on rapid mass transit planning, initially by the LACTC, is a waste of money that should go instead towards buying more buses and increasing the number of bus lines.

At first, I see the LACTC, with its focus on rapid mass transit, as more esoteric. It is made up of the visionaries along with an interesting coalition of professional planners, transportation gurus, and business interests whose economic and psychological well being is associated with increasing alternative forms of transportation and seeing the economic good created by heavy and light rail, electric vehicles, and other options. The visionaries busy themselves planning for the future and considering every conceivable method of transportation that can get people out of their cars and off the freeways. That supplies an environmental good and during this time L.A. has a well-deserved reputation as the smog capital of the world because of all the exhaust from buses, trucks, and cars.

The parochial view of the RTD, when it is an entity unto itself concentrating solely on the bus system, runs contrary to the alternative methods of transit that national leaders keep talking about.

The two sides are constantly battling and sniping at each other, sometimes blocking progress. It doesn't matter what you tell them about how we are all stronger when we work together with common objectives. If you spend a dollar on planning, that's a dollar bus advocates feel they are losing. If you spend a dollar on buses, that's also a waste since it doesn't deal with reducing traffic gridlock, or cleaning up the environment. The closest consensus you can get is the debate between clean-diesel versus regular diesel buses or electric-powered versus polluting diesel buses. I'm for fighting for a better bus system in an economically sensible way. I also learn from the other side that planning is needed to solve a serious regional transportation dilemma that will ultimately impact people in my district and other communities that have a need for a transit system embracing a variety of alternatives. Freeway and roadway congestion is worsening year after year. That's affecting the quality of life for everyone. During this time we have to deal with threats that federal funds are going to be cut off because of a lack of progress in reducing congestion and pollution. In short, we need a mix.

Relations between the RTD and the LACTC are at an all-time low at the time the merger is passed in Sacramento. But we have great employees in both entities and they deserve an opportunity to work together. The question is how will that get done? How will both entities function as one organization responsible for all transportation needs throughout the region?

Things don't change much until the consolidation that forms the MTA is completed. Then the bus policymakers and the mass transit policymakers are forced to work together in a merged agency with good leadership and political support. At that point we begin to make inroads and progress that honors the importance of both approaches. I never play the game of making one side more important than the other. Both are important and have to be supported.

Bringing in the right leadership starts when I hire Wally Karabian, a former assemblymember, an L.A. attorney and my political mentor, as a legal advisor to the steering committee because of our long-term relationship and because I know he will help facilitate the objectives I set forth for a successful merger. The merger gets done.

Leading the LACTC is its executive director, Neil Peterson, who is a genius in terms of futuristic thinking. My first take on Neil is that he's arrogant. But the more I work with him, the more I like him. If he says he'll do something, he does. He figures out how to take an idea and make it a reality. He also has a brilliant political sense. Neil is always thinking and studying. He assembles some of the best transportation minds in the country. He marshals the manpower to research and write the proposals and goes after the monies available for L.A. in Sacramento and Washington, D.C. We work closely together through the LACTC and the MTA to build L.A.'s mass transit network. He knows how to involve government with a private sector that has a vested interest in seeing rapid mass transit succeed because moving people around more effectively is key to creating jobs and business and expanding the economy. A good transit system is a great economic engine for any city or state.

When you look at other cities, you see high-density housing in and around the transit lines and stations. You see multi-use properties for nearby businesses that are attracted to the people and the foot traffic. That is why I want to explore the options of extending mass transit east into my district. The most critical factor is what happens to the economy when the system is completed and growth occurs. But what happens during the process is also crucial through the creation of jobs and the revival of neighborhoods.

When I first come on board with the MTA, the blue line, opened in 1990, is a light rail route going from downtown L.A. to downtown Long Beach. Two other systems open in 1993: The red line is a heavy rail subway going from Union Station in downtown L.A. initially to Vermont and then in a second phase to Hollywood (and eventually into North Hollywood). The purple line is also a heavy rail subway running between downtown L.A. and the mid-Wilshire district. Three other important light rail routes are yet to be built or completed at that time: The green line, which opens in 1995, will link Redondo Beach and Norwalk, with indirect access via shuttle bus to LAX. The gold line, operating by 2003, will run between Pasadena and East L.A. via downtown L.A. The Expo Line, opened in 2012, now runs from downtown L.A. to Culver City.

The Pasadena link of the blue line, built in the late 1980s, goes through parts of my 14th District. "Richard played a key role in getting it authorized, funded, and built," Gerard says, "using voter-passed half-cent county sales tax monies and California Transportation Commission funding." Despite month-to-month opposition from opponents, it is an opportunity for people living in Lincoln Heights, Highland Park, South Pasadena, and farther out to have access to alternative forms of transportation.

Keeping the Expo Line alive going west from downtown is my crowning glory. It's supposed to be heavy rail heading west, eventually hitting the sea in Santa Monica. Studies are done. Plans are made. Then there's a methane gas explosion around Fairfax Avenue and Wilshire Boulevard. Congressional legislation is developed by U.S. Representative Henry Waxman that stops plans for construction underneath these heavily Jewish neighborhoods, which are up in arms over the gas blow up. Rational discussion gets lost. Subway construction gets a black eye. They stop it from being built. Instead, light rail—going above ground—replaces heavy rail going underground. If it is possible to find a way to mitigate the gas problem—which can be done—there would be heavy rail taking riders to the ocean and saving billions of dollars in the process.

All planning for alternative transit and the economic vitality that comes with it seems to be focused on heading west, south, and north. Nothing up to that time is discussed about aiding the most transit-dependent communities, Chicano neighborhoods, to the east. As early as the 1980s, when Ed Roybal is representing East L.A. in Congress, rail transportation is envisioned to also head in that direction. My aim is to change the debate so it begins to include the places I represent to the east of downtown L.A. I begin bringing along more people on the boards of the RTD and LACTC to support this idea and to buy into the economic good that will result from construction.

I make the gold line to Boyle Heights a top MTA priority in the agency's "Call for Projects," its capital construction program. I personally win a full funding agreement in the language of a congressional bill authoring the building of the gold line, first to Boyle Heights and then to Atlantic Boulevard in the county of L.A. Planning and fundraising begin in the late 1990s. Construction of the gold line link, heading east, starts at Union Station in the 2000s.

Building the East L.A. extension of the gold line into Boyle Heights carries with it huge economic impacts on the communities it goes through. Downtown people can hop on light rail and go east to shop or enjoy real Mexican food. People on the Eastside will have greater access to downtown, where they can make connections to other parts of the city in all directions. A housekeeper or a nanny on the Eastside can take the gold line to Union Station and then make transfers to wherever. Factory and service workers can more easily reach their jobs downtown or farther out. It significantly improves working people's quality of life by cutting down on commute times from riding buses or spending money on gas.

I initially envision construction of a heavy rail subway from downtown that would end up at Atlantic Boulevard and eventually move on to parts east. I organize community support from Boyle Heights and East L.A. for the idea of an underground subway with five or six station stops, including Japantown, Mariachi Plaza, and the corner of Soto Street and Cesar Chavez Avenue. It takes a lot of advocacy to get the support of other board members, many of whom have their own, sometimes competing, agendas. Mine is one of the highest on the food chain because I have already done so much of the work.

I'm eventually successful in winning agreement on full funding from the federal government with help from President Clinton's secretary of transportation, Frederico Peña, who I know going back to when he serves as mayor of Denver and through our joint involvement in Democratic Party politics. But be-

As chairman of the Metropolitan Transportation Authority, Richard pushes construction of the extension into East Los Angeles of the gold line light rail route because of the economic benefits and improved access to public transit for residents of his 14th District.

cause of political backlash against subway construction on the Westside of L.A., what is going to be a subway heading east is delayed and eventually can only move forward as a light rail, above ground system.

Since the MTA board includes the five members of the board of supervisors and the eastward construction of the rail system will emerge from the city into county jurisdiction, it is important to get the county on board too. "Richard forged consensus through [County Supervisor] Gloria Molina because it was in her supervisorial district," Gerard says. "Gloria got to cut the ribbon at the grand opening, although Richard, out of office by then, attended briefly."

We also make real progress on building the other links in the new transit system. A new part of the vocabulary is coming into fashion: multimodal. We set up a multimodal transportation system that becomes my whole attitude towards mass transit through the MTA. We combine improvements to traditional bus service with new heavy and light rail systems, all linked with conventional train service from outlying parts of the region and ultimately making the connection with LAX. I recognize early on what it takes some of my colleagues longer to realize: the opportunities created by multimodal transportation. They include environmental (curbing congestion and pollution), economic (resulting in business and economic growth), and convenience (improving people's quality of life by supplying them with new transportation options) opportunities. That's why I come to be seen by many people who are in the midst of the transportation fight during the 1980s and '90s as the godfather of the MTA.

"Richard got the MTA to treat his constituents like clients rather than numbers," Gerard Orozco says. "That was a new thing. Other elected officials really didn't do that much before, at least on the Eastside of town. Richard brought with him sensitivity to his constituents' needs. Take how he authorized and pushed through one of the first local circulators—or DASH routes. These are local bus systems or neighborhood shuttle services. In Boyle Heights they take people from the Mercado on Lorena and First streets to the County-USC Medical Center in Lincoln Heights and then on to Union Station downtown. They made it easier for people to get to certain commonly used destinations from which they can link through public transportation to other parts of the city."

We dedicate a number of buses that go to destination points heavily traveled by people living in Boyle Heights. We identify places buses should originate and how and where they should circulate in that community. During the day and through the early evening, people can more easily and quickly get to work or obtain goods and services. Then they don't have to make multiple transfers on buses, often going far out of their way. We work with community groups to determine where large numbers of people need to get to and from for work, commerce and service needs. It is still heavily used.

Because of various construction delays, as time goes on the money it takes to build each mile of the heavy rail—or subway—system becomes prohibitive. So we eventually turn to light rail.

"As chair of the MTA, Richard sets the policy directives and pushes to make things happen so Neil Peterson could do his work," Robin Kramer, my first council chief of staff, recalls. My philosophy is not to stop, to keep on planning and get ready for when the money is made available to build mass transit. Others argue that we should wait for the money and then do the planning. I ignore them. When we have the votes on the MTA board to approve a particular link in the system, we are ready to go—and it just gets done when the money shows up. So plans are approved and as soon as the federal dollars and our matching funds from the local sales tax and the state get put together, the construction begins. That approach is not without controversy because planning is not free; it costs money. So we're spending money on construction project plans for which complete funding is not yet all there. We tap the half-cent sales tax money for planning since it frequently takes much longer to get funding from the state or federal governments for a lot of reasons.

My philosophy of planning and how I see decision-making taking place at the state and national capitals through my interactions with Neil Peterson comes down to this: You dig a hole in the ground. Once the hole gets dug, you can't stop—and neither can the state and federal officials who are putting up their share of the construction financing. They have to see it through to the end. Neil and I joke about it: We get the first hole dug. Once that happens we find the money and everything else needed to finish the project.

I'm convinced we can get the funding. It obviously can't be supplied just from the sales tax money. The biggest pot of money comes out of Washington. I discover that Congress and later the Clinton administration are more interested in other forms of transportation than just buses. I also learn that offering Washington the kinds of projects it is interested in funding is the most critical factor in moving L.A. transit projects along. I also know Secretary of Transportation Peña, which helps.

In the meantime, I carefully watch Neil Peterson perform since my early service on the LACTC board. He is a master at public policy, but he is also very adept at knowing where the federal money can be found and how to compete for it. What begins as mistrust and suspicion turns into admiration and respect for his intellect and thorough knowledge of transportation issues. He has a big vision that transcends bus service. He believes the buses will take care of themselves—that they will get their chunk of the money anyway. Now it's his and my job to get L.A.'s fair share of federal funding for rail lines and subways despite tough competition with other cities that are building or expanding their systems that are usually further along than ours.

Finding the funding is just one step. We also have to round up the votes on the transit agencies' boards—later on one board, the MTA panel—to approve the projects themselves. I become pretty good at doing that. There are 13 members when I'm on the board of the Los Angeles County Transportation Commission. There are the five members of the county board of supervisors. There are four appointees by L.A.'s mayor, then Tom Bradley. And four other members are named by the independent cities of the county other than L.A. The secret is getting to seven votes, the simple majority needed to approve anything.

I start with the biggest numbers. About a year or two after being elected to the council, Tom Bradley asks me to serve as one of the four council representatives he appoints to the board. He trusts me because of the relationship we have.

I figure out the mayor can get his other three appointees to agree with my agenda, which is not inconsistent with Tom's. He lets it be known to the rest of them that they should follow my lead on important issues. That gets me to four votes.

Few county supervisors, all of whom belong to the LACTC board, pay much attention to it. They look at it as one of many committees they have to serve on when they are very busy with other duties. Transportation isn't that big a deal at the time, so the supervisors usually send their chiefs of staff or some other designated person to go to the LACTC board sessions.

Supervisor Kenny Hahn names Mas Fukai, his chief of staff, as his representative. Mas is a friend of mine from many years before. Supervisor Mike Antonovich, who I know since we are both students at Cal State L.A. in the 1960s, appoints Nick Patsouras, one of Antonovich's political allies and a developer of housing and other projects in the San Fernando Valley. Nick and I know each other since I'm in the legislature, and he contributes to my campaigns. Marv Holen is Supervisor Ed Edelman's representative on both the LACTC and RTD boards. He's a liberal Democrat and a staunch supporter of the bus system. I have a good political relationship with Marv. He respects me because I never double-deal him and I am always honest with him. Gerard Orozco, my deputy, works on him a lot, knowing Marv is an old political warhorse—and selling him on the fact I will be fair and do the right thing by everyone concerned. Plus, Marv knows I represent a transit-dependent constituency as well as downtown L.A.; both Marv and I want to convert the old Union Station into the hub for a multimodal transit system where all lines—bus, regional train (Amtrak and MetroLink), and light and heavy rail—come together. I also maintain good relations with the two remaining supervisorial appointees. (A new rule for the merged MTA board says county supervisors have to be there to vote on certain items; a representative can't just show up and cast a supervisor's vote. If a supervisor can't make it for an important vote, his or her designee has to have a letter authorizing the person to cast a vote on the matter.)

Then there are the League of City types from the smaller independent municipalities. Usually mayors or city councilmembers, they get appointed or reappointed every two or four years. They are consistently policy wonks. Like anything else, everyone has his or her own selfish interest. These four representatives all have needs. I help them out whenever there is an opportunity. And I develop a reputation among them as someone who is fair and can be approached to get support from the LACTC board for their particular transit concerns.

I serve on both the LACTC and RTD boards. The appointment structure is almost the same. I religiously work relationships with both sets of board members over a number of years. That's why, when the law merging the two groups passes the legislature, I'm the perfect consensus candidate for chairman of the merger steering committee and later become the first chair of the MTA.

The upshot is that from the beginning of my service on the RTD and LACTC boards, I pay a lot more attention to what's going on than my fellow elected officials. That helps me get my agenda through. When Tom Bradley leaves office he is replaced by Dick Riordan, with whom I have even more influence.

There are numerous unresolved issues as the merger is implemented such as distribution of funds, determination of assets, and employee pension plans. Employees of the two agencies have different pension systems. The merger creates conflicts over rights. The RTD, an older agency, has its own retirement benefits and protections. The LACTC is more recently created with its own pension benefits and rules. The two agencies' rights and privileges have to be combined into one system. There are also disparities over salaries and job descriptions.

The staffs of the two entities don't trust or like each other. We work with the employee groups to identify issues they care about. One of them that attracts my interest has to do with providing for domestic partners when it comes to insurance, medical care, and retirement. I recruit the best and the brightest authorities, including actuarial and employment experts, and let them whack it out with the parties. When they can't make decisions, I make them—which gives them an incentive to work things out themselves. We develop equality of pay and benefits for like positions and work out all the other issues. It is very complicated and tedious.

The most difficult challenge comes with the union contracts. There are two separate work forces, bargaining units, and sets of union contracts that need to be merged into one. That takes a long time. But I have great relationships with all the unions so I can help mediate disagreements.

A couple of new policies I help hammer out during my chairmanship of the MTA steering committee stand out.

Once both entities are merged together, we're talking about multibillions of dollars that are on the table for massive transit projects. It involves everything from research and engineering to construction and management. The MTA has to tightly control and facilitate a process that makes sense in terms of transparency and openness of government. My thing about ethics is to force everyone to report everything, set limits, and have transparency. Once those guidelines are set out then the lawyers can work out the details.

Some of my detractors like to point out my skills at the backroom deal, which is not a secret. Yet I help get the steering committee to adopt one of the strongest ethics policies of any transit agency in the nation. It restricts gifts to appointed and elected officials, provides for full disclosure, and requires lobbyists to register, which hasn't been done before.

Since we're creating a new agency with new policies, I see the opportunity to break some new ground and right some old wrongs. So under my chairmanship, the steering committee adopts a domestic partners benefit policy years before most other public agencies act in places like San Francisco. It goes back to my initial campaign for the assembly in 1971, when I become the first L.A. politician to openly court and win the gay community's support. I later get a call from U.S. Representative Barney Frank (D-Mass.), saying congratulations. "That was quite a feat and I think it will be replicated by other agencies of government around the country," he says. We meet through national Democratic politics.

Other transit agencies across the country start taking note by looking at L.A.'s groundbreaking ethics and domestic partner policies. I also use the merger process to set in motion innovative practices that open up a lot of access for qualified women, Latinos, blacks, and other minorities, to make sure they have opportunities to be hired at all levels of the new agency. Billions of dollars in contracts will be issued in the coming years as a result of our lobbying for transit funds in Sacramento and Washington. Teams of outside consultants, contractors, and subcontractors will be put together to perform the work. One of the hallmarks of my tenure with the RTD, LACTC and MTA is opening up access for qualified women and minority small-business firms—to guarantee they will be full participants in the planning and construction processes.

This access is across the board and applies to the many new employees who will be hired by the merged MTA, from the lower levels to the upper echelons of agency managers and supervisors. I particularly advocate for upward mobility for people working there, covering new positions that will be created over time. It's important that women and members of ethnic and racial minorities be fully represented in terms of whom we hire and where we spend our money.

We make these policies clear in the transition document. I know Tom Bradley will support it. I know the liberal wing of the board of supervisors will support it. And I know—and make sure—that the other appointees to the boards of the transportation entities will not object.

At that point, we can get away with setting quotas for minorities. When the federal courts throw them out, we accomplish the same result by calling it something else that doesn't violate judicial rulings. Those hiring and contracting objectives remain bedrocks of how the MTA operates today.

"A big deal with the MTA is growth of Latino-owned engineering and planning firms that know the community and work on the gold line, which goes through the Eastside," my deputy, Gerard Orozco observes. "Once they get and work those contracts, they can replicate the work they did in bidding on future projects in L.A. or on transit projects in other communities. They can boast that they got experience planning these complicated urban routes; just look at the gold line, they can say. By ensuring that qualified Latino and other minority-owned firms get their fair share of the business by participating in the planning and designing and construction, these firms built up their book of experience and resumes using the MTA. It was all because Richard set in motion an outreach and sensitivity that drew them in."

When the merger forming the MTA takes place, there is already a transit authority police force covering the RTD buses. When the combined entity emerges, there's an attempt by the LAPD to take over all law enforcement duties involving transit in L.A., including underground subways, light rail, and buses. I see it as featherbedding by the city cops. Since it requires city council action and I'm convinced the MTA needs its own police force, I stop it by getting the agency board to agree with me.

Now we need to select a new MTA police chief in 1993. I champion the candidacy of the first woman to head a transit police force. Sharon Papa is a consummate professional, the former police chief for the city of Santa Monica. She is the best-qualified candidate and the rank-and-file officers in Santa Monica like her. I line up the votes on the MTA board to hire her.

Eventually, the MTA transit police force and the LAPD merge. Many of the younger transit cops think there is more glory and opportunities for advancement if they're part of the LAPD. Yeah, a lot of them will be able to join the LAPD, we tell them. But a number of older transit police officers won't qualify by meeting the LAPD's higher standards and will be left out in the cold. Once the merger takes place Sharon Papa joins the LAPD at the rank of commander. She becomes the city police department's highest-ranking woman.

"First, Richard is forward looking in how the planning takes place," Robin Kramer says. "He also has the ability in general to see and understand things on a big scale. He had already seen how using a policy decision like reapportionment could change people's lives in a big way. When doing transit policy, you have to understand how to act on big horizons and levels of scale, in both money and time. Even though he didn't grow up with a lot of money, he's not intimidated by multibillion-dollar budgets."

How the process moves towards making decisions and all the intricacies that lead up to it is what interests me the most. When we're fighting in Washington for funding of the red line, I closely observe—and come to understand and respect—how Neil Peterson spends money on hiring legislative advocates and getting the lobbying done to win the necessary funding. He understands how both Democrats and Republicans work, how the committees that control the money and policy on transportation make decisions on both the short and long term. He knows who is in power and how we can get to them, which lobbyists have the best relationships with which committee chairs or with the U.S. secretary of transportation. It doesn't matter whether the person we're targeting is a Democrat or a Republican. We hire a Democratic or Republican lobbyist depending on who will have the greatest influence.

It all pays off, whether we're lobbying for money or on policy issues. We always have access to the right people. "Since Richard worked on reapportionment with [U.S. Representative] Phil Burton in 1981, there are all kinds of members of Congress whose districts he helped create and whom he knew," Gerard Orozco says. "He'd arrive on Capitol Hill like a rock star. I'd staff him. The MTA had several big-time D.C. lobbyists on retainer. Richard would come in and out perform them. They're used to having clients come to them when they're in town to meet senators or representatives and ask, 'What do I do?' Richard was completely in his element, completely in control. He mastered every meeting without using any notes.

"The MTA's lobbyists were like, 'We got a nuclear weapon here.' That was a lot of fun."

Part of the reason I'm successful navigating Capitol Hill and at the state Capitol in Sacramento is that I do my homework at the board level. Most board members never grasp the importance of the position they hold—the magnitude of the power from the votes they cast for projects creating light and heavy rail lines. For most of them, especially if they are mayors, city councilmembers, or county supervisors, it's just another of many boards and commissions they have to sit on and spend time with. It's the same thing for the other council people who are appointees of Tom Bradley.

Like my fellow mayoral appointees, I have the responsibility of voting the way Tom Bradley and later Dick Riordan want. But I position myself with both mayors, earning their trust. They know I will never do anything to embarrass them. I will (nearly always) act in ways that are consistent with their interests. They are convinced of that fact and consequently give me the authority to cast my vote the right way. They also give me the ability to sway my colleagues on the board who know I'm acting for the mayor. I don't abuse that authority. Therefore, when it comes to issues that are important to my agenda and the agenda of L.A., I always have the votes on the board I need.

Likewise, when I arrive in Washington or Sacramento as a member of the RTD and LACTC boards, and later as chairman of the MTA board, lawmakers know I'm speaking for the mayor who appointed me. And they know because of my relationships with the other board members, I'm never seen on Capitol Hill or at the state Capitol as an individual board member advocating for myself; they always see me as representing the entire board of the agency.

Doing your homework means I go into every meeting with a specific agenda. I know what I'm advocating on behalf of. The state and federal lawmakers or transportation department officials I'm meeting with know it is an agenda endorsed by my regional agency and its board. As an assemblymember in Sacramento, the policy part of legislating is never high on my list. Politics—how you get things done—is. But if there is an area where I develop a measure of expertise when I return to L.A. to serve on the city council it is transportation. I learn to master the subject matter.

Since decennial reapportionment—what lawmakers' districts will look like over the next decade—is the nearest and dearest thing to the hearts of any state or federal legislator, I have a great advantage since I shepherd assembly and congressional redistricting in 1981. There are also the relationships I develop over 14 years at the state Capitol—many with colleagues who now serve in Congress. Those relationships in many cases become cemented for life. I tap all them for the RTD, LACTC, and MTA when I make trips to Sacramento or Washington.

We're fortunate to have very good lobbyists on retainer from GOP and Democratic firms. Following Neil Peterson's example, I know what my job is. I know whom we need to get. And I focus like a laser beam on getting that job done. For example, I'll go and meet with Dianne Feinstein, California's senior U.S. senator with much clout when it comes to transportation. My relationship with her goes back to when she is mayor of San Francisco after the 1978 assassination of my friend, Mayor George Moscone. I will seek out her advice on the best way to proceed. Then I also develop a great relationship with Senator Alfonse Demato, a Republican from New York who chairs the Senate Transportation Committee, through one of our lobbyists who is Italian American. Joe Cerrell, one of my political advisors and a friend from early in my legislative career, also has contacts with Demato. Nothing moves out of Demato's committee unless he agrees.

There is also a broad base of construction contractors who work on MTA projects and who have their own extensive D.C. connections. We invite key senators or representatives from both parties who chair or sit on the right policy or appropriations committees or subcommittees—and make transportation decisions and can vote to give us funding—to visit L.A. under the guise of showing them our latest plans and projects. The official idea is to let them see the great progress we are making, for example, on the red line. We have them meet policymakers at a breakfast. We schedule a similar meeting during a luncheon. But the real reason for the trip is a reception the MTA contractors organize in the evening to raise money for the lawmakers' campaign treasuries. We do the same if, say, someone important from Capitol Hill arrives in L.A. to attend a Super Bowl or for some other purpose, hosting a reception with representatives from all the construction companies who wine, dine, and contribute—or do whatever it takes to make their stay in our city more comfortable. When I'm in D.C., in addition to whatever else is on my plate, I drop by to pay respects to a particular chairman, even if we have nothing in front of him at the time, to acknowledge his prerogatives and ask how things are going. It's also often an effective way to pick up useful intelligence about certain developments.

For me, the most captivating element—beyond the billions of dollars that are at stake—is learning how to play the game of getting our agenda through and how to gain access and influence a decision to produce a positive outcome for L.A. From having worked in Sacramento, billions of dollars don't intimidate me. Getting the money is just a function of who has it, who makes the decisions on how to allocate it, and how to influence them—all of which I learn early during my political career. The rules of the game are nearly always the same. What's important is understanding the decision-makers you're dealing with and finding out what's important to them.

One day I'm in Washington and need to catch up with Dianne Feinstein in her Senate office. So I'm not able to make a scheduled meeting with U.S. Representative Nick Joe Rahal (D-West Virginia), chairman of a House transit appropriations subcommittee. I get my deputy, Gerard Orozco, to go take care of the meeting with the chairman. Gerard is a little nervous. I just tell him, "You know, be like me." It turns out that he takes it literally.

Gerard gets to Representative Rahal's office, accompanied by two of the MTA's in-house lobbyists. "I walk in and before I could say anything to the congressman, he looks at me, smiles and says, 'Hi Richard, how're ya doing? How can I help you today? I only got five minutes, Richard. I'm just going to do some work while you tell me what you want.' He just keeps talking, not letting me get a word in. Finally, I say, 'L.A. needs this much money'—and I tick off what we need, covering the whole request for funding of the gold line in Richard's council district.

"Nick Joe Rahal looks up at me. 'I like you,' he says. 'You got a deal. We're going to help you out. Have a good day, Richard.' Then he slaps me on the back and escorts us out of his office. Ever since then when the two MTA lobbyists see me they call me 'Councilman Alatorre.' Richard's reputation had preceded him. Big time.

"The lesson for me was you don't send Richard Alatorre in to speak at length about public policy or philosophical issues. You send Richard in to bring consensus and get action, which means votes."

Even before the MTA merger takes place, we start working on an assessment of where the high-rise administrative offices of the combined RTD and LACTC should be located. The boards of both groups ultimately agree that the headquarters should be consolidated in one location for efficiency of operation and financial advantage. We discover that many millions of dollars are being spent housing each of the transit agencies on properties they don't even own. No economic benefit comes from paying a whole lot of rent.

My council district includes the historic Union Station, adjacent to Chinatown and Olvera Street just north of downtown. Built in the early 20th century, this grand old structure is the terminus of the transcontinental railroads. I know that is a logical place for the central headquarters building. Land-use decisions like this one are made easier because, except for Chinatown, few people actually live in the area. So a councilmember has a freer hand in making a decision that will change the face of the neighborhood.

I work before with Catellus Development Corp., the real estate wing of the Santa Fe Pacific Railroad (now the Burlington Northern Santa Fe) that owns Union Station, on development projects in my district. Two principals in the development company are Nelson Rising and Ira Yellin, who I know and have also worked with. I am aware of Catellus's interest in making this downtown property the transportation hub for southern California by locating the new headquarters facility in back of the old railway station on Alameda and what is now Cesar Chavez Avenue. The company knows both the RTD and the LACTC are interested in constructing a building to house both entities in one place.

I begin building consensus behind the Union Station site. Catellus puts together a package of incentives for the MTA to choose the location. I work with the boards of the RTD and LACTC. We're in the middle of the merger process and the process of deciding on location of the headquarters. Low and behold, Tom Bradley calls me and wants to meet, asking that we look at other options for the headquarters location—in particular a large parcel west of the 110 or Harbor Freeway, southwest of downtown. The mayor wants that piece of property entered into the mix and ultimately selected for the new MTA building.

The idea of locating the headquarters west of the Harbor Freeway will spearhead a renaissance in that depressed area, the mayor argues. I know Tom is acting on behalf of Ray Watt, a major civic leader, philanthropist, and contributor to his campaigns. He also is a big property owner and owns the land in question.

That creates a big problem for me. I'm already so far down the line, building a lot of support for the Union Station site in my district, I tell the mayor.

"This is important to me," the mayor says to me. "It's the least I can do for him [Ray Watt]."

I'm on the spot. I'm an appointee of Tom Bradley. I'm also not going to give up on my idea. A lot of traction has been built up for the Union Station location, which is logical both from a policy and economic view. I have to figure out a way to placate the mayor.

I tell Bradley, "Why not look at two buildings" as potential headquarters for the MTA? "Let's get the west of the 110 freeway site in the mix and get an economic study done on the feasibility of whether to create two sites or one site." I make it clear that it will be hard to have two MTA headquarters. "You should have come to me earlier and I would have gone in a different direction," I add. At least the mayor has something to tell his benefactor.

I learn over the more than three decades we know each other that Tom Bradley is a great man, truly a man for his times. He cares more than most people will ever care about his city and dedicates himself to making it a better place. He's not an electrifying public speaker. Maybe he's not the smartest when it comes to making political decisions or interpreting policy. But you never have to worry about his motivations. They are pure in my eyes. He trusts the people he likes and works with. By and large, people reciprocate that trust.

Dealing with him one on one never takes a lot of time if you know your agenda. I get it right out when we're together. We don't spend a lot of time talking or philosophizing. Most of the time it is all about business. It's even better if I don't have to see him in person and can handle it over the phone. I just do it: Boom, boom, boom. I'm not a man of many words. Neither is he.

"The relationship between Bradley and Alatorre was cordial," Robin Kramer observes. "But Bradley in many ways is regal and can be stone faced although he's publicly very cordial." The closest to real power I have is when Dick Riordan is mayor and I'm sitting with the inner circle on all the big meetings where decisions get made.

The study we commission is done. The conclusion is that it makes no economic, policy or historical sense to put the MTA center west of the 110 freeway. The mayor still persists with his proposal.

I quietly work with the Marv Holens of the world—the transportation policy wonks—and with the other board members to kill the mayor's idea. "It's a great idea whose time has *not* come," I tell them privately. And it never does. I'm sure Tom Bradley is not happy, but what is he going to do? The boards of the two agencies make the decision; it's primarily the board of the LACTC because it holds most of the money. The new MTA headquarters goes behind Union Station, which boosts its status as the transit hub for the entire region.

We buy the property where the MTA building will sit, but also the adjoining parcel, which will be developed to bring in added revenue for the agency. We know the Metropolitan Water District has outlived the usefulness of its building on nearby Sunset Boulevard and is looking for a place to build a new corporate headquarters. Since this is my district too, I start negotiations with the water district and we end up building to suit a new structure next door to the

Richard maneuvers transit officials, Mayor Bradley, and the city bureaucracy to build the new MTA headquarters that now towers over historic Union Station just north of downtown L.A. The site becomes the region's transit hub.

MTA headquarters that the water district leases with an option to buy. The district owns it within five years.

On top of the two agency headquarters, land is left over to build new housing units. They initially plan the parcel as for-sale housing, but when the economy goes down the toilet, the development gets turned into beautiful market-rate rental units overlooking Olvera Street and downtown L.A.

I handle the responsibility for making it all happen first because they are all my ideas and second because I'm a member of both the RTD and LACTC boards, and the councilmember for that district. I'm on the committee overseeing construction of the MTA headquarters. I help obtain the zoning changes and get the required city permits. I pave the way for the mixed-use housing that goes up adjacent to Union Station. The California Endowment also decides to locate just north of there. A short distance away is Homeboy Industries, run by Father Greg Boyle, whom I know and support.

Right across the street from Union Station is the old Terminal Annex U.S. Post Office facility. Once the main post office for U.S. mail service in L.A., it outlives its usefulness. The question is what should go in there. My idea is to get someone to buy it and develop the property into something benefiting the area.

When the Los Angeles Rams leave the Coliseum in Exposition Park and L.A. is left without a professional football team, a group of people interested in attracting an NFL team is searching for places to build a new stadium. One idea we play around with is constructing a football stadium on top of the train tracks at the Terminal Annex site. It's perfect. You won't have to go to the game in your car. You can take one of several different modes of transportation instead: MetroLink, subway, light rail, or bus—all letting you out at the same place right next to the stadium.

I have a conflict. While I like the idea and think it is viable, I also represent Dodger Stadium not far away. The O'Malley family, still owners of the Dodgers, also want to host an NFL team by building a stadium on their sizeable plot of land on a bluff overlooking the city. The space is big enough for the existing Dodger Stadium, a football stadium plus plenty of room for parking. We discover the stadium-on-the-tracks idea is too complicated. So I concentrate on the Dodger Stadium alternative. But Peter O'Malley blinks in the face of opposition from a committee of about 10 residents seeking to preserve Elysian Park. If not for that, I believe a stadium would be built and an NFL team attracted. I believe the stadium would be there today under Walter O'Malley, Peter's father. But he's dead.

Through my council office and the MTA, we work on a daily basis to maintain transit services that are safe and reliable, especially with the city's bus system. "Richard was always on top of the field operations guys and the management leadership at the MTA," Gerard remembers. "It was a constant thing. Because he was always accessible and constantly out in the district, Richard would hear about problems from constituents. His network among neighborhood residents was amazing. 'Hey, this bus line off the 60 freeway has been running late,' someone would complain. Richard would bug the right MTA officials to fix the problem. You couldn't bullshit Richard about whether something had gotten done because he would find out for himself."

I'm on the street, at the store or in a restaurant. People gripe to me about a particular bus line. No one has to tell me how hard it is to be a member of the working public and a bus rider because of the safety concerns, the inconvenience, and the periodic cuts in service. You're talking about poor, low-wage earners who ride the bus out of simple necessity, not because they want to make a statement about how politically correct they are.

As long as I have influence at the MTA, when complaints come directly to me or to one of my offices, I immediately make sure they are turned over and pursued with the MTA, and I ask for reports on the results. I make it plain to MTA managers that when one of my staff members calls with a constituent complaint, he or she is calling for me. My staff knows to always get back to me. If the complaints are egregious or if they aren't being resolved, I make calls myself to the MTA executive director. I explain the problem and ask him to get back to me with a report on how it is being addressed. If I get on the phone over a complaint, the MTA officials know it is serious—and I always have their attention.

They respond not just because I'm bitching about something, and I chair the MTA board. They do it because they know I'm consistently their biggest champion and supporter on the MTA board—and at the state and national capitals for management's construction agenda. I also know being a bus driver is a difficult and arduous job. I'm always a big supporter of their union and its bargaining demands. So the MTA staff is responsive to me on the natural. That's how I get things done. They know I support them and so they respond to the needs of my constituents when I bring them up.

This kind of teamwork helps create a transit authority for L.A. that becomes a model for the nation. The MTA is named the Outstanding Transportation System for 2006 by the American Transportation Association. Most MTA buses and trains are affixed with "America's Best" decals.

Mass transit isn't the only form of transportation advocacy my council office and I undertake. The 110 freeway, known as the Pasadena Freeway, is the oldest freeway in L.A. and the nation. It rests on a very small footprint compared to the freeway construction of today. Motorists have to come to almost a complete stop to negotiate some off ramps. There are lots of accidents or near misses. Since it is so old, the Pasadena Freeway doesn't go in a straight line; it winds and curves, making it virtually impossible to add lanes. I ask my staff, "When are we going to get to this, to fix this damn thing and make it safer?"

My office does research to prepare a project study report, the first step in finding out what is feasible from an engineering standpoint to make the 110 safer.

My staff comes back to me during the study. "We're limited in what we can do because it's an historic freeway," Gerard says.

"God damn these fucking NIMBY people," I reply.

"It was state legislation that created it as an historic freeway," Gerard says. The law is tombstoned, or named in honor of its authors, then-Assemblymembers Richard Alatorre and Mike Roos.

Gerard shows me a copy of the law. "What a brilliant piece of legislation," I remark, "with such a far-reaching affect." In truth, I push for the historic designation to thwart efforts by people in neighboring South Pasadena who oppose extending the 710 freeway north into their city. Instead, they want the 710 moved west through the low-income community of El Sereno that I represent in the state assembly. The South Pasadena NIMBY activists propose that the 710 freeway eventually hook up to the 110 freeway that is already overused and congested. To stop this move, I discover that the wash along Arroyo Seco Creek paralleling the 110 freeway is an historic landmark, meaning no construction can take place on it. So my law extending historic status to the Pasadena Freeway works and South Pasadena has to give up on the scheme.

We get state funds to improve the egress and ingress by widening some of the 110 freeway entrances and exits, and installing better signage on the portion going north from Lincoln Heights all the way to the city of Pasadena where it ends. But there are limits to what can be done because of the small space—with houses and apartments abutting right up to the freeway—and the historic landmark status.

Chapter 13

Finding Redemption

The tail end of my service on the city council sees me go from the heights of political power to the depths of personal shame. It is the hardest time of my life. But thanks to the people I love, I find the strength within me to come back. And the whole thing ends up saving my life.

"Richard was one of the most powerful people in the region," my last chief of staff, Hillary Norton, says. "He was chair of the council's Budget and Finance Committee and around the same time chair of the MTA [the Metropolitan Transportation Authority]. But he was having these personal challenges of Greek proportions."

My problem with addiction begins when I'm in junior high school and growing up in East L.A. I'm going to a school dance with a friend. We make arrangements to buy a half-gallon jug of cheap wine we think we're going to split, drinking it before heading over to the dance. Neither one of us have any experience with drinking.

We find someone to make the purchase for us. But the wine doesn't arrive on time. We take off for the dance. One of our other friends is a guy much older than us who's graduating from high school. They're having a party for him.

I'm probably 13 years old, and have no idea what my tolerance is for liquor. Oh, I've started to dabble in drinking a little bit of beer. I like wine for some reason.

I'm the youngest person there. Everyone else is out of high school. Kids growing up are dared to do all kinds of things. They dare me to drink, to chugalug the jug wine. I want to be accepted by the guys, so why not? I proceed to do it, never realizing the ramifications.

I don't remember much after that. It is getting late, 1 or 2 in the morning. I know I'm in deep trouble. But I'm so drunk I can't walk. The one thing my friends at the party fear the most is my father. They find a way to get me home so they can wash their hands of having anything to do with me getting so wasted. So they put me in a car and dump me at the house next door to mine. First, they ingrain in me over and over again, "Don't tell him [my father] you were with us. Tell him someone forced you to drink this wine."

Meantime, my father and mother are looking for me all over the neighborhood. They fear for my life. They find me at 2 or 3 a.m. My father is panic-stricken. "Are you all right?" he asks. "Are you hurt?"

"Yeah, a little bit," I barely get out. Then I go right ahead and repeat the company line.

He is putting me in the car to drive me to the emergency room when a Sheriff's Department patrol car pulls up, which panics me. A deputy opens up the back door of the car and sees me all collapsed. All I remember is the flashlight glaring at me and the deputy with this smirk on his face asking what's going on. I give him the company line too.

The cop knows I'm lying to him, which I am. But I'm not going to admit to anything else in front of my father, who I fear more. The deputy looks at me suspiciously with his shit-ass grin.

My parents take me to the emergency room at a hospital in East L.A., on Arizona and Whittier. It's more like what we call an urgent care facility today. They examine and X-ray me. My mother, panic-stricken too, believes my story, she being my mother. My father isn't buying it at all, but it's very late and he doesn't want to deal with it then. So they take me home.

I wake up later that morning. All I can smell is the reek of wine, which I think is the most disgusting smell in the world. I'm so sick. I think I'm going to be able to sleep it off. Well, that's a mistaken thought because my father wakes me up and tells me to get dressed.

"What for?" I ask him.

"We're going to try to find that wino" who gave me the wine and made me drink it, according to my story. My father puts this big wrench in the car. He tells me he's going to avenge what the wino has done to his son. We drive around for a while, but return home because I'm not feeling so good.

"I get the distinct feeling you're lying to me," my father tells me. "I don't want you to lie to me. You better not lie to me if this involves some of your friends."

He talks to some of my friends who live next door. They all say they don't know anything. But my father keeps on and on. "He's not feeling good," my mother says, "let him sleep it off."

"Nope, I think he's lying to me," my father persists. I try to walk back to my bedroom. But he's not having any part of that. He pushes me up against the wall: "I don't want you to lie to me. There's something you're not telling me. Tell me the truth and I won't do anything"—he gives me that line.

So I finally decide to come clean. That doesn't produce a real productive result either. He hits me—"that's for lying," he says. "If you'd been man enough, you'd have told me the truth. You thought you were a man by going out and drinking. If you were a man, you'd have said the truth—and this wouldn't happen." He threatens to punish and penalize me for the next 30 years or so it seems the way he's coming at me.

All I can think is how my first outing of any kind where I'm drinking isn't a lot of fun. I swear to myself and to my father that I'm never going to have another drink in my life.

Two weeks later another young guy is taking off for the service and they're having a party. I don't remember how my parents let me get out of the house, but I tell them something. I'm back at it again, drinking with my friends. This time, it's not wine. They have cases upon cases of beer. I have some, but decide to moderate my drinking. I only get buzzed.

From hindsight, which is always 20-20, that first experience should teach me I have a problem as it relates to drinking. But at 13, that doesn't occur to me at all. I just want to have fun and be accepted by my friends. Acceptance, especially among my friends who are older, is very important because I'm the little kid in the group. I believe doing things at an earlier age than normal is part of growing up in this community.

My drinking to gain acceptance takes its course over many years until it becomes a very destructive addiction. Of course, at the time the only addicts I know are dope addicts, guys who shoot up with heroin, or out-and-out winos you see on the streets. In my eyes, that isn't part of my life and never will be.

For all my fear of him as a kid, my father pretty much becomes my rock as far as it involves the direction my life will take and encouraging me to make something of myself. He's always concerned about what will happen to me—whether I'm going to finish college. He knows how tough it is. I'm married with a pregnant wife and I'm working full time at an East L.A. jewelry store while going to college full time at Cal State L.A.

My father and I have just begun to be able to talk with each other, him treating me like an adult for the first time. We have these long conversations about what we're going to do together. I know he will play a tremendous, positive role in the rearing of my kids; I look forward to it, especially given my own insecurities about being a father. This newfound ability to talk is short lived; it only lasts six months before he dies on the very day my first son, Derrick, is born. I'm not even in the middle of getting my college education. Now I have nobody I can talk with and rely on—except myself. The impact of his death lasts for a long time.

I'm very young in relation to my fellow employees at the jewelry store. At least a couple of the salesmen like to drink. I find myself starting to go out with them during breaks to one or two of the local dive bars on Whittier Boulevard. Instead of eating dinner, we drink our meals with a minimum amount of food, if any at all. I proceed to drink more than ever after my father's death to help get through.

My father gives me a lot of good advice. Although not formally educated, he is well read and informed. He gives me my interest in politics and public service, and in someday doing something so the community where I grow up finally has a say over its own destiny. He is also very traditional in his role as head of the family. I start realizing more and more after he's gone that now I'm the head of the family—for my mother and sister, and for my wife and young son (soon to be two sons). I remember him emphasizing the importance of ensuring that no matter what happens in the family or at home, it is kept there—that you never discuss your family or personal business with anyone else. I also remember him telling me, "You make your bed and you lie in it. Don't blame anyone but yourself for your problems, and do the best you can." Those words stick with me. I take them literally.

I do a great job of honoring my father's advice. I never discuss with anyone what the loss of my father does to me or the resentment of losing him when I'm so young and being forced to become head of the household, knowing how unprepared I am for the responsibilities.

I learn to never communicate my real feelings or what is bothering me with anyone outside the family—or inside it either. People are flabbergasted that here's this 21 or 22 year old who shows no emotion. I do such a good job of hiding my feelings that whenever someone asks, "What's going on in your life?" all I can say is "Nothing," or "Everything is fine"—whether that's true or not. People tell me during my political life that I have no blood in my veins because nothing seems to faze me. I learn much later that this is a classic sign of a person with some deep-seated problems. And it's a sign of the emotional hardening that is one of the stages of alcoholism.

Work hard. Get an education. Take care of your family. Be a good provider. Watch your kids grow up and teach them the values that are important. I work hard at doing everything my father teaches me. What person in his right mind gets up in the morning to go to school full time, taking 15 units a semester, then leaves campus to be at work by 11 a.m., getting off at 9 p.m. to go home, maybe watch the news and study until 2 or 3 in the morning? I have a kid who's crying at night while I'm trying to do my homework. I have a wife as young as I am who knows as little about parenthood as I do. Then add on worrying about my mother and sister. I do all that with the exception of one college semester day in and day out for three years.

I'm viewed all of a sudden as having grown up fast and having become so wise that I don't let things bother me. It's all a façade. But I do such a good job at the façade that it becomes a reality in my mind too. Still, it takes its toll. I'm not superman. I take pills to keep me up late at night to study. By then I'm drinking more but it's very controlled. I usually drink on weekends, not during the week, which is dedicated to work and school.

By the time I graduate from college and begin my activism with the Chicano movement in the mid- to late-1960s, I really enjoy drinking as a social outlet in my eyes. It becomes a pleasant release after working hard all day, sometimes seven days a week, in an era where the world is changing and I'm a part of it. Eventually, I begin a political career that is my life's ambition and the fulfillment of aspirations I share with my father to be elected to represent my community in public office.

Much about politics is social. It's about going to events, functions, and dinners. After joining the legislature in 1972, I discover the environment in Sacramento is very collegial, much more so than today. Even if you fight during the day with your political opponents, lawmakers, including some Republicans, come together after hours to attend fundraisers and receptions or just go out to a string of bars and restaurants around the state Capitol. As a matter of fact, a lot of business and many deals get hammered out in these places. We also socialize, have fun—and drink.

Going out to the bars I develop a great tolerance for a high volume of liquor. I rarely drink beer. Since my first experience with drinking at the age of 13, I can't stomach wine, fine or otherwise. I mostly drink hard stuff, Canadian Club Whisky and Seven Up, martinis, or, as I get older, cognacs and finer liquors.

I make a commitment to myself that drinking will only go on in the evening hours. During the day at the Capitol or when I'm in my district attending meetings or events, I rarely partake. I'm never impaired during an assembly committee hearing or floor session. Some people may believe I am because of my earthy language; I don't always speak the queen's English all the time. But I never am. I take my public responsibilities very seriously.

A lot of people think all I do is party at night. I do some. But more times than not I head over to my apartment or to my room at the Marina Inn Motel in West Sacramento, across the Sacramento River. There, I watch television, read—and drink.

I know a lot of people. I can walk the Capitol corridors or walk or drive around my district and countless people I know come up to say hello, exchange pleasantries, or ask me questions. But very few know very much about me, including those I meet at the Capitol or the women I take out. I'm very outgoing in the halls of government or in the community. Yet my basic nature is as an introvert, which isn't very consistent with political life.

The 1980s are a time when it's popular for people to experiment with what comes to be called recreational drugs. Using that name doesn't sound as serious as the heroin of my youth in East L.A. I'm introduced to recreational drugs—cocaine—when it's kind of the thing among young people wanting to explore. Cocaine is not viewed as addictive; it's something you can do, or not do, as you wish. It is readily available among many of the professional people I interact with all the time. One thing I am careful to maintain is anonymity. I drink in public because it is acceptable. When it comes to using drugs, I'm a loner, a private consumer. I never do drugs around anyone with the exception of a small handful of people. I satisfy my addiction in the privacy of home late at night after work. Like drinking, I never use during the day—until the drug begins to lead me by the nose and really controls me more than alcohol.

Cocaine isn't to my liking when I first try it out. My drug of choice is always alcohol. I view drugs as addictive but never see alcohol the same way. I later learn this notion is not very correct or rational.

From when I start drinking at age 13 to when I finally begin confronting my addictions in my mid-40s, they are never anyone's fault except my own. Acknowledging that fact is the first step in changing. All of my addictive behavior catches up to me and eventually forces me to look at what I am doing to myself and to the people I love. I come to feel deep shame and regret over it. It takes me 30 or 40 years to understand it myself. So I offer this story of my addictions not as an excuse, but as an explanation.

My entire political life is dedicated to the premise that politics is the most effective way of bringing about constructive change and wide-ranging impacts on the daily lives of the people I grow up with and end up representing. I like to think I'm a part of my times. I begin my activism and arrive in political office when some of the most exciting events of my day are unfolding, from the start of the contemporary push for Chicano civil rights, bilingual and bicultural education, health and human services, opening up higher education for Latinos and other minorities, the struggle of Cesar Chavez and the farmworkers, the first gains in equal representation for Latinos through reapportionment and the battle for immigrant rights. I don't think it is boastful to say it is my great privilege to play a hand in shaping these and other worthy causes during my activism and tenure in office.

That comes with a price. I sacrifice, as do many politicians, to be in public life: Time with my children and family as well as time to develop my own interests outside of public service because of the long hours and days it takes to be, and stay, in elected office, particularly if you want to make a difference. For me, the career means everything because it is a vehicle to help the people I care about.

Over the years, especially after getting elected to the council in 1985, the pressures of the job increase. As a state lawmaker I spend four days a week in Sacramento in a very controlled and cushy environment and then return home to be with my constituents over a long weekend. You don't deal with people's daily burdens and problems day after day as a legislator. That changes as a councilmember, when I'm constantly in the middle of the district. I take very seriously the demands of the people who rightfully turn to me for help. That's my job, a job I covet and love.

It is fashionable to dismiss someone by calling him or her a politician. The very word can be a term of derision. There are plenty of politicians who deserve the contempt. But many go into public service for all the right reasons and they have to give up much to meet the demands of the job. For those who want to do the job right—which is even harder representing a poor and diverse community with multiple legitimate needs—you can begin internalizing the challenges and pain felt by the people you're trying to help. There aren't many opportunities to talk about such pressures. It can be seen as a sign of weakness, especially by political opponents. As my political life progresses, the people who say I don't have blood in my veins don't see the pain I'm hemorrhaging every day of my life.

Let me repeat: None of this is offered as an excuse. Still, nobody can ever say I complain or whine about anything I do or what happens to me. Whatever road my life takes, good or bad, I'm thankful it eventually gets channeled into something positive.

Yet, I sometimes think about how things could be different if not for these secrets I live with—about what more I might be able to accomplish. My conclusion is I could probably do more, but I'm at peace with what I am able to get done.

"Richard is one of the finest people I've ever known," Hillary Norton says. "But I will never stop being a little disappointed at what could have been if he had not succumbed to some of his demons. Still, I have the grace of knowing him now."

One of my closest friends who figures out my problems over time is George Pla, successful CEO of Cordoba Corporation, a civil engineering firm. I come to look at him as a political advisor. "Can you take care of this problem?" I ask George. "Can you tell me what this situation is about?" "Can you help me raise this money for that campaign?" George never works for me; he is never on my staff. He's just a friend—which says a lot.

"I thought so highly of Richard and what he had done and could do," George says. "I got frustrated when he sometimes didn't show up for an event or came late. He was like that often. For a long time I didn't know why that was. I knew he drank, but didn't know about the drug addiction for years. In Sacramento, he didn't miss floor sessions or committee hearings. But it was different on the city council, maybe because his addiction had advanced; he was probably using and drinking more. It took me a while to catch on to what it was, but I eventually figured it out.

"A small group of us among Richard's closest friends held an intervention with him around 1988, including Lou Moret, Andy Camacho, Ernie Camacho, and myself. Richard tried. He got professional help. He'd make progress. Then he'd con them too, going on and off booze and drugs for a number of years.

"What made the difference were Richard's wife, Angie, and his daughter, Melinda."

I first meet my wife of now 25 years, Angie, in 1973, my first year in elected office. She is also born and raised in East Los Angeles, graduating like me from Garfield High School. At the time we meet, she is working as office manager for the East Los Angeles Retarded Children's Association, helping developmentally disabled kids and their families through programs and services with an entire unit of social workers, a medical director, and an activities person. She is a liaison for the Mexican Olympic team in Los Angeles and organizes events during the 1984 games. She spins that off into her own business out of downtown L.A., Eventfully Yours, planning and organizing events and fundraisers for nonprofit groups and elected officials.

What attracts me to Angie then—and now—are the very traditional Mexican values I grow up with and the beautiful human being she becomes. We go together for two or three years in the mid-1970s, and remain friends afterwards. Angie helps convince me to run for the city council and spends time helping me improve my Spanish. When I get elected in 1985, she stages my big 16th of September Mexican Independence Day observance, taking up the entire south lawn of City Hall. She handles my political fundraising, including putting on events, when I'm on the council.

We start dating again in 1988, and get married in 1991.

I remain close to Angie's family from the time we meet in 1973. Her family openly welcomes me and always sees me as a part of it, even after we stop dating and get married to other people. When Angie loses a brother, I'm a pallbearer at the funeral. Her older sister, Belinda, has a daughter, Melinda. I'm there when she is born in 1988, and remain an important part of her life as she is growing up.

Melinda teaches me humility and what it means to be unselfish. A young child forces you to take time away from what you think is very important—like politics—and to spend some of it doing things I never do for my own sons. After we get married, Angie and I take Melinda to the movies, shopping, and on our vacations. We are there when she starts school; we enroll her in Catholic school.

Tragically, Angie's sister is diagnosed with colon cancer. Angie and I take care of Melinda. Sometimes she stays at our house. I drive her to and from school. Eventually, Belinda calls Angie and me together and asks us to raise her daughter if she passes away.

"We had a proxy drawn up to take care of all of Belinda's affairs," Angie says. "Belinda wrote and signed a letter that Richard had drawn up by John Karns, an attorney friend and partner of Wally Karabian, making it clear that she wanted sole custody of Melinda to go to Richard and me."

Angie and I love taking care of Melinda and doing things for her. I have that responsibility for my own two sons who by then are already adults. My life is fairly well defined. Angie and I have a nice condo in the Monterey Hills that Angie designs to meet all of our needs. It's perfect for us and we love it. It's not too big, which is fine. We don't have the burden of keeping up yards and landscaping. Angie has her own business. I have my political career. It's a great life.

But after Belinda passes, our condo isn't appropriate for a young girl, especially one who fears being alone after losing her mother. Our bedroom is upstairs and Melinda's is downstairs. We decide to buy a larger one-story house, which we find in Eagle Rock, so Melinda can have her room next to ours.

In the meantime, after decades of denial I become very disillusioned and disappointed with myself because the standards I set for my conduct during the workweek are gradually becoming compromised. My addiction is increasingly evident. I'm not the only one who notices the changes. I finally get on the road to sobriety in 1988. Change doesn't happen overnight. It's a struggle I wage—with victories and defeats—over a decade.

I start seeing a doctor who specializes in addiction. Later, he recommends I spend some time in an out-of-state treatment center, which I do for 24 days. John Ferraro, president of the city council, is aware of my problem and the battle I'm waging. He does everything he can to encourage my recovery and make it possible for me to get the time away because he has a son afflicted with a similar problem. I will never forget his kindness and help.

The treatment center helps you understand the addiction, what brings you to it, and what you have to do to avoid it. I gain a lot more insight about what makes me tick and what I have to do for myself to get and stay clean and sober. When you first start down the road to recovery, you become very self-righteous; it's easier to talk about it than to really do it. Also there are no temptations in the highly controlled environment of a treatment center. You might dream of drinking and getting high, but it's not going to happen there. All the temptations come back when you return to the real world and the streets you know so well.

I make the decision to go all the way in participating in the activities. The day is totally controlled by the staff. You hear the speakers and attend group sessions. There is free time to read and do your chores. There is individual therapy. Then you do more group sessions. I continue attending Alcoholics Anonymous meetings. (I learn that while I use drugs too, I'm really an alcoholic, and I have a family predisposition towards the disease.)

The big revelation for me are verbalizing things I never talk about in my life and hearing the stories of other alcoholics and finding out how similar they are to mine. A common belief held by alcoholics is that nobody will understand their problems. That's why you use. There's a boy at the treatment center who comes to understand more about what is going on with himself at 14 than I do at 40. That's rather embarrassing, but it demonstrates how we convince ourselves to believe we are the victims of something no one else will understand only to discover we all have the same thing in common: We abuse and we're very good at hiding it—or we think we are.

The week before I'm getting out, on a Saturday, my sponsor comes from L.A. to speak at the treatment center AA meeting. He shows up early and we have dinner. All that week I have this epiphany, which keeps me awake at night, working it out in my head: I'm going to go public, hit the speaking trail, go on TV talk shows and talk about myself and how I overcome drugs and alcohol. "Look at me now," I'll declare. I figure I can do so much good for people with the same kind of affliction. I share my epiphany with some of the guys in my group at the center and they think it's brilliant, the greatest thing that can happen because they know I'm a public official.

I tell my sponsor. He interrupts me: "Can you just stop for a minute?" I think he's going to tell me what a great idea it is and maybe help me flesh it out some more.

"Do me a favor," he says. "You're sick. Don't think about it for a year. Because whatever comes out of your mouth right now is absolute shit. Because you don't have the capacity to think or reason or make decisions. So just shut the fuck up." It's the most devastating thing I can hear in the world. I think I'm going on Oprah. But what I'm thinking is ludicrous.

I never go public when I get out of the treatment center, thank God. At a session I attend there with my sponsor he says, "The one thing all of you dope fiends and alcoholics have in common is you *will* go back to your addiction. You will fail. But from every failure, hopefully you will move a little bit more forward. Then, hopefully, the lapses won't kill you." He is correct in everything he says, including the one thing we're really good at, which is relapsing because it is to be expected from someone moving towards sobriety.

I go to AA meetings for years, taking the 12-step program very seriously. There's pain, especially when you have to go apologize to people for being the prick you've been towards them and for what they suffer because of your addiction and selfishness. I'm okay most of the time after the initial stint at the treatment center.

During the two weeks of the child custody hearing before Judge Shafford, my late sister-in-law's desires are clearly spelled out in her letter asking Angie and me to raise Melinda, who very much wants to stay with us.

The judge is about to issue his ruling, and the day before I learn from our attorney that it will be in our favor. I think it's in the bag. Then I think, "Shit, I deserve to reward myself."

My battle to escape both drinking and drugs is a number of years old. I know it isn't behind me yet. The fact I even entertain the idea of going out and getting loaded again—and then do it—proves that.

The next day we go to court to receive the judge's decision. I stay in the courtroom while my attorney and the opposing attorney representing the natural father meet with Judge Shafford in his chambers. Much time elapses. Back in the courtroom, the judge informs the attorneys he is prepared to rule in our favor. The attorney for the natural father demands I be drug tested before the judge issues a final decision. The judge agrees. The other side happens to have a technician handy. I refuse at first. The judge makes it clear that if I don't do it, he will not give me custody.

I know I'm screwed. It is a stupid act by a stupid person who is totally irresponsible. That's what addiction does to you. You're basically dealing with two separate personalities and individuals in one mind and body. There is the sick Richard Alatorre who has to drink and use mind-altering substances. And there is the Richard Alatorre who functions, serves responsibly, and cares about people.

None of this would become public or more complicated except for the attention from the media. From the early 1990s until I leave office in 1999, it's as if everything I do as a member of the city council and chairman of the MTA is the subject of a vigorous investigation, mostly by the *Los Angeles Times*. A series of news stories infer that I'm controlling the allocation of millions of dollars of contracts to private vendors seeking work with the MTA or city agencies, that I'm intervening on their behalf to get them the contracts, and that I'm personally profiting from it.

It seems as if I sometimes get stories on the front pages of the newspaper once a week. They make it sound like I'm this evil person who has all this influence and I'm only using it to help out my friends. The reporters are very clever. They contact me just before each story appears, asking me for comment. They call right at 4 p.m., letting my office know they're writing a story that will be published the next morning, revealing part of what it will say and asking for my side.

I don't comment. I follow a simple practice from early in my political life. You listen to what they want to talk with you about and then ask yourself a question: Is there anything I can add to this story that will turn it from being a negative story into a positive story? I conclude 95 percent of the time that there is nothing I can say that will help. They're determined to go ahead with whatever line they wish to use no matter what facts I or anyone else will provide.

Take for example a prominent story in the *L.A. Times* about a new Spanish-tile roof that goes up on our house in Eagle Rock. The old roof needs replacing after we move in. I speak with my friend of 30 years, David Lizarraga, head of TELECU, the East Los Angeles Community Union, which develops multi-family housing. David is a friend of mine since middle school.

David recommends a roofing contractor who I also know for 20 years, and he agrees to do the work. The contractor, to my knowledge, has never sought or obtained work from the MTA or any city agency; he's just not interested. But the *Times* story makes it sound like I'm attempting to enrich myself by employing a contractor who I can later reward with contracts or who I can receive kickbacks from. Every accusation that is humanly possible to make comes out over a nearly five-year period in the pages of the *Times*.

Most of the coverage centers on my chairmanship of the MTA, the influence I do have with the agency, and the fact many people who are close to me, allies and friends, seem to get looked upon favorably in the awarding of contracts. The truth is that I'm sure many people and firms I know do get contracts from the MTA because they are good providers of the services that are sought.

"The *Times* was saying transportation contractors seeking contracts at the MTA were contributing to golf tournaments and fundraising events for Richard's nonprofit, El Sereno Youth Center, that was turning around and paying Angie money," Hillary Norton says. "Angie had a fundraising and event business, Eventually Yours, that worked with the El Sereno Youth center. She had been doing it for years and was very good at it."

While Angie and I are waging our struggle for custody of Melinda, the attorney for the natural father leaks information to *Times* reporters on strategic occasions during the hearing. So the *Times* reporters know when to show up and write about the proceedings that are supposed to be closed because they involve a minor child. Because I'm a public figure and the subject of numerous newspaper "exposés," the custody fight becomes a media circus too. The father's attorney anonymously leaks other allegations to the *Times* so its reporters are in a position to write stories they can't prove because there is no evidence.

Exhaustive investigations of me by the FBI, the U.S. Attorney's Office, the L.A. County District Attorney's office, the state Fair Political Practices Commission, the city ethics commission, and the inspector general of the MTA, a neutral watchdog office, follow the newspaper coverage. The *Times* dutifully reports on the investigations. Nobody, including me, is ever charged, prosecuted, or convicted over any of the allegations of wrongdoings that appear in the *L.A. Times*.

The feds in particular are convinced I'm enriching myself as a public servant and that I'm doing it, in part, through my wife's successful event planning and fundraising company, which she continues to run. They're convinced I have money squirreled away in Mexico or in other foreign countries or the funds are being held in the names of other people. After years of investigation and exhaustive auditing and subpoenaing of my records and those of my friends, relatives, and associates, the feds conclude I don't have any money other than what I earn from my job with the city. In fact, I don't have any assets except my house. They never find any evidence I receive any profits from any of the transactions they investigate. They are unable to pursue any of the allegations that are brought up.

The only charge that does emerge from the U.S. Attorney's Office is that I have not reported income of $32,000, which is a loan from a wealthy apartment house developer I use several years earlier for the down payment on our house in Eagle Rock. The federal grand jury in L.A. holds closed-door hearings on a wide variety of issues involving me. The developer who provides the loan testifies under oath that I never ask him for any money and that he never gives me any money; it's a loan, not a gift or a bribe. No other evidence proving allegations of impropriety are presented to the grand jury. If they can uncover any credible proof of this or any other alleged wrongdoing, they would not hesitate to file charges against me.

The developer sticks to his testimony until the feds get the goods on him over an unrelated income tax evasion. Federal authorities offer to help him out on his income tax problem if he will help them get me. So the developer changes his story, claiming the loan to me is not a loan and that I did force him to give me the money.

My attorneys assure me we can easily impugn the developer's integrity and beat the charges.

At that point, the U.S. Attorney's Office informs my lawyer that unless I accept a plea bargain on the nonreporting of income, the feds are prepared to go after Angie too since she also signs the income tax returns that we jointly file as husband and wife. My attorney says we will be found innocent if it ever gets to court. But going after my wife is too much for me. And Melinda is about seven then. Her mother has recently died. Angie and I don't want Melinda to have to suffer more than she already has.

I agree to the plea bargain. The fed's case is so weak that under terms of the agreement, I just have to pay the back taxes and interest. Because of my precarious financial situation—the fact I have very few personal resources to show after 28 years in public life—no fine is imposed. I never lose my right to vote.

I go from celebrating a great victory one day—anticipating the judge's decision to give us custody of the little girl who becomes a daughter to Angie and me—to the next day enduring the worst humiliation I experience in my life. I take the drug test in the courthouse and fail it. I can honestly say that is when I hit bottom.

"Richard had me and Luisa Acosta, his deputy chief of staff, go pick up the judge's ruling at the courthouse in the Mid-Wilshire District," Hillary Norton recalls. "So we go to pick it up. I'm pregnant at the time.

"Richard has us open up the ruling at the courthouse. We read it and sit there and cry our eyes out. The judge expresses his disappointment that Richard failed the drug test. His order says Richard can't go within 500 feet of Melinda. This is just devastating. Luisa and I are more than Richard's chief of staff and deputy chief of staff. We are like his kids. He had married Gerard and me.

"I'm driving back to City Hall thinking how mad and sorry I am for Richard at the same time. We were profoundly disappointed in him too because we knew what a great man he was and what a great thing he was doing for Melinda. And we were disappointed because he risked everything he was doing to set his life right. We met with him in his office. He could see something was wrong when we walked in because we must have looked terrible from the crying. I remember him crying too.

"It was one of the worst days of my life because I just felt so bad for him and Angie," Hillary says. "I was so angry because [the natural father] just wanted to get at Richard politically."

"Richard was devastated, embarrassed, humiliated," Angie remembers. "He wasn't angry with anyone but himself. I have vivid memories of him finding a slope in Eagle Rock Park where he could park his car nearby, get out, set a folding chair in the grass and watch Melinda play flag football on the field down below, obeying the judge's order to stay 500 feet away from her. I was with Melinda, pointed Richard out to her in the distance, and she waved to him. She always wanted him around.

"I could see the pain. At one point I did get angry over the stupidity of it all. Maybe subconsciously he welcomed getting that final kick in the butt that would finally force him to give it all up. Interestingly, throughout this difficult time, aside from the normal crowd of Alatorre haters most of his constituents and political associates, even those who were not always his supporters, showed a lot of compassion. By then, people began to realize addiction is a disease and it affects a lot of people. I doubt there's a family that doesn't have a loved one who's been hit."

"This crazy Greek tragedy wouldn't be believable if it was an opera," Hillary continues.

It is customary in custody proceedings for minor children to be represented by their own attorneys, to look out for their interests. Melinda's lawyer goes back to Judge Shafford not much later and sees him in his chambers. "I'm not a well man," the attorney tells the judge, "but I'm begging you—you're not doing this little girl any good. This is a terrible thing. You're taking her away from the only father she has ever known. He's gone to rehab and will do anything to get her back. Don't let me die knowing Melinda, my client, isn't going to be taken care of." The judge can see the attorney is heartbroken.

The judge brings Melinda in to speak with him in his chambers. He wants to know how she's doing. They engage in the kind of small talk you have with a seven year old. Melinda tells the judge she doesn't want to keep going on required visits with her natural father and that she wants to live with Angie and me. That plays a big role in convincing the judge to change his mind.

I appear again before Judge Shafford. He is pretty stern with me. He knows Melinda is better off with us. He will give me another chance, but if I relapse one more time it's over. I have to keep going for treatment and be regularly tested. All the test results and reports on my treatment will go directly to the judge. "Don't disappoint me again," the judge says. "Make sure I'm not making a mistake."

A few weeks later, Melinda's attorney is working on another case at the courthouse when he has a heart attack and dies.

I enter an outpatient treatment program after working hours four days a week. Some days I go from 4 to 10 p.m. Sometimes it's from 6 to 10 p.m. I get tested several times a week too since some drugs remain in your system for only a short while. That lasts for close to a year. It becomes less rigorous over time as I make progress and the therapist sees I'm doing better. One time I need surgery and the pain medication the doctor prescribes that I temporarily use shows up on the drug test. The therapist sticks up for me, saying it is clearly not a violation of the court order. The judge agrees.

I never miss any of my therapy or group sessions. I meet all the terms and conditions set out by the court. Eventually, Angie and I are awarded full custody of Melinda.

Judge Shafford follows our daughter's progress and stays in touch. He goes to her middle and high school graduations and to her graduation from Cal State L.A., my alma mater, coming to the house afterwards for the graduation party. He still mails Christmas cards every year. Angie sends the invitations along with the most recent photos of Melinda. The judge once writes back in a note, "Boy, we did this one right."

"Richard dedicated himself to making it right," Angie says. "From that point on there was no hesitation in what he needed to do so all of us could be a family again. He was not a happy person for a long time. He had to confront his own demons that were with him from childhood, from growing up in East L.A., and from the early death of his father. For many years, Richard was a private person who never talked about himself. He could face and fight many battles on behalf of other people, but he was not willing to face his own pain, insecurity, and lack of self-confidence. The custody battle—the struggle to win back Melinda—motivated him to finally face and understand and learn from the disappointments he experienced and caused.

"He hasn't had a drink in 28 years."

"People sometimes ask me why do I look up to Richard Alatorre, why he is such a good friend?" says George Pla. "They know his reputation as kind of a bad-ass; some know about his problems with addiction.

"I start with: 'Do you understand what he did with redistricting and the impact it had on California, with respect to Cesar Chavez and the farmworkers, and with changing the face of Los Angeles while on the city council?' Then I add, 'Let me ask you, Do you know why he pleaded to [the income-tax allegation]? Because he wanted to protect his wife and daughter.' David Ayon, an author, professor and historian at Loyola Marymount University of Los Angeles, said, 'That was Richard's finest hour.'"

"Richard became the leader he taught his students to be when he taught at UC Irvine, Cal State Long Beach, and Terminal Island prison," Hillary says. "But he also became the man he taught them to be when he came to terms with himself and confronted his own ghosts."

Finding redemption and grace: Richard Alatorre with his wife, Angie Alatorre; daughter, Melinda; and sons, Derrick (left) and Darrell. (Photo: Raymond Kwan)

There are so many years of denial. You tell yourself, I can handle the drinking and the coke, the on-and-off addiction. But AA teaches that you can't be an on-and-off alcoholic or drug addict. You have to give it up.

I keep going to AA, learning the meaning of living one day at a time. I learn about humility, how to reach out and talk with other alcoholics, how to verbalize things that concern me (contrary to how I'm raised), the need to go to AA meetings on a regular basis, and the things I need to put into practice day to day. I still practice the principles of AA to the best of my ability. Now I go to AA meetings when I feel the need. Because of all that, I'm clean and sober since that dreadful day in court.

I sink to the depths of humiliation on the worst day of my life. But it ends up saving me. With help from those I love the most, I discover the power within me to find redemption, and in the process for the first time in my life I also find peace and grace.

Index

Note: Richard Alatorre is referred to as RA throughout the index. Photographs are indicated by italicized page numbers.

A

Abortion issue, 227
Acosta, Luisa, 425
Acosta, Oscar, 44–45
Adelante Eastside Area, development of, 375–377
The Advocate (gay newspaper), 100
Affirmative action, 86
AFL-CIO, 189, 358–359
African Americans. *See also* Racial discrimination
   Chicanos' needs vs., 36–38, 293, 305
   city council reapportionment and, 298
   in L.A. population, 293–295
   LAPD relations with, 320–321
   RA relationship with, 305
   voting rates of, 297
   War on Poverty funding and, 36
AFSCME (American Federation of State, County and Municipal Employees), 339
Agnos, Art, 206, 211, 231, 385
Agricultural Labor Relations Act (1975), 172, 175, 194
   elections following passage of, 199
   failure of enforcement of, 199, 208, 228
   passage by assembly, 197
   RA's role in, 203, 205
   signing of, *198*
Agricultural Labor Relations Board (ALRB), 155, 208, 209, 227–228
Ahmanson, Caroline Leonetti, 342–343

Alatorre, Angie, 311, 315, 353, 420–421, 424, 427, *428*
Alatorre, Antonio (uncle), 10
Alatorre, Cecelia (sister), 4, 6, *7*, *9*, 90, 206
Alatorre, Darrell (son), 26, 186, 421, *428*
Alatorre, Derrick (son), 26, 186, 421, *428*
Alatorre, Francisca (grandmother), 7–8, *9*, 10, 351
Alatorre, Jose Paz (father), 4–7
   connection to "the barrio," 12
   dealing with RA's first intoxication, 414–415
   dislike of his employment, 6, 12, 15–16
   early death of, 6, 11, 27–28, 415–416
   guilt over RA taking job while in high school, 16
   importance of education for his children, 6, 12, 13
   as inspiration to RA, 6, 18, 24–25, 28, 233, 415–416
   personality of, 12
   photographs of, *9*, *17*
   racial discrimination experenced by, xi, 10–11, 233
Alatorre, Maria Martinez (mother), 4–6, 10, 12, 200, 234, 315, 414
Alatorre, Melinda (daughter), 420–423, 425–427, *428*
Alatorre, Richard (RA)
   Alcoholics Anonymous meetings, attendance of, 421–422, 429
   alcoholism of, x, 413–418, 421, 427, 429

in Assembly. *See* Assembly
Belvedere home of, 5
birth of, 1
Boyle Heights home of, 3–4
Budget Committee chair (L.A. City Council), 326–335, 341–342
career choice of, 16, *17*
Chicano movement role of, 23–50. *See also* Chicano movement
childhood friends of, vii–viii
city council membership. *See* Los Angeles City Council
closeness to and responsiveness to L.A. constituency, 340–341, 410–411, 419
clothes and, 13
college education of, 23–29, 426
committee memberships and chair posts. *See* Assembly committees; Los Angeles City Council; *specific committee*
corruption investigations of, 424–425
criticisms of, 218–219
divorce of, 52
drug addiction of, 418–419, 421, 426
as educator, 51–84. *See also* Teaching career
failure to be handy, 12
family background of, 4–8, 28
farmworkers, involvement with, 183–200. *See also* Chavez, Cesar; UFW
father as inspiration for, 6, 18, 24–25, 28, 415–416
federal grand jury hearings on, 424–425
financial status of, 387, 425
Ford Foundation Fellowship, 87, 91

gang membership of, viii, x
graduate school education of, 87
high school employment of, 13–16
internship with Karabian, 87, 89–90. *See also* Karabian, Walter
intervention by friends, 419–420
jewelry store employment of, 26, 28–29
LACTC board member, 391–392, 401. *See also* Los Angeles County Transportation Commission
LAPD and, 317–325. *See also* Los Angeles Police Department
leadership and problem-solving style of, 20, 147–148, 341–342, 388–389, 427
Los Angeles City Council member, 274–289. *See also* Los Angeles City Council
marriages of, viii, 416. *See also* Alatorre, Angie (second wife); Alatorre, Stella (first wife)
Melinda's child custody hearing and, 422–427
motivation for public service career, xi, 346, 419
move to Eagle Rock, 421, 424
MTA chair, 391–412. *See also* Metropolitan Transportation Authority
partier and carouser reputation of, 177–178, 417
personality of, 16, 200, 342, 390, 416–417
photographs of, *7, 9, 17, 53, 73, 90, 123, 141, 192, 195, 197, 198, 207, 211, 216, 277, 283, 304, 314, 323, 328, 366, 378, 428*

playing basketball, 12–13, 20
public school education of, 8, 12–13, 18–21
public speaking skills of, 284
reapportionment and, 220, 238–272. *See also* Assembly Elections and Reapportionment Committee; Reapportionment
reflecting on best times, 200, 233, 274, 282
RTD board member, 391–392, 401
in treatment programs, 421–422, 427
UFW, involvement with, 183–200. *See also* Chavez, Cesar; UFW
Alatorre, Stella, 26–27
Alatorre-Berman-Dunlap-Zenovich Agricultural Labor Relations Act of 1975. *See* Agricultural Labor Relations Act (1975)
Alcoholics Anonymous, 421–422, 429
Aldrich, Daniel G., 52, 55, 64–66, 125, 168
Alinsky, Saul, 3, 110, 180, 278
Alioto, Joseph, 149, 201
Allee, A. Y., Jr., 181
ALRB. *See* Agricultural Labor Relations Board
Alvarez, Sal, 221
American Farm Bureau Federation, 185
American Federation of State, County and Municipal Employees (AFSCME), 339
American Transportation Association, 411
Animal use in medical research, 166–168
Anti-immigrant sentiments, 270, 271, 276, 358
Antonovich, Mike, 383, 400

Areias, Rusty, 184
Arguello, Dan, 262
Arnett, Dixon, 110
Arywitz, Sigmund, 358–359
Asa, Oran, 17, 18
Asian American community of L.A., 296, 298–299
Assembly (1972–1984), 115–178
  Agricultural Labor Relations Act (1975), 172, 175, 194
  animal use in medical research, legislation to terminate, 166–168
  art and culture, legislation to fund, 163–164
  Berman vs. McCarthy for Speaker (1979–80), 170, 204–206, 209–213. *See also* Speakership war
  bilingual contracts legislation, 136–141, *141*
  bill limits, 156
  Brown as speaker, 116–117, 170
  budget bills, review of, 153–154
  Chicano Caucus, 121–122, 127, 149–150, 159, 183, 203
  committee assignments, 124–126, 149
  Democratic Caucus, 202, 205
  district demographics, 117
  drug testing on prisoners, legislation to change, 160–162
  farmworkers legislation (AB 3370, 1974), 191–194
  freshmen members' relationship with lobbyists, 159
  human medical experimentation on prisoners, legislation to change, 160–162
  Latino Legislative Caucus, 271
  mandatory retirement age, legislation to change, 159–160
  McCarthy as speaker, 116, 169–170, 201–202

medical practice, legislation to include podiatrists and other medical professionals, 163–164
Moretti as speaker, 115–116, 118–121, 201
persons with disabilities, legislation to recognize rights of, 162–163
public safety, legislation to fund, 165
public school funding and programs, 156–157
RA as master of back-room politics, 146–148
RA punished by McCarthy for not supporting him, 169–170, 197–198
RA's political philosophy, 112, 117–118, 157–158, 385–386, 418
RA's record of introducing and passing bills, 177
RA's sources of information, 159
RA's staff, 126–127, 158. *See also* Trigueiro, Toni
speakership war (beginning 1974), 201–231. *See also* Speakership war
UFW's comprehensive farm labor bill (AB 1, 1975), 195
videotaping of court proceedings, legislation to introduce, 165
women's empowerment issues and, 128–132
Assembly (first campaign, 1971), 85–110
campaign movie, 96–97
campaign strategy, 101–103
funding, 94–95, 113
gay community and, 97–101
loss to Republican opposition, 103–104, 109–110
Moret's role in, 102–103
primary victory of RA over Ralph Ochoa, 92–102
promotional mailings, 97
Raza Unida's role in, 103–105
redistricting and, 266
Republican dirty tricks and, 106–109
Assembly (second campaign, 1972), 111–113
campaign strategy, 113
funding, 113
victory against Republican opponent, 113
victory in Democratic primary, 113
Assembly Criminal Justice Committee, 203
Assembly Elections and Reapportionment Committee, 148, 203, 220, 238–272. *See also* Reapportionment
Assembly Governmental Organization Committee, 166, 186, 281
Assembly Human Resources Committee, 149, 170, 203, 240
Assembly Insurance Committee, 186
Assembly Labor and Employment Committee, 170, 203, 221, 222, 227
Assembly Majority Consultants. *See* Assembly Office of Majority Services
Assembly Office of Majority Services, 77–78, 89, 170, 181, 223
Assembly Revenue and Taxation Committee, 203
Assembly Rules Committee, 169
Assembly Select Committee on Farm Labor Violence, 186, 189–191, *192*, 208

Assembly Select Committee on Prison Reform and Rehabilitation, 160, 173
Assembly Ways and Means Committee, 82, 83, 86, 124, 152, 178, 182
Association of Mexican American Educators, 30, 32–34, 36, 43, 48, 144
Avila, Ed, 278–279
Avila, Gil, 282
Ayala, Ruben, 269
Ayon, David, 427

B
Baca, Dick, 33
Baca, Joe, 269
Banks, Ronald, 285–286
Barry's Jewels, 26
Battle of Chavez Ravine, 376
Becham, Jim, 275–276
Bella Vista, housing discrimination in, 11
Belvedere Citizen, 17–18
Belvedere neighborhood (East L.A.), vii, 4, 6, 11
Benitez, Francis (aunt), 5, 9
Benitez, Juan (uncle), 9
Berman, Howard
  campaign strategies of, 146
  Chavez in support of him for speakership, 209–212, 237
  congressional race of, 225, 256–257
  farm labor law and, 175, 187–188, 197, 198
  as political insider, 150
  RA in support of him for speakership, 212, 237, 316
  RA's relationship with, 385
  RA transferring his support from, 213–221
  in speakership war with Brown, 215, 237
  in speakership war with McCarthy, 170, 202–204
Berman, Michael, 205, 212, 213, 215, 242, 246, 250, 259, 260
Bernson, Hal, 380, 386
Beverly, Bob, 134, 158, 203
Bilingualism and biculturalism, 30–31, 32, 52, 117, 126
  Assembly Bill 86 for bilingual public services, 132–136
  bilingual contracts legislation, 136–141, *141*
  bilingual education legislation, 141–146
Billy the Kid (William H. Bonnie), 10
Bird, Rose, 175, 195, 196–197
Birk's jewelry store, 26, 28–29
Black Panthers, 57
Bloody Christmas (1951), 3
Boalt Hall School of Law (UC Berkeley), 85–87, 125, 152
Boatwright, Dan, 203, 268
Bonanno, Salvatore, 78, 80
Bonnie, William H. (Billy the Kid), 10
Bowler, Michael, III, 95–96
Boxer, Barbara, 384
Boycott. *See also* Grapes boycott
  lettuce boycott, 188
Boyle Heights (East L.A.), vii, 1–3, 344–349
  absentee landlords in, 346–347
  Adelante Eastside Area, development of, 375–377
  Breed Street Shul, preservation of, 379–382, *381*
  business startups in, 2, 349–350
  changing Brooklyn Avenue to Cesar Chavez Avenue, 350–351
  Chavez Ravine, eminent domain used to take property in, 376
  commercial development, 367

436 Index

council redistricting and, 291
County-USC Hospital, rebuilding
    efforts for, 382–383
DASH routes in, 399
description of neighborhood mix,
    1–3, 350, 379
freeways in, 392
gangs protecting community
    against 1992 rioting, 309
infrastructure needs of, 345–346
Jewish immigrants and businesses
    in, 1–2, 349, 379
LAPD and, 317
Mariachi Plaza, revitalization of,
    377–379, *378*
public housing projects in, 373–
    374
Puente Learning Center, 306–307
rail transit (gold line) and, 397–
    399
as RA's home district, 1, 3
substandard housing for immi-
    grants in, 372–373
Bradley, Tom, 87–89, 104, 228,
    280, 282–283
1969 mayor race, 87–88, 303–305
business and, 367
ethics problems of, 386
homelessness, dealing with, 348–
    349
LACTC appointments by, 400
LAPD discrimination and, 317
mass transit system and, 391, 393,
    404, 407–408
personality of, 305
photographs of, *89, 304*
RA and, 303–305, 408
veto of council reapportionment
    plan, 300
Bravo, Francisco, 318
Breed Street Shul, preservation of,
    2, 379–382, *381*
Briggs, Judith, 255–256

Brody, Bonnie, 328, 348
Brokaw, Tom, 62
Bronzan, Bruce, 184
Brophy, Bill, 103, 109, 111, 236
Brown, Anne Gust, 176
Brown, Jerry
    Agricultural Labor Relations Act
        (1975) and, 194–197, 208
    Aldrich and, 65
    California Arts Council and, 164
    at Century Plaza fundraiser, 127
    Chavez and, 172, 195–196, 229
    on drivers' licenses for undocu-
        mented immigrants, 268
    education reform and, 145
    in governor race (Democratic
        primary 1974), 94, 148, 201–
        202
    Patino appointed to judgeship by,
        166
    photographs of, *172, 174, 198*
    RA's relationship with, 170–177
    on unemployment benefits
        for farmworkers, 213
Brown, Kathleen, 362
Brown, Pat, 43, 87, 172
Brown, Willie
    animal use in medical research,
        legislation to terminate, 168
    appointing RA to reapportion-
        ment committee, 148, 220,
        238–239
    appointing RA to Ways and
        Means subcommittee on
        higher education, 82–86
    Burton and, 259
    at Century Plaza fundraiser, 127
    Chavez and UFW working with,
        229–231
    consenting adults bill and, 98
    Cory-Wood bill (1971) and, 182
    ideological alignment with RA,
        94

leadership style of, 274–275
LGBT voters and, 100
photograph of, *216*
picketing of, 262
RA in City Council and, 282, 294, 384
reapportionment and, 242–243, 245–246, 248–250, 252, 254–255, 259–260, 268
as Revenue and Taxation chairman, 203
San Francisco school district and, 156
as Speaker, 116–117, 170, 198, 237, 384
in speakership war, 116–117, 149–150, 201–202, 213–220
Waters and, 273–274
as Ways and Means chairman, 124–125
Brown Act, 297
Brown Berets, 48, 84, 317
Budget and Finance Committee (L.A.), 313, 326–335, 340, 370
Bugliosi, Vince, 97
Burke, Bill, 393
Burke, Yvonne Braithwaite, 383, 393
Burt, Marina, 143, 145
Burton, John, 93, 94, 119, 127, 148, 184, 191, 267, 385
Burton, Phil
  Berman and, 256
  Patino and, 167
  photograph of, *239*
  reapportionment and, 238–239, 240, 242, 258–259, 268, 269, 280, 404
  speakership war and, 225
Bus Riders Union, 394
Bustamante, Cruz, 266, 362

C

CABE (California Association of Bilingual Educators), 144–145, 217
Cain, Bruce
  council reapportionment, 274, 292–301
  legislative reapportionment, 240–241, *241*, 243–253, 257–266, 268–271
Calderon, Chuck, 223–225, 229, 231
California Arts Council, 164–165
California Constitution, 236
California Department of Education, 33
California Endowment, 409
California League of Cities, 384
California Medical Association (CMA), 163–164
California State Polytechnic University, Pomona, 25
California State University, Long Beach, 51, 56
California State University, Los Angeles, 23–29
Californios for Fair Representation, 262, 264, 268
Cal Tech students working on reapportionment, 247, 263
Camacho, Andy, 419–420
Camacho, Ernie, 46, 47, 64, 107, 419–420
Campaign fundraising, 126–127, 202, 226, 278, 281–282
Campbell, Bill, 158, 252
Capitol building (Sacramento), 354
Carpenter, Dennis, 139–140
Carpenter, Paul, 102
Carrillo, Luis, 86, 317
Carter, Jimmy, 204, 279
Castellanos, Leonard, viii
Castro, Sal, 40, 42–46, *44*, 48–49, 56

Castro, Vicky, 48
Catellus Development Corp., 407
Catholic Church and schools, 84, 108, 306, 330, 353–354, 362
Catolicos por La Raza (Catholics for the Race), 84
Cavala, Bill, 259
Cedars Sinai Medical Center, 2
Cedillo, Gil, 267
Centro de Ninos Inc., 128
Century Plaza Hotel fundraiser (October 1973), 126–127
Cercedes family, vii–viii
Cerrell, Joe, 89–90, 312
Chacon, Peter, 121–122, *123*, 142–144, 149, 202
Chandler, Norman, 60
Chatfield, LeRoy, 195–196
Chavez, Cesar, 177–200
  Berman and speakership war, role in, 209–210, 215–218
  in Boyle Heights, 3, 4
  Brown (Jerry) and, 172, 195–196
  Brown (Willie) and, 229–231
  CABE and, 144
  Calderon and, 225–226
  changing Brooklyn Avenue to Cesar Chavez Avenue in Boyle Heights, 350–351
  Church of the Epiphany and, 48
  Commonwealth Club of California address (1984), 179
  communication skills of, 180
  Community Service Organization and, 39
  complimenting RA, 200
  Delano grape strike and, 52, 67
  Dodger Stadium and, 376
  farmworkers legislation and, 191–199. *See also* Agricultural Labor Relations Act
  Gallo demonstration (1975) and, *195*, 195–196
  Garcia and, 228
  Grossman and, 66, 151
  health problems of, 193
  Karabian and, 183
  Maggio Inc. v. United Farm-Workers judgment, 175
  McCarthy and, 208, 210
  Meany/AFL-CIO and, 189
  nonviolence principles of, 188
  photographs of, *192*, *195*, *197*, *207*, *211*, *283*
  on "poverty warriors," 38
  RA in Assembly and, 117, 187, 206–207
  RA in City Council and, 282
  RA's first meeting with, 180
  Torres and, 209–212, 217–218, 222, 225, 227, 228
  undocumented immigrants and, 110–111
  Waters and, 155
  worry about antifarmworker amendments to weaken Agricultural Labor Relations Act, 208
Chavez, Fernando, 210, 229
Chavez, Helen, 379
Chavez, Paul, 227, 230
Chavez, Richard, 229
Chavez Ravine, eminent domain used to take property in, 376
Chella, Lou, 82
Chernin, Rose, 42, *43*, 44–47, 63
Chicana Service Action Center, 128
Chicano 13 (1968), 45–46, 47, 48. *See also* High school walkouts
Chicano Moratorium (1970), 46–47, 58, 60–64, *61*
Chicano movement. *See also* Student activism
  beginning of organizing, 39–42
  Chicano 13 (1968), 45–46, 47, 48

Mexican American Action Committee, 39
Mexican American Political Association (MAPA), 39, 40, 42–43
RA's awakening and early role in, 23–50, 52
War on Poverty funding and, 36–38
Chicanos. *See* Latinos
Childcare centers, 128–130
Children's services and budget, 326–330, *328*. *See also* Education
Chinese Exclusion Act, 358
Chrisman, Michael, 65, 66
Church of Scientology, 160
Church of the Epiphany (Episcopal church), 48, 49
City Council. *See* Los Angeles City Council
City Hall, L.A., 354–355, *355*
Civil rights issues, 39, 50, 51, 84, 104
Clinton, Hillary, 2, 380
Clute, Steve, 184
CMA (California Medical Association), 163–164
Cocaine, 418
Cohen, Jerry, 175, 181–195, *187*
  Agricultural Labor Relations Act (1975) and, 191, 193–194, 196–198
  Teamsters-UFW negotiations, 199
Collier, Bud, 253
Colorado Boulevard development, 368
Comisión Feminil Mexicana Nacional (National Mexican Women's Commission), 128–132, *129*
Commission on Children, Youth and Their Families, 330

Committee for the Defense of the Bill of Rights, 42, 44, 47
Committee to Protect the Bill of Rights, 2
Committee to Reelect the President (CREEP), 106
Communists/communism
  Bradley called "communist," 305
  Committee to Protect the Bill of Rights and, 2
  LAPD investigation of, 41
  Monroy as communist, 40
  RA called "communist," 277
  RA's knowledge of, 24
Community Concerned (nonprofit), 80
Community Redevelopment Agency (CRA), 375–377
Community Service Organization (CSO), 3, 39, 40, 92, 235, 278, 317
Commuting
  automobile, 393
  subway system. *See* Metropolitan Transportation Authority
Comrie, Keith, 337–339
Condit, Gary, 184
Congressional races, 225, 256–257
Congressional relations, help for L.A. from, 384
Contreras, Miguel, 310, 358, *360*, 360–363, 365
Contreras, Rufino, 175, 208
Coro Foundation, 287
Corona, Bert, 39, 43, 46, 104, 110, 111, 304
Corporal punishment at school, 18–19
Corrections, California Department of, 160–162
Corruption, 279, 424
Cortines, Ray, 157
Cory, Ken, 82, 83, 125, 158, 181
Cory-Wood bill (1971), 181, 182

Costa, Jim, 184, 221
Council of Mexican American Affairs, 30
County-USC Hospital, rebuilding efforts for, 382–383
Cowan, Geoff, 386–387
CRA (Community Redevelopment Agency), 375–377
Cranston, Alan, 60, 62, 108, 384
CREEP (Committee to Reelect the President), 106
Crime, 36, 276, 293, 327, 329, 330, 345, 346, 357, 358, 374. *See also* Prisoners
CSO. *See* Community Service Organization
Cultural Affair Department (L.A.), 165, 328
Cunningham, David, 283, 294
Cutdowns of Hoyo Mara (gang), viii, x, 12
Cuthberston, Peg, 60–63

D
D'Agostino, Carl, 212, 242, 246
Daniels, Stella. *See* Alatorre, Stella
D'Arcy, Brian, 335–336
Davis, Angela, 57
Davis, Ed, 41
Davis, Gray, 177, 268
Deaton, Ron, 354
Decade of the Hispanic, 116
de Leon, Marcos, 32, 33–34
DeLeon, Rudy, 321
Demato, Alfonse, 405
Democratic National Committee, 384
Democratic National Convention (1972), 118–119, 132, 165–166
Democratic Party
  Agricultural Labor Relations Act (1975) and, 194
  Assembly staffs, 169–170

Chicanos and, 103–104, 111–112, 236
growers vs. farmworkers and, 184–185
liberalism and, 147
reapportionment and, 103, 251, 257, 265
Riordan and, 310
rural Democrats, 221, 267
Demographic change, 117, 293–295, 304, 326. *See also* African Americans; Latinos
Deukmejian, George, 177, 199, 226, 228, 245, 273, 280
Diaz, Eddie, 18, 40–41
Disabled persons, legislation to recognize rights of, 162–163
Discrimination. *See* Racial discrimination
Districting. *See* Reapportionment
Dixon, Julian, 170
Dixon Arnett law, 111
Dodger Stadium, 376–377, 410
Doolittle, John, 145
Downtown L.A.
  African-American influence over, 293–294
  homelessness in, 348–349
  infrastructure needs of, 346
  RA's childhood memories of, 351
  revitalization of, 306, 314, 348, 351–354, 371
  transportation to, 376. *See also* Metropolitan Transportation Authority
Drake, Jim, 180
Drug testing on prisoners, legislation to change, 160–162
Duffy, Gene, 83
Duffy, Gordon, 125, 168
Dulay, Heidi, 143, 145
Dunlap, John, 198
Duran, Mike, 48

Durazo, Maria Elena, 358, 360, 363, 364, *366*
Dymally, Mervyn
  bilingualism legislation and, 132, 139
  Bradley and, 303–304
  internship program set up by, 87
  Patino and, 190
  photograph of, *198*
  RA in City Council and, 282
  RA race against Ochoa for assembly nomination and, 93, 94
  as role model for RA, 104
Dymally-Alatorre Bilingual Services Act, 132

E
Eagle Rock
  Cultural Center, 369, 370
  electoral role of, 275–277, *277*, 279
  Historical Society, 369
  infrastructure needs of, 346
  RA's move to, 421, 424
  revitalization of, 367–371
  Snyder and, 343–344, 370
Earthquakes, 308–309, 356, 380
East Los Angeles. *See also* Belvedere neighborhood; Boyle Heights
  childcare centers in, 128–130
  Kennedys and, 5
  Latino politicians from, 235, 266
  poverty programs and, 36
  public schools, 20, 30–31. *See also* High school walkouts
  rail transit and, 376, 397–399, *398*
  RA's attachment to, 16, *17*
  RA's representation in assembly, 97
  Reagan in, 137
  reapportionment and, 18
  Rodney King riots and, 309

voter registration drive in, 90
Echo Park, 11, 47, 97, 98, 102, 117, 296, 343, 344
Economic and Youth Opportunities Agency (EYOA) of Greater Los Angeles, 35, 36, 38
Edelman, Ed, 312, 401
Education
  bilingual education legislation, 141–146
  Chicano student protests over, 58–60. *See also* High school walkouts (1968)
  deaf and blind children, schools for, 162–163
  delivering services to children through schools, 326
  demand for more minority teachers, 50
  dropout rate in California public schools, 32
  gifted program, 154
  importance in RA's family, 6, 12, 13
  lobbyists, 156–157
  RA's college education, 23–29, 426
  RA's graduate school education, 87
  RA's public school experiences, 8, 12–13, 18–21
Educational Resource Program of the Teen Posts of Southern California Director, 34–36
EERC (Executive Employee Relations Committee, L.A.), 335–337
El Sereno, 117, 344, 370
  infrastructure needs of, 346
  proposed park, 307–308
  Youth Center, 327, 424
Ely, David, 297–298
Eminent domain, 376

EMR (educationally mentally retarded) classes, 8
Erickson, Charlie, 30, 33, 59
Esparza, Moctesuma, 43, 48–49
Ethics law, 386–388
Ethnic awareness, 38. *See also* Racial discrimination
Eventually Yours (event business of Angie Alatorre), 424
Executive Employee Relations Committee (EERC, L.A.), 335–337
EYOA (Economic and Youth Opportunities Agency of Greater Los Angeles), 35, 36, 38

F
Fair Political Practices Commission, 386, 424
Farmworkers' rights, 67, 179–200. *See also* Agricultural Labor Relations Act; Chavez, Cesar; UFW
FBI, 424
Federal Correctional Institution at Terminal Island, 70–81, *73*
  class structure and curriculum, 72–73
  inmate life at, 73–74
  inmates with drug-related offenses, 72, 74
  prison industries strike and prison lockdown, 77–80
  RA's bringing in outside entertainment to, 74–75
  RA's first visit to, 71
  women's side of, 71–72, 75–77
Federal grand jury hearings on RA, 424–425
Feinstein, Dianne, 384, 405, 406
Feliz Navidad project, 327, 344, 374–375, *375*

Fenton, Jack, 149–150, 202, 203, 213
Ferraro, John, 93, 94, 97, 102, 311–316, *314*, 334, 339, 354, 383
Ferraro, Margaret, 315–316
Fiesta Broadway, 352–353
Finn, Howard, 300–301
Fishman, Hal, 23–24
Fitzsimmons, Frank, 185, 207
Floor jockey, 139
Fong, March, 149, 182–183, 186
Ford Foundation Fellowship, 87, 91, 303
Foundation of Mexican American Studies, 30, 36
Frank, Barney, 402
Frontlash, 359
Fukai, Mas, 400
Fundraising. *See* Campaign fundraising

G
Galindo family, vii–viii
Gallo wines, 186, 188
  March on Gallo, *195*, 195–196
Gang of Five, 224
Gangs
  anti-gang alternatives, 35–36, 38, 80–81
  culture of, viii–x, 13
  RA as member of, viii, 12
  today's violence and, x, 357
Garcia, Alex, 121–122, *123*, 149, 182, 202, 225, 227–228, 269
Garcia, Miguel, 268
Gates, Daryl, 308, 319–322, *323*, 356
Gay community, 97–101
Gerrymandering. *See* Reapportionment
Getty, Ann, 164–165
GLAD (Greater Los Angeles Council for the Deaf), 162

Goldberg, Jackie, 364
Gonzales, Henry, 378
Gonzales, Paul, 374–375
Gonzales, Ray, 121–122, 149, 159, 184, 202
Gonzales, Rodolfo "Corky," 67
Governor. See also specific governor by name
  Democratic primary (1974), 148–149
Grapes boycott, 67, 181–182, 187–188, 191. See also Chavez, Cesar
  Contreras and, 358
  resolution of, 197
  secondary boycott strategy, 188
Gravel, Mike, 119–120
Grodin, Joseph, 175
Grossman, Marc, 65–68, *141*, 150–151, 182, 208, 222, 225, 228–230
Gutierrez, Jose Angel, *106*

H
Hahn, Kenny, 391, 400
Hallett, Carol, 214, 215, 220, *237*, 252, 254, 265
Hammer, Armand, 371
Hawkins, Gus, 273
Head Start program, 4, 7, 29–30
Healey, Dorothy, 40
Henning, Jack, 170, 203, 226
Herald Examiner, 17
Hernandez, Enrique (Rick), 319
Hernandez, Fernando, 51
Hernandez, Hank, 317–319, 322
Hesburgh, Theodore, 181
Highland Park, 343–344, 346, 367–369, 396
Highland Park Historical Society, 369, 370
High school walkouts (1968), 40, 43, *44*, 49–50, 52, 53, 84, 184. See also Chicano 13

Hill, Frank, 167, 252
Hoffa, Jimmy, 14
Hoffman Packing Company, 13–16
Holen, Marv, 401
Holland, John, 275
Homelessness, 348–349
Honorof, Ida, 186
Hospitals
  bilingual services, 135
  UCI teaching hospital initiative, 81–84, 125, 158
Hotel workers, 364–365
Housing
  absentee landlords, 346–347
  discrimination, 11, 233
  expensive real estate, effect of, 393
  homeless and, 348–349
  need for affordable housing, 372–373, 376, 383
  public housing projects, 373–374
  substandard conditions for immigrants, 372–373
Housing and Urban Development (HUD) office in San Francisco, 384–385
Huerta, Dolores, 119, 155, 209, 215, 216–217, 221–222, 225, 229
Human medical experimentation on prisoners, legislation to change, 160–162
Humphrey, Hubert, 107, 108, 118–119

I
Immigration and Naturalization Service (INS), 384
Immigration Reform and Control Act (IRCA, 1986), 270–271
Industrial Areas Foundation, 3
International Brotherhood of Electrical Workers Local 18, 335–336
Irvine Corporation, 52, 65, 66

J

Jackson, Henry "Scoop," 93
Jalisco, Mexico, 378–379
Japanese Americans, 2, 3
Jett, Lee, 70–71, 78, 79
Jewish Federation of Los Angeles, 37
Jewish Historical Society of Southern California, 379
Jews, 1–2, 28, 47, 88, 260, 288, 289, 304, 349, 350, 397
    Breed Street Shul, preservation of, 379–382, *381*
John Paul II (Pope), 353
Johnson, Lyndon B., 34, 103
Johnson, Ross, 220, 269
Joint Committee to Oversee the Agricultural Labor Relations Board, 209
Jones, Opal, 38–39
Jordan Downs project in Watts, 384–385
Justice Department, U.S., 263, 292, 294, 296, 298, 321

K

KABC-TV channel, 160–162
Kantor, Mickey, 371
Karabian, Walter, 87, 89–96, *90*
    background of, 89–90
    Brown (Jerry) and, 171
    Chicano Catholic cleric used by Republicans in campaign against, 108
    Ferraro and, 102
    funding RA's campaign for Assembly, 94–95
    fundraising ability of, 126
    Moret and, 113
    motivating RA to run for Assembly opening, 91, 93–94
    political sense of, 96
    RA as campaign manager for, 90–91
    in speakership war, 214–215
    trust of RA, 91
    UFW and, 183
    Waxman and, 148
Karanga, Ron, 112, 180, 305
Karns, John, 420
Katz, Kenny, 95–99, 107
Katz, Richard, 391
Kennedy, John F., 5, 97
Kennedy, Robert F., 43–44, 46, 87, 96–97, 182, 303, 318–319
Kennedy, Ted, 108
Kent State shootings (1970), 58
Ketchum, Stuart, 354
Keveles, Daniel, 243–244
Kim, Paul, 285–287
Kimbrough, Ted, 156
Kindel, Maureen, 287
King, Rodney, 308–309
Kirk, Nancy, 227
KMEX-TV channel, 59, 60, 64, 138–139, 284
Knabe, Don, 383
Knights of Labor, 358
Koransky, Louis, 26, 28–29
Kovner Publications, 16–17
Kramer, Robin
    on Bradley-RA relationship, 408
    Breed Street Shul preservation and, 379–380
    on budget process, 331
    on Cain, 295
    as chief deputy in RA's city council office, 284, 390
    on children's services, 326, 329
    on EERC, 335
    on Ferraro-RA relationship, 313, 316
    on housing developments, 371
    on MTA, RA's role on, 399, 404
    photograph of, *288*

as public policy expert, 376
RA hiring, 287–289
on RA's influence, 383
on reapportionment hearings, 297–298
on Woo, 299
KTLA TV channel, 47

L

L.A. Best program, 329
L.A. Conservancy, 353
L.A. Labor, 358, 359, 361–365
L.A. Mirror, 17
LACTC. *See* Los Angeles County Transportation Commission
Lady, Al, 190
Lambert, Bill, 156
Lanterman, Frank, 214
La Opinion (Spanish-language daily), 17, 284
LAPD. *See* Los Angeles Police Department
La Raza newspaper, 48
La Raza Unida Party, 103–106, 110–111, 118
Latino Police Officers Association, 321
Latinos. *See also* Chicano movement; Racial discrimination; *organization names starting with "Mexican"*
  bilingual programs for. *See* Bilingualism and biculturalism
  in Boyle Heights area, 2, 20, 102, 349–351. *See also* Boyle Heights
  Chicano Caucus (in assembly), 121–122, 127, 149–150, 159, 183, 203
  empowerment of, 116, 278. *See also* Chicano movement
  as farmworkers. *See* Agricultural Labor Relations Act; Farmworkers' rights; UFW

as focus of RA's efforts, 37, 43, 117–118, 126–127, 133, 148, 155, 186, 287, 305, 321. *See also* Reapportionment, assembly initiatives; Teaching career
  "good Mexicans," 146
  housing and. *See* Housing
  intermarrying of, 270
  LAPD and, 41, 285–287, 317–321
  mistrust of government, 235
  political experience of, 111–112. *See also* Assembly (first campaign, 1971)
  population growth of, 271, 293–295
  protests. *See* Chicano movement; Grapes boycott; Student activism; UFW
  RA's work in jewelry store and, 28–29
  redistricting and influence of, 148, 220, 222–223, 250–252, 257, 261–270. *See also* Reapportionment
  voting rates of, 297
Lehman, Rick, 184, 221, 269, 385
Lehnhardt, William B., 175
Lettuce boycott, 188
Levine, Mel, 269, 385
Levitt, Herman "Blackie," 358, 360
Levy, Herman, 195
Liberals, 147–148, 173, 303
Libraries, 325, 344
Light rail transit construction. *See* Metropolitan Transportation Authority
Lincoln High School, 48–49, 154
Lindsay, Gil, 294, 352, 353
Linka, Wendy, 231
Living wage ordinance, 364–365, 366
Lizarraga, David, 34–35, 423

Lockyer, Bill, 173, 255
Lopez, Art, 322
Lopez, Rene, 228
Los Angeles City Council (1985–1999), x, 3, 274–289
　Becham considering running against RA, 275–276
　bilingual education proposal, 143
　Bradley veto of reapportionment plan, 300
　budgetary process, 326–335
　business taxes, 367–368
　campaign funding and, 281–282
　City Hall restoration, 354–355, *355*
　ethics law, 386–388
　importance of, 284
　LAPD and, 285–287
　living wage ordinance, 364–365, *366*
　RA's decision to run first time for, 280–282
　RA's first term, 282, 287–289, 291
　reapportionment, 291–302. *See also* Los Angeles City Council reapportionment
　restoration of Broadway, 351–354
　Roybal as first Latino council member, 278
　Snyder and, 275–281, *277*
　Spanish-language media and, 284
Los Angeles City Council reapportionment, 291–302
　civil rights suit against based on violations of Voting Rights Act, 292–293, 296, 301
　demographic changes in L.A. and, 293–295
　Eagle Rock voters, 275–277
　hearings, 297
　legacy, 301–302
　plan 1, 291, 295–300
　plan 2, 300–301
　RA as chair of council reapportionment, 295–301
　Woo and, 296, 298–299
Los Angeles Convention Center, 353
Los Angeles County Board of Supervisors, 295
Los Angeles County District Attorney, 424
Los Angeles County Federation of Labor, 358–359, *360*, 394
Los Angeles County Human Relations Commission, 48
Los Angeles County Sheriff's Department, 321
Los Angeles County Transportation Commission (LACTC), 391–392, 394–396, 400–401, 408
Los Angeles mayor
　1969 race, 87–88, *89*, 303–304
　1973 race, 88
　1993 race, 310
　expectation that RA will run for, 283, 288, 308, 312
　power of, 312, 331, 383
　RA's endorsement of Riordan for, 310–311
Los Angeles Police Department (LAPD)
　Boyle Heights and, 317
　Chicano Moratorium (1970) and, 60–64, *61*
　Highland Park substation, 369
　Hollenbeck Police Station, 356
　immigration enforcement, 356–357
　Justice Department setting integration standards for, 321
　Latino community and, 41, 317–319
　police brutality, 39, 40, 59

prosecution for beating Latinos (1951), 3
racial discrimination in, 317–321
racial discrimination in hiring and promotions, 285–287, 317–321
RA's relationship with, 317–325
Salazar's reporting on, 60
Special Order 40, 356–358
union negotiations, 338–339
Los Angeles Police Historical Society, 370
Los Angeles Rams (football team), 410
Los Angeles Redevelopment Agency, 359
Los Angeles Times, 17, 58, 354, 423–424
Los Angeles Unified School District, 30, 33, 34, 157, 262, 326
budget for L.A. Best, 329
Puente Learning Center and, 306
RA's close relationship with, 156
sit-ins, 46
Luce, John, 48

M

Maddy, Ken, 158, *192*, 203, 252
Maggio Inc. v. United Farm Workers, 175
Mahony, Roger, 353, 362
MALDEF. *See* Mexican American Legal Defense and Education Fund
Mandatory retirement age, legislation to change, 159–160
Manibog, Monty, 223, 225, 229
Mankiewitz, Frank, 43, 46, 60–62
MAPA. *See* Mexican American Political Association
Mapistas (members of MAPA), 42
Mardirosian, Vahac, 42
Mariachi Plaza, revitalization of, 377–379, *378*

Marquez, Richard, ix, x, 35
Martin, Albert C., Sr., 354
Martin, Chris, 354
Martinez, Marty, 213, 269
Mayor. *See* Los Angeles mayor
McCarthy, Dan, 161
McCarthy, Eugene, 45–46
McCarthy, Leo T.
Berman vs. for Speaker (1979–80), 170, 204–206, 209–213
Brown (Willie) working against, 149–150
Chavez and, 208, 210
desire for higher office, 203
personality of, 201
punishing RA for not supporting him, 152, 169–170, 197–198, 203
as Speaker, 116, 169–170, 201–202
McCarthyism, 47
McGovern, George, 118–119
McIntyre, James Francis, 84
Meany, George, 189
MEChA (Movimiento Estudiantil Chicano de Aztlan, or Chicano student movement of Aztlan), 51, 58, 84
MediCal coverage for deaf and blind children, 162–163
Medical practice, legislation to include podiatrists and other medical professionals, 163–164
Metropolitan Community Church, 98, 99, 101, *101*
Metropolitan Transportation Authority (MTA), 340, 363, 385, 391–412
bus advocates vs. rail advocates, 394–395
daily operations and service complaints, 410–411
DASH routes, 399
downtown lines, 353, 396

Eastside neighborhoods and, 397
equal opportunity for jobs and minority-owned firms, 403
Expo Line, 396
funding and use of lobbyists, 404–407
gold line to Boyle Heights, 397–399
headquarters location, 407–410, *409*
merger of RTD and LACTC to create, 394–396, 401–402
MTA police chief, selection of, 403–404
MTA police force, 403–404
multimodal transportation system and, 398–399
Outstanding Transportation System (2006), 411
Pasadena link, 396
RA appointed as chair, 394
union contracts and, 402
Mexican American Action Committee, 39, 43, 84, 92–93
Mexican American Legal Defense and Education Fund (MALDEF), 39, 170, 171, 297
Mexican American Political Association (MAPA), 39, 40, 42–43, 110
Mexican Americans. *See* Latinos
Mexican Mafia, 80
Mexican Revolution, 7
Meyers, Marcella, 162
Miller, John, 149, 202
Mills, James (Jim), 94, *198*, 227
Minser, Shirley, 276–277
Molina, Gloria, 128, *129*, 301, 383, 398
Monroy, Sol, 40–42, 44, 47, 59, 317
Montes, Phil, 30–37, *31*, 39, 43, 46, 48, 52, 58–59, 70, 144, 173, 180

Montoya, Bob, 158
Montoya, Joseph, 121–122, *123*, 149, 202, 223, 269
Moreno, John, 235
Moret, Kathy, 287–288
Moret, Lou
  in Calderon campaign, 224
  in city council campaigns, 278–279
  at Democratic National Convention (1972), 119, 132, 165–166
  RA intervention, role in, 419–420
  as RA's administrative assistant, 126–127
  RA's first campaign for Assembly and, 91, 93, 95, *95*, 96, 100, 102–103, 104
  RA's second campaign for Assembly and, 113
  running for city council, 279
  in Torres campaign, 277
  on UFW involvement of RA, 183, 186
Moretti, Bob
  appointment of RA to Ways and Means Committee, 124–125
  at Century Plaza fundraiser, 127
  Cory and, 82
  in governor race (Democratic primary 1974), 139, 149, 201–202
  Ochoa endorsed by, 92–94, 101
  photographs of, *119*, *187*
  RA's admiration for, 148
  RA's election and, 103
  as Speaker, 115–116, 118–121, 198, 201–202
  UFW strikers and, 186–187, 208
  Waxman and, 148
Mori, Floyd, 209
Moscone, George, 83, 94, 97, 139, 148, 201, 312

Mount Sinai Clinic (East L.A.), 2
Movimiento Estudiantil Chicano de Aztlan (MEChA, Chicano student movement of Aztlan), 51, 58, 84
MTA. *See* Metropolitan Transportation Authority
Munoz, Carlos, 53, 66
Munoz, Rosalio, 58
Murphy, Frank, 165
Muskie, Edmond G., 107, 108

N

NAACP Legal Defense and Education Fund, 39, 51, 52, 66, 181
National Chicano Moratorium Committee, 58
National Labor Relations Act (1935), 187
National League of Cities, 326
Nava, Yolanda, 128, *129*, 217
Navarro, Mike, 95
Navarro, Ruben, 74–75
Naylor, Bob, 220, 245, 253, 254
Nestande, Bruce, 252
Newman, Frank, 85–87, 125
Newspapers, 16–18. See also specific newspaper
  coverage of RA, 423–424
  Spanish-language, 284–285
NIMBY activists, 311
Nixon, Richard, 104–106
Nonviolence principles, 188
Nordstrom's, 368
Northeast Newspapers, 17
Northridge earthquake (1994), 308–309, 356, 380
Norton, Hillary, 308, 339, 367, 376, 379, 388–390, 413, 419, 424–425, 427

O

Obledo, Mario, 170–171
Ochoa, David, 43
Ochoa, Ralph, 43, 92–94, *93*, 101, 118, 234
O'Connell, Jack, 225, 282
Office of Legislative Counsel, 91
Offshore oil drilling, 371
Olivares, Father Luis, *207*
Olympics (1984), 155, 279, 280, 358, 378, 392–393, 420
O'Malley family, 410
110 freeway, 411–412
O'Neal, Ryan, 75
Operating Engineers Local 3 (San Francisco), 226
Orange County jail, 40
Orozco, Gerard, 300, 342
  MTA role of, 393–394, 396, 398–399, 401, 403, 406, 410, 411

P

Padilla, Gilbert, 180
Papa, Sharon, 403
Papan, Lou, 252
Parker, William, 40, 41, 317, 318
Parker Center (L.A.), 356
Parks, Bernard, 285, 321, 322, 324–325
Parks and recreation centers, 325–326, 344
Parks and Recreation Department (L.A.), 307–308, 328
Pasadena Freeway, 411–412
Patino, Lorenzo, 119, *123*, 132, *141*, 165–169, 189–191, *192*
Patsouras, Nick, 400–401
Paz, Octavio: *Labyrinth of Solitude*, 74, 75
Peace, Steve, 184
Peña, Frederico, 397, 400
Perry, Troy, 98, 99, 101, *101*
Persons with disabilities, legislation to recognize rights of, 162–163
Peterson, Neil, 396, 399–400, 404, 405
Pitches, Peter, 39

Pla, George, 267, 319–320, 419–420, 427
Polanco, Richard, 48, 271–272, 282
Police. *See* Los Angeles Police Department (LAPD)
Police and Fire Committee (L.A.), 319–321, 370
Police Protective League, 322, 335, 338, 339
Politics. *See also* specific parties and candidates
  Chicanos, politicization of, 111–112. *See also* Chicano movement
  friendships in, value of, 147, 385
  image vs. substance in, xi
  as motivating factor in RA's career choice, xi, 418
  RA's political philosophy, 112, 117–118, 157–158, 385–386, 418
  social aspects of, 417
Polka, Sandi, 282
Pollution from vehicles, 393, 395, 399
The poor, 5, 36, 330, 343, 365, 372–373, 410. *See also* War on Poverty program
Prescott, Ron, 156
Priolo, Paul, 134, 158, 214, 252
Prisoners. *See also* Federal Correctional Institution at Terminal Island
  drug testing on, legislation to change, 160–162
  prison reform, 40, 70, 117, 173–174
  rehabilitating, 80–81
  seeking RA's advice or help after release, 389
Proposition 13 (1978), 214, 331
Proposition 22 (1972), 182
Proposition 98 (1988), 157

Proposition 140 (1990), 168, 224
Proposition 187 (1994), 146, 258, 270, 271, 362–363
Proposition 209 (1996), 258
Proposition 227 (1998), 146, 258
Proposition U (citywide measure), 371
Public Safety Committee (L.A.), 313, 317, 319–321, 325, 330–331, 358, 370
Puente Learning Center, 306–307
Putnam, George, 47

Q
Quevedo, Enrique "Hank," 39
Quezada, Leticia, 262
Quinn, Joe, 88

R
Racial discrimination. *See also* Civil rights issues; Reapportionment
  AB 3370 farmworkers bill and, 192–193
  affirmative action, 86
  Boalt Hall Law School (UC Berkeley), 85–87, 152
  city council, civil rights suit against based on violations of Voting Rights Act, 292–293, 296, 301
  housing discrimination, 11, 233
  in LAPD hiring and promotions, 41, 285–287, 317–321
  MTA jobs for minorities and women, 402–403
  RA's father experiencing, xi, 10–11, 233
  redistricting and, 263, 264, 270–271
  restaurants refusing to serve Mexicans, 10–11, 233
  UCI School of Fine Arts, 54–55

UC system undergraduate and professional schools, 152–153
in Yorty-Bradley election (1969), 87–88
Rafferty, Max, 30, 32, 33
Rahal, Nick Joe, 406
Rail transit construction. *See* Metropolitan Transportation Authority
Ralph, Leon, 149, 202
Ramos, Mando, 75
Rathburn, Bill, 357–358
Reader's Digest (1974), 80
Reagan, Ronald
 bilingual services act legislation and, 132, 135, 137–138, 140, *141*
 Century Plaza tribute dinner for, 127
 election as governor (1966), 43
 election as president (1980), 204, 273, 362
 farm labor legislation and, 193, 213
 Proposition 140 opposed by, 168
 reapportionment and, 109, 236
Reapportionment, assembly initiatives, 18, 103, 109, 148, 219, 222–223, 225, *235*, 236, 238–272. *See also* Assembly Elections and Reapportionment Committee
 Brown (Willie) and, 242–243, 245–246, 248–250, 261
 Cal Tech students working on, 247
 census data used in, 247–248, 264
 computerization and, 246–248
 congressional races and, 256–257
 Democrats cutting deal with Republicans (1982), 269–270
 discriminatory practices, addressing of, 262, 264
 dispersal approach in, 257, 264–265
 Latinos and, 222–223, 250–252, 261–262
 odd-looking districts, 260
 press reaction to, 261
 RA's critique of process, 251
 Republicans and, 18, 103, 220, 245–246, 248, 252–257, 260, 265–266, 268–270
 secrecy of process, 258, 260, 262
 suburban growth and, 245, 266–267
Reapportionment, council initiatives, 291–302. *See also* Los Angeles City Council reapportionment
Redistricting. *See* Reapportionment
Redwood Room (downtown L.A.), 58, 60, 64
Reinhardt, Stephen, 197
Republican Party
 Agricultural Labor Relations Act and, 228
 Assembly staffs, 169
 bilingual services bill and, 135–136
 growers vs. farmworkers and, 184
 newspapers and, 17, 18
 Proposition 187 (1994) and, 362
 RA's relationship with, 147, 168
 La Raza Unida Party and, 104–106
 reapportionment and, 18, 103, 220, 245–246, 248, 252–257, 260, 265–266, 268–270
 Riordan and, 310
 in speakership war, 202, 205, 212–216, 218–221, 223, 227, 237
 splintering Latino support for Democratic candidates, 106–109
Respect for institutions, 316

Restoration and revitalization
  Adelante Eastside Area, 375–377
  Breed Street Shul, 2, 379–382, *381*
  City Hall, 354–355, *355*
  County-USC Hospital, 382–383
  downtown L.A., 351–354, 371
  Eagle Rock, 367–371
  Los Angeles Redevelopment Agency, 359
  Mariachi Plaza, 377–379, *378*
  South Central, 357
Reynoso, Cruz, 175
Rico, Charlie (uncle), 14–15, 124
Riles, Wilson, 32, 33, 173
Riordan, Richard
  business tax reforms and, 365, 367
  children's programs and, 330
  city hall renovations and, 354
  election campaign of, 365
  Gates and, 322
  influence on RA, 303, 306–312
  labor relations and, 335–339
  mass transit system and, 401, 404
  photograph of, *366*
Roberti, David, 91–94, 101–102, 113, 166–168, 227, 229, 312
Robertson, Bill, 359
Rodda, Al, 142–145
Rodney King riots (1992), 308–309, 322
Rodriguez, Antonio, 43
Rodriguez, Arturo, 212
Rodriguez, Steve, 279–282
Ronstadt, Linda, 173, *174*
Roos, Mike, 117, 155, 168, 266, 273, 274, 311
Roosevelt High School, 49
Rose Institute of State and Local Government (Claremont McKenna College), 243, 257, 262, 265
Ross, Fred, 3, 278
Ross, Richie, 223–224, 225, 229, 255–256, 272, 279, 281, 282
Roybal, Edward R.
  Brophy and, 109
  business support for, 18
  Community Service Organization and, 39, 278
  election to L.A. City Council, 3, 234
  liberal support for, 304
  Moretti and, 94
  photographs of, *93*, *283*
  rail transportation and, 397
  reapportionment and, 269
  retirement of, 280
  Roberti and, 92
Roybal-Allard, Lucille, 269
Ruiz, Raul, 104–105, *106*, 110, 111
Russell, Pat, 283, 292–294, *293*, 298, 312

S
Sacramento Municipal Court, 166
Safer, Morley, 167
Salazar, Ruben, 58–64, *61*, 138, 284
San Antonio Winery, 357–358
Sanchez, David, 48, 317
Sandoval, Rafael ("Chispas"), ix, 71, 75, 78, 80
San Fernando Valley, 298
San Francisco school district, 156
Santillan, Lou, Sr., 376
Santillan, Richard, 268
Save America's Treasures project, 380
Schwarzenegger, Arnold, 177, 240
Scott, Gene, 352
SDS (Students for a Democratic Society), 65, 68
Secondary boycotts, 188

Segretti, Donald, 106–107, *108*, 109
SEIU (Service Employees International Union), 339
Sewell, Sandy Serrano, 128–131, *129*
Shriver, Maria, 34
Shriver, Sargent, 34
Smith, Al, 362
Snyder, Arthur K., 275–281, *277*, 295, 341, 343, 370, 386
Social Action Training Center, 180
Social activism and advocacy, 36, 85. *See also* Student activism
Song, Al, 87, *90*
Soto, Phil, 235
South Central, 36, 122, 180, 291, 293, 294, 297, 309, 330, 357
Southern California Rapid Transit District (RTD), 391–392, 395, 401
South Pasadena NIMBY activists, 311
Spanish language
   media coverage of politicians, 284–285
   RA speaking at home and with his grandmother, 8
   school punishment for speaking on school grounds or in classroom, 8, 31–32
Speakership war, 201–231
   Berman vs. McCarthy for Speaker (1979–80), 170, 204–206, 209–213
   Brown in, 201–202, 213–221. *See also* Brown, Willie
   Chavez involvement in, 209–210
   divided Democratic Party as result of, 237
   Huerta and, 215, 216–217
   job of speaker to help members get reelected, 204
   McCarthy's revenge on Brown and RA, 203
   McCarthy's surprise election to become Speaker, 201–202
   RA not interested in reconciling with McCarthy, 203
   RA's position in McCarthy-Berman contest for speaker, 206
   RA's support of Brown, 215–216, 219
   Republican Party in, 214, 215, 219, 237
   rural Democrats in, 221
   strategy to oust McCarthy and its failure, 202–203
   Torres in, 206, 209–212, 214–218, 222
Speaker's Office of Majority Services, 223
Staples Center, 353
Steinberg, Jonathan, 292–293
Stevenson, Adlai, 5
Stirling, David, 228
Student activism
   antiwar activism, 57, 62, 65
   Brown (Jerry) and, 171
   Chicano activism, 58–60, 84, 111. *See also* High school walkouts
   fleeting nature of, 84
   grapes boycott and farmworkers' rights, 67, 181
   importance of, 56
   UMAS (United Mexican American Students), 51
   Vietnam War protests, 58
Students for a Democratic Society (SDS), 65, 68
Suburban growth, 245, 266–267

T
Tapia, Abe, 39
Target department store, 368
Taxation, 367–368
Teaching career, 51–84

454 *Index*

at Federal Correctional Institution at Terminal Island, 70–81
at University of California, Irvine, 51–60, *53*, 69–70, 81
Teamsters, 14, 183–189, 193–194, 199, 207, 356
Teen posts, 34–36, 48, 84, 319
Terminal Annex U.S. Post Office facility, 409–410
Term limits, 121, 168–169, 224
Texas Rangers, 180–181
Textbook reform, 173
Thompson, Steve, 83
Thurman, John, 184, 221
Tijerina, Reies Lopez, 52, 67
Tombstoning of names on bills, 142, 198, 311
Torres, Art
  bilingual services legislation and, 132
  Brown and, 174
  on campaign fundraising, 105–106
  Chavez and, 111, 182, 209–212, 217–218, 222, 225, 227, 228
  city council candidates and, 278–279
  election of, 159
  Garcia vs., 227
  Patino and, 190
  photograph of, *211*
  as RA campaign worker, 96, 100
  RA's support for, 227
  on Segretti's campaign tactics, 109
  Snyder and, 277
  social skills of, 146
  in speakership war, 170–171, 206, 209–212, 214–218, 222
Torres, Esteban, 269
Transportation. *See* Los Angeles County Transportation Commission; Metropolitan Transportation Authority
Trigueiro, Toni, 134, 135, 140, 142, 145, 150–156, *151*, 158–159, 162, 165, 169–170, 177–178, 258–259
Tucker, Jim, 244

U
UFW (United Farm Workers), 67, 110–111, 179–200, 228. *See also* Chavez, Cesar; Grapes boycott
  Agricultural Labor Relations Board and, 155
  Bradley supported by, 228
  Central Valley strike, 185
  Coachella Valley strike, 185, 189
  farmworkers legislation (AB 1, 1975) and, 194–199. *See also* Agricultural Labor Relations Act (1975)
  farmworkers legislation (AB 3370, 1974) and, 191–194
  Imperial Valley strike, 208
  influence in legislative races, 226
  Maggio Inc. v. United Farm Workers, 175
  March on Gallo, *195*, 195–196
  representation elections after passage of Agricultural Labor Act (1975), 199, 207
  Salinas Valley strike, 181–182, 188, 208
  single unit (industrial) bargaining vs. craft units bargaining, 192
  in speakership war, 208–210, 215–218
  strikes and strikebreakers, 111, 180–181, 208
  UFW Citizenship Participation Day Fund (PAC), 208

violence associated with strikes, 185–191
UMAS (United Mexican American Students), 51, 84
Undocumented immigrants, 110, 111, 136. *See also* Proposition 187 (1994)
  drivers' licenses for, 267
  INS raids on businesses, 384
  IRCA amnesty provisions for, 270–271
  Special Order 40 (LAPD), 356–358
Unions. See also UFW; specific government agencies
  county federation, 360–363
  RA's father in support of, 10
  RA's uncle as organizer for, 14, 124
Union Station, 407, *409*
United Farm Workers. *See* UFW
United Mexican American Students. *See* UMAS
United Parcel Service (UPS), 357–358
University of California, Irvine (UCI), 27, 51–60, *53*, 64–65, 69–70
  Aldrich as dean, 52, 55, 64–66, 81–83
  Chicano faculty at, 53
  Chicano students at, 54–56, 69–70
  Cinco de Mayo event (1969), 68
  courses RA teaches, 54
  description of campus and location, 52–53, 65
  RA as faculty sponsor for MEChA at, 58
  RA's teaching approach at, 56–57
  student ratings of RA, 81
  teaching hospital initiative, 81–84, 125, 158

University of Southern California, 87, 376
Unruh, Jesse, 92, 95, 198, 226, 236
Unz, Ron, 146
Urban Affairs Institute, 303
U.S. Attorney's Office, 424–425
U.S. Commission on Civil Rights, 48–49, 52, 66, 180
UTLA (United Teachers of Los Angeles), 131, 156

V
van den Noort, Stanley, 83–84
Vasconcellos, John, 83, 125, 148, 256, 266
Vasquez, Angie, 280
Vicencia, Frank, 213, 237
Vietnam War, 58, 62, 66–67, 84
Villa, Pancho, 7–8
Villanueva, Danny, 59, 138–140, *140*, 284
Villaraigosa, Antonio, 176, 288, 362
Viva Bradley campaign, 304–305
Voter registration and turnout, 271, 359
Voting Rights Act (1965), 220, 263, 292, 295–296, 301

W
Wachs, Joel, 283, 299–300, 312, 386
Waldie, Jerry, 194, 201
Walters, Rita, 352
Wardlaw, Bill, 311
War on Poverty program, 34, 35–36, 38, 52, 180
Water & Power Department (L.A.), 335–337
Watergate, 106–108
Waters, Maxine
  Brown and, 117, 125–126, 168
  congressional election campaign of, 269

on Democratic control of state
    legislature, 273–274
as governmental organization
    subcommittee chairperson,
    152, 154–155
on minority politicians, 68–69
at RA's city council induction
    ceremony, 282
reapportionment and, 385
Ways and Means Committee and,
    256
Waters, Norm, 184, 221
Watt, Ray, 407
Watts, Jordan Downs project in,
    384–385
Watts Riot (1965), 34, 36, 309, 322
Waxman, Henry, 146, 148, 202, 397
White, Joe, 51–52, 70–71
Williams, Willie, 285–287, 321–
    324, *323*
Wilson, Pete
    farm labor legislation and, 228
    as governor, 177, 245, 273, 310
    Proposition 187 and, 146, 270,
        271, 361–362
    as senator, 384–385
Wisely, Jim, 244–245, 251, 263,
    264
Women
    Comisión Feminil Mexicana
        Nacional (National Mexican
        Women's Commission),
        128–132
    training for nontraditional occupa-
        tions, 128
Woo, Mike
    on city council, 296, 298–299
    ethics ordinance and, 386–388
    in mayoral race (1993), 310
    photograph of, *300*
Woo, Wilber, 299
Wood, Jim, 90, 310, 359–361
Wood, Robert, 181

Y

Yaroslavsky, Zev, 283, 309, 312,
    313, 331, 371, 380, 383
Yellin, Ira, 351–353, 407
Yorty, Sam, 87–88, *89*, 228, 303,
    305, 318
Young Citizens for Governor
    Brown, 43
Younger, Evelle, 43

Z

Zanelli, Jerry, 91, 113
Zenovich, George, 198, *198*
Zoot Suit Riots, 3

*Then he answered and spake unto me, saying,
This is the word of the Lord unto Zerubbabel, saying,
Not by might, nor by power, but by my spirit,
saith the Lord of hosts.*

Zechariah 4:6

To Hélène,
without whom this book
would never have been written,
with all my love.

A New Day of Small Beginnings
By Pierre Courthial

Translated by Rev. Matthew S. Miller

Copyright © 2018 Zurich Publishing Foundation, Inc.

Published by:

Zurich Publishing Foundation, Inc.
2236 Capital Circle Northeast
Suite 102
Tallahassee, Florida 32308
www.zurichpublishing.org
Office: 850-893-6570

Unless otherwise indicated, Scripture is quoted from the New King James Version® of the Bible. Copyright © 1982 by Thomas Nelson, Inc. All rights reserved.

Scripture quotations marked (ESV) are from the ESV® Bible (The Holy Bible, English Standard Version®), copyright © 2001 by Crossway, a publishing ministry of Good News Publishers. Used by permission. All rights reserved.

No part of this publication may be reproduced, stored in a retrieval system, or transmitted in any form by any means, electronic, mechanical, photocopy, recording, or otherwise, without the prior written permission of the author and publisher, except as provided by the United States copyright law.

Courthial, Pierre, 1914–2009

Originally published in 1996 under the title: *Le jour des petits recommencements. Essai sur l'actualité de la Parole (Evangile-Loi) de Dieu* in the Collection Messages by Éditions L'Âge d'Homme in Lausanne.

Interior Design by Kyle Shepherd
General Index by Lauren LaFleur & Shelby Shepherd
History Index by Madison Cormick

ISBN: 978-0-9843785-3-1
Library of Congress Catalog Number: 2015935984
Printed in the United States of America.
First printing, Spring 2018
Second printing, Fall 2018

A New Day of
Small Beginnings

PIERRE COURTHIAL

Translated By
Rev. Matthew S. Miller

Zurich Publishing
Tallahassee, Florida
Lausanne, Switzerland

A NEW DAY OF SMALL BEGINNINGS